The Making
of a Market Guru

The Making of a Market Guru

Forbes

PRESENTS **25** YEARS OF

KEN FISHER

Aaron Anderson

WILEY

John Wiley & Sons, Inc.

Published by John Wiley & Sons, Inc., Hoboken, New Jersey.

Published simultaneously in Canada.

For general information on our other products and services or for technical support, please contact our Customer Care Department within the United States at (800) 762-2974, outside the United States at (317) 572-3993 or fax (317) 572-4002.

Wiley also publishes its books in a variety of electronic formats. Some content that appears in print may not be available in electronic books. For more information about Wiley products, visit our web site at www.wiley.com.

ISBN 978-0-470-28542-8

Printed in the United States of America

10 9 8 7 6 5 4 3 2

Contents

Introduction

Twenty-five years is a long time to do just about anything. It's a particularly long time to make stock market forecasts for all the investing world to scrutinize—over and over again. Sticking your neck out inherently involves certain risks, like getting your head chopped off (figuratively, of course. This isn't eighteenth-century France) by readers, investors, editors, or anyone else. But that's exactly what Ken Fisher has done over the last two and half decades, monthly, in *Forbes*. Ken's columns have included his views on investments, the economy, market misperceptions, specific stocks, financial planning, the news, politics, and politicians—anything and everything impacting capital markets. His tendency to go against the investing public's prevailing opinion has made him more susceptible to criticism than most—over the years, Ken has probably received far more hate mail than love letters. It may seem masochistic, but the contrarian in him wouldn't have it any other way. The wisdom of good advice often isn't apparent until well after it's offered.

Twenty-five years makes Ken the fourth-longest-running columnist in *Forbes* history (as of this writing). An impressive tenure, but in his columns Ken has been clear about his ultimate goal. "My goal? To be number one. To be still writing this column when the issue of August 30, 2016 comes out." ("Rummaging in the Attic," December 18, 1995.) At that point he would overtake Heinz Biel who wrote for just over 32 years—from November 1, 1950 (the month Ken was born) until December 20, 1982, just before Ken starting writing columns for *Forbes*.

The magazine has had more than 100 columnists come and go. Few endure long. A very few, like current columnist Gary Shilling, have come and gone and come back again. That a select handful of columnists *have* had such longevity with *Forbes* is just unusual. Very few columnists in publishing history have such a long run—in *Forbes* or anywhere. It's a testament to both the quality of the magazine and those few columnists that have lasted so long. After all, there's no reason to keep publishing columns unless the publication and the advice therein is relevant. This is simply the mark of a guru. Imposters get chewed up and spit out quickly.

25 Years of Relevancy

How do we know Ken's advice is relevant? There are several ways. One could be to just trust *Forbes* to know what it's doing. If advice is no longer relevant, long-time readers won't read it, and *Forbes* wouldn't need to run the column.

Next, look at the history of Ken's stock picks in his column. About half of each column (on average) has been economic and market commentary and

TABLE 1 Fourteen-Year History of the Forbes Report Card[1]

Year	Ken Fisher's *Forbes* Stock Pick Returns	S&P 500 Returns
1996	13.90%	12.10%
1997	23.00%	33.00%
1998	14.90%	14.90%
1999	20.53%	11.53%
2000	0.00%	−10.00%
2001	−2.50%	−11.40%
2002	−6.00%	−3.00%
2003	31.64%	17.64%
2004	12.60%	7.60%
2005	14.30%	3.40%
2006	15.70%	8.70%
2007	0.90%	−0.50%
2008	−25.80%	−24.70%
2009	44.44%	20.92%
Annualized Return	9.94%	4.71%

forecast (which is primarily what this book focuses on) and the other half has been specific stock recommendations along with justifications for them. Since 1997 *Forbes* has issued a "report card" on its columnists each year (starting with calendar year 1996 returns). It tracks columnists' stock picks (less 1% to simulate transaction fees) versus the S&P 500 (with no fees deducted)—as if equal-sized investments were made in both on the date of magazine publication. Through 2009, Ken's average annual return was 9.9 percent, compared to 4.7 percent for the S&P. (See Table 1.)

This book comes out in 2010, and no doubt many will still be focused on 2008—and Ken's record includes that terrible year. That year Ken lagged the S&P 500—though just by a scant 1.1 percent—a whisker. In fact, overall, Ken's picks have only lagged the S&P three years in this derby—which is a stunning fact by itself. He also lagged in 1997, when his picks were positive, but not as positive as the S&P 500, and 2002.

On the topic of stunning: 2009 was simply spectacular for Ken. The S&P surged 20.9 percent (as measured by *Forbes*)—a sharp market rebound he predicted in his columns early that year. But Ken's stock picks did 44.4 percent after adjusting for a 1 percent brokerage haircut, beating equal money in the S&P by a huge 23.5 percent.[2] Not a bad way for Ken to end this 25-year period.

Over the long haul, if you can lag by not much in a few years and still annualize a 5.2 percent spread over the S&P 500, you're not just doing okay, you're killing it. Hence, the making of a guru.

Yet another way to know Ken's advice is still relevant is to look at how his peers and other legitimate third parties rate him. His *Forbes* report card is all about how his stock picks have done, and it's a great record. But CXO Advisory

Group, a third-party research group that rates professionals who make public forecasts, measures Ken's more macro calls on broad market direction, as stated in his *Forbes* columns. Since they've been keeping track, Ken's continuously been one of their top-rated (if not the top-rated) most accurate forecasters. (You can find their rankings at www.cxoadvisory.com.)

Ken's also won the prestigious Bernstein Fabozzi/Jacobs Levy Outstanding Article award for one of his scholarly papers on behavioral finance. He's appeared on *Investment Advisor's* IA-25 list—their ranking of the 25 most influential investors. And, in 2009, Ken and Charles Schwab were awarded the two inaugural Tiburon CEO Summit Awards. Ken won the "Challenging Conventional Wisdom" award, and Schwab won for "Maintaining a Focus on Consumer Needs." When being recognized by your peers, that's not bad company to keep.

Money Where Your Mouth Is

As Ken explains in his columns, it's one thing to write about investments and quite another to put your and others' money where your mouth (or pen) is. He's also said managing money is much harder than writing about it—which is why there are few investment newsletter writers that are successful at managing money. Yet, Ken has had good fortune doing both. During his 25 years as a *Forbes* columnist, he and his employees have built his firm, Fisher Investments, into arguably one of the largest independent and founder-run money management firm in the world. When 2009 ended, Fisher Investments was managing over $35 billion for institutional clients—large state pensions funds, major name corporations, sovereign nations, large endowments—and about 24,000 individual high-net-worth clients. *Investment Advisor* magazine called his firm in 2007, when it had only 18,000 clients, "the most successful RIA (registered investment advisor) in the universe."[3] Over the years in his columns, Ken has offered guidance on how to reach the *Forbes* 400 list of wealthiest Americans. His own firm's success landed him on the list for the first time in 2006—where he's remained since.

But Ken doesn't just write for *Forbes*. As of this writing, he's penned six books, three of which are *New York Times* best sellers. He also writes regular columns in Britain and in Germany's *Focus Money*. He has written or co-written more than a dozen published scholarly papers. And he has spoken all over the world. But his prime venue for public expression—and he has been very clear about this—has always been his monthly *Forbes* column. Ken has said there is simply no venue like it anywhere, combining wide readership, high credibility, consistency over time, and an organization that's easy to work with. Every month Ken comes back to his roots to focus on what he wants *Forbes* readers to read next month—but that he is also willing to have them look back on one, 10, and even 25 years later.

Evolution of the Guru

As you read Ken's columns, you'll undoubtedly notice a number of changes in Ken's writing and investing style over the years. When Ken started writing for *Forbes* in 1984, he was focused almost exclusively on small US firms. Today, Ken's focus is global and has been for many years. Ken no longer subscribes to some of the advice he offered in his earlier columns, at least not as steadfastly as he once did. He's simply adapted to the times and evolved as an investor. Even so, Ken is a firm believer that capital markets don't fundamentally change over time. The mechanics of investing might be different—folks rarely exchange physical stock certificates anymore, trades can be executed in fractions of seconds, information is available with the click of a mouse, myriad new investment products are offered now that weren't dreamt of decades ago. But investors still invest for the same reason they always have. Firms raise capital for the same purposes. Basic economic principles haven't been altered by time. So even though some of Ken's views have changed and some center around then-topical issues, much of the wisdom contained in Ken's columns is timeless—as applicable today as it was when he wrote it.

Ken columns, from his first in July 1984 through 2009, are reprinted in this book just as he wrote them, save one feature—Ken's stock picks. When Ken has been outright bearish, he advised avoiding stocks, so his columns don't include any individual stock recommendations. When he's bullish, he typically offers three or four (sometimes less, sometimes way more) in his monthly column. The individual stock picks have been removed, unless they were central to the column's message. Why? First, it would nearly double the length of the book. But more important, a stock pick with a price 20 years old is virtually meaningless. Heck, a two-year-old stock pick might be meaningless. The stocks he mentioned may have split, had subsequent offerings, gone bankrupt, or been acquired. In the interest of getting all of Ken's higher-level commentary on markets, I decided to take out what is really, after all these years, the least important part of his commentary. You won't miss the stock picks. And if you do, you can find his columns since 1997, in full, online at www.forbes.com/fisher. And, the stock picks since 1984 are listed at www.makingmarketguru.com.

Plus, stock picks do not a portfolio make. Ken makes that point, repeatedly, in his columns. A portfolio should never be a loose conglomeration of stock picks. A well-crafted portfolio should be driven by your individual long-term goals, return expectations, and cash-flow needs.

And, as the years have worn on, Ken has become more decidedly top-down—focused on the higher-level factors affecting stocks more than individual stock nuances. Ken's stock picks have become more examples of higher-level themes he's highlighting. If he's writing about rising energy prices, he's likely to recommend several Energy stocks. If it's foreign commentary, his stock picks are likely overseas. You get the picture.

A Road Map to 25 Years

Can you remember what you were doing 25 years ago? How about 10 years ago? I sure can't. So preceding Ken's columns each year are a few pages of commentary. The goal was to provide some context for Ken's columns, highlight some of his notable market calls—both good and bad—point out areas where his perspective has changed over the years, and sprinkle in tidbits about Ken and his investing philosophy that deserve extra attention or insight.

I've included some other comments for you in the columns themselves—to underscore some material call Ken got right as well as some he got wrong. Or maybe I'm just noting an area where Ken has evolved or would evolve. And sometimes, my comments relate to something investors today should keep in mind.

Compiling this book at the end of 2009 and into 2010, in the wake of one of the largest recessions and bear markets in history, has provided me invaluable perspective. As Ken points out in his December 14, 2009, column, "The Old Normal"—the final column of 2009 and of this book—the fears investors face this time around are scarcely different from those faced during many of Ken's 25 years writing for *Forbes*. Somehow, folks think the world is a different place today. It is in some ways, but our short memories have many believing the future will be far different from the past. It won't. Case in point, the past 10 years—bookended by two steep bear markets—have been awful for stocks. From 1999 through 2009, the S&P 500 posted slightly negative returns. But over the entire 25 years Ken has been writing in *Forbes*, the S&P's average annual return is about 10 percent—almost exactly the long-term average. With time, the more things change, the more they stay the same—at least when it comes to investing.

Seeing history through the eyes of a market guru has been illuminating and fascinating for me. I hope it is for you too.

1984

A Not So Orwellian Year

> "
> *I specialize in out-of-favor small cap growth companies, which*
> *means, by definition, ones with problems. They can be good buys if*
> *those problems can be solved.* "
>
> "Cherchez the Sales Rep," July 16, 1984

> "
> *The uncanny degree to which successful intermediate- to long-term*
> *performers come from the ranks of low PSR [price-to-sales ratio] stocks*
> *bothers some investors because it seems to have nothing to do with*
> *earnings, which everyone has been trained to accept as the driving*
> *force behind a stock's price.* "
>
> "Why Glamour Doesn't Pay," August 13, 1984

Nineteen-eighty-four was quite a year. Fortunately, it didn't involve nearly as much government oppression or book burning as George Orwell's *1984* foretold, but it was eventful nonetheless. Ronald Reagan trounced Walter Mondale to secure his second term as president, the Cold War was in full swing, the Olympics were in Los Angeles sans the Russians and many of their comrades, and Larry Bird's Boston Celtics defeated Magic Johnson's Los Angeles Lakers to win the NBA finals. Heck, Michael Jackson's hair even burst into flames in a Pepsi ad (he also won a record eight Grammys that year, so it wasn't a total loss for the King of Pop). And a relative newcomer, managing just $60 million, started writing for *Forbes* magazine.

From an investing standpoint, 1984 was a bit of a bore. In the US, the S&P 500 was up a paltry 6.3 percent.[1] Foreign stocks rose only slightly more, just 7.9 percent—both well below their long-term averages.[2] 1984 oil prices were still elevated relatively, but were trending down from their 1980 peak. And you could still buy a US government bond with a double-digit yield—though those too were falling. In some ways, Ken Fisher's first "Growth Stocks" column published in *Forbes'* July 16 edition came at a rather inauspicious time.

Longtime readers of Ken's *Forbes* columns might sense a typo. Ken's popular "Portfolio Strategy" column was originally titled "Growth Stocks." The new title didn't come about until years later. The eventual name change reflected several interesting evolutions in Ken's writing and investing philosophies over the past two-and-a-half decades. You see, in 1984 and for years thereafter, Ken's focus was on a much narrower universe of stocks than his global view today. His specialty at the time was beaten-up, small domestic companies. Very soon, Ken would be instrumental in defining what is now known as the "small cap value" universe—a major investing category today, but not yet well-defined in 1984. So "Growth Stocks" was a bit of a misnomer since Ken wasn't looking for growth companies—what he sought was value.

To identify out-of-favor companies, Ken did something fairly radical. While most investors then (and even now) focused on the price-to-earnings (P/E) ratio, he saw that P/E ratios could be misleading. Temporary conditions like management slipups or a spike in input costs can weigh on earnings. That causes the P/E ratio to jump, raising red flags to investors fixated on P/Es. These firms' stock prices often suffer as a result.

But as long as sales remain stable, those temporary problems can be fixed, potentially leading to outsized returns in the future. So Ken focused instead on a stock's price relative to its sales—calling it the price-to-sales ratio (PSR). Low PSRs often identify companies with solid sales, but brutalized earnings. Ken saw that sometimes a firm with very low or even *no* earnings (therefore a high P/E stock) could be hugely profitable. Once the problems were fixed, an explosion in earnings could drive stock prices sky-high. The key was finding them before that happened. As he puts it, "They [PSRs] are an almost perfect measure of unpopularity, whereas low P/E multiples aren't always so (an unpopular stock with a temporary low earnings usually sells at a high price/earnings ratio)." ("Why Glamour Doesn't Pay," August 13, 1984.)

Today, PSRs are a widely used analytical tool, but back then, they were unheard of. The PSR is an early example of what Ken refers to as "capital markets technology," or tools he and his employees at Fisher Investments develop to analyze stocks and the stock market differently from other investors and analysts. Ken and his firm have come up with many such tools throughout the years, several of which Ken has written about in *Forbes* and will be highlighted in this tome.

It was Ken's long and heavy earlier research into PSRs that was the backbone of his first book, 1984's bestselling stock market book, *Super Stocks*. And it was very much *Super Stocks* that caused long-term *Forbes* editor James Walker Michaels (who edited *Forbes* from 1957 to 1999)—the then-dean of American business journalism—to give Ken a shot at doing a column. Michaels loved the PSR and gave *Super Stocks* the following endorsement: "Ken Fisher has produced the first worthwhile new investment ideas in years."

But PSRs alone can't identify great stocks. Ken references a number of other factors that make firms and their stocks successful. Two attributes Ken highlights in his 1984 columns: Strong marketing and high relative market share. Ken emphasizes the importance on marketing in his first-ever column, "Cherchez the Sales Rep." (July 16, 1984.) Neat new products aren't worth a lick if customers don't need or want them. As he puts it, "The prizes usually go to the company that finds a need and fills it." High relative market share is important because it allows a company to spread costs out over more products, so "a company with a high relative market share will usually be the low-cost producer." ("High-Tech Checklist," September 10, 1984.) That can mean better profit margins and the ability to weather difficult times. As you'll read, these are just a few attributes distinguishing good investments from bad Ken points out in his inaugural year—1984.

Incidentally, Ken's initial July 1984 column was thought of (by him, at least) as a one-time-only event. His first five columns too—Ken had no inkling he'd be a regular columnist. It wasn't until the December issue that Jim Michaels gave Ken an ongoing monthly production schedule—which has continued ever since.

Ken and Jim became increasingly close over the years—particularly after 2000 when Jim stepped down as editor. Ken introduced Jim to one of his major hobbies—California coastal redwoods—taking Jim on a few tours. With their spouses they visited the Scottish highlands and enjoyed martinis late into the night. But it all started in 1984.

Cherchez the Sales Rep

July 16, 1984

Most investors make a big mistake when investing in small growth companies. They get intrigued with technology. What a hot little gadget those guys have! It's not the hot gadget that puts small companies over the top but hot marketing. The prizes usually go to the company that finds a need and fills it.

The odds are much against an outfit that goes the other way, inventing a product and then trying to find a market for it. Take Lynch Communications, which dropped a bundle and whose stock plunged, when it had to write off its Atlas answering service product. Atlas was state of the art—a terrific gadget. But the customers couldn't finance it, which Lynch didn't find out until it was too late. Lynch put too little emphasis on market research; it lacked and lacks dedicated top-notch marketing savvy.

I specialize in out-of-favor small growth companies, which means, by definition, ones with problems. They can be good buys if those problems can be solved. If a troubled company is strong on marketing, it is a good bet to solve its problems, and its stock will almost certainly come back. So I like companies run by a top-notch marketing person, or companies with one close to the boss' elbow and ear.

Recent research done at Stanford University by Modesto Maidique and Billie Jo Zirger shows the importance of marketing. Among electronics executives they surveyed, marketing was cited over technology and research by a margin of 10-to-1 as the prime factor in success.

Okay, but how do you research marketing prowess? It's not something the standard stock services cover. One way is by getting out and talking with sales representatives. Sales reps are out on the firing line and in the trenches. At trade conferences you can meet reps from most companies (check out upcoming events in trade journals). They are very friendly and like to talk.

You can ask about things like how their competitors' reps (perhaps the company you are interested in) are compensated. Do they use their own sales force or independent reps? Sophisticated big-ticket products usually do best with a dedicated, in-house sales force. Ask how long their typical rep has been with them, ask about his prior job, his next job, how he gets his leads, how he qualifies prospects, how long it takes to close a sale and on and on.

Indirectly, you can learn his attitude toward his superiors. Few firms thrive without an upbeat attitude about management. Does management listen to the reps? After all, reps have customer contact and thereby the market's pulse. ∎

The Vital Importance of Marketing and Sales

In this column, Ken emphasizes the importance of having a great sales and marketing operation for any firm. It's a theme that appears throughout his writings—including some of his later books, like 2008's *The Ten Roads to Riches*.

Why Glamour Doesn't Pay
August 13, 1984

When most folks think about buying West Coast stocks they think of Silicon Valley. I have news for them. Most of California's recent big winners bear such non-high-tech names as Marathon Office Supply, Chesapeake Industries and RV Weatherford.

Table 1.1 lists the ten top-performing California stocks of 1983 (with sales over $10 million). Only three are high tech, and even they aren't exactly household names. With price increases ranging from 213% to 1,100%, these stellar performers defied most conventional means of identification.

What did these star performers have in common? Not low price/earnings ratios. As a matter of fact, most of them had no earnings at all. The list doesn't show it, but only one paid a dividend. Likewise, you couldn't identify this group based on a percentage of book value—it just wouldn't work. In short, you couldn't have picked them on any of the more popular measures of value.

What they did have in common is what I call low price/sales ratios (PSR). That is, they were stocks where the total market capitalization was a small proportion of annual revenues. (To figure the PSR simply multiply the stock price by the number of shares outstanding and then express the resulting sum as a percentage of revenues. Thus a company whose market capitalization was $100 million and revenues were $200 million would have a PSR of 0.5.) It's just like a P/E ratio but uses total sales instead of earnings. Note in the table that of last year's big California winners all but one started the year with a PSR of 1.0 or less—usually much less.

The uncanny degree to which successful intermediate- to long-term performers come from the ranks of low PSR stocks bothers some investors because it seems to have nothing to do with earnings, which everyone has been trained to accept as the driving force behind a stock's price.

TABLE 1.1   The Top Ten

Rank	Company	Price (1/1/83)	1983 Gain	Sales* ($ millions)	PSR (1/1/83)	P/E Ratio (1/1/83)
1	Marathon Office	$0.50	1,100%	$21.5	0.04	d
2	Chesapeake Industries	$0.38	833%	$15.4	0.06	d
3	RV Weatherford	$1.29	636%	$43.6	0.05	d
4	Marshall Industries	$5.94	435%	$118.0	0.18	d
5	First Lincoln Financial	$4.12	367%	$94.8	0.10	d
6	Wherehouse Entertainment	$3.63	348%	$83.4	0.17	16
7	Anthem Electronics	$8.59	255%	$38.7	0.79	23
8	International Rectifier	$5.19	247%	$119.2	0.25	d
9	SYM-TEK Systems	$5.00	215%	$12.4	0.48	9
10	Servamatic Systems	$1.06	218%	$18.5	1.48	d

* Fiscal 1982   d: deficit

Ken Fisher. "Why Glamour Doesn't Pay." Forbes. August, 13, 1984

As David Dreman has repeatedly pointed out, the fact that a company is poorly regarded now doesn't mean it will be later. That's why u n p o p u l a r stocks frequently out- p e r f o r m popular stocks, and that's why low PSRs work so well: They are an almost perfect measure of unpopularity, whereas low P/E multiples aren't always so (an unpopular stock with temporarily low earnings usually sells at a high price/earnings ratio). Simply put, unpopular stocks of good companies perform well.

Whether in California or in Michigan, whether among big companies or small, whether among high tech, low tech or no tech, big winners tend to come from among the ranks of low-price/sales-ratio stocks. My research, contradicting what most people would expect, shows that this has been true for generations—all the way back to the 1920s and 1930s.

What is a high PSR and what is not? Looking at California's 1983 winners, six out of the ten sold at prices valuing whole companies for less than 20% of their annual revenues. Only two sold for more than 75% of sales.

By the same token, the top five performing stocks of the Dow in 1983 all had PSRs below 0.20. In 1983 the low PSR quartile of the DJI increased 56.1%, vs. 28.7% for the low-P/E quartile, and 20.3% for the DJI as a whole.

Of course, low PSRs alone won't guarantee success. You still need to sort quality from garbage. ∎

High-Tech Checklist
September 10, 1984

From my mail and telephone calls I gather my recent columns confused some readers. I stressed the relative unimportance of technology when it comes to investing in small companies and then proceeded to recommend some small technology companies. Later I crisscrossed again, showing that many of the best buys aren't high tech.

I wasn't arguing against high-tech stocks; indeed, they are my specialty. My point was simply this: Leading-edge technology is not critical to successful investing. Certainly *appropriate* technology is needed; you can't sell buggy whips. But the really critical factors are not technological. The critical factors are a low stock price and good marketing.

One risk-reducing marketing-oriented sign to look for is high relative market share. It helps, too, if there are no heavyweights trying to muscle in to the market. The champ is a lot safer when up against lightweight competition, and so are you. It's about as close to monopoly power as society allows.

Investors often get this backward, buying low-market share and figuring the company has nowhere to go but up. It's possible, but it's a risky strategy. A company with high relative market share will usually be the low-cost producer, because it spreads its costs over many more units, and being the low-cost producer is a big advantage. In tough times it can drop its prices lower than the competition and still make money.

High relative market share also provides selling economies in advertising and public relations, since you have more units to spread your cost over. In strategic planning the big guy can afford more gray matter—like market and feasibility studies by outside consultants. You can maintain your own sales force instead of relying on independent sales representatives, who may cover many other different lines or be hard to control.

Of course, high relative share doesn't guarantee success. General Motors and US Steel are classic examples where management squandered the advantages of its market dominance. But in General Motors' case, at least, that huge market share enabled the company to remain strong, in spite of decades of management mistakes. ■

The Lion and the Mouse
October 8, 1984

"You make the most money with the least risk in small, well-managed companies aimed at big, fast-growing markets." Right? Wrong. Long-term risk/reward is maximized by investing in companies aimed at markets appropriate to their size. Small companies should address small markets. Big companies should address big markets. Rarely should the two meet.

I began to get a feel for size segmentation, an important and often misunderstood marketing issue, some time ago. I was probably the only kid on the block eager for bed. My old man told great bedtime stories. My favorite was the lion and the mouse. Remember? The lion gets caught in a trapper's snare. At first he wants to eat the bait that had lured him, the mouse. But slowly, persistently, the mouse chews through the trap to set the big guy free. They become fast friends. Everybody has his place in life.

Thus, it's no surprise that when the huge microcomputer market developed, the likes of Texas Instruments, Hewlett-Packard and Digital Equipment jumped in. As $4 billion giants, they need $400 million of growth to increase their size by 10%. But it was IBM, the giant of them all, that made the biggest splash—and in the process covered lots of little guys with mud. Companies that were considered healthy microcomputer prospects only last year—Fortune Systems, Osborne, Vector Graphic, Victor Technologies and a host of other look-alikes—now look sick or crippled.

There are more casualties to come. Why? Small outfits like Apollo Computer and Compaq have a long fight ahead against IBM. And the giant also-rans like DEC, H-P, and Texas Instruments show no signs of fatigue. As the market matures, rest assured that those champion nonpioneers, the Japanese, will show up.

Huge companies rarely address small markets, and do poorly when they do, because they can't afford to waste their best brains on them. Will a big outfit send its stars into a small market where, at best, they might get a 30% market share? No way!

Can they justify price-warring their way into markets dominated by entrepreneurs who are close to the customer? Can a lion hunt for mice the way a cat can? Why should it bother with mice at all?

Enter the smaller company, which can put its top people on the smaller market and get meaningful results—partly because it runs into few large competitors, and partly because the few giants it encounters usually do poorly and lose interest.

The same is true of the dreaded Japanese, who do great in big markets like steel, autos, TVs and the like, but poorly in small markets—particularly where there is a lot of sophistication to the selling process or where service support is required. Consider the small laser market, which is made up of a number of niches based on different technologies. The Japanese have coveted lasers for years without success. The US is a major and growing net exporter of lasers to Japan.

I ran a company supplying these markets. I loved the very names of the products—Argon, CO_2, diode, eximer, HeNe and, my favorite, yttrium aluminum garnet (YAG) lasers. The only things missing were Buck Rogers and large markets. At first the markets were so puny that people said lasers were "solutions looking for problems to solve."

Slowly the growing markets became dominated by a few independents like Spectra-Physics, Coherent and Control Laser. The few big firms in the business, such as Raytheon, have not done well. Recently, giant Allied Corp. made a big push into lasers, but Edward Hennessey's troops have precious little to show for the effort.

So remember the lion and the mouse. Stick to companies that address growing markets, but markets appropriate to their size. ■

Blind Pessimism
November 5, 1984

There is a good chance that Ronald Reagan will be reelected and that the Republicans will retain Senate control. If so, Reagan will be the first second-term President since Truman to have a house of Congress controlled by his own party. Most second-term presidents have faced hostile legislatures.

Why is this important? A second-term president doesn't suffer the short-term political pressures faced by one seeking reelection. Thus he can afford to prescribe sound but unpopular "medicine." But he can do so only if Congress will go along. A second-term president with at least one house held by his party can do more than a president confronted by two hostile houses. We have had 2½ two-term presidents in the postwar era—Truman,

Eisenhower and Nixon (the half). Only Truman was in a strong position to counter second-term opposition stonewalling from Congress. Reagan, reelected and supported by at least a Republican Senate, could make enough local interest deals with Democratic House members to pass lots of controversial legislation. Reagan could afford to trade short-term popularity for a long-term viewpoint—to ensure his good treatment by historians.

There are several simple and logical actions that together could balance the budget and reduce governmental spending as a percentage of GNP. Putting public and private employee retirement systems on comparable terms would be one. Simplifying regulation would be another: Why should state and federal watchdogs cover the same territory in so many areas, ranging from income taxation to securities regulation? Recent presidents haven't been free from reelection worries to take on this kind of thing. But that's the kind of fight Reagan loves.

Interest on the federal debt is two-thirds the federal deficit and is greater than the combination of the deficit and the municipal surpluses. Reagan could slash interest expense by offering lower-coupon, gold-backed Treasury bonds, or inflation-adjusted bonds tied to the CPI.

In short, a Reagan second term with a malleable Congress could change the economic and social picture—and very much for the better. It could take us from an atmosphere that has been hostile to capital and to equities into one that could be extremely bullish. But the market remains gloomy.

We have a whole generation of investment pros who are too skeptical. They can't see potential progress. Most institutional investors are more like bureaucrats than investors. It isn't their money. They mostly want to preserve their jobs. To them, safety is success.

They are conditioned by 30 years of one-termers and Democratic domination. They can't believe anything else is possible. Talking with these guys can be a nightmare.

Mention any topic and they can show you a potential disaster in the making. Their predisposition to safety lets them rationalize pessimism into anything.

The Republicans will probably keep the Senate. They lead by six now. There are only eight vulnerable Republican senators—in Illinois, Iowa, Minnesota, Mississippi, New Hampshire, North Carolina, Tennessee and Texas. But the Democrats have a few up for grabs, too. Yet, a front-page *Wall Street Journal* feature (August 22) echoed what's commonly heard on The Street by headlining: "If Reelected, Reagan Might Find Problems Tougher Than in 1981—Political Climate, Moreover Could Be Even Harsher." Among the investment pros I know, 90% agree.

With institutionalized skepticism so thick, any good news on the federal spending front from a president freed of short-term constraints is apt to catch the investment pros by surprise, pushing up stocks in a longer and more violent buying spree than the August 1982 or 1984 rallies. I wouldn't be surprised to see the DJI at 2200 by 1989. That would still leave it at levels consistent with the long-term past, about 12 times earnings and 1.5 times book value. Moderately priced growth issues could rise more. ∎

How to Cash In on Whizzers
December 3, 1984

You are on vacation in California and notice that strawberry-coated whizzers are all they rage—kids are lining up for them everywhere. But back home in Peoria, they are unknown. Returning from vacation, you quit the factory and start up the state's first whizzer stand. If you are aggressive, you might dot the whole Midwest market with whizzer stands before any big competitor gets a whiff of what you are up to.

By the time competition shows up, you have lots of hard-to-overcome advantages. For instance, on the basis of market share in your region, you can amortize the cost of regional advertising over your various stands. The latest whizz to come along can't. You are on local radio and in the regional newspapers and magazines. Smaller competition isn't. By capitalizing on your early start you have made yourself the whizzer king of the Midwest and are well on your way to joining the *Forbes* 400.

Since you are buying for all your stores, you can get freight-rate breaks, based on volume and central warehousing, that a Johnny-come-lately can't afford. So your costs per unit are lower. Operating in this mode, you get many of the advantages of a national firm without losing the human touch of being local. By the time you have lost that local touch, you are big enough to cash in your chips and head for Hawaii.

This principle is inherent in any new idea—you don't need to be first, only first in your region. After Colonel Sanders proved that folks would buy fast-food chicken in Kentucky, S. Truett Cathy exploded out of Atlanta with Chick-Fil-A restaurants and his boneless fried chicken sandwich. Cathy has built 280 outlets in 31 states—and a fortune to boot. But he still concentrates heavily in the Southeast. Even with the big three fast-fooders (Burger King, McDonald's and Wendy's) now in the chicken business, Cathy holds his own with his strong regional base. The big national chains don't have that many advantages over a regional giant. Wendy's decided to go into the chicken business, but its national status hasn't helped much. Its Sisters Chicken & Biscuit chain has struggled up to 49 outlets and is still losing money.

Sometimes the big guys simply overlook fertile markets. For example, Seattle-based Nordstrom pyramided an unexciting shoe business into a major regional retailing chain with a national reputation because it was good, but also because the national chains hadn't exploited the Pacific Northwest the way they could or should have. By the time the nationals caught on, Nordstrom was king of the mountain. Along the way, its stock increased fivefold in value.

While retailing is one prevalent place for regional segmentation, there are lots of others. Regional focus is fundamental to cost-conscious commodity producers, particularly those with heavy, freight-intensive products. Cement producers, burdened by the need to truck wet cement to remote building sites, have always marketed locally. Inland steel producers, far from water, have been relatively protected from the full brunt of cheap foreign steel. And even low-cost steel producers such as Nucor and Chaparral (50% owned by regional cement producer Texas Industries) carefully operate along regional lines to maximize profits.

Hotel, restaurant and supermarket chains, along with distributors, insurance companies and airlines, are just a few of the areas in which regional segmentation has paid off as a means for little guys to build up good-size businesses without suffering at the hands of bigger, more powerful national competition.

Investing in regional segmentation offers additional advantages for individual investors. You can check them out at home. What are the kids lining up for in your area? What burgeoning local products have you been buying that didn't exist five years ago? No New York-based security analyst is likely to beat you to such bargains.

A nifty tool for checking out regional up-and-comers is Ward's Directory. It's great, available in many libraries, and yet, like most good things, it's largely unknown on Wall Street. Ward's spotlights the 55,000 largest US corporations—public and private—by ZIP code. It shows the location, phone number, corporate sales and number of employees, as well as whether the stock is publicly traded. By looking at several years' editions, you can spot unknown emerging companies in your own backyard—or anyone else's. ∎

Ward No More

Of course, Ward's is long gone now, replaced by myriad superfast online directories and search tools. But the idea is the same: You can use publicly available information to spot advantages others haven't thought of yet—if you know how.

Big Bloopers of 1984

December 31, 1984

Nineteen-eighty-four was not a banner year in the stock market but it was an exceptional year for me—exceptionally bad, my worst yet. But one learns from mistakes. So, here goes a dearly learned lesson:

My biggest bloopers were: Charter Co., a $12-to-$2 nosediver; Storage Technology plunged 50% before I sold out; System Industries dropped sharply from $9 to $3.

Charter and Storage Technology both went into Chapter 11. While System Industries didn't, it came close. What happened? How can future repeats be avoided?

Charter came first. I was bewildered at its sudden crash to bankruptcy. Sure, it was leveraged and troubled, but management seemingly understood the problems. The company had sufficient finances (just barely) to buy enough time to sell or close the unprofitable oil refineries and insurance businesses (beclouded by the Baldwin-United debacle) and to push its large, profitable oil marketing operations.

The bankruptcy was announced on Friday, April 20. I was stunned. Shorting sharpshooter Alan Gaines, of Gaines & Berland, had been screaming for months that Charter was a goner. I laughed, but he laughed last. Yet the suddenness surprised even him. Only 58 days earlier, accounting giant Peat Marwick signed audited financials showing stockholders' equity making up 34% of total assets, and a current assets-to-liability ratio of 1.1—not great, but hardly immediate bankruptcy material.

I spent the next weekend reviewing the prior decade's bankruptcies. With the exception of the freakish Johns-Manville case, I couldn't find a single bankruptcy coming on the heels of such strong financials. By past standards Charter should not have gone bankrupt. Often companies were allowed to have current liabilities exceeding current assets—and still the banks kept them alive. But not Charter. Why?

Media attention, for one thing. The *Wall Street Journal* vigorously pursued negative news on Charter. This negative press seemingly created a flood of Charter insurance policy redemptions, generating deteriorating financials, creating still more bad news, which the *Journal* printed. Finally, citing these articles, Charter's oil trade creditors suddenly became unwilling to continue extending credit. Chapter 11 was the only choice.

There is a pattern to a stock's action prior to bankruptcy. For months the stock moves slowly lower. Then one day a not too significant announcement will drop the stock about 30% to 50% within the day. At that point, caution is preferable to courage. A few days or weeks later comes the bankruptcy announcement, which tumbles the stock one more 30%-to-50% notch. From there it goes nowhere for months or maybe years. Charter, for instance, has traded between 1½ and 2½ since April, having been at 11 only weeks before bankruptcy.

Storage Technology also got negative press every time it sneezed. It, too, had financials superior to historic bankruptcies. Again, bankruptcy descended from out of the blue. When larger than expected third-quarter losses toppled Storage Tech from 9 to 6 in one day, I recognized the pattern and sold out. A few weeks later the bankruptcy came, and Storage was at 2½.

System Industries just escaped bankruptcy. Being smaller and more obscure, it never much attracted the media's gaze. When this computer-memory manufacturer's financials slowly deteriorated, its bankers, Chase Manhattan and BankAmerica, became increasingly nervous. But this time the board of directors moved in advance of Chapter 11, replaced the chief executive and, to calm the bankers, raised capital at distressed prices.

Bankers, disturbed over mounting loan losses, increasingly are nervous and won't renew credit for troubled companies the way they once did. When that happens, companies must seek Chapter 11 protection. There has not been such a sustained gush of bankruptcies since the 1930s. What is interesting is that this is happening during prosperity. Why? As I mentioned, media attention has something to do with it, speeding up the process.

What I learned from my mistakes was that in this new world of nervous bankers and eager journalists, the threshold of bankruptcy is much narrower than it formerly was. Balance sheet tolerances must be tighter than before. Companies don't go bankrupt unless they have a lot of debt. I also learned to steer away from troubled companies where the troubles make good press. ■

1985

A 30% Yawner

" *Most of the mistakes I have made in my career have come from trying to tackle something too complicated. The successes have all been simple and well within my grasp.* "

"Don't Be Too Smart for Your Own Good," July 1, 1985

" *Here is the key to why stocks have done better than other investments through the decades. As the world changes, gold doesn't change, bonds don't change, real estate changes hardly at all. But a company can and must evolve, little bits at a time, year to year, forever—or die. If it can evolve to conform to a changing world, it will prosper and grow. The more successfully it evolves, the faster it grows.* "

"Emulating America's Richest," October 28, 1985

Almost a mirror image of 1984, 1985 was a humdrum year with stellar stock market returns. Sure, 1985 saw the Plaza Accord signed by the US, UK, France, West Germany, and Japan to stem the rise in the US dollar. Microsoft released Windows 1.0. And New Coke launched, then thudded. But global events were generally mundane—except stocks. Stocks like boring because it means there's less for investors to worry about—as evidenced by this boring year with a big 31.7 percent S&P 500 return.[1] Even those outsized gains were bested by foreign shares—rising 56.7 percent.[2] That made one of Ken's main 1985 themes fitting: Keep investing simple.

In Ken's view, as shown this year, investing needn't be complicated. In fact, the more complicated you make it, the worse the results can be. Too often, investors are drawn to high-flying stocks or unnecessarily complex strategies. Whether it's individual stocks or whole stock categories, the flashy ones rarely turn out to be long-term winners. In "Half Buck Bargains" (November 4, 1985) Ken illustrated this with an analogy between book buying and investing: "I have trained my eye to bypass the bright, colorful spines, preferring the drab, often discolored ones that most folks never notice. . . . Just as I have found the best books misclassified and overlooked, so are the best stocks found."

The same applies to investing strategies. "Wall Street is full of supposed shortcuts that really end up giving your wallet a wallop. . . . If you don't understand it cold, forget it. If it sounds complicated, circuitous or the least bit fast-buckish, forget it. Let some other sucker tackle it and learn the hard way." ("Don't Be Too Smart for Your Own Good," July 1, 1985.)

Ken's 1985 columns also hint at a big difference in the way stock research was done compared to today. Most importantly, the Internet didn't exist then as it does now. Prodigious amounts of information are now just a mouse click away. Back then, things weren't so simple. Getting timely information on stocks really required some work, especially the small stocks Ken favored. But if you were good at finding—and understanding—information, it could be hugely profitable. That hasn't changed. Today, it's more about weeding out the noise, whereas then, it was about just finding the info.

And the dearth of readily available information about small, sometimes obscure companies resulted in myriad market inefficiencies to exploit. Dedicated analysts could sometimes uncover information that wasn't widely digested by other investors and, thus, not reflected in stocks' prices. This wasn't necessarily true for the biggest stocks, which were covered by scads of Wall Street analysts. However, it was certainly true for the universe of small stocks Ken favored then, before he broadened his purview. Instead of focusing nearly exclusively on small US firms as he did in the mid-1980s, he now invests globally, and has for over two decades.

You'll undoubtedly notice in 1985 Ken recommended researching stocks at the local library. Libraries might seem antiquated now, when waiting more than a few seconds for information seems too long. Ironically, the San Francisco Business Library Ken had used for over a decade and referenced in columns has been shuttered—it exists no more. Yet libraries are still great places to get tons of information about stocks and the stock market. In "Gifts of the Gurus" (June 3, 1985), Ken recommends several of his favorite books. Many of these were decades old when Ken wrote the column, but the wisdom therein is timeless. Ask Ken what investing books he finds most useful today, and virtually all those he recommended then will still be at the top of his list.

In a prelude to his own 2008 book (and *New York Times* best seller) *The Ten Roads to Riches: The Ways the Wealthy Got There (And How You Can Too!)*, "Emulating America's Richest" (October 28, 1985) offers some advice on build-ing mega-wealth and getting on the *Forbes* 400 list of America's richest. As you'll read in "Pipe Dreams" (October 27, 1985), Ken didn't believe he'd ever make the list himself, nor did he care to. "I don't ever really want to be that rich. I have other values that touch my life besides money," he wrote. Apparently, Ken's wealth-building tips were better than even he expected, eventually landing him on the *Forbes* 400 list for the first time in 2006, and he's repeated every year since. Though, as Ken stated in that 2008 book, big wealth was never a goal, but instead the result of having done what he wanted to do—nothing more.

Big Companies, Fragile Stocks
January 28, 1985

Some folks are uncomfortable with the little, off-beat stocks I often recommend. They prefer big names, the ones synonymous with corporate America. Still, most of the same fundamental investment principles apply to both. The main difference? With so many professional analysts scrutinizing these big names and focusing on their all-sacred earnings' projections, there isn't much value added by detailed security analysis.

Forget all that juicy Wall Street gossip about these Goliaths. It's already in the stock prices. Instead, keep things simple and a bit more in the here and now. If you buy depressed, unpopular stocks with a lot of value, in time, prices will rise to match — even if short-term profitability isn't robust.

My favorite approach is buying financially strong companies selling at low price/sales ratios (a.k.a. PSRs — the price divided by revenue per share). Why? Because PSRs measure popularity almost perfectly. The best-performing stocks are the unpopular shares of good companies. Until PSRs started popping up in *Forbes* last year, the concept fell on virgin ears. Precious few have caught on, even now.

But Mark A. Byl and Michael J. Hill did. At Arizona State University's finance department they undertook a five-year PSR study using NYSE stocks. From a random list, annually they "bought" the 20% with the lowest PSRs. They totaled the results and applied standard academic mumbo jumbo to determine so-called risk-adjusted rates of return (total return adjusted for beta).

According to the efficient-market theorists who have dominated academia in recent years, the risk-adjusted return should be zero for any such random grouping. To their great surprise, Byl and Hill found risk-adjusted returns of 3.8% per quarter on their low-PSR stocks. According to their statistical processes, there was less than a 5% probability that this could have been a result of chance.

Most folks can't buy 100 stocks. They buy just a few. And there's the risk that some unpopular, low-PSR stocks could go broke, bringing down their overall results. So how does one pick out the right few? Easy. Buy only financially strong companies. Companies with strong balance sheets seldom go bankrupt. Here's a quick rule of thumb:

Take a stock's current ratio from the balance sheet (current assets divided by current liabilities) and divide it by 4. Then, divide shareholders' equity by total assets. Add these two numbers together. They should add up to at least 1 to indicate a strong balance sheet. If they total less than 0.80, it's a rather weak balance sheet.

Consider the 30 stocks in the Dow Jones industrials — America's old standards. By this measure, 12 have wimpy financials. They include (from weakest to strongest): International Harvester, American Express, Chevron, Sears, US Steel, Bethlehem Steel, Allied Corp., Westinghouse, American Can, Texaco, United Technologies and AT&T — which, as the strongest, sports a current ratio of only 1.55, with equity making up less than 40% of total assets.

What's more, many of the DJI stocks with the strongest balance sheets are priced too high. Merck and IBM, for instance, are financial fortresses but also sell at price/sales ratios above 1.5. Only a few stocks have ever rendered above-average, long-term results from such levels. It's best to avoid stocks of big companies if the PSR is above 0.80. The goal is to find them closer to 0.20. For comparison's sake, the DJI currently has an average PSR of 0.45.

TABLE 2.1 Low PSR Stocks—1985

Company	Recent Price	Price/Sale Ratio	Current Ratio	Equity/Assets	CR/4*
Goodyear	26	0.28	1.91	0.56	1.04
Woolworth	37	0.21	1.83	0.47	0.93
Union Carbide	37	0.29	1.84	0.51	0.97
General Foods	56	0.33	1.88	0.50	0.97
Owens-Illinois	40	0.35	1.86	0.48	0.95
Du Pont	49	0.33	1.79	0.46	0.91

*A stock's current assets divided by current liabilities, then divided by 4
Source: Disclosure II; Ken Fisher. "Big Companies, Fragile Stocks." *Forbes*. January 28, 1985.

There are only six stocks in the DJI with strong balance sheets and low PSRs. They are listed in Table 2.1.

These are all strong companies. Goodyear and Owens-Illinois are classic examples of high relative market share, which is so important (see my September 10, 1984 column). General Foods and Du Pont are synonyomous with quality. Is Woolworth really worse than highly leveraged but more popular and pricey Sears? Don't play the "What-are-next-quarter's-earnings?" game. Take a long-range focus on value. Buying the unpopular stocks of good, financially strong companies pays better and runs less risk than buying popular glamour issues or financially shaky cripples. ■

Pint-Size Powerhouses
February 25, 1985

Institutional investors have all the advantages. Right? Wrong! Why? Simply put, the institutions can't touch most of the stocks available to the little guy.

Consider the world of stocks according to their market capitalizations (market cap equals stock price times total shares outstanding) Small cap companies greatly outnumber large ones. The market values more than two-thirds of the country's actively traded companies at less than $15 million. After all, everyone can't be IBM. So what?

The institutions can invest only in the bigger cap stocks. Why? Liquidity. Institutional managers tend to avoid stocks whose market caps are less than the amount of money they manage. Suppose I am some smallish institutional yo-yo, perhaps one managing $150 million for "Sillycorp." Take a stock the market values at $150 million. If I buy $1.5 million worth, I own 1 % of the company. If the stock fizzles, I may have too much to get out without disrupting the market. So I don't buy more to avoid illiquidity.

To fill my portfolio, I would need 100 such stocks. It's hard to manage so many. If I buy stocks with market capitalizations of only $15 million, I would need 1,000 to fill my portfolio, clearly a managerial nightmare. So I would stick to larger capitalization stocks. Almost all professional investment (a.k.a. institutional) interest is focused on stocks with market caps a good notch above $15 million.

As a finicky eater, I am uncomfortable in a restaurant with a limited menu. With a big menu, I almost always do fine. On the investment menu, most of the entrees are companies with market capitalizations too small to attract professional investment interest. The institutional guy is much disadvantaged. He has a tiny menu to choose from, compared with the little investor. In terms of liquidity, the small investor can buy stocks the big boys only dream about.

But most folks pass up this advantage. They think smaller capitalization stocks have more risk than do bigger ones. After all, don't the GMs and Du Ponts have a lot further to fall before going under than some obscure Peoria peanut? And, a la Continental Illinois and Chrysler, doesn't Uncle Sam bail out the big guys when they hit the wall? In my opinion, this is all wet. To me, Chrysler (with its carload of debt, a small market share and a bevy of big, tough foreign competitors) is riskier than a small, obscure no-name with little or no debt and a high market share in some small, hard-to-enter niche.

The point is to buy unpopular stocks of sound, well-financed and fundamentally strong companies—regardless of size. Slowly their quality will be seen by others, and their popularity will rise—and with it the stock price. Additionally, with small cap stocks, you can avoid the up-and-down volatility of the stocks that are subject to institutional stampedes in and out.

Look Out Below
March 25, 1985

It will pay readers well to read and reread *Forbes'* annual "Who's Where in the Stock Market" (January 14). It shows the top-performing stocks for the five years ended December 1984. What kind of stocks perform well? Take the top 25. Go back five years to January 1980—the beginning of the period. Calculate the 1980 price/sales ratio (PSR) of each. This is easy to do. Just take its January 1, 1980 price, multiply it by the total shares outstanding, then divide by the prior 12-months' revenues. The resulting figure tells you how many dollars or cents were paid in the stock market for each dollar in sales at that time.

The results of this exercise are eye-opening. The top-performing stocks all had extremely low PSRs; that is, you could have bought $1 worth of their sales quite cheaply at the start of the period. The highest 1980 PSR from among these winners was only 0.44. That is, its total stock market value was only 44% of its annual revenues. Nineteen of the top 25 started 1980 selling for less than 20% of revenues. Study after study points to the same conclusion: Precious few high-PSR stocks (for our purposes, above 1.0) ever offer above-average long-term performance.

Not only that, high-PSR stocks carry oodles of risk. At the peak of the technology bull market, the Hambrecht & Quist Technology index had an average PSR of 4.05—and you know the free-fall those stocks suffered. They fell because they were too richly priced. If a company is earning 5% after tax and selling at 80 times earnings, it has a PSR of 4.0 (4 times revenues).

PSRs measure popularity. "How much will the market pay for a dollar of sales of this company?" If it will pay a lot, it thinks well of the company; the stock is popular—rightly or wrongly. If the market won't pay much, it's unpopular. High-PSR stocks are already too popular and pricey to perform well, even if the companies do exceptionally well.

If investors did little other than weed the high-PSR future disasters out of their portfolios, their average performance would improve. ∎

Follow the Wino's Lead
April 22, 1985

Who has more continual access to tidy investment tidbits, stockbrokers or hobos? The hobos, it seems. As a kid I used to hang out in the San Francisco Business Library—just blocks from the brokers. All winter long the hobos and winos flooded in to keep warm, but there was rarely a broker in sight. For top investment results, try following the winos' lead.

From Seattle to Tampa, from Boston to Los Angeles, without doubt, there are better research facilities in any medium-size or larger city library than in most brokerage firms. Of course, you have to be willing to spend time and effort at it, but the information is there to make you an informed investor.

And it's free. Many folks are unfamiliar with the dandy tools they could use if only they would hang out with the winos and bums. I have never met an unhelpful librarian, so ask for aid. But, to get started, here are some of my favorite gizmos.

Standard & Poor's Corporation Records is a must. I couldn't last two days without it. Its seven huge volumes have a ton of basic knowledge on almost every publicly traded stock. When readers write for the address of some obscure stock I have mentioned, I do them a favor by insisting they learn how to look it up themselves in the *S&P's*. It might not have enough data for you to decide to buy a stock, but it often has enough to convince you to avoid one. *Standard & Poor's Stock Guide* gives you recent pricing information, including price/earnings ratios, dividends, yields, etc.

The F&S Index is the best-kept secret since the $64 question. It's like a customized reader's guide to everything in print about a company or industry. In minutes you can track down years of magazine and newspaper articles on a stock—and dig more deeply than most stock buyers and sellers ever take time for. It covers publications ranging from the big financial press to obscure industrial trade journals (available through interlibrary loan if your library doesn't carry them).

By the same publisher (God bless them) as the above is *Predicasts F&S Index of Corporate Change*. It will pilot you through years of organizational gyrations, such as joint ventures, bankruptcies, liquidations, reorganizations, name changes and subsidiary changes. For instance, I like the seemingly fruitless but at times rewarding search for bargains among bankrupt companies. That would be ever so much harder without this source. The *Wall Street Journal Index* covers what the *WSJ* has run by company, industry, topic or whatever. Pick a subject. Quick as a wink, you could check out anything they had printed—either on the subject or specific companies.

The Wall Street Transcript is a great source of what the Street is thinking, feeling and doing. It covers brokerage firm research reports, publishes text from newsletters, has regular interviews with a host of security analysts and money managers. Best of all, it indexes all mentions of stocks from previous issues. If a stock isn't here, it probably isn't in Wall Street's eye (and by contrarian logic might be a good buy). When a stock is mentioned, you can get a quick and dirty assessment of what the Street thinks of it.

Ward's Directory lists—by Zip Code—almost every corporation, so you can check them out regionally. There was a paragraph on *Ward's* in my December 3, 1984 column, but it is so useful, it's worth a second tout and more than a second of your time.

How would you feel about a stock where the insiders bailed out? The SEC's *Official Summary of Insider Transactions* gives a monthly breakdown on officers and directors who have been buying and selling their own stock. Do you need a quick scan on recent articles about a business, person or subject—maybe Texaco, John Templeton or tender offers? *The Business Index* from Information Access Corp. covers articles from over 800 publications.

There's too much at the library to do all of it justice here. Maybe you blow a boodle on newsletters. Try reading them at the library. Did you get 300 shares of American Widget when Uncle Morris died? Do you need its price on the date of his death for estate taxes? Try Standard & Poor's *Daily Stock Price Record*. You need to know about all the publications in a certain field, like chemical processing; you can learn about them from *Cahners*. ∎

Library Gems

It's hard to imagine a time when we didn't have massive amounts of data, instantly available, free, right on our desks. Or even on our mobile phones! But Ken Long has preached the importance of wading through all available information to discern the noise from the valuable news—it just used to take longer and required a library card.

Bankruptcy Bargains
May 22, 1985

There are investment bargains in bankruptcy. The problem is, most folks buy stocks before the firms go into bankruptcy. The trick is to wait until afterward.

Take *Charter Co.*, which went into bankruptcy last April and was $1 at year-end. By mid-February it was up 300%. You can't get results like that from IBM. Bankruptcy investors in Penn Central, Miller-Wohl or Toys "R" Us made fortunes. And those who bought Wickes, Saxon Industries or even Equity Funding didn't do too badly, either. This happens often because, like leprosy, most folks are so scared by the word "bankrupt" that panicky sellers push these stocks far too low.

Sure, it's risky. Fortunately, there are tricks to improve the odds. First, spread the risk. Diversify. Buy lots of different bankruptcies. Second, recognize the way the stocks trade. While they plummet in the months before bankruptcy and drop another 30% to 50% in the first few days of bankruptcy, after a few weeks the stocks usually go to sleep. They may drift slowly lower at year-end as individuals take tax losses.

If a company is actually going to die, the stock will keep drifting lower. But if the company is to survive with a new, reorganized future, it will take longer than anyone imagines, and the stock will stay adrift. Vulturous lawyers drag out the process at their pace—they are being paid by the hour. No one speeds it up. So you need patience. There's lots of time. Let the months go by to see if the stock stabilizes. Buying stocks that have been in bankruptcy for a year or more is safer than buying those that have just filed.

When first in Chapter 11, companies struggle, reshuffle management, write off assets, dodge the media, reassure scared customers, placate bankers and generally salvage whatever they can. Survival may become foreseeable after about 12 to 18 months. Someplace in there the stock may climb precipitously. It also may not.

What separates the wheat from the chaff? Cash flow and dilution. If there is enough cash flow so that creditors may be paid off slowly, even at some modest discount from full value, there won't be the need to create more shares. And then the stock almost always does well. Why? Creditors know that as the dust is settling on bankruptcies they often get a dime on the dollar. The possibility of getting at least a half-dollar encourages them to sit tight as management goes to work.

Most Wall Streeters focus on earnings. But, the key to bankruptcies is cash flow—earnings plus depreciation and amortization. In this game, the company with lots of producing assets is at a great advantage.

Another risk reducer is the company with profitable divisions. If a significant part of a company's business is profitable and the losses are confined to divisions that can be shut down, management's resurrection activities are much simpler.

Sometimes there are two chances for investors—one in bankruptcy and one right after bankruptcy. Again, like leprosy, bankruptcy's aura is so strong that it lingers after the event has passed, providing for after-the-fact bargains.

Often you can buy a preferred stock or bond that is convertible into common stock. This has been a traditional way to reduce risk while trading off only part of the upside potential. It works. Risk is reduced because, if the company is liquidated, the preferred comes before the common stock. But I often recommend the common; if the company can't be saved, usually there isn't much left for the preferred stock- or bond-holders, either.

Finally, don't pay too much. A typical industrial bankruptcy usually has a tiny total market capitalization (price times total shares outstanding)—less than 10% of its annual revenues. ∎

Gifts of the Gurus
June 3, 1985

Would you like to learn firsthand from the greatest investors of all time? It's easy. Read their books. My April 22 column covered the library as an investment research center. But some readers correctly noted that a library's main function is lending books—a fact I omitted. You can gain some great investment savvy from books, too.

Which books? Most say the same old stuff. But try these. They are my all-time favorites.

- *How to Buy Stocks* by Louis Engel (Bantam Books, 1953). This is the introductory stock market book. Using simple language, it covers basics like "What is a stock?" Yet it is deep enough to cover most of the lingo you will ever need. Once it's digested, you will be ready for the others listed below.

- *The Intelligent Investor* by Benjamin Graham (Harper & Row, 1949). You shouldn't buy stocks before reading this book. Its easy lessons let you avoid common screw-ups that regularly trip Wall Street. Graham, the father of security analysis, was an investment manager and professor who made a bigger impact on investors than anyone before or since him. He eases you into the art of value investing: Those immersing themselves in his book are the intelligent investors.

- *Security Analysis* by Benjamin Graham and David Dodd (McGraw-Hill, 1934). Graham is the only author to make my all-time-best list twice. *Security Analysis* is the bible of security analysts. Most were weaned on its 778 pages. While not exactly light, it is straightforward, easily understood and authoritative—a text to which I still refer regularly.

- *Common Stocks and Uncommon Profits* by Philip Fisher, coincidentally my father (Harper & Row, 1958). This was the original gospel for growth stock investors and was the first stock market book ever to make the *New York Times* bestseller list. It is still used in classes at Stanford's Graduate School of Business. It covers 15 basic points in analyzing growth stocks.

- *Extraordinary Popular Delusions and the Madness of Crowds* by Charles Mackay (L.C. Page & Co., 1841). You will see between its staid lines (written in ye olde English, and as ponderable as Buddha's navel) that, despite what the media says, nothing really important has changed in centuries. Mackay spirits you through the Mississippi Scheme, the South Sea Bubble, Tulipmania and other preindustrial versions of 1929–1932, 1980's gold bubble or 1983's technology stock orgy.

- *The Templeton Touch* by William Proctor (Doubleday, 1983). This little-known gem is a biography of the greatest mutual fund manager ever. You will learn how in 30 years John Templeton multiplied megadollars 40-fold by buying 40-cent dollars.

- *The Contrarian Investment Strategy* by *Forbes* columnist David Dreman (Random House, 1980) relieves you of your reverence for Wall Street "pros." And you will be glad. If Dreman suddenly started babbling, I would still read his *Forbes* columns just because of his book's impact on me. It makes you skeptical of analysts' earnings projections.

- *The Money Masters* by John Train (Harper & Row, 1980). When it came out, *Forbes* said: "Read this book carefully, and in a couple of pleasant weekends you can get as good a perspective on investing as you could get at Harvard or Stanford in a full school year for $10,000." Train chronicles the investment lives of nine legendary postwar investors (including Fisher, Graham and Templeton).

- *Reminiscences of a Stock Operator* by Edwin Lefevre (George H. Doran, 1923), supposedly the *nom de plume* of the legendary plunger Jesse Livermore. Here is Livermore, perhaps the all-time short-term trader, in disguise. In real life he made and lost fortunes repeatedly, ending broke and a suicide. Without meaning to, his book conveys the futility of in-and-out short-term trading.

These books are gifts of the gurus. Old though some may be, they are timeless. Reading them, you realize there is no one path to stock market success, but several. As an individual, you may find some approaches more congenial than others. ∎

Don't Be Too Smart for Your Own Good
July 1, 1985

The way most people end up with $1 million in the stock market is to start out with $2 million. That's right. They don't have to, but most folks lose money. They commit three common mistakes: They overpay, buy businesses they don't understand and neglect to take a long-term approach. These three fatal errors account for most stock market failure. By avoiding these three you are almost certain to generate reasonable results. How best to avoid the treacherous trio? By keeping things simple.

I first learned this at the tender age of 12 from Clarence K. Bennett, who made his fortune in the 1920s and 1930s opening most of John Hancock Insurance west of the Mississippi. By the time I came along, he was long retired and mainly interested in his gardens and orchards. As a kid I did agricultural labor for the kindly old Southern gentleman. He would give me a task and I would cook up some cute trick to get it done faster or fancier. When my shortcuts became disasters, he would pat me on the back and in his slow drawl remind me of his rule for success: "Keep it simple, stupid." Over the years Bennett's phrase has hit home again and again. Most of the mistakes I have made in my career have come from trying to tackle something too complicated. The successes have all been simple and well within my grasp.

Wall Street is skeptical of simplicity. It prefers complex rationalizations for gains and losses. The Wall Street kind of mind seems instinctively to reject the simple explanation and to seek something more devious or complicated —insider wheeling and dealing, for example. But in the long term, insiders can't drive a good stock down, or a bad stock up.

Okay, but how do you keep the stock market simple? The answer is, don't do things you don't understand. Wall Street is full of supposed shortcuts that really end up giving your wallet a wallop. Short sales. Options. Puts and calls. Straddles. Convertibles. If you don't understand it cold, forget it. If it sounds complicated, circuitous or the least bit fast-buckish, forget it. Let some other sucker tackle it and learn the hard way.

Recall the three fatal errors to stock market success: overpaying, overtrading and over-your-head. In each of my next three columns I will focus on one of these factors in detail. In a nutshell, I will argue for buying unpopular stocks of good companies. This is the simplest kind of investing to understand—too simple for some folks. Because these stocks are unpopular, their prices are depressed. You get value. Because they are good companies, you can comfortably hold them for a few years or longer. With time, their quality will be more widely recognized and the stocks will become more popular. As that happens, the stocks go up. It's that simple. ■

IBM Drove a Tough Bargain
July 29, 1985

From the coverage, you would think the recently announced alliance of IBM with MCI is the greatest thing for both sides since sliced microchips. It looks to me as if IBM has cut itself a very fine deal. Not so for MCI; the deal renders MCI extremely vulnerable.

Let's review the facts. IBM gets a 16% (45 million shares worth $360 million) stake in MCI. IBM also gets $105 million worth of warrants for the purchase of another 7 million MCI shares, and can acquire as much as 30% without MCI's approval. What is IBM paying for this $465 million stake in MCI? Most of IBM's shares in Satellite Business Systems (SBS), a communications carrier owned by IBM and Aetna Life & Casualty Co. Parse the deal and you must conclude that IBM drove a very tough bargain.

The alliance, most press reports had it, will create a powerful challenge to AT&T and speed the integration of telecommunications and computers by hooking MCI's ground-based voice communications to SBS' fast computer-grade satellite system. Because IBM bought a piece of Rolm and then came back to take it over, lots of folks think IBM will buy out MCI.

That is all well and good. Buck Rogers may take over the Tooth Fairy's job, too. But meanwhile there are immediate results that are good for IBM and less so for MCI.

For one, IBM is shedding the burden of SBS and passing it to MCI. SBS, remember, was created a decade ago in a $1.3 billion joint venture among IBM, Aetna and Comsat. After a decade of disappointments, Comsat dropped out. Aetna has made no secret of its desire to dump the hemorrhaging hemophiliac. IBM was holding the bag.

Now 60%-owned by IBM, SBS had $290 million in sales last year and, by IBM's own admission, is running losses of about $100 million a year, pretax. By selling SBS to MCI, IBM traded a major money loser for 16% of a liquid, publicly traded stock.

IBM also immediately increased its aftertax profits by the amount of SBS' losses, which it will no longer suffer, about $50 million for IBM. With the market valuing IBM at 10 times earnings, that alone should be worth about $500 million to the company's shareholders.

Allowed to cherry-pick SBS' assets prior to the deal, moreover, IBM is hanging on to soon-to-be launched satellites and an SBS unit that provides communications to office buildings—the part of the world IBM addresses best. Finally, IBM got flexibility. With its option to buy more stock and the right to buy still more after that without MCI approval, IBM can easily increase its stake in MCI if the long-distance discounter prospers, or cut its losses if MCI gets its buttons pushed by AT&T. Put simply, IBM is getting, at modest cost, a long-term call on MCI. MCI gets a powerful new partner, but at a cost. IBM drove a hard bargain.

What did MCI get out of the deal? MCI got, as its chairman and chief executive, William McGowen, described it, "A wealthy shareholder." It also got to take on a headache that couldn't be handled by Comsat,

Aetna or IBM. It got $290 million in sales to add to its existing $2 billion. But it also got $100 million of losses, which will clobber its current $50 million pretax profits.

Moreover, although its shareholders' equity increases by $465 million, its cash position doesn't increase at all. Its earnings coverage of its debt decreases immediately and substantially because its net earnings evaporate. Were I an MCI creditor right now, I would be getting nervous.

All of this comes on top of already stretched financials. Were it not for one-time extraordinary credits, MCI would have suffered losses in the first quarter. MCI's equity is only 30% of total assets—38% after this deal is done. And its steadily deteriorating current ratio has slipped below 2.0 for the first time in years. Overleveraging might be fine if MCI were king of the mountain, but it controls only about 5% of the long-distance market, which on a relative market-share basis is peanuts, compared with AT&T's 85%.

Regular readers know I often use price sales ratios (PSRs) as a quick and dirty first stab at interpreting events. Just before the deal was announced, IBM was 120%, which meant the market valued it at 1.6 times the prior year's revenues (PSR, 1.6). MCI sold at 8, which meant the market valued it at 91% of the prior year's revenues (PSR, 0.91).

By contrast, MCI paid $465 million worth of its own shares to buy SBS' $290 million sales (PSR, 1.6). With a PSR of 0.91, MCI paid a PSR of 1.6 to buy SBS—or almost twice its own market multiple. That looks like a stiff price for a money-loser that three major corporations turned their backs on.

MCI's McGowen boasts that IBM is saying, "MCI runs a better telephone business than we do." Again, maybe so, but IBM, unlike a lot of other companies in making acquisitions these days, was careful to get the best bargain it could for its own shareholders. ∎

Where Are They Hiding?
August 26, 1985

If you want to hold on to your money, you could do worse than developing the habit of holding on to your stocks. A long-term orientation may sound stodgy, but it is as important to investment success as picking stocks or pricing them. My last column highlighted what I call investing's three fatal factors that make or break results. They are: Understand what you buy, don't pay too much for it; and, just as important, hold on for the long term.

Most investors get this backward. Encouraged by reduced capital gains holding periods and the market's volatility, short-term investing is all the rage. The growing newsletter industry is based on it, as are most commission-oriented brokers. And pension plan managers, who have

their lives measured via quarter-to-quarter performance, find it easier to keep their jobs if they avoid having bad quarters, even if it means missing the good ones, too. It all spells short term.

But few see the more penetrating question. If you could make good money with short-term approaches, there would be lots of visible folks who had done so. Where are those who have made fortunes as short-term traders? Not Joe Granville—he let his bankbook ride and slid several times. Not the most famous of them all, Jesse Livermore—he killed himself, a broke alcoholic.

Who made and kept big bucks in the market? Take a look at John Train's book *The Money Masters*. One thing you will see in common among the big successes—however their style may vary—is that they bought stocks to hold for several years or longer. Warren Buffett, John Templeton, Ben Graham, T. Rowe Price, Phil Fisher—they bought long term. They bought and held long enough for a big move to unfold. They waited for stocks to double, triple or even multiply 10-, 20- and 100-fold in value.

You wouldn't buy real estate thinking, "What could I sell it for in three months?" You wouldn't buy into the corner shoe store thinking, "What could we liquidate for next year?" You would buy them to hold for the long haul. But for some reason folks go fruitcake with stocks.

Stock represents fractional ownership in a business—that's it. If you buy right, you buy an unpopular and much depressed stock of a good business. In time the firm's quality will be recognized by others, and then the stock will become more popular and rise. But no one can tell just when this will happen. A stock can be too cheap and go nowhere fast or, even worse, decline. Some of my best buys have been stocks that didn't perform for some time. Why? Because stocks move based on the simultaneous action of countless unacquainted investors acting independently. You may be dead right that a company is good and cheap, but if lots of folks mistakenly feel otherwise, your choice won't rise until after their selling is done.

Worse even than in-and-outing stocks is trying to outguess the stock market. I have never ever seen anyone who could consistently outguess the market's direction. There are many who claim they can, but none delivers with consistency. The fellow who is spectacularly right once or twice is going to trip up sooner or later—probably sooner; a little luck just sets you up mentally to get whipsawed all the harder next time. Remember the old saying: "The market is God's gift for teaching humility; it builds you up only to let you down." I have always felt sorry for folks who sell good stocks because they think the market is headed south. Usually, they sell out near the bottom instead. At the bottoms, most folks think the market is going lower, and at the tops they think it's headed north.

It's easier to hold a stock through all the market's jiggles, if the business is good and you bought it at a reasonable price rather than at a P/E that discounts the hereafter. ∎

How to Get the Real Lowdown
September 16, 1985

Whom would you call before buying a growth stock?

a) Your broker?
b) Your banker?
c) A stock analyst?
d) The company's president?
e) The president's secretary?

The answer is "e," the president's secretary. Why? The president's secretary always knows who is the best person to answer your questions and has the clout to motivate him or her to help you. I usually open with something like, "Hello. My name is Ken Fisher. I handle investments out here in California. I've become interested in your company, and am hoping you can put me in contact with the right person to answer some questions and help me beef up my knowledge."

Folks often grouse, "That's fine for you. You run an investment firm. But they'll never talk to me, I'm just an investor." Well, you handle investments, too. The truth is, in the decade I have used this technique, no one ever asked how large my firm is or even if I have a firm. The secretary usually likes to help and virtually always puts me in touch with someone having more answers than I have questions.

Folks often buy stocks without understanding what they are buying and end up sorry later. My July 1 column highlighted three fatal factors that predetermine investment disasters: overpaying, overtrading and, just as important, failing to understand what you buy.

A stock is nothing more than fractional ownership of a business. If you don't understand the business' basic nature, you are flying blind. Before blowing a boodle on a stock tip, plus a bunch in broker's commissions, try spending $5 or $10 on telephone calls to understand something about the business.

Great Questions to Ask

One wonderful part about *Super Stocks* is the questions Ken provides are still great ones to ask (and answer) before making an investment. And today it's even easier to get the answers; publicly traded firms provide copious information online now.

Okay, so what do you ask the president's secretary? Folks often underestimate their skills and common sense. They gripe, "I wouldn't know what to ask. And if I did, I wouldn't understand the answers." One lady at an investment conference recently told me: "I couldn't invest in growth stocks. Why, I wouldn't know a microchip from a potato chip." Lady, you don't necessarily need to know that.

At the same conference I heard the talented Charles Allmon, owner of the newsletter *Growth Stock Outlook,* ask an audience of 200 if they had a can of WD-40 in their homes. Eighty percent of them raised their hands. He asked if that same can was there two years back, and if it was there, to raise their hands. Again, virtually everyone's hand went up. Allmon quickly saw that WD-40 had saturated its market and was no longer a good investment. Allmon is good essentially because he asks the simple questions.

My book (available in most libraries) listed 35 major questions to ask while interviewing managements. The most important ones are about the company's markets and marketing. Here are some for starters: "What exactly does your product do for your customers? Why do they buy your products instead of your competitors'? What is your market share by product area? Who are your leading competitors and what are their market shares? How important is pricing to your customers? Service? Product features? How is the selling effort conducted?"

After 15 minutes on the phone you should understand the company better than you ever thought possible. If you don't, then don't buy the stock. ∎

How to Shoot in the Dark, Safely

October 7, 1985

How do you avoid buying a stock that's too high? Simple. Don't pay too much. "Thanks a lot," you say. "Now please tell me how to know when a stock is too expensive." Okay, I will. I suggest tripod pricing. I'll explain:

When I was a sub-teenager, much of the money I made working for Clarence K. Bennett went into photography gear. I was a nature photography nut. Dusk and dawn found me wandering Bennett's woods, stalking wildlife. The problem was that the critters came out the most when the light was the worst. This required slow shutter speeds, where my slightest jiggle blurred the shot. Any camera buff knows that the solution is a tripod to stabilize my movements.

Investing is pretty much the same—particularly since many folks feel as if they are shooting in the dark, too. Hence tripod pricing. Your stock purchases should be balanced securely on three basic pricing "pods": Don't pay high prices in relation to earnings, book value or, my favorite, to the company's sales size.

Start off by seeing how much the stock market says the whole company is worth: Simply multiply the stock price by the total number of shares. Then compare that market value with the company's earnings and revenues in the last 12 months and to its current book value. A reasonable price in relation to all three standards says you are unlikely to be paying too much. What's reasonable? A total market value less than 75%, or less, of sales; 12 times, or less, of earnings; 1½ times book value, or less.

Regular readers know I often preach the merits of a low price/ sales ratio. A low valuation in relation to the sales size of a company, right or wrong, means an unpopular stock. Most stocks increase in value, at least significantly, by slowly becoming more popular. If it's an unpopular stock of a good company, in time folks decide it's not such a bad outfit after all—like Chrysler since 1979. Then they bid it up, thinking it's worth more in relation to how big it is.

In a recent study at the University of North Carolina, George A. Walker made a heck of a case for low price/sales ratios. Over the past 18 years, he found, you would have made out three times as well had you bought the 20% of New York Stock Exchange issues with the lowest price/sales ratios rather than having bought the market as a whole. So, you can see what a strong tripod low price/sales ratios are.

As David Dreman correctly, repeatedly and wisely points out in his *Forbes* columns, study after study shows above-average returns using low-P/E stocks.

Why buy low in relation to book value? Well, you could go back 50 years to Ben Graham's logic in his legendary *Security Analysis*. In essence you are buying a dollar's worth of assets at a discount. With subsequent inflation it may be discounted further. Is this antiquated thinking? Then try *Forbes'* more recent and almost as

Top-Down Considerations

Today, Ken would say it's important to consider a firm's valuations relative to its peers—all of them that are available—but larger themes have greater impact on a stock's performance. For example, if you are picking from among Tech stocks in an environment when Tech is unlikely to do well, even the best Tech stock might badly lag the overall market.

famous "loaded laggards" for testimony to the power of book-value bargains.

Each of these screening techniques is good and useful by itself, but each can, by itself, lead you astray at times. A low P/E can merely mean the company's earnings have temporarily bulged. A low price/sales ratio may signal tough times for the next few years—or longer. And a low price-to-book-value ratio may camouflage an over-inflated book value, owing to needed but untaken asset writedowns.

Hence, the tripod: book value; earnings; sales. ∎

Emulating America's Richest
October 28, 1985

Virtually everyone on the *Forbes* 400 got there one of four ways—inheritance, oil, real estate or being a founder-builder of a major corporation. These are the big four of wealth wagons. You can count the exceptions on your fingers and toes. Note this: Only a handful made the list through speculating in stocks (the three Allens, Ivan Boesky, Warren Buffett and maybe a few others—all considered true sharpshooters—hardly role models the average man on the street could hope to emulate). Clearly, trading in the stock market isn't the easiest or the safest way to build a boodle—it isn't even a likely way.

The best way to do that is by building your own company and continuing to own much of the stock. That's how such folks as David Packard, Ken Olsen, Norton Simon, Frederick Smith and Art Nielsen Jr. made the *Forbes* 400. Each ran a public company long before he would have qualified for his *Forbes* 400 listing. While they made lots of money building their firms before the companies went public, they also made lots more afterward. And you could have ridden along with them.

Traders these people were not. They held the stock of growing outfits. They held it for a long, long time, and they didn't have to pay too much for it.

Even for those of us who are unlikely to build a major company, and just want a good return with liquidity, there are lessons here. The first is that the market as a whole has done pretty well, and much better than most investors. So how do you get good results? These three axioms—buy growth, buy low, hold—virtually assure stock market success for anyone. Consider each separately.

Growth: In a single lifetime, from nothing, each of these founder-builders built a sheikh's ransom—which requires skill, time, freedom and flexibility. Here is a key to why stocks have done better than other investments through the decades. As the world changes, gold doesn't change, bonds don't change, real estate changes hardly at all. But a company can and must evolve, little bits at a time, year to year, forever—or die. If it can evolve to conform to a changing world, it will prosper and grow. The more successfully it evolves, the faster it grows.

And growth fuels your compound return. If you allow $100,000 to compound at 20% per year, it becomes $150 million in 40 years. And that's how you make the *Forbes* 400. Gold won't grow at that rate. Bonds won't return that kind of money. A growing company can.

The founder-builders didn't buy today and sell tomorrow, wheeling and dealing their way through life. They focused on building their companies and letting the stock ride, slowly building in value.

They let time and compounding work in their favor. Unfortunately, most folks today shoot themselves in the foot trying to outguess the market. Precious few do it, as highlighted by the lack of stock traders on The Forbes Four Hundred.

Lord knows enough wheeler-dealers have tried. There are more than 80,000 stockbrokers in America. There are tens of millions of investors. As the old saying goes: Where are the customers' yachts? Only the Ivan Boeskys, the Allens and the Sol Steinbergs have had the nimbleness and luck to navigate their yachts through the stock market's treacherous waters. Most folks trying that get shipwrecked.

The founder-builders held growing companies a long time, and they also didn't pay too much for their stock (because, not only did they get in at the ground floor, but they also laid the foundation). While most folks can't do that, they can make sure they don't pay the kind of outrageous prices that ensure failure.

Aha, you say. But how can I buy the stock of a growing company at a low price? My answer: Most firms, particularly rapidly growing ones, at some point in their long evolution stumble badly. They "grow" problems for themselves, like poor inventory control or unstable production processes. Purging the problems involves writedowns and restructuring, which stack costs on top of lack of profits. Just then Wall Street usually gets much discouraged and hammers the stock down. Since most investors figure value based on price/earnings ratios, when the earnings disappear, so do most investors. This is when the best bargains crop up: when a good company stumbles. Often insiders, like our founder-builder, will be buying the stock.

To recognize these bargains I advocate using price/sales ratios—or the market value of the whole company compared with the firm's total revenue. You can use PSRs to value good outfits that are temporarily unprofitable. Low PSRs flag the unpopular stocks whose dollar of sales the market values at only 25 cents. With PSRs, patience and an eye to quality, you can do much the same thing the founder-builders have done—make good money while avoiding much of Wall Street's foolishness. ∎

Half-Buck Bargains
November 4, 1985

Visitors often get it wrong. They see my library of hundreds of investment and business books and assume that I spent a bundle accumulating them—particularly the classics, like my 53-year-old first printing of Robert Rhea's *The Dow Theory*. It's in mint condition and worth over $50. It was one of the seminal books for chartists and is still quoted regularly. My cost? Fifty cents.

Virtually all of my library was bought slowly over the years at library book sales and for under a buck each. My secret? Attending library sales. Not only did this save me some money, but it also taught me several good investment practices: the value of patience and what to look for while sniffing out a bargain.

Take Rhea's classic as an example. It showed up at a sale sponsored by the Friends of the Palo Alto Library—one I will never forget. I was frustrated. We had arrived late from dropping our son at a dance. I hate being late. I am always sure that the bones will be picked clean by the early birds. As always, I rushed to the reference table, because it goes first. I bagged a new copy of the Commerce Department's *US Industrial Outlook—Prospects for Over 3oo Industries*. Then, as always, I next moved to the "Business and Economics" table. There were a few buys, but it was pretty well picked over.

With little left, I moseyed over to the larger general nonfiction tables, where I have often found bargains, such as *Extraordinary Popular Delusions and the Madness of Crowds* and a host of others whose unclear titles led the volunteer sorting staff into miscategorizing them away from Business and Economics. Do you think your average Joe Doc volunteer worker cares if *The Dow Theory* is a book on investing, psychology, anthropology or religion?

I have trained my eye to bypass the bright, colorful spines, preferring the drab, often discolored ones that most folks never notice. As John Shedd, noted Chicago merchant, once said, "Opportunities are seldom labeled." By now you are getting impatient to know what all this has to do with stock investing.

Just this: You can't get these classics by sauntering into your local B. Dalton's. Same with good buys in stocks. You are not apt to find the best buys on your brokerage firm's recommended list. Just as I have found the best books misclassified and overlooked, so are the best stocks found. A broadly typecast "growth stock" will be overpriced, or else everybody will be shocked when its growth prospects subsequently do the fast fade.

Just as bargain books don't have colorful spines that jump out at you, the best stocks don't announce themselves either. You have to train your eye to look for the ones others ignore. At book sales I never know what I will find—maybe nothing. The stock market is just that way. When you find a bargain, buy it. If you don't find one, hang on to your money and keep looking. You needn't buy something merely to buy. That's foolhardy. Come back tomorrow. Or the day after.

One of the best points about buying book-sale bargains is that at half a buck a pop you can blunder without feeling much pain. Investing is the same way. By sticking to bargain-basement pricing, you can afford a few bad picks without getting hurt too badly. And when you do find a doozy priced like a discard, your financial return will be sufficient to make it all worthwhile.

Our libraries are among America's most underrated assets (see my April 22, 1985 column). So, if you want book bargains, try library book sales for miscategorized and overlooked gems. You will save lots of money and help build a national resource. ■

Modesty Is the Best Policy

December 2, 1985

People can be such fools. They too often do not realize that the bigger the promise, the more certain you can be that the offerer is a huckster. Take a pitch that recently came my way for *Predictions,* put out by Financial Intelligence Reports. It popped my cork. The publisher's letter claims he has found and packaged 18 men who consistently predict virtually everything, almost to the penny. The very stridency of the pitch would put off any sensible person.

Its misleading verbiage is couched in phrases that may be legally defensible but certainly aren't realistic. After reading 17 pages of extravagant promises, you are to believe that for only $42 a year these geniuses will show you which way interest rates, silver and gold are headed, which banks will go down the tubes, which stocks will soar, and even "how to make a quick killing in palladium."

For example, the letter claims that one of its experts, Bert Dohmen-Ramirez, has been "right on target" with gold, inflation, stocks and interest rates. If that's so, wouldn't his *Wellington Letter* be right at the top of the newsletter heap? According to newsletter scorekeeper Mark Hulbert, the *Wellington Letter* is distinctly middle of the pack.

Predictions claims Doug Casey is "America's foremost expert in selecting obscure (but often wildly profitable) penny stocks before they become known." That may be true, probably isn't, but more important, the penny stock approach is too dangerous a track for even the most agile folks to ride without crashing.

Few *Forbes* readers would fall for this kind of baloney, but I cite it because it represents an extreme example of the type of pitch to which all of us are vulnerable: a promise of certainty in an uncertain world.

So don't waste your money. When you hear a bold promise, shy away. You will save the direct cost of the advice, the disastrous indirect cost of following the advice and the pain of discovering you have been duped. The professionals who really perform well don't make outrageous claims and don't offer their services for $42 a year. Top-ranking newsletter writers like Al Frank *(The Prudent Speculator)* and Charles Allmon *(Growth Stock Outlook)* promise less than they deliver. Superperforming money managers like Mario Gabelli and John Templeton charge big bucks for their worthwhile efforts. You would, too.

All of this brings me to me. Sometimes folks misunderstand what I am doing when I recommend stocks. Usually each column recommends three stocks that I think will do well over three to five years. I am not saying *you* should buy these stocks. I don't think anyone in a magazine or newsletter can tell you what to buy without knowing your circumstances and your temperament. What I'm saying is that these are stocks I have checked into and that they make sense to me. You might check into them to see if they make sense to you, too. If they do, then buy them. You have to be responsible for your own decisions. I think you should apply that same self-determination to any adviser, anywhere. The ultimate decision should be yours.

No, I'm not trying to wriggle out of responsibility for stocks I have touted that have gone wrong. My next column will review some of my recommendations that have worked out well, and try to figure out why they have. The column after that will cover suggestions that haven't worked out well, and why.

My point is simply this: Whether I suggest a stock or someone else you respect does, don't buy it unless it makes sense to you. By all means listen to ideas. But don't follow them blindly. ∎

Keep Your Worms Warm
December 30, 1985

Some folks keep fine-tuning a simple mechanism until it's a broken gadget. There are easy-to-use principles that virtually assure stock market success. Stick with simplicity and don't overrefine proven methods until you are broke.

Take my January 28 column, which used price/sales ratios (PSRs) and balance sheet adjustments to ponder the 30 Dow industrials. It ruminated on which to buy if you could choose among only those 30 corporate giants. The resultant choices were the most unpopular six, relative to their financial strength. They were Goodyear, Woolworth, Union Carbide, General Foods, Owens-Illinois and Du Pont.

By now, those six stocks are up an average of 55%, three times as much as the whole Dow Jones average. They were picked using only strong balance sheets and low PSRs (price times shares outstanding, divided by the outfit's last 12 months' revenues). The highest stock on the list sold for 35% of revenues. Easy enough, but most folks can't stick to such an ordinary tactic.

Instead, they hedge and overrefine. They may reject one cheap stock because it lacks sex appeal. Others because they are too risky. They would have gassed Union Carbide, owing to its Bhopal disaster and the supposed legal snafus to follow. Next they would nix General Foods because "the food stocks had run up too much." Owens-Illinois may be the best in its field, thought many, but with glass bottles losing out to plastics, who wants to be in a dying field? Woolworth was thought "Woolworthless" because of its 1950-ish ho-hum image.

All of this reminds me of the boy catching dozens of fish on a frozen northern lake. As passersby asked him about his luck, he mumbled incoherently. Finally, one guy kept hounding the closemouthed boy about the secret to his success until the boy spit a wiggly clump of worms into his hand and groused, "You have to keep your worms warm." Most folks can't stomach putting the market's worms in their mouths, much less keeping them there long enough for good results.

The predictions of that column worked because of plain rules tied to long-term value. Consider what happens to people who go for glamour instead. My March 25 column, sadistically labeled "Look Out Below," pinpointed 12 "overpriced beauts just bound to bomb." Using high PSRs, it picked pricey stocks to avoid—ones where the market valued $1 of sales ten times higher than with any of the 6 stalwarts from my January column. These glamour issues were heavily touted by brokers and advisers everywhere. Since then, all but 4 are down, 3 are down at least 50%, and on average they are down 12% in a market up 17%.

Note that neither column put all the chips on one or two selections, but instead spread the risk over a number of stocks. I would be eating crow until Christmas if I had only slammed Stratus and Cray. Even when armed with sound principles, there is safety in numbers.

Simple but proven methods let you avoid getting overrefined or too cute for your own good. To sum up: Diversify, buy long term, buy strong balance sheets and buy unpopular, low-PSR stocks.

Lest you fear I am feeling too clever, next column I will review my biggest bloopers of this year and what they have taught me. ■

1986

Global-dy Gook

" *If my mistakes recently have been many fewer than my successes, it does not change the fact that one learns more from one's mistakes than one's triumphs.* "

"LESSONS FROM MY LOSERS," JUNE 30, 1986

" *The odds are overwhelming I will end up richer aiming for a good return rather than for a brilliant return—and sleep better en route. Folks who seek a killing usually get killed. Gunslingers get shot—often in the foot—with their own guns.* "

"BE CONSERVATIVE, NOT CONVENTIONAL," SEPTEMBER 22, 1986

In his first 1986 column, Ken makes the point stocks can shrug off even the very worst news. Turns out, 1986 was a year of very, very bad news. Not so much for stocks—stocks did well in 1986, especially overseas. The S&P 500's 18.7 percent gain seemed paltry compared to the 69.9 percent gain in foreign shares![1] Even though 1986 was a fine investing year, it wasn't so great otherwise.

The year began tragically as the space shuttle Challenger, carrying school-teacher Christa McAuliffe, exploded shortly after takeoff. Just a few months later, the Chernobyl nuclear power plant disaster rocked Eastern Europe and the world. In the US, as 1986 was winding down, the Iran-Contra Affair was making headlines—a scandal threatening to make it all the way to the Office of the President.

But financial markets events were more cheerful. In the UK, 1986 was the year of the Big Bang—the financial one, not the cosmological version. The dereg-ulation of Britain's financial markets reinvigorated London as one of the world's most important financial centers, eventually rivaling—and some say surpassing—New York.

As for stocks, Ken's opinion was they were getting to be quite expensive. "In case no one told you, this market is high," Ken wrote in "Bombs Away" (April 21, 1986). "Using many valuation methods, it's higher now than it has been in about 70 of the last 85 years." But Ken wasn't calling for a big drop in the market—not yet. One consistent theme through the years is Ken has said just because stocks are high doesn't mean they can't go higher. So he focused on finding cheap stocks in good companies, but those were increasingly hard to come by in 1986. That was okay with Ken. To him, patience and discipline were more important than a quick buck. In the midst of a raging bull market, ebullient investors can be tempted to adopt wild strategies to squeeze every cent possible out of the bull. Ken's advice: "Be comfortable and conservative but not conventional. Conventional means going with the fads and following the in-crowd hotshots, who will lead you to disaster. Why try to double your money in a year with horrendous risk when an achievable long-term return will make you rich without exposing you to potential poverty?" ("Be Conservative, Not Conventional," September 22, 1986.)

Ken's 1986 columns also shed a little more light on his affinity for small stocks. It wasn't the smallest he was after—it was stocks just out of reach of big institutions. Large investors typically don't bother with tiny stocks; they can't buy enough to make a difference to their portfolios without owning a sizeable a portion of a company. That usually inhibits their ability to buy or sell shares when they want—too illiquid for them—so they steer clear. Ken looked for cheap companies with good prospects on the cusp of being big enough for big investors. Those stocks might rise slowly at first, but if they became big enough for the institutions to take notice, the stock prices could soar as institutional money flowed in.

Throughout his career, Ken has advocated not blindly following the investing crowd. In that vein, Ken's October 6, 1986, column, "Myths to Frighten Children," debunks some commonly held investing concerns. Interestingly, many of the concerns Ken debunks then are the same ones on people's minds in 2010. Things like government debt, deficits, and lackluster savings rates got folks' hackles up then as they do now. Ken would remind today's worrywarts not only were these factors not disastrous then, they preceded 15 nearly uninterrupted years of stellar stock market returns.

In "Lessons From My Losers" (June 30, 1986), Ken reflects on some of his recommendations to date that didn't go as planned. To this day, Ken espouses the humbling notion he can and will be wrong. There's no way around it. No one can expect to be right all the time. The key in investing is to be right more often than wrong. Over time, that can add up and result in outsized returns. If you're mindful of the fact that mistakes are an inevitable part of investing, it's possible to keep those mistakes from taking too heavy a toll, so you aren't wiped out before realizing the benefits of your successes. (Incidentally, Ken does still take stock of his losers each year, though over the last decade or so, he does so early the following year.)

Lastly, Ken finishes the year arguing against the benefits of investing overseas—a stark contrast to his viewpoint today. (Soon after this column, he would flip this stance around to be among the first of the fully global investors.) At the time, many investors were jumping on the foreign investing bandwagon because foreign shares had been outperforming US shares. In Ken's view, when too many people start following a fad, that fad's run is about done. Not to mention information on foreign stocks was much harder to come by in 1986, and foreign accounting standards weren't as robust. Both those concerns are largely non-factors today. Information on foreign stocks is readily available, and international accounting standards are at least as good as those in the US. These changes, along with other foreign-investing benefits outlined in later years, have contributed to the change in Ken's global-investing tune.

The investing game isn't about creating rules and sticking blindly to them—it's about evolving as conditions warrant. The ease and importance of investing globally has grown dramatically, and global investing is one important issue where Ken has evolved.

The Case for Madness

February 24, 1986

On January 28, 1985 this column suggested Union Carbide at $37. Carbide had a 9.3% yield, a P/E of 7, sold at 25% of its revenue, 53% of book value and 3 times cash flow. Oh, sure, Carbide had this little disaster in India, so buying the stock also earned you free psychiatric sessions from spouse, relatives and friends.

Looking for another stock like this? One that is cheap but untouchable in the eyes of the crowd? Try Texaco. Everyone or nearly everyone will tell you you are crazy, just as they would have had you bought Carbide last year at this time. I have never bought a stock that outraged my clients more than has Texaco. Everyone's read the papers about Pennzoil's $11 billion judgment from a seemingly kangaroo court in Texas. The bonding requirements and the bankruptcy banter. Pennzoil's swaggering chairman, J. Hugh Liedtke, and his brimstone Texas talk. It's scary.

And haven't oil prices been falling rapidly? As a result, investors have difficulty seeing how Texaco gets out of this one whole.

All of which makes the stock cheap. Whether it's Carbide in 1985 or Ronald Reagan's presidential prospects in 1978, society's collective wisdom is worthless. The fact that everyone is so down on Texaco is exhilarating. I feel like climbing the Alamo's walls and shouting, "Remember the Union Carbide." Texaco has a 10.7% yield, sells at 5.5 times earnings, half of book value, 15% of sales and 1.6 times cash flow. Disaster is discounted. Everything is discounted.

Now, let's look at the numbers. Texaco's book value is $13.5 billion, or $57 per share, and backed by one of the better balance sheets among the oils. Compare Texaco's current ratio and long-term debt-to-equity ratio with that of its peers. It stacks up better than Arco, Chevron, Diamond Shamrock, Mobil, Occidental, Phillips, Unocal and, yes, even Pennzoil.

Texaco earns more than a billion bucks and has $4 billion a year of cash flow, even with low oil prices and high legal fees. Think of it as an LBO (leveraged buyout) artist would. Start with the company's market value—$6.9 billion. A rule of thumb is that the banks will finance LBOs up to about 5.5 times earnings, before interest and taxes–less the company's long-term debt. For Texaco that is $4 billion times 5.5—minus $10 billion. This means that a T. Boone Pickens could easily pay $12 billion for Texaco—$50-plus per share. That would still be cheap. He would get Getty at the price Texaco paid for it and the rest of giant Texaco (valued at $7 billion 15 years ago) for only $2 billion.

But what about the Pennzoil $11 billion judgment? I almost forgot. You should, too. It is patently silly. If Carbide stock could perform so well with the liability of thousands of folks dying, Texaco ought to be a real gas. Why?

First, it hardly seems that Pennzoil suffered any irreparable damage. There wasn't death, or maiming, or a plant buried in volcanic ash. At worst Texaco could give the company the Getty assets at the price Pennzoil initially proposed paying. Next, both sides at first agreed that the case, while tried in Texas, would be settled by New York law. Can you imagine a bunch of New York attorneys swallowing the notion that an uninked billion-dollar deal is binding?

Finally, Texaco has time. The reported courtroom shenanigans alone seem enough to assure that the case will be heard on appeal through the 12th of never. For example, there is the Pennzoil attorney's campaign contribution to the judge, and the head juror's failure to disclose his long-standing hatred for his father (a long-time Texaco employee). Then there is the juror who failed to disclose a spousal firing at the hands of a major oil company. There is the amazing judge who reportedly let the hometown boys testify about what happened at meetings they didn't attend, but refused to let Texaco's side testify about these same meetings, which they did attend. If this is justice, they had better rewrite the dictionary.

Wiser heads will prevail. Before this is all over, a reasonable settlement (or no settlement via a new trial) will result in Pennzoil's getting, at best, a token compared with its current demands. Liedtke and various Pennzoil board members very well could,

and should, lose their positions over spurning settlement offers that are huge in relation to Pennzoil's assets.

My guess is that when the dust settles Pennzoil will get less than $500 million—1½ months of Texaco's cash flow. Texaco's P/E, PSR and price to book will probably average about 40% less than the Dow Jones industrials, which at current levels would put Texaco at about $50 a share. While waiting you can bank a 10% yield.

The lesson? Remember, when mania prevails, sanity cannot be too far behind. Stick to value and simplicity and you can make money when others succumb to hysteria. Afraid your friends and loved ones will think you are crazy for buying Texaco? Buy it, but keep quiet. ∎

Rigged
March 24, 1986

The whole thing is nuts. The argument as to whether you do better buying stocks of big companies or tiny ones has raged for decades, mostly peppered with nonsense. Some guys like big companies, thinking they are safer and more is known about them. Others prefer small outfits—the hope of catching the next ascending Xerox or DEC. The "small fry" fans have gained ground since the 1970s, particularly when University of Chicago studies provided solid empirical underpinnings to what is now labeled the "small-firm effect."

But the label is a misnomer. You see, the studies were mum on "small firms." They proved something else—that small market capitalization stocks (price times total shares—the market's valuation of the whole company) have outperformed large cap stocks over the years. But even a moment's thought tells you that small cap doesn't necessarily mean small fry.

As often as not a small market cap comes from a good-size firm with its stock price in the dumps. A big market cap can come from a big firm, or from an overloved little darling whose sky-high price discounts Nirvana. Confusing? To make sense of this, start by considering the hierarchy of market caps.

IBM has the largest market cap—$90 billion. There are about 350 companies that the stock market now says are worth $1.5 billion or more. What's below that? About 1,300 businesses valued at between $150 million and $1.5 billion each, and 2,400 more companies valued at between $15 million and $150 million each. Finally, there are another 5,000 actively traded issues valued by the market at less than $15 million each. Simple arithmetic shows that all 5,000 of those outfits added together are worth a bunch less than IBM.

Now consider how institutional money managers operate. They tend to avoid buying more than 2% or 3% of the owner- ship of any company. Why? To avoid illi- quidity should things sour. Next—and this is the part few folks reckon with—money managers have tremendous difficulty buy- ing stocks whose market caps are a lot less than the amount of money they manage.

Owning those stocks is a managerial nightmare and can't do them much good. Imagine a $100 million money manager pondering tiny (say, $20 million) market cap stocks. Buying 2% of each, he would need 250 of them to fill his fund. He prob- ably couldn't even remember all their names. And suppose one of them ended up a real winner, rising 1,000%. Since he would buy only $400,000 worth of it (2% of $20 million), his fund would rise a mere 3.6%. So why waste the effort? If he tried instead to buy only 50 of these tiny cap- pers, he would need to own 10% of each firm to fill out his portfolio. No liquidity!

So big-buck managers concentrate on big cap stocks, mainly the 1,650 with market caps above $150 million. Most won't even consider anything too small for them. I run a small firm, managing only $35 million, and even I can't waste time on stocks with market caps below $20 million. If I'm limited, think of the poor guys with billions. Perverse but true, as a stock and its market cap rise, and get overpriced, more and more money managers can initially consider it. If you always thought the market was rigged against the small guy, think again. It's rigged against the biggies.

So, here's the trick. Buy unpopular, undervalued stocks of good companies, ones with market caps that arc low in rela- tion to the company's size and a tad too low for the big-buck boys to ponder.

As more folks like you spot the bargain, they will buy it, too, along with the outfit's customers, competitors, suppliers and hometown enthusiasts. The good news is that as these buyers push the market cap up enough for megabuck managers to take notice, it will still be cheap enough for the institutional Goliaths to jump on the bandwagon without break- ing its wheels—and take you along for a pleasant ride.

Want proof? Just count the results from the annual *Forbes* 500 feature "Who's Where in the Stock Market," which ranks the performance of stocks over the prior five years. Recently I participated in a study based thereon, examining the top 25 performing stocks from each of the last five years' editions—125 top winners. We calculated their market values at the beginning of each of those five-year peri- ods. It turns out that only 12 of the 125 (15%) started their five-year streaks with market caps of less than $15 million; none started with market caps of over $1 billion. A whopping 90 (72%) started at between $15 million and" $150 million. Were these outfits tiny? No way. The average com- pany on the list had sales of $609 million. They were good companies about to be discovered. ∎

Bombs Away
April 21, 1986

In case no one has told you, this market is high. Using many valuation meth- ods, it's higher now than it has been in about 70 of the last 85 years. Consider the price-to-dividend ratio of the Dow Jones industrials. The ratio rose from 14 times dividends to more than 29 in three years. The Dow Jones averages haven't ever sold for more than 34 times dividends. Ever. And only 11 times before have they risen to 29.

The last time was 1973. You know what happened then. Only when one looks at book values, does the market seem anything shy of the extreme high end of normal.

No, I am not predicting a decline. No one can outguess the market's short-term moves with regular success. But I do predict that good stock selection will be a lot more important in the next year than it was last year. The easy money is over.

Or worse. Folks forget that stocks can drop as steeply as they rise. They also forget caution. Why not? Who needs it? For months the only thing seeming to matter was whether you owned stocks. Virtually everything went up. Since it hardly mattered what you bought, stock-picking seemed pointless. A year ago (March 25, 1985) I wrote a column called "Look Out Below," which highlighted 12 overpriced stocks to avoid. Since then, on average, the 12 are about flat. What do you suppose might have happened to them if the overall market hadn't risen 40%?

Some folks need memory pills. Do you recall Kodak's 70% nosedive between 1972 and 1978? That you could have lost 90% of your boodle in stalwart but overpriced Polaroid in just 12 months, starting in mid-1973? Extreme? Yes. It is more common to suffer smaller losses—like 25% in Digital Equipment (12 months starting in 1976), or 45% (1981), or 50% (1983). Oh, I almost forgot, 60% (1974).

If I sound pessimistic, don't get me wrong. I love stocks and buy a bargain whenever I find one—whether the overall market is up, down or dribbling. But now, with prices up, it's time to be extra careful. ∎

Ready-to-Go
May 5, 1986

Fisher, you're always spouting about how folks should buy unpopular stocks of good companies," a reader of this column groused, "but how in the devil are we supposed to find them? If they're unpopular, they aren't exactly earmarked and ready-to-go in the local paper." That's true. But unpopular stocks *are* labeled. Most folks just don't know how to read the labels and where to look for them.

A company's popularity is reflected almost perfectly by its stock's price/sales ratio (PSR). When a stock sells at a low value in relation to its sales per share, the market thinks poorly of that company's future ability to wring profits from its business. But such a company may be unpopular for poor reasons. In time you will make money with a stock that is wrongly unpopular.

Of course, you need more than unpopularity as measured by PSRs to make a winner. You need quality, too—but PSRs are the way to start your search. But our reader groused about that, too. "What good does that do me?" he wrote. "Where can I find them? Not even the *Wall Street Journal* lists those ratios you like."

Where do you find low-PSR prospects? There are five simple ways I have done it. Four of them involve using a computer to scan databases. For about $500 you can buy a used but fully functional IBM-compatible computer. There's a glut of them, and price shouldn't be an obstacle. Lots of folks pay almost that much for a newsletter. Computer-less investing makes about as much sense today as camping without matches. It's too much work.

Then you can spend a lot or a little on databases. The most elegant approach is to use Micro/Scan, published by ISYS Corp. in Cambridge, Mass. It accesses the largest stock market database, Disclosure II, yet is so easy to use a gorilla couldn't goof it. With it you can, for example, ask your computer to "Show me all the companies that are in the following geographical regions and in the following industries; have PSRs under X and more annual sales than Y; have current ratios better than Z"—and whatever else you want to throw in, hundreds of variables. With Micro/Scan, in short, you can create a complex model of whatever you are looking for and then have it dished up for you. The problem is that Micro/Scan's $15,000 m i n i m u m annual cost is enough to gag almost anyone. For between $245 and $735 you can use StockPak II from Standard & Poor's (in New York). It will do much of what Micro/Scan does with only a little more difficulty.

To spend even less, you will have to throw in $100 for a used modem to connect to databases via your phone line. Another $200 gets you a subscription to The Source, a product of *Reader's Digest.*

With it you will pay for the time you are "on line." The Source won't play the complex modeling games that Micro/Scan or StockPak II will, but it will let you scan industries inexpensively, and it lists PSRs (calling them "% Mkt to REV").

IP Sharp, a Toronto-based database, lets you do everything Micro/Scan does—the whole banana. But a warning: No monkey is going to manage this routine. It is difficult to learn and frustratingly error-prone. Why consider it? IP Sharp charges you only for your usage. Although you pay a lot per minute for data, for most users it is a lot cheaper overall.

What do I use? At my firm we use all of them except Micro/Scan, plus some odds and ends of our own devising. Of course, our computer gear is more sophisticated and expensive than most nonprofessionals', which makes our job faster and easier, but no more accurate than what you can do with a cheap computer.

Once you have a list of unpopular stocks, of course, it still takes lots of labor to determine which are good companies and which are good grief. But to find the winners you have to start looking among the unpopular. If you want to find cheap stocks, buy a computer.

For those who are too stubborn to step into the 20th century, I have two suggestions.

First, I still find *Value Line* a good introductory source of data for many stocks. It's available at most public libraries. Along with lots of other useful data, it shows price and sales per share for about 1,800 of the most actively traded stocks. You can scan the whole thing manually, page by page, in about two hours, which ought to generate lots of ideas. Second, and this is the easiest and least expensive approach of all, keep reading my columns. I don't recommend stocks unless they have low PSRs. ■

Witch Doctors

June 2, 1986

Witch doctors sometimes make people feel better but often prevent them from seeking more useful treatment. So it often is with professors of finance. Take beta, that academic concept that was supposed to measure risk in investing. Take it as far away as possible, and leave it there. The academics who pawned beta off on us as a useful risk-measurement device set investment thinking back decades.

Beta is a simple and, by itself, harmless concept. It is also useless. A stock's beta is a number representing its past volatility relative to the overall market. The higher a stock's past volatility, the higher is its beta. If a stock's volatility perfectly matched the market, its beta is 1.0. So far, so good. Also, so what?

Fact is, beta tells you very little. Academics went on from there to assume—without any sound reasoning—that if a stock has been more volatile than the market as a whole, it is also more risky. They served up beta as the measure of a stock's risk, and the world has swallowed it hook, line and sinker. The problem is that prior price history has nothing whatsoever to do with future stock performance. Nothing!

Gurus like William F. Sharpe of Stanford and Jack L. Treynor, formerly of the University of Chicago, weakened the world's wisdom by teaching folks to measure a portfolio's risk via its average volatility. Then, they reasoned, you could compare "risk-adjusted" true performance of past portfolios. According to these eggheads, you can beat the market only by taking extraordinary risks via high beta stocks.

For example, consider a recent paper by doctors AJ Senchack Jr. and JD Martin, of the University of Texas at Austin. They studied a random sample of 500 stocks, ranked both by price/earnings ratios and price/sales ratios. They annually broke the PSRs into quintiles (five groups ranked lowest to highest) and compared them with quintiles for the 500 stocks based on P/Es.

It turns out that you could have made good money buying the lowest P/Es or lowest PSRs. If you annually had invested $1,000 in the low-P/E grouping, sold at year-end and reinvested in the new low-P/E quintile, you would have gathered a tremendous $10,804 at the end of the decade (forgetting taxes and commissions). Buying the lowest PSRs, you would have gained an additional $2,595, totaling $13,399.

In all the studies I have seen, low-PSR groupings have averaged far better than the market. This latest study shows that, but then concludes that the return from low-PSR stocks was achieved at the cost of high-risk exposure—buying high-beta stocks—and that adjusted for risk, low-PSR stocks weren't so hot.

Horse manure! If the low-PSR groupings regularly appreciate more than the market, do they really have higher risks? Of course not. It just happens that stocks with high historic earnings in relation to their price also have low historic volatility, and so have low beta—so the studies have a built-in statistical bias favoring low P/Es over PSRs. The real problem is that using beta to measure risk is nonsense.

If you took beta seriously, you would have to say that Avon at 120 in 1973 was less risky with a beta of 0.9 than the next year at 19 with a beta of 1.3. It was Avon's free-fall that gave it the high beta—and made it cheap—and reduced its risk. Buying after a big drop means a higher beta, but it has to be less risky than before the drop. A real long-term winner quickly develops a high beta, too, just because it has been moving more than the market over a prolonged period.

Academics use beta, despite knowing that there is no theoretical or empirical evidence to support beta's centerpiece—the notion that past price action relates to the future. If the witch doctors of finance are to believe the voodoo of beta, they should accept its cousin, the equally voodooish concept of predicting stock prices based on charts, which they rightly abhor.

The worst part? In the papers I have read, it seems that many professors start with a point to prove instead of an unbiased quest for knowledge. Take the hatchet job on PSRs that was presented recently to a Southwestern Finance Association meeting. It baffles me how the authors reached their convoluted and backward conclusions, which were wrong, based on the data—and the data were wrong based on prices that didn't match the periods involved. But what do you want from witch doctors?

Which leads me to my biased conclusion: Ignore the witch doctors of Wall Street. Forget beta. Diversify among unpopular stocks, ones that are already down and have the real risk wrung out of them. Buy low P/Es, or low PSRs, or both. Buy for the long term, and only if the company has a sound position in its business and a strong balance sheet. If you restrict yourself to unpopular stocks of good companies, you won't find lots of buys in this pricey market, but you needn't fret over the few available. ∎

Lessons From My Losers
June 30, 1986

Recently, someone checked into every "buy" stock I had "specifically" recommended in *Forbes*—over 22 months and 26 columns, through April 30—56 stocks in all.

My buys had increased at a 38.8% average annualized rate, far faster than the 25.9% average annual rate turned in by the S&P's 500 during the same period. Twenty-six, almost half, were up more than 50%, ten of them had more than doubled, and only five were down.

If I seem to be bragging, it is only because I want to devote this column not to boasting of my successes but to learning from my mistakes. If my mistakes recently have been many fewer than my successes, it does not change the fact that one learns more from one's mistakes than from one's triumphs.

Several of my columns had no buys. And there were two "theme" columns that weren't included (May 20, 1985 on bankruptcies and February 25, 1985 on micro-cap stocks). In these two columns I gave lukewarm endorsements, but endorsements nonetheless, to 24 stocks. Precious few were big winners, and 10 were down. Only one stock doubled. The rest were lackluster.

Mistake number one: Suggesting a long list of stocks. When anyone does this, steer clear. Sloppiness loves company. When I'm mentioning a large group of stocks it is hard to have the conviction, not to mention the background research, that I routinely have with just two or three stocks. When I wrote a full-page column recommending just one stock, Texaco, at $28 (February 24), you could have disagreed, but you couldn't dispute the fact that I had reasons and convictions. You should have powerful reasons and convictions, too, for anything you buy.

Mistake number two: Recommending a broad thematic category of stocks, such as oils or utilities, or bankruptcies or micro-cap stocks. In investing you buy companies, not themes or concepts.

The bankruptcy theme turned out badly. Since my May 20, 1985 column, I served on the Equityholders' Committee of the Charter Co. bankruptcy proceedings, acting for a time as head of the reorganization subcommittee. It was the only bankruptcy stock our firm actually owned, and a waste of time and money, as it turned out.

Through that process I concluded that creditors as a group are much more sophisticated in wresting equity dilution from bankruptcy shareholders than was true just a few years ago. There are too many powerful but conflicting forces in a big bankruptcy for anyone to know how it will unfold. So my experiences have taught me that bankruptcies, on the whole, should be avoided.

My micro-capitalization theme didn't work either. The February 25, 1985 column listed ten nice enough little companies, with total stock market values under $15 million. I called these micro-cap stocks and reasoned that since two-thirds of all publicly traded stocks fall into this category, the large menu would give investors a chance of finding a few undiscovered bargains. It sounds good, but it doesn't work. Micro-cap stocks just don't get bid up very far. But when there is a problem, they drop fast.

As I found out in a recent study (see my March 24 column) most big-time winners come from unappreciated and under-discovered medium-cap stocks of big companies—the kind that institutional investors can adopt when improvements unfold just right. Few come from the micro-cap world because micro-caps are too illiquid for institutional investors to buy. Without the institutions wading in,

you don't get enough "greater fools" willing to bid them up to crazy valuations and maximize previous holders' returns.

Apart from these two broad mistakes—too many stocks and too much concept—what about my other losers of the past 22 months?

There were five: Halifax Engineering (selling at 5 on November 5, 1984; now 4), Tesoro Petroleum (15, August 13, 1984; 11), Rogers Corp (27, October 8, 1984; 22), Ramtek (7 October 8, 1984; 6) and N.B.I. (16, September 16, 1985; 11). Halifax was a micro-cap stock, too—enough said. Tesoro? Its foreign-based reserves took a double blow from falling oil prices and the falling dollar, and I would avoid it today. If you want an oil stock, Texaco is a lot better deal.

The remaining three stocks got clobbered by the too-fast-changing computer situation. NBI, for example, suffered as its word-processing customers shifted from specialty machines to networked micro-computers, using specialty software. Rogers found the inventory needs of its computer-making customers bouncing like yo-yos, and Ramtek found the market for its computer graphics equipment drastically curtailed.

But I still like all three of the latter. I hope they will turn from mistakes to successes. I have reviewed their problems with each of their managements, and would hang on to them.

In investing as in anything else: Small mistakes don't kill you; not learning from them does. ∎

A Time to Buy, a Time to Sell
July 28, 1986

Recently a reader groused, "You're always recommending what to buy, but then, after I've bought, you never say when to sell." That's a justified gripe. I recommend about three stocks per month but haven't provided any follow-up advice on these picks. Last month I mentioned that someone compiled a ranking of all my buy recommendations. I am proud of the list's 38% average annual price gain, but I was taken aback by some of the names that today I would avoid.

Why? It varies. But first off, the market is way up, yet hardly a peep is heard about how the Senate's tax bill butchers business and investor interests. There's the near unanimity that interest rates will fall—when you and I know that whatever everyone expects to happen won't. Scary? Add it up and it's time to decide whether the stocks you own are stocks you would buy today if you were starting fresh.

Why did I wait until now to talk about selling? Because for the most part, it hasn't been necessary. Over and over again I have stressed buying only for the long term. It is most unlikely that after making a buy recommendation I would recommend selling that stock a couple of months later. (I stated on February 24 that I liked Texaco and specifically said that falling oil prices helped make my case; it baffled me when nervous readers wrote in March asking if I still liked it as oil prices dropped further.)

Yes, I still like Texaco, up only about 14% since I mentioned it. But Union Carbide, which I recommended a full year and a half ago, has tripled. Meanwhile, in thwarting GAF's takeover attempt, Carbide evolved from a financially muscular industrial powerhouse into a debt-laden rummage sale with some of the best bargains picked clean. What once sold at 7 times earnings, 25% of sales and half of book value now sells at 2 to 3 times those levels. Farewell, UK.

Next to overpaying, the world's worst investment mistake is hanging on to stocks, even good ones, that have become too overpriced. It's hard to make a boodle, even with the world's best little growth company, if it averages above 20 times earnings, 2 times book value and 1½ times revenues.

Why the finickiness on pricing? To make sense of it, try looking at it backward. Instead of a P/E, think about an E/P, or an earnings yield, which is a lot like a bond yield—the income as a percent of what you must pay to get that income. A P/E of 25 is an earnings yield of 4%. How do you make a bundle buying that? Even if earnings increase 25% per year, its yield in three years will rise to only 8%. You can get that with a virtually risk-free Treasury note.

Freaks and quirks excepted, to make big money a stock's earnings yield must be 15% to 25% or higher—based on what you think earnings will be two or three years from now. It doesn't matter much whether you get that yield with a low P/E, high-yield stock where earnings remain flat or with a no P/E, profitless outfit that is about to turn around and now is selling at low PSRs and low price to book value.

Some stocks I have recommended I would avoid now because I was wrong then—they didn't produce the earnings I thought they would—yet they have gone up in this bull market anyway. They have had continued business deterioration, coupled with a rising stock price.

The rest of the stocks I have recommended still seem okay to me. If a bear market unfolds, most of them will drop, too, but maybe not as far as the market, and in another bull market they should bounce back further. Remember, in any long list of names like this, there will be places where I am wrong, so think for yourself. Review your stocks to make sure they make sense to you. Not understanding what you own is the best reason of all to sell. ∎

Sell? Or Hold?

August 25, 1986

When key market indicators point to rough water ahead— as they have recently—is it best to sell out and wait for a better market? No. At least it hasn't worked that way for me, because selling out and waiting for clearer weather means trying to call market turns. Precious few market timers get it right for long. After a few years' hot streak, their tea leaves fade, the old crystal ball glazes over and they end up sidelined with Joe Granville. Can you think of even a single seer with a lifelong record of accuracy as a market timer? I can't find one. So why play a game no one has ever won?

Instead of focusing on market timing, I have participated in major up markets and avoided getting clobbered in most down markets another way. You can, too. It's what I call "the un-cola" of market timing. Here's how it works. To un-time the market, you have to start with simple but specific rules for stock selection and portfolio management. The first of these is my 5% Rule.

This is a portfolio diversification rule with a hidden benefit. It states that you will never—never—spend more than 5% of your portfolio on any one stock. A stock can become a bigger piece of your pie—if it goes up a lot. But you never spend more than 5%. This way, to be fully invested you are going to have at least 20 stocks in your portfolio, maybe more. Here's the hidden benefit of this kind of diversification:

If you start with some skinflint-tough buy-and-sell criteria, as a bull market rages you will find ever fewer stocks that meet your purchase criteria and ever more that meet your liquidation standards. When the market is too high, you won't be able to find the 20 stocks needed to be 100% invested. As single stocks rise further, you will sell some, be unable to

buy more, have fewer stock positions and an ever bigger hoard of cash for upcoming bargains when the next bear market de-hibernates. But note: You are not trying to call market turns; you are letting your account liquidate itself as prices get too high. Currently, I can find some good stocks that meet my buy-and-sell criteria, but not enough to fill out my portfolio.

Why not just conclude that the market is too high and pitch everything? Remember, no one successfully times the market. Just as important, the few stocks that meet tough buy criteria are worth holding—even in a down market. Remember the real bruiser of a bear in 1980, 1981 and 1982? My portfolios were up because of ample cash and three big winners.

So how do you set strict buy-and-sell criteria that un-time the market? Here they are, the ones I use. Modify them any way you like. They cover the qualitative aspects, what I call the "quantitative qualitative" and valuation, or pricing.

First, qualitative. I don't like junk. Ideally, I want to buy a company that is clearly recognizable as either the biggest or best at what it does—better yet, both. At worst, if its industry is fragmented, I want the outfit to be no smaller than third in the pack. And if the firm is diversified, it better not be in more than four industries. (On how many fields can any top management keenly focus at once?) As a kid, I was taught by my dad that if a widely diversified outfit enjoyed good markets—and good management—it would sell its weak sisters and concentrate on its best few business segments.

Then comes the quantitative qualitative. Get out the outfit's financial statements or Value Line. Weed out the potentially risky small fry by considering only stocks where the price times total shares outstanding exceeds $20 million. Then look for rock-steady balance sheets. Common shareholders' equity should be at least 45% of total assets. Current assets divided by current liabilities should exceed 1.8. Finally, year-end inventories should have grown no faster over the last three years than did total annual revenues. Bulging inventories are management's prime pocket for hiding upcoming losses.

Now for valuation and pricing. Only buy a stock selling for less than 35% of its prior year's revenues (price/sales ratio). Then, review the last decade and average the outfit's three highest years' net margins (profit divided by revenues). If it had those margins on today's sales, would its P/E be less than 10?

Damn few stocks meet all of the above criteria right now. So it's hard to fill up via the 5% Rule. Following my rules, then, would assure lots of liquidity now, which could help if stock prices fall in the coming months.

What about selling? The qualitative factors seldom change fast, but if they do, sell. Sell, too, if the quantitative qualitative criteria are violated. Or if a rising price or sagging business causes the PSR and price-to-book value to average more than 1.5 times that of the Value Line Composite. (Its PSR is now 0.55, and it sells at 1.5 times book value.) ∎

Be Conservative, Not Conventional
September 22, 1986

Here's a paradox: The odds are overwhelming I will end up richer by aiming for a good return rather than for a brilliant return—and sleep better en route. Folks who seek a killing usually get killed. Gunslingers get shot—and often in the foot—with their own guns. While there is always some guy around on a red-hot streak, his main function is to tempt the rest of us into becoming fools and paupers.

Don't get me wrong. I'm all for above-average returns—if they're achievable over the long haul. Plenty of pros have double-decade-long and highly visible records, ranging from 15% to 20% annually. But 40%? Peter Lynch of the Fidelity Magellan Fund has done almost that well for a decade, but he is alone. He was sound, skillful, lucky and is humble enough to tell you that the odds of repeating his spectacular performance in the next decade are remote. And you don't need it anyway.

A return of 15% to 20% annually is a lot more than most folks realize, or need. If a 30-year-old with $10,000 in an IRA gets 15% annually, he'll be a millionaire before normal retirement. That's the power of compound interest. If that same 30-year-old were to sock away another $2,000 per year at 15%, he would end up as a 65-year-old $3 million fat cat. At 20%, it's an incredible $13 million.

That's a lot, but it's not too much to ask. The two most definitive studies ever on long-term returns, the Ibbotson/Sinquefield and Fisher/Lorie studies (available in better libraries everywhere), both point to average annual returns for the stock market of 9%-plus per year going back to the mid-1920s. So 15%-to-20% per year is really 66%-to-100% better than the market as a whole. That's tough but doable.

Consistency is the key. Regularity. It is close to impossible to get a good, long-term rate of return if you suffer serious negative numbers en route. It's in the math. A single year that is down 30% means you have to get 30%-per-year positive returns for the next four years to get back on track for a 15% annual average. Or, if you score 20% annually for four years and then suffer a 30% decline, your five-year annual average return is only 7%.

It brings me back to some early lessons—ones that were learned in my first years as a professional. I assisted my father in preparing an obscure book, now long out of print, called *Conservative Investors Sleep Well.* My biggest contribution to the book was the title. But its contributions to me were numerous. Working on it taught me that getting a good return does not necessarily require extra risks.

If you buy unpopular stocks of good companies, most of the risks have already been wrung out. Most important, it taught me that most folks do better when using a comfortable style, allowing them to sleep well at night—partly because people think more clearly when they are comfortable.

But don't confuse comfortable with conventional. Conventional means following past rules blindly. Conventional folks took horrendous after-inflation losses buying bonds in the 1960s and 1970s.

Conventional, no, but conservative, yes. By conservative I mean trying for two-base hits rather than swinging for the fence. It means combining knowledge and procedure to minimize risks relative to potential.

Take a lesson from longtime newsletter writer Charles Allmon, a grizzled and grouchy old-timer who has never had a year when he topped the Hulbert newsletter ratings. Yet his long-term record is right at the top because he has done pretty well regularly and avoided the boom-bust cycles that most of the single-year top performers have suffered. The very same knowledge that avoids pitfalls helps build returns through buying undervalued securities without taking fliers on the latest fad.

Take a reverse lesson from the flamboyant and famous Freds—Fred Alger, Fred Carr and Fred Mates, who, along with Gerry Tsai, were the top-performing "go-go" mutual fund gunslingers of the mid-1960s. After a brief stint as shooting stars, they were driven from the mutual fund world as their booms busted. Mates, for example, who was among the top performers of 1968, was among the worst in 1969, and lost investors 90% of their assets in the next six years. Easy come, easy go. Alger is back, with a multimillion-dollar advertising campaign that claims a great 20-year "audited" performance record that somehow seems to ignore the disaster of his 1960s mutual fund.

That's why I say: Be comfortable and conservative but not conventional. Conventional means going with the fads and following the in-crowd hotshots, who will lead you to disaster. Why try to double your money in a year with horrendous risk when an achievable long-term return will make you rich without exposing you to potential poverty? ■

Myths to Frighten Children
October 6, 1986

When you get events like last month's 80 plus point, one-day crash in the Dow on record volume, people panic. But don't let mass hysteria throw you off course from a sound long-term investment program. The most severe and real problem for most investors should be finding stocks with real value— particularly so in a market that is up 130% in four years. Stick to unpopular stocks of good companies.

But—some people say—isn't the federal deficit so bad that it threatens the entire economy, unpopular stocks included? Not so. While you read lots of media hype about the deficit, and politicians babble about it no end, the deficit/federal debt hysteria is just one of many scarecrows needlessly frightening folks from sound investment policies.

The crucial issue isn't the deficit's size or total federal debt, but our ability to service that debt. The fact is, total federal debt is a smaller percentage of GNP than it was in the mid-1960s, and lots lower than in the 1950s. Public debt as a percentage of GNP reached a peak of about 120% during World War II. For the next 30 years we shrank that ratio. Even in years when we ran budget deficits, debt shrank relative to GNP because real growth and inflation raised the ratio's denominator more than the deficits raised its numerator. Inflation was a big force, boosting our repayment power by lowering the debt's value.

By 1955 the 120% had dropped to 58%. By 1965 it was 42%, and by 1975 it reached a 40-year low of 25%. Since then, things have worsened. Yes. That much is true. The deficits have grown, and the ratio has risen. Risen to where? Only to the low 40s. Nothing like what we lived with years ago.

Another way to look at the deficit is to compare it with those of other countries. Over the last five years our deficit has averaged about 3% of GNP. Other countries? In Japan it's 7.4%; in Germany, 2.5%; in France, 2.6%; in England, 3.5%; in Canada,

Myths That Still Frighten Children

Since this column's publication, not much has changed. People still fear federal debt, thinking it is too big and unmanageable. In 2010, though elevated historically, federal debt is still smaller than many would think relative to GDP—and smaller than it's been at points in the past that most would regard as being overall fine and not troubled by too much debt.

5%. But the worriers say the deficit and debt load are worse for us because our savings rate is lower. That, too, is exaggerated. As Susan Lee demonstrated in a compelling article (*Forbes*, December 16, 1985), the differences are mainly in accounting and how we do our savings now—like pension plans.

It isn't clear to me that the much heralded deficit even exists—if you account for it right. If Du Pont kept its books the way Uncle Sam does, that stalwart chemical giant would have run deficits virtually nonstop for decades. But Du Pont rolls right along, and with good company. Why? When a business builds a plant, buys a car or a computer, it capitalizes the item on its balance sheet and slowly counts it as expense over the asset's estimated life. But Uncle Sam doesn't keep a balance sheet. When it buys those same items, it expenses them immediately. A major portion of the companies in the *Forbes* 500 would run deficits if their books were kept via the government's ultraconservative cash basis.

Our major airports are worth a few billion bucks each. Ditto for the highway system. The military system. The Postal Service. The parks and forest lands. There's also the small stuff, like computers and trucks. The government is, by far, the largest buyer in every major category of big-ticket items, but these purchases are all expensed immediately—even raw land.

Then there are the huge budget surpluses generated by states and municipalities—which total almost half of the official federal deficit, but are financed by federal government transfer payments of $ 100 billion-plus. The states and municipalities also understate their surpluses, because they don't capitalize their asset purchases either.

So if you lumped the federal government, states and municipalities together, and treated all their asset purchases the way corporations do, you would either have vaporized the government "deficit" or come damn close. As a percentage of GNP? It would be so small, it wouldn't be worth mentioning.

Don't get me wrong. There are real problems—like the growth in government spending. Since 1965 federal spending has risen 11% per year. Worse, it grew from about 18% of GNP to 24% now. If those relative growth rates continue, it would take only a shocking 96 years for the government to take over the whole GNP—everything. And President Reagan's 11% annual profligacy is even higher than Carter's was, once you adjust for the lower inflation during Reagan's terms.

If you want to worry, then, worry about the trend in government spending. But despite a frightening-sounding federal deficit and scary air pockets in the stock market, our world is not coming to an end. It will continue to reward folks who buy good stocks when they are cheap and hold them until the market recognizes their merits. ■

Pipe Dreams
October 27, 1986

It takes less than you might imagine to qualify for the *Forbes* 400. What would it take to put you on the list? Only six things, really—longevity, discipline, common sense, above-average brains, a financing source and a financial calculator. Most folks have two of the six already. A good many have three. Every *Forbes* reader can afford the calculator, so you may well be closer than you might have dreamed. With those elements in place, the only question is, do you sincerely want to be rich? If so, here are three simple ways to do it.

Method 1: is the hardest: Become rich through compound interest. Let's say you are 30 years old. Your financing source? You just inherited $250,000 from Uncle Sedrick. Seem like a lot? It's merely the value of the rundown old downtown house he died in. To make the list by age 80 your calculator says you must make your investments grow 13.6% annually, net of taxes and inflation. Tack on 5% for inflation and divide by 72% to adjust for a 28% tax rate, and you need 25.9% annual growth—year in and year out. It's not impossible, but it would qualify you among the top 1% of all money managers. The big roadblock is inflation and taxes. Without them, you could get there with the 13.6% return, or about half the results.

Method 2: Change your strategy and your financing source to take advantage of taxes. Forget the inheritance. Become a doctor. Plan to work until you are 70. Make a few hundred grand a year. Incorporate and fund a tax-deductible and tax-deferred "defined benefits" pension plan. Your calculator says that if inflation is 5%, you will need $1.72 billion when you are 80 to make the *Forbes* 400 list.

To accumulate that, starting at age 30, you must contribute $566,896 per year to your retirement plan and generate at least 18% average annual returns on your savings, again putting you toward the top of the pack of all money managers. While that might seem like a bundle to save, and it is, it is only one-third of your $200,000 annual income, which still leaves lots more left over than most folks ever see. The key is above-average—but not uniquely incredible—investment management skills, coupled with what most folks would consider draconian savings skills.

Method 3: Build a business that takes advantage of compound interest. Suppose you still think you can generate 18% returns but want to skip the heavy savings bit. You might start your own money management firm. Look at mine. We manage about $60 million. We charge clients 1% per year of the assets managed. That's the financing source. If we increase our clients' assets by 18% annually, we increase our revenue that much, too.

And if, like lots of other businesses, we generate good results and then spend 20% of our revenues on marketing, we ought to attract more clients. Adding new clients at the rate of 17% per year would bring our overall growth rate to 35% (18% + 17%). Consider the awesome potential. If inflation averages 5% annually, then our 35% is cut to 30% "real" growth, which, the calculator says, would turn our current $60 million of managed assets into $7 billion in just 18 years, $14 billion in 21 years. At our 1% billing rate, that would be revenues of $70 million to $140 million per year. Since very few large investment management businesses are sold for less than 250% of revenues these days, that would value the business at $175 million to $350 million—easily enough to make The Forbes Four Hundred. Seem like a pipe dream? In the next few years, a number of money managers, such as Batterymarch's Dean LeBaron, should easily make the list this way. Of course, there is a fourth method, which, rather than relying on one method, combines all three. Someone might inherit a little, manage it pretty well *and* build a business that takes advantage of the nature of compound interest *and* also salt away a big chunk of yearly savings in a retirement plan. He would be listed among The Forbes Four Hundred far younger and with a lot more room for slippage.

Do I look forward to being on the *Forbes* 400 list one day? No, because, like most folks, I don't really want to be that rich. I have other values that touch my life besides money. If I accumulate $20 million to $30 million of real purchasing power in my lifetime, that's far more than I'll ever need to do every single thing I would ever possibly want to do. That kind of wealth, my calculator says, is far from unachievable in my lifetime.

The point is that the real limits to your wealth are as much a matter of determination and willpower as of skill. An important key to driving is knowing where the road leads. So, instead of recommending stocks this issue, I suggest you buy a financial calculator and learn to use it. My favorite is the Casio BF-100, which costs about $30—less than the commission on a stock trade. It will help you navigate what's possible and what's not better than any investment guru's crystal ball. ∎

Smoke, Mirrors and Suckers
November 17, 1986

You have seen the syndrome. An outfit reports good profits and seems reasonably priced on the basis of those earnings, but the stock keeps dribbling downward, even as the outfit announces another quarter of good earnings. Six months later the blood-red ink gushes forth. The stock collapses.

Was somebody hiding something? In many cases the answer is yes. Management was hiding declining earnings. Hiding them how? With inventories, receivables and the like, a sure sign is a deteriorating balance sheet.

Masking declining earnings isn't all that difficult. You see, quarterly earnings aren't audited, so the reported numbers are mostly whatever management says they are. In my 15 years as an investment professional I have yet to see a brokerage "research" report say, "Sell this stock because the balance sheet is deteriorating and losses probably are ahead." Instead, everybody talks about earnings and the income statement and forgets that reported earnings are nothing more than a large mass of compound assumptions filtered through the balance sheet via some very broad accounting policies that give management tremendous temporary leeway.

Quarterly financials include undisclosed assumptions about how much inventory was consumed in making products and how much was destroyed through bad production. Once management decides how much was wasted, that amount is expensed against income. Estimates, at best. At worst, it's a great place for deception. A too-low assumption about inventory consumption can boost reported profits, even in the midst of a real loss. The only warning is the sky-high pile of paper "inventory" remaining on the balance sheet afterwards.

Doesn't management realize that such tricks will catch up with it in the end? It rationalizes that maybe the loss can be made up later on and that investors will never know the difference. How do you detect this chicanery? Beware of inventories that rise relative to sales. It is worse if sales are falling while inventories are growing.

The same thing can be done with bad receivables, just keep them on the books at 100 cents on the dollar and pray. Normally, managements keep inventories and receivables as low as possible relative to their sales. After all, why add too much? They will have to borrow from the banks to finance any excess which means more interest expense and lower real profits. Other classic tricks include decreased pension plan contributions (only visible at year-end) and increased non-operating income.

The same way a deteriorating balance sheet warns of trouble, improving balance-sheet quality often foreshadows long-term improvements in earnings. Here again you catch the crowd sleeping. When an outfit has had problems, then does all the right things to fix them, it will simultaneously deal with its balance sheet, initially writing off the ballooned inventory, receivables and what-have-you that impairs the balance-sheet quantity but improve its quality. The quantity improvements are likely to follow close behind. ∎

Greener Grass?
December 15, 1986

An ever-increasing army of investors has come to believe that one can reduce risks and broaden opportunities by diversifying overseas. The message is blared at us from all sides: in advertisements, in articles in the press and through TV commentary. But no matter how many people repeat the message, it still boils down to one word: baloney.

It all started in 1975. Since then the Dow Jones industrials have yielded investors an impressive 15% annual rate. But the world's non-US equity markets increased even faster. In the last decade America's share of the world's stock market fell from 58% to 48% because the booming overseas markets overwhelmed our own good results.

Only five badly battered countries didn't beat our market. It isn't surprising that the Japanese stock market beat ours, but markets in places such as Malaysia beat us, too. Even the Italians and English outdid us—by a wide margin.

Predictably, Americans have jumped on the bandwagon. Government statistics say that we bought $4.25 billion worth of foreign stocks in 1976; by 1985 we were spending 10 times that much; and by early 1986 we were gobbling foreign stocks at an $80 billion annual clip.

People notice a trend only after it has been going on for a long time, and they jump on the trend just about the time it is ending—right about now. What almost no one understands is that most major markets around the world tend to rise and fall at about the same time. They don't necessarily move the same amounts, or at exactly the same time, but the variations in timing are truly small. It has been that way almost forever.

For example, markets boomed all around the world in the 1920s, and all crashed in 1929 within months of each other—first in Berlin, then London, Paris and, finally, here. Even England's legendary South Seas Bubble of 1720 burst within weeks of France's equally bizarre Mississippi Scheme. Financial liquidity flows over international borders more easily than most folks conceive—always has.

So when this aging bull market someday goes bust, the billions that have been poured into overseas markets will go bust even worse—pretty much the way the speculative over-the-counter market usually rises a lot more than the New York Stock Exchange during a bull market, but then falls more freely in a bear market, too.

Compounding the problem is the fact that you don't know what the devil you are buying overseas. With a tad of effort you can learn lots about US companies through company documents, SEC filings and, best of all, the library. The Ivan Boesky insider trading scandal notwithstanding, our markets are, generally speaking, much better policed and regulated than those overseas. With foreign stocks you have to deal with horrendous accounting differences. It's like learning many new languages. Then there are currency fluctuations. Still worse, most large overseas outfits are small by US standards. You would recognize very few of their highest-valued stocks. Folks feel fine owning just about anything when the price is rising, but how would you feel in a major bear market or in a time of international turmoil owning Hutchinson Whampoa, Hong Kong's fourth-most-valued company?

I'm not suggesting that overseas investing can't be done intelligently. Of course it can. But the folks who do well overseas will be the few who know what they are doing, not the many who are along for the ride or the newcomers to the game.

So, besides the potential headaches, the only real benefit of overseas investing is that your menu to choose from has been boosted by a few thousand stocks over the 10,000 you already could access here in America. But if you don't know enough to know what you are doing here, how in the world are you going to know enough to beat a bouncing market in, say, Malaysia?

And if you do know what you are doing, why lust for the seemingly greener grass overseas? So, stick to stocks you can find out about and understand. Focus particularly on unpopular stocks of good companies—ones that are on the outs with investors so they are statistically cheap. Stick with quality characteristics that provide growth potential. ∎

1987

Crash!

" *Good money management starts with sticking to a good long-term strategy. That doesn't mean rigidity and inflexibility. But, then again, it doesn't mean jumping into stocks to chase rising prices—and jumping out at the first sign of crisis.* "

"WHAT GOES UP . . ." JUNE 15, 1987

" *Nothing new of any real importance has happened in the market for centuries. So, if financial history doesn't include a type of event, it probably won't happen.* "

"THE 2% RULE," DECEMBER 14, 1987

Nineteen-eighty-seven started out like any other year in a raging bull market. It wouldn't end the same way. The S&P 500 jumped 1.8 percent on the first trading day and didn't look back. By the end of January, it was 13 percent higher. By the end of February, the S&P 500 was up 18 percent. Then 21 percent by March's end. On August 31, the S&P 500 was up a whopping 39 percent year to date.[1]

As the year progressed, Ken became increasingly concerned a bear market was approaching. Too many people were finding it too easy to make money in stocks. Suddenly, everyone under the sun was a stock market forecaster. The easy gains of early 1987 had taxi drivers, hairdressers, and carpenters—who had never been investors—forecasting stock prices to whoever would listen. "With a formal academic background and years of professional study, I never know where the market is going, but 'they' do. What is more interesting is that 'they' never used to care. But they do now . . . The time will come again when John, my carpenter, will cease to be a market seer, and he will return to the sports pages. The stocks I want to buy today are those that will still be good when that happens." ("Back to Basics," February 9, 1987.)

Exceptionally bullish sentiment wasn't confined to amateurs. Professional investors too were over-the-top optimistic—there weren't many sharing Ken's cautious outlook. Measuring sentiment is often more art than science, but Ken got a powerful indication of professional investors' bullish outlook when he was asked to appear on the popular *McNeil-Lehrer Report*. Ken wondered why he was invited instead of some more well-known investing hot shot. The answer: The show couldn't find another bear. "Our war-room staff joked about my August 13 debate on *The McNeil-Lehrer Report* against Dan Dorfman. He was bullish. I was bearish, saying the market was grossly overvalued and headed for a long-term 40% drop." ("Diary of a Money Manager," November 16, 1987.) A dearth of bears was a warning sign to Ken folks were too optimistic.

All this bullish sentiment had stock valuations through the roof. That left very few stocks cheap enough to pique Ken's thrifty interest. To ensure portfolio diversification, Ken utilized Benjamin Graham's 5% Rule. "Never spend more than 5 percent of your boodle on a single stock. This means you need at least 20 stocks to get fully invested." ("What Goes Up . . ." June 15, 1987.) In early 1987, 20 sufficiently cheap stocks were hard to find. Rather than reach for more expensive stocks, Ken preferred to hold cash, so he'd have money to spend when prices fell as he expected they would. "Right now I can't find enough bargain stocks that meet my long-standing, penny-pinching criteria to fill my portfolios via the 5% rule. So I'm keeping lots of cash in all my managed portfolios."

Interest rates were also on the rise. Ten-year US Treasuries yielded about 7 percent when 1987 began. In October, they peaked above 10 percent.[2] And it wasn't just the US. Interest rates were rising worldwide. Ken viewed these rising rates as a sign of scarce liquidity. "Interest rates are rising all around the world in a rather steady trend. Japan. England. France. Germany. Everywhere. A key point I stress over and over in my new book, *The Wall Street Waltz*, is that major booms and busts occur worldwide. The whole world is now seeing rising rates, which means there is a worldwide shortage of liquidity, not an excess of it." ("Double Damned," October 5, 1987.)

Together, Ken's bearishness, expensive stocks, and the 5% Rule had the portfolios Ken managed in defensive positions. Turns out, that was a good place to be.

In 1987, the S&P 500 peaked in early August. Stocks' decline was relatively orderly at first. From the market peak in August through October 5th, the S&P 500 was down a modest 2.4 percent.[2] But the orderly retreat wouldn't last long. The bear market started to gather steam. Over the next nine trading days, the S&P 500 lost almost 14 percent—an average of 1.6 percent per day.[3] Then came Black Monday.

On Monday, October 19, stocks plummeted. The selling started in Asian markets. The Nikkei 225 index in Japan fell 14.9 percent. Hong Kong's Hang Seng Index dropped 11.1 percent. In Australia, the All Ordinaries Index lost 25 percent. Selling spread to Europe. Germany's DAX index lost 9.4 percent. France's CAC lost 9.6 percent. And in the UK, the FTSE 100 slid 10.8 percent.[4] By the time US markets were set to open, sell orders for many stocks overwhelmed buy orders. Many stocks didn't begin trading until well after the market opened. By the end of the day, the S&P 500 was down over 20 percent.[5]

A number of factors contributed to Black Monday's massive decline. One was a strategy known as "portfolio insurance." Portfolio insurance made use of computerized trading to sell stocks and futures contracts in falling markets to minimize downside risk. Instead, the use of this strategy by many investors on a large scale had the opposite effect—precipitating market declines as trading programs sold more and more stock into already falling markets.

Ken expected a market drop, but nothing like this. Yet with lots of cash on hand in the portfolios he managed, Ken was well positioned and feeling "cocky." Ken and his clients fared well on Black Monday, but even they didn't come through those tumultuous days unscathed. In his November 16, 1987, column "Diary of a Money Manager," Ken recalls the events of Black Monday, and closes with some hard-won advice. "I learned that no matter how well you are trained, how smart you think you are, how good your game plan is and how many advantages you may have, when a freight train is coming, get off the tracks."

Bag a Bargain
January 12, 1987

What do you buy in a market that's up 150% in four years, while average P/E multiples have risen from 7 to 19? Why not try shopping among the stocks that have fallen amidst the rise? While the bull market has been broad and powerful, and most stocks are now far from cheap by any reasonable historical basis, there are a good many that have fallen through the cracks, and that's where the best opportunities for the next two to three years lay hidden.

Of course, most of these companies have had rough times in recent years. That's why they are down. So you have to be independent-minded and ready to buy things that are bruised and unpopular.

Take the mobile home industry. It has been "shaking out" since 1981, and the stocks have been falling since 1983. About 20% of 1981 capacity has been shut down, weeding out the little guys to where the top five now have 40% of the field. They are still profitable, but margins have eroded badly for the biggest players, and immediate profit prospects aren't rosy.

But the long term still holds growth. Folks are learning that conventional houses are too expensive. Here in northern California a quarter of a million bucks buys what was known back in the 1960s as a tract house. A shack goes for a hundred grand. So, as folks retire, they can buy a nice lot in the woods and bring in a modern mobile home—not the kind from the 1950s—and save a bundle. Ditto for vacation homes and younger buyers. This won't be everybody, but only a tiny population shift can make a huge swing in mobile-home demand.

Of course, it's an easy-entry business, so anyone with a few million bucks can build a plant in an upturn. The real key is "Who has the distribution?" The answer is the big guys do. Fleetwood is a fine company. But for half the price you can buy Redman Industries, which, having gained market share, is now number two. It was $27 four years back, when it sold for 100% of its revenue, 32 times earnings and 4 times book value. Today, at 20% of sales, 20 times depressed earnings and less than book, it's cheap. You get a brawny balance sheet, a 4.5% dividend yield—and James Redman to boot.

Moving up the alphabet shifts you from mobile homes to motor homes, those oversize gas-guzzlers everyone abandoned back during the energy crunch. With inflation-adjusted gas prices now down enough to be cheaper than when I was a kid, it's a new ball game. America seems about to rediscover its long-dormant affair with heavy-duty vehicular vacations. Along the way Coachman Industries may reverse its three-year slide from $40. It's number one in recreational vehicles, with the broadest line and dynamite financial strength. It sells cheap—at the same approximate valuations as Redman.

Oneida has fallen by more than half since 1981. But you can read between the lines of *Forbes'* November 17 story to see reasons for optimism now. Despite strong market share and the leading product image in flatware, it was hamstrung by lousy production costs. When you add in its new and aggressive young chief executive, Samuel Lanzafame, with his proven low-cost manufacturing skills, you begin to see the light at the end of the tunnel. Roughly one-third of the business has been generating two-thirds of the profits.

While things may not get better in a hurry, Lanzafame's got enough financial muscle in his balance sheet to buy the time he needs while he pares the production costs. By 1988 profitability should be more uniform. Here, too, the outfit sells for 30% of sales and about book value. The P/E looks high now, because the earnings are so depressed. While I don't expect the company to get back to its old 6% net profit margins, it should get back to 4%. That would put the stock at about 7 times earnings, which should be cheap enough.

A higher risk, higher reward possibility is Convergent Technologies, also covered in the November 17 issue of Forbes This formerly high-flying microprocessor-based computer firm took a nosedive, its stock dropping from $40 to $4. Back in 1983 it sold for an outrageous 10 times sales and 30 to 70 times earnings. Since then earnings vaporized as did orders from its biggest customer (AT&T). Value Line estimates Convergent will lose $25 million this year on $265 million in sales.

But all is not lost. The speculative froth is gone. You can buy it for book value now. Profitability and sales growth will return. Along the way you get top products, an experienced management and absolutely no debt. Chief executive and former Hewlett-Packard star Paul Ely Jr. recently brought in his old HP cohort Cyril Yansouni as president and chief operating officer. Convergent is ultra-high-risk because the industry is so cutthroat, but the potential is large. The stock could rise fivefold in the next five years.

Why take the risk of buying stocks that are down so badly? Where else in a heady upmarket can you still bag a bargain? ∎

Back to Basics
February 9, 1987

John, who has been doing carpentry for us for a few months, recently started foretelling the market's daily movements. How did he know what was going to happen? He based his judgment on what he heard on the TV morning news. One day he said, "Well, they say the Dow's goin' over 2000 today." And it did.

With a formal academic background and years of professional study, I never know where the market is going, but "they" do. What is more interesting is that "they" never used to care. But they do now.

As Bernard Baruch's autobiography said of 1929, "When beggars and shoeshine boys, barbers and beauticians can tell you how to get rich, it is time to remind yourself that there is no more dangerous illusion than the belief that one can get something for nothing."

Maybe I'm a 36-year-old fogy, but I can't get myself to buy based on a bull market. I can only do it the way we did it back in the static markets of the 1970s. We tried to buy things you were content to hold, whether the market rose or fell.

The way I learned it, the really big moves for a stock come from the differences between what Wall Street thinks a company is and what it really is. When Wall Street is wrong, it pays. When an outfit is better than Wall Street thinks it is, the market pays up, via a higher price. Likewise, when expectations for a firm exceed reality, the stock falls in proportion to the gap.

In those days you were supposed to scratch around among the more unpopular stocks, looking for good companies, ones where Wall Street was pessimistic—perhaps because of short-term industry trends or temporary internal problems—but ones where the outfit had growth prospects and a real niche to protect it from big, bad competitors. You wanted outfits with a real advantage, like low-cost production or novel products or superior service. And since you couldn't assume rising stock prices before a recession might appear, you also wanted a strong balance sheet so your company could weather tough times.

Has all this gone by the board? Only temporarily. For those who still want to invest the old-fashioned way, my firm's computers point out pockets of unpopularity, as statistically measured by low ratios of stock price to sales, earnings and book value, among the auto and the oil-related stocks, the nonresidential construction stocks and the mobile home shares. The market seems to envision a downtrend in building because of existing overcapacity and the new tax law, which takes away most of

nonresidential real estate's longstanding tax goodies. Folks also expect the traditionally cyclical auto world to crash after 1986's record sales. But each of these factors also has opposite possible consequences. Slower new car sales may help auto replacement parts outfits, which are in the market's doghouse, too. Low-income folks can't afford many new cars now at $8,000 to $20,000 a crack, but Uncle Sam's new tax bill helps them fix up their old clunkers. More than 60% of the new income tax cuts come as windfalls to folks who earn less than $20,000 per year.

The time will come again when John, my carpenter, will cease to be a market seer, and he will return to the sports pages. The stocks I want to buy today are those that will still be as good when that happens. ■

Betting on the Dow—Partly
March 9, 1987

The Dow Jones industrial average has done so well lately that not even the 30 Dow stocks themselves could keep up with it. For example, the DJIA gained 27%, including dividends, in 1986. But if you bought an equal dollar amount of each Dow stock in January 1986 and held it to year-end, your gain was only 18%, dividends and all.

How did the parts manage to do less than the whole? Simple. The DJIA counts a measly seven-buck gain in a $100 stock, 7%, for as much as it would a $7 gain, 100%, for Navistar. So when the high-dollar Dow stocks outperform the low-dollar Dow stocks, the index outperforms the stocks. That's what happened in 1986.

This statistical discrepancy is part of why folks, professionals included, fared poorly at keeping up with the Dow Jones in this banner year. CDA Investment Technologies Inc., a research group that tracks investment advisers, reported that the

average money manager gained just 17% in 1986.

If the pros gained only 17% in one of the best years on record, who makes really big profits—and how? The truly big rewards go to long-term holders of stocks that end up making big moves. The trick, of course, is identifying them. In all of my columns I have recommended only seven DJIA stocks—ever. The first six were in my January 28, 1985 column. Those six—Goodyear, Woolworth, Union Carbide, General Foods, Owens-Illinois and Du Pont—did so well that they provided more than 75% of the DJIA's total 1985 return.

Each has provided at least a 100% total return. General Foods was taken over, for a 145% gain. Goodyear and Union Carbide were reorganized to ward off raiders at big profits, and Owens-Illinois was the best-performing Dow stock of 1986.

I recount all this, not to brag, but to make a point. What did these stocks—plus a seventh I recommended later—have in common? (The seventh, Texaco, appeared in my February 24, 1986 column.)

What they had in common was 1) they were all well-financed companies and 2) they were out of favor for one reason or another when I recommended them. The first six were picked simply because they then had the Dow's best combination of unpopularity, as measured by low price/sales ratios, and strong balance sheets. Texaco didn't qualify then, but it did 13 months later, as it sunk because of the Pennzoil litigation and falling oil prices.

How can you assess balance-sheet strength? My favorite approach, as detailed in that January 1985 column, is a two-step process. First, divide a stock's current ratio (current assets divided by current liabilities) by four. Then divide equity by total assets. Add the two numbers together. You want the resultant sum to be 0.80 or higher—the higher, the better. This ratio trades off working capital against total debt, much the way a corporate treasurer would in managing his firm's coffers. If you divide a stock's price/sales ratio by this debt-adjusting factor, you can rank its popularity relative to its financial muscle—exactly the way I did in that column. ∎

Bull in Bull Markets
April 6, 1987

I was a newcomer in the investment business at the time. It was at a three-day American Electronics Association conference, during a dinner contest to see who could predict most closely the next day's move in the Dow industrials. Hundreds of folks were to turn in cards with their name and forecast.

So I guessed the Dow would fall 5.39. Then I noticed the gent next to me jotting down a 35-point plunge. With the Dow then around 800, a 35-point drop would make headlines. I asked him why he expected such a crash. He said he hadn't the foggiest idea what might happen.

Then he explained: "If you win, the crowd will think you were lucky to beat everyone else who bets on minor moves. But if my extreme call wins, they'll be dazzled." Dazzled they were, because the market dropped 29 points the next day. That afternoon folks bombarded the winner for details on how he had foreseen the crash. He obliged them all, embellishing his "analysis" more with each telling.

That night, when I saw him alone, he had convinced himself that he had known all along, and became indignant as I reminded him that his call was based on showmanship.

Later, on a much larger scale, Joe Granville seemingly did the same thing. Now we have Robert Prechter. The media are full of him and his supposedly brilliant recent market calls. *Fortune* recently put this sage on its cover, calling him "the champion market forecaster."

Champion? Prechter is noted for long-term, to-the-point predictions for the Dow, and for years has been predicting a straight-up ride to a 3600 peak—3686 to be exact. Last September he swerved momentarily to predict a brief correction on the route to 3686, and we got the swerve. Hallelujah! For that, a mass of media mental midgets see him as near-immortal rather than lucky. Yes, Prechter's extreme forecasts have been closer to the mark than most others' in recent years. But that doesn't mean he's found the secret that has eluded people for centuries: how to predict the future. It just gives him something in common with my former dinner mate.

The hoopla moved me to review Prechter's self-published book, *Elliot Wave Principle*, which details his methods and those of his mentor, RN Elliot. On careful reading, it becomes clear that Prechter's use of the Elliot Wave is internally inconsistent. He admits the Elliot Wave isn't useful for single stocks—only for indexes—and in his book makes only meager mention of two stock indexes other than the Dow.

Yet, if you know how the Dow is devised (detailed in most basic college investment texts), you also know that the Dow's level can often be more a function of stock splits than of stock movements. While few folks understand this, the Dow is a price-weighted index. After a split, a "divisor" is adjusted to keep the index' overall level steady, but the stock's weighting is split also, altering future performance. The Dow's structure is skewed with every stock split. To put it simply, how well the Dow does depends as much on how often its component stocks are split as it does on stock prices. How then can any "scientific" method know the market's future level? Can it foretell the frequency and timing of stock splits?

For example, if the six Dow stocks that had 1986 splits hadn't done so but still yielded their same, actually incurred, 1986 percentage value gains, the Dow would have been another 224 points, or 15%, higher in 1986 than it was. That's a 15% boost to the averages but not to shareholders' purses.

There's more. As I mentioned last month, the Dow's performance varies vastly from that of its underlying stocks, depending on how the high-priced Dow stocks do in relation to the low-priced ones. Last year, because the high-priced stocks beat the pack, the Dow industrial averages did almost 10% better than the Dow's underlying stocks.

So, if you can't predict the components and the splits, as Elliot Wavers can't (by their own admission, since they ignore individual stocks), then you can't be close to piercing the veil of the future on precise Dow levels. It has always seemed silly that *Wall Street Week* makes such a big deal about its yearly Dow guessing contest. The guesses and guessers are absolutely meaningless. I'm not against the Elliot Wave, but I am against applying it to the Dow, and particularly against those who have made accurate Dow calls with methods inappropriate to the Dow—and who now think they are more than just lucky.

And maybe my argument isn't so much with the Prechters and the Granvilles as with the naive media people who hype these alleged geniuses. The important point is this: Don't let yourself be mesmerized by prophecies and prophets, especially in this ebullient 1987, where fools are making fortunes. Stop worrying about where the Dow is going, and when, and keep looking for stocks that are true holds with underlying value and depressed prices. ■

Spread on Thick
April 27, 1987

It's the hidden transaction costs that kill short-term traders, particularly short-term bargain hunters. I'm not just talking about brokerage commissions. Precious few folks think in terms of the spread between a stock's bid and ask prices. Most investors hear that a stock is 22 and think they could buy or sell it for that. They can't.

You can only sell to bids, and buy offerings (a.k.a. the ask price). That's the real world that few folks consider. If a stock's last sale price is 22, its bid and ask are probably quoted at about 21¾ by 22¼. You can force a sale at 21¼, and a purchase at 22¼. But that's it. If you want to sell one stock that sold last at 22 to buy another "22" marvel, you must sell at the bid and buy at the offering and eat the spread. The spread in this example is half a point, or 2.3%. So you are that much in the hole before you even factor in brokerage commissions.

Can't you do what many do? Put in a lowered offering at 22 to sell your old dog and a raised bid at 22 to buy your new sweetheart, and skip all this spread baloney? Only if you are lucky, and not if you are smart. Here's why. Your old dog was 21¾ bid, offered at 22¼. The most anyone would pay for the mutt was 21¾. Now you want to offer yours at 22. You are welcome to, but to get your sale "off" you still need buyers to step up one-fourth of a point to 22—an effective price rise.

Ditto in reverse if you hope to buy your new darling at 22. You are welcome to split the bid and ask price. But you still need a price drop to buy your stock. What's wrong with that? Just this: To complete your sale you need the "good" stock to go down and the "bad" stock to go up sufficiently to get your price. So if your dog is really a dog and your new darling really is a sweetheart, trying to skimp the spread is absolutely penny-wise and pound-foolish—because you never end up owning the right stocks.

Of course, spreads vary, but 99% of all stocks have at least a one-eighth point spread, more than half have a one-fourth point spread or more, and lots have a one-half or three-fourths point spread—or worse. The worst damage often comes with the biggest bargains because the spreads are largest as a percentage of the trade in the low-dollar-per-share stocks.

Take a $30 stock with a one-fourth point spread, which then falls on tough times and Wall Street disfavor. It nosedives to $5. If your sniffing around smells good times ahead, be prepared to eat a huge spread, because during the stock's descent, the spread probably broadened to half a point—now 10% of the price. Most stocks under $10 have a half-point spread or more.

Don't get me wrong. I love low-priced, beat-up bargains and have put scads of them in these columns, but always for the long term so that transaction costs can be amortized over a big move. Think of the effects of trading. If some hot-shot, market magician has a system using $5 stocks with half-point spreads, in which he trades once a month, his system needs to yield 120% per year gross returns after the spreads (12 × 10%) just to break even. If he miraculously gets 50% gross annual returns, he goes broke quickly—in less than 2½ years. If instead he trades $10 stocks every other month, he still must get the stocks to rise at least 60% annually to come out whole. Egads!

And that's before brokerage commissions, which ain't cheap even when they are cheap. Commissions at discount brokers average about seven-tenths of 1% of what you are buying or selling. To in-and-out should cost you about 1.5% on top of your spread. At a full-service broker that might be 3% or more.

The market is a zero-sum game in the short term. For you to win, someone else must lose. Think of the problems pension plans suffer. Surveys say that the average pension plan pays 1.1% commissions, three-fourths of 1% in investment management fees, one-half of 1% on bank custodian fees, and rebuys its portfolio about once a year. If its average stock is $25 with a one-fourth point spread, it loses 1% there. All told, that's 3% per year—a lot, since it comes out of the market's overall return. Last year—a good one—the S&P's 500 gained just 17%. It's a miracle a lot of these pension funds aren't broke.

To avoid going broke yourself, minimize your ins and outs and make them only after careful analysis. Then buy bargains for the long term—unpopular, beat-up stocks of good companies. ∎

15% With Little Risk
May 18, 1987

Here's the deal. You get 8% annually, cash in hand. You get a good shot at 15% or more in total return, and with no more risk than if you were buying high-grade corporate bonds. Interested? You're probably not, because everyone now makes 25% per year in the stock market, probably you included.

But if you haven't lost touch with reality and if 8% to 15% with safety still sounds sensible to you, I have a suggestion: Take a look at convertible bonds. Not all convertible bonds. Buy convertibles where the premium to investment value is small or nonexistent.

Let's step back a bit. A convertible is a corporate bond with the right to swap the bond for a specified number of shares of the corporation's stock at the holder's option. If the stock rises enough to make the shares worth more than the straight bond value, the convertible will thereafter rise in exact proportion to the stock.

Most folks buy converts with the stock already above that "conversion value" so the bond trades based on the stock. Buyers think the bond is just like the stock but with, in many cases, a much better yield.

The trouble is you double-expose yourself to the current high level of stock prices. The bond will drop if the stock does, but so may the bond's underlying value. The reason: Stock declines are often worse as interest rates rise, making bond prices fall. In such an environment converts commonly drop significantly more than their underlying stocks.

Some folks dislike converts because technically they are subordinate to straight corporate bonds in a bankruptcy. But if you study the history of companies emerging from Chapter 11 proceedings, you see that statistically the bond repayment characterization of converts in reorganization varies only insignificantly from other corporate bonds (almost all of which are also general faith unsecured debt).

Here, then, is the kind of convert I like: Imagine one that isn't trading above conversion value and has the following five features. First, the underlying issuer has a balance sheet that won't quit. Next, to reduce risk further, see that the convertible issue you're considering is a big part of the outfit's total debt—so there aren't lots of other mouths to feed if tough times crop up. Third, is the yield to maturity competitive with nonconvertibles of companies with similar balance sheets?

Fourth, the spread between the stock price and the conversion price should be small enough so that the stock needs to rise only a few percent per year over the bond's life to put you "in the money." Finally, see that the stock sells at a low price-to-sales ratio so you know the stock has room to rise.

With a convert like that, you're getting a competitive bond return. But if, over the bond's life, the stock rises more than a few percent annually, you get any and all additional appreciation. Since numerous studies show that stocks have, on average, returned about 9% annually over the last 60 years, it isn't hard to see why you might make 15%-plus per year. That's 8½% yield upfront, plus 9 minus 2 (2% to get in the money), or 7% annually from potential appreciation. If you pick your issues carefully, you may do even better. ■

Will Rogers Was Right
August 1, 1987

Will Rogers had it right when he tongue-in-cheeked that "Stocks are easy—you buy 'em and when they go up, sell 'em." When he was asked what happens if they don't go up, he responded, "If they don't go up, don't buy 'em."

The Fisher corollary to the Will Rogers principle: Don't buy 'em unless they can go way up. Since there is always risk, I want to own stocks only where the potential gain far outstrips the potential loss.

Which means I never buy preferred stocks. Why the devil they're called *preferred stocks* is beyond me. No one in his right mind would prefer them. Folks buy them for a supposedly safe dividend yield. Reality is, preferreds pay less than bonds yet aren't as safe as common stocks. Few folks understand that preferreds are even riskier than common stocks. Preferred holders buy all that hogwash about those shares being senior in liquidation rights to common and so, therefore, less fundamentally risky. That's a pea in the shell game. Anybody who has ever worked his way through a big-time bankruptcy reorganization knows that. In court, the preferred shareholders' only voice is subordinated to the common shareholders' through majority rule vote on the equityholders' committee.

The weak link with preferreds is that their very nature violates a key cornerstone of sound investing: The only worthwhile investments are those where the maximum upside is very large in relation to the maximum potential loss.

When you buy any stock, preferred or not, the potential loss is 100%. Without the prospect of making at least several times that with a particular investment, the reward-to-risk ratio isn't high enough.

This same principle underscores why I have been bearishly biased against some of the supposedly safest common stocks, like the Baby Bells—and virtually all regulated utilities—because the potential returns are too low relative to the potential losses. The politically driven regulatory process gyps you of any big upside, but provides no real protection from financial disaster. Sure, you can make money in utilities if and when interest rates fall. But you can do just as well with the most ultrasafe bonds. Who needs the 100% risk for a few measly percent in dividends?

All the more reason for concentrating your investments in unpopular stocks of good companies. The thing that determines the big market moves is the difference between expectations and reality. So with time the unpopular stock of a good company will gain popularity as Wall Street realizes it's not so bad after all. It will then rise in price en route to reflect reality.

The trick is to buy companies meeting two criteria. First, stick to above-average quality through the now almost forgotten skills of measuring balance sheet strength and then looking for real world signs of fundamental business advantage. What would those signs be? Features like high relative market share, low-cost production, superior service organization, unique product quality (rare), unique technology (rarer still), topflight marketing or freight-oriented regional dominance. If a company has any two of these traits, it is almost certain to average good profitability and growth over the long term.

What do I mean when I talk about unpopular stocks? I compare the whole company's price tag—its market capitalization—to that of the market as a whole. Right now the market sells at about one times underlying revenues. I like to buy companies at about one-third of that—35% of sales—or less. This way, if our unpopular but above-average-quality outfit rises to average popularity, our stock triples. Yes, it's still possible to lose everything, but you can also make six times your money if the stock by chance rises to become twice as popular as the market. ■

Medium Is Beautiful
August 24, 1987

Where's a bargain hunter to turn? As the bull market pounds along, stocks of big companies selling at low price/earnings ratios have become virtually extinct. To see just how rare they now are, I asked our computer to scan the Standard & Poor's Compustat Tapes to see the S&P 500's current P/E makeup. At June 30, exactly half of the S&P 500 stocks sold above 19.4 times their trailing 12-month earnings, and half below that. Given the market's latest advance, this median average is even greater now. Ten years ago the market's average P/E was only 7, and scores of stocks sold far below that. So we have had a virtual trebling of P/E ratios for the big stocks.

But here's the killer. Only 32 sell for less than 10 times earnings. Only 6 of those sell at less than 6 times—and the only one with a balance sheet I would willingly show my mom is Chrysler (recently 36).

I next asked my computer to spit out all S&P 500 stocks selling below 10 times earnings, with a ratio of current assets to current liabilities greater than 1.6 and with less long-term debt than stockholders' equity. The computer came back with just six names: American Standard, Nacco Industries, Singer Co., Textron, Tonka Corp., and Trinova Corp. When I notched the current ratio screen up to 2.0, the computer gave me no names. Farewell high-quality, high-capitalization, low-P/E stocks.

If the easy hunting in big-cap, low-P/E stocks is gone, where is there still value? Try stepping down to stocks with medium market capitalizations. First, some definitions. There are about 375 publicly traded companies that the market values at more than $1.5 billion each. This is the traditional big-cap universe.

At the other end of the spectrum, there are around 7,000 companies the market values at less than $100 million—the small-cap stocks. Between the two extremes are the medium-cap stocks: the roughly 1,800 companies that the market says are worth less than $1.5 billion but more than $100 million.

Rigorous academic works like the Ibottson-Sinquefield and Fisher-Lorie studies have found that medium-capitalization stocks generally outperform big-cap stocks. If, over the last 60 years, you ranked all NYSE issues by market cap and annually bought the 20% with the lowest caps (which is roughly the same as medium cap as defined above), you would have averaged 3% per year better than with the average of all NYSE stocks.

In the last few years, however, things have flip-flopped. Big-cap stocks have been outperforming medium-cap stocks—and by wide margins. Take the year ended last June 30, and take the 100 stocks that had started 12 months earlier with the lowest market cap among the S&P 500. These 100 companies advanced, on average, only 6%, vs. a 25% gain for the overall S&P. The 100 companies that began the year with the largest market caps climbed 28%. So it has been an aberrational period.

But will big continue to be beautiful? I doubt it. There is so much more value among the medium-cap stocks today—those with total values of between $100 million and $1.5 billion. There is a bigger menu here, with lower valuations. The analysts have picked over fewer of these and the prices haven't risen so much and aren't so high.

For example, if I tell my computer to search for companies selling at less than 10 times earnings, with current ratios better than 1.6 and less long-term debt than equity, and I am willing to accept companies with market caps as low as $100 million, then instead of the 6 stocks I extracted from the S&P 500, I now get 26 companies. ∎

Fair-Weather Genius
September 7, 1987

Some folks say bull markets don't end without a heavy speculative phase, and that this market's bubble hasn't happened yet. Maybe. But to see a speculative mania today, you need only look at the mutual funds.

First, there are too many funds. There are more mutual funds than stocks on the New York Stock Exchange. Back in the 1960s there were a few hundred funds. By 1980 that had roughly tripled. Now there are more than 3,500 (including unit trusts). Since 1983 we've added new funds at roughly 25% per year. That's 75 new funds a month now.

Natural resources? Australian bonds? Mexican stocks? They're all prepackaged and ready to buy. There are style funds for almost everything—indexing, low P/E, low market cap, high market cap, high yield—you name it.

From its beginnings in the 1920s, it took until 1980 for the fund industry to amass $100 billion of assets. It now has more than $825 billion. That's 30%-plus growth per year. Not madness? Turn your TV to Financial News Network and watch a steady stream of relative newcomers forecast which no-load, telephone-switchable funds will perform best next week. Not next year. Next week.

In the go-go days folks got awed by gunslingers with hot-shot year-to-year returns. Now the game is seemingly to speculate which no-load funds will do best right now, and to switch out of the cold ones and into the hot ones, as if they were faucets to turn on and off.

Everyone seems to have forgotten what mutual funds were for: long-term investments for those without the wealth, skill or desire to build their own diversified portfolios—almost the opposite of speculation.

In a bear market, pain will appear. With so many new funds, many of the managers are too young and inexperienced to have flinched their way through even one bear market. This scares me—some of these youngsters will panic.

Nor are the older names in the business aloof from the frenzy. For example, who would expect Fidelity, with all its size and success, to have funds headed by relatively inexperienced 26-year-olds, almost straight out of business school? I don't care how bright or learned or highly paid a 26-year-old is; people that young shouldn't be running publicly traded mutual funds.

And make no mistake about it. In bear markets, funds get clobbered by redemptions. When they wake up each morning, they don't know what their redemptions or their cash balances will be. As reborn bears ask for their bullets back, funds are forced to sell—expensively, having to hit bids, knocking down stocks. Redemption-based sales cause prices of the fund's stocks to fall, lowering their net asset value, causing fundholders to freak out. That causes more redemptions—a vicious cycle.

Net fund redemptions will not only be the result of the next bear market but also will be among its fueling causes. In a bull market, this downward cycle is broken by the many bidders who step in to buoy up falling stocks. Bull markets have bids. In a bear market, bids simply vanish. The potential buyers are still there, but they hibernate. That is what a bear market is all about. You must experience it to know the feeling. My prediction is one of the next bear market's bloodiest sectors will be in these new mutual funds.

Don't get me wrong. Mutual funds are great. But with stock prices and valuations at record levels, my advice for mutual fund fans is to get old-fashioned. Stick with very old funds. Read the fine print in the prospectus and shop for management, management, management—where the top honcho has been there for decades, with a record of survivability through bad times. Even if you must pay full load fees, do it, but buy proven management and hold long term, the way funds were originally meant to be held. That way any load fee won't hurt much. It may even make you hang on through tough times and not flush yourself out at the bottom when your no-load friends do. ∎

Double Damned
October 5, 1987

If there is so much liquidity floating around to fuel higher stock prices, the way the superbulls claim there is, then why the devil are interest rates rising? With excess liquidity you would expect rates to be flat or down. Not so. Interest rates have been rising steadily, depending on which you look at, for the last 6 to 13 months—all of them.

Five-year Treasury rates bottomed out way back in August of 1986. Commercial paper and CD rates started rising in early September—last year. Long-term corporate and municipal bond rates didn't really start up until the January-to-March period. Since April we have had seven boosts in the prime rate. Take five-year Treasurys; they have risen from a hair over 6.5% to more than 8.75%—a 35% rate hike.

So where is all that excess liquidity? Overseas? Balderdash! Interest rates are rising all around the world in a rather steady trend, Japan. England. France. Germany. Everywhere. A key point I stress over and over in my new book, *The Wall Street Waltz*, is that major booms and busts occur worldwide. The whole world is now seeing rates rise, which means there is a worldwide shortage of liquidity, not an excess of it.

And eventually that will hurt stocks. Interest rates play off against stock prices through P/Es. It's confusing, but the way I have always simplified it in my mind is to invert the P/E into an E/P, which can be thought of as an earnings yield. Then it's a yield, like an interest rate, that can be compared with bond yields. The way I do it is to compare the market's earnings yield with the yield on long-term corporate bonds.

For example, right now, even after September's sinking spell, the Dow Jones industrials sell at about 20 times earnings. So the earnings yield is 1/20, or 5%. For a moment, forget about stocks per se, and consider how you would value businesses if there were no stock market in which to trade. The question is, would you buy a business for a price that would return 5% on your money when you could earn 10% in bonds? The answer is, only when corporate earnings will rise fast. You need at least a doubling in earnings to justify the valuation.

But rapid growth over the next few years is unlikely. This boom, which started in 1982, has just now become the longest continuous economic expansion in history. Along the way we have built unrealistically high expectations into our economy. Perhaps most unrealistic of all is Beryl Sprinkel, President Reagan's chairman of the Council of Economic Advisors.

Sprinkel is among the world's most highly educated ignorant men. He believes that "economic expansions don't die of old age, they die of inappropriate economic policies." Well, they do die of old age sometimes. Other times they die because of what's happening in other countries. And, again, as I detailed in my book, when the global economy starts going down, the policies of a single country can't keep that country from going down, too.

And that's when we really get it. Because, as if rates weren't high enough now, they will almost certainly rise more when our economy sours. Few ever expect this, but rates usually rise early in a recession. Why? Because sales fall, so inventories build up—which are financed through unanticipated borrowing. That's where stocks get double-damned, caught between falling earnings and rising rates.

If you now think I'm predicting the world's demise, relax. I'm not. But I'm also not predicting happy-ever-after, either. We will have a recession in the next year or so, and it will be a lot like others we have had. And along in there somewhere, stocks will fall, because there is a liquidity shortage and because the earnings yield on stocks is very low relative to bond yields.

So I'm not saying run for the hills, because I don't believe anyone can precisely "time" the market. What I am urging is to own only those rare stocks whose earnings yield over the next few years will be much higher than the bond yields against which stock valuations must compete. That means either low P/Es or low price/sales ratios, coupled with a big earnings rebound ahead. ■

How to Take—and Keep—Unfair Advantage

October 26, 1987

Posted by my desk is a sign saying, "All I want out of life is an unfair advantage." That's what I want out of stocks, too: companies with definable unfair advantages.

No, I don't mean companies that cheat, rifle rivals' files or bomb competitors' premises, bribe officials or sell shoddy products. I mean companies that are so firmly entrenched in their markets that their competitors are at a permanent disadvantage. Envision a product where one guy makes 40% of the widgets and the next biggest player has an 18% market share. Number three has only 12%, and the rest you could put in your eye.

The 40% fellow has as close to monopoly power as law allows. He can really whump his smaller brethren whenever he wants, even if they are bigger companies in other fields. Or he can let 'em live by setting prices high to keep them breathing—and him fat. Other things being equal, the big kid on the block ought to be able to beat up on the little kids almost every time.

Suppose the big guy wants to drop his production costs. Funding a study on how to do that costs him less than half as much per widget as it would for his next smallest competitor, because he can amortize the cost over his twice-as-large production base. Advertising costs him less per unit. Or he can hire lobbyists to cajole the rulemakers and amortize those costs as well over his market share in ways his smaller brethren could never afford.

But high market share alone doesn't give the unfair advantage I want. For example, if two guys each had 35% of a market, they might really hurt each other. I'm reminded of when Ali and Frazier fought. At the end of each bout even the winner was pretty beat up. No, I want high "relative" market share. I mean I don't want Frazier vs. Ali; I want Frazier vs. a featherweight. If my stock has 40%, I want to see the contender with 20% or less.

Mind you, the bigness I'm after doesn't require a giant company—just dominance in a few areas: It can actually be a quite small company.

Market share isn't the only good unfair advantage. It could be any basic business trait that allows a company over the long term to make above-average profitability or to have above-average growth: low-cost production, superior service capability, regional dominance, unique product (rare), unique product technology (rarer still).

Of course, having one of these advantages doesn't ensure success. The management must understand it has the unfair advantage, and it must understand what to do with it. General Motors and US Steel both had high relative market share going their way for decades, and successive managements were too dense to use it properly.

One more unfair advantage I require: to buy the shares of the companies that have unfair advantages at a cheapo price. The key to long-term stock investing is buying unpopular stocks of good companies—companies with unfair advantages but which are temporarily out of favor. In time the world appreciates the quality, and the stocks get more popular and rise in price.

My basic technique for identifying stocks with an unfair advantage is through price/sales ratios and price/earnings ratios. (For those who have forgotten, a price/sales ratio is the market price of the stock divided by the revenues per share.) Right now the market, depending on exactly which measure you use of it, sells for between 85% and 100% of its underlying revenues—a price/sales ratio of 85 cents to $1. That's rich for me: I want to stay with stocks selling at less than half that—and/or less than half the market's current P/E of 20. ∎

Diary of a Money Manager
November 16, 1987

Morose Monday—October 19, 1987, 7:30 a.m. West Coast time. I felt pretty good, pretty darn good. When my traders told me the Dow had gap-opened below 2200, we were cocky and excited. Our clients' portfolios had lots of cash. Our value-oriented, unpopular stocks had suffered only lightly compared with the largest-capitalization stocks.

By 11 a.m. the Dow broke below 2000. Our war-room staff joked about my August 13 debate on *The McNeill-Lehrer Report* against Dan Dorfman. He was bullish. I was bearish, saying the market was grossly overvalued and headed for a long-term 40% drop, taking the Dow to perhaps 1700. I hadn't expected it all so fast, but now it was here. Euphoria. More cockiness.

But our stocks were off only 8%. Throw in our hefty cash, and our portfolio looked super. Now we were getting ready to take advantage of the drop. We planned to buy from among the most bloodied big-cap stocks, but only those with the most value. Ones like General Motors at 50, with a $5 dividend, a 10% yield and a P/E of 5.

Tuesday—October 20, 6:15 a.m. West Coast time. We're positioning orders for the opening. Big-cap names: GM, Exxon, Sears, Federated, Ames Department Stores, National Intergroup, Pulte Home, Peoples Energy, Inland Steel, General Dynamics, United Technologies, Nacco Industries, Grumman and Fluor. All beat-up but with strong balance sheets and cash flows and low valuations relative to sales, earnings and asset value. Our kind of stock and—now—at our kind of prices. Then we throw in a few smaller-cap old favorites like those you have seen in my columns in recent years.

The market opens, but many big-cap stocks don't trade. For example, indications from the floor show GM at 55 bid, offered at 65, with a last sale of 50. My traders say it will probably open about 58. Now I'm feeling less cocky. Are they going to get away from us? GM finally opens at 65, right at the top of its spread. En route, its ultra-cheapness faded.

Now we had either to chase them or say good-bye. We did some of both. By midmorning the Dow was up 200 points, and we ended up paying much more than we had hoped before dawn. Just then stocks sank again. And we were there to catch them. For example, we loaded up on GM at 58 and 55. But it roared right through us to 51. Along the way the stocks we bought were now at losses. But only small losses. We still felt pretty good.

When the key news came, it barely creased our consciousness. They had temporarily suspended futures trading in the Chicago market because of an order overflow (and purportedly to stop program traders and portfolio insurers from pummeling the S&P stocks with their chicanery). Sounded wonderful. It wasn't. It was murder.

Some shrewd program traders, cut off from their heroin, figured they could get similar relief from options on the Value Line index, traded in Kansas City. The Value Line includes 900 stocks, all equally weighted, so it reflects the kinds of medium-market-cap stocks we usually hold (see my August 24 column).

Suddenly the medium-cap Value Line stocks started collapsing—big. The whole Value Line was down 8% in minutes—while the Dow and the S&P were rising. The normal owners of these secondary stocks, individuals, were paralyzed with fear from Monday's debacle. There were virtually no bids at all. These kinds of stocks can't take institutional punishment, because they aren't used to the phenomenal trading volume. The price declines extended the fear but broke the paralysis, as individuals panicked into a selling mode, dumping not only the Value Line stocks but other smaller-cap issues as well.

Within minutes, and on light volume, many of our same stocks, which held up so well Monday, fell 20% to 40%. When the dust settled, the Dow and S&P were up 5% to 6% for the day, while the Value Line fell that much. And we got hurt. I sure didn't expect such pain in these stocks. NBI, for example, fell 32%, from 7 to 4¾. And that with $8.50 of book value per share and a rock-steady balance sheet.

Tuesday, October 20, 11 p.m. Most folks bemoan Morose Monday. We suffer Terrible Tuesday. Until today we did great, and since August, I suppose we have done far better than most. So, we live to fight again—but not so cocky now. You keep learning—the hard way these days. I did.

Every stock in this column is fundamentally too cheap, by a wide margin, and is a long-term value. This must be a time to buy. But I learned that no matter how well you are trained, how smart you think you are, how good your game plan is and how many advantages you may have, when a freight train is coming, get off the tracks. ∎

The 2% Rule
December 14, 1987

As history is my guide, stock prices should move higher through the spring. Then they should drift lower for a very long time. In this prediction I differ from most money managers. Since Meltdown Monday most forecasts call for either straight down or a rebound to new highs in 1988 or 1989. To me, both possibilities are unlikely. Why?

My views owe much to my childhood hero, Yogi Berra, the alltime best bigleague catcher and great folk philosopher. "Sometimes you can see a lot just by looking," he once said. Just looking at what has happened in the past has convinced me that markets follow similar patterns. Nothing new of any real importance has happened in the market for centuries. So, if financial history doesn't include a type of event, it probably won't happen.

That's why I think the market won't free-fall. We've never done that—ever—where you had a sudden huge collapse rear-ended by a second collapse. You can see that via something my second book called "the 2% rule." The 2% rule says that from absolute peak to trough, major bear markets tend to fall at predictable average monthly rates of about 2%. For example, the famed Panic of 1907 was a 49% drop spread out over 22 months. That's 2.2% per month, with lots of big bounces and jiggles en route.

The 1987 Dow dropped 36% to its October low. That's a bear by anybody's standards—lots more than a "correction." According to the 2% rule, that's about 18 months' action compressed into two months.

My 2% rule meets Yogi's test. If you extend the 2% rule to consider average monthly declines of between 1.5% and 3%, then you include virtually every major bear market (except for 1937 and 1962). My point is that duration is just as important to bear markets as is magnitude. A bear market not only scares bulls with short, sharp drops but also wears them out with sucker rallies followed by prolonged, Chinese-water-torture-like declines that eventually cause most folks to believe that stocks will never again see a big bull.

Put it this way: Bear markets don't just suddenly turn into bulls. Dismalness and dullness are the stuff of which market bottoms are made. When the optimists can't remember why they were optimistic, the selling is complete.

When the selling is over, stocks have gone from selling at above-average valuations to below-average valuations. What does that mean? During the last 75 years, average P/Es were about 13. Average price-to-book ratios were about 175, price to-dividends were 22, price-to-cash-flow averaged 7, and price-to-replacement-cost-of-assets were about 90%.

If these averages were applied to the current Dow, the market should sell somewhere between 1500 and 1700. So the market should fall to below 1500 or even to 1200 before the bear is over. But it will, if history is a good guide, take a long time to get there—at least 15 months.

In between we should see some sharp minibull rises that give the bulls cause to hope and the bears a rally to sell into. Through year-end I'd expect more volatility, some of which will be fueled by tax-loss selling in the most beat-up stocks. But starting in January prices should rise, just as they did in early 1930. The economy won't have started to weaken—yet. And folks will begin to think maybe October really was what President Reagan called it—"just a stock market thing." Interest rates will be falling as the Fed tries to pump money. Reports of Christmas sales won't be great, but they will exceed November's expectations. The new year won't look too bad.

Folks who missed the 1982–87 rise will jump in, as will those who waited in 1986–87 for "a correction." Maybe the Dow will hit 2250 by June. That would realign us with the 2% rule's average trendline. But after that begins the Chinese-water-torture-like bear market that takes a very long time and drops today's Dow equivalent index to well below 1500. In the long term prices want to fall because, even now, they're still too high and because we've got a big economic decline coming, which I'll discuss next month.

What about the exceptions to the 2% rule? In 1937 and 1962 we had short, sharp major bear markets at rates much faster than 2% per month. Those two drops were followed by fast bounce-backs. This strengthens rather than weakens my case for expecting a rally in this bear market. If you want to participate in the 1988 bounce-back rally, do it with stocks that are liquid, too cheap and terribly beaten up. ■

1988

Ear to the Ground

> " *Why did stocks do better [than Treasuries or inflation] over the last 60 years? Probably for the reason I expect them to do better over the next 60 years. Stock represents business ownership. And businesses are run by adaptable people who can change with a changing world.* "
>
> "Anything That Can Happen . . . Probably Will," October 24, 1988

> " *Fear is highest around market bottoms, when it's the best time to buy. . . . The essence of money management is weighing possibilities against probabilities and going against your gut.* "
>
> "Anything That Can Happen . . . Probably Will," October 24, 1988

Nineteen-eighty-eight offered a few distractions from the Black Monday hangover. One major part of the world was rapidly changing. In the USSR, Mikhail Gorbachev was implementing dramatic social and economic reforms known as "perestroika"—a first step in the dismantling of the Soviet Union. In the US, George H. W. Bush defeated Republican contenders, including Bob Dole and televangelist Pat Robertson, to win the presidential nomination and eventually the presidency over Democrat Michael Dukakis. Sports offered some memorable moments as well. Hobbled Dodger Kirk Gibson hit his dramatic bottom-of-the-ninth-inning homerun to win Game One of the World Series. Still, all the distractions in the world weren't enough to make folks forget the stock market crash.

Ken was still short-term bullish. "There are so many short-term bullish signs now that it's a miracle everyone seems so bearishly blind to them." ("The Quiet Bull," March 7, 1988.) But he didn't expect that bullishness to last through year's end. In his view, most stock market prognosticators either believed Black Monday was a temporary event from which stocks would quickly recover, or they thought it was the start of an even more massive downturn. Few believed they'd see something in the middle—a bounce-back bear market rally followed by a renewed downturn. That was Ken's initial forecast. "Stocks have a good chance of moving higher through spring in a kind of reflexive rally, tied to the fact until then there won't be visible signs of recession." ("The Coming Recession," January 11, 1988.)

One of Ken's concerns was rising interest rates. Long-term interest rates rose in 1988, but not much. The more interesting change was in short-term rates. Prior to 2003, the Federal Reserve's discount rate—the rate at which banks borrow directly from the Fed—was lower than the fed funds target rate—the rate at which banks lend to each other in the fed funds market. (Today, the opposite is true—the discount rate is above the fed funds target rate.) This might seem like an easy opportunity to borrow cheap money from the Fed and lend it out at higher rates, profiting from the spread. But the hitch was (and is) only distressed banks can borrow directly from the Fed at the discount rate. That created a perverse incentive for banks to pose as troubled to get access to cheap funds. To remove this incentive, the discount rate had to be raised. Ken saw tightening monetary policy as a risk that could weigh on stocks.

Ken also believed too many economic soothsayers dismissed the impact of the bear market on the economy. They'd argue recessions lead to bear markets, not the other way around. As Ken saw it, years of economic expansion was partly fueled by people and businesses using their assets as collateral for debt. When asset prices fell, debt became undercollateralized, which forced folks to sell any liquid asset they could. In 1987, that was stocks. When the dust settles, scared firms favor liquidity over growth. They sell their less-liquid assets and rein in spending, sowing the seeds of recession. But that takes time. In the interim, stocks would rally. Ken thought a cautious business sector would eventually lead to mild economic contraction and a renewed stock market downturn.

But no forecast is ever set in stone. A few months into the year, Ken noticed the negative factors he thought sure to weigh on share prices were being offset by bullish signs—first and foremost: negative investor sentiment. Overly optimistic sentiment frequently precedes big stock market drops. Folks get giddy, forgetting the risks of investing. That sets the stage for disappointment when people figure out stocks and the economy aren't as bulletproof as expected. That euphoria was decidedly absent in 1988. In fact, most investors were extremely cautious if not outright dour. "I keep hearing about how 'the other shoe has to drop,' and this from folks who never had an inkling of the first shoe . . . Bullish. For the market to implode, investor sentiment should be more greedy and less fearful."

"You see charts in the press comparing the market's 1987 fall and post-November rally with 1929 and early 1930, leading to the inevitable conclusion that a late-1930 type drop is just ahead. You don't see anything in print suggesting a 50% market rise, or a 150-point up day. Simply no big optimism anywhere. Bullish." ("Frankly, I Am Confused," May 16, 1988.)

With compelling reasons to be both bullish and bearish, Ken saw stocks stuck in a rut. "It seems to me the market is trapped. It appears to be blocked on the high end by excessive valuations and high and rising interest rates that will put pressure against truly big gains. It is unlikely to fall far and fast because investor sentiment is so extremely negative." ("Three Stocks for a Dull Market," July 11, 1988.) But all was not lost. "The good news is that a flat market can be great for a good stock picker. In a bull market, almost anyone can make money. But in a basically sideways market, a good stock picker can make money when no one else does."

Ken thought stocks would rise in 1988, but was fairly cautious on the market overall. The S&P 500 rose 16.6 percent—better than the long-term average but below the bull market average of about 22 percent per year.[1] Foreign stocks again beat US stocks, rising 28.6 percent.[2] But it was a choppy year of fits and starts for the market. The S&P 500 experienced a 6.8 percent drop in a single day in January and several other significant pullbacks and jumps throughout the year.[3]

The Coming Recession
January 11, 1988

Since the crash, most economists have been chanting, "No recession ahead." The media have echoed the message. Even *Forbes* has joined the chorus (November 30, 1987). A *Wall Street Journal* survey of 40 leading economists shows 37 calling for no recession in 1988. It is fashionable to joke, "The stock market forecast nine of the last seven recessions."

I disagree with this consensus. As usual, the economists don't understand the economy.

Economic theory misses the mark by assuming that Main Street affects Wall Street, but that Wall Street's effect on business is only through interest rates. At times Wall Street helps or hurts Main Street directly through securities prices. That's why the stock market is a good economic forecaster—it's a major trigger mechanism to prosperity and recession.

Historically, when the market has tanked, a recession, as officially defined by the National Bureau of Economic Research (NBER), has usually followed. What about 1962, which is often cited to prove that stocks and economics aren't linked? That was mostly a US stock decline. It was triggered by President Kennedy's attempt to scare the steel firms into line on wage rates.

But if you look at global market busts, instead of just US bear markets, and correlate them to major worldwide economic declines, the linkage is effectively 100%. When the world stock market goes down big, the economy follows in 6 to 12 months. Given the global nature of the market crash, history portends a recession.

To see why stocks can trigger recessions, envision a classic bull market. Early on, some folks borrow to get more assets to make more money. As they succeed, they become ever more adventurous, as do their previously timid friends. They borrow against real estate to buy stocks, against stocks to buy real estate and against both to build widget plants. Then they borrow against their "wealth" to buy bigger houses and fancier cars. Bull markets encourage big-ticket spending—and big-ticket borrowing.

As worldwide private-sector debt rises relative to GNP, the banking system becomes strained. So the central banks, one by one, readdress their main function, protecting the banks by raising interest rates—which is what we saw last year.

At first higher interest rates don't slow the borrowing; few care if money costs 8% when they are making 25% in stocks. At first. But eventually, it happens. For whatever reason, stocks fall a hair. The debt level stays fixed. That causes relative under-collateralization of the debt, which generates a worldwide scramble for liquidity, which is what October 1987 was all about.

Investors sell stocks because that's about all you can sell fast. That selling, in turn,

---

Some Things Change, Some Stay the Same

While much of this is still true, better technologies do allow firms to better respond to trouble they see brewing. Technology has drastically improved inventory management, which is why inventories remained lower relative to history in the 2001 recession and exceptionally low, relatively, in the 2007–2009 recession.

But it remains true as ever that the market is a leading economic indicator—it drops before recession is even thought of and starts rising well before the recovery is felt—and much before it's seen in official data.

pushes stocks lower, increasing the under-collateralization. When the panic settles, folks and firms think in a different mindset, with liquidity now foremost in their thoughts. To regain liquidity they eventually sell real estate, factories and whole corporate divisions. They will close plants and fire workers. These things generate recession.

But it takes time. You can't sell a division overnight, and you can't close a plant fast. Bureaucracies, like those of most S&P 500 outfits, couldn't plan their way out of a paper bag in less than three months.

Because of the time lag, we won't see visible signs of this market-crash-generated recession until the later part of 1988.

And what you don't see is what gets you. Economists never see a recession until we are well into it. Remember Gerald Ford's WIN (Whip Inflation Now) buttons? He was pumping for an anti-inflation tax hike in September 1974, fully a year after we entered a whopper. Do you recall who was Ford's chairman of the Council of Economic Advisers? Alan Greenspan.

Perhaps recession can be averted through money creation and central bank cooperation, but the banks have rarely cooperated before. Nationalism is now on the rise, building political pressures to keep them from cooperating. And our 1988 elections won't help in terms of encouraging meaningful world economic cooperation.

So a recession is coming. They rang a bell in October—all around the world—and announced it. This coming recession won't end until we have repaid or written off a double dose of debt, which also takes time—probably not until late 1989.

Short term, as I explained last month, stocks have a good chance of moving higher through spring in a kind of reflexive rally, tied to the fact that until then there won't be visible signs of recession. ∎

Tighten Up, But Don't Panic
February 8, 1988

No, the sky is not falling. But, as I have said before, we entered a bear market in August that will most likely last until late 1989. With it will come a recession, starting maybe in the summer. But this will not be the end of the world.

In magnitude and style this event will be much like most other cycles we have faced before. So understanding the history of bear markets and recessions is vital to success.

The short, sharp bear market rallies we can expect will be great for nimble traders and speculators. With each new tumble will come increased doom-and-gloom babble. Bear markets cause folks to seek reasons to justify the decline. They usually miss the real ones and collectively harp on phonies. The mass of myths accumulates and turns most people bearish precisely when they should be bullish—at the market's eventual bottom.

Why do I say the sky isn't falling? Because most of what you hear is much believed but it's just talk, not reality. Take, for example, the hoopla about Uncle Sam's debt and budget deficit. They are blamed for the trade deficit, the October crash, the fallen dollar and for perhaps a coming depression. We may or may not have a depression, but not because of these deficits.

Consider the debt crisis. You have often heard that Uncle Sam has $6,700 of debt for every man, woman and new child born in America. That's true, but not so bad. The interest cost of carrying that debt is about $600 per capita per year. GNP is about $4.5 trillion. There are about 225 million Americans. You do the math. GNP comes to about $20,000 of average income per capita. Does $600 out of $20,000 sound like a crisis to you?

Actually, Uncle Sam is the richest entity in the world. If you count the 750 million acres of land he owns (even with Nevada desert), plus built assets, if he wanted to he could sell assets and pay off the debt many times over. His raw grassland in Washington, DC alone, not the memorials and buildings, but the raw grassland, is worth about 40% of his debt at average undeveloped Washington, DC real estate prices.

Or try the budget deficits. First, I don't think they exist. Uncle Sam supposedly blows about $180 billion per year. But he pays about $100 billion to our local governments, and collectively they run surpluses of about that amount. You plop all of government together, and it's out of one pocket and into the other. The other $80 billion of deficit is mostly mirrors too. Uncle Sam doesn't depreciate purchased assets the way the private sector does. He writes them off immediately. But he is the largest buyer of capital assets in almost every category. By my figures, if the government started doing its books the way private industry does, that $80 billion of deficit would vanish too.

Interestingly, if America's largest outfits, as represented by the 900 biggies in the Value Line Industrial Composite, kept books the way Uncle Sam does, according to Value Line statistics, industry would be running a $60 billion deficit this year and would have run a deficit in every single year of the last 20.

But even if the budget deficit is real, it's no larger in relation to the size of our economy—or ability to shoulder it—than that of our major trading partners. Why are our deficits supposed to be so bad while their deficits go hardly noticed?

Which brings us to the much-discussed trade deficit—also often credited for the October collapse. If the trade deficit is bad for us, shouldn't it be good for the foreigners? But look at what happened to their stock markets since October—just as blotto as ours—or worse.

No, the trade deficit is a result of our business expansion being too strong. The only thing that will reduce this deficit will be a recession, which ironically will also boost Uncle Sam's budget deficit, as income and taxes fall. Wait until you hear the doom-and-gloomers then. I predict that a potential $400 billion budget deficit will emerge and keep most folks from buying—right at the market's bottom.

Then there's the drivel you hear today, mostly from older folks, about how we don't save anymore. That's a basket of manure. We save plenty, only we don't do it the way we used to. Today its done via state, municipal and private pension plans. Why, the California teachers' retirement system alone has saved about 40 billion bucks. Pension savings recirculate through the economy just like any other savings.

Finally, there's the myth that big-cap stocks are okay, but you must avoid smaller-cap, o-t-c stocks like the plague. You can see the signs of this most recently among the people quoted in Susan Lee's January 11 column. But I predict that for nimble sellers, the biggest 1988 profits will come from second-tier stocks. ∎

Deficient Thinking

Here Ken points out that America's big trade deficit is frequently, and wrongly, derided as a major negative. It's not. If it were, stock and economies of countries with trade surpluses would be inherently better than those with trade deficits. They're not—as Ken points out in his 2006 book, *The Only Three Questions That Count*. The trade deficit is a recurring fear that pops up through the years. And America's big trade deficit doesn't hurt us any more now than it did then. In fact, it's likely more a symptom of economic health.

The Quiet Bull
March 7, 1988

Stocks have been rising nicely—since December. True, the Dow and the S&P 500 are basically flat, but they measure only part of the market. The Value Line Composite, by far the best measure of the average stock, rose 16.5% from December 4 until January 30. The O-T-C Composite, another broad gauge, was up 17.7%—a rally by anyone's standards. The most bullish feature of this bear market rally is that no one notices it. They see only part of the market.

There are so many short-term bullish signs now that it's a miracle everyone seems so bearishly blind to them. The fact that sentiment is so awfully negative is in and of itself positive. In talking to investors, I continually hear about "when the other shoe drops." Everyone can envision another big down day, but few seem able to imagine a 200-point up day. We have more than 100 clients, and I interact with lots of pros. Not one in ten thinks stocks can sustain any significant advance. That's bullish as the devil.

So is the fact that insiders—top managers and board members—are on a buying spree of almost unprecedented magnitude. Big insider trading has usually had uncanny accuracy in being on the right side of big moves. Normally, there are at least two insider sales for every buy. Since October this ratio has flip-flopped. Buys lead sales almost 2-to-1—mostly in second-tier stocks. To eyeball this yourself, get *Vicker's Weekly Insider Report* (Post Office Box 59, Brookside, NJ 07926), which details all insider trades—right off government filings.

The current blindness to the rally started with the view that stocks bottomed on October 19 and then rebounded. Pure fiction. The market as a whole didn't bottom until early December. The rest is mirrors.

First, look worldwide, where the big moves always occur. For speed's sake, look at the back of *Investor's Daily*, which graphs stock trends in markets around the world. The bottoms came in early December.

Then look at American stocks, but do it the way few do, with some smarts about how the indexes work that measure our stocks. First, forget the Dow Jones industrials. Yeah, it bottomed on October 19, but it's a silly index. It covers only 30 stocks, and in a most bizarre and often dramatically misleading manner (detailed in my April 6, 1987 column).

Then skip the also much overused S&P 500. As I see it, the index doesn't exist. It's really what I call the S&P 151. It's a "market capitalization weighted" index. It covers 500 stocks, but each one's influence within the S&P depends on what the market says the whole outfit is worth (price times shares outstanding). So, by chance, the top 100 market cap stocks make up about two-thirds of the S&P 500's results. If the bottom 20% (or 100) of the companies in the index dropped off the face of the earth, it would drop the S&P 500 by only about 2%.

Turn instead to the Value Line Composite. It has two big advantages. First, it covers the same stocks as the S&P does, but it also covers another 1,200 smaller stocks that the more commonly watched indexes miss.

Second, Value Line is unweighted—meaning that each and every stock has about the same impact on the index, which is much the same way a portfolio works. So when the 1,700-stock, unweighted Value Line Composite moves, it is our best reflection of the average American stock. Its bottom? December 4.

Now here's the key. Think of the Value Line in two parts—the S&P 500 part and the non-S&P, smaller-cap part. When the

Value Line bests the S&P, it means the non-S&P part of the Value Line must be doing much better than the S&P segment.

Since early December, and for the first time in years, the Value Line has outperformed the Dow and the S&P every week. That means smaller-cap stocks are whomping larger-cap issues. And that's classic behavior for a bear market's first countertrend rally. As long as the Value Line rides high relative to the Dow and S&P, this bear market rally probably has life.

While on bullish signs, note that no matter how hard the Fed tries, it can't prop up interest rates. Since December the Fed has held Fed funds, its prime tool, tight

as tamales. T-bills, the flip side, haven't budged, either. But market competitive rates have been silently drifting down— CDs, commercial paper, utilities, muni bonds, even the prime rate. Lower interest rates alone don't ensure higher stock prices, but they can't be bad.

How long will the rally last? I don't know—maybe until April or May. As I have said for months, we are in what seems like a major countertrend rally to a several-yearlong bear market. En route we should have a rather regular but big recession. The world won't come to an end. And 1988's best investment results will come to those who are nimble at holding and knowing how and when to sell. ∎

By the Book
April 4, 1988

Reader James W. Barlow of Clearfield, Utah, writes, "Back on June 3, 1985 your column was entitled 'Gifts of the Gurus.' I greatly enjoyed your selections. Could you expand your list on other investment books to read?" I hasten to respond with some new suggestions. (At the end I will repeat the titles of the books I recommended earlier.)

The Too Jones Averages by Bennett Goodspeed (EP Dutton, 1983). This book teaches you to overcome man's irrationality through the eyes of ancient Lao Tsu's Taoist teachings. Not only is Goodspeed's writing witty and entertaining, it also bubbles over with wisdom that lets you pierce much of what you read and hear about on Wall Street by teaching you inferential thinking.

Once I picked it up, I couldn't put down *How to Lose $100,000,000 and Other Valuable Advice* by Royal Little (Little, Brown & Co., 1979). Little humbly shows you his mistakes along the road to building

giant Textron through acquisition. His business buying blunders, which he unabashedly unfolds in open-kimono style, are mostly the same ones folks make when they buy stocks. Reading this book will help you avoid them.

The Stock Market Crash and After by Irving Fisher (no relation—The Macmillan Co., 1930) is available only in better libraries or through book finders, but it is a fascinating account of the 1929 crash. Fascinating because it was penned in the midst of the decline by the greatest of America's pre-Depression economists, who incorrectly thought the market would promptly rebound. From his grossly mistaken analysis one learns valuable lessons about 1929 and about how wrong famous forecasters can be.

There have been a lot of personal financial planning books, most of which were obsoleted by the 1986 tax revisions. William E. Donoghue's *Lifetime Financial Planner* (Harper & Row, 1987) is the best of the new post-tax-bill planners. Its wide scope ranges from retirement plans and insurance to custodianships for your kids and taxes. Full of sound advice and easy reading, it's ideal for anyone who wants to plan his or her financial future, which should be just about everybody these days.

While obviously biased and a bit of the braggart, I wouldn't have penned my two books if I didn't think I had something to say. My *Super Stocks* (Dow-Jones Irwin, 1984) covered new turf by introducing the world to price/sales ratios (PSRs). If you have been intrigued by PSRs in my columns, this book was the first detailed coverage of the subject.

My *The Wall Street Waltz* (Contemporary Books, 1987) seeks to give perspective to an overview-starved world in the easiest format to grasp—a detailed picture book. Each right-hand page is one of my 90 favorite long-term charts, in color. Everything from stocks, interest rates, real estate, commodities, government finance and quackery, spanning centuries. On each left-hand page is an analysis, in a format similar to my columns, explaining the source, how to read it, and what it means and says about the past, present and future.

Every investor should read one of the great graduate investment texts. Far and away my favorite is Frank Reilly's *Investment Analysis and Portfolio Management* (Dryden Press, 1985). Reilly is the business school dean at Notre Dame. He is also exhaustive without being wordy. For example, not one professional investor or journalist in ten really understands how the Dow, S&P and other indexes actually

work. Yet, everyone babbles about them. You can get them all down cold in just 12 of Reilly's 895 pages.

Another key reference is Mike Lehmann's *The Dow Jones-Irwin Guide to Using the Wall Street Journal* (Dow Jones-Irwin, 1984). It's sort of a "How to be your own economist by reading the paper." Lehmann explains how the leading indicators work and puts them in perspective.

Each year I am one of the few Americans who actually read a little $11, one-inch-thick mind-calmer called *Budget of the US Government* (available from the Government Printing Office in Washington, DC). While the plot is thin, you will be amazed. Read it. It reveals to me that there isn't really any federal debt crisis—the federal deficit doesn't really exist if you count it right—and Uncle Sam is superrich.

Those are my newer choices. My favorites remain: *How To Buy Stocks* by Louis Engel (Bantam Books, 1953); *The Intelligent Investor* by Ben Graham (Harper & Row, 1949); *Security Analysis* by Ben Graham and David Dodd (McGraw-Hill, 1934); *Common Stocks and Uncommon Profits* by Phil Fisher (my father—Harper & Row, 1958); *Extraordinary Popular Delusions and the Madness of Crowds* by Charles Mackay (L.C. Page & Co., 1841); *The Templeton Touch* by William Proctor (Doubleday, 1983); *The Contrarian Investment Strategy* by *Forbes* columnist David Dreman (Random House, 1980); *The Money Masters* by John Train (Harper & Row, 1980); and *Reminiscences of a Stock Operator* by Edwin Lefevre (George H. Doran, 1923). ∎

And the Last Shall Be First

April 25, 1988

In 1988's first quarter the Value Line Composite, which reflects smaller stocks, rose 14%, versus a measly 3% for the Dow 30, which reflects the corporate behemoths.

The irony is that so few expected this divergence. The swings between these two groups is a seldom studied but key factor in understanding market movements.

There are two rules here. First, big-cap stocks—the kind you always think of as big, safe names—are usually less volatile than smaller-cap issues, in both up and down markets. If the market plunges, you probably lose less with the big names, but if the market rises sharply, you usually make more by diversifying among lesser names.

It doesn't always happen that way, though. At times, as in 1986–87, 1972 and 1929, the smaller-cap stocks don't rise like the big boys at the tail-end of a major bull market. This is what technicians call "decreasing breadth," meaning a few big-cap stocks are carrying most of the advance, which is generally considered bearish. This 1987 phenomenon conditioned folks to thinking of big-cap stocks as the best way to make money. When the big caps fell less in late 1987 than the smaller fry, it reconfirmed the wisdom in most folks' minds of owning only big-cap stocks.

And that's just when you should remember rule two: In the very long term, smaller-cap stocks provide higher returns than the big guys.

Another way to think about it is that most of America's economic growth has come not from industrial giants but from emerging firms that end up becoming giants. (Think back on the emerging Apple Computers, DECs and Wal-Marts.) The same will be true in the future. To the innovators go the spoils, and generally the big guys are the status quo, not the innovators.

Much of this is statistically documented at length in a wonderful little book entitled *Stocks, Bonds, Bills and Inflation: The Past and the Future* by Roger G. Ibbotson and Rex A. Sinquefield. Often referred to in the industry as the Ibbotson-Sinquefield study, this work was commissioned by the Financial Analysts Research Foundation and is updated yearly. Skip the expensive updates. I got my 1985 edition for $ 1 at a library book sale. The historical data are just as good.

Starting with January 1926, the authors compare the monthly results of buying the average New York Stock Exchange stock with buying only the 20% of those NYSE stocks with the lowest market caps. Over the last 60 years the smaller-cap stocks did, on average, about 3%-per-year better than the average of all stocks. Since the smaller caps did better than average, the largest caps did worse.

But the most telling aspect is to consider when the smaller caps did their doing. Take 1929. In that fateful year the average NYSE stock fell 33% from its August peak, on an inflation-adjusted basis, to a short-term low in November. But the smaller-cap stocks peaked earlier (in July) and fell longer (until December). En route, the little fellows dropped another 15%, losing almost half their purchasing power. Sound like 1987? You betcha.

Then in the 1930 countertrend rally that peaked in April, the average NYSE stock gained 22%. In the same rally the smaller-cap stocks peaked earlier (in March) but climbed 35%. In the bust the big guys did better, but in the subsequent rally the little guys led the way and peaked out earliest.

Same thing at the 1974 bottom. In 27 months, coming off the September bottom, the average NYSE stock gained 62% in real buying power. But the smaller-cap stocks, which didn't bottom out until December, gained 140%.

Which is exactly what I have been predicting will happen this year: a bear market rally with leadership by the smaller stocks, which will then falter, with leadership taken over by the bigger stocks, until the latter, too, run out of steam.

Once we suffered a big-stock decline in the fall, it was easily predictable that the next big up-move, whether a major bull market or a countertrend rally, would be led by second-tier, low-cap stocks.

If what we are seeing is just a countertrend rally—as I envision—you need to plan to sell soon, which brings up the question of how far this rally can go. An old saw runs, "Bull markets end with a whimper, not with a bang." That's true. This peak will almost certainly be a relatively quiet six-to-eight-week event in which stocks fall ever so gently. As this occurs, the smaller-cap-oriented Value Line Composite will regularly, but perhaps only slightly, underperform the S&P 500. Likewise, the O-T-C Composite will lag the O-T-C 100 (the o-t-c's largest caps). When this happens—when the smaller caps stop thrashing the big caps—the end is near.

My fear is, that may have already started, as the second-tier stocks stopped booming in mid-March. If that continues for a few more weeks, I would sell any stock, big cap or small, unless you are ready to own it throughout a bear market. ∎

Frankly, I Am Confused
May 16, 1988

Everything I know about valuations, financial history and economic cycles says last fall's market crack should have been the first leg down in a long-term, two-year bear market. This view is consistent with the strong countertrend rally that started last December in the secondary stocks, and that I have been discussing continually since then.

But my readings of investment sentiment give a different picture. The big runup in secondaries should have made investors relatively upbeat on stocks. It hasn't. In a contrarian sense, that's optimistic. In talking to folks, I hear tremendous pessimism. I keep hearing about how "the other shoe has to drop," and this from folks who never had an inkling of the first shoe. As my firm has taken profits from this rally, our investors have been *too* glad. Bullish. For the market to implode, investor sentiment should be more greedy and less fearful.

Insider buying continues to run at close to alltime record highs. Executives and directors are packing away big bunches of their own company's stock week after week. Bullish. In my career I have never seen an insider buying spree like this one—ever. While deluges of insider buying and selling are often early, they seldom are on the wrong side of major market moves.

The world seems to acknowledge the recent rally led by the secondary stocks but seems to expect it to fade away. You see charts in the press comparing the market's 1987 fall and post-November rally with 1929 and early 1930, leading to the inevitable conclusion that a late 1930-type drop is just ahead. You don't see anything in print suggesting a 50% market rise, or a 150-point up-day. Simply no big optimism anywhere. Bullish.

Also bullish is the action of the overseas stock markets. Foreign stocks are rising. In Denmark they have risen steadily since November. In Sweden it's since December. In Japan since January. Australia went nowhere until February but has been straight up since. Canada, France, Germany, Hong Kong, England, Norway, Switzerland—they have all had major 1988 rallies, and keep rising. Bullish.

Yet, for all these bullish indicators, I can also make a strong bear case. There are strong signals coming from both the bull side and the bear side.

I have listed the bullish factors above. Now for the bearish ones. First, stocks aren't cheap. There are two ways to see this. The market indexes all average at about 15 times earnings. While that isn't outrageous, it is on the high side of long-term historical norms. At a P/E of 15, the market has an earnings yield of 1/15, or 6.6%. That's hardly compelling, compared with high and rising bond yields of 9% to 10%. Other valuation measures, like price to book, cash flow, sales and dividends also say that the market is a bit too high.

Second, there's not a lot that's selling much below the average of the market. There were lots of cheap secondaries, but the really super 1988 rally in this class of stock raised most all of them a lot—

beyond cheapness. There are still some cheap tertiary tiny-cap stocks. But if the market were to head lower, their already minimal liquidity would vanish completely. Who needs it? Big-cap stocks? There are about 350 companies the American market values at more than $1.5 billion each.

Also bearish: Interest rates resumed their 1986–87 upward march in February, and the dollar resumed its weakness. Rates have been rising worldwide. If the dollar hadn't fallen, our rates would be higher still. Meanwhile, after the longest peace-time economic expansion in history, and at a time I'm fearful of recession, our monetary officials are talking about fighting inflation. Scares me.

Finally, as discussed in my March 7 and April 25 columns, the secondaries have finally stopped outperforming the big-cap stocks. The end of this superior relative performance seems to date to March 9. If you review those two columns, you will see why I think this is so bearish.

All told, I am confused. Investment sentiment, being negative, suggests stocks should rise, but a big advance would get stocks awfully overvalued. A recession from here could drop stocks another 40%-plus by late 1989. Being confused, here is how I am structuring my portfolios: 25% big-cap stocks, 25% secondaries, 50% cash—and waiting and watching. ∎

Stormy Weather Stocks
June 13, 1988

You probably are going to continue owning some stocks even though you fear a bear market. What kind of stocks should they be? By my thinking, they should be dirt cheap and have high relative market share in their industries.

What has market share to do with the stock market? In a bear market,

plenty. My authority for this is history and a gentleman named Charles Schwab—not the famous discount broker of that name but the long-deceased steel magnate. In a cutthroat era, when steel prices had fallen steadily for decades, this Charles Schwab got JP Morgan to back him in buying up steel outfits at about five times depressed earnings. By putting companies together, Schwab knew he could dominate certain markets. He knew that market share had a worth in and of itself, particularly in tough times. Thus was US Steel born.

Schwab quit and started what is now Bethlehem Steel, again concentrating on market share, this time in steel specialties and subspecialties. He knew he didn't have to dominate the whole industry to be the kingpin in certain parts of it.

Kenneth Iverson proved that again in the early 1970s when he started building market share. His *Nucor Corp.* made steel joists and was America's largest consumer of angle iron. So instead of buying angles, he started making his own, using new technology with lower costs—which he both used himself and sold to others. His internal use allowed him quickly to become the big kid on the block, and gain dominance in angle iron.

Over the years, Iverson plowed his above-average profits back into transferring his low-cost skills into other steel products, but always mindful of his relative market share. His goal, as he told me then, was quickly to gain 35% market share and be twice as big as the next guy in any product. Nucor has become far and away America's most successful steel firm, and Iverson is an industrial legend.

Iverson used new, low-cost production technology to help build market dominance. Another version of the same game is to build low-cost distribution. Another is to pick off a geography that isn't well served by others. New and improved product features work, too, sometimes, but the goal of all these strategies is to gain market-share dominance and keep it.

Why is market share so important? Nothing mysterious. Many activities, like advertising, information accumulation and governmental regulation and compliance, cost a big guy little or no more than they do a little guy, but the big guy can amortize the costs over his much larger unit volume.

What has all this to do with which stocks to own if tough times are ahead? In a downturn everyone suffers, but on average the guys with lowest relative market share get hurt worst. As things get bad, the weak get weaker, and eventually many can't take the heat and get out of the industry.

As that happens, everyone who remains picks up a little market share. Competition is now a hair less intense. When the decline is over, the survivors make bigger profit than before. That's what capitalist cycles are about—building supply when needed and purging supply when it's not—and purging the weakest (usually the smallest), so those that produce the product at the lowest cost can thrive.

I have rarely lost money when I've bought high relative market share at a cheap price. Every other thing can work against you, and you still usually come out okay. ■

Three Stocks for a Dull Market
July 11, 1988

Was the June rally for real? Is the market finally coming out of the doldrums? I wouldn't bet on it. But I wouldn't exactly expect the market to drop either. It seems to me that the market is trapped. It appears to be blocked on the high end by excessive valuations and high and rising interest rates that will put pressure against truly big gains. It is unlikely to fall far and fast because investor sentimentis so extremely negative.

Some folks see lots of value in today's market. But this market looks reasonably priced only if you look at P/Es and nothing else. Last summer the market sold at 22 times earnings. The market is now down 30%, and earnings are up 15%. But that still leaves you at 15 times earnings, smack dab in the middle of historical valuations. Bulls argue that the Dow (ones industrials' earnings will rise another 20% in the next year, to about $175, 12 times next year's earnings. So what?

A P/E of 12 is an earnings yield of 1/12, or 8%. Why is that so attractive when you can buy a bird-in-the-hand bond with a 10% yield? A future P/E of 12 isn't terrible, but it's not great either.

Then there is the market's dividend yield, which is about 3.4%. Another way to say that is 29 times dividends, a level that has always led to lower prices long term. Normally the market averages about 22 times dividends, and every decade or so you can buy it below 17 times. It has always been worth the wait.

Then there is book value. The S&P 500 is now at 3.25 times its book value. To my knowledge, the only years of higher prices in relation to book—ever—were 1987 and 1928–30. Otherwise, 2.5 times book was the peak, which is the DJI's current price to book. Since 1920 stocks have averaged only 1.5 times book. Of course, bulls will argue that inflation has perverted asset values

Flip It to See It

Flipping the P/E on its head and looking at the earnings yield and how it compares to other comparably liquid investment alternatives is something Ken had been doing for a long time and is still doing today. Too many investors focus on the P/E, but the P/E alone gives you no context. If you can compare an earnings yield (the E/P) to, for example, a bond yield, then you can begin deciding if a stock is attractively priced, relatively.

and that stocks should now sell at higher price-to-book ratios. But the 1910–25 era saw high inflation, too.

Looking at the other side of the coin, there are equally strong suggestions that the market won't drop much. Take the bearishness that prevails among so many investors. A fresh poll of the American Association of Individual Investors shows only 23% of its members as bullish. Before October's crash, 65% were. Or consider *Investors Intelligence*'s ranking of market newsletters: Recent readings show 55% of them are bearish, which is the highest level of bearishness since August 1982, when the bull market began.

Of course, a small advance may be enough to swing sentiment, which would end the rally. And that leads to my Forecast du Jour, which calls for the market to go nowhere fast—just where it has been headed all year. If it rises too far, it will run into a wall of hard valuations and high interest rates. If it drops much, it sees a world that is still so scared from last October that it panics too many sellers too fast, and creates an oversold condition, and a sentiment-based bottom.

The good news is that a flat market can be great for a good stock picker. In a bull market, almost anyone can make money. But in a basically sideways market, a good stock picker can make money when no one else does.

How do you get to be a good stock picker? The road to good stock selection is lined with value. Buy the unpopular and beat-up issues of fundamentally good companies. The key is in combining the cheap with the good. I particularly like to measure popularity using low price/sales ratios.

If the market stays flat for a while, a stock like that will do well. Why? Because it is a special situation—a justifiable takeover and/or turnaround. If it's really cheap, someone can take it over without being a greater fool. And if its earnings have vaporized but it has a strong balance sheet and unique product, high market share or low production costs, the inevitability of its turnaround will soon be obvious to all on Wall Street.

How do you find such bargains? First, don't waste time on anything that isn't statistically cheap and unpopular—I won't linger on anything that sells for more than half the market's price/sales ratio.

Then comes quality. It's harder, but look around Wall Street's garbage dump for telltale signs to ease your search. Gems are often labeled with signs like, "the largest producer of XXXXX." Another sign is where an industrial outfit's plant and capacity average five years old or less—which spells modern—which spells efficient. Brand name dominance is good, too. ∎

Thanks, Dad
August 8, 1988

I learned a lot about the investment business from my father, Philip Fisher, described by *Forbes* just last year as "one of the seminal figures of modern investment thinking." When I worked for him in the days before I struck out on my own, he drummed a great lesson into my head. "No, no, no!" he insisted. "You just don't understand. When you read an annual report, start in the back, with the footnotes to the financials. Then move forward."

The years since have again and again shown me the wisdom of his advice. The back of the report, the footnotes, is where they hide the bad stuff they didn't want to disclose, but had to. Whether it's in a limited partnership, an initial public stock offering prospectus or just an annual report, they bury the bodies where the fewest folks find them—in the fine print.

When I worked for dad, we analyzed companies to see how reflective their accounting was. You do that in the footnotes. We liked conservative ones because emerging problems were easier to understand and seen faster than with their looser brethren. It seems creative accounting is used mostly by those inclined to hype images of phony profits or to hide real losses. For us, when warnings popped up among the crazy accounters, it always

spelled disaster. The few times we ignored the warning, we were sorry.

One time it was Amrep—1972. The world was crazy for recreation and retirement. Amrep had both—through Florida land development. It also had gimmicky accounting and sales schemes. We ignored the gimmicks because we bought the "story." We got killed in the stock. They finally put Amrep's chief executive, Howard Friedman, in

jail. He has been out for years now, and ironically is back heading Amrep.

This was an extreme case, but there were others where we went into a stock—in spite of the red lights that flashed in the footnotes. Take Measurex. It is a good outfit, but in 1973 it used mirrors to boost sales, profits and return on investment by getting its venture capital backers to create a separate third-party leasing firm for sweetheart, low-interest financing for Measurex customers. Million-dollar sales on leases at below-market interest rates didn't really reflect the events. But Measurex booked the sales, showed phony profits, and the stock rose—and then collapsed. I have since made good money buying Measurex—but not when its financials were inflated.

I repeat: Always read the fine print. And read Abraham J. Briloff's *Unaccountable Accounting* (Harper & Row). It's a classic for anyone wanting open eyes. In the bear market following 1972, his unheeded lessons cost investors dearly. As Briloff made clear, success includes remembering that just because a company adheres to "generally accepted accounting principles" (GAAP), that doesn't mean its audited financials even resemble reality.

Also well worth reading—but ultraexpensive—is *Behind the Numbers*, a nitpicky accounting newsletter that is put out by David W. Tice, a Dallas-based CPA and a chartered financial analyst. He rebuilds financial statements to show how the numbers would look if stated more conservatively.

He shows how some big and respected firms realistically aren't earning even half what they report. That's what scares me about folks who buy low P/Es without further homework. It's too easy to get bagged by numbers that aren't really as good as they look.

Let's face it: Careful analysis is a lot tougher than just buying stocks on stories or on a superficial look at the numbers. But if you are not willing to do the analysis, you shouldn't be investing on your own.

Where to start? Hit the backs of annual reports and get the yearly SEC Form 10-Ks (available from the company usually, or from the SEC). Here are a few things to look for: unconsolidated finance subsidiaries, changes to depreciation policies, and inventory costing. Then look for pension plan assets that are less than promised or where the plan has reduced actuarial assumptions—both common smokescreens for lost assets.

A loss that pops up lots now is the company that bought back stock just before the price fell, and has the stock on the books at cost. A microcomputer and a simple spreadsheet program, like Lotus, actually can track this before the quarter ends. Then look for changes in non-operating income and how it's accounted for, decreases in the tax rate, and rising capitalized expenses. Some managements would capitalize hot air if they could, and so would their auditors (even among Big Eight firms). In the real world auditors are picked by management. The slimiest managements find the slimiest auditors. ■

Too Little, Too Late
September 5, 1988

"**W**e are ripe for a discount rate hike." That was the opening line of the column I submitted for this issue shortly before the Fed's August 9 boost. Events got ahead of me and I rewrote the column. But its basic point remains: Interest rates are going higher. We are ripe for at least one more discount rate increase, despite the Fed's recent ratchet.

Why? The Fed's boost wasn't big enough. It raised the discount rate one-half point, but a full point was needed to close the arbitrage possibilities that exist for banks to borrow from the Fed and then lend the bucks back out at higher market rates. The arbitrage spread is smaller now—one-half point or so—but that's plenty to keep the game going and to force the Fed into another rate ratchet, at least.

And that's scary, because multiple discount rate increases often foretell liquidity crises—which could make the market's recent knee-jerk reaction seem like child's play. When the Fed has raised the fee it charges to lend reserves two or three times in succession—without a cut in between—it has been doubly damning for stocks.

It was only in those extraordinary late 1950s and early 1960s that multiple rate hikes didn't correctly warn of disaster. More frequently they have—as in 1921, 1929, 1947, 1972, 1981—and many smaller debacles enroute. Usually, repeated discount rate hikes have preceded savage bear market maulings.

As a refresher, recall the primary purpose of the discount window: a vehicle to lend funds to troubled banks that are short on legally required reserves, but which hope to be healthy again soon. So the Fed likes to keep the discount rate relatively low—hence the term discount—because those troubled banks can't afford high rates.

But at times like these, with short-term interest rates far above the discount rate, and rising, the discount window begins to look like a honey pot to healthy banks, too. If they can borrow bucks from Uncle Fed at low discount rates and, in turn, lend those dollars out at higher market rates, they can pocket the spread at absolutely no risk.

Right now, for example, they could borrow at the 6.5% discount rate and with the proceeds buy risk-less short-term 7% US Treasury bills and make a 1/2% annualized profit. The regulators would never figure out the difference. At only

negligible risk they could pick up an extra 1/2-point-plus on top of that by lending into the A1P1 commercial paper market. That's 1%-plus at almost no risk. Not too shabby, huh?

I would borrow every dollar I could that way. So would they. With so many banks posing as crippled beggars, the Fed can't tell the real cripples from the fakes. Finally, the Fed has no choice but to raise the discount rate. But in so doing, it risks a liquidity squeeze by making reserves more scarce. The banking system now scrambles to pull in loans to build reserves, which ripples out through all near-liquid assets—including, and especially, stocks. The tightening of mid-August was modest enough, but it does rein in some lending and investing.

In my mind, the only thing that will prevent another discount rate hike would be naturally falling interest rates. And that seems unlikely with interest rates rising worldwide. If the current spread between the discount rate and other short-term rates remains for even another month, count on another hike.

Usually, this chickenhearted approach of raising discount rates, but not enough, has eventually required more and bigger hikes. Painful examples of this too-little, too-late approach include 1929, 1955–56 and 1967–68. At times, back-to-back rate ratchets have rippled faster than you can say, "Greenspan is gagging." By my count, 1973 saw seven boosts. Remember 1974?

So, until the liquidity picture clears, I am reluctant to put further funds in stocks. There may well be a snap-back rally in the next few weeks as the hysteria over the Fed's feeble action passes, but I would use such a rally to seek liquidity.

Some folks insist stocks must do well because of the elections and political self-dealing. Not so. As Yale Hirsch details in his nifty and educational annual appointment calendar, *The Stock Trader's Almanac*, stocks have historically averaged downward starting about September in election years in which the incumbent party loses. With Dukakis ahead in the polls, this is something to think about. (Hirsch's *Stock Trader's Almanac* for 1989 costs $25.50 from Six Deer Trail, Old Tappan, N.J. 07675-7124.)

Maybe I'm too cautious, but I am also reminded that September and October are often wretched. Skipping 1987's debacle, the decade before that saw only two September/October combos when stocks did well (1982 and 1986). The rest were break-even or, more often and worse, breaking down badly.

So I'm not recommending new stocks now. I'm holding those I suggested recently, and a lot of cash, and waiting for better monetary and interest rate conditions. If they don't come, better bargains will. ∎

If It's Too Complicated, Forget It
October 3, 1988

In a letter to *Forbes*, B. Philip Chenok, president of the American Institute of Certified Public Accountants, called my August 8 column, a "cheap shot" at auditors. It was not meant to be. The column warned investors to be skeptical when they read annual reports and to pay close attention to footnotes.

Chenok was especially outraged by two statements: "The slimiest managements find the slimiest auditors"; and "Some managements would capitalize hot air if they could, and so would their auditors." As spokesman for the accounting group, Chenok claimed that a recent poll found that auditors have "the highest credibility and trust."

Yes, Mr. Chenok, most company managements and auditors are honest, but like all groups, at one end of the bell curve are folks who are honest to a fault, while at the other are the con merchants. No certification or association—CPA or otherwise—eliminates all con artistry.

The minority of con artists get away with things in auditing because it is specific but imperfect. Imperfect because there is no solidly real number on any financial statement except for the item marked cash. The rest is calculated via assumptions, and the closer you get toward net income per share and shareholders' equity, the more the assumptions and errors compound.

To standardize methodology, accounting has decades of rulings from the Accounting Principles Board (APB) and more recently the Financial Accounting Standards Board (FASB). Auditors are supposed to examine reality and apply correct accounting based on the APBs and the FASBs. But this permits the bad guys to study the rules looking for loopholes and then plan transactions that, by their nature, require accounting that paints the financials in an unreal shade of reality.

So, with due respect to Mr. Chenok and his fellows, I still advise paying careful heed to the often overlooked footnotes.

Will reading the footnotes enable you to spot deliberate misrepresentation? Only rarely. But reading them will help you better understand the financials. It did recently for me. Sequa Corp. surfaced on my firm's computer's value screen, and its annual report rippled onto my desk for review. Its footnotes detailed information that modified what anyone could see from the financial statements alone. For example, the financials showed rapid growth, with sales tripling in three years—while earnings from continuing operations rose from $12 million in 1985 to $28 million in 1986 to $50 million in 1987. Wow!

Now to the footnotes. Footnote number 3 showed that the growth came mostly from the way in which acquisitions were accounted for. For instance, in December 1987 Sequa bought Atlantic Research for $325 million. It used the "equity method" of "purchase accounting"—as required by 1970's APB number 16—all quite correct, but also confusing. A legally required "pro forma" (in the footnote) shows that if Sequa had accounted for the deal as if Atlantic Research had been owned for both years, the combined operations—what is there now—would have shown an earnings decline, from $64 million to $36 million—almost the exact reverse of what its income statement shows.

Sequa got our computer's attention with a balance sheet that exceeded a formula based partially on "equity." But the financials show that $365 million of its $674 million of equity comes from "goodwill." The footnotes further show that $200 million of the $365 million of goodwill hangs on the Atlantic Research takeover. Sequa paid a fancy price (about 24 times earnings and 2.7 times book value). Maybe the goodwill is worth that much. Maybe it isn't. But my point is that you couldn't begin to figure it out without studying the footnotes.

Read on in this same report. Sequa has 21 major footnotes, more than giants IBM, Exxon or Sears— including $150 million of unconsolidated subsidiaries, a $21 million nonrecurring pension plan gain, $80 million of unbilled receivables—all proper but also all altering how you perceive Sequa.

Don't get me wrong. I'm not saying Sequa or its auditors engaged in fraud or misrepresentation. Quite the contrary, the annual report includes three pages of unrequired disclosures, and the "President's Message" clearly points you toward the notes. And the company was quite open in speaking with me. This is not a case of sleight of hand, but rather one of such complexity that I, for one, cannot grasp what the numbers really mean. Who could? My point in highlighting Sequa is to show the absolute importance of footnotes.

Precious few individuals will read all those notes, much less understand them. My advice is: Unless you think you're the next Ben Graham or John Templeton, think five times before buying any stock with lots of complicated footnotes. The more of them and the more complicated, the more trouble you will have distinguishing the phoney from the merely complex. ∎

Anything That Can Happen . . . Probably Will
October 24, 1988

Imagine how David Packard would feel today if he had sold his Hewlett-Packard stock the first time he ran into a potentially dicey stock market. Bill Hewlett would have laughed at him for decades—all the way to the *Forbes* 400.

Investor sentiment toward stocks is amazingly low these days, maybe rightfully so. But in the long term it never pays to be a bear. In pondering this issue's list of the 400 richest, it is wise to note that they didn't get there by being holders of cash, or even bonds. They did so by owning either a business (equity) or real estate. Note Messrs. Walton, Kluge, Perot, Packard, Buffett. They were all long-term bulls.

And then look at two who aren't on the list—professors Roger G. Ibbotson and

Rex A. Sinquefield. They engaged in a classic study, which is available in most libraries, sponsored by the Financial Analysts Research Foundation. Starting in the mid-1920s, before the Great Depression, it shows quite clearly that the average New York Stock Exchange stock did about 6% per year better on average over the last 60 years than did Treasury bills, long-term government bonds or inflation.

Why did stocks do better over the last 60 years? Probably for the reason I expect them to do better over the next 60 years. Stock represents business ownership. And businesses are run by adaptable people who can change with a changing world.

How similar is Hewlett-Packard's product line today to 20, 30 or 40 years ago? About zip. Pick a retailer—any retailer. How similar is its inventory today to a generation back? Industry by industry and firm by firm, you see the same thing.

Don't get me wrong. I'm not suggesting throwing caution to the wind. But don't let bearishness override your long-term best interests. Unless you can turn on a dime, which darn few can

do, big bearishness will hurt you. Meet some of my social friends.

These are folks with tiny stock positions now selling out completely. A year ago they loved stocks, but since the crash they have become ever more bearish. Their rationale includes all the standard stuff: pre-election jitters, postelection tax hikes, upcoming recession, high interest rates and a world that's headed to hell in a handbasket.

One of them got some kind of feeling in the middle of the night—woke up and decided he didn't need "this kind of risk." Another thinks it too risky to own anything that might be "high risk," regardless of how small the position. A third decided he would buy stocks again, but only after interest rates come down "to maybe 4%." He couldn't quite get that by the time rates fell that massively, stocks would already be much higher.

Invariably they feel they can buy stocks again later, "when the future is clearer." But my question to my friends is, "If you will be able to see when to get back in, why couldn't you warn me of the risks in stocks last year at much higher prices? You loved them then. And why weren't you buying big after the crash? You started your selling then."

They don't get it. Fear is highest around market bottoms, when it's the best time to buy. But they won't be able to. The essence of money management is weighing possibilities against probabilities and going against your gut. Years ago, John Larson of Brobeck, Phleger & Harrison, who thinks more like a businessman than any lawyer I have met, told me, "Anything can happen—probably will." By that he meant that the most probable event is usually less likely than the sum of all other possibilities.

That's what a portfolio must deal with. If I am bearish, I think the odds are greatest for stocks to fall. But that doesn't mean they will. Anything can happen. So despite what I may fear as the highest probability, I don't

Be a Bull, Most of the Time

This column is chock full of great wisdom that was true in 1988, 1998, 2008, 2038, and forever. Ken points out, rightly, that investors tend to be most nervous about risk when risk is actually least—right at the end of a bear market. And, he points out it's better to be bullish, most of the time. It's generally better to bet wrong as a bull and suffer some downside than bet wrong bearish and miss upside. Long-term market averages include big down years. But if you miss a lot of upside, that's really tough to make up.

sell out completely. I protect myself from my own foolish inclinations so that if I'm wrong my portfolio won't suffer too much.

Since spring my firm has been relatively bearish because, as medium-capitalization stocks rose much more than larger-cap stocks, the valuation spread between these two largely vanished—we couldn't find many stocks meeting both our quantitative and qualitative screening rules. Not finding many stocks to meet our needs, we bought few. By me, that's bearishness. Arthur S. Bechhoefer, a reader, recently groused in a letter that he was stunned to learn that "Ken Fisher in his September 5 article had gone from a bull to a bear to a chicken."

Well, Mr. Bechhoefer, I have always been a chicken, and proud of it. And I have usually been a bull. And even when I'm not bullish, I'm eager to hold unpopular, beat-up stocks of good companies in small positions in a well-diversified portfolio. And if I could find new ones right now, despite any and all bearish factors, I would be buying them.

As I said last month, I'm holding the stocks I have suggested recently, and a lot of cash—and waiting. If more bargains appear, hallelujah. If not, at least I have some of what made the *Forbes* 400 special—equity. ∎

Ownership Counts
November 14, 1988

Other things being equal, it is better to invest in an outfit with heavy managerial ownership than in one where the top bananas take theirs mostly in salary. You want management that thinks the way an owner would. After all, as a shareholder you are an owner, and you want someone running your company whose interests are the same as yours. An owner-manager isn't likely to overpay for a merger just to make a bigger empire; he isn't likely to let overhead swell out of control—it's his money. All too many managements that are not substantial stockholders run their companies bureaucratically in an after-me-the-deluge spirit.

For this reason I find that *Forbes'* annual listing of the 400 richest Americans offers an investment moral. It is chock-full of folks who made themselves fabulously rich by making their other shareholders rich, too: Warren Buffett, August Busch,

Bill Gates, Ron Perelman, Milton Petrie and on and on.

This richness issue parallels a general management issue key to all investors: Who are today's most effective business leaders? The answer will weigh heavily on which stocks will perform best in the next few years. Yet the issue is addressed by many who miss the integral link between an owner-manager's self-interest and general shareholder interest. Business wealth is created through effective management, and the best way to keep someone focused is to provide him financial incentive for focus.

The shining light in this respect is Sam Walton of Wal-Mart. Starting with nothing, through 25 good years and bad, Walton created 200,000 jobs—half as many as the total work force of Ford or IBM and more than the total work force of Du Pont or Exxon. He created value for tens of millions of customers and 18 billion bucks of stock value, some of which is his, but most of which belongs to 79,000 of his co-investors. Now, that's an effective business leader.

Of course, in considering who are America's most effective business leaders, many folks focus too much on who has done well recently. First of all, it is good to remember that even Sam Walton's career was not without its early failures. Second, whatever the recent success of a company, the past is already reflected in the stock, so it does today's investors little good. And third, today's best leaders may not be today's popular heroes but instead the unknown legends of the 1990s.

Fortunately, *Forbes'* focus is fully on the added plus of the owner-manager. (It is full of articles like George Gilder's October 24 home run explaining why entrepreneurship and good management are a duo.) I believe that a substantial share of America's most effective business leaders are either among The Forbes Four Hundred—or more likely, folks who aren't, but who through success will be one of 1998's Forbes Four Hundred—which gets us back to the investment lesson. You will make more in the long run investing in cheap stocks of good companies where the managements have ownership incentive to perform for you than you will any other way.

Again, take Wal-Mart. Every year from 1975 through 1982, before it was popular, you could have bought the stock at bargain valuations of less than 50% of its trailing annual revenue per share—that's equivalent to a P/E of 10 for a company that happens to be earning 5% net profit margins. En route, you would have owned

Sam Walton's wisdom, energy and "Thank God, it's Monday" motivation. Forgetting dividends, a dollar dropped into Wal-Mart stock in 1982 is $13 today. A 1976 dollar would be $80 now.

By contrast—and with relatively few exceptions—it's hard to find heavy management ownership among America's largest publicly traded corporations.

And that's why, despite what anyone tells you, you shouldn't turn your back on potential investments in stocks of medium-size firms that are well run by folks with a big stake that parallels your best interests. That's where the future Wal-Marts will come from. Of course, all the traditional investment rules still apply. Manager-ownership alone certainly doesn't insure success. You have to look for those outfits that are doing something different and better than the next guy. You must be ever mindful to buy on the cheap. And it's often best to buy them when they have had short-term reverses that scare others away.

What fills the bill? Dollar General might. The Turner family sure hopes so, because it has committed its fortunes to the company, owning 40% of the stock. (I'm very happy with the $2.50 power ties I bought there—you couldn't tell them from your more expensive ones.) Likewise, many folks see the Adolph Coors family as too stodgy for the stock to do well, but the second generation is bubbling with enthusiasm and hopes to prove the pessimists wrong. And the next time you are camping, remember that Coleman is a stock, too. You can bet Sheldon C. Coleman will never be able to forget it. ∎

Unburying the Footnotes

December 12, 1988

Recently I did two columns attacking funny forms of accounting—each of which made some of the folks doing the accounting mad. So, I figure, why quit when I'm on a roll? Here is number three. This column's focus is on a good change in the accounting rules, which will make some stocks look bad, mainly some of the more blue-chip, big-capitalization ones.

The Financial Accounting Standards Board's new FASB 94 requires companies with majority-owned subsidiaries to consolidate the assets and liabilities of those subs into the parent's balance sheets. That means next spring's deluge of December 31 annual reports may hold a few surprises—negative ones.

Let's say you sell big-ticket items; years ago you created a separate financing subsidiary to help your customers finance their purchases. You borrow money and lend it to your customers so they can buy your product. The money you borrow is a liability and your loan to your customer is an asset.

The old accounting rules let you exclude your sub in preparing your balance sheet, as long as you detailed it in the footnotes to your financials. So that's what most folks did. The problem is, in many cases, these unconsolidated subsidiaries grew to become huge relative to the main business, so that not including them could be an inaccurate portrayal of reality.

Enter FASB 94. Companies that appeared to have conservative balance sheets will in some instances now look very much more leveraged. Many will look as if they got hit by a tidal wave of debt. Nothing will have actually changed—except appearances. Now all debt will be highly visible, like a wart on the nose, whereas before it was buried in the footnotes, back

in the back—which, by my reckoning, only about one out of five investors ever studies in any detail.

One of the more extreme examples is PHM Corp., the old Pulte Home, which consolidated its subs in 1987. In 1986 its balance sheet showed a current ratio of 2.4-to-1, $18 million of long-term debt, and $188 million of equity. After consolidation, its current ratio was only 1.3, long-term debt had mushroomed by more than $2 billion, with equity gaining only $37 million. Nothing had changed really—only the accounting. PHM was extreme—and thus shocking—in that there was so much unconsolidated debt in a smaller company. Usually anything smaller than corporate giants have little in the way of unconsolidated subs. Perhaps the new visibility of the debt helps explain PHM's drop from 24 to 8 in the strong stock market since 1986.

The PHM Corp. example shows just how much debt is floating around out there in the footnotes that most folks never know about.

But you have to discriminate. Few cases will be like PHM's. Take Fleetwood Enterprises, America's leading producer of mobile homes and recreational vehicles. It has a finance subsidiary, an unconsolidated insurance sub and a real estate development sub, all of which will have to be consolidated in Fleetwood's next annual report.

But in Fleetwood's case, as with most non-giant companies (its revenues are about $1.5 billion), the unconsolidated subs are small in relation to the overall business. By my count, the inclusion of Fleetwood's unconsolidated subs won't affect its overall balance sheet presentation by even 15%.

Recently our firm did a review of all the companies we either owned or are researching to buy for our clients. We wanted to see exactly where we stood on the FASB 94 issue. The review covered 43 mid-capitalization stocks (ones with market caps between $100 million and $1.5 billion) and 18 big-cap, blue-chip-type stocks.

Fleetwood was the only one of the 43 midcap stocks to have an unconsolidated finance subsidiary. Nevertheless, of the 18 big-cap stocks we owned or were reviewing, 8 would see some material change in their balance sheet because of FASB 94. I'm talking companies like Honeywell and JC Penney. Most were not too bad. The worst, by far, of our holdings was General Motors, because come next spring you will see the $90 billion of debt from General Motors Acceptance Corp. consolidated into GM's balance sheet for the first time. The other domestic automakers should suffer even worse impairment to the appearance of their balance sheets.

Other big-cap blue chips that probably will have the look of their financials particularly affected in almost shocking ways include Deere, General Electric, ITT, Navistar, Tenneco and Westinghouse.

I'm not suggesting that you sell these stocks—just be prepared for the changes FASB 94 will create in their balance sheets, and be sure you are comfortable with them. My advice is: Check every stock you own to make sure this year's footnotes don't catch you by surprise when the new annuals come out in the spring. ∎

1989

The End Is Nigh

" *What all this nonsense about US weakness overlooks is that we Americans are far and away the world's best marketers. No one else comes close. The marketing feature that distinguishes us, and gets too little press, is the Yankee merchant's ability to anticipate markets and innovate based on market feedback. In a capitalistic world, innovation is the only real future.* "

"Right Under Your Nose," July 24, 1989

" *I am usually a very patient, long-term holder of unpopular stocks of what I see as good companies. But if I'm right on this downturn, the only stocks that won't be pounded in 1990 are those few that are free from normal economic vagaries. There aren't many. Cyclical stocks— and most stocks are cyclical—are going to be hurt.* "

"Early Casualties," December 25, 1989

The world was busy in 1989. The Soviets fled Afghanistan after nine years of occupation. In Europe, the Berlin Wall came crashing down (figuratively and literally). In China, students clashed with tanks in Tiananmen Square. Americans viewed their first *Seinfeld* episode. Researchers at the University of Utah claimed to have achieved cold fusion, possibly solving the world's energy problems. (They didn't.) The 7.1 magnitude Loma Prieta earthquake rocked Northern California. And the US Savings & Loan crisis was hitting a crescendo, with hundreds of thrifts going under.

Yet, none of this held back stocks. The S&P 500 soared 31.7 percent, walloping foreign shares (although foreign was up a decent 10.8 percent).[1] US stocks went nearly straight up until a 6.1 percent drop in the S&P 500 on October 13.[2] But the major indexes quickly regained their upward momentum, finishing 1989 just shy of the year high.

Ken was relatively upbeat as 1989 began. He started the year with somewhat unorthodox advice on researching stocks. Everyone has access to quarterly reports, earnings statements, and balance sheets. Those are valuable, but Ken advocated going several steps further and calling competitors, customers, and suppliers to gain greater insight into a firm's advantages and disadvantages in the marketplace. It was an idea he borrowed from his father, Philip Fisher—a legendary investor himself and author of the investing classic *Common Stocks and Uncommon Profits*, the first stock market-related book to make the *New York Times* bestseller list. "What one looks for in all these calls is a consistent pattern showing that the company concerned has the strategic strengths that are necessary for superior performance over its competitors—what I like to call 'unfair advantages.'" ("Getting the Lowdown," January 9, 1989.)

Again, before having evolved to a fully global investor, Ken warned against investing abroad. Too many folks saw foreign as the Holy Grail of investing, offering better returns with less risk. It wasn't that Ken was particularly averse to foreign investing, but from his perspective it had become faddish. From 1984 through 1988, foreign shares rose more than three times as much as US shares.[3] As a result, overseas valuations were through the roof—nowhere more so than Japan. Japan's Nikkei 225 Index reached an all-time high of nearly 39,000 in December 1989—up tenfold over the prior decade.[4] In 1989, Japanese stocks accounted for over half the value of the world's stock markets! (By comparison, in 2009, Japanese stocks were 10% of that of the developed world.)[5] And it wasn't just stocks. At its peak, Japan's Imperial Palace was said to be worth more than all the land in California. To Ken, overseas meant over-inflated. The result—1989 was the first year in four US shares beat foreign, and by a wide margin. And most people know what happened to Japanese stocks after their bubble burst. Over 20 years later, the Topix (a market-cap weighted index and therefore a better gauge of Japanese shares than the Nikkei 225) is still over 60 percent below its 1989 peak.[6]

But in 1989, markets were rising both here and abroad. Investors were gaga. So were economists. All were too giddy for Ken's liking. By the end of the year, he was turning outright bearish. He outlined some of the reasons for his bearishness in his September 18, 1989, column "The End Is Nigh."

First, there was simply too much optimism. The 1987 bear market gave people a scare, but stocks had moved steadily higher since with nary a correction of over 10 percent. The eventless market had lulled investors into complacency. Second, institutional investors seemed tapped out. Their cash on hand was at "its lowest level in four years." A leveraged buyout (LBO) craze was also sweeping the market. Nineteen-eighty-nine was the year LBO firm Kohlberg Kravis Roberts & Co. (KKR) completed the $25 billion ($31+ billion, including assumed debt) acquisition of RJR Nabisco—adjusted for inflation still the largest LBO deal to date (and the basis for the well-known book *Barbarians at the Gate: The Fall of RJR Nabisco*). LBOs weren't new, but Ken noted in 1989, "Today's LBOs occur at valuations 300% above those prevailing when LBOs first appeared ten years ago." As mentioned, foreign stock valuations were sky high too.

Not only were investors overly optimistic, economic fundamentals didn't support their optimism. Ken noted a number of economic indicators—including the Index of Leading Indicators, retail sales, inventories, the Purchasing Manager's Index, durable goods orders, truckers' shipments, and construction spending—showed signs of weakness despite low interest rates, which normally spurs the economy. Inverted yield curves (short-term interest rates above long-term interest rates) around the world were another ominous sign for the economy and stocks.

Even as his pessimism grew, Ken wasn't ready to bail out of stocks just yet. The market momentum was still clearly to the upside, and market trends tend to last much longer than most expect. Ken's advice: "Since I believe in stocks more than I believe in anybody's forecast, mine included, I don't suggest getting out of the stock market. I do recommend concentrating in defensive, cheap stocks of companies that are well positioned, where their customers won't easily stall purchases in tough times and—most key—where companies have little debt." ("The Quiet Bear," October 16, 1989.)

Calling a bear market correctly is no easy task. It requires seeing the conditions for a bear correctly when others don't and timing it right. Getting out of the market entirely is risky business for long-term, growth-oriented investors, and it's only effective if you do both the seeing and the timing well. Getting out too early or being wrong about the bear can seriously damage a portfolio's long-term growth prospects. And even if you correctly get out of the market ahead of a bear, you've got to get back in at the right time too. The moral of the story: Unless you're a world-class market forecaster with some market insight others don't see, resist the urge to purge your portfolio—odds are you'll be better off staying invested.

Getting the Lowdown
January 9, 1989

In 1958 my father's *Common Stocks and Uncommon Profits* became the first stock market book ever to make the *New York Times* bestseller list. Its brief but bold introduction of "scuttlebutt" as a new means for picking stocks gave investors some unorthodox advice. By this he meant going beyond the published figures and talking with customers, competitors and suppliers before buying a company's stock. The idea was radical then. Funny thing is, it is still seldom done.

Most investment research—then and now—is done by reading reports and talking to the company in question. Quantitative and computer-driven analyses have been steadily on the rise. But depending on numbers without knowing something of what lies behind them can leave you vulnerable to surprises.

Scuttlebutt lets you get beyond the numbers to find out whether the company you plan to invest in has certain necessary strategic advantages, things like low-cost production skills or low-cost distribution. The advantage can be something like regional dominance or location or a reputation for superior service. For my own firm I have developed what I call the "12-call" process for gathering useful scuttlebutt. Here's an example of how it works:

We assigned MBA ex-journalist Sally Allen to apply the system to Fleetwood Enterprises. Her assignment was to complete 12 telephone calls, 4 each to customers, competitors and suppliers.

Of the customers she was to ask "buying" questions like: "What swings your decision to buy from Company A versus Companies B, C and D—price, quality, service?"

Of the competitors she was to ask a set of "sell" questions like: "Why do you sometimes win when you sell against Company A, and what makes you sometimes lose?"

For the suppliers she needed to pose questions you would normally ask a Wall Street expert because, in a very real sense, suppliers are the best experts. They spend most of their lives analyzing what makes their customers tick. Here Allen might ask derivatives from, "Who tend to be the leaders and followers in this industry and why?"

What one looks for in all these calls is a consistent pattern showing that the company concerned has the strategic strengths that are necessary for superior performance over its competitors—what I like to call "unfair advantages." If you don't hear much consistency in the 12 calls, you can safely assume no such advantage exists.

Of course, to complete 12 calls, we might have to make 40. But once completed, 12-call feedback provides a portrait of a company that makes any normal Wall Street qualitative analysis seem colorless.

An easy process? No. First, you have to figure out who to call. Then you have to figure out how to get them to talk.

Allen easily got the names of competitors from Fleetwood's public documents. Customers were easy, too—from the phone book—they are dealers. Suppliers are tougher, both because they are often harder to identify and they are much harder to get talking. They don't want to say something bad to you that might get back to their customers. Allen had to do what we call "building bridges" by asking the customers and competitors who the suppliers were and getting names back in ones and twos.

How do you get all these folks talking? Well, no surprise—some won't. But, believe it or not, most folks love to talk—eat it up—if you can get them going and they don't feel threatened. The key is: Ask for no sensitive information and only five minutes of their time. Once loosened up, most people enjoy being treated as experts. One guy went on for an hour with Allen and in a follow-up call to me told me how much he enjoyed the time with her.

So, what did Sally Allen's 12 completed telephone calls tell us about Fleetwood? We already knew from the numbers that Fleetwood has dominant market share in mobile homes, motor homes and travel trailers and has been increasing its lead. What we learned from working the telephone was that this dominance was no accident but could be traced to superior distribution and below-average production costs.

We also learned from suppliers that Fleetwood's production cost advantage is reinforced by its dual dominance in both motor and mobile homes. This allows it to get volume discounts in costly items like appliances, which are common to both product lines—whereas the top also-rans tend to be in either one product line or the other, and hence competitively a step behind. In short, we learned that the dominance is not only secure but likely to grow over the next few years as Fleetwood continues to gain market share by taking it away from its smaller and weaker brethren.

You add up major advantages like that and you know you have a good company, one with a solid future, despite the fact that its industry has been in the doghouse for years. And that makes Fleetwood cheap at 35% of sales and 8 times earnings. ∎

Security Analysis Updated
February 6, 1989

In my last column I described the 12-call checklist my firm uses before reaching a decision as to whether to buy a stock. It told about the work our Sally Allen did on Fleetwood Enterprises and the mobile home and recreational vehicle industries. Her 12-call file sits 2¼ inches thick with the results of 27 phone calls necessary to complete 12 meaningful calls—4 each to Fleetwood's customers, competitors and suppliers. The results tell a lot, not only about Fleetwood but about some of the ingredients we think must go into a sound investment decision. Here are some of the highlights of the research:

The first Fleetwood customer contacted was Hadden Smith of Media Camping Center in Media, Pa., who deals in recreational vehicles, carrying Winnebago, three Fleetwood lines and several others. While he emphasized Winnebago's top quality, he stressed Fleetwood's "real touch in the marketplace. They know both what the public wants and what it will buy . . . real pizzazz . . . and always timely." In travel trailers, for example, he would prefer it if Fleetwood's Prowler line, his top seller, had a high-quality aluminum frame instead of wood, but he just loves Fleetwood's design and cabinetry.

Jerry Ashford, customer number two, of Travel Trailer Exchange in Everett, Wash. carries only Fleetwood's mobile homes. Why? With Fleetwood's broad multiple product lines covering all price points, and its co-op and warranty dealer programs, "Fleetwood is there when we need them . . . gives our customers the best line for the money." But, because of its dominant market share, dealers are at some disadvantage negotiating with the giant.

"Fleetwood won't allow a dealer to have more than one of its travel trailer lines," Ashford told us. It splits lines up among dealers in a town (although a dealer can carry multiple Fleetwood mobile home

Stock Picking Is Storytelling

This column and the one from January underscore the depth professionals go to when evaluating stocks. While technology makes analysis so much easier today in many ways, it doesn't short-cut the analysis process. Money managers must still gather data and try to understand what it means—building a narrative that helps them understand if the stock is likely to outperform its peers moving forward.

lines because mobiles cover a very much wider price range, and the lines vary with the different prices).

Butch Johnson of Johnson Motor Sales in Spokane, Wash, comes under the heading of unhappy ex-customer. He and brother Bruce, who run a "high-end" dealership, with extra emphasis on service, used to carry Fleetwood and stopped. Butch said, "They don't protect dealers like they should. They are the General Motors of the RV industry." He groused that Fleetwood builds different makes of the same model to get penetration higher. The result: "Six Spokane dealers carried the same product . . . makes dealers hostile toward each other . . . nonprofessional . . . there is no service left, the customer suffers."

Finally, Dean Ford of Dean Ford Centers in Moses Lake, Wash., noted Fleetwood's dominance—even in used RVs, where 40% of the used vehicles he sells are Fleetwoods. His point is: "There seems to be customer loyalty. People stay with what they buy the first time, a real edge for Fleetwood." Ford doesn't mind the same multiple-dealers-in-a-town problem that gripes Butch Johnson. If he were a car dealer he would be glad to sell GM's line.

Note this: Almost every competitor paid deference to Fleetwood. That's unusual when 12-calling. Winnebago saw itself as the RV trendsetter, but everyone else in mobile homes and RVs saw Fleetwood as the main innovator. For example, Dale Gonzalez of Kit Manufacturing, which really has come on lately on Fleetwood's own California home turf, called it "the class outfit . . . done a lot for the industry . . . innovative." Then there was Wayne Dahl and Dan Walters of the Holiday Rambler division of Harley-Davidson—both very proud of their dominance of the ultra-high end of RVs but also acknowledging Fleetwood's number two position with a much inferior product because of all its other advantages. In essence, they are saying Fleetwood sales rank can exceed its product-quality rank in almost any product category in the industry.

Suppliers are always tight-lipped. They won't bad-mouth a single customer and thereby endanger future sales. Four talked, but only on the promise of being "off the record." One appliance maker was most telling as he referred to Fleetwood's 21% share of appliances sold to RVs and mobile homes combined—triple that of number two Winnebago and five times that of anybody else. "You almost wouldn't introduce a product if you couldn't get them to take it, too risky," he said. That's power. It's the power to create product "standards" for style that lesser vendors must live with.

With an unpopular and depressed stock like Fleetwood, selling at 35% of sales, ten times earnings and a discount to the market's price to book, not only does Main Street feedback demonstrate industry dominance and real value, but it also gives you comfort to hold on for the long haul, where the big gains come. You can do the same kind of digging yourself, whenever you want, and I believe you will find your results not only better, but more comfortable when you do. ■

All in a Name

March 6, 1989

Investors often complain they can't do the kind of in-depth research I advocate. But on a limited scale they can. They can start right in their favorite supermarket.

Names like Coke, Revlon and IBM are obviously golden. But there are oodles of smaller, still substantial, midsize companies that own strong brand names. Why bother to seek them out? Most consumers will pay a premium in the store to buy a name they trust rather than buy an unknown imitator. In that premium is an advantage for the name's owner. The stronger the name, the stronger the edge. Strong brand names tend to have staying power—for decades or longer.

Folks seem to feel more comfortable with the familiar, and brand names are nothing if not familiar. Coors, for example, recently found that when it changed its familiar yellow can, it lost sales. Folks thought the beer must have changed. Not so, but Coors' diehard fans wouldn't buy the new label. While some folks see that as a sign of failure for Coors, I see it as tremendous power. Cheap stock.

Outboard Marine demonstrates the same principle in reverse. Chief Executive Charles D. Strang is quite open and honest about the fact that his famous Evinrude and Johnson brands are today identical, except for the paint and nameplates. But the customers think they are different, and by offering both OM gets extra sales. Clearly, both names are worth money. Yet OM stock doesn't reflect the value of these franchises, selling at 35% of sales, eight times earnings and a hair below book value.

Oneida demonstrates another of the advantages brand names can carry. Food tastes the same to me no matter whose fork it's on, but consumers who want "the best," whatever that means, do pay a premium to have the Oneida name stamped on their tableware. Oneida gets a fatter profit margin and return on equity than do competitors.

Huffy, the bicycle kingpin, not only has a leading brand name, which is recognized by kids everywhere, but it also has high relative market share in its field—a great double whammy. None of this, much less Huffy's dynamite balance sheet, is reflected in the current stock price.

Or take Holly Farms. Not to brag, but I recommended it here last June 13 at 33. As the dominant brand name in chickens, it was clear the stock was worth more than the 130% of book value that it was at then. Since then ConAgra and Tyson have been clubbing each other in a billion-dollar takeover tussle to get control of Holly at prices on the high side of 60. Why? They both want Holly's very visible name for their own high-volume but no-name chicken operations.

There is still another way brand names can work. Stanley Works shows it. For all the reasons already stated, most folks will pay a slight premium for Stanley's tools. But because the hand tool industry is so fragmented, with so many types of tools, Stanley is able to grow by adding new products with the Stanley name and instantly gain a leg up on older, more entrenched firms. It doesn't matter what type of tool it is, most folks feel safer with a Stanley. Its stock is currently just a hair too high for my cheap tastes, but if it should drop 20%, it would make a very nice tool in my portfolio.

Another plus for brand names, in this era, is their value to corporate raiders: Whether it's Revlon several years back or the recent RJR deal, brand names have been more than heavily represented in recent takeover tussles. And again, not just big names. From when I started to write this column, two of the stocks I intended to include—SSMC Corp. and Formica, whose name is generic for its product—have both seen takeover announcements. Ditto for Coleman, which was up $20 the day this column went to press because Sheldon Coleman just made news taking it private.

Getting back to brand name research for the average investor: There are two parts to it. First, talk to store employees. For example, for a firm like Coleman, go to about five sporting goods stores, including ones that don't carry Coleman. Ask why they carry the lines they have—what's good about them—and what their customers think. Getting folks to open up is an art, not a science, but almost anyone can do it if he keeps at it. The more you ask, the more you will think to ask.

Then, as if you were an election pollster, conduct exit polls. It takes courage to approach folks, because half of them will think you're nuts, but after a while it's fun. Stand outside a store and, one by one, ask a handful of customers what they think of the products. If you smile, focus on them and seek their views, more will talk than not. The benefits? Learning where your own biases are in conflict with those of the average consumer. Better still, it will help your picking of unpopular, cheap stocks and make you feel far safer owning them. There's gold in them thar brand names—and not just in the big, obvious ones. ∎

I Call Them "Takeaways"
April 3, 1989

Leafing through my columns of recent years you might think I love takeovers. Not so. I have had more than my share, but I have come to hate them. While they may give a quick boost to the coffers, they eventually make a money manager's life miserable. More important, takeovers defy the most basic precept of portfolio management. "Takeaways" is more like it. Here's why.

When I was a kid my father drummed into my head this bit of age-old wisdom: "Let your winners run and cut your losses short." But it's tough to let your winners run when they keep getting taken over at small markups to the market. Take my March 6 column on brand names as a strategic advantage. The column as submitted named eight stocks for your consideration. By the time the column "closed," two weeks later, takeover bids had been made on two of them, SSMC Corp. and Formica—each with a gain of less than 50%. The morning after the column closed, a deal came on a third, Coleman. We broke into the print run to reflect the news.

A markup of nearly 50% only sounds good. Here's the rub: Really good holdings are the kind on which you might make several hundred percent over a number of years. If you give those up for a quick 30% to 50% gain, it's hard to find equally good things to replace them with. Result: Your average portfolio quality tends to fall, and so will your long-term results.

Admittedly, losing three of eight picks in one column is unusual. Nevertheless, the recent bludgeoning from takeaways has been relentless. According to *Buyouts*, a newsletter from Venture Economics of Wellesley Hills, Mass., there were 304 leveraged deals totaling $98 billion in 1988, most of which were some form of takeover. Only 17 separate deals out of the 304 were valued above $1 billion.

Fully 124 takeaways, or 41%, were in the $100 million to $1 billion region, just where I have most often found both liquidity and value. That's 124 reasons my life has gotten tougher—yours too. At that level they took away 8% of what was out there at the start of 1988. And you can bet those takeaways weren't the worst 8%.

I can't say that all of those 124 takeaways were great deals for the buyer. But I can say that on average the takeaways focus on firms with the kind of strategic advantages— like high relative market share, low-cost production or leading brand names—that make for a good long-term holding and that offer the fat profits that will pay off the debt needed to do the takeaways.

The Coleman takeover teaches another lesson. Sheldon C. Coleman, the firm's chief executive, is taking it private. He already effectively controlled Coleman through his and his family's 24% ownership. If he thought the company might do poorly, he certainly wouldn't want to boost that considerable stake.

So why is he taking it private? He must agree with me that it's worth a good deal more than he is paying. And who could know better than Coleman, with his access to inside information? My point is that takeaways rarely are done on a fair playing field, and rarely done at the highest price for the shareholders' best interests. If they were, there would be nothing left for the takers.

Our problem now, in any case, is that there aren't many great stocks floating around out there, and fewer all the time. What's a great stock? My definition is simple: It's the very unpopular stock of a very good company. That means a firm selling at low valuations, but also one that has strategic attributes that allow it to make above-average profit margins or above-average growth. When you can find them, you can get a double whammy as the company does well, grows, makes profits, and the stock market comes to appreciate the unexpected quality—and bids it up in popularity and price.

But, sadly, the market is simply too damn efficient to allow for lots of-those. They exist only if they have fallen between the cracks somewhere. If they take away too many more I may soon have to talk *Forbes* into letting this column be a tip sheet on the race track. At least more ponies are bred every year. ∎

Stock or Cash? Or Both?

Don't take this column to mean that Ken thinks M&A is always bad for stocks. Quite the contrary, as he'll explain in the very next column. For more on Ken's more recent views on how to play the M&A field, check out his 2006 best seller, *The Only Three Questions That Count.*

Few Is More
May 1, 1989

When does less equal more? Charles Schwab knew the answer. I'm not referring to the discount brokerage king, but to the man behind putting together US Steel and later Bethlehem Steel. He knew the key: Acquisition binges that shrink the number of players in an industry, and thereby the competition, allow for vastly more profits for the survivors. It's almost surefire.

While Schwab actively created his desired goal of industry consolidation, you can apply the same principle to investing in stocks: Invest in industries where the number of competitors has fallen to a handful.

Look at the airline industry as a 1980s example. Deregulation led to price wars, which led to red ink, which led to a myriad of takeovers, causing much increased concentration. And that has led to tremendous rate hikes recently. You can feel it when you fly. The price you pay for a ticket will reflect the reduction in competition.

And the rate hikes bring huge profits. The overall industry should earn well over a billion bucks this year, up from under $100 million in 1986. The trend has made the airline stocks strong. At first, investors were scared to death. AMR Corp., for example, the parent of American Airlines, sank to 1980 prices of $7 to $12, which meant it sold for only 5% to 10% of revenue. In 1988, by contrast, it sold for between 26% and 45% of sales. En route, stockholders got almost a tenfold gain in price.

While the airline consolidation trend is near its end, Delta still has room to rise. More conservative than other majors managerially, Delta hasn't seen its price rise as much, either. At 36% of sales, seven times earnings and a hair over book value, it is selling at a nice discount to industry averages, yet has by far the best balance sheet of the majors, the most modern fleet and strong regional dominance. You aren't going to see Delta's loyal work force pull an "Eastern," either.

Where can you see hot-off-the-press mass consolidations to tip us off on fat future profits? The clearest sign I see is in the auto parts market, with particular emphasis on replacement parts. When my firm runs computer screens on Standard & Poor's Compustat database looking for ideas, recently acquired companies pop up with a full row of "N/A" (not available). The auto parts field shows N/As galore. By my N/A count, about 19% of the industry has consolidated in the last 18 months. According to various other estimates, in the last five years the auto parts industry has lost between one-third and one-half of its participants.

When I look through the purchase accounting footnotes in annual reports of auto parts firms, lots of these outfits look like snakes that just ate several rabbits. I haven't seen a single major independent that hasn't made at least one good-size acquisition in the last three years. Sure, maybe I missed somebody, but the point remains: It has been very much an acquire-or-be-acquired world.

One reason is that, at the original equipment level, the big three automakers have signaled they want fewer and higher-quality suppliers, a la Japanese-style management. But perhaps the main cause is simply that there has been too much competitive price bashing—too many bashers. Retail prices for replacement parts are too low. To take one example, I can buy a standard muffler from my auto parts store for $18. How does anyone coin a buck vending a big hunk of expensive and precisely shaped metal for $18? It's too cheap.

But remember, the darkest hour is just before the price goes up. Here's the telling aspect: After recent mergers, the three biggest players make up over 75% of the muffler market—original equipment and replacement. There may be a little more consolidation, but not much, and soon thereafter you can expect higher prices for mufflers, especially for the big kids on the block. Who is the kingpin of mufflers? After recently acquiring Maremont, Arvin is the clear market share leader. According to my research, Arvin has more of the combined original equipment and replacement market for mufflers than the second- and third-largest vendors put together.

By my estimate, once prices start going up, Arvin's earnings per share could double. Since it sells at 25% of sales, nine times earnings, and dead even with book value, it's hard to see how you won't do well with Arvin over the next five years—at least matching its 1987 peak of $40, plus dividends.

The whole trend to concentration in auto and replacement parts verges on, and is likely to become, what introductory economics texts call "oligopoly"—the nearest thing to monopoly power the law allows. Higher prices on Main Street should translate directly to higher prices on Wall Street. ∎

Buy 'Em When They're Not Hot
May 29, 1989

Now is the time to buy defense stocks—when no one wants them. Sure, defense spending will be hammered by all the forces you hear about—primarily federal budget deficit pressures and the public's new view of less need for spending because of the Russians' recent dovish cooings. But these stocks have over-discounted the bad news. They are much too cheap.

Recently I was talking with a professional investor who was down on General Dynamics, whose earnings he estimated would fall 35% by 1991. That appears unlikely to me, but even if he is right, my response was, "So what? That would move GD from six times earnings up to nine times earnings." Still a substantial discount from the market.

At $57, the market says GD is worth about $2.3 billion—a hair's whisker over book value. With $300-million-plus of yearly earnings and $350 million of depreciation, it sells at less than 3.5 times cash flow, which is a cash flow yield of more than 28%. Beat that!

Of course, all defense stock P/Es aren't that low, but earnings alone, out of context, can mislead. That's why my favorite way to see what is unpopular is to look at price/sales ratios (PSR)—what will the market pay for the firm's revenues?

You figure PSRs by taking the company's total market value—stock price times number of shares—and expressing it as a ratio to sales. Thus if a company had a market cap of $2 billion and sales of $5 billion, the PSR would be 0.4. And when you look at PSRs, the defense stocks seem even cheaper than their already low P/Es indicate.

As a routine monthly fire drill, my firm takes the Standard & Poor's Compustat group of 7,180 stocks and ranks by PSR those with market capitalizations above $150 million, and then breaks all of these down into deciles—10% groupings from lowest to highest—to see where the bodies lie.

Where does defense fit into this popularity spectrum? Smack dab in the lowest 10% group, which tops out at 33 cents on the sales dollar. General Dynamics, for example, sells at 25% of its annual sales, Grumman 18%, Lockheed 26%, McDonnell Douglas 20%.

Should these stocks really be considered among the worst 10% of all companies? No! They have above-average balance sheets, cash flow and proprietary products. They also possess massive electronic know-how, which could be redeployed into nonmilitary products. Sure, with their low-growth or no-growth future these firms are far from the best companies in America, but they are also far from the worst.

How deeply will we cut the defense budget? Not too deeply, I think. We're not going below $300 billion. That's enough for the cutters and the stocks. Defense spending is at 7% of GNP—not high by any long-term historical standard. The "Reagan buildup" was merely a reaction to under-spending in the two prior decades, when defense spending fell from 12% of GNP to 5%. Because defense is such an emotional issue, it's one where there is always more extreme talk than reality.

Take Grumman. Everyone is sure it has no future since it has a lack of new prime contracts and because Defense Secretary Cheney proposes burying its classic F-14. Yet new systems cost a bundle to develop, both for Uncle Sam and the developer, and provide no benefits for years. As a penny-pinching Congress awakens to the costs of futurism and the jillions saved by upgrading the existing fleet of proven tac-tical equipment—including Grumman's F-14—there may be a much better day for Grumman than is commonly envisioned.

There are hundreds of F-14s on carriers right now that need upgrades yesterday.

Sure, no one wants old toys in an unlimited budget environment, but in our world, modernizing is a high-payoff alterna-tive. If I'm right, this very unpopular stock of a good but not great company is quite cheap at 85% of book value. Interestingly, in the 24 hours after Cheney announced killing the F-14 budget, Grumman stock bounded up a point—a full 5%.

In fact, the defense stocks as a whole have been acting nicely through this period of dismal news—more sign that the bad news is already overdiscounted in the market.

Remember, the time to buy a stock is when no one wants it. It's hard to make yourself step into the breach, but it's one of the surest ways to make money. For defense, the time is right now. ∎

Big Fish in Small Ponds
June 26, 1989

Where do bargain stocks hide? Try Siloam Springs, Arkansas, or Belpre, Ohio. Why? Wall Street has a perverse tendency to bypass firms that serve primarily out-of-the-way little towns. There are stocks of good compa-nies tucked away in places—maybe up to 30,000 in population—you or I rarely hear of, but the firms are doing good business, growing and, best of all, selling for cheap.

Wall Street, perhaps because it is so isolated and parochial, tends to think that only big cities matter. But there's a lot more to America than just New York, Chicago, Los Angeles and a few dozen other big cities. Check out a bunch of smalltown-only retailers. It takes a knack to hack it in small-town America.

Kmart, for example, is a fine firm, but it doesn't have that knack. Thousands of

towns are too small to support its size. Its 2,250 stores do almost $30 billion. Compare that with Dollar General, with 1,300 dinky stores in tiny towns, selling a mere $670 million—only about 2% of Kmart's volume with half the stores, 1/25 as much per store. Dollar General thinks small, selling relatively few items at very low prices. Yet it has comparable returns on sales and equity to Kmart's, while grow-ing somewhat faster.

It's not easy handling all those small stores—a different merchandising and dis-tribution orientation from that of a larger mass-market store. But by thinking "small town," a firm can be a big fish in lots of small ponds.

Dollar General, for instance, has dou-bled its store count over the last decade while maintaining an ultra-conservative balance sheet. From a shareholder's viewpoint it's pretty safe, combining small-town defensiveness with the inherent conservative approach of Messieurs Cal Turner, senior and junior, who own 40% of the stock and are clearly on your side. With a current market capitalization of only 33% of annual sales, 180% of book value and 12 times historically depressed earnings, the stock is cheap compared with the market.

Ditto for twinlike Family Dollar, which has a similar style in similar towns and a slightly more aggressive financial approach, oriented toward faster growth than Dollar General. At 44% of sales and 175% of book value, its market capitalization is just as cheap.

Competition? Sure, but the only big guy to really make it in small towns, with staying power, has been Wal-Mart. It's the exception that proves the rule, because Wal-Mart is itself a product of small towns, not an outside invader.

Lowe's is a good example. Although mainly in small southeastern towns, it is America's largest vendor of home building products. Wall Street loves its more urban competitors, Hechinger's and Home Depot. These urbanites do a wonderful job with their larger warehouse-type "superstore" approach, which features stores averaging on the high side of 60,000 square feet, versus Lowe's 15,000-foot size. They each have about 80 stores, against Lowe's with 300.

But, tailoring its methods to lower store volumes, Lowe's does very well. In its relatively small stores Lowe's actually sells more per square foot than anyone else in the industry. Sure, some of those sales are lumberyard and contractor call-ins, which the city boys don't have, but every little bit helps. And, even after deducting "outside" sales, Lowe's still sells per square foot in the store as much as or more than anyone. And it does so while pricing at low average gross margins, making it doubly tough for new competitors to slip into town.

The best part is: Lowe's stock is cheap, selling for 32% of revenues, versus about 80% for the urban duo, 6 times cash flow, versus a 12 times multiple for the others, and even a lower P/E at 10, versus 14 and 23 for Hechinger's and Home Depot, respectively. With Lowe's barely outside the Southeast, it can grow for decades in tiny towns and rarely ever compete with the city slickers. Lowe's is a stock to tuck away for years and start worrying about if and when it ever tries to invade downtown. ∎

Little Lowe's, and Not-Quite-So-Huge Wal-Mart

While a lot of the commentary in these columns is still valid today, it's also worthwhile to read these to provide some historical context. Once upon a time, Wal-Mart wasn't the big-box behemoth it is now, and Lowe's was a much smaller, more regional player. Over time, some stocks zoom, and some implode.

Right Under Your Nose
July 24, 1989

Which foreign stock market is the best bet now? None. I say stick with the American. Yet each year fewer folks here invest in individual American stocks.

At the same time, buying globally is fashionable. Witness the gush of new "packaged" mutual funds in this area—and even the dozens focusing on single countries, and many of them not the world's biggest or most industrially successful countries. In the seemingly sophisticated institutional world, most large pension funds have jumped overseas with both feet.

They fool themselves into thinking they are reducing risk by diversifying by geography. Know it or not, what they are doing is the ever dangerous game of chasing prices—in this case the vastly superior gains in the 1980s of foreign stock markets relative to ours.

This passion for investing abroad is no different from any other market mania. All of them, from the days of tulipomania and the South Sea Bubble to now, have been disguised as, and supported by, some form of sophisticated poppycock. Like this: Japanese stocks are a bargain at 60 times earnings because their accounting is more conservative than ours and understates their results.

Not only is that untrue in aggregate, it's patently silly and fails to account for history and for the explosive tripling in Japanese P/Es in the last seven years, while ours merely have treaded water.

Rather than being an argument for owning Japanese stocks, this should be an argument for owning US stocks: Ours have lower P/Es.

But the trend extends beyond the Japanese. These days America rarely gives itself its due relative to foreigners. When I was a kid, we believed America was the world's best at everything. Now, it seems, we count our inferiorities instead of our strengths, whether educational, mercantile, moral or political.

Why this America-bashing mood among US investors? Lots of reasons, none of them very good. Perhaps it erupted in reaction to guilt over racism and domestic poverty and a lousy war in the 1960s. It was certainly fueled by Watergate and corporate kickback scandals in the 1970s. And more recently by an unending stream of misguided media drivel about our "twin" trade and budget deficits, not to mention insider trading.

What all this nonsense about US weakness overlooks is that we Americans are far and away the world's best marketers. No one else comes close. The marketing feature that distinguishes us, and gets too little press, is the Yankee merchant's ability to anticipate markets and innovate based on market feedback. In a capitalistic world, innovation is the only real future. While our schools may not turn out the best engineering students and we may not always be the low-cost producer, or the quality producer, virtually every major product or service feature innovation comes from America. The entrepreneur with a dreamlike idea and more courage than currency is an almost completely American phenomenon.

Whether microcomputers, computer software, fast-food restauranting or services such as the one Federal Express pioneered—innovations spring from America. Ditto for another aspect of marketing—retail distribution. Whether it's the Toys "R" Us or Home Depot-like superstores, or distributed discounting such as Wal-Mart pioneered, America leads and others follow.

So, whether you look at P/E ratios or marketing ability, the US is a good place to invest.

Some people will tell you that investing abroad will protect your portfolio against a market crash here. Ask them what happened after October 19, 1987. The debacle was worldwide. The big busts have always happened globally.

Finally, you can learn lots about American stocks because you are here. But it is hard to get the straight skinny on foreign stocks. Two of my favorite columns (January 9 and February 6) detailed the need to cross-check Wall Street ideas with Main Street reality. In America you can talk around and get the low-down. So I'll bet on American stocks, where the valuations are lower, where the innovation is higher and never-ending, and where you can dig deeper and understand more about what you are doing. ■

The "S" Factor
August 21, 1989

I am getting increasingly keen on the stock of Greyhound Corp. It's got what I call the "S" factor—the possibility of a big surprise tied to a stock so cheap you should make money even without the surprise.

Stocks that have the "S" factor can make you big money. The big swings in stocks come when most folks are surprised, either for good or bad. What's the potential surprise in Greyhound? The fact that few folks know what a good company it is. Nobody knows what it does. Ask most professional investors what Greyhound does and you will get a yawn and a joke about a "doggy" company. Greyhound doesn't run all those buses all over America anymore—but few know what it does instead.

Yes, it still makes buses, but that's only about 13% of revenue. Much more important is a long lineup of great consumer names: Dial soap, Purex bleach, Brillo soap pads, Sno-Bol toilet cleaner, Parson's ammonia, 20 Mule Team Borax, Boraxo and Borateem. All wonderful consumer franchises—and unrecognized on Wall Street.

Those are names on which mega-bucks have been spent on advertising over many decades—ingraining them in our minds. Who can purge themselves of: "Don't you use Dial? Don't you wish everybody did?"

Once in the habit of buying a toiletry brand, folks tend to stick with it.

If Greyhound's consumer products were priced on Wall Street the way other leading consumer products firms are, you would be getting the rest of Greyhound for free. The biggest chunk of that remainder is another unique franchise. Go eat at an airport and get outraged at the high price of your food. Then slowly appreciate that the bottom of your receipt often says in little letters, "Dobbs." Greyhound is Dobbs, which by my count is also worth about as much as the market's current price tag for all of Greyhound.

Anything wrong with Greyhound? Sure. Too much debt. Its tiny finance subsidiary has more debt than parent Greyhound has total equity. As with most small finance subs, this one makes no sense; Greyhound should sell it. Then if it sold the busmaking line, I think you would see an almost instant 50% stock price bounce. At 36% of revenue and a hair over book value, Greyhound is too cheap.

Another surprise is apt to be Coors. My firm recently surveyed a handful of brewery competitors and suppliers. We heard a clear consensus: that Coors suffers from having a single plant and low market share relative to Budweiser and Miller—so Coors' advertising and transportation costs per unit are high. True, but untrue. Anheuser-Busch and Philip Morris have gained market share for Bud and Miller, but Coors has boosted market share, too. More important, a less competitive market probably looms for beer. After decades of consolidation, brewing has shrunk from hundreds of firms to a handful.

Anheuser-Busch has gained market share steadily to just over 40%. Any good student of competitive strategy knows that it's a powerful plus to get and keep high relative share, but, that as share starts exceeding 40%, gaining more probably costs more than it contributes. Bud will have little incentive to pursue profitless further growth.

Another ricochet-type surprise may come soon from Miller. Coors may be a huge winner from the RJR leveraged buyout, which could dampen competition in beer. Why? Philip Morris has decided to use RJR's LBO-induced weak financial condition as an opportunity to gain permanent yardage against it in tobacco, Philip Morris' prime turf. But stretched thin by $13 billion of its own debt and an earnings-sensitive stock market, Philip Morris almost must, despite protestations to the contrary, become less aggressive with Miller beer, going for maximum cash flow rather than for maximum growth, as it did in the past. Instead of blowing big bucks on market-share-oriented ad campaigns, Miller is apt to be a new voice speaking to less competitive pressure in beer.

I wouldn't even be surprised to see Philip Morris sell Miller before too long. If it did, there would be only a few logical buyers, and who tops the list? You guessed it. If debt-free Coors bought Miller, it would be the ultimate surprise—a whole new ball game, with 30% market share, and a stock that would move almost overnight from selling at 40% of sales and 65% of book value to twice those levels—and even then still be at deep discounts from Bud's valuations.

Don't think stodgy old Coors could be that aggressive? Look at what it's doing now—buying assets from number three Stroh's.

To make really big gains, work the "S" factor. Look for whopping surprises, which by definition are the kind few people expect. But stick with stocks so cheap that if the surprises don't work out, you could make money anyway. ∎

The End Is Nigh
September 18, 1989

A good many analysts have become more bullish with the market hitting its all-time high, but I see a peak. As I write, the market's momentum is clearly upward, but warning flags are flying for this bull market's death, and soon.

Bulls correctly note that major bull markets don't end without speculation, and they haven't seen it yet. But I do. Optimism is back in the air. A recent *Barron's* interview had all five of its five market seers envisioning the Dow at 3000 within 12 months. Then see the widely read, but often wrong, *Bank Credit Analyst*, with its new "Dow 5000" forecast. And, amazingly, it's not alone. Where will the buying come from? I don't know, because institutional cash, as measured by Indata of Stamford, Connecticut, is at its lowest level in four years.

The speculative format changes form with almost every new market peak. That way you don't notice when it is upon us. Afterward, all bubbles seem silly.

When the postmortems are in, the LBO craze will be seen as a key aspect of the speculative froth that accompanied this top. Note the bubble's growing size, which in 1989 will total several hundred billion dollars worldwide—virtual 100% leverage. New York's Kohlberg Kravis Roberts has already done about $40 billion of LBOs this year. Today's LBOs occur at valuations 300% above those prevailing when LBOs first appeared ten years ago. Without a resurgent stock market to justify prices that let the LBOers liquidate their flotsam later at profits, this game of monopoly would have ended back in 1987.

Another obvious bubble is the flood of institutional money being thrown at foreign stocks. These supposedly sophisticated folks absolutely do not see that they are speculating. They see themselves reducing risk by "diversifying globally." But the vast bulk of the bucks heads for countries with steep valuations and hot price action (Japan being number one). Remember, the dollar value of Japan's market alone is fully half that of the world's total. The ultrahigh Japanese valuations coupled with justifications for even more remind me of America's elite "one-decision" big-cap stocks of the 1970–72 mania. You recall what happened after that.

Much of this could have been said last year, but with less force. Lending urgency to my concern is a host of very current events. The Index of Leading Indicators is down for the fourth time in five months. Retail sales have been weak since April. Inventories continue building.

The Purchasing Manager's Index has fallen by 25% since 1988 and hasn't been this low since the last recession. Durable goods orders are falling—right now. Ditto for truckers' shipments in many areas. Construction spending has fallen since January, despite recent lower interest rates. Look out below!

In the midst of all this, buried in August 1 newspapers: The Conference Board's Consumer Confidence Index hit its highest level since 1969. And you tell me that we are not in a period of speculation?

Then, too, the "yield curve" inverted in May. In English, that means short-term interest rates are now higher than long-term rates, just the reverse of how they normally arc. The yield curve is now inverted in every major nation except West Germany. Whenever the curve has pointed downward worldwide, a few months later we've seen a recession and bear market. Why should this time be different?

Finally, it has been much too long since we have felt any sustained weakness in stocks. Since December 1987 we've been lulled by steadily rising prices without any real hiccups. Another danger signal.

All this stock market euphoria in the face of these dismal facts reminds me of John Templeton's famous phrase that the four most dangerous words ever spoken are "This time it's different."

Do I therefore recommend ditching all stocks now? No. The momentum is still on the upside, and a few months can seem like forever at a market peak. Also, I'm a believer in stocks. And I could be wrong. Timing markets is always treacherous. But remember: The stocks that do well in a rising market aren't the same ones that shine later. Use the market's current strength to get your portfolio ready for a very different kind of market than has prevailed in recent years.

My favorite defensive stocks are the defense stocks. Unpopular, almost to the dirty-word stage, defense is dirt cheap—as detailed in my May 29 column. And as the economy weakens, government orders won't, giving these stocks the superior earnings momentum relative to other stocks that they lack now. ∎

> ## Land of the Rising Sun and Falling Stocks
>
> Ken's view on Japan here was spot on. After flying high for much of the 1980s, Japan did dismally in the 1990s and still has yet to fully recover.

The Quiet Bear
October 16, 1989

Since my forecast last month of tougher times ahead, the stock market dropped 3%, junk bonds recoiled from their worst-ever shake-out and foreign money markets marched to even higher rates and more steeply inverted yield curves.

But, no, this is not Armageddon. The bear market I predicted in my September 18 column will probably be a painfully slow, gradually sinking affair, not an October 19, 1987-like panic. Most folks fight the last war, and since 1987 was so terribly wild, everyone tends to be wary of a repeat. But things don't work that way. The 1987 crash was foreshadowed by volatile markets with 100-plus-point intraday swings. The subsequent recovery has been much more orderly and so, I suspect, will the coming decline be orderly. This time the old saw will once again be true: "Bull markets die with a whimper, not with a bang."

It is that good-feeling, long-lasting seduction made of nonvolatile, small and steady price fluctuations and relatively light trading that characterizes both the last gasps of most bull markets and the first two-thirds of most major bears.

Why do I expect problems when the government economic statistics sound as good as they do? Because I put little stock in government numbers. GNP, employment data, trade deficits and all the rest are constructed with a planned potential error of about 5%, often more than the conclusion cited. Then, in the next few years, to get them right, they are revised more often than my son visits home from college.

But even if they were accurate, interpretation is tricky. Take last month's headline of the trade deficit at its lowest level since 1984. Sounds good. Is it? Well, if it's accurate, it's a sign of recession, because it supposedly came from our exports' falling less than imports.

Our big trade deficit of recent years merely has reflected our economy's being too strong. We have bought everything we made, and much of what everybody overseas made. As our economy declines, so will our foreign buys, and the trade deficit headlines will sound seductively good to most folks—at first.

Then comes Wall Street's seductive warming. The market letters have become bullish—laced, of course, with safety net-like calls for microcorrections, but still basically bullish. There are few predictions of big stock market declines. Then, too, there is the telltale danger sign, capitulation by long-term professional bears who have been pressured to throw in the towel. Most recent has been Dean Witter's bearish chief strategist, John Mendelson. When he wouldn't cave in, his firm capitulated for him by publicly firing him—front page and all.

There is just too much good news and too many good numbers. Tough realities are only distant memories. Yet as I said last month, the economy appears to be sliding right now.

What should the investor do? Since I believe in stocks more than I believe in anybody's forecasts, mine included, I don't suggest getting out of the stock market. I do recommend concentrating in defensive, cheap stocks of companies that are well positioned, where their customers won't easily stall purchases in tough times and—most key—where the companies have little debt. This way, you can't get hurt too badly in a bear market, but will profit if my bearishness is wrong. ∎

Three Easy Steps

October 30, 1989

"Yes," I reassured the reader, "underwear and shoes are both basics, and will surely continue to be used in the tougher times I envision ahead." But right now, I went on, I would much rather own stock in America's largest shoe firm, Brown Group, than our underwear king, Fruit of the Loom. Why? In a word: safety.

In my October 16 column I mentioned my fears for stocks with too much debt, should a bear market be around the corner. Since then, several readers asked me to explain how to measure what is "too much" debt. These two apparel outfits will serve to illustrate my points well.

In many ways the two are similar. Both midsize. Both top dogs in two defensive consumer product niches. Both sport leading brand names. But there is one huge difference: debt.

In a nutshell, a balance sheet shows what a firm has bought, and how everything was paid for. All that wasn't paid for by floating stock or retaining earnings was paid for by borrowing—and that means extra risk. To put that risk in context, I look first at equity as a percentage of total assets. The higher that ratio, the less the risk. Ideally it should be about 50% or higher. The lower it is, the more I worry.

Brown Group's ratio here is about 47%, versus a meager 22% for Fruit of the Loom. Other things being equal, that makes Brown about twice as safe as Fruit of the Loom.

The next thing I look at after equity is working capital, which is actually often more vital. The word "corporation" derives from *corpus*, the Latin word for body. Working capital is the blood pulsing through business. Folks go bankrupt when they can't get enough to pay their bills and nobody will give them a transfusion. We're talking about the excess of current assets, cash, salable inventories and receivables versus bills you have to pay out in the next year. With lots of working capital, another day is assured. Without it, mere survival is a scramble.

Think of working capital as insurance. Brown Group has about $300 million of working capital, versus current liabilities of about $225 million. That's a coverage of about 130%, which is great. American industry as a whole averages only about a 40% coverage right now. But Fruit of the Loom has no coverage. It has negative working capital: Its current liabilities exceed its current assets by about $60 million.

Closer scrutiny of the two firms' working capital brings out another difference. Brown's $225 million of current bills, or accounts payable, is only about 12% of its $1.9 billion of sales. That's good. It's safer when a firm's current obligations are low relative to its size. Fruit of the Loom is quite a contrast. Its $530 million of short-term IOUs come to more than 40% of its $1.3 billion in sales. That's far too high.

Finally, after equity and working capital, I examine "nonearning cash flow." By this I mean how much cash a firm has pouring in from "expenses" that don't actually involve cash outlays—basically depreciation and amortization. I want to know how large that cash stream is relative to its long-term debt burden. I express this coverage in years.

For example, Brown has about $35 million of annual nonearning cash flow that pours in on top of normal earnings, versus about $130 million of long-term debt. While that cash is usually used to replace old plants, it could, in a recession, be used for anything. If Brown was just breaking even in tough times, it wouldn't need more plant and capacity right away. It could then use this cash flow to repay all its long-term debt in less than four years. Brown's four-year "debt-down" is about average for industry as a whole today. I worry when I see seven-year debt-downs. But it would take Fruit of the Loom fully ten years to pay down its $960 million of long-term debt from non-earning cash flow.

What, then, is the conclusion on Brown Group and Fruit of the Loom? Brown Group's debt picture is consistently strong, whereas Fruit of the Loom looks consistently overleveraged. And this despite Brown Group's selling at 34% of revenue and 175% of book value, as against Fruit of the Loom at 70% of sales and 265% of book value. While Fruit of the Loom has done well in the strong market of recent years, its price seems to me not to be reflecting accurately its degree of risk should tough times hit. ∎

What You're Not Reading About
November 27, 1989

Following October's decline it is wise to note that 1) a month doesn't make a market, and 2) the history of Octobers is a portrait in abnormally violent and often out-of-phase declines. The next few months should be kinder.

Does this mean I am abandoning the bear market call I made in my September 18 column direly titled "The End Is Nigh"? No. I am basically bearish, but if the market kept falling at October's rate it would be worth absolutely nothing at all by year-end 1990. Not too likely. More likely is a bear market that starts with slumps, followed by persuasive recoveries and more slumps.

Good portfolio strategy is based on perspective and patience and keeping the odds on your side, which is tricky. One important way to keep the odds favorable is by trying to anticipate surprises; it's surprise that swings the market. An important happening, ignored at first, can cause a dangerous surprise. Here, then, are some possible surprises I see lying in ambush that helped swing me toward a bearish persuasion for 1990.

Take the worldwide illiquidity and yield-curve inversion (jargon for short-term interest rates rising above long-term rates) that started this summer in every major foreign country. Only the US' yield curve is not inverted. Elsewhere, ugh. With US short-term rates almost exactly mirroring our long rates, you add it all up and you get a global inversion that shrieks with pain. Yet you read and hear basically zip here about this nasty buildup.

It has been driven by a rapid worldwide rise in short-term interest rates—ironically just when every dodo in America seems fixated on how our rates are falling and on what a great job our Fed is doing. We seem blinded to the worldwide picture by our fallen dollar. Otherwise, our rates would be inverted, too. The historical link between global inversions, bear markets and recessions is very strong.

So it should come as no surprise that recent months have seen the first really noteworthy downtrend in foreign stock prices since 1987. But you see little on that here.

That there is so little notice here of the major multimonth price drops going on everywhere but Japan makes these declines doubly noteworthy. Japan may be the exception proving the rule. Folks have cried wolf on Japan for so long that people take for granted its outlandish stock prices.

As the first shall be last, Japan may avoid buckling until it's too late for anybody in Japanese stocks to do much about it. Just another surprise.

Still another? George Bush. If a President's popularity rises, our boosted confidence tends to push stocks up, too — and vice versa. We tend to believe in a new top banana and lose faith as his first year passes, when he actually does things and proves himself to be human — and that hurts stocks. Bush kind of reversed things. His immediate postelection popularity was so low that when he wasn't a disaster, he got a long, strong, reactive and contrarian honeymoon, which helped stocks.

But now, according to Gallup surveys, his approval rating has risen to top any recent President at this stage of his term. Unless the public has suddenly become less fickle, Bush's popularity will probably now regress toward the historical mean — above 1988 levels but below current ones — and that, too, should push stocks downward in 1990.

Finally, folks may be surprised to see how high we are. Yes, unlike 1987, P/Es aren't at record highs, but that is because earnings are too fat from our longest-ever economic expansion. A tip-toe through history's tulips of P/Es and price/sales ratios (PSR) shows that valuations have risen amazingly since 1980.

At 1981's major market peak the S&P 400's P/E was only 10.5, versus today's 15. Scarier, but seldom seen in print, it sold for only 35% of annual revenue then, versus August's whopping PSR of 80%. Its 1987 peak PSR was 84% — only microscopically above 1989's. As recently as 1985 the S&P sold at a PSR of 45%. There is a lot of muck and slosh before touching terra firma.

But I am always mindful that my market views can be wrong. Even if I'm right, I may not be right again for you at the bottom, when you have to own stocks. For now, I would stick to defensive stocks, where, if my bearishness is right, you can't lose too much, but if I'm wrong, you will still make money.

That means cheap, unpopular, well-financed stocks that aren't wedded to the business cycle. Sadly, the only recent one I have seen fitting my bill is Thiokol, a spinoff from Morton Thiokol. Everyone hates it, but it's cheap, the leader in its field, and if the economy goes to hell in a handbasket, Thiokol's earnings should rise anyway.

P.S.: Correction: My brief October 30 use of Chris-Craft in a handful of examples of financially weak firms was in error. I absentmindedly flip-flopped it in my draft with another firm and didn't catch the mistake in proofreading. Chris-Craft is quite strong financially, and I apologize to all involved. ∎

America the Beautiful . . . and Small.

This column is a good reminder to not be so US focused. One nation, even one as large as the US, may have a positive yield curve. But if the rest of the world is inverted, that's a powerful force that Influences the whole world. America's big, but it's not that big. Never fail to consider what's going on outside our borders when making investment decisions.

Early Casualties

December 25, 1989

The reader was angry. My May 1 column recommended Arvin at 23, and he loaded up. Now the stock was at 16. What should he do?

First, what he shouldn't do. He shouldn't pick a single recommendation from many and load up on it. My long-term stock-picking record is a good one, but like everyone I have misses. The intelligent reader will realize this, and, like most savvy investors, spread his bets.

Okay, but should he continue to hold Arvin? That depends. It depends on his view of what lies immediately ahead. If he is relatively optimistic about the near future, Arvin is a cheap stock. I continue to be content with my May 1 wording on Arvin, which said, " . . . at 25% of sales, nine times earnings and dead even with book value, it's hard to see how you won't do well with Arvin over the next five years—at least matching its 1987 peak of 40, plus dividends." By mid-1994, 40 seems like a darn good bet and a great return, from either May's price or today's.

Arvin is a fine firm with an improved strategic position, as detailed in my May column. What I said then should work out just fine. The key phrase is "five years."

But, as my readers know, I have turned bearish on the overall market since I wrote that Arvin recommendation. Had I been as bearish in May as I was in September, I never would have recommended the stock in the first place. In a bear market and recession, Arvin could see 10 before it sees 40. A patient, long-term holder might be content to sit with Arvin for a further dip in order to be holding it when it comes back. But an investor who wants to be in a defensive position if the market collapses will probably want to sell the stock. The questions are: How long is your investment time horizon? And how tolerant are you of temporary but potentially good-size paper losses?

My September 18 column, entitled "The End Is Nigh," foresaw a coming bear market and recession, and advised avoiding anything that wasn't defensive. Arvin is certainly not defensive. Its original-equipment auto parts business is heavily affected by classic business cycles.

Since my May Arvin recommendation, there has come the ticking of a time bomb, including significant summer speculation, a sharp break in secondary stocks, a long list of smelly indicators and, most telling, a drastic and startlingly rapid drop in liquidity overseas. Recent production and employment indicators show the tip of an economic iceberg. As retail sales fall, inventories pile up—scary. Look around.

Anyone who travels moderately can see that airport parking lots are less full, as are most planes. But auto dealers' lots are too full. New cars can't be moved, even with incentives. If you are in America's geographical center, in all but a few states you should be able to see the economy sliding all around you. Finally, there are lots of recent major layoffs by huge firms; plenty of small ones, too—probably in your area. Hardly a propitious market for a cyclical stock like Arvin.

Okay, the angry reader wanted to know, but why hadn't I said: Sell Arvin? Perhaps I should have, but the words I would apply to Arvin fit most every stock I have ever recommended. Most firms are heavily wedded to the economy and can't escape the major recession I see looming. If the market goes, they'll go with it, no matter how good the company and how cheap the stock.

I am usually a very patient, long-term holder of unpopular stocks of what I see as good companies. But if I'm right on this downturn, the only stocks that won't be pounded in 1990 are those few that are free from normal economic vagaries. There aren't many. Cyclical stocks—and most stocks are cyclical—are going to be hurt. Because the auto industry is already feeling the cold breath of recession, Arvin has been hurt.

What bothers me more than Arvin are my recent "defensive" picks, which have bombed. I thought the defensive nature of Ames' geographically niched customer base in small-town discount retailing would be perfect for tough times, and that should have offset -the extra debt it added by buying Zayre. But in today's context investors have their sights on Ames' short-term earnings difficulties. Ames and Dollar General are both good discount retailers in defensible special niches. But 1990's economy may make the phrase "discount retailers" redundant.

And the defense stocks should be defensive. They are way too cheap and discount more than any proposed budget cuts. Long term, they are almost sure winners. But right now, short term, they are victims of psychology, and in trouble. Like Arvin. Be careful. Even where stocks look cheap. ■

1990

A Sneaky Bear Market

> *In the long term, America and the stock market have a wonderful future. As history as my guide, things clearly get better over the generations. Always have. Always will. Technology improves pervasively. Work ethics swing back and forth, and right now are swinging forth. I sure wouldn't want to go back to any prior decade—any.*
>
> "A Sitting Bull," February 19, 1990

> *Sprinkled throughout my bearish columns of the last 15 months are long-term reminders to my readers that the Nineties will be a fine decade and that bearishness cannot be justified longer term. That's still my opinion. . . . Yes, we are in a recession, but remember: Stocks always bottom out long before the economy does.*
>
> "Buy Now," December 24, 1990

Ken called for a market top in his September 18, 1989 column "The End Is Nigh," and he got it right. Only most people didn't know it yet. "The start of the bear market since October has been quiet, and twice as big as most folks realize. I am unusually proud of my September 18 bear market call, featured on the magazine's front cover. It was right." ("A Sitting Bull," February 19, 1990.) Virtually all US stock market averages peaked just a few weeks after Ken's prescient column ran, but the downturn in the Dow and the S&P 500 didn't last long. In fact, they were hitting new highs by the first trading days of 1990.[1] The next few months would be choppy, but the Dow and the S&P 500 didn't reach their ultimate 1990 peak until July.[2] Was Ken's bear market call too early? Not for the smaller stocks he coveted. At the beginning of 1990, Ken saw that the market was already in the early stages of what would become a steep bear market—it just wasn't showing up in the major indexes yet. Smaller stocks were falling, and more stocks were falling than rising—despite the biggest stocks that were driving the S&P's rise.

The big stock market indexes are heavily weighted to big stocks. The Dow, with only 30 stocks, is all big. It's not made up of just the mega caps, but the

Dow constituents are definitely among the stocks most would consider large. The S&P 500 is much broader with 500 constituents (give or take a few as companies merge, go out of business, or the index is reshuffled). So it includes a fair number of midsize and smaller firms. But since it's weighted by market size, the big companies have much more influence on the index than the little guys. Instead of the Dow and S&P 500, Ken focused on a different index—the Value Line Index.

Throughout his columns so far, Ken has referred to the Value Line Index. Even the savviest stock market watchers might not be familiar with it because it's not strewn across headlines daily. The Value Line Index is produced by the Value Line investment research firm. Like the Dow and the S&P 500, the Value Line tracks the performance of US stocks. But there are some important differences between these more well-known indexes and the Value Line. First, the Value Line is broader. As mentioned, the Dow has only 30 constituents—hardly representative of the entire US stock market. As the name implies, the S&P 500 has 500. That's fairly broad, but it pales in comparison to the Value Line Index's 1,700 stocks. The Value Line includes the 500 stocks in the S&P 500 plus 1,200 too small to make the S&P 500's cut. The inclusion of these smaller companies alone makes the Value Line more representative of smaller stocks than the S&P 500 or the Dow. But the way stocks are weighted in the Value Line index also skews it smaller. Value Line is an equal-weighted index.

Ken's February 19, 1990, column, "A Sitting Bull," aptly describes the three basic types of stock market indexes: price weighted, market-capitalization weighted, and unweighted (aka equal-weighted). To be fair, there are other index-weighting structures, like fundamentally weighted indexes, which weight stocks based on factors like earnings or dividend yield. But these are few and mostly intended for purposes other than tracking market performance.

Price-weighted indexes are inherently flawed. The Dow is price-weighted and a relic. "The Dow is our worst index. No one will ever build a price-weighted index like that again." ("A Sitting Bull," February 19, 1990.) It's true—no new indexes are price weighted, none worth mentioning anyway. Not even new Dow Jones indexes, of which there are many. Those tend to be capitalization weighted.

Market capitalization–weighted indexes (aka cap weighted) make much more sense than price-weighted indexes, but even cap weighted indexes have their plusses and minuses. On the plus side, they represent how money is actually invested. To see where money is being made or lost in aggregate, cap-weighted indexes do the trick. Today, Ken favors cap-weighted indexes. Not only is Ken far less focused on tiny stocks than he was decades ago, cap-weighted indexes are more useful for analyzing the composition of global markets. But few investors market cap weight their portfolios. Using the 5% Rule Ken introduced in 1986, a well-diversified portfolio would have at least 20 stocks with roughly the same amount in each. So an equal-weighted index, like Value Line, better reflects how folks actually invest.

In 1990, the unfolding bear market was evident in the Value Line but not the Dow or the S&P 500. The Value Line peaked in October 1989 along with the others, but it didn't rebound. Instead, small cap stocks fell through most of

1990, eventually declining almost 30 percent below their 1989 peak[3]—a steep bear market by anyone's standards. And it wasn't just US small caps sliding. Foreign shares were suffering too. As the year rolled on, more and more foreign markets were starting to fall. Eventually, big US stocks followed suit. From the July 1990 peak through mid-October, the S&P 500 dropped 20 percent.[4]

By year-end formerly jolly investors, pummeled by the bear and worried about the looming onset of the Persian Gulf War, had soured. Ken took that as a positive sign the bear was ending. "Doom and gloom has now grown to proportions I haven't seen since 1974." ("Buy Now," December 24, 1990.) In 1990, the S&P 500 finished down 3.1 percent, the Value Line dropped 16.8 percent, and foreign shares slumped 23.2 percent.[5] Nineteen-ninety-one would turn out much better.

In 1990, Ken continued to call for an extended stretch of US outperformance. "A major theme I will harp on in columns this year is that the 1990s will be America's era." ("America's Decade," April 16, 1990.) And he did. Ken dedicated three consecutive 1990 columns to the reasons he believed US stocks would trounce foreign stocks in the decade ahead. And indeed they did.

Ken saw foreign central banks tightening monetary policy significantly. In most cases, rising short-term interest rates had risen above long-term rates, inverting yield curves worldwide. But investors had become too enthralled with the notion foreign economies were somehow permanently superior to the US to notice. Ken disagreed. He saw restrictive monetary policies abroad weighing on foreign stocks and economies in the short term. Over the longer term, Ken noted demographic shifts favored the US. And most importantly, Ken disagreed with the idea foreign business practices had lapped the US. "America's biggest strength is its market-driven creativity. Almost everything new and novel comes from here. Always has, always will . . . it is vital to remember that the real innovators of the 1990s will come out of America—and, just as in the past, usually from the smaller and more midsize firms that can pick up the opportunities and run to market fast." ("There's Life in the Old Bear," May 14, 1990.) Ken's advice on owning domestic shares was worth taking. Foreign shares doubled during the 1990s; US shares quadrupled.

It's Here, Folks

January 22, 1990

Don't be too heartened by all the year-end, no-recession forecasts you see from economists. As a group, economists have never seen recessions coming. As fellow columnist David Dreman pointed out in his classic 1980 book, *The New Contrarian Investment Strategy*, the economists missed the 1973–75 debacle completely. Only 1 out of 32 correctly foresaw any economic decline at all before that worst-since-1937 worldwide crunch.

According to National Association of Business Economists' data, they did it again with their forecasts for 1982. Interestingly, and again based on NABE data, the consensus of economic forecasts looks very similar every year. Economists always say there won't be a recession in the coming year, but that maybe one's coming the next year or the year after or the year after that. There never has been a time when even 15% stood up and screamed, "We're about to go over the cliff." But sometimes we do go over.

Economists, in my view, rely too much on ivory tower and office tower input and too little on gutsy, right-now Main Street sightings. You can't foresee a decline by fixating on government data and hanging around corporate office buildings. Government statistics tend to be 5% off reality, then revised often in the next two years, and thus worth less than zip in forecasting.

And when economists poll their corporate sources about how business is going, they get rosy numbers, because sales forecasts tend to come through the sales force, a group that is always optimistic—never pessimistic.

So, here goes my own, seat-of-the-pants, count-the-customers, watch-the-parking-lots forecast: We started a recession about May, and it won't be generally recognized until about next May. Recessions rarely are seen as such until they are almost over. Remember Alan Greenspan and Gerald Ford's WIN buttons in September 1974? They were trying to fight inflation and raise taxes fully a year after a major recession was rolling downhill.

The beginning of most recessions is so gradual you can't feel it. The steep part comes as much as a year later. I first felt this one during Labor Day weekend.

I live in a remote, giant-redwood-studded part of the San Francisco Bay Area called Kings Mountain, which is mostly parkland. Each Labor Day I do my community bit by driving one of the shuttles that whisk flatlanders a mile from their cars in to our local fundraising art fair. This September our visitors weren't carrying back as many purchases as during past years.

I travel about three nights and five flights each month. It was hard to miss the airport crowds thinning out this fall. Except for Thanksgiving, I haven't been on a full plane in months. The other day I was on a Boeing 757 that wasn't 10% full.

In early December I drove down Route 30 from Tennessee to Dallas in two midnight runs. All the standard roadside hotel parking lots were empty, Just nobody! I finally slept in Little Rock, Ark. and Sulphur Springs, Tex. You could have rolled bowling balls through their hotels and never hit anybody.

Finally, I haven't found a parking space on the second floor of Hillsdale Shopping Center in San Mateo, California, during a midweek night of Christmas season for years—until this one, and there were plenty.

Impressionistic economics? Sure, but better than working from inaccurate government data and too rosy corporate forecasts. Some regions, like the Pacific Northwest and Great Lakes states, seem unaffected so far, but even ever-strong California is sagging now.

I think this recession will have engulfed our entire geography by early in 1990. But the real boot will be when Europe kicks in. While our Fed may have been trying to engineer a "soft landing," not so overseas, where foreign central banks have been slamming on the monetary brakes very hard since last summer. There is a classic inverted yield curve liquidity squeeze going on everywhere but in the US, and foreign interest rates have climbed, often to double-digit levels.

Even Japan, which is legendary for cheap money, is in the midst of this whirlwind, with short-term rates rising from 4% to 6% in 1989.

This is not the end of the world. Just a normal recession. But until more people understand we are in it, there are a lot of investors still to be surprised and hurt. As I have been saying since September, were I you, I would be very careful.

I expect 1990 to be a bad year for stocks and one in which darn few will buck the trend. If you are patient, with a very long time horizon, don't bother selling current bargains, even though they too probably will fall. After a few hiccups, they will do just fine over the next five years. But if you have a shorter time horizon, sell now to have cash to be able to buy more and better bargains in the months ahead. Whatever you would like to have in stocks when the market is really cheap, at least half of it should be in cash now—and waiting. ∎

A Sitting Bull
February 19, 1990

I guess with a column entitled "The End Is Nigh" (September 18, 1989), I should have expected it, but I have been surprised by the number of letters accusing me of being a gloom-and-doomer. I'm not.

In the long term, America and the stock market have a wonderful future. As history is my guide, things clearly get better over the generations. Always have. Always will. Technology improves pervasively. Work ethics swing back and forth, and right now are swinging forth. I sure wouldn't want to go back to any prior decade—any.

But that doesn't mean there will not continue to be cyclical swings. Since September I have been looking for a downswing in the market, a mild recession here and a rougher one overseas. It's clear to me that both have already started.

It's scary how few folks realize the big, quiet slide we have had since October. Most folks see the Dow's January peak and recent minor hiccup, and shrug. Misleading! Whereas the Dow fell 8% through late January, America's average stock peaked in October and is now down 12%. To see how badly stocks have done, you must look to better indexes than the Dow. There are three basic index types, based on how they are weighted.

The Dow is our worst index. No one will ever build a price-weighted index like that again, since this type is dominated by events having little to do with the average moves of the stocks. Then, too, the Dow Industrials covers 30 stocks only—all huge firms—and too many cyclicals. There are more than 7,500 stocks in America. At least 1,800 of them are liquid enough for anyone. The Dow 30 gives no measure of the more n u m e r o u s, midsize issues. So most "sophisticated" investors look to the S&P 500—our second-lousiest index. It's a misnomer. It's really 100 similar stocks and a "tail." Right now it is moving in line with the Dow; they mostly measure the same thing differently, our few biggest issues. Neither depicts well America's average stock.

The S&P 500 is a market-capitalization-weighted index rather than a price-weighted one. A stock's impact is based on that stock's market cap—how much the market says the whole outfit is worth (price times shares outstanding). In the S&P 500, the biggest-cap stocks are so much larger than the smaller ones that the latter hardly count.

For example, Exxon's $60 billion market cap has a 2.7% weighting in the S&P 500. In all, the biggest 100 S&P stocks have two-thirds of the effect, and the smallest 100 count for less than 2%. If one day the biggest 400 went up 2% while the bottom 100 disappeared off the face of the earth forever, S&P freaks might never know the difference.

The best indexes are unweighted. That means they act like a portfolio that starts by "buying" equal positions in each stock, so they all have the same future impact. There aren't many of these, because they are hard to maintain—there is inordinate housecleaning involved.

For most folks the most accessible is the Value Line, quoted daily in the Wall Street Journal. It may be our most useful index, covering 1,700 of our most liquid stocks, including most of the S&Pers, but all equally. It gives the best snapshot of the average American stock. The Value Line peaked on October 9, and has slid almost straight down, so that by late January it was down 12%.

Then there are various indexes like the Russell and the Nasdaq Composite, which supposedly depict secondary stock action, but they have their flaws, too, all tied to their market-weighted construction.

When I want to see how the smaller stocks are doing, I get my computer to take the S&P stocks out of the Value Line and look at the results of what remains—the bulk of America's midsize stocks—all on an equally weighted basis.

When the S&P is beating the Value Line, the non-S&P Value Line stocks are doing even worse. Consider this: While the S&P 500 was up 31.5% in 1989, the more representative Value Line was up only 11.2%. Startlingly, by my count, the 1,200-plus non-S&P 500 stocks in the Value Line were up only an average of 2.5% in all of 1989.

How's the market? Which market do you mean? Judging by the non-S&P Value Line stocks, 1989 was a lousy year for stocks even though it was a great year for the S&P 500.

The start of the bear market since October has been quiet, and twice as big as most folks realize. I am unusually proud of my September 18 bear market call, featured on the magazine's front cover. It was right.

Behind it all is an emerging recession here and the unabated climb in overseas interest rates and their inverted yield curves—which I have been screaming about since September. Foreign central banks are slamming on the brakes hard against inflation. The scariest thing is how few folks seem to notice. I expect our recession to be mild compared with theirs. But we will feel it. Later in the year I expect to do a lot of buying, but not now. Don't call me a doom-and-gloomer. Call me bullish—just waiting. ∎

Backwater Bargains
March 19, 1990

Remember when real estate was dirt cheap—with very heavy positive cash flows? In the old days you would buy a building only if its cash-on-cash return was better than a mortgage interest rate. If money cost 10% then you would pay $1 million for a building only if it threw off $100,000 a year in net rent, after operating expenses.

I'm a stock market guy. Always have been, always will be. But today's real estate pricing lends a lesson for all markets. There is a general consensus in the media and in the minds of financial types that residential real estate is overpriced nationally, and particularly so in pockets like California. That may be true. But the market is huge, and there are also obscure pockets where prices have already been beaten down so low as to bring safe bargains. Whether stocks, real estate or whatever, you measure for safety by the acid test of secure and high future cash flow yields.

In recent decades real estate speculators have paid up for a property simply because its price was rising—just as regularly happens with stocks. They cut prices loose from any rational relationship to sales or earning power—for a while.

Here in the San Francisco Bay area, where I live, the speculative premiums have become legendary and simply crazy. Mortgage payments typically run at least twice what you could rent out the house for. A middle-class home sells for $500,000. Not so everywhere.

Even during an era of rampant speculation, bargain niches can exist where prices are low enough in relation to earning power to, in essence, let a purchase finance itself. Case in point: Small-town residential real estate where the trend to national corporate restructurings has killed the local job market.

Consider Arkadelphia, Arkansas. Don't laugh. It's a wonderfully cute little college town—about halfway between Little Rock, Arkansas and Texarkana, Texas, and minutes from Hot Springs National Park. I saw the want ads and couldn't believe my eyes. Free cash flow. So I looked up the local Coldwell Banker franchisee, Scott Tatman, who showed me the town—which didn't take long.

About half the 10,000 residents are students or employees of the two nearby colleges. You can find perfectly nice three-bedroom, two-bath homes for less than $35,000, which rent for $350 per month. At 100% leverage on the $35,000, the fully amortized carrying costs are about $290 monthly, which gives you $60 per month for repairs, property tax and insurance. Free money. Why so cheap?

Arkadelphia got hit by corporate streamlining—the Reynolds Metals rolling mill and a Textron bearings plant shut down, taking out 900 jobs. Why, then, haven't the rents fallen comparably? Because of the two colleges and their effect. There are plenty of folks who want houses and can pay the rent. But students, or untenured faculty, or a host of other unbankable locals don't have the kind of income streams that qualify for a mortgage.

Owners, of course, take more risk than renters. If the colleges fold, you're dead meat. But beyond that, the risks are remote. There are no more major plants to close. And you handle risk as does any good portfolio manager—via diversification. Don't just buy Arkadelphia. Buy a portfolio of towns with similar attributes. Anyone can find them. I set a green 22-year-old college graduate onto it. She used the IMS Ayer Directory of Publications, which lists newspapers by city, detailing both paper and city. She focused on small towns with a college and phoned, asking "Any plant closings lately?" From there she contacted real estate agents and collected prices.

We quit after being convinced that there are plenty of towns where corporate gamesmanship has created imbalances between rents and bankable buyers.

Consider Ely, Minnesota, (population: 5,000). For a while after Reserve Mining went bankrupt, houses got so cheap that outsiders were actually lifting them off their foundations and hauling them away. You can get a nice home, in town, for under $30,000—some for under $15,000. And again, nicely positive cash flows exist because the remaining local mortgageable income base is small. Ely is a recreational wonder, amid 1,000 lakes, hunting and skiing. It's a town, too, with a hospital, schools, jet airport, department stores, banks and a college. Nice place.

Then there is Glendive, Montana, hit by a Halliburton plant closing but a nice college town. Pawhuska, Oklahoma and Holly Springs, Mississippi are particulary interesting. Holly Springs bills itself as "the cheapest place to live" in America.

You won't make a quick killing on backwater bargains, but you can rest assured that they will hold up over the 1990s better than hot-market properties trading at 30 times annual rental value. Ultimately, values of all assets come into line with their income streams. That's the lesson. A bargain has a low price relative to future cash flow yields. Sooner or later, greater-fool buyers lose out. ■

America's Decade
April 16, 1990

Today individuals hardly count in the stock market. The bucks, buy or sell, are institutional—and are mainly from a clique of the 1,000 largest pension plans; they total about $1.9 trillion. Scarier, the top 200 have about $1.4 trillion. To know today's market you must know how these few Goliaths work.

The top 200 themselves are of four types: the very biggest corporate, union and state pension plans, and a few huge churches. The smallest plan among the top 200 has $1.6 billion in assets. There are 35 with more than $10 billion each. Most have trouble figuring out what to do with all their money. They don't think, "Is GM a good stock?" They think in asset classes: stocks versus bonds versus cash versus real estate. Then they think "subsets."

In equities they usually think "core" versus "aggressive." Core means big-cap stocks often "passively" selected via indexation to clone the S&P 500. Aggressive means everything else, including the "micro-sets" of small-cap stocks, foreign stocks and venture capital. Within aggressive they figure where to place bets and then mostly hire specialty investment managers for selection and timing.

Every year these pension funds get more cash flow from their work force and have to put it somewhere. If a consensus forms on the best place to invest, a disproportionate amount of their collective cash flow goes to one micro-set, making prices there surge. Perversely, other competitive micro-sets get starved. Darn few funds bought foreign stocks ten years ago. Now it's the rave hot item. Aggressive equity cash flow has fed foreign stocks and pushed them up, while starving smaller-cap American stocks, so last year they were basically flat, while the S&P 500 was up 31%.

By itself California spent $3 billion on foreign stocks last year. This mania for anything foreign is just that—manic. First, note that these guys didn't get in early on foreign stocks. Stocks almost everywhere overseas have left America in the dust in the 1980s superbull market. Our Goliaths jumped on the band-wagon late, chasing prices—usually in the hottest markets, most heavily in Japan. They didn't place their bets before the foreign markets surged. They bought late in the game, and their very buying has formed a top in foreign stocks.

Note that, as always, you can see the mirror image of this speculation in the mutual fund world. Single-country closed-end funds now sell at tremendous premiums to their underlying stock holdings.

With every mania comes intellectual rationalization. In this case it is the notion of a low correlation between stock price movements in differing countries. Most pension plan giants believe they are reducing risk within their aggressive asset subset by diversifying globally.

Yes, most of the time the correlation between differing foreign markets is low. Prices may be rising in one place and falling elsewhere. But, as I documented in my second book, the link is quite high between major foreign markets at the most critical time, that is, at major cyclical peaks and troughs. You couldn't avoid 1929's peak by buying British or French or German stocks.

But, as history shows, neither common sense nor history will stop the truly sophisticated when they get carried away with a fad. If that were not so, the smart money would already be pulling away from overseas stocks. In the last two years interest rates have been skyrocketing overseas, rising almost daily, and yield curves have inverted. But the big guys just blink and buy. Few anywhere seem to notice or pay heed. I am very proud to say my September 18, 1989 column was the first time you could find in the US print media any major mention of this foreign monetary phenomena. Foreign central banks are feverishly applying the old-time religion to fight their fear of future inflation. As the noose tightens, our biggest funds will get hung on their foreign buying and finally panic.

The history of headlines clearly shows that any consensus ends up being wrong. Headlines as 1989 ended said that just as the 1980s was the decade of Japan, the 1990s will be Europe's decade. So I bet not. A major theme I will harp on in columns this year is

America's Time to Shine

Ken rarely makes long-term forecasts of any sort, preferring to look just 12 to 18 months ahead. But his 1990 prediction America would have a great decade was spot-on. America blew away foreign stocks overall during the entirety of the 1990s.

that the 1990s will again be America's era. While I have predicted since September a declining stock market and a mild recession, I have also envisioned more brutal batterings overseas. I predict the big boys will be burned by foreign equities for years.

And then smaller American stocks truly can shine relative to other asset classes—for the first time since 1983. As the next bull market begins and the giant asset allocators look within their aggressive allocation, they will divert cash flow away from foreign to other micro-sets. US smaller-cap stocks are the logical next wiggle for the big investors. Buying strong but smaller American firms that their managers can really know, visit and understand will seem safe. My advice: In the 1990s buy good small-caps and mid-caps—made in the USA. ∎

There's Life in the Old Bear
May 14, 1990

If you believe, as I do, that a bear market started in October, then beware of these countertrend up periods, which encourage the bulls and make the bears nervous.

I remain bearish for the near future because—with the exception of the junk bond bubble's having burst—all the negative points I made in my September 18 column, "The End Is Nigh," still pertain.

Springtime is particularly treacherous, which folks have come to forget since in the 1980s' superbig bull market almost every season was a winner. But as Yale Hirsch notes in his valuable 1990 *Stock Trader's Almanac*, May has been a down month for stocks 17 out of the last 25 years. Between 1965 and 1985 there were only 5 years when May saw advancing stocks.

Another nifty point Hirsch notes is that when May doesn't get you, June often does—like a one-two punch. Finally, I note that whenever January has been down, as per this year, it has never been the market's real bottom—which almost always comes in the spring, or later.

If you look just at the Dow Jones industrials you cannot realize how much damage has already been done to the stock market, both here and overseas. The broad Value Line Index is down much more than the Dow, and so is the S&P 500. Much attention has been given to the 25% drop in Japanese stocks, but more interesting is that stock prices have been falling in most countries—in some worse than others. Only France, Germany, Hong Kong and Norway have escaped the downdraft. Most countries are off about 8%—some much more, like Sweden, down 15%, Spain, off 18%, and Taiwan, off 24%. We won't swim against the tide for long.

Interest rates have skyrocketed all around the world. Foreign central banks have engaged in restrictive monetary policy. Two-year English government notes have risen from 11% to 14%. German long-term rates have risen from below 7% to over 9%—above ours.

In every major country rates have risen, and in most places short-term rates are higher than long-term rates—almost always the precursor to a credit crunch and recession. "Won't the opportunities in Eastern Europe cancel all this out?" you ask. No time soon. While most folks look excitedly at the demise of the communist bloc and see Europe getting major benefit from the "1992 Europe" concept, I see a can of worms. Most of these countries have never gotten along very well. Why are we to believe it will be different now? Human nature doesn't change that fast.

In the 1990s I see demographic weakening, too, in a pair of economies that have been everyone's envy: Japan and Germany. Germany's retirees-to-workers ratio is barely higher than ours is now, but it will double relative to ours in the coming two decades, making a society of nonproducers. Japan, which is used to having few retirees and lots of workers, will soon see its demographics become worse than ours as its large bulge of 50-to-60-year-olds retire. It should crimp its output and savings rate.

So I see trouble for the markets here and abroad over the next few months. After that? I see good things for the US market.

We've got the baby boomers coming into prime earning age and into the post-family-formation stage, so savings will rise relative to consumption. For the first time in decades, compared with these other countries, we will find ourselves with a low ratio of retirees to workers and particularly to peak-income-age workers. We'll be on top.

Then there is a contrarian aspect. Note how fashionable it is now to assume that American businesses aren't as good as their foreign competitors. There is a non-stop barrage of articles these days depicting how much we have to learn from all the foreigners. Are we really that bad?

It all depends on the product area. It is a very competitive world today, and it is key to recall that America's biggest strength is its market-driven creativity. Almost everything new and novel comes from here. Always has, always will. As Japan's plant and capacity get older, and as the Europeans themselves age, it is vital to remember that the real innovations of the 1990s will come out of America—and, just as in the past, usually from the smaller and more midsize firms that can pick up the opportunities and run to market fast.

All this leads me to think the 1990s will see more focus on and interest in smaller, more midsize American stocks. The mania that exists now for foreign stocks will fade, choked by interest rates and deteriorating fundamentals. America will be the place to be. But our big-cap stocks had their run in the 1980s, and we will rediscover how good mid-America really is.

For all my optimism about America's long-term future, I'd hold off on buying until the current bear market, which is still young, has run its course. But then be prepared. For the smaller-cap American stocks, which did so poorly in the 1980s, the best is still ahead. ■

Don't Sell America Short
June 11, 1990

When I stand at a formal pension plan committee review and start stating the case that the 1990s will be America's decade and a great era for smaller-cap American stocks, I'm met with stark disbelief and blank stares. Then silence, furrowed brows and several questions asking whether I hadn't heard about Japan, Germany and every other nation that supposedly is now better and more resourceful than we.

Yes, I've heard about them and I have heard all the other negatives, and I still think the 1990s will be our decade. Because many nations have done so well relative to us recently, we have come to see them as better than they are, and yet the big trends are now starting to shift against our overseas competitors.

Twenty years ago we were fearful of the communists. We were fresh from campus protests, civil rights and the start of a nonstop string of political ethics inquisitions. But back then we also thought we were pretty darn good at business. Our big stocks sold at P/Es of 20. And the Nifty Fifty at 40 and 50. Why? Because they were going to grow at high rates forever.

As a result of the inevitable letdowns and coincident foreign successes, we think too poorly of our own business skills. Instead of premium valuations, our stocks, and particularly secondary stocks, sell at discounts to global averages. But our prospects are about to get better.

Why do I say so now, when our self-regard is at a nadir? One reason is that demographics stank. Soon they won't. I'm on the old edge of the baby-boom crowd— those born from the late Forties to the early Sixties. By our mass we have dominated US trends and will for decades. We have been a huge drain on America's bottom line. In our youth we merely consumed as America invested in us. In our early adult years we spent our way through the typical family formation stage, which is a low-income, mass-buying binge. But in the 1990s we enter our peak earning years, and that will have a big and positive impact.

Folks in the 45-to-54-year-old age group—which we baby boomers are entering—earn more than anyone else. For example, this age bracket historically averages a huge 60% to 75% more income per capita than the 25-to-34 year olds. This productive 45-to-54-year-old group will grow 46% in the 1990s, according to Bureau of the Census estimates. Meanwhile, the unproductive pre-25 age group grows by only 1% and the 25-to-34-year-old family formation generation will actually shrink by 16%. This means higher savings and productivity per capita.

Looking at it another way, ten years ago there were 70 million folks in the productive years between 35 and 65 supporting a larger group of 103 million folks from the largely unproductive ages of under 25 or over 75. Ten years from now there

should be fully 105 million folks in the 35-to-65 age group supporting a like number of youngsters and oldsters. As the worker-to-consumer ratio improves, so will our profits, our image and our stocks.

Won't we continue to have problems with drugs, bad schools and varying forms of social decay? Of course, but so will other societies. Take Japan. It will be particularly hard hit. First, it faces a massive demographic problem almost identical to that we are now leaving behind. Then, too, it faces an onslaught from the Pacific Rim where many more hungry countries are now, for the first time, generating more college graduates per capita than does Japan. Those countries will be going after the markets Japan took away from us in the last 20 years. That competition will insure us cheap imports while beating the stuffing out of export-dependent Japan and its still overinflated stock and real estate prices.

In the last 15 years the non-US stock market has mushroomed from being worth $500 billion to $6.3 trillion. Half that value is in Japan, even after the recent decline. By contrast, the total US market is worth about $3.7 trillion. Japan's market is overdiscussed and still overpriced. But right now most of the other $3 trillion overseas is vulnerable, too, and relatively illiquid.

What should an investor do? My advice right now is: Wait. Despite the recent all-time highs in the Dow Jones industrials, most American stocks are nicely below their October peaks. I think we are early in a major global bear market. It's too soon to buy yet. But the worst damage and smallest subsequent recovery should occur overseas. When the time docs come to buy, the place to be will be here. And the stocks to buy will be the world of smaller-capitalization midsize companies that were largely ignored in the last eight years.

As Bill Lowery of Performance Analytics showed me, in only two of the last six decades did America's biggest-cap stocks beat the average of all stocks, one of them being the 1980s. In four of those six decades smaller-cap stocks did best. The recent experience was unusual. The 1990s won't be. The 1990s will be an American decade, and one when small-cap stocks lead. ■

Dad, You Were Right
July 23, 1990

Society has become too quantitative lately in all aspects, but particularly in stock analysis. The real value added in the 1990s will be in qualitative stock selection.

As a green college graduate I was trained by my father to analyze quality. That was his obsession. He was an un-numbers man. No charts or tables. When he had to deal in numbers, he used an old hand-crank adding machine. What interested him then and interests him still is quality—what could be called the two "Ps," people and position. Meaning, how good are the people? And how well is the firm positioned in its field? No matter how good the numbers looked, he wasn't interested in a stock unless he saw exceptionally skilled and dedicated people running a firm with natural competitive advantages.

Not that quantitative analysis didn't have its day. When computer power was hard to get, there was a real value in number crunching. I remember paying a major brokerage firm $15,000 in the mid-1970s for a one-time computer ranking of the New York Stock Exchange stocks with the lowest price/sales ratios. It was a bundle for me then, but it was worth it to get the cheap-stock ideas no one else would have—giving me a competitive advantage.

Today, for about $350 a year you can get a floppy disk each month that will do that, plus dozens of different screens you can set to your own parameters. It's all so cheap. Now, for about $50,000 a year, which isn't much more than my $15,000,

adjusted for inflation, our firm buys the top-of-the-line Compustat product, which runs on a PC and allows screening I never imagined possible just a few years ago—like screening by market share—plus literally hundreds of precise user-determined screening factors combined any way I want—plus statistical back-testing.

Not surprising, it being so cheap, that most stock analysis today is quantitative. Most investment management firms are buying low P/Es or in my firm's case, low price/sales ratios or low price to cash flow—or low something to something. One new fad is high historical dividend yield. Another is "asset allocation models" that tie valuations to interest rates and technical analysis to create electronic market timing—all quant driven. The quants rule Wall Street.

It's hard to find green college graduates who even want to do qualitative stock analysis. Too unscientific. They're all brainwashed by their professors to believe they are supposed to do quantitative work, dealing with output and data and statistical techniques. The Catch-22 is, since quanting is now so common, it's less important.

You can see the result in valuations. A pretty big chunk of the market used to sell for less than half the market's average valuation and an equally big chunk sold for twice the market's valuation. A statistician would say the Gaussian distribution around the mean was relatively flat. You could make money in that era simply buying the low-priced stocks and selling short the high-priced ones. Regression to the mean would give you a nice profit. But

today fewer stocks are at steep premiums or discounts. The quants have picked over both ends. The few steep discounts tend to be bad companies that deserve it.

So how will one make money in the 1990s? By making smart judgments on the two "Ps"—people and position, and separating the superior from the mediocre. Is management determined and motivated? Are their sales skills top-notch? Ditto for motivational skills? How deep is management?

Then, what is the firm's cost position relative to competitors? Is there growing demand for its products? What makes it hard for competition to outdo the firm? Does it dominate, based on geography, brand name or special niche?

Yes, numbers still matter. But I think we will soon return to a time when Wall Street relearns an appreciation for the two "Ps"—quality in management people and strategic position. Quality, not quantity. ∎

Growth or Value?
August 6, 1990

Too many folks posture themselves as either growth or value buyers—as if the two were separable. They aren't. History clearly demonstrates that stocks with good growth potential are worth paying up a bit for. The problem comes when you pay too much for a given level of growth or assume future growth that never materializes.

Valuing growth is easier than forecasting it. There is an old growth-stock investors' saw that runs, "Buy 'em at half their growth rate and sell 'em at 1.5 times their growth rate." It's an amazing value formula. It means: If you expect a firm to grow at 20% annually, you get a good value if you buy at a P/E of 10 (half of 20). Then you hold until the stock gets fashionable and

sells at a P/E of 30 (1.5 times 20). Adding growth in earnings to the P/E expansion can allow for a very big gain.

Watch out, though, for excessively high growth rates. They are almost always unsustainable. I never invest in firms that try to grow at more than 30% per year. I prefer a 20% growth plan, or even a 15% or 10% growth plan, properly priced to a 30% growth plan—because with extremely high growth goals you take on the double risk that both the growth does not occur and the company actually gets into serious difficulty trying to stretch beyond its capabilities.

For example, if a firm tries to grow at 35% a year, with normal 15% attrition, after a year half the employees are new and don't really know the lay of the land. After five years, 90% of the workers are new. With so many new employees the odds are much higher that some are deadwood, or worse. Problems in business tend to pop out all at once, and fast-growing firms that are more oriented toward hiring employees than keeping an eye on them often don't spot problem employees until after a crisis arises. It takes a phenomenal management to keep things on track when growth is extremely high and so many employees are new.

However, if you pick real growers and don't overpay, you can hardly lose. Even if the P/E never rises above 10, a 20% growth rate virtually ensures the stock will double within four years. If the P/E does rise to 150% of growth, you'd have a stock that would septuple. This formula works because it ties the P/E to growth rates and never lets you pay extremely high P/Es. If anything, the formula is too cheap. There are darn few firms that grow 30% annually, and even for those few, the formula lets you pay a P/E of only 15. That hardly seems like overpaying with the Dow at 3000 and with the whole market selling at a 15-times-earnings level.

But that's the beauty of the formula: It prevents you from overpaying for growth. The formula also protects its rigorous user in times like 1972 and 1983, when the world goes growth-crazy. It forces you out. With it you would never have held on to those 40-times-earnings gee-whizzers, whether they were 1972's quality big-cap variety or 1983's explosive high-tech marvels.

Fine, but can you find suitable stocks in a market that sells at 3000 on the Dow? Yes. First, note that smaller capitalization stocks are still nicely below their peaks of last fall. Second, you need to find a way to look between the cracks via some additional tools. Partly because everyone else is looking at the world through the eyes of P/Es, when I'm looking for growth bargains I like to use my old friend the price/sales ratio. For example, if you expect a firm to grow at 10% per year, you double that number and want to buy it at 20% of its annual revenues. A 20% grower you would buy at 40% of annual sales, and a 30% grower at 60% of revenue.

This helps identify companies that due to one-time events aren't making any profit at all right now, and seem to have no P/E. Or they may be just barely breaking even and have a P/E of 100, or 1,000. Sometimes they even have great cash flow but because of funny-money modern accounting don't appear to have earnings. This apparent lack of earnings happens from time to time in most young growth companies, sometimes after they've previously tried to grow too fast and suffered from internal hiccups. ∎

Right Around the Corner
October 15, 1990

I keep hearing the same question from institutional clients: "We thought value-type stocks would be defensive if the market sold off. But they have fallen more than high-P/E growth stocks. Why?"

Fair question. The answer, based on history, is: Value stocks show their defensive strength in the late stages of a bear market, not in the early stages. Investors make the mistake of presuming that what is true point-to-point—from peak to trough—also occurs steadily en route. Untrue. Markets are wicked. They love to deceive. Stocks with low P/Es, low price-to-book ratios and low price/sales ratios usually get hit first in a bear market. Value stocks best the market only in the later half of a bear market and the first phases of a bull market. They tend to underperform toward the end of a bull market and in the beginning of a bear market.

That's what's been happening the past year or so. Conversely, growth-type stocks do relatively best in the late stages of a bull market and the following first phase of a bear market. Take recent history. From 1972 to 1976 value stocks underperformed the two-tiered Nifty Fifty stocks in the beginning of the decline, 1972 and 1973, then made up for it in the ravages of 1974 and surpassed the market in 1975.

Again, off the market's bottom from 1982 to 1986, value-type stocks did so well they became faddish among institutions. But in the post-1987-crash era, growth stocks started doing best. In 1989, as you will recall, the fad became stocks that could grow through the expected "soft landing"—i.e., the big, high-P/E, consumer products companies—ones thought to have "safe" growth, so their already high P/Es could bid up "safely."

But a bear market started last October. The Value Line Arithmetic, by far the most reflective index of America's average stock, has fallen rather steadily since then and is off 20% from its peak. Bear markets are seldom recognized until we are well into them—part of what makes them so wicked. Hence the Dow Jones industrials and S&P 500 hit new all-time highs in July, confusing most folks fully nine months into this major decline.

So, in the first half of a bear market, most folks are still playing bull market—fighting the last war. So they sell their value stocks, which were doggy in the late exciting stages of the rise, pushing them down in the first phases of the bear market. At the same time, folks hang on to growth stocks—their good recent performers.

As this goes on, the value stocks get oversold early in the bear market, setting the stage to do much better than the market late in the decline. As the bear market drags to its conclusion, people lose faith in growth, and the growth stocks are shunned. It's a pattern that repeats again and again: Value stocks do badly early in a bear market and then come into their own late in the bear market and in the early stages of the succeeding bull market. Growth stocks, vice versa.

The action of these last 12 months has not been particularly unusual for early in a bear market. For example, as the S&P 500 rose to a new high this year, more stocks fell than rose—even within the 500 S&P stocks—a kind of index illusion. And big-cap stocks did much better than smaller-caps—another typical early bear market behavior. Hence, while the big-cap S&P 500 is now down about 10% since last October, the broad-based but small-cap-oriented Russell 2000 index fell steadily—fully 25%.

And, as said before, high valuation growth stocks did better than value issues. Whether looking at 1990 to date or only looking at the few weeks after Iraq rocked the financial markets, value stocks have sunk sadly. For example, even among the very largest market cap stocks there has been about a five percentage-point spread favoring high valuation stocks as the market stagnated and then slid.

But the good news is twofold. First, most major bear markets only last between 12 and 24 months. Two years is a very long bear market. Only the 1929–32 drop lasted longer. This one is a year old now, suggesting that it is soon to be time for the value stocks to start doing their thing—which is the second part of the good news.

The first signs of change are happening in the high-glitz growth areas. Case in point: previously red-hot Oracle Systems, which has done a $23 to $7 nosedive in just 75 days. To my thinking, this year's fourth quarter and the first quarter of 1991 will be the time to start spending cash and loading up on value stocks. Not just yet, but in a few months, they should be coming into their own again. This fall I would focus on smaller-cap value stocks, particularly those that may suffer tax-loss selling pressure from earlier 1990 losses. ∎

Buy Small, Think Big
October 22, 1990

A helpful stock market lesson for the 1990s pops right out of the *Forbes* 400. It's what I call buying small and thinking big. Looking at the self-made centimillionaires who have graced the lists over the years, note that many of them got there buying things no one else wanted, that didn't take much of their money and for which they could see huge futures. Then they patiently realized those futures. They typically did not make the list buying well-recognized, quality properties at fancy prices.

No one exemplified this better than Donald Trump. While much is written on him, to me the most interesting part is seldom stated. He made his money buying small and thinking big and lost it by doing just the reverse. Trump's troubles started as he bought what he himself came to call "trophy properties"—the ones the world wanted most, only Trump paid more for them than anyone else would.

The same buy-small, think-big principle applies to the stock market: The real money is rarely made in buying premium-priced stocks—and the rule will apply even more in the 1990s than in recent decades. The really big opportunities in the 1990s market will be in smaller-capitalization stocks, where the companies have huge opportunities ahead, opportunities not yet capitalized in the price of the stock.

According to a recent survey, pension plans with assets over $100 million each, which in total have over $2.1 trillion, have reduced their allocation to small-cap stocks during the 1980s because of poor performance. Less than 5% of their assets are allocated to US stocks with market caps below $2 billion. About 60% of their total assets are allocated to stocks, so only 8% of their stocks are small-caps.

Yet small-cap stocks in aggregate make up about $680 billion, or 21%, of the $3.2 trillion US equity market. Pension plans are clearly and significantly underweighted in small-cap stocks.

To see the potential for small-cap stocks, imagine this: If, by the end of the decade, pension plans increase their small-cap allocations to reflect small-caps' current 21% share of the US equity market, then by the year 2000 those pension plans will have increased their overall small-cap allocations from 5% to 12.6% of total assets. That doesn't sound too wild. But if at the same time nationwide pension plan assets grow modestly at, say, 10% annually, by the year 2000 they will have bought an additional $630 billion of small-cap stocks—93% of all outstanding shares at today's prices.

After eight years of poor small-cap stock performance, few initial public offerings, lots of LBOs, buybacks and takeovers, there is now a very inelastic supply of small-cap stocks. Even a small allocation increase from pension plans will have a stunning price impact.

But to carry the *Forbes* 400 analogy further, you don't want merely to buy small-cap stocks. You also want to buy ones that are cheap, and you want to think big in terms of potential.

A stock I think fits nicely is Applied Magnetics, the leader in magnetic disk heads (to computer memories what needles are to record players). It was the third stock I ever mentioned in *Forbes*, back in 1984. Since then it has doubled in size, and the stock had a nice run.

But since 1987 Applied Magnetics has gotten the tar beaten out of it, falling from $20. Since I first wrote about the firm, it has established clear dominance over its competitors, while remaining financially rock-solid. Computer memories will continue to grow, and with 40% of the market for recording heads, Applied Magnetics will get its share. Future growth should be 15% to 20% per year; yet with a total market value of $125 million it can be bought for just 33% of its annual revenues of $375 million and 80% of book value.

Be careful. We are in a bear market. But it has been going on for a year now. And a quarter or two from now this bear market will be awfully darn old. If it isn't over by then, it will be close enough that it won't much matter looking back on it a few years from now. All of these stocks could have heavy tax-loss selling pressure in November and December, and I would plan on that time frame as an opportunity to buy. I would also want to be fully invested before getting very far into 1991. The next bull market should be exceptional for "buy-small, think-big" stocks. ■

It Kinda Sneaked Up On Us
October 29, 1990

Make no mistake about it. The last year has been a serious bear. The worst since 1974. Worse than 1981–82. And it didn't start with Saddam Hussein. It has lasted a full year and has dropped stocks more than 25%. It is now scaring people who didn't even know it was happening before the invasion of Kuwait.

What this means is that the bear market is now much closer to its end than its beginning. Based on historical durations, it will probably be over by midspring and some parts of the market are likely to bottom by year-end.

Most stocks—but not the widely watched averages—started falling a full year ago. Take the S&P 500. If you take the same 500 stocks and equal-weight them—that is, envision an equal dollar amount of each stock, the way a portfolio tends to work—their July 1990 prices never got close to their January averages, and January never got close to last October. The last year has been a full 20% downride.

The Value Line Arithmetic is America's best overall stock index because its 1,700-stock coverage is by far the broadest of any readily available index that equal-weights stocks. It has fallen 26% since its peak last October. And it fell steadily all July, well before Hussein did his thing, as did the 500 S&P stocks, equal-weighted.

The reason most people didn't notice that silent rout was that they were watching only the big averages and the big stocks. These got hit only after the Kuwait invasion.

Then, too, few folks have any sense of the foreign bear market. Note that Japan peaked in December 1989. Britain and Ireland in January. Austria and West Germany in March. Sweden and Switzerland in June 1989. France was a late bloomer in May. None of these markets made new highs in July, as the Dow Jones industrials and S&P 500 did, and most are now down 25% or more from their peaks—some much more—and most wiped out three to four years of gains.

Or, look at the long bond. The 20-year government note double-peaked at 142 in September and November 1989. Then it fell steadily, to 128 by April, rose to 134 in July and has fallen ever since, but only to 128 — back to where it was.

What I'm saying is: By the time most people knew we were in a bear market, the bear had already done most of the damage it would do.

I have been saying all year that the 1990s will be exceptional for small-cap stocks. Not only did they do poorly in the 1980s bull market, but they were beaten up much more than big-caps in the bear market. They are like a depressed spring waiting to explode. Historically, big-cap stocks and small-caps have had vacillating periods of performance. When big-caps did well, small-caps often didn't, and vice versa. After all, why hassle owning small-cap stocks when it's easy to make money in big-caps?

But take the 1972–82 period as an example. Big-cap stocks did terribly tied to two major recessions, two oil shocks, stagflation and Watergate. Yet small-cap stocks yielded high double-digit returns. The 1990s are likely to be similar.

Another way to see the "depressed spring" is via Ibbotson & Associates' monthly historical price data for the lowest 20% of market-cap stocks on the New York Stock Exchange. Since World War II, out of 11 bear markets, the average small-cap decline has been 32% and lasted nine months. This current decline is 31% and almost 13 months. Only the 1970 and 1974 bears were longer for small-caps.

Small-caps' time is soon. And there-in lies the opportunity. At any time in the last few years, most folks would have loved the notion of a chance to buy good companies at 1982 prices. Well, now you can. This bear market has unwound most if not all of the 1980s bull market.

But watch out. This bear may still have a way to go, particularly in the biggest stocks that haven't suffered nearly as much or for as long. And there will be plenty of market-depressing tax-loss selling. (Folks who do tax-loss selling have not thought through the poor math of it, but that doesn't stop them.) But before 1990 ends, I want to be fully invested for the next bull market. When small-cap stocks come under pressure from year-end tax-loss selling, I want to be buying them. ∎

Knee-Jerk Selling
November 26, 1990

A host of puzzled readers wrote or phoned wanting elaboration. Why did I write in my October 29 column, "Folks who do tax-loss selling have not thought through the poor math of it, but that doesn't stop them"?

The readers were planning to sell stocks before year-end so that they could chalk up capital losses to offset capital gains or to store up for future use. What was wrong with that? I'll explain:

Think it through. Suppose you have a $10,000 gain already and have another $20,000 original-cost stock position that has fallen in half in the market. You figure your $10,000 of paper loss can be sold to wipe out the gain you realized and eliminate your tax. You are in a 28% bracket and live in a state with about a 6% tax rate. After the one tax is offset against the other, your combined federal and state tax is about 32%. So most folks assume that if

Tax Tails

In this column, Ken makes the point to not let the tax tail wag the portfolio dog. Another way to put that, don't cut off your nose to deny the IRS relative pennies. The market tends to move higher over time. While no one likes paying taxes, you're usually better served staying in the market as much as possible.

they don't do the tax-loss sale Uncle Sam's capital gains bite next spring will be $3,200, and that they can save this amount by offsetting the capital gain with a capital loss.

It ain't that simple. Let's suppose you still like the stock and plan to buy it back next year. The odds are heavy you'll pay a good bit more than you'll get selling now even if the stock doesn't move. That's because brokerage costs and the bid/ask spread will take a nice bite.

If a stock is $10 bid, offered at $10.25, to do your tax loss, you sell at $10, buy back at $10.25 and lose 25 cents in the round-trip plus brokerage. While that doesn't sound like much, it's really 2½%. Brokerage racks in another percent—as a percent it typically rises as the price per share falls.

What is worse, if the stock goes against you in the midst of your tax maneuver—even by a few percent, one-eighth or one-quarter of a point, which can happen in a few minutes—you are clearly net-behind, regardless of the tax aspects. What you have done, instead of taking tax losses is added to your losses.

Still, you say, a bird in the hand is worth several in the bush. If I take my losses, I pay Uncle Sam a lot less come April. Yes. Or you can take your loss in any future year. Unless the stock rises, you still have your potential tax loss available any time you want to take it. At worst, you lose

a year's interest on that $3,200 in taxes—a couple of hundred dollars at most. That's your real savings from acting now, not the full $3,200. Why risk thousands to save a few hundred? At best, your stock goes up and you are materially better off for not having sold it.

Remember this: The stocks that have been banged down the most by November, the ones with the most potential "tax savings," are the ones that see the most tax-loss selling. This drives them down more, and irrationally, as everyone is trying to get out the tax-loss door at the same time. Historically, the stocks with the heaviest year-end tax-loss selling have bounced back nicely right after the tax-loss selling season.

The documented "January Effect" among smaller stocks is directly correlated to how poorly the stocks behaved the prior November and December under tax-loss selling pressure. Years like 1990, when there was no January Effect, follow on the heels of 1989, when there was little tax-loss selling because few people had big paper losses after the up markets of 1988 and 1989. In early 1990 folks realized gains, and after the big down market, they are now gagging on their paper losses. And particularly so among the smaller-cap stocks, which have been beaten up so much more than the big-cap stocks and are much less owned by tax-free institutions.

Because they hate to pay taxes, a lot of people make irrational investment decisions. Don't be one of them. Go against this irrationality. Instead of selling your biggest losers this late in the year, look around for other big losers. Consider buying them now, before tax season is over. Pick strong companies that are hammered to the point of being statistically cheap. By February you are likely to see some nice gains, which, after all, is the basic goal of this whole stock market thing.

Particularly now, after stocks have been falling for more than a year, and smaller stocks are down fully 30% from their peaks, you want to recall that bear markets don't last forever and that the biggest January gains for smaller stocks often come on the heels of times just like this. There are lots to choose from. Fully 25% of the market's stocks now sell below their July 1982 prices, and almost half the market sits below its December 1985 prices. Remember: Knee-jerk selling is still jerk-selling. This tax-loss season is the time to be buying. ∎

Buy Now
December 24, 1990

Human affairs are admittedly in a deplorable state. This, however, is no novelty. As far back as we can see, human affairs have always been in a deplorable state." So begins Berkeley Professor Carlo Cipolla's humorous but insightful treatise, *The Basic Laws of Human Stupidity*.

In spite of the deplorable state of its affairs, the human race has done pretty well for itself since World War II, yet people love to worry. A recent *Newsweek* magazine cover shows a man with a huge pencil piercing both his chest and a "terminated" memo. The title: "How Safe Is Your Job? The Warning Signals—How to Cope." *Newsweek* is a pretty good contrary indicator. It's the sort of publication Wall Streeters refer to when they say: "When the covers get bearish, it's bullish." Doom and gloom has now grown to proportions I haven't seen since 1974.

What clinched it for me was a recent front page of my *San Francisco Chronicle*. It was loaded with phrases like "risking a financial avalanche, widespread proliferating misery, carnage, painful readjustment, confronted, double-digit unemployment, continued free-falling real estate prices." It warned that "Americans have never before been so heavily in hock."

Yes, there is $13 trillion of debt in America. No, that isn't as much as it seems. The total value of US homes is itself about that big. Add in commercial real estate, timber and farm land, public land, factories, stocks and bonds, and our immense accumulated knowhow, and you end up with an asset pile that dwarfs the debt. Despite the doom-and-gloomers, our nation's overall balance sheet is quite strong. Fact is, net interest payments as a percent of corporate cash flow stand at about 28%, just exactly where they were in the 1973 and 1982 recessions—not any higher.

In terms of servicing debt, then, we are in no worse shape than we were in previous recessions. While little talked about, our debt-servicing capability is stronger than perceived because nonearning cash flow, principally depreciation, is at record levels relative to earnings and debt. This is because of the much underreported 1980s capital spending boom. If our affairs are in a deplorable state, the state is no more deplorable than at previous recent bottoms.

My columns have been largely bearish since the September 18, 1989 one entitled "The End Is Nigh." Although the big averages kept rising until well into 1990, most stocks have been declining since early October 1989, and are down vastly more than the Dow or the S&P 500—even within the S&P 500 the average stock is down 23% from its 1989 peak. The smallest 100 firms in the S&P 500 are down 33% over the last year. The next largest 100 stocks are down 28%. The middle 100 by size-are down 24%. The second-largest 100 are down 19%. The largest 100 stocks—the ones that get all the weighting in the market-cap weighted average—are down only slightly; that's why the averages don't show how rough this bear market has been.

Meanwhile, short-term interest rates clearly peaked in March and have fallen gently ever since. Classic reveille for stocks to rise after a prolonged bear market.

If you look at the midsize range of stocks, they are amazingly cheap—not as cheap as in 1974, but cheaper than in 1982, when the great Eighties bull market started. Via the Compustat database, we looked at the smallest 40% of America's 1,500 largest stocks. Of those 600 stocks, 36% are actually selling below their July 1982 prices.

Sprinkled through my bearish columns of the last 15 months are long-term reminders to my readers that the Nineties will be a fine decade and that bearishness cannot be justified longer term. That's still my opinion. With stocks down big, value stocks down bigger, short-term rates falling, and gloom and doom at almost all-time record levels, now is the time to buy. Yes, we are in a recession, but remember: Stocks always bottom out long before the economy does.

What about Iraq? War? Oil prices? Too much is made of it and all of it is already fully discounted in the market. Iraq has no major allies, isn't all that powerful and will be costly to us but not nearly as costly as Congress is regularly. For perspective consider this: The Iraq/Kuwait combo has a population a little smaller than California's and, shockingly, a GNP that is only about half the size of Exxon's.

What to buy? I would focus on smaller stocks of good companies that have been pounded in this bear market and have been under tax-selling pressure. ■

1991

Unbelievable Bull

> "
> *I am never absolutely sure about anything. Portfolio strategy is an odds game. You figure the most likely outcome, the odds, the penalty that may attach to being wrong, and act firmly but watchfully. My bullishness, while firm, is not unmovable.* "
>
> "A Contrarian's Mailbag," February 18, 1991

> "
> *Staying with this bull market, or any bull market, is sort of like hanging on to a horse when it's bucking; it keeps trying to toss you off. But hang on. Don't listen to the beaten-up bears who seize on every correction to trumpet the long-awaited end.* "
>
> "The Bucking Bull," November 25, 1991

Near the turn of the nineteenth century, Lord Nathan Rothschild offered this investing advice: "Buy to the roar of cannons, and sell to the sound of trumpets." In other words, buy stocks when war begins and sell when it ends. A few minor details aside (substitute laser-guided missiles for cannons, for example), Rothschild's old adage proved half correct in 1991. Tensions in the Middle East had been escalating rapidly since Iraq invaded Kuwait in August 1990. In early January 1991, chances of a peaceful resolution were fading fast, adding to investor anxiety. In the first nine trading days of 1991, the S&P 500 lost 5.3 percent.[1]

Then, on Saturday, January 12, Congress authorized the use of military force in Iraq. True to Rothschild's advice, stocks didn't look back. The next week saw both the beginning of UN military action and the start of a two-month, 20 percent S&P 500 rally.[2] But Rothschild wasn't entirely on the mark. The Gulf War lasted just a few months. The bull market would last nearly a decade.

As is always the case in the early stages of new bull markets, there were many stock market doubters in early 1991. The war was just one concern. The US was also in the midst of a recession, the S&L crisis left hundreds of failed banks in its wake, and the US debt and budget deficit were troublesome to many—just to name a few. Ken was aware of all these perceived problems, yet he was bullish. Why? Because he knew everyone else was aware of them too.

In Ken's view, virtually all the concerns that top financial headlines each day don't count for much when it comes to market forecasting—unless you are confident things will turn out differently from what everyone else expects. It's the things investors *don't* expect that move markets. "A most basic truth is that whatever most folks are fretting about never much impacts stocks in the long term. The market is driven mainly by surprise. That so many have visibly focused on banking and real estate problems for so long almost guarantees their impact being less than a surprise and already fully 'in the market.'" ("Dumb Bears," August 5, 1991.)

This perspective often results in Ken being labeled a "contrarian." Heck, he labels himself as such in his columns. In Ken's February 18, 1991 column, "A Contrarian's Mailbag," he responded to readers' disbelief in his bullishness by writing, "With due respect to my readers, these howls of outrage make me feel good. They are kind of a contrarian indicator that I am likely correct. . . . For you who remain resolutely bearish, I can only say: Write on! Keep those letters coming. In my contrarian way, they make me feel better than if you agreed."

But Ken isn't a contrarian in the classical sense (i.e., he doesn't doggedly go against the crowd, come what may). In his view, what the crowd expects is least likely to impact the stock market, so you only gain an advantage over other investors by identifying unheralded information or analyzing known information differently. This is especially true when investor sentiment is at an extreme—positive or negative. Too many bearish investors increase the likelihood their too-dour expectations will be greatly exceeded, boosting stocks. The opposite occurs when people are too bullish—reality ends up falling short, and stocks can plummet. In 1991, folks were too bearish in Ken's view, which made him bullish.

To an item, Ken saw the stock market impact of the day's popular concerns differently from most. It's true the US was in a recession during the first months of 1991, but as he put it, "Recessions are buying opportunities. The stock market always bottoms long before the economy does." ("The Year of the Small Caps," January 21, 1991.) There are two main reasons stocks move before the economy. First, stocks discount future conditions. Even in the middle of a recession, investors see the recession's end at some point in the not-too-distant future and bid up stock prices in anticipation of better times ahead. Then there's monetary policy. The standard and appropriate central bank response to a recession is usually to loosen monetary policy, making cheap money available to businesses. But firms often aren't looking to build new factories or hire workers when the economy is contracting, so a fair amount of that cheap money flows to stocks and bonds before making its way to the broader economy, which it does eventually, stoking the economy and fueling the bull market. "The perverse beauty of this lag is that the more and longer the economy weakens, the more the Fed reacts with even looser money, which mainlines its way to Wall Street. Less is more. The less economic strength there is, the more Wall Street gets injected, unintentionally, with bigger doses of money. Count on it." ("The Young Bull," March 18, 1991.)

Similarly, the continuing wave of bank failures most people feared only made Ken more bullish. "Wouldn't a rash of bank failures put a huge damper on credit creation, thus rippling through the entire economy and hurting healthy banks as well as unhealthy ones? I doubt it. That's carryover thinking from the Great Depression days. Folks forget that the Fed consciously shrank the money supply by 30% from 1928 to 1932. That would kill credit today. But the central bankers will never make that mistake again. They will expand the money supply; the strongest banks will pick up the slack, pumping credit back into the economy." ("Who Cares About Bankers?" September 2, 1991.) Or to put it more succinctly, "If 250 banks fail, the market will rise. If 750 of our 10,000 banks fail, the market will explode upward. Fundamentally, we have too many darn banks." ("Dumb Bears," August, 5, 1991.)

The national debt was and is another topic Ken usually sees differently from the crowd. A lot of people hate debt. They see debt as bad and more debt as worse. Ironic, since most successful companies have some debt, and so do most people. Granted, the dollar amount of US government debt was huge in 1991, and it's huger still today. But so is the size of our economy. Scaled against our gross domestic product (GDP), the national debt in 1991 was no higher than it had been at many economically vibrant times in the past in the US. "No, overall we don't have too much debt. We have too little and have had too little since first becoming a modern society. Which is why for 60 years we have been adding debt relative to our economy's size. And will for maybe 30 more years." ("Dumb Bears," August 5, 1991.)

Ken's advice for 1991 was to stay invested and focus on small value stocks, his bread and butter. That might seem a bit self-serving, but he had good reason. Not only had large-cap stocks outperformed small cap for a record 13 years leading to 1991, small stocks suffered considerably more than large stocks during the 1990 bear market. He liked value stocks over growth stocks because when banks aren't lending money freely, growth companies with higher valuations can often raise cash by issuing shares. Value companies with slimmer valuations don't have that luxury. Without access to bank capital, they're stuck. As the Fed became more accommodative, small-value companies would get the greatest benefit initially.

Amid all the fear, Ken's bullishness paid off in 1991—stocks soared, finishing the year with the S&P 500's best-ever December (+11.4 percent for the month).[3] For the year, US small-value stocks (+41.7 percent) underperformed small-growth stocks (+51.2 percent), though value would do better over the next several years. Both trounced the larger S&P 500 (+30.5 percent).[4]

The Year of the Small Caps

January 21, 1991

If you didn't buy secondary stocks in the fourth quarter, when the new bull market started, don't be too disconcerted. Although you have missed a nice move, it's still not too late. This bull will be big and long. There will be steep countertrend pullbacks, as in every bull market, and they will offer further buying opportunities.

The media and a lot of the players have missed the start of this bull market because it has been concentrated in the smaller second-tier stocks, bypassing the big blue chips that led during the 1980s. Sort of like the mid-1970s, when big-cap stocks staggered sideways and smaller-cap stocks exploded.

Why do I say the bull market has started? Because from their lows around October 19, 1990 smaller-cap stocks are already up over 20%. This while the Dow Jones industrials and S&P 500 have scarcely moved. It is the first time in several years that small-cap stocks have done better than big-cap stocks for even as long as a few weeks.

Ironically, the big-cap-oriented Dow and S&P 500 aren't capable of measuring small-cap-led rallies. To see that correctly, note the astounding feature that the ten largest stocks in the market-cap-weighted S&P 500 have 50% more impact on the index's overall movements than do the 300 smallest stocks (which make up 60% of the index)—all combined. So, even when the smaller S&P stocks move a lot, as they have recently, the S&P 500 index feels it almost not at all.

Historically, small-cap stocks and big-cap stocks have often moved out of sync with each other for cycles lasting several years, one group rising while the other marks time.

Four such sweeping broad cycles are measurable. Recently, my firm took the monthly returns of the smallest 20% of stocks on the New York Stock Exchange and plotted them against the monthly returns of the big-cap S&P Composite—going back to 1932—(all on a three-year moving-average basis to eliminate statistical noise).

Doing so lets you see on both an absolute and a relative basis when big caps have bested small caps, and vice versa. The conclusion is: Both big and small have had periods of 4 to 12 years when they have done best, followed by the reverse.

We are now coming off a 13-year period—the longest ever—when every single year big caps have bettered their position over small caps compared with the year before. Small caps' day is overdue and now.

It's kind of commonsensical. When big caps are doing real well, folks don't need to scratch around among smaller caps to find good returns, so they don't, and small caps aren't bought. But when big caps start to not perform, perhaps with a little time lag, investors start looking for other ways to turn a buck, which leads them to smaller stocks, which they bid up.

In the 1980s big-cap stocks had just about their best decade ever, so if history repeats, the 1990s will be much tougher for them, which is quite good for small caps.

Most folks wrongly suppose that small caps can't do well unless big caps do, and that recessions and other tough times are too tough for small caps to buck. It just isn't so. Recall the decade from the 1972 peak to the 1982 trough. We had the two largest recessions since World War II, another small one, two major oil shocks, double-digit stagflation, Spiro Agnew's demise, and Watergate. Yet over that period, small caps returned more than 15% on average annually, much of it in the first half of the decade, when the economic and political sledding was toughest. Adverse times are when small becomes beautiful.

Recession? Yes, we are in one. But it is clearly the most ballyhooed recession I have seen or studied. Recessions are buying opportunities. The stock market always bottoms long before the economy does.

Could this recession turn into a recession or even a depression? If we were to have a depression, or anything close to it, you wouldn't see so much talk of it in the media now. In 1929 and 1930 the vast bulk of the press wasn't bearish. It was bullish. Ditto for all other major busts.

When your local paper and the general-interest magazines carry so much gloom and doom, the worst is almost over. Real economic busts don't reveal themselves in advance to TV pundits and headline writers. Bull markets have always "climbed a wall of worry."

This year will probably see pull-backs. Buy into them. You need not buy the smallest stocks, but don't buy the biggest. And don't confuse small cap with small-sounding but big-cap, high-tech stocks having fancy prices, as so many folks do. Buy good, solid small-cap firms, but ones that are cheap. ∎

A Contrarian's Mailbag
February 18, 1991

How can I be so bullish with a war on and a recession just starting?

A spate of hate mail has poured in recently from bearish readers who object to my recent bullishness. With due respect to my readers, these howls of outrage make me feel good. They are a kind of contrarian indicator that I am likely correct.

Still, just because folks say I'm nuts doesn't make me right. Besides, I am never absolutely sure about anything. Portfolio strategy is an odds game. You figure the most likely outcome, the odds, the penalty that may attach to being wrong, and act firmly but watchfully. My bullishness, while firm, is not immovable.

Having issued that caveat, I repeat: To my thinking we are in the early stages of a small-cap-led bull market that started in October. I have heard all the arguments for a capital R recession and/or a depression. There is the supposed debt crisis and the related federal budget deficit. Then, too, there is the much presumed imminent banking-failure crisis and the related

imploding of real estate prices that is supposed to further sink the banks. I even watch CNN's coverage of the Iraqi war. While all these are much discussed, as I have said in times past, as economic disasters they are mostly myths and at worst won't sink America's economy.

Try as I have over the years, I have never been able to fully forget my formal training in economics, and I still recall the error of confusing major microeconomic hiccups like these phenomena with what happens to the overall macroeconomy.

Instead of dwelling on negatives, consider the positives. First, as I have said often, we have been through a much bigger and longer bear market than most folks realize. The 13-month decline that ended in October wasn't as big as the 1972–74 decline but was far larger for most stocks than the 1982 bear market—a fact few appreciate, even now.

Then note the bear market divergence between big-cap and small-cap stocks. Within the S&P 500, the 10 largest stocks were up 13% in 1990 and flat from the market's 1989 peak. Yet the 338 smallest S&P 5oo stocks, which merely equal the big 10 in weighting within the index, were down 17% in 1990 and down 37% from the market's 1989 peak—an amazing and little-noted "they-went-that-a-way" head-spinning spread.

This is important because, as I said last month, since October's bottom, smaller stocks have steadily bested their bigger brethren for the first time in years: Surprise—opportunity via depressed prices and value, followed by subsequent price performance in a part of the market where few are looking for it. Not only were smaller stocks up big in November and December, when the biggest stocks weren't, as I cited last month, but in January's decline they also fell less. For the first time in years the market has "breadth," and not even the "technicians," who are supposed to watch out for such things, have noted it as they remain fixated on the biggest-cap Dow and S&P indexes.

Third, note that interest rates peaked last March and have fallen ever since, and the Fed is vocally clear about keeping us on track. I give them a B+, better than any Fed-recession relationship ever. The correlation between loosening monetary policy and bull markets is very high and hard to refute.

Then there is sentiment. It is hard to find bulls. Almost everyone is bearish—including the folks who take pen in hand when they read my column. Yet look at the war reaction. As Humpty Dumpty would have said of January, "All Hussein's tanks and all Hussein's men couldn't put the bear market back together again." A major bullish feature is that there is almost no one who isn't familiar with the negatives. They're discounted.

This has been the most broadcast recession ever—because the media industry and the Northeast were the last sectors to suffer the decade's "rolling recession" before the national recession began. The media was more recession sensitive than when going into any prior national decline of the 20th century. The result? As I wrote early warning words to America's heartland, folks started battening down the hatches early, which has accelerated the decline but will diminish its depth through lightened inventories, reduced middle management, debt pay-downs, etc.—all of which is healthy and quite bullish.

So I'm still a raving bull about all but the biggest stocks. In the next five years I see nice double-digit small-cap returns accompanied by small single-digit returns for the 100 largest stocks. For you who remain resolutely bearish, I can only say: Write on! Keep those letters coming. In my contrarian way, they make me feel better than if you agreed. ■

The Young Bull
March 18, 1991

The bull market isn't over. Not that it won't be punctuated with short, sharp pullbacks occurring almost kamikaze-like at the most unpredictable times. It will. The first such pullback came during the first half of January. I have no idea when the next will arrive. These early-cycle bull pullbacks can gut-wrench you as badly as any amusement park roller coaster ride. But, normal for a bull market, corrections are almost designed to scare you away. Don't let these pullbacks spook you.

A business writer for a local paper called the other day and expressed the confusion of many when he said, "How can this market be so turbo-charged when the economy is so clearly dismal? Is there no reality to this thing?" But, yes, it is for real and rooted in reality.

First, folks forget that stocks have always, simply always, rallied long and strong in the middle of recessions. Market bottoms happen long before economic bottoms. Sometimes bull markets begin just a few months before a recession ends. At times it has been as long as a year, but stocks always head up while the economy is still seriously tanking.

And by my measurement, once the market has made a major up-move in mid-recession, stocks have always stayed strong until at least a year after the recession has died. If you study market history you won't be surprised by this bull market that was spawned mid-recession, nor the likely next spring-like up-leg, probably starting this spring. Ultimately, this small-cap-led bull market will probably last two to five years, and small-cap stocks will probably advance 200% to 300% before it is over.

There is no mystery as to why the market should turn up before the economy does. It's because of the long lag between changes in monetary policy and economic results. After a long expansion, as money tightens and the Fed fights inflation by tightening further, we get recession. When the Fed figures that out and loosens, it does so while business is terrible—right here and now—and Main Street has no immediate use for the Fed's money with aggregate demand in rugged recession.

So, the only place the new money can flow is to Wall Street—via lower interest rates, which lead to higher bond prices. The money flow is through banks using their Fed-injected liquidity to buy Treasury securities, which for them is the least risky of all loans. And when bonds rise after a long bear market, stocks explode.

Mass psychology improves, and eventually the money works its way around to Main Street. By then the improved business conditions are more than enough to sustain the bull market. But long before it stimulates the economy, the easier money stimulates the stock and bond markets.

The perverse beauty of this lag is that the more and longer the economy weakens, the more the Fed reacts with ever looser money, which mainlines its way to Wall Street. Less is more. The less economic strength there is, the more Wall Street gets injected, unintentionally, with bigger dosages of money. Count on it.

Bears seem fixated on debt, the federal budget deficit, fears of a banking failure crisis, imploding real estate prices and another shoe dropping in the war. Maybe even depression.

None of these worn-out old arguments will drag down this bull market. As I have said in the past, we don't have too much debt. We may even still have too little. While the debt-doomers will think I'm nuts, I think they're nuts. By my count, I'm sure our society can shoulder at least twice the debt it has now before running into the threshold level where any real debt problems arise.

Massive banking failures before this recession ends? What's wrong with that? We have massively too many banks now. Bankruptcies always abound before recessions end. That's partly what they're

Liquidity Tsunami

To anyone who witnessed the huge global boom in stocks in 2009 from their March low, this will all sound familiar. After a major global recession in 2008 the world's central banks unleashed a massive wall of liquidity—never before seen in terms of its size and near-coordination. A lot of that made its way to capital markets, helping goad stocks higher even as the recession wore on.

about. The war? Study the history of stocks during wars: bullish. And we will no more have a depression in 1991–92 than I'm going to be heavyweight champion of the world.

I'm very proud of my market calls in this cycle. Starting with my September 18, 1989 column, just weeks before the broad market's peak and running through 11 subsequent monthly bearish columns, I argued for falling prices. Since October 22, 1990 five successive columns have urged being fully invested, and most important, doing so in smaller-cap stocks. En route I have recommended 50 small-cap names.

At the risk of tempting fate, I'll say that despite the breathtaking runup to date, it's not too late to get on board the small-cap express.

We just ended a four-year period of flat small-cap stock returns. After prior such four-year flat periods, the subsequent average annual three-year and five-year returns for small-cap stocks have been slightly better than 25%. So, despite the 35% small-cap runup since October, if you're not in now, use any material pullback as a chance to load up. If you are in, hang on, and use pullbacks to upgrade your holdings for the next up-leg.

It's Early in the Game
April 15, 1991

In one respect the bears are correct: The S&P 500 is far from cheap. But they are also wrong, because the rest of the market is exactly at levels from which major advances have historically continued. Weighing the big stocks versus the small stocks in judging whether the market is too high, the small stocks are a better yardstick because there are a lot more of them. The bulk of the S&P 500 reflects only about 100 to 150 stocks out of a multi-thousand-stock US market. And those few giants that dominate the S&P are about 70% of a particular type—big-cap growth stocks.

In short, while the S&P 500 is a bit better bellwether than the Dow industrials, it still doesn't tell the whole stock market story. Looking at the biggest stocks, the market is fairly dear. But the further down the list you go in size, the cheaper they get.

Skip the 500 largest stocks and look at the next 1,500 stocks as a group. Within

these 1,500 study the distribution of valuations and match that distribution against that of the comparable 1,500 stocks at the market's important past turning points. Doing this, my firm creates bell curves of the market's valuations at various key points in time. It is a quantitative but also visual snapshot of what "shape" the market is in. Here, the results are simply stunning, because the bell curve is consistently very differently shaped at major tops and bottoms.

For example, with P/Es at or near major market bottoms the bell curve has a classic shape with a bulge in the middle and a downward slope at beginning and end.

At market bottoms the bell curve bulges, because right then most stocks are worth about the market's average, with relatively few worth a lot more or less than the average. But at major market tops the bell curve of P/Es for the 1,500 simply looks flat. There is little or no bulge in the middle. At the tops there are far more variations in valuation among the 1,500 than at the bottoms. Many stocks then sell materially above or below the average. At tops the market is cocky and thinks it knows how to discern value—how to tell which stocks should be worth a lot and which aren't so hot. At bottoms it has no such confidence in itself and so prices all stocks about the same way.

In October 1990 the 1,500 showed similar average values to those of August 1982, and the distributions were almost identical to 1982's. And the similarity continues today. That is, the bell curve is now almost identical to that which existed five months after the 1982 bottom.

The pattern of valuations among small stocks today, therefore, is parallel to that which existed just as the market took off on one of the greatest bull markets in history.

Ultimately, valuations only count relative to the cost of money, and any comparison of current P/Es to the past must be adjusted for the cost of capital. Here, too, small stocks come out winners: Interest rates are a lot lower today than in 1982, so by this measure small stocks were much cheaper this time than in 1982—fully 25%.

Skeptics may remind you that there was a small-cap crash in 1983, but they are only partly right. That crash was among hot, high-priced small cap growth stocks; it didn't bring the whole universe down with it. I expect similar parallels in the next 18 months, with small-cap value pulling nicely ahead of growth.

So this small-cap-led bull market is nicely on track. ∎

Bell Curve Technology

Creating a bell curve to measure distribution of valuations and subsequent market returns is just one of the many examples of capital markets technology Ken has shared with *Forbes* readers.

Sell Growth
May 13, 1991

My April 15 column keeps haunting me. It suggested similarities between this small-cap-led bull market and the 1982–83 bull market. What haunts me now is the growth stock butchering of 1983–84, and that it might happen again soon. If recent history repeats, now is the time to sell growth stocks selling at high multiples of sales and earnings, and to reinvest the proceeds in small capitalization value stocks, those selling at relatively low valuations of sales and earnings.

What's a small-cap stock? My definition is: Skip the 500 stocks with the largest market capitalizations (stock price times shares outstanding) and look at the next 1,500. In the three years starting July 1983, the most expensive stocks—the 40% of that 1,500 stock group that sold at the greatest price-to-sales ratios—provided a total return to investors of only 2% per year. By contrast, in the same period, the cheapest stocks—the 40% with the smallest PSRs—generated a very nice 17% annual return. Small value stocks beat growth stocks by a wide margin, which is what I believe will happen again.

Why? For one thing, as I discussed in my last column (*Forbes*, April 15), the distribution of valuations of small-cap stocks has evolved to be now almost identical to January 1983. For growth stocks, that's scary.

Another problem is the appreciation of what I call "small-cap illusion" stocks. These are stocks thought of as small growth companies, though their market capitalizations are very big. My firm's research shows that the way small-cap illusion stocks perform in relation to how small-cap value-stocks perform often warns of whether growth stocks or value stocks will do best in the coming few years. Right now this points, as it did in 1983, to problems ahead for growth stocks, and opportunities in value stocks.

A classic example of small-cap illusion is Amgen, a fast growing West Coast biotech firm with latest-12-months sales of $299 million that is almost universally considered a small-cap growth stock. That's the illusory part: The market says Amgen is worth $5.3 billion, making it the 128th-largest American stock, by market value, on March 31. Amgen hasn't been a small cap stock since 1989, when it sold at under $30.

This market is full of such small-cap illusion stocks. Software vendor Novell has just $500 million in revenues but a $4.1 billion market cap. Others are Lin Broadcasting, Sun Microsystems, Tele-Communications and US Healthcare and, among listed stocks, Alza Corp., Home Depot and US Surgical. They are all generally thought of as small-cap stocks, yet are in fact big-cap stocks.

The confusion is so prevalent that there is even an almost pure small-cap illusion index regularly mis-cited to depict small stocks: The O-T-C Composite (a.k.a. the Nasdaq Composite). Half its market-cap weighting is made up of small-cap illusion, huge-cap o-t-c names from among America's 500 largest stocks. Far from small!

Here is the key point: In the stock market, leadership rotates. Big- and small-cap stocks, growth and value stocks each have their days in the sun—and the rain. Market trends tilt between favoring small versus big, and growth versus value. Sometimes the market leaders are small growth stocks. Other times small-cap value stocks lead—or big-cap growth, or big value stocks. Since last October, growth and small-cap stocks have been hot. Before that it was growth and big-cap stocks. But the growth-style tilt is getting old.

My firm's recent research shows a two-part trick for seeing when market leadership is about to shift from growth stocks to value stocks, or vice versa. When the small-cap illusion stocks have done well for several years, as they have now, you have the first part. And if small-cap value stocks also did poorly for years (as they did until October), and then suddenly small-cap value stocks take off (as they did five months ago), then you have the signal of an upcoming demise of all growth stocks, big or small. This phenomenon occurred in 1970–71 and 1982–83, I think it is happening now. (It works just the reverse if small-cap value stocks shine for years and then small cap illusion suddenly takes off—signaling the demise of value stocks and the rise of growth stocks—witness 1964, 1978 and 1986–87.)

To avoid a 1983–84-like growth stock butchering, use the coming months as a chance to move out of high-P/E, high-PSR growth stocks, big-cap or small-cap. Happily, small-cap value stocks have just entered into their up-cycle, after years of lagging. Relative to sales and earnings they're still cheap, and if the 1982–83 parallels continues they can rise nicely for years, even if their small-growth brethren stall. ∎

Watershed

June 10, 1991

Last year I beat the drum long and hard to the tune that 1990 would see small-capitalization stocks—those with market capitalizations below a billion bucks- start besting big ones for the first time in years. Starting late in the year, the market vindicated my judgment. But now, in my opinion, small-cap stocks are at a watershed. One part of the small-cap universe has had its day. The other part still has a great deal of life left in it.

But first, some definitions: Size-wise the 500 largest stocks make up the big-cap world, and the next 1,500 in size compose the tradable portion of the small-cap world. The 1,500 now span from about $1 billion down to about $80 million. Anything smaller than that is too illiquid for safety. Then, within the 1,500 are two general types of stocks: growth and value.

Small-cap growth stocks are already richly priced, currently at levels essentially identical to those existing before the great 1983 small-cap growth stock collapse. Right now the typical small-cap growth stock sells at 20 or more times earnings, 4 or more times book value and has a market cap of 200% or so of sales. By contrast, small-cap value stocks are very much cheaper. Maybe 8 to 12 times earnings, 125% of book and a market cap equal to maybe 35% of sales.

More important, small-cap valuation distributions (the percentage of the small-cap world that sells within any given range of P/Es or price/sales ratios) are mirror images of distributions from the spring of 1983. For example, in April 1983, 18.3% of the small-cap world had P/Es between 25 and 150. Now 17.4% does. That level compares with 8.2% and 7.2% at the market bottoms in 1990 and 1982.

Another parallel with 1983 is the flood of new stock offerings. In the two weeks ended this April 30 there was $3 billion worth of new stock certificates. The new stock is being offered mostly by growth companies with high valuations. The current level of new issues is about three times that of recent years—and again on a par with 1983.

So I am convinced that market leadership in the small-cap sector is about to rotate from the growth stocks to the value stocks. Partly my faith is based on what has happened among the 1,500 stocks I look at during periods of similar past monetary conditions. On April 30 the Fed cut the discount rate for the third time in recent months. There have been five times since 1970 that the Fed has cut the discount rate three times within a 12-month period. Each time, there was a clear market effect in the next 6-, 12- and 24-month periods.

All stocks, even the 500 largest, did pretty well—but on average small-cap stocks did better than big-cap stocks and value stocks beat growth stocks. In the first year after the third rate cut, the 1,500 stocks performed 8.5% better than the 500 biggest stocks. Most of that superior performance was accounted for by the stocks selling for low multiples of earnings and sales.

This makes sense. In the right money conditions preceding discount rate cuts, those firms least threatened by their bankers are the biggest growth firms. What banker in his or her right mind would cut off IBM or Merck? Smaller growth firms fare less well but, because of high valuations, they can usually get capital if needed from new equity offerings without it being too costly and painful in terms of" the amount of new shares they have to offer to get the money.

But the low-valuation, less-regarded smaller firm can't get new capital from the stock market. Their low valuations ensure that raising money from new stock sales would require so much new stock that earnings per share would get decimated by the avalanche of all the new shares. At the same time, in tight money periods these unexciting corporations are the most likely ones for a bank to abandon when trying to upgrade the corporate quality of its loan mix.

So, as the Fed loosens monetary conditions, it is the small-cap value stock that feels the most incremental access to capital. It is like releasing a depressed spring. ■

Surveillance
July 8, 1991

You know how essential reading *Forbes* is. But what else should you be reading? As a professional money manager I must pore through all the really big business and financial magazines and newspapers, so I speak with some experience in the field.

Here are my less-well-known favorites and what it is about them that might help you with your investing:

Pensions & Investments, a biweekly from Grain Communications ($135 per year—if that is more than you want to afford, most libraries have or should have *P&I*). The big beasts in Wall Street's herd mentality are the 1,000 largest pension plans that together own one-third of the stock market, plus much more. *P&I* is the only good source specializing in what these Goliaths are doing. From it you can gather the guts of crowd thinking plus upcoming trends.

You read a publication like this as much to know what to avoid as to know what to do. For example, *P&I* regularly chronicles what styles of money managers the plans are hiring and firing, so you can sense when they are taking a good thing too far. Case in point: Reading between its lines convinces me that foreign equities will lag in the next few years—the contrarian in me senses that the big institutions have gotten too carried away with those stocks since 1989.

You can also see what they aren't buying, which, if it's cheap, is often the hot fad a few years down the road. Reading *P&I* keeps you tuned in to the relatively invisible but huge institutional world. Otherwise, darn few of you will recognize even 10% of the 200 multibillion-dollar-plus managers. Who is Miller, Anderson & Sherrerd? With $20 billion, it just might matter if MAS is the largest shareholder and then sells a stock you own.

Money Market Directory ($895 per year; ditto on studying the library's copy). It ranks, slices, describes and localizes the big plans and managers. Who does David Dreman or Ken Fisher really work for? And how big are our firms? What managers handle General Motors' plan? Here is where to find out. You can also find the scoop for relatively small pension plans of all types in your area. Unless you spend at least a few hours with the *Money Market Directory*, you can't know how money management is evolving in the arena where the really big bucks change hands *Morningstar* ($490 per year). A rather new publication in a two-part format, it is far and away the best mutual fund coverage ever done. Awe-inspiring is the only way to describe the detail it offers in a very concise format. What have been the-hot and hurting funds of any style in recent years? Easy. But you can also see exactly what each one owns and all other key details you need—at a glance—sort of the Value Line of mutual funds.

The Economist ($110 annually) gives you foreign perspective on what is going on here and around the world, which helps avoid blind spots.

Another form of blind spot can be avoided by checking *Vickers Weekly Insider Report* ($40 per year). This catalogs insider buys and sells in an easy-to-follow fashion. There is a long history of insider selling preceding stock price implosions.

Electronic Buyers' News ($89 per year from CMP Publications). This one keeps me up on the tech world, an ever growing slice of Main Street, and a good chunk of what I both own and recommend in *Forbes*.

Wall Street Computer Review ($65 yearly from Gralla Publications). This magazine's coverage ranges from retail packages you might want to add to your PC arsenal now,

to expensive new professional programs and gear that offer a glimpse of what may be skinnied-down and available to you in a few years—and there will be a lot.

The annual *Nasdaq Fact Book* ($16 from Nasdaq in Washington, DC) and its cousin the NYSE Institutional Investor Fact Book ($10 from the stock exchange). Packed with data on what trades, what doesn't, what's big and small and who owns it all.

The Stock Traders Almanac ($28 from the Hirsch Organization in Tappan, NJ). It has a calendar, appointment book, monthly analysis of historical market trends and wealth of investment data, as well as daily and lively quotes from famous financiers.

So, what does my perusing all this paper plus our own research tell me? That I expect small stocks to best big ones and statistically cheap stocks to do better than high-priced growth issues. ■

Dumb Bears
August 5, 1991

Supporting most bears right now is a bunch of bull: namely the notion that too much debt will bite us in the butt. Ever since last fall, the guts underlying gloom-and-doom market forecasts have been disproven one by one. Excessive debt is the main argument that the bears still hug.

Which is one reason the bull market has a good long way to run; the bears are basing their case on a wrong argument. Debt doomers come in varying styles. There is the banking crisis style and the real estate implosion style—often linked, as in "falling real estate prices will bankrupt the banks, which will cause chaos." Then, too, are those noting the "tapped-out consumer" who can't or won't borrow more—thereby causing an anemic recovery,

or no recovery, or finally, the pseudo-sophisticated favorite—the "double dip" recession.

Don't get me wrong. I don't recommend going into debt. Personally I owe virtually no money. Certainly there are individuals, firms, industries and municipalities that are too heavily and stupidly leveraged and will pay for it dearly (as is always true).

However, in aggregate, debt levels won't hurt the economy or the stock market in the 1990s.

A most basic truth is that whatever most folks are fretting about never much impacts stocks in the long term. The market is driven mainly by surprise. That so many have so visibly focused on banking and real estate problems for so long almost

Debt Doldrums

Readers will note that back in 1991, investing fears were much the same as today. Investors feared America had too much debt and consumers were "tapped out." Yet, despite those fears, stocks soared through much of the 1990s. Remember that whenever you hear anyone fretting tapped-out consumers and massive debt. Those fears are nothing new, and typically don't have the impact most think.

guarantees their impact being less than a surprise and already fully "in the market." Trust me: If 250 banks fail, the market will rise. If 750 of our 10,000 banks fail, the market will explode upward. Fundamentally, we have too darn many banks.

And the tapped-out consumer? Historically silly. Consumers have always reacted conservatively to tough times — recoveries have never been fueled by consumer borrowing. Despite all you read, consumer debt as a percent of personal income has always been flat to down in the 18 months after a recovery's birth. That so many otherwise seemingly intelligent and educated seers seem to have so overlooked this fact is astounding. Consumer debt won't impede this recovery just as it didn't fuel past ones.

Don't believe me? Hit your library and get the Department of Commerce's Business Conditions Digest, a great statistical source. It will show you that consumer debt as a percent of personal income is only a hair higher, maybe 2%, than it was in 1980 — up to 16%, from 14%.

In aggregate, the net carrying costs of America's total debt of all forms are only about 9% of US personal income.

Yet, you or anyone with a semisecure job and minor savings, could borrow five times that amount relative to your income at most banks — home mortgage, car loans, credit cards, etc. Far from "tapped out."

For all the chatter about indebted America and indebted Americans, our total societal debt of all forms — corporate, individual and government debt — is less than that of most Western nations, relative to GNP. And less than they had two recessions ago. If they evolved past prior recessions with higher debt loads, I suspect we will do just fine now.

No, overall we don't have too much debt. We have too little and have had too little ever since first becoming a modern society. Which is why for 60 years we have been adding debt relative to our economy's size. And will for maybe 30 more years.

Why? A better but seldom considered question is: What is the right amount of debt for a society to carry? The answer? Well, look at good old America in total. Our total societal $13 trillion of debt is relative to about $5 trillion of total income. Our total assets are worth some $30 trillion to $40 trillion (depending on how you value our land, etc.). That gives us an overall return on assets of 13% to 17% (5 ÷ 35 = 14%). As long as our societal return on assets is handily higher than the top sustainable interest rates imaginable (averaging long and short term), borrowing will slowly rise.

As long as society can borrow at 5% to 9% and generate 13% to 17% returns on the borrowed bucks, we have too little overall debt. And somebody somewhere who isn't too leveraged will cook up a scheme to turn a buck or buy some cheap assets, and debt levels will rise. It doesn't matter much even if the borrower is Uncle Sam or your state, because statistically their borrowing is a mere "transfer payment" of cash that ultimately ends up in private hands anyway.

Since debt won't bag us, you might find something better to worry about, like which stocks to put in your shopping bag. For all the reasons I have discussed in recent months, I would focus on second-tier stocks (in terms of size), selling at value discounts. ∎

Who Cares About Bankers?
September 2, 1991

If lots of banks fail, stocks will go up. I don't expect lots of banks to fail, although I'm sure some will. The market will not mind in the least.

Why? Two reasons. The total cost of bank failures is less than most folks envision. For $50 billion of private sector losses, we can wipe out the ten biggest banks. For another $50 billion we could dust the next 150. Impact? Lose $100 billion and it's about one quarter's GNP growth or about the same as two Iraq wars—perhaps enough to cause a recession in our $5 trillion economy, but no more. Even that might be a modest price to pay to get the better class of banker that will emerge from any wave of failures. The current wave of bankers created their own stupid loans. Let them suffer from their own actions.

Today's major economic problem is that money is still far too tight, despite a series of minor loosening efforts by the Fed since last Fall. If failures erupted, the Fed would loosen instantly and massively. I suspect Alan Greenspan knows he will need Bush's reelection to get reappointed and has been holding his holy powers back, waiting for the right political moment.

Some uptight people fear that a loosening by the Fed would unleash inflation, the dollar would fall, and the Fed would have to raise rates again to defend it. I disagree. There's too much excess capacity around, and easier money wouldn't drive up prices; it would simply cause the velocity of money, or turnover, to fall.

The economy would pick up mildly and inflation would be mute.

Wouldn't a rash of bank failures put a huge damper on credit creation, thus rippling through the entire economy and hurting healthy banks as well as unhealthy ones? I doubt it. That is carryover thinking from the Great Depression days. Folks forget that the Fed consciously shrank the money supply by 30% from 1928 to 1932. That would kill credit today. But the central bankers will never make that mistake again. They will expand the money supply; the strongest banks will pick up the slack, pumping credit back into the economy.

Much has been written lately questioning how much the Federal Reserve is really in control of the country's financial system today. One bearish fellow points out that the Fed has cut the discount rate three times, but to little avail.

I disagree. The Fed has loosened some, but so far its actions are like a fever dropping from 105 degrees to 103—too little. The Fed could cut rates much more, with almost no inflationary impact. And if you get the cost of money down, there will be lots of borrowers.

The mere fact that so much ink has been spent on "impending" banking failures tells you that actual failures, should they come to pass, won't move the market. The fear is already fully discounted. The thing that moves the market is surprise. And the big surprise is likely to be how little bank failures hurt overall. ∎

Geographical Biases

September 30, 1991

After being bullish for 11 straight months, I am especially watchful for bear market warnings.

The scariest evidence I see seems virtually unnoticed: Yield curves are now inverted outside the US (meaning short-term rates are higher than long-term rates). And in almost all non- English-speaking nations, all rates have nudged higher and higher for months. The duo of inverted yield curves and rising rates has historically warned of oncoming bear markets. Pay attention. If foreign stocks sag, it will be hard for ours to do well.

And here's a truly macabre note: A bright young man named Holger Berndt points out his murder rate indicator has an amazingly uncanny 30-year forecasting record as a reverse barometer of stock action. I've checked. It's scary.

Using FBI data on murders per 100,000 Americans, Berndt notes: The current peak of 9.5 murders per 100,000 population rivals slightly higher peaks in 1973–74 and 1980—times when stocks peaked.

Am I joking? Not entirely. This is as valid as the much-watched Super Bowl indicator, maybe more so. And right now it suggests 1991 could end badly for the markets.

However, there are more hopeful straws in the wind than scary ones, Note that the economic recovery started without much monetary pump priming by the Federal Reserve. Few folks notice that M2, the Fed's top money supply measure, has grown at less than 3% annually for two years. With inflation running nicely above that, it leaves Alan Greenspan lots of room to loosen the monetary noose and drop interest rates. And facing 1992's elections, that would be an awfully considerate way for Alan to thank President Bush for reappointing him recently, while helping set the stage to be reaffirmed once again, by George, in 1994.

Bears see little economic rebound. And it's true, of course, that second-quarter GNP was recently revised downward. Yet home resales have rebounded to pre-recession levels. New factory orders are higher than almost anyone's forecasts. The July boost in consumer durable orders was the largest percentage gain in 21 years.

The Purchasing Managers' Index, which forecast the recession so well, is now rising and is above out-of-recession levels for the first time in 18 months. And, though fewer folks pay heed to the leading economic indicator series these days, it's bullish.

Noteworthy news from my back yard: Most bears have long expected California's high real estate prices to implode—as northeastern real estate did. In the recession, prices dropped some, volume dried up and the inventory of homes for sale mushroomed—warning of more price drops to come. But from what I see out here, prices are surging once again, to new highs. Prices of recently completed sales have boggled my mind—and I wasn't bearish on California. My home state is often a trendsetter, so real estate may do better nationally than folks expect. Bullish.

While on regionality, I see a heavy geographical warp I've not noted before when I talk to money managers, journalists and business leaders—one with contrarian meaning. The farther north and east you go, the more rock-solid pessimism people have. In Boston and New York gloom and doom is spread on thick. The moods of folks I chat with there range from deep, dark depressionism to simple disbelief in the possibility of any bright future.

Northeasterners have been hit by a real estate collapse, failed insurance firms and banks, brokerage scandals and fear of a banking crisis. They also suffer from disastrous politics and cities that have been deteriorating steadily for decades. Out here in the West, these things loom less large. So optimism per capita increases in a straight line as I talk west and south. In New York folks think I'm Pollyannaish. Maybe. After all, I'm a Californian. Or it may be that most of Wall Street is too bearish.

I still think stocks will continue to do nicely well into 1993. The Dow and S&P 500 may do less well, but they are dominated by a very few, very big and mostly growth-oriented stocks and aren't too reflective of America's average stock. The smaller and less-growth-oriented stocks should lead the market through 1993. Measure the overall market's progress by watching that of the Value Line Index (the "arithmetic" one, not the geometric one). ∎

Unloved and Undervalued
October 21, 1991

Each year some folks join the *Forbes* 400, and others drop off it. The dropouts fall into three main groups. First are the Disasters. Donald Trump and the Hunt brothers come to mind. From a position most folks would call "having it all," these dropouts shoot big, have big egos and make visible, non-diversified and risky moves, usually on leverage, to try to become richer than rich. Eventually they push their luck too hard, and . . . disaster strikes. Goodbye to the 400.

Then comes the Slow Bleeder variety of dropout. This includes most of the great fortunes of the early 20th century—the "shirtsleeves to shirtsleeves in three generations" crowd. These heirs often try to justify their position in life by running their investments without any real know-how—usually steering their assets on a different route from Daddy's so they can put their own mark on their wealth, making it "theirs."

As often as not, these people are swayed by lavish lives, pride, vanity or social issues and not by acumen. Their wealth dwindles slowly but surely and may even vanish. Finally come the Passive—the rich who get richer, but too slowly to keep up with the Joneses. Tending toward too timid, these folks won't allow themselves heavy exposure to wealth-building assets for fear of taking a risk. They may be rich, but their kids probably won't be after inflation and taxes.

What's the moral here? I think it is quite simple: Stick with things you know and understand and do them aggressively enough so you can keep up with the Joneses. If you want to invest outside your own expertise or don't have any expertise, get professional help so you don't one day find yourself feeling like a member of the formerly rich. ∎

Surprise
October 28, 1991

In May I started saying that so-called value stocks—those at cheap statistical valuations—would do better than recognized growth stocks selling at fancy prices. It hasn't happened yet. The so-called growth stocks have continued to outperform the others.

In the third quarter they did more than twice as well as the value stocks. The OTC Composite index, which basically measures medium-size growth stocks, was up more than 10%. Meanwhile, the Value Line Arithmetic index, a pretty darn good proxy for America's average-size stock with average valuations, was up only a hair over 5%. By simple math, the hard-to-measure value sector must have lagged even more.

It's the old story. Trends go to extremes. The big pension plans, the guys with all the bucks, and often the greatest fools, have thrown allocations at "growth" this year like mud at a wall. But it's a little late now. We are five years into the growth fad. In 1986, when the growth stock bull market began, the big boys were buying the value stocks that had been hot in the prior four years, and have done zip ever since. Just as they got on the bandwagon late, they will be late in getting off. Don't be like them.

My advice to my readers is: Buy into the next five years' value cycle before the big investors do. Not growth. Expectations for well-recognized smaller-growth names are at levels I have seen only in 1983—higher than those of 1972—and both of those were simply disastrous times to buy recognized growth.

The reason I think value stocks will do better than recognized growth is simply that among those value stocks will be some that provide unexpected growth. ∎

The Bucking Bull
November 25, 1991

Staying with this bull market, or any bull market, is sort of like hanging on to a horse when it's bucking; it keeps trying to toss you off. But hang on. Don't listen to the beaten-up bears who seize on every correction to trumpet the long-awaited end. Ever since the initial rally started in October 1990, folks have grasped for reasons to get off early.

With each correction or setback in the trend to higher prices the arguments grow in volume, if not logic: First was the Gulf war, then recession, then the weak economic recovery or no economic recovery. Last month folks feared another October massacre. They are always afraid we have too much debt and that P/Es are too high. While each correction is followed by new strength from the bull, I find investors still nervous.

I explain to them that interest rates have fallen and will continue to do so. That Treasury bills are at their lowest in 14 years; and that the yield curve slopes steeply upward—very bullish. That it has always been smart to buy stocks in a recession and hold them for several years. And finally, I remind them that it has usually been great holding stocks in the year before a presidential election.

Folks will acknowledge all that, but they think that this time it's different. Why? Too much debt, they say. Nonsense. I have never believed America is overindebted. Everyone says so, but that doesn't make it true. Contrarians know that. As I have pointed out before, society's total return on assets is nicely higher than the cost of capital, and as long as that is true, we will keep adding societal debt.

John Templeton is famous for, among other things, saying that "the four most dangerous words in the English language are: 'This time it's different.'" It's always different, and yet at the same time, always the same. Each time is uniquely scary.

It sure was different in 1974-75, with massive commodity price inflation and an oil embargo, at the same time as the biggest worldwide recession since the 1930s. And we paddled through those perilous waters with a President who hadn't even been elected Vice President, and who rammed an anti-inflation tax hike down our throats in the very depths of the recession.

It certainly was different in 1981–83, when the AA corporate-bond rate hit 16% and short-term rates hit 20%, while the federal budget deficit and national debt exploded. Based on my study of history, I can't think of a single early bull market period that didn't have its own unique differences that scared the heck out of investors and caused most of them to shy away from rising stock prices.

Now this one is different, too. The media companies got hit badly this time, which is different, and you can feel it in the way they report the economic news. The media's pessimism makes most investors, who can't think for themselves, too pessimistic. That is in itself bullish.

Some people think it's different to see a bull market proceed when the P/Es of the Dow and S&P 500 are so high. Not so. Just as it is this time, the recessions of 1974 and 1982 made P/Es for most stocks temporarily high as earnings disappeared—not a comment on how high stocks were but a standard mechanism the bucking bull uses to scare investors away. Are valuations of the few very biggest stocks—the ones that get noticed—very high? Yes, that much is true. But smaller stocks are not, Despite what the bears may babble, valuations of most stocks are nicely lower today, relative to the cost of money, than they were at most times in the last 15 years.

Many people see another difference. They think the economy won't respond to monetary loosening by the Fed. They fear the banking system is too tied up in knots to lend as the Fed loosens. I doubt it. But even if I'm wrong, it's still bullish, because it means to get a mere scent of stimulation the Fed must force interest rates vastly lower. Put short rates at 3% and stocks will rise, even if the Fed can't get the banks to lend a penny.

So hang on, despite the corrections and the litanies of gloom. It's a bull market, and the way to make money in it is to own good stocks and stick with them. ∎

Stay With It
December 23, 1991

In the early phases of every bull market investors think stocks are getting too high, that the economy won't expand and that this time things really are terrible and "different" because of vast new societal problems. There's lots of such talk around these days, especially after the market's November tumble.

In my view this frightened attitude is a sign that the bull market isn't over. Most signs I see are bullish. For example, most smaller stocks are historically cheap relative to the cost of money, while investors are scared away by the few hundred largest stocks' seeming not so cheap. Then, too, it is usually profitable to buy stocks in a recession or early in a recovery. And it has usually been a good idea to buy stocks the year before a presidential election.

We have had five successive discount rate cuts in a year. Every other time that has happened stocks have done well when you are looking back two years later—except after 1930. All the "usuallys" didn't work then. It truly was different that time.

Pessimists love the 1929–30 parallels. Weren't the 1920s and 1980s decades of speculative excess? Kondratieff Wave fans note that the Great Depression came just ten years after inflation peaked in 1920—and didn't inflation peak again 11 years ago? Finally, the pessimists note, total debt—public and private—as a percent of GNP is now higher than at any time since the Great Depression.

And all that debt! Then and now we were up to our eyeballs in the terrible stuff. All this is mythology, a selective and inaccurate interpretation of the past designed to justify a pessimistic view of the present. Contrary to today's almost universally dogmatized myth, and as I have explained in past columns, debt levels aren't too high now in relation to our assets and our gross national product. While they are higher than they have ever been before, 10 and 20 years from now, they will be higher still. Our total societal return on assets is too high relative to the cost of money for us not to use more debt in the long term.

Whether I'm right or wrong about debt loads now, one thing the bears certainly have wrong is thinking that the Great Depression was caused by excessive debt. It wasn't. Total societal debt rose during the Depression, even as the economy fell. There was no scramble to repay excessive debt loads because, simply, debt wasn't excessive then—or now.

No, 1929–32 wasn't caused by debt. It started overseas with worldwide trade barriers and central banks unwisely shrinking the world's money supply. The Fed made matters worse by shrinking the money supply in absolute dollars by 30% from 1929 to 1932. It won't ever do that again. The Fed was 16 years old in 1929. Most of its high-volume activity started only in the 1920s. And in 1930 it had a new and unprepared chairman. Today's Fed is more experienced and has better tools at its disposal.

The differences between 1991–92 and 1929 32 are greater than the similarities. Our economy is immeasurably broader and more balanced. Not even autos or housing is singularly important the way those industries were even 25 years ago; but in 1929 we were still almost half a farm economy. So inflation-impacted commodity prices were critical. Ditto for the impact of the bad luck 1930s drought.

In 1929, contrary to myth, P/Es were pretty low—about 12 on average—because for years earnings grew faster than stock prices. As profit margins exploded in the late 1920s, investors were suckered into thinking stocks weren't too high. That is exactly the reverse of the last four years, when earnings and profit margins have fallen as American corporations scrambled for competitiveness. Investors are now scared off by the resultant "high" P/Es. Stock prices too high today? Goldbugs should note that the market's current value divided by the price of gold is less than half the level of 1929.

Stocks, of course, hit a much higher peak in 1929 than ever before—that's a parallel of sorts. But, contrary' to myth, it was a narrow rally. Smaller secondary stocks peaked in 1928 and did little in 1929's big-stock peak. Narrow rallies led by big stocks are usually a warning of tough times ahead. But, confounding the pessimists, this year the smaller stocks hit exciting new highs in a quite broad rally encompassing all the indexes. Unlike in 1929, big stocks have been the laggards this year,

In 1929 and 1930 few people were very worried. Today you can't read a paper that isn't filled with gloom-and-doom-slanted stories. No, it's not at all like 1929–32. It's still fairly early in this bull market. ■

1992

Times, They Were a Changin'

> "*You can always find things wrong with the world. There is never a shortage of problems. Never has been. Nor a shortage of people who love to fixate on them. The only thing that really counts is: Will the problems hurt stock prices now?*"
>
> "Fear of Falling," March 16, 1992

> "*The nature of corrections is they come at you out of the blue and last ten days to two months. They cost most stocks 5% to 10% and disappear as quickly as they came, yielding to the next up leg of the market. You can't really protect against corrections, and they aren't really worth worrying about.*"
>
> "Going Up," May 11, 1992

The geopolitical winds of change were blowing hard in 1992. Just days before the start of the year, the Supreme Soviet formally dissolved the Soviet Union, ending the Cold War. A bit farther west, the European Union (EU) was founded with the signing of the Maastricht Treaty.

But all wasn't well across the pond. Before the EU was formed, most major European countries joined the European Exchange Rate Mechanism (ERM). The purpose of the ERM was to maintain stable currency exchange rates within Europe. Unlike today's European Economic and Monetary Union (EMU), countries in the ERM had their own currencies and monetary policies, but they agreed to heavily manage their currencies' exchange rates to keep them within narrow bands. The UK was reluctant to join the ERM, but finally did in 1990. This was until Black Wednesday (September 16, 1992) when, after raising interest rates dramatically and spending billions to support the pound sterling, the UK was unable to prop up its currency and was forced to exit the ERM. Currency speculators, including George Soros, famously made a fortune betting the pound sterling would fall.

Political winds were also blowing in the US. Bill Clinton defeated George HW Bush to become the first Democratic president since Jimmy Carter, which scared Republicans silly—and most investors too. Actual winds were blowing here too as Hurricane Andrew tore across southern Florida and Louisiana, causing dozens of deaths and tens of billions of dollars of damage—the costliest, hurricane on record until Hurricane Katrina in 2005.

As for stocks, 1992 was a slow, slogging year. After a roaring finish to 1991, stocks listed aimlessly for much of 1992. As Ken would be the first to note in his early 2009 columns, election years when a Republican wins tend to have above-average returns, but a Democrat winning tends to mean below-average election-year returns. That impact flip-flops in the inaugural year, when Republicans tend to have lousy returns and Democrats are typically double-digit positive. Such was 1992—lackluster, followed by a pick-up in 1993.

Major indexes suffered a minor correction to start 1992. The S&P 500 slid about 5 percent for the year through early April.[1] The smaller stocks Ken was recommending fared better, rising by a few percent during the same period. But even their returns were unspectacular. In fact, stocks across the board were pretty much flat for the year well into October.[2]

Ken remained bullish. He still saw far too much pessimism. "Too many people are too pessimistic. I find myself almost shunned as a moral outcast for expressing the view, which I believe firmly, that the later 1990s will be better than average for the American economy." ("Fear of Falling," March 16, 1992.) Much of the pessimism was fostered by the media. Many folks turn to print or broadcast news for information on the state of the world. So if the news is gloomy, people often are too. Ken saw that people in the news business had reason to be gloomy, but most others didn't. Media companies were falling on hard times, and that was reflected in their reporting. "I suspect much of the gloom owes to the fact that the media businesses are in the toughest economic times they have seen since the Great Depression. They feel bad, and figure you should, too. They report it as they feel it." ("Misery in the Media," January 20, 1992.) The resulting dour sentiment contributed to the stock market malaise.

One of investors' main concerns was stock valuations. Ken noted the Dow was trading at a P/E of about 30 in early 1992—historically rather high. But it was also based on trailing earnings, or earnings over the past 12 months. The US was still recovering from a recession that caused earnings to drop, as most recessions do. So the elevated P/Es were the result of lower earnings, not skyrocketing stock prices. When earnings recovered, which Ken believed they would, normalized P/Es wouldn't seem so out of whack. In fact, Ken pointed out buying stocks when P/Es are high following a recession is usually a good bet. "Anyone who ever bought whenever the market's P/E got above 25 looked pretty darn smart in a few years . . . the current high valuations aren't scary at all. They simply reflect the fact that earnings are still depressed." ("Worry, Worry," July 6, 1992.)

Ken explained that the market P/E alone isn't a good indicator of where the market is headed. Not only have stocks often done very well following periods of high P/Es and poorly after P/Es were low, stock market P/Es only matter relative to other investment options. To gauge whether the market is over- or under-valued, Ken suggested flipping the P/E ratio on its head to get the E/P (earnings-to-price ratio, or earnings yield). Instead of simply looking at the absolute P/E level, Ken judges the stock market's relative value by comparing stocks' earnings yield to the yield on a another similarly liquid investment option— long-term government bonds, for example. (This later came to be widely known as "The Fed model," but Ken had long used it and referred to it before—and has continued to use it off and on over the years.)When the earnings yield is high relative to bond yields, stocks are cheap, relatively. But earnings yields don't have to be above bond yields. Corporate earnings grow over time, so "the earnings yield from owning stocks will rise, but the interest yield from bonds bought today is stagnant forever." ("Fear of Falling," March 16, 1992.) Stock market valuations are just one factor to consider when divining how stocks will do in the future, but in 1992, Ken saw perceived high valuations as an unwarranted investor concern.

Up until 1992, Ken's columns had a bottom-up bent to them. In other words, his views on the direction of the overall market aside, Ken usually offered advice on ways to identify attractive individual stocks. Most of those fell into the small-cap value universe, since that was his specialty (despite the term not yet being widely used in the investment community—that came later). But Ken knew that his penchant for small, cheap stocks didn't mean small-cap value stocks would always be the best performers. In his February 17, 1992 column "Ripe for Rotation," Ken hints at a more top-down approach, or identifying the type of stock that will do best at varying times. "The market has four basic stock groups [big-value, big-growth, small-value, and small-growth]. Market leadership rotates among them. The key is sensing which groups are leading, lagging and which will soon take the lead . . . Each group has its day, rises, gets frothy and fades— to be followed by another group. That's what market rotation is all about." Big-growth, big-value, and small-growth had traded off leadership over the prior decade. Ken though it was small-value's turn to shine. This top-down approach is much more in line with Ken's approach to investing today.

But in 1992, the style-box concept was very far ahead of its time. The first institutional small-cap value peer group, developed by Callan Associates, was only three years old then. And its existence was due in large part by Ken's lobbying to Callan directly to create such a peer group. Mutual fund rating groups didn't yet categorize funds into this kind of style-box category, as they all do now, particularly since Morningstar took the lead in doing so.

Despite the lackluster start to 1992, stocks eventually jumped. From October 9 through year-end, the S&P 500 rose 9 percent and posted a 7.6 percent increase for the year—decidedly middling, though still positive. But as Ken predicted, the Value Line Index did much better, gaining 15.1 percent in 1992.[3]

Misery in the Media

January 20, 1992

Folks are much too pessimistic—which is very bullish. Don't get me wrong. Yes, we have had a rough recession and face plenty of problems. We all know that. But we have faced much worse problems before and will deal with these, too. It's surprise that moves the market, not what we already know, and I am sure that the surprises will be mostly good ones. If you routinely read the dire news in the press or, worse, hear it on network news—if all your friends already know about it and if politicians blithely assume it—it simply doesn't count. Forget it. Look elsewhere for events to move the stock market.

I travel a good deal, talking with the people controlling our largest pension plans—most of America's liquid assets and therefore most of the money that moves the market. I see and hear darn little optimism for the economy or the stock market. Consumer sentiment numbers show the same from the guy on the street. Too much debt, lousy politicians, the fading consumer, deteriorating social and moral values. More and more you hear and see things like the recent *New York Times* headline that this isn't a recession but a depression.

Depression? In depressions there is massive unemployment, 20% or 25%. In big recessions like 1975 and 1982 we got 9% and 10% unemployment. In this one we never got more than 7% unemployment. And yes, Martha, it has been getting irregularly better, not worse, despite all you read about layoffs. Employment is rising. It's just that everyone who isn't unemployed is so God-awful gloomy.

I suspect much of the gloom owes to the fact that media businesses are in the toughest economic times they have seen since the Great Depression. They feel bad, and figure you should, too. They report it as they feel it.

The networks, with the exception of Turner, are losing big bucks—they have never done that before. The big newspaper chains have seen drastic profit declines, and lots of little newspapers actually died this year. While it isn't possible to get a handle on it, I think magazines as a whole are losing money—all for the first time.

Much of the media's problems are of their own making, not the economy's. First came two decades of over-expansion. Think of how many more specialty magazines of every type there are than there were 20 years ago. Look at all the new TV capacity through cable. Even newspapers, with comers like *USA Today* and *Investor's Business Daily.*

Meanwhile, in the get-lean-and-mean craze of the late 1980s, a major change began in the way many advertisers, primarily those with relatively mature products, viewed advertising. They learned that they could cut two bucks of name maintenance advertising, add a dollar of in-store promotion and maintain revenue and boost profits. It worked. Falling ad volume has hobbled the media.

But the country, possibly as opposed to some media businesses, isn't going to hell. I think this recovery will be modest but solid. So the surprise will be pleasant. Earnings will turn up nicely and stocks will do just fine, particularly smaller ones. As the decade progresses, demographic shifts will be the most powerful and positive force America has felt in decades, as our most productive age groups swell and the least productive age groups fall relative to total population. Savings and consumption will both grow nicely, which happens only at this one phase of the very long-term demographic cycle. If recent years felt like rowing upstream, the late 1990s will feel like a raft ride down the Mississippi—quiet, powerful and unending.

As I write, the Value Line Arithmetic, our best index of America's average stock, is at 310. By the year 2001 I expect it to be nicely above 1,000. ∎

Ripe for Rotation
February 17, 1992

The other day syndicated columnist Herb Greenberg asked me: "Doesn't the stock market's heavy speculative tone mean it carries an unusually high risk level?" I replied: "Not this time, Herb." Why not? Because the fervor he worries about is limited to just one part of the market. Unless the froth encompasses at least several market sectors, it will fade.

The market has four basic stock groups. Market leadership rotates among them. The key is sensing which groups are leading, lagging and which will soon take the lead.

One way to dissect the market is by market cap—stock price times number of shares outstanding. Generally, the 500 largest stocks, running down to about $1 billion in market value, are considered "big cap." Below that in size there are about 1,500 liquid "small-cap stocks."

A second way to cut the market is by relative value. Here, stocks are arrayed by a valuation tool, like P/E or price-to-book. The lower half are "value" stocks. The higher half are "growth" stocks—they must grow fast to justify their premium pricing.

Combining these two cuts produces the matrix shown here. In it, stocks are arrayed vertically by market cap—"big" or "small"—and horizontally by valuation—"growth" or "value." The upper left box comprises one group: 250 big-cap/value stocks—big-caps and low price-to-book ratios. Think of Dow Chemical, GM, ITT, or these days even IBM.

The upper right-hand box represents a second grouping: 250 big-cap/growth stocks. Examples are Coca-Cola, Gerber or Merck.

The lower right-hand box represents a third group: 750 small-cap/ growth stocks—ones like Circon Corp., Kaydon Corp. or Xilinx.

The lower left box comprises the fourth basic group: 750 small-cap/value stocks—ones like those I have been recommending recently.

America's 1,000 largest pension plans, which now control most of the money in the market, parcel it out among these four groups. First, they decide what they want allocated to each group. Then they hire specialty managers to beat the category by stock-picking from within it. Asset allocation is a bit more complicated than this, but only a little.

Here's the key: Each group has its day, rises, gets frothy and fades—to be followed

The Best Kind of Agnosticism

This column contains an important lesson many miss: No one style is best for all time. Leadership shifts, and investors who stay loyal to one size or style can miss out on years of better performance. This points to the value of being style agnostic.

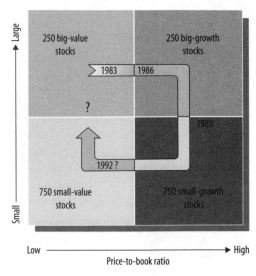

FIGURE 9.1 Four Basic Groups

by another group. That's what market rotation is all about.

From 1983 to 1986 the market was led by the big-cap/value pack. Pick up a 1986 copy of *Pension and Investments,* the leading journal for institutional investors, and you see that big-cap/value was all the rage.

But then the lead rotated to the big-cap/growth stocks. This group led the market through late 1989.

Then the lead rotated again, to small-cap/growth. This group held the lead until this January; now the small growth group has begun to look both frothy and a little tired.

To where will leadership rotate next? To the only group that hasn't done well for years—the small-cap/value stocks. Relative to the other groups, these stocks have been out of fashion since the mid-1980s.

I thought this shift would start last summer (see my June 10, 1991 column), but no, I was too early. Now, while I'm not 100% certain, I think January rang the starting bell. Why? Because the big-cap/growth group is the mirror opposite of the small-cap/ value group—and big-cap/growth stocks fell from second place in performance last year to last place in January. In a telling shift—for the first time in years—lots of leading big-cap, big-growth names like Merck, Coca-Cola, and Gerber dropped sharply in January, while the market rose. Meanwhile, small-cap/value stocks climbed in January. ∎

Fear of Falling
March 16, 1992

Instead of feeling euphoric about the bull market, many people are simply scared. How can stocks be so strong when the economy seems so soft?

The Dow Jones industrials is at 30 times trailing earnings, and other indexes have similarly high P/Es. The market looks historically high by many other value measures too: price-to-book ratios, for example.

Then there is the worry that when recovery docs come it will shove up interest rates and this will pull money out of stocks.

But don't let these kinds of fears drive you out of a market that still has a long way to go. First, P/Es aren't as out of line

as they seem, because they are based on recession-depressed earnings. Over the long run corporate profit margins tend to average about 6%. They bounce around, but overall they always end up right back at those levels within a couple of years. Based on normalized earnings, the market has a P/E of about 13. If you wait for the earnings to be realized, it's always far too late. The market is a discounter and moves far ahead of earnings—always has.

A P/E of 13 is an earnings yield of about 7.7% (1 divided by 13 = 7.7%), which is just fine compared with yields on government bills and bonds, which run from just below

4% for short-term paper to 8% for risking 3o years (with a median yield of 6%).

The earnings yield on stocks doesn't have to be quite as high as bond yields for stocks to rise. Remember, in the long term, businesses in aggregate will grow in sales, continuing to average those 6% profit margins. En route, the earnings yield from owning stocks will rise, but the interest yield from bonds bought today is stagnant forever.

What about other signs of high valuations, like that historically high price-to-book ratio? Disregard them. Price-to-book is no longer useful in measuring the market's value relative to its past because of too much inflation distortion in recent decades. It is biased by inflation to the high side. Most other measures that now signal prices are too high also have their own quirks, which cause them to mislead investors to the painfully wrong conclusion that this market is too rich.

As for the threat of higher interest rates, a rising economy doesn't necessarily force rates up and usually hasn't done so early in a recovery. There is usually a time lag. In fact, often interest continues to fall well into recovery. Demand for short-term money often falls with less need to finance inventory and receivables—and demand for long-term money can fall because of the capital expenditure cycle, which always lags the economy on both sides of the business cycle.

You can always find things wrong with the world. There is never a shortage of problems. Never has been. Nor a shortage of people who love to fixate on them. The only thing that really counts is: Will the problems hurt stock prices now? Weak foreign economies? Deficits? Tax cuts? Hikes? Congressional stupidity? Pat Buchanan? IPO mania? Good grief!

While these are all real problems, they are amply discounted in stock prices. Too many people are too pessimistic. I find myself almost shunned as a moral outcast for expressing the view, which I believe firmly, that the later 1990s will be better than average for the American economy. But even if they aren't—if they are a bit worse than average—the bull market will prevail. The market has dealt so many times before with vastly worse problems than those we face now. Count on it to do so now. Buy cheap stocks of good firms from which investors don't expect much, and then be patient. ∎

Overripe
April 14, 1992

If you own mutual funds that invest in common stocks you should seriously consider getting out. Does that sound strange coming from a columnist who has been pound-the-table bullish for 17 months and remains so?

Let me explain what seems like an apparent contradiction.

Hardly anyone has noticed that mutual funds' portfolios are now filled with the market's priciest stocks. It has been a slow drift over time from funds being market-like to the present condition, where, on average, mutual funds' stocks trade at much higher multiples of sales and earnings than the market as a whole.

Last summer I predicted that the high-valuation growth-stock fad, the dominant market theme since 1986, would end soon. I was early, but not wrong: Since December most classic big-cap growth names are down while the market is up; stocks like

Gerber, Merck and Wal-Mart are currently lagging and actually sagging. They haven't finished sagging.

But in the prior six years, this type of stock as a group was the hottest-performing part of the market and simply got out of line with stocks as a whole. By the end of 1991 it accounted for a much higher percentage of the total dollar value of the US stock market than normal. It is most important that you avoid this group of stocks in the next few years. They are overvalued and overbought; the value stocks are underbought.

What do I mean by "growth" stocks? In this instance I mean stocks that sell for more than the median price-to book-value ratio for large stocks as a whole. That midpoint ratio is currently 2.7. So let's say stocks selling above this ratio are growth stocks and those selling below the ratio are value stocks. Those above the median are ones where investors expect above-average future growth to justify the above-average valuations. The ones below the median are stocks folks think of as too cheap compared with the market—hence, value stocks.

Now let's take America's 500 largest stocks (which, contrary to many investors' perceptions, are not the same as the S&P 500). Take the combined market value of the 250 stocks above the median price-to-book for each year of the past 20 years. You find that in total they averaged 45% of the dollar value of the entire US stock market (the whole market includes small stocks, too).

This figure has ranged from a low of 36% of the total market value in 1984, to a high that plateaued in the 50%-to-55% area in the early and mid-1970s. Note the significance of the swings in this ratio: After the mid-1970s, when the ratio was very high, growth did poorly for many years. It was overbought and had nowhere to go but sideways and down. In 1984, when the ratio was low, growth stocks were underbought and on the verge of a mighty and long-lasting rise.

The ratio is now at 50%, after a December peak, of 53%. This says to me that the big growth stocks are materially overbought, have peaked and have much further to fall—perhaps to where they again total less than 40% of the market.

By contrast, the 250 large value stocks that in aggregate make up the bottom half of the price-to-book ranking now account for only 32% of the overall market's capitalization. That puts them very close to the bottom of their 20-year range of 30% to 41%. Which is why I am now extremely leery of equity mutual funds. If the big-cap growth sector of the market has peaked—as my calculations indicate—so have most mutual funds, because the funds are overwhelmingly overweighted in big-cap growth issues.

Data from Chicago's *Morningstar* show that funds have piled headfirst into big growth stocks. Of the 98 pure no-load big-cap equity funds, fully 79 have average price-to-book ratios above the overall market's average. That is 80% of the mutual funds and 85% of the dollars in the funds.

Few people have noticed that, but it really shouldn't be a surprise. Retail investors bought the hot funds that owned the hot stocks; the incoming money was recycled into more growth stocks. At the same time, other and lesser-performing funds piled into growth stocks, trying to chase their hot performance.

Just when big-cap growth stocks got too overbought, the mutual funds pigged out on them. Whereas mutual funds currently own about 10% of the US stock market, they own about 20% of the big-cap growth stocks—100% overweighted now in the wrong sector at the wrong time. When these funds start to sell, it'll be too late to get out. Take heed.

My advice is: Get rid of any fund whose average stock has a market capitalization above $2 billion and a price-to-book ratio averaging above 2.7, *Morningstar* shows these numbers. Get it at your library. And if they don't have it, get them to get it. ∎

Going Up

May 11, 1992

You can't have a healthy bull market without some sharp corrections, and it's good news for the stock market that we have just had one, even though most people didn't even notice it. Now we can move on to this bull market's next up leg.

March was a rugged month. The first half of April, too. You hadn't noticed? That's because you were paying too much attention to the Dow Jones average or the S&P 500. The 500 dropped 2%, but all the truly broader indexes dropped much more, in the range of 5% to 10%. The are Composite, for example, which is heavily dominated by midsize growth stocks, fell 5%—followed by another 3.5% drop in early April.

What caused the correction? Fear of Japan's falling stocks, fear that Bush might not get reelected, and fear that the Fed wouldn't loosen further, choking the economy.

None of these are really worth worrying about. The Fed? We don't need looser money to sustain this bull market. Japan? Japan's problems contributed to our 1989–90 bear market. It isn't a risk now. Most of the air is out of that bubble in the 55% multiyear drop that is history. If there is a bit more, don't worry; it won't blow all the way over the Pacific.

Mr. Bush? As a third-party candidate Ross Perot might or might not cost Bush the presidency, but with all due respect to the President, he doesn't have much impact on my market forecast. Nor Mr. Clinton.

I think the years ahead will likely show a stock market a bit like the Carter years: Folks who are fixated on the Dow and S&P 500 will find little to cheer about. They may never note the magnitude of this quiet bull market. But those willing to root around among the smaller and cheaper stocks will have a heck of a fine party.

This small-cap bull market started in October 1990. We had a January 1991 correction just before the Iraqi invasion. We had a second one last November and December in a double-dip recession head-fake. This one—March–April 1992—was the third.

There will be at least several more. I don't know when. The nature of corrections is that they come at you out of the blue and last ten days to two months. They cost most stocks 5% to 10% and then disappear as quickly as they came, yielding to the next up-leg of the market. You can't really protect against corrections, and they aren't really worth worrying about.

What is worth worrying about is that this is a bull market for most stocks, despite not being reflected in the Dow industrials and S&P 500. Bull markets that were led by smaller-size stocks, whether

Correction Behavior

One theme Ken has repeated through the years is the futility of trying to time a market correction. Corrections are fast, steep, and scary. But they're usually driven more by sentiment than fundamentals, making them impossible to see coming. And because they are so fast, in Ken's view, you are better off gritting your teeth and sticking with your stocks through them. Soon enough, it will be over and a mere memory. But if you try to maneuver around them, you might end up getting whipsawed—never a good strategy.

growth stocks or value stocks, have typically lasted three to four years. Having started in October 1990, this bull market is only about halfway through its life—maybe even a bit less.

So get ready for the fourth floor on this elevator. It's going up for smaller stocks selling at low ratios of P/E, price-to-book and price-to-sales. ∎

Two to Avoid
June 8, 1992

While I continue to be a bull, I'm nervous about some groups of stocks.

The utilities are one such. They had a heck of a fine last decade, but tougher times lie ahead. Expect the exact reverse of trends that benefited these stocks for years. In the Seventies' era of rising interest rates and hostile political regulation, they hadn't done well, so people came to assume they were hopeless. Surprise.

Falling interest rates and weakened oil prices combined to give the group a big boost in the Eighties. So did the national conservative swing in politics. The public utility commissions and the Federal Energy Regulatory Commission' became more reasonable about profitability, rate increases and rates of return. The stocks have done wonderfully up to now.

Money managers and investors used to own utilities for their yields and safety. They still see utilities as safe, but the last decade's returns have also led investors to perceive them as top-performing stocks—competition for the most successful sectors of the stock market. Today it is quite common to find aggressive equity managers overweighted in this sector. That's scary enough by itself.

Take a stodgy old name like Detroit Edison. Sales almost doubled since 1982. Earnings slightly more than doubled. And the stock tripled. Throw in dividend yields that got as high as 14% per year and the compound annualized return for the decade was an incredible 32%. A real winner by any standard.

But after the last decade's huge drops in interest rates and oil prices, these two haven't that much further to fall. On the political front, based on sources within the Federal Energy Regulatory Commission, I believe the Beltway gestapo are out to punish utilities, and you can bet the local public utility commissions will quickly catch the mood next.

I remember recently riding a taxi to see people at Memphis eight, Gas & Water. The crabby cabby babbled about how they kept raising his bills, "while those guys on the top floor make millions and don't pay a penny in income tax." The statement is hardly factual, but it is the kind of noise that politicians heed.

Detroit Edison now sells at 1.3 times annual revenue, a 60% premium to the stock market. The P/E doesn't seem high, but that's because its profit margins are so comfortable. If those margins get squeezed, I doubt the stock will continue to sell at 130 cents on the revenue dollar. Most big electric and gas utilities could suffer this same whack.

The drug sector is another one full of sitting ducks. Investors have been lulled by 20 years of one-way stock price action into seeing little risk here.

Take Eli Lilly, which makes 24% net after-tax profit margins, up from 13% in 1982. Since then, revenues doubled while profits rose fourfold. Meanwhile, its stock rose from 11 to an 85 peak—23% annually—before an annual dividend yield that ranged from 3% to 5%.

In the not-quite-so but by any standard still fat-category are Bristol-Myers, Pfizer, Schering-Plough, Upjohn and Warner-Lambert. They all make about 15% net after tax, having doubled those margins in a decade. Expect drug margins to shrink for a long time. And with them, stock prices.

There is no way the so-called populists in Congress will resist attacking the pharmaceutical companies, with their life-or-death products and high profit margins. The result, of course, will be bad for everyone, but that won't stop Congress. Never does. Reminds me of the joke about how many regulators it takes to perform surgery. Answer: five—one to wield the knife and four to bury the body.

Congress is not the only threat to pharmaceuticals. Contrary to public perception, old folks—the prime marker for drugs—grow in number more slowly now. In the Eighties we added 5.8 million post-65-year-olds to a base of 25 million. That's 20% growth. In the Nineties we will add 3.4 million post-65-year-olds to a base of 31.4 million—10% growth. The growth rate falls in half.

These drug stocks' valuations are simply absurd: 3 times sales, 4 times book and a lulling 20 times earnings that is the equivalent of 50 times earnings if the profit margins shrink to appropriate levels. Avoid these stocks. They are as vulnerable now as the Nifty Fifty were in 1973–74. ∎

Worry, Worry
July 6, 1992

With the Dow at record highs, some folks are afraid of the market's high P/E, others of its price-to-book of 2.5 and still others of its meager 3% dividend yield. Don't worry.

A simple but little-known fact: Anyone who ever bought whenever the market's P/E got above 25 looked pretty darn smart in a few years. Contrary to common myth, buying when the market's P/E is ultrahigh forces you into recession and postrecession periods like 1982–83, 1975, 1932–33, 1921 or 1895.

Looked at this way, the current high valuations aren't scary at all. They simply reflect the fact that earnings are still depressed. The right time for real caution is late in an economic expansion, when the Dow's P/E is in the not-so-scary 12-to-18 range—coupled with too-fat profit margins. The most classic example is early 1929, when P/Es actually averaged only about 12. Amazingly low.

Today's supposedly low 3% dividend yield is another common worry. While a high dividend yield for the market has always been a bullish omen, the reverse has not always been true. Here's my rule: If yields are low before a recession, it's risky; if low during or just after a recession, history shows it's probably not a risk. Normally, dividends aren't increased much late in an expansion. They are actually cut back in and just after a recession, dropping the market's dividend payout ratio and yield.

Yields aren't a risk now. Within a few years both earnings and dividends should be much higher. But stocks always move ahead first. By my calculations the market is currently about ten times normalized earnings and would yield 5%, based on normalized payouts. Compared with current interest rates, that's pretty good.

Then comes the "high" price-to-book ratio illusion. Based on simple data history, today's price-to-book does look high. But this phenomenon is among the rare exceptions to John Templeton's famous phrase that our four most dangerous words are: "This time it's different." Two decades of huge inflation truly and fundamentally changed this measuring stick. So price-to-book *should* be higher now than ever before.

The "book" in price-to-book isn't asset value but original accounting cost. The last 20 years of unprecedented levels of inflation boosted the real value of corporate assets, plant and capacity, but didn't adjust book. The market reacts to real asset values, not paper accounting entries that don't change with a changing world. A 1972 dollar is now $4, yet today's price-to-book of 2.5 is only 38% above its 20th-century average of 1.8. There is a lot of complicated finance in adjusting net present value of book for asset replacement rates versus inflation, but by my numbers the 1.8 long-term average should adjust up to about 3. So it isn't too high now.

Almost all studies show that the market in the very long term has a total return of about 9%. Before dividends are added back in, the Dow's compound price appreciation since 1945 is 6.3%. Since 1955 it's 5.4%. Since 1965, 4.6%. Since 1975, 7.5%. It doesn't vary too much over very long periods. At 3400 the Dow is not out of line with long-term returns. At a mere 5% per year from here, it will hit 5000 by the year 2000. The Dow isn't too high if you look at it historically and use an extremely long term prospective.

I continue to be a bull. Particularly so on smaller stocks that are economically sensitive (although I would stay away from overvalued growth stocks).

But while being bullish, be careful. Lots of stocks do sell at simply silly levels. For example, one froth-filled fad sector is all these trendy new restaurants. A new menu of these entrees flames out about every 20 years. It's the shareholders who are apt to be broiled. Reminds me of when Sambo's and Denny's were hot. ∎

My Favorite Indicator
August 3, 1992

Consensus thinking says the economic recovery is terribly weak—so weak that a ferocious bear market lies ahead. If we aren't already in it.

Last month (*Forbes,* July 6) I explained why the stock market's current valuations aren't really as high as most people believe. Let me now introduce my single favorite economic indicator, and one that has given excellent advice on the stock market's direction for 40 years.

Pick up the Department of Commerce's *Survey of Current Business* (found at most libraries, or available by subscription at $76 a year). Find the *Survey's* Series 940, the "Ratio of Coincident Index Indicators to Lagging Index Indicators." When this ratio is rising sharply, always be bullish.

When it is rising moderately, be cautious and look elsewhere for further guidance. When it is falling, adopt your most bearish posture, except for the rare times when the ratio is falling during a widely recognized recession. (Whenever you are in a commonly perceived recession, always be bullish.) History shows this hybrid is a pretty darn good leading indicator not only for the economy but for the stock market, too.

Skeptical? Check out this ratio's record. It would have kept you on the right side of most major moves. In mid 1982, for example, the ratio began a steep rise, a nice tipoff to the 1982–86 bull market.

Right now? The ratio keeps rising sharply. Better times ahead.

While perusing the *Survey of Current Business,* note some other data that confirm Series 940's bullish signals. Series 77, for example, shows that the powerful inventory-to-sales ratio is at its lowest—and most bullish—level in 25 years. Series 95 contradicts the popular myth that consumers are too indebted. Even Series 90, the ratio of people employed to the work force (and a much better economic indicator than the media's favorite, the unemployment rate) is now rising and bullish. ∎

The Cool Shall Be Hot
August 31, 1992

For mutual funds, the next few years won't look anything like the last few when it comes to which funds do best, The hot investment styles of recent years—recognized growth stocks and Japanese stocks, for example—are already out of favor and will stay out of favor.

Oppenheimer Global Bio-Tech was down 28.6% in the first half of 1992, but its prior two years were so sizzling it still has a 26% three-year average annual return. Don't expect much in the next few years from this kind of previously hot fund. Growth stocks are out. Value is in.

So, many stocks with poor long-term records and the funds built from them are starting to shine. The funds buying mundane value are doing well. Among the leaders this year have been sector funds specializing in single boring industries like autos or banks.

To wit: Fidelity Select Automotive was up 31.7% in the first half, more than any other fund—stodgy old autos. By my count, four out of the five top performing domestic equity funds were specialists in bank and financial stocks. So should you jump on this new bank built bandwagon? No! Its run is about over.

Smaller bank stocks have had a heck of a rise since 1990—not surprising in a time of steeply falling short-term interest rates. Banks are in the business of borrowing short term and lending long term and profiting from the spread between the two—a dangerous practice, but one that works exceptionally well when short rates fall much more than long rates.

We have just had the most favorable shift in interest rates, from a bank's viewpoint, in the 20th century. In 1989 short-term rates were higher than long-term rates. It's reversed now, and so much so that the spread between long and short rates is the largest it has been in 40 years. With such a shift already behind us, there is little more move, if any, still potentially ahead of us.

Au contraire. Expect it to go quite the other way. As we speak, long-term interest rates appear to be starting to crack materially, and I predict they will continue to decline irregularly for several years at least. As this happens, banks' lending margins will shrink. And bank stocks will lag.

Who will be doing well in an environment of lower long-term interest rates? Companies that can refinance their long-term debt at lower interest rates. And those are value stocks, which by their nature tend to have more debt than growth stocks. That's because they sell at low P/Es and low price-to-book ratios and can't easily sell equity to raise money.

Forbes has said it again and again, but it bears repeating at a time when so many publications run surveys featuring the currently hottest funds. By and large it pays to avoid most funds with hot performance histories. Buying these funds now is like trying to drive forward while looking backward. Right now the mutual fund industry as a whole—and especially many of its hottest funds—is overweighted in high valuation growth stocks by a factor of about 2-to-1, compared with the overall market's weighting in these stocks (see my April 13 column)—and they have

built those overweightings at just the wrong time.

Before you buy a fund, read carefully *Forbes'* mutual fund survey. Then, before making a final choice, consult *Morningstar* at your library. If it shows the fund has an average price-to-book over about 2.4 and a P/E over about 18, it is overweighted in growth stocks. You should avoid it. ■

Value Will Out
September 28, 1992

I recently had the good luck to speak with Richard Nixon, who is a lot smarter about politics than I could ever hope to be. The former President said he didn't know who would win in November. He thought that if Bush could take both Illinois and Ohio—two bellwether states—he would win, but lose either and Clinton would be President. It could go either way.

So what should the investor do? Not to worry.

Clinton is clearly a moderate front for a liberal future Cabinet and Congress—a

Playing Politics

Ken writes frequently about the impact of politics on the stock market. People tend to think the politicians they favor ideologically are best for stocks. Not so—neither party is better overall for stocks, though the impact can differ some from year to year. For example, as Ken points out here, the first year of all Democratic presidents' terms is positive—save Carter's first year. But Carter turned out to be a one-termer. And Clinton's first year in 1993 was indeed a fine year for stocks.

classic nightmare. So if he appears to stay ahead in the polls, the market is likely to remain lackluster through November.

But as happened after Jack Kennedy's 1960 election, the market could give Clinton a sweet 15-to-20-month honeymoon. The stock market fares better under Democratic administrations than most investors can possibly imagine, especially early on. A market honeymoon has been afforded all newcomer Democratic Presidents except Carter. And the smaller, value-oriented stocks that I have been urging you to own always did particularly well during these periods and even did pretty well in the early Carter era.

Why so? Hopes for a looser Fed, a bit more inflation and a flatter yield curve historically have caused stocks selling at valuation discounts to out- shine perceived growth stocks, as they did throughout Carter's reign.

With a Bush victory would come initial market strength this fall as he rebounds in the polls. If Bush wins, as in 1988, it would be less because voters like him than that they reject Clinton, and would be followed by an early 1993 recoil at the notion of four more years of an uninspired Administration. Later would follow an okay market, as per his first term. The market has no heavy fears or misgivings about Bush. He is a "known."

Either way, the level of stock prices in 12 to 18 months will have less to do with who is elected this fall than it will with traditional economics. The economy's rebound may have shown little zip to date, but below-average early recoveries are historically linked to above-average later recoveries and to ones that are longer than usual. Since the market always moves in advance of the economy, stop worrying about November. Focus on basically good, sound firms selling at cheap prices that will benefit as this economic recovery slowly builds. ∎

Profitable Reading
October 26, 1992

With Christmas still eight weeks away, here's my gift to you now: a listing of good new investment books for yourself or as gifts for friends and relatives. Plus some books to avoid wasting time and money on. If you think I didn't work hard to prepare for this column, you have no idea how many dreadful books I had to read.

I cameoed my all-time favorites in two columns—June 3, 1985 and April 4, 1988—see your library's old *Forbes* for those shopping lists. Now I catch up on more recent ones, having read 32 in all. Here are the best from the Class of '92.

The Practical Forecasters' Almanac by Edward Renshaw (Business One Irwin) will help anyone, novice or professional. Renshaw simplifies 137 indicators, like inventory-to-sales ratios and interest rates. My only gripes: His writing is dull, and you could see his points better if many of his tables were graphs.

I never cared for Martin Mayer's books and in his newest, *Stealing the Market* (Basic Books), I dislike his views, but love the book. Ignore his wrong and reactionary views, which suppose Uncle Sam can best discern how Wall Street should work. You know better. But read it for a great account of changes in Wall Street methodology. You will be more in-the-know on contemporary key evolutions like AutEx, Instinct, the Dot and SuperDot

and much more. It is full of fascinating nuts-and-bolts history worth knowing.

Relative Dividend Yield by Anthony E. Spare with Nancy C. Tengler (John Wiley & Sons) introduces the concept of investing via relative dividend yield—a new, valid approach to value investing—of which Spare was a pioneer. Any value investor should know about it. But like any single "system," it isn't a panacea. Spare and Tengler, of course, run a shop based on the concept. I have known and respected Tony Spare as a friend for 20-plus years, so this is hard to say, but his writing is drier than you deserve.

Global Investing, edited by Sumner N. Levine (HarperBusiness), is yet another Levine tour de force, blanketing a vast subject, and this time in only 652 pages. While the book was intended for professionals, anyone tuned to this trendy subject will benefit from this new bible. With chapters from a host of leading luminaries like Robert Arnott, Geoffrey H. Moore and Fischer Black, and ranging in subjects from analysis to techniques to specific countries, this book is hard to skip.

Wealth 101 by John-Roger & Peter McWilliams (Prelude Press) isn't on market techniques but the psychology of wealth, both getting and keeping it. It is fun, funny, and full of piercing quotes and insightful wisdom. At times it is too cynical. But it will boost your comfort with money and managing it.

Few folks embrace turf as tough as *Bankruptcy Investing* by Ben Branch and Hugh Ray (Dearborn Financial). But this book simplifies this usually hard-to-fathom field.

Gerald Krefetz's *The Basics of Stocks* and *The Basics of Bonds* (Dearborn Financial) are perfect for first-time or soon-to-be investors. These two cover all the basic subjects with overview—and without heavy biases, which is rare. The glossaries alone are valuable for novices.

The Money Bazaar by newly arrived *Forbes* columnist Andrew Krieger (with Edward Claflin, Times Books) explains currency trading. It is fun, fast and breezy. Krieger has been there, trading billions of bucks—and other moneys. This is his insider's view of a trillion-dollar-a-week market that impacts everyone on earth. In Story-book fashion you learn lingo like the cable, handle, fill, spot, old lady and how to "square up."

Among 1992's financial planning books Paul Merriman's *Investing For a Lifetime* (Business One Irwin) and Mike Stolper's *Wealth* (Harper Business) are good, but sell between-the-lines too hard on their advisory services. My pick of the litter is *Get Rich Slowly* by William Spitz (Macmillan). He has a better background, covers more and isn't selling anything. Besides, it is easy to read and makes simple sense.

Capital Ideas by Peter Bernstein (Free Press) and *Money of the Mind* by James Grant (Farrar) both attracted lots of favorable notice in the press, but are apt to mislead you. They package history and phony sophistication to mask perversely wrong ideas. ∎

Buy American
November 23, 1992

The election is over, and for better or worse that uncertainty is behind us. What now? Let's look for clues in the action of the stock market, the market being a discounter of the future. What is it telling us now? That whereas in the 1980s foreign economies generally beat the American economy, in the 1990s America will come in first.

European bankers believe they must keep interest rates high to defend their currencies and fight inflation. They think we should, too. And that our dollar is "too high."

But the stock markets don't seem to agree with the tight-money-obsessed Europeans. The stock markets of high interest rate nations are doing terribly. Germany, the philosophical leader of the high interest rate crowd (but not actually with the highest interest rates), has seen a 10% drop in its stock market this year. Markets like those in Italy, Spain and Sweden, with the dearest money, are down more than 25%. The higher the rates, the worse the stock markets. It's perverse.

Britain's interest rates are middlish-high yet slightly lower than most. So their stock market is flat this year, beating the other Europeans. We have lowered our already low rates, and the mere 3.3% gain in our S&P 500 is leading the world's major markets.

As always, among US stocks, some are doing better than others. The primarily domestic ones are besting those with high foreign revenue, and on average by about 8% this year.

I think this trend will continue. Reasons? First, our interest rates will keep falling under the new Administration. Note: The big drop to date came via zero growth in the money supply in the last three years—actual tight money—despite dropping rates. So the Fed can print money now without causing inflationary pressures. By my figures, a one-time 10% boost in the money supply in the next two years brings the last five years' average growth in the money supply up to a mere 1.9%. Hardly high and inflationary.

And if short-term rates merely don't rise, long rates must fall, as they have been, because the spread between long and short rates is at record levels historically.

For the first time in decades, we have the world's cheap money, with that trend certain to continue under the new Administration.

So prospects for the domestic economy look better than those of a lot of foreign economies. Focus now on stocks doing business mainly in America. ∎

Damn Lies
December 21, 1992

Long Treasurys are yielding 7.5% these days. Do they tempt you? If not, it's probably because you think inflation is 3%-plus and at risk of going a lot higher. And if that's what you think, get a copy of Darrel Huff's *How to Lie With Statistics*.

What does Huff's classic, first published in 1954, have to do with Treasury bonds? At first blush, nothing. Huff doesn't even mention bonds. Rather, what he does, in 142 small pages and simple words, is show the fallacies behind official-looking statistics. Huff will help you fathom how the official government statistics on price indexes are drastically overstating inflation. Officially, consumer prices are 3.2% ahead of where they were a year ago. I can't tell you exactly how much that 3.2% is overstating inflation, but I know that it is.

To a great extent the surveyors in the Bureau of Labor Statistics who compile the Consumer Price Index rely on published figures, such as list prices, rather than actual transactions. They are smart enough to know car buyers can do better than sticker prices. But they don't know how much better, so they estimate. But lately, estimates have gotten screwy, because of the abnormally large amount of discounting—particularly on big-ticket items.

Nobody pays retail anymore. Discounting, including under-the-table discounting, is more common than it was a few years ago. Do the bureaucrats at BLS have a handle on this? I don't think it is possible.

Another reason for the exaggeration involves what the economists call substitution. If the price of one type of meat stays high while others fall, consumers shift to the cheaper meats. If movie tickets are steep, viewers shift to video rentals. But the statisticians compare prices for the same cut of beef one year to that cut's price the next, even

> ## Inflation's Inflated
>
> This is something else that hasn't changed. Our "official" inflation reading, CPI—like any official government data—is as flawed as ever, measuring a quirky basket of goods that likely don't replicate your experience of prices in the real world.

though consumers might be buying more of a cheaper cut. Likewise with movie tickets and many other items. They only "rebalance the product mix" once per decade. As a result, the surveyors miss the central fact that protein is getting cheaper and filmed entertainment is getting much, much cheaper.

Statisticians, moreover, are slow to pick up the cost-reducing benefits of new products. Think of just a few from the 1980s: light beer, CNN, mountain bikes, voice mail, ATMs, baking soda toothpaste. Each is a price-to-benefit improvement over what it replaced; otherwise, the new product wouldn't have succeeded. Since 1989, new products have been introduced at a furious pace. Tied to optimism late in the last business cycle's expansion, corporations went on a frenzy of new-product development that came to market in the post-1989 recession. But their impact won't show in indexes for years to come.

Again, you can't tell exactly how much less inflation is running than the indexes show, but it's a lot. Actual inflation may well be zero right now.

For investors, this means many things, all of them bullish. First, it means real (inflation-adjusted) interest rates are higher than they appear, and have further to fall than is commonly presumed. At zero inflation, a 7.5% long bond rate is too high and should fall—bullish.

Zero inflation means the economic recovery is stronger than presumed because it is calculated by subtracting inflation from gross numbers. It means monetary policy is a bit looser than it appears, which is bullish, although it is clearly still too tight. Zero inflation means that Americans are slightly richer than they think, which is bullish for consumer spending.

As I have said for more than a year, consumers and voters are grumpy and fixated on negative news. But investors shouldn't be. This is a time to own cheap common stocks of good firms that will prosper as the economy continues in an expansion that will be stronger than commonly expected. ∎

1993

A Taxing Year

" *In setting your cerebral scales to balance between bullish and bearish, never let your views of government, positive or negative, be more than about 10% of the weight of your thinking. Other things should weigh heavier, always.* "

"THE CLINTON FACTOR," MAY 10, 1993

" *What distinguishes highly successful investors from everyone else is what the smart ones don't do as much as what they do. Really sharp investors don't get sucked in by the trend du jour.* "

"FOUR DON'TS AND SOME DOS," DECEMBER 20, 1993

Nineteen-ninety-three was an average year in the stock market. Literally. The S&P 500 returned 10.1 percent on the year—almost exactly the stock market's long-term average, which is quite unusual. Most years, market returns are extreme—up big, up bigger, or down—and far from average. But the year wasn't average for all stock categories. Large US stocks lagged in 1993, hence the S&P 500's middling returns. The Value Line Index—heavily weighted to smaller stocks—jumped 18.1 percent.[1] And foreign stocks did even better, rising 32.9 percent.[2]

Newly elected President Clinton took office in January, ushering in an era of "Clintonomics." Hallmarks of President Clinton's new economic plan included higher corporate, income, and fuel taxes—enacted in 1993—and NAFTA, the North American Free Trade Agreement, signed in 1993.

Remaining politically agnostic is essential in investing. Biases in general lead to poor investment decisions. Political biases are no different. Politicians of all stripes have proven abilities to muck things up. It's the policies, not the politicians or political parties in power, deserving investors' attention. Ken's view of the new administration's policies was clear. "Certainly our economy would be better served by the exact reverse of Clinton's direction." ("The Clinton Factor," May 10, 1993.) But even Ken's negative view of Clinton's policies didn't diminish his enthusiasm for stocks. "Bad politicians," he said, "happily do not make bear markets."

Even so, the bull market was aging. Every day of a bull market is a day closer to the next inevitable bear. Seem overly dour? Maybe, but it's a fact. The stock market moves in bull and bear market cycles—always. A bear market follows every bull and vice versa, each of varying lengths. Permanently bullish and permanently bearish forecasters are both proven wrong at times, though the permabulls have the upper hand since stocks tend to go up more than they fall, and overall move higher over the long term.

Ken's now third year of stock market optimism in the face of general pessimism had some pegging him a permabull. He made the case he's not a perma-anything but bases his forecasts on where he thinks the market is headed in the near future. "I've been bullish so long that some readers write complaining that I'm a Pollyanna. Not so. Dig out my columns from late 1989 to late 1990. Nonstop brutal bearishness—but always laced with the caveat that the time to turn bullish would come. In time, therefore, I will become a bear again. But the time is not yet." (Stay Bullish," August 2, 1993.)

Ken's stock market optimism had been rewarded with good returns in the prior several years, but his optimism about the economy wasn't. The 1993 economy wasn't stagnant, but it wasn't much to write home about either. "I have been too optimistic since 1991 on the economy. While recovery started in mid-1991, and my timing on that was very good, I expected more oomph than occurred." ("The Other Dow Theory," January 4, 1991.) What was holding the economy back? Sentiment was one thing. Ken noted sentiment's power to overwhelm fundamentals for a time, but not forever. "We live in a world where perception can overwhelm reality for quite a while. . . . Respect media power and crowd psychology, even when you know they are long-term wrong."

Ken wrapped up the year by again warning against investing fads. One fad Ken highlighted was the rush into emerging markets stocks. "The emerging market movement is a classic bubble building. You don't want to be there as it bursts." ("Four Don'ts and Some Dos," December 20, 1993.) The emerging market bubble didn't burst in 1993 per se. But returns in emerging markets stocks, although positive, significantly lagged developed markets for the next few years.

The Other Dow Theory
January 4, 1993

"Never promote a man who hasn't made some bad mistakes, because you would be promoting someone who hasn't done much." I quote Herbert Dow, that brilliant business manager who founded Dow Chemical. I'm decades too young ever to have met Dow, but when my dad caught me doing something wrong he would quote Dow to me and then insist on analyzing what I had done wrong in the interest of learning from it.

In that spirit I confess my recent mistakes to you my readers and seek to draw some lessons therefrom.

I have been too optimistic since 1991 on the economy. While recovery started in mid-1991, and my timing on that was very good, I expected more oomph than occurred.

One thing that has held the economy back is the perception that consumers and business owe too much money. I think this perception is wrong, but it exists and I should have remembered we live in a world where perception can overwhelm reality for quite a while. The media have browbeaten a debt-based gloom into us (January 20, 1992) and made it politically incorrect to speak optimistically.

Lesson? Respect media power and crowd psychology, even when you know they are long-term wrong.

I still expect our economy to do better in 1993 and 1994 than most folks do—in the end reality will prevail over false perceptions.

The good news? My mid-1991 optimistic call for smaller, value-oriented stocks was vindicated in 1992. As I write, the S&P 500 is up 4% year-to-date, but the Value Line index, full of smaller stocks, is up more than 12%.

If that call was right in general, I made a serious misstep in my March 16 column.

I failed to see that the small stocks had risen so much in the early months of 1992 that they were due for a reaction. All of March's stocks are off a bunch since then.

Turning to individual stocks, my prize boo-boo was JWP (19 when I recommended it March 16, 4 now). I knew the outfit was heavily in debt, but I thought its excellent prospects outweighed the debt. I was dead wrong. As internal management problems arose that finally toppled JWP's president and culminated in November in large-scale accounting irregularities and writeoffs, JWP's debt was an anchor around its neck.

What is the lesson to learn here? Playing with fire gets you burned. Even if you think you know a situation cold, there are too many ways things that can go wrong for a highly indebted firm not to be a high-risk stock. My mistake here—and most investors have done this at some time or another, and I hope I don't do it again—was to think I knew enough to justify that high debt load. Wrong.

What should you do if you bought the stock on my say-so? It's risky, but I would hang on. It still has too much debt, but the bad news is out, cash flow is good and JWP should be able to pay down its debt. Of course, I was wrong before. It's your decision.

Less a disaster but still an unhappy experience was M/A Com (4—also recommended on March 16, at 7—down 40%). Here I'm more confident holding the stock, despite its sad results to date. My mistake was in underestimating how difficult change is. M/A Com has been moving from defense markets into commercial ones. And it's done well at that, but at the price of far less short-term profitability than I expected. It sort of falls into the Murphy's sub-law category of: "Everything takes longer and costs more than you expect."

But at 75% of book value, 25% of revenue and 8 times trailing earnings I would hang tough here. It is far from a leveraged company. Nonearning cash flow, mainly depreciation, is huge—enough to pay off all debt in only two years. And the management has a clear mission moving forward.

I suggested avoiding several stocks this year, and did okay there, but Outback Steakhouse (cited July 6) is up 99% since then. I simply thought it was vastly too pricey and didn't appreciate the priceless momentum of a fad.

Of course, among my 35 1992 stock picks I also had a few winners. In a fairly flat year for the S&P 500, only 8 of my other picks were down, and none as much as 10%. The average of all my 1992 picks is up 11.5%, which is much better than it sounds, because on average these picks are slightly less than six months old. I had 13 picks that were up double-digit amounts, including: SCI Systems (16—cited at 6 on January 20—up 165%), Applied Magnetics (11—cited at 7 on February 17—up 57%) and Mueller Industries (21—recommended at 14 on July 6—up 47%). So, I'm not at all ashamed of my overall results.

But as Herbert Dow would have said, and as my dad did his best to beat into my dense brain, you learn much more from examining your failures than from doing so with your successes. In facing the future, I count each lesson learned from my mistakes as being among my successes, and never expect to avoid all mistakes, or hope to stop learning. Happy New Year. ∎

Acres and Acres of Bargains
February 15, 1993

For all the talk about this being a high-priced stock market, I find more cheap stocks out there than I can shake a stick at.

Regular readers know I have been a rabid long-term bull for the last 27 months. I still am. Furthering 1992's trend, I expect the best part of the market will continue to be smaller, cheap stocks of firms that are fundamentally strong in their underlying business. Hard to find?

There isn't space here to detail all the good, small stocks that look darned cheap to me. So many that, ranking them alphabetically, I run out of space even before I get to D. Starting with A:

The market values computer giant Amdahl at merely $875 million. Five years ago? Value: $2.5 billion. It had $1.8 billion in annual sales then. Now? Sales: $2.8 billion. Yes, the company has hit some snags lately, like almost everyone in computing, but I think it can earn $150 million in a few years and keep growing. It's a strong firm.

At 38% of trailing revenue and 65% of book value, Amdahl is darned cheap. More so as you note that its balance sheet looks like a rock. Its depreciation is so large relative to long-term debt that if it chose to, it could use this source of cash flow to pay off all its debt in just nine months. Most firms would need at least five years to do this.

Amax (18) was well regarded 12 years ago at 65—or $4 billion for the whole natural resources firm. Now, down 75%, its total price tag is $1.5 billion, but it's still a fine company. At the current depressed price, it is a cheap stock today at just 42% of revenue and 72% of book value.

American Maize-Products is likely to be taken over before long—if not by its peer, Archer Daniels Midland, which seems likely, then by someone else. At 25% of sales, a P/E of 10, and 85% of book value, American

Maize shares should do well whether taken over or not.

Ameron, a leader in concrete water and sewage pipe, has had tough times lately with the economy and the budget woes of local governments. It should see pickup in demand ahead, and increases in its currently modest foreign sales. Selling well below its 1988–90 peak prices, at 14 times earnings, 30% of revenue, 90% of book value, and with a 4% dividend yield, it could well hit 50 by 1995.

I cited Black & Decker two years back (June 10, 1991) at 12. It broke through 26 and has now given much of that back, retreating from the big-cap world again. But 32% of revenue, 1.1 times book value and 9 times what I think it can earn in 1994 is simply too cheap for a truly great consumer products franchise. Expect a 100% rise by 1995.

I'm not politically correct, because I love the logging industry, having studied at forestry school before switching to economics. I love the woods, the smell, the sound, the thud and the feel of a big tree felling. And I love Blount and its role as perhaps the world leader in commercial logging products. Its $169 million total price tag is too low for its logging line; but you get its sporting equipment and construction lines, too—$700 million in sales all told. I think by 1995 Blount could earn $20 million and the stock be at 30. It was at 20 a decade ago.

CDI leads in two areas that should be hot in the years ahead. Its temporary employment services will hum—from the economic upturn—and from tax incentives to hire long-term "temps" instead of "permanent" help. In a cost-conscious world, contingency-fee executive search (CDI is the biggest) will gain share from the "retainer" side of the industry. Valued at $175 million, cm sells at 20% of sales, 1.6 times book value and 11 times what I think it can earn next year. Hold out for 15.

If you want 15 stocks to put away and not worry about, don't own Comdisco. But if you own 75 stocks and watch them closely, this computer leasing firm is a good risk, despite the debt inherent in leasing. At 27% of sales, 8 times earnings, 95% of book value and with potential for fat profit margins, Comdisco should hit the high 20s by 1995.

Commercial Metals. Times have been tough for the metal industry, and with over 50 plants this firm has had more than its share of the troubles. But at 23% of sales, one-third over book value, and 10 times its basic earning power, the stock looks cheap.

Property and casualty insurers are becoming too cheap. An example?

Continental Corp. At 29% of revenue, 75% of book value and with a 4% yield, it's at less than 10 times what it used to earn in the casualty cycle's last upleg. The stock is half its 1986 price and be low where it was ten years ago. The company is well run, and the stock could easily hit 50 by 1996.

No cheap stocks left out there? What do you call these? All from A through C. There are about 100 more between D and Z. Out of space. ∎

Design Your Own
March 15, 1993

Last year brokerage firms put software on their terminals and now sell "asset allocation" for big fees to folks like you. It's a great revenue producer for the brokers. A billion bucks is going into it monthly. They charge you about 3%—every year. In return, they regularly adjust the allocation and help you parcel out money into appropriate asset styles among a screened list of specialty money managers or mutual funds.

Two questions arise. First: Should you bother? Yes. Smart asset allocation can do as much for investment performance as the choice of money managers or stock selection. And using asset allocation protects you from indecision and timidity. Too many investors, on their own, penalize long-term results by keeping too much of their savings or defined contribution plans, like 401(k)s, in cash.

Recently I heard SEC Commissioner J. Carter Beese Jr. grousing on the SEC's fear that the fast-growing area of individual-controlled defined contribution plans will keep growing but generate poor investment returns because folks hold too much cash—and accordingly won't do well enough to afford retirement. Sticking to a fixed-asset allocation plan protects from this danger.

Second question: Do you need a broker who eats up a good chunk of your return in fees? No. You can easily allocate your own assets.

The first step: Don't be awed by this fancy term. It simply refers to how you spread your available assets among stocks, bonds and cash based on your age. I'm going to show you how you can do it on your own and save those 3% fees.

Most corporate pension fund asset allocations end up at about 54% stocks, 32% bonds, 14% cash. Pension funds pay fat fees for extremely fancy studies that tell them to do this. Since they all end up with very similar asset allocations, what do they get from these studies? Litigation protection. They have a legal fiduciary responsibility to employees to cross every "t" and dot every "i" (i.e., the corporate pension plan can be sued).

These corporate plans are based on a simple algebraic formula for how much of varying asset categories to own, based on the ages of the participants. In your case, there is only you, so it's very much simpler.

Here's what you do: How old are you? If you are 20 years old and just starting, hold 90% equities. If you are 80, you can't risk much, hold only 10% equities. If you are in-between in age? It's a straight-line function; as your age increases, cut back equity. At 40 you are down to 63% equities. At age 60 you are down to 40%.

Until you are 40, as you slowly cut back equity, year by year, it all goes into bonds, which in the longest term also beat cash. After 40, as you age and slowly cut equity exposure, half of what comes out of equities goes into cash and half into bonds. So, for example, at age 65, you are 30% equity, 54% bonds and 16% cash.

Assuming you don't want to make studying the stock market a major part of your life, use good no-load mutual funds for the bond and equity portions. Fund families like Vanguard, Fidelity or T. Rowe Price have good no-load products.

Within equity you break it by style. Here, too, to make it easy and cheap, you can use no-load mutual funds, all with annual fees of 1% or less.

Unless you are an active and shrewd investor, in which case you don't need my advice on asset allocation, I wouldn't suggest putting all your equity eggs in one basket. Split the equity money according to market segment. For details on mutual funds, study the *Forbes* mutual fund survey. The latest annual one is August 31, 1992; the latest interim one, February 15, 1993. Or *Morningstar* at your library.

Each year adjust your equity, bond and cash balances by the formula. Then be patient and relish the 1.5% or more per year you saved by doing it yourself. By using these no-load mutual funds you will be paying annual management fees of 1% or less, not the 3% brokers will charge you. And you don't need expensive studies. After all, you are most unlikely to sue yourself. ∎

Henry's Cattle Prod
April 12, 1993

Henry B. Gonzalez chairs the House Committee on Banking, Finance & Urban Affairs. Firmly entrenched with Hispanic votes, Gonzalez is a force to be reckoned with in Congress. His views are important to investors at this time. Why? Because Gonzalez is out to get Alan Greenspan—and more specifically the independent Federal Reserve. Gonzalez is the recent author of HR 28—the Federal Reserve System Accountability Act of 1993. This might better be called the Making-the-Federal-Reserve-Do-Congress'-Will Act. The bill hasn't passed and probably won't. It need not to be a potent weapon for Gonzalez all the same.

As far as I am concerned, this is a good thing. Gonzalez and HR28 will cattle-prod Alan Greenspan into loosening money a bit. Money has been too damned tight for years. As Milton Friedman warned decades ago, the Fed usually, and this Fed now, confuses the path of interest rates with the tightness of money.

Monetarists know that a real noninflationary money policy would be several large notches looser than Greenspan's deflationary path. It means annual M2 growth of about 4.5%, versus the sub-2%

he gives us now. Fixing that shortfall will boost the economy and stock market tremendously.

Greenspan is and for all of his career has been fixated on inflation. Too much so. But like any Fed chairman he is even more fixated on keeping the Fed free from political interference. My guess is that, with Congress and Henry Gonzalez baying at the Fed's door, Greenspan will ease credit to keep the wolves away.

Until 1993, he didn't have to worry. Whenever the President and control of Congress come from different parties, the Fed doesn't have to worry. It knows the two parties much prefer fighting each other to fighting it.

But now the Democrats run the whole shooting match—which means Gonzalez wields a big stick. Gonzalez is almost a Friedmanite. He waxes wonderfully Friedmanesque on money. He would mandate steady, noninflationary money-growth rates to the Fed. With Democrats controlling the whole Washington scene, Gonzalez can use HR 28 to force Greenspan to do his bidding.

That means slightly easier money, and that is bullish for stocks. ∎

The Clinton Factor
May 10, 1993

Too many investors take a wrong read on how President Clinton should affect their view of stocks and bonds. Since they don't like Clinton, they are bearish. Certainly our economy would

be better served by the exact reverse of Clinton's direction.

But fortunately, even Clinton's crew can do only limited harm to our economy. In setting your cerebral scales to balance between bullish and bearish, never let your views of government, positive or negative, be more than about 10% of the weight of your thinking. Other things should weigh heavier, always.

Like what? Like the existing general direction of the economy, monetary policy, interest rates, foreign impact, inflation, the dollar—and underlying fundamentals like changing demographics, investor sentiment (in a contrarian sense) and, of course, securities valuations. Even $200 billion worth of Clintonesque fiscal foolishness is a minor ripple in the rising or falling tide of our huge combined $6 trillion GDP and $10 trillion stock and bond markets.

I see Clinton and crew on a 1-to-10 scale as a bearish 7. But George Bush wasn't great either—maybe a 4. Lyndon Johnson's Great Society was a 10 for terrible. But note, other things were bullish, and it was wrong to avoid stocks during his watch. Nixon wasn't so hot—peacetime wage-and-price controls and all that "I'm a Keynesian now" nonsense. Ford and Alan Greenspan and their WIN-button brigade boosted taxes big time at the bottom of the worst economy since the 1930s. The market rocketed up.

Bad politicians happily do not make bear markets. After a long expansion tires, bad Washington policies can be the straw that breaks our economy's back. But that's not now. I have been a raving bull for several years now. I'm still bullish but not raving. Prices are higher and the bull is older. ∎

A Near Sure Thing
June 7, 1993

I've never been much of an enthusiast for investing overseas; there are plenty of opportunities here at home. But European government bonds look good right now and so does one European equity market—Britain.

The European opportunities are a consequence of Germany's mounting problems. Germany's economy is in a virtual free-fall that hasn't yet hit publishable statistics. Expect big declines this year, with no recovery in sight. The German situation is worsened by German arrogance: Those folks just can't admit that Germany can have major problems. I recently heard the Bundesbank's chief economist, Reiner Konig, claim that recent German economic weakness is mainly caused by bad prior policies in other nations. Germany at fault? Never. As elsewhere, until Germany fears its recession greatly, it won't be over.

The Germans constantly lecture us on our fiscal folly. Our deficit is about 4.7% of GDP. Yet their budget deficit is half again as large—a hair above 7% of their GDP. A whole series of other problems drag them down longer term: deadly demographics this decade, the costs of unification, tumultuous 1994 elections, future corporate restructurings and sky-high labor costs. Worst of all is a never-ending anti-inflation, tight-money fetish that strangles commerce. It is like dealing with the obese via starvation rather than via a continual supply of the right amount of healthy nutrition.

So how do German problems make French and Danish bonds a buy? Here's how: Germany must loosen credit, and as it does, as the anchor of the European economy, others will be able to do what they have long wanted to do—lower their own interest rates. There is a long row to hoe with this, just as there was with the US rate decline. Prices of European bonds will rise, inevitably so.

For 20 years the world has waged a war against inflation, slowly killing it.

That war is ending now in front of our eyes. Yet most observers don't want to believe it. Inflation is dying, if not dead. The rest of the 1990s will see looser money worldwide—plus less inflation.

For investors wishing to cash in on this near-inevitability I recommend the Benham European Government Bond Fund. It's a well-defined and easy-to-buy no-load fund that started late last year. Its bonds have a seven-year average maturity with an 8.5% yield. Benham's bonds are about 20% dollar-hedged—meaning you have some protection against a strong dollar erasing your gains. This should be a long-term commitment, say for five years. Let it be volatile and bounce as much as it wants. You should find your patience rewarding.

I would stay away from most foreign equity markets. Japan has done well this year, but it's still overvalued, has lots of competitive problems ahead and is heavily a trader's market, mainly oriented to short-term swings.

All the global gurus say you simply have to own the rest of the Pacific Rim—and South America—which says to me, via contrarianism, you probably shouldn't.

Just before the German economy bottoms will be a wondrous time to buy German equities, but that time isn't here yet.

The one exception to my skepticism about overseas markets is good old England. And, fortunately, you can buy these stocks right here in the USA, via New York Stock Exchange ADRs. Britain is in an upturn, leaving many of its well-publicized problems behind—about 18 months behind us in an economic recovery. It's now time for its cyclical stocks, which are simply too cheap. ■

> **Going Global**
>
> Here is another very important lesson: Even if you are a single country investor (against Ken's recommendation for most investors), you must pay attention to what's going on outside your borders—even for investors in a single economy as big as the US. The world is more connected than you think; major events outside your borders can impact what's going on within them.

Your Board of Directors
July 5, 1993

Since investment management is my business, I probably see far more financial reports and data than the typical reader of *Forbes*. Nevertheless, I value highly the opinions of *Forbes* financial columnists. (And not just for the pleasure of seeing my name among them.) Why so, when I am saturated with numbers and views?

Envision us columnists as imaginary members of your board of directors whose biggest value is to expose you to different viewpoints. That we may sometimes contradict each other should not bother

you. What matters is that opposing views can force you to examine, defend, and, if necessary, adjust your own conclusions.

Imagine getting a call from Board Member David Dreman, chiding you for panicking out of Philip Morris at its April lows—against his good advice. So you mention: "Oh, by the way, David, on May 10 Mark Hulbert was warning me to be cautious on the market because, as he put it, 'The [advisory] letters clearly anticipate relatively weak stock and bond markets in the 1990s.' Yet, David, you say you are cautiously bullish."

Then you say to David, "In fact, two weeks later, on the 24th, Mark warned me that most advisory letters expect short-term interest rates to rise—maybe as high as to 6%. Scary, isn't it?"

Imagine that David responds by saying: "Well, remember, I'm known as the Contrarian. If most advisory letters are bearish, and expect rates to rise, bonds to sink and stocks to dawdle, what does that say to a contrarian? It says: 'Buy.' "

So, both Hulbert and Dreman are rendering you a service. Hulbert is reporting from the market letter front, which is bearish; Dreman, as a contrarian viewer, would be bullish. The contrast benefits you—and me.

Reading the opinions of all my fellow columnists, I continue to be bullish. I think the recent uptick in short-term rates is a temporary blip, or at least is discounted in current stock prices.

The crowd has said for three years that the 1990s won't be as good as the 1980s. So far the 1990s have been pretty darned good in the financial markets. Far better than most seers foresaw. So much for the crowd.

Too many people are still too bearish for us to be on the verge of a bear market. For all the reasons I have laid out since 1990, I expect this decade to be just fine on Wall Street—punctuated with a couple of normal bear markets and a recession or two. But don't expect the next downturn until more seers turn optimistic.

Good, and Getting Better All the Time

Ken says here, "So far the 1990s have been pretty darned good in the financial markets. Far better than most seers foresaw. So much for the crowd." He also reminds readers in this column that in 1990, he'd predicted the 1990s to be a great decade for stocks. And, a fairly lackluster 1994 aside, the 1990s would be great, particularly for US stocks.

Though I side with the bulls, I am still most grateful to Hulbert for keeping me posted on what the investment letters think. I need that outside input to keep testing my own views. So should you.

Since I am still bullish, what stocks do I like?

Trans World Music is a half-billion-dollar (sales) retailer of records, tapes and video products that the market sees as worth only $150 million. As the economic recovery builds, so will consumer confidence and Trans World's earnings. But after three years of consumer pessimism, investors are tired. The stock is half of its 1987 or 1990 peaks, selling for 1.3 times book value, a P/E of 12 and 35% of revenue, with very little debt.

Strawbridge & Clothier is another recession-impacted retailer I like. Its mid-Atlantic department stores saw earnings hit harshly. The stock followed suit, tailing 50% from its level of five years ago. I think earnings will rebound. If it achieves 3% net margins—as I expect—based on the current stock price it is less than ten times earnings. It currently sells at book value and 25% of annual revenue. This is a fine department-store chain at bargain-basement prices.

If you believe the bull market still has life, then expect brokers to do well. You will like the Baltimore brokers. They have had a good run, but I see them only about halfway through it. Alex Brown is a great firm, with a strong investment banking arm, yet sells at 1.2 times book value, and has a P/E of 6. I may be wrong, but it should hit 40 before this bull market is over. Legg Mason is a similarly cheap Baltimore broker—1.3 times book value and a P/E of 7. And again, a price target of 40.

Of big brokers, Paine Webber is almost irresistible—at 1.5 times book value, 7 times earnings and 42% of revenue, the market values it at $1.4 billion. But much of that could be realized if it sold off its Mitchell Hutchins money management subsidiary, particularly now that it lured in Frank Minard as boss. ∎

Stay Bullish
August 2, 1993

We are about halfway through a bull market in stocks. It started in late 1990 and may end about the start of 1996. Long-term bond prices should do fine until about then also. Short-term rates will probably behave well until sometime next year.

I've been bullish so long that some readers write complaining that I'm a Pollyanna. Not so. Dig out my columns from late 1989 to late 1990. Nonstop brutal bearishness—but always laced with the caveat that the time to turn bullish would come.

In time, therefore, I will become a bear again. But the time is not yet. Not until certain signs have appeared. Short-term interest rates should have risen for at least a year. The excess of long-term rates over short-term rates should have fallen for at least 18 months—the yield curve will have flattened; right now it is quite steep.

The economic expansion should be old. And about four years will have elapsed from the bottom of the last bear market.

What will really clinch things to start the bear market will be a vocal excess of bullishness.

None of these factors is present yet.

Quite the contrary. Reading the press, or listening to investors, you hear a preponderance of voices expecting poor stock and bond results. You would expect gloom at or near bear market bottoms. But the only time in my 20-year-plus career with quite such thick pessimism so long after a market bottom was between 1977 and 1979—a great time to buy stocks, particularly value stocks.

Newsletters, Barron's institutional investor poll, and consumer confidence are all gloomy. Mutual fund and institutional cash balances are at highs. Bears adorn magazine covers. Bulls don't. And there are any number of professionals being quoted everywhere with bearish forecasts, but darned few bulls.

But since the bearish crowd is so noisy right now, let's examine its premises. They include: 1) The 1990s can't be very good for securities because the 1980s were so great—aka the party must be over; 2) P/Es and the like are so high that stocks must fall far to get back to a normal range; 3) We are at or near a bottom for interest rates; 4) The 1990s will be a slow-growth decade on Main Street, tied to debt, deficits and taxes and a tapped-out consumer; 5) Clinton.

> ### Hibernating Bear
>
> Ken would become a bear again, but not until 2000. He turned bearish on Tech stocks in these pages in March 2000, and bearish on the market as a whole in early 2001. And, as Ken predicted, there was a vocal excess of bullishness on Tech stocks in early 2000.

As detailed in prior columns, I view all these arguments as a bit off base. For example, while the later 1980s were great, they merely got us back to normal after the dismal decade of 1972–82. Almost everything is more normal now than most folks realize. But even were all the bears' points basically right, they are still not bearish if the market has already discounted them, which it has.

It's surprise that moves markets, and only surprise. All the bearish arguments are too old and well digested not to be fully in the market already. It will take new and bad surprises, or time to forget the old arguments, before the bear begins. ■

He's Still Hibernating

August 30, 1993

Even my most casual readers know that I continue to be bullish on the bond and stock markets and do not expect a serious bear market until about 1995–96. Looking beyond that, I expect nasty corrections, but all within another good bull market.

I realize that long-term forecasting is extremely iffy and that readers have an inconvenient habit of remembering. Nevertheless, I will put my neck way out. By my reckoning our last bear market was in 1990. That one was mostly in value stocks. This next one, starting in 1995 or 1996, will correct excesses on the other side, in growth stocks. Bear markets led by growth stocks are the most scary kind. That bear market should spell the doom of Mr. Clinton's reelection prospects; presidents are rarely re-elected close to bear market bottoms.

On the bear market's heels should be a rather normal recession—likely bigger than the one in 1990–91, but it won't seem so. Why? Last time, the media got hit hard and early and cried loudly. Next time it will suffer less and broadcast the misery less.

By then Mr. Clinton will have picked the next Fed chairman, and he or she will go down in history as among the best. Alan Greenspan has squeezed so much juice from the monetary sponge that his successor will have, it easy, arriving at a near perfect point in history.

After the 1995–96 bear market and recession, even a monkey or a moron at the Fed's helm will make it look easy and will be backed up by one big, broad bull market in stocks that will carry through into the new century and put the Dow Jones industrials nicely above 5000.

That bull market will be backed by an economic recovery that will be all the things this one hasn't been: big, fast and growthy, with rising revenues and fattening profit margins, giving business a two-fer.

The expansion will be backed by the best shifts in US demographics to occur in my lifetime. Too, it should be backed by rising productivity and a once-in-a-generation secular shift downward in the velocity of money.

Velocity is simply how fast money turns hands. It correlates well with major, slow demographic shifts. That means there will be a shift from your lifetime experience in terms of how much money can be printed relative to future price levels (i.e., inflation). We will print more money in the late 1990s than you are used to, without generating inflation. That will surprise most folks and will be bullish for interest rates and stocks.

In short, I expect the 1990s to be very different from the 1980s, but just as good. Oh, by the way, I expect by then the 1980s finally will be seen for what they were, a

---

Market Call Mania

Eerily, Ken's 10-year prediction in this column was spot on. Value did lead for the front part of the 1990s bull. 1994 wasn't a bear market, but it was a generally lackluster year. Then, in the back portion of the bull, growth stocks led decidedly.

Through the years, Ken has attracted a lot of attention around his bear market calls—calling the 1987, 1990, and 2000–2002 bear markets. But as important for an investor are recommendations to remain bullish. Perhaps more so, since over time stocks rise more than fall.

mere catching up after the dismal decade of 1972–82.

Even further out, we could have a monster bear market and real depression sometime around the year 2015. What would bring such disaster? A deadly demographic backlash as the baby boomers retire. Truly terrifying shifts. I hope I will still be writing here then and that *I* will call its coming in time to get my readers out. But that's inthe dim future. ∎

Housecleaning Time
September 27, 1993

Now is the time to sell anything you aren't content to hold for the next few years. I'm still overall bullish, but as I write, the market seems a bit ahead of itself, some stocks in particular.

While the big averages haven't moved up much—3.3% in the latest quarter for the DJI and 2.4% for the S&P 500—the smaller indexes have made good moves. The Russell 2000 and the Wilshire 250 (a wonderful new index) were both up 6% after a big first quarter and a huge fourth quarter last year. Not a bad time to begin pruning your portfolio.

Why now? Because my firm's momentum studies show that the demand for stocks is strong right now and may become less so in the months ahead. I'm not predicting a bear market, just a mild correction. But if you have some weak sisters, why not sell them when the market is strong and stocks are liquid?

My firm's trading department has built a series of real-time computerized models aimed at predicting upcoming liquidity shifts. They dice and slice the market by style and sector to try to figure out the future balance between supply of stocks and the demand for them. Right now the market is simply screaming for sellers. Our studies suggest that in a few months there will be a somewhat reduced demand for stocks and an increased supply of sellers.

So why not oblige the eager buyers now by giving them some of your tired merchandise? Don't sell the stuff that still looks cheap. Don't sell the companies you think are magnificently managed and worth holding for a long time. But where you are in doubt about a stock, sell it now. You may have to sell for less if you wait until later in the year.

So seek out those holdings you aren't really happy with. You're probably going to sell them eventually. Do it now rather than later. ∎

The Bubonic Plague Technique

October 18, 1993

In the 1300s plague killed 25% of Europe. Many of those spared had been fortunate enough to have avoided the two main transmittal mechanisms: human interaction and the rats that bore disease-ridden lice.

Clintonomics is a spreading economic plague, but, like all diseases, this one will run its course. I suspect he is a one-termer, and that repudiation and reversal of his policies will be rapid. We always rejigger taxes every few years whether we need to or not, and the outrageous 1993 tax bill surely won't endure past 1997.

As per the plague, self-made fortunes that made it to the *Forbes* 400 have avoided the various tax plagues of the 1960s and 1970s by simply avoiding taxable interactions. How so? By making investments for the very long haul and staying with them: no sale, no tax on the gains. That's how smart folk like Sam Walton, Warren Buffett, David Murdock kept compounding their wealth.

No matter how tax rates are raised, it won't hurt you if you don't sell the asset. Or if you must sell in part to repay debt or for other reasons, try waiting for one of the inevitable lower-tax periods, a la Kennedy comes along. They wait, Carter—they wait. Clinton's is just the latest of many major social assaults on property rights, competition and incentive. Wait the rascals out.

Admittedly this takes discipline. You will have to forget timing this bull market or the next bear phase. Try to buy assets cheaply enough and good enough that you can hold them through ups and downs for a very long time. With interest rates on Treasurys ranging from 3% to 6%, a 12% annual return through 1998 would be respectable. That's not unachievable. Just find a firm that grows 6% annually and is now 25% under-priced. Such stocks don't grow on trees, but they are not entirely scarce.

And here are some wrong ways to react to the current tax plague: Don't just dump good stocks because you don't like Clintonomics. You will just pay a lot of taxes and miss out on a bull market that may be strong enough to overcome the results of goofy economic policies from Washington.

Don't try to avoid tax on dividends by owning high-multiple growth stocks. If a stock is cheap enough, you want to own it, even if it does pay a large taxable dividend. Conversely, if a growth stock is pricey now and misses an earnings estimate in 1995, you will face a capital loss.

So, pick 'em carefully, hold them long and you needn't worry about falling victim to the latest wave of redistributionist politics. ∎

Love the Sinner
October 25, 1993

Think biblically: Love the sinner—hate the sin. In investment terms, buy tobacco stocks—hate smoking.

It's not for me to pass moral judgment on smoking. My job is to identify good investment ideas. Right now US investors have a bearish wrong read on tobacco-related firms.

The stocks started sagging as they saw Clinton coming—now down on average 30%-plus from prior peaks. Yes, he will escalate the war on smoking, not only via tax but also via social disdain. The EPA's new edict that secondhand smoke is a major cancer cause is a new, dubious, yet strong weapon in the antismoking war.

Simultaneously the stocks suffered from Main Street pressures. The trend to discounting everywhere else in our economy finally hit tobacco. Nowhere was this more visible than when Philip Morris cut prices earlier this year to retain market share, hurting itself, competitors and suppliers. For several years the trend has been for premium brands to lose market share to no-name discounters.

But everybody knows all this. The worries are reflected in the prices of the stocks. What is not reflected are some strengths.

Overseas, tobacco is a growth business. As poor people rise above subsistence in places like Africa and Asia, where most of the world lives, the first thing they do is reach for alcohol and a cigarette, because they like it.

Lung cancer? Medically mysterious as it sounds, many people in poor nations would love the implications of lung cancer. Right now they are not likely to live long enough to contract it. My point? They won't deny themselves what small pleasures they can afford. Expect tobacco use outside America, and so in the overall world, to grow slowly for 20 years.

In America, usage will shrink—but slowly. Tobacco demand is inelastic, which, if you recall your economics, means a big price rise, by taxation or otherwise, causes only a small drop in use. If the last 20 years' antismoking war has cut demand only a little, the next few years will at most cut it only a little bit more.

But the stocks are dirt cheap, and the market seems not to have focused on who can reap advantage from the non-US growth trend. I would focus on those firms primarily. ■

For Giving and for Reading
November 22, 1993

As I did last year (October 26, 1992), I have again browsed the bookstore shelves, inspecting the year's crop of new investment books. This year's books are not, in my opinion, as good, on average, as those of recent years, but do offer some profitable reading and worthy Christmas gifts.

Any new Peter Lynch book is newswor thy. *Beating the Street* (Simon & Schuster) is also wise, witty and well written. Since the book is simple and easy to read, beginners will learn lots from it, but so will veterans. Ever eclectic, Lynch can be self-contradictory; for example, when he says you can buy a stock only knowing a bit about it, and 240 pages later urges you to know the story better than Wall Street does. But he pokes fun at himself, offers introspection into his analysis, and is wonderfully quotable, as in: "Never invest in any idea you can't illustrate with a crayon." Highly recommended for keeping and for giving, for pleasure and for profit.

Martin Pring's *Investment Psychology Explained* (John Wiley & Sons) also benefits novice and veteran. Novices will gain from Pring's ring lore and overview, gained over a long career. Veterans will like his chapters on contrary thinking, and one on pride's role in making mistakes — far and away the best I have seen on that subject. The last chapter — trading rules from classic traders — is worth the 25 bucks by itself.

William Eng's *The Day Trader's Manual* (Wiley) is the best book I have seen on trading. Covering volatility, spread scalping, stochastics, relative strength and so much more, it's at times too technical, as are many of the Wiley finance books, but it's a great tutorial on technique.

Clearly I'm biased to like *The Stock Market Explained For Young Investors* by my son, Clayton Philip Fisher (Business Classics). For high school and college students, it's a handy gift item. Clay wrote it while still in school and in kids' lingo, so his peers could fathom this usually daunting subject. He offers a unique viewpoint gained from growing up day-to-day inside a 30 person money management firm. Give it to young people you want to instruct about markets.

Leo Melamed on the Markets, by Leo Melamed (Wiley) is great coverage of financial futures. With a stirring foreword by Nobel Laureate Milton Friedman, this book is so vital because it's by Melamed, who built the Chicago Mercantile Exchange and was one of a small handful of men who made financial futures what they are today. The book's top-notch trading advice applies to any form of speculative market.

I admire Robert Sobel's historical writings, and never more so than with his new *Dangerous Dreamers* (Wiley). Great book. He focuses insightfully on junk bonds and takeover artists. Easy, fun, yet detailed, it depicts Milken as a necessary product of our times who was done in by an Uncle Sam who has always been threatened by and "out for" significant pioneers of finance.

It's a Sure Thing, by Robert Metz and George Stasen (McGraw-Hill). Each of 75 short-story-like chapters ties a cartoon by Henry Martin to a two-page story challenging the good and bad of some aspect of investing. There is a lot of wisdom in small bites here. Each story ends with an easy-to-read lesson of a few lines.

The Prudent Investor by James P. Owen (Probus) winds you through the good and bad of asset allocation, consultants and picking money managers. Owen was a legend in money management sales, and knows his turf. His insights, overview and focus on mistakes to avoid are worth the book's price.

Since there were fewer than usual good books on investing published this year, it's not a bad time to revisit some of the classics. Not all of them are in print, but you can find them in any good library:

The Intelligent Investor by Ben Graham (Harper & Row, 1949); *Security Analysis,* also by Graham (McGraw-Hill, 1934); *Common Stocks and Uncommon Profits* by my father, Philip A. Fisher (Harper & Row, 1958); *Extraordinary Popular Delusions and the Madness of Crowds* by Charles Mackay (L.C. Page & Co., 1841); *The Templeton Touch* by William Proctor (Doubleday, 1983); *The Contrarian Investment Strategy* by David Dreman (Random House, 1980); *The Money Masters* by John Train (Harper & Row, 1980); *Reminiscences of a Stock Operator* by Edwin Lefevre (George H. Doran, 1923) — and Frank Reilly's *Investment Analysis and Portfolio Management* (Dryden Press, 1985). ∎

Four Don'ts and Some Dos

December 20, 1993

What separates the men from the boys in investing, the big winners from the also-rans? After doing a great deal of thinking and research on the subject, I have come to a simple conclusion. What distinguishes highly successful investors from everyone else is what the smart ones don't do as much as what they do. Really sharp investors don't get sucked in by the trend du jour. By avoiding high-tech stocks, Warren Buffett missed Microsoft. Poor Warren.

This bit of wisdom is good to keep in mind at this stage of a bull market that started way back in 1990 and will probably run until late 1995 or 1996. Four trendy traps to avoid: (1) "emerging markets" (2) "new" REITs (3) IPOs and (4) faddish eateries. Let's dissect these traps, one by one.

The emerging markets movement is a classic bubble building. You don't want to be there as it bursts. No sector has been hotter, longer. Foreign markets are heavily herd-driven, much more so than domestic equity markets. And the herd has charged long and hard into the non-Japan Pacific Rim and the hot Latin American markets.

Americans have bought about 5% of the dollar value of these countries cumulatively each year for years. We are now illiquid in these markets. When the bubble bursts there will be no one left to sell to.

On a smaller scale, REITs evolved fast from an unpopular, cheap way to buy real estate with dividend yield into a hot fad. The real estate boys are responding with an ample supply of new properties that will soon quench this newly hot market. Illiquid real estate partnerships are rapidly repackaged as REITs and sold to a naive public. The trend even sports a moniker: "securitization" of real estate. It also sports a high level of gimmicky accounting. Avoid them like the plague.

A similar trap is to be found in faddy new restaurants. There are too many to list, dozens of them, and most of them will be big losers by 1997. Checkers, Starbucks and Outback Steakhouse are examples. If you hadn't heard of the chain three years ago and its P/E and price-to-book and sales are high, it's very likely a trap.

This same perversion, in an earlier incarnation, saw Sambo's and Denny's at 40 times earnings in 1972. Trendy eateries become old and everyday and same-store-sales drop, and with them the stock. Much of the high profitability they show now is, like the REITs, accounting gimmickry aimed at supporting stock offerings.

As bad or worse is the whole realm of initial public offerings, I once wrote that IPO should mean "It's Probably Overpriced." IPOs are priced to provide cheap capital to the investment banker's clients—which means expensive to you. We are close to the end of an IPO cycle. Beware.

Avoid all these manufactured securities. As John Moody, the founder of Moody's Industrial Manual said in 1904, "Old and tried securities, like old friends, are likely to be the truest and best." Doing so should enable you to enjoy the last half of this bull market. Diversify among stocks of good firms that are cheap because of some bits of temporary bad news. ∎

1994

The Calm Before the Storm

> " *Each year for ten years I have written about 14 columns and picked about 50 specific stocks. My overall* Forbes *record is good but certainly not perfect. I make bad picks. I'll make others. I hope each time to learn from my mistakes.* "
>
> "Nolo Contendere," January 17, 1994

> " *A simple market truism: Old arguments, even correct ones, don't move markets (at least not until they are forgotten, and then they can have real power). Something new must arrive—a surprise or catalyst, because it is a surprise, and only that, which moves markets.* "
>
> "Jell-O Versus the Facts," February 14, 1994

"Plan for a great year in stocks" was Ken's opening line to his February 14, 1994 column "Jell-O Versus the Facts." The start of the big bull market Ken was predicting was less than a year away, but a great year 1994 wasn't—though it wasn't terrible either. Foreign stocks gained just 8.1 percent in 1994.[1] The S&P 500 price level fell 1.5 percent but actually posted positive returns.[2] How? Dividends. Just looking at changes in the price of a stock or stock index tells only part of the story. Gains on stocks come not only from stock price changes but also from dividends. In any given year, the stock market's total return results from the change in stocks prices plus dividends reinvested in stocks. So stocks' total return will always be a little bit higher than just the price changes. Most years, that means total returns will be slightly more positive or slightly less negative than price returns. But in an exceptionally flat year like 1994, price and total returns came in on opposite sides of zero with a positive S&P 500 total return of 1.3 percent.[3] Of course, whether stocks are slightly positive or slightly negative is virtually meaningless for investors.

Even though most would prefer positive to negative, investors shouldn't position portfolios differently if they expect the market to be down a little. Ken has often said, in any given year, stocks will have one of four outcomes: up a lot, up a little, down a little, or down a lot. That's it. And only the last scenario—if you think "down a lot" is most likely—warrants getting out of stocks. Accurately forecasting small stock market moves is simply impossible to do consistently.

Plus, what if you're wrong and stocks move up a little or a lot instead of falling? Riding out the little downturns is a small price to pay to ensure capturing the big stock market upswings, which are far more common. From 1926 through 2009—84 years—the S&P 500 has had calendar year losses of 20 percent or more only six times, and half those came during the Great Depression. By contrast, the S&P 500 has been up big 32 times during the same period—38 percent of the time the market is way up.[4] Historically, the risk of getting out of stocks far outweighs the gains. So investors should turn defensive only if they're very certain a big downturn is ahead. Trying to avoid small drops just isn't worth the risk.

In 1994, Ken warned against trying to time short-term stock market moves and introduced his "7% Rule." "Bull markets die with a whimper, not with a bang. A plunge off a broad peak . . . is scary, but it's the way corrections act, not how bear markets usually begin." ("The 7% Rule," May 9, 1994.) To avoid overreacting to quick, steep market drops, Ken's 7% Rule says to buy (equally important, *not sell*) when stocks fall 7 percent or more in two calendar months. Those types of moves are typical of emotionally driven, short-term market drops. Stocks can recover from those quickly. Again, only the big bear markets are worth trying to avoid.

One reason for Ken's 1994 bullishness was the shape of the yield curve. A yield curve is a graphical representation of yields on bonds with different maturities. Typically, yields on short-term bonds are lower than those on long-term bonds, meaning the yield curve is positively sloped. Banks tend to borrow money at short-term interest rates and lend money at long-term rates, so the steeper the yield curve, the more profitable it is for banks to make new loans. That makes money more readily available and is generally positive for the economy. In 1994, interest rates were rising (the US Federal Open Market Committee raised short-term rates for the first time since 1989), but the yield curve remained quite steep. "With long-term interest rates much higher than short-term rates, banks become eager to lend. They can make fat profits borrowing short and lending long term. Rising rates don't choke booms so long as long and short rates and the spread between them stays wide." ("A Bullish Spread," July 4, 1994.)

Ken also offered advice on avoiding market whiplash. Market leadership changes over time. Today's big winner can be tomorrow's loser, and vice versa. Too often investors are tempted by high-flying investments or discouraged by investments that have done poorly, so they buy near the top and sell near the bottom—not a good investing strategy. The easiest way to avoid whiplash, Ken said, is portfolio diversification. "This isn't the path to instant riches," Ken explained, "because when one group shines, another will hold you back; but it's the path to steady growth. It's a sure way to avoid whiplash." ("Avoiding Whiplash," August 29, 1994.)

Away from the stock market, the tabloids had a heyday in 1994. Ice skating became a contact sport when skater Tonya Harding's goons clubbed rival Nancy Kerrigan to keep her from competing in the Olympics. Football players were trying their hand at auto racing as former NFL pro OJ Simpson sped down a freeway in a white Ford Bronco. And a massive political shift unfolded as the Republican Party wrested control of both the House and Senate from the Democratic Party in midterm congressional elections. On Wall Street, the heyday was just beginning. 1994 might have been a mediocre year for stocks, but patient investors would be paid handsomely in the years to come.

Nolo Contendere
January 17, 1994

Reader Charles Lipshitz of Skokie, Ill. nailed me last May. How could I be so dumb, he asked, as to recommend Amdahl at 8 in my February 15 column shortly before it dropped to 5? The answer is simple: I was wrong.

Each year for ten years I have written about 14 columns and picked about 50 specific stocks. My overall *Forbes* record is good but certainly not perfect. I make bad picks. I'll make others. I hope each time to learn from my mistakes.

As Mr. Lipshitz wrote, Amdahl cratered right behind me. It was cheap, but I didn't see the impact Europe's receding economy would have on its mainframe computer sales—further worsened by a very strong dollar. Mainframes sell with the hair-trigger economic sensitivity of any other big-ticket capital good. With a bit of a time lag they are very heavy overreactors to economic swings. I should have seen this coming at me—and you—but I didn't.

Okay, so what do you do if you own Amdahl? Hold on. It sells at 35% of book value and 85% of annual sales. Despite its current losses, its balance sheet is quite strong. With time, sales and earnings should rebound. I still think it can earn more than $1 per share in a few years.

None of my readers wrote to chide me on an even bigger blooper. American Maize-Products fell 30% (also cited on February 15). I thought American Maize would be taken over, and it still may be. I thought it would do well if it weren't taken over; it sure hasn't.

This firm's main product line is high-fructose corn syrup, which is heavily dependent on the demand for soft drinks. It has suffered very weak pricing, killing its sales and earnings. Here, too, hang on. Fine firm. Good cash flow. Cheap at 75% of book value, 30% of sales, a P/E of 15 on depressed earnings, and a 4% dividend yield. In the long term it is a play on the growth of Coke and Pepsi. Its second product area, tobacco, is also timely, as I discussed in my October 25 column. Obviously it will take longer than I thought, but American Maize's stock still has big potential.

Having confessed my bloopers, may I point out some of my winners? Despite these two major strikeouts, gains from my winners were big enough that my overall first-quarter average stock pick was up 27% by December 15. The time-weighted average of my first-quarter recommendations was up even more—an impressive 32.5%, easily bearing the S&P 500 or any other stock index. Among those 11 stocks were Amax, which was taken over in November for 24—up 35%; Blount (up 86%); CDI Corp. (up 33%); Comdisco (up 30%); Commercial Metals (up 33%); and M/A-Com (up 100%).

The only one of these that seems cheap enough to me to buy now is Comdisco. I wouldn't necessarily sell the others and pay the capital gains tax—they just seem to me to be fairly priced now and unlikely to do a lot better than the market as a whole. But Comdisco is still a buy. It sells just above book value and at 34% of its annual sales. It is about 9 times my estimate for 1994 earnings. And finally, it sells for 1 times annual depreciation; very few stocks sell that cheaply. The same forces that will come back to aid Amdahl—a pickup in computer sales tied to an economic upturn—will also help here.

Another stock from my first-quarter 1993 list that I still like a lot is Continental Corp. It is up only about 6% since I recommended it and was too cheap by half then. This is a broad-based insurer selling below industry multiples at a time the industry is selling too cheaply. It sells for 72% of book value, 12 times earnings, 30% of annual sales and sports a nice 3.6% dividend yield. I think earnings will double in a few years and the stock will be north of 60.

Ameron is up only 10% since I recommended it, and 1994 should be its year. Earnings should come along nicely in both its major areas: coatings and nonresidential piping.

Its fiberglass piping is the right product at the right time. Its stock hasn't been, and still sells at book value, 32% of annual sales, and 10 times 1994 earnings, with a 3.5% dividend yield. Ameron should earn about $12 million this year but could earn $25 million in a few years. Valued at only $140 million, the stock could easily join Continental at 60.

Since I am in a confessional mood, let me note that, while my first-quarter picks were good on the whole, my second-quarter picks were much less so; I'll address that in a subsequent column. But even with that, a bad quarter and all, overall for the first half I did okay, with a 14% average return and a 22% time-weighted return.

So forgive me my transgressions. They are part of the game. And I try to learn from each, so as not to make the same kind of mistake twice. ∎

Jell-O Versus the Facts
February 14, 1994

Plan for a great year in stocks. In 1993 stock indexes posted 10% to 20% returns. Expect no less now. I am optimistic because I meet so many pessimists these days.

As I travel reviewing accounts or soliciting new ones among institutional investors, I hit a psychological morass that feels like moving 20 pounds of Jell-O with no bowl. They all have the same mildly bearish views, and each time I push bullishly one way, out ooze blobs of pessimism. I sometimes feel these days like the star in a sci-fi nightmare movie titled *Return of the Jell-O Heads.*

And they are just that: blobs. All mushy and slippery.

"Okay, you had a good 1993," one client told me, "but with the upside potential now gone from the market, what are you going to do now?"

The client recited the common wisdom. Valuations are too high. Interest rates must rise from here and inflation, too. Clinton is a disaster. It is too long since we have had a big correction. Too much debt. The recovery is so anemic earnings won't grow

Same Old, Same Old

As much as things change, they stay the same. Here Ken points out an enduring market truth: Investors tend to fret over things that are either old news or don't typically have the market impact they fear. In 1994, investors feared debt or deficits as much as they had the previous year and the year before that (and pretty much all through the history of mankind). Yet the nation's big debt didn't make stocks fall in 1992 or 1993. Why 1994? And why this year? Some fears replay continuously through the years, but that doesn't mean they should suddenly start impacting the market in a way folks think when previously they hadn't.

much. Too much IPO-type speculation—the list goes on and on.

This endless litany of woes is a mixture of things that are either untrue—such as that we have too much debt—or things that may be true but are already fully discounted in stock prices—like the weak recovery.

You could have heard all of them in virtually the same format 12 and 18 months ago. A simple market truism: Old arguments, even correct ones, don't move markets (at least not until they are forgotten, and then they can have real power). Something new must arrive—a surprise or a catalyst, because it is a surprise, and only that, which moves markets.

Here's the countervailing good news: Interest rates fell further than most people expected. The economy nicely exceeded forecasts in the second half. And NAFTA passed.

I know from history that when the tone is biased to pessimism and ignores an expanding economy, surprises tend to be on the positive side and stocks do very well indeed. What surprises? I don't really know or they wouldn't be surprises. Count on them nonetheless. ∎

False Glitter
March 14, 1994

When the Fed raised interest rates on February 4 the stock and bond markets panicked, but the drop has had absolutely no follow-through.

Don't rising rates kill markets? Sure. Eventually. As I have said in the past, it takes a long time—a year—maybe two, or more, plus a lot of other conditions must be met. They haven't been yet. During most of history rising rates have paralleled rising stock prices. Bull markets die with a whimper, not with a bang.

In short, I expect the bull market to continue until 1995 or 1996.

Of course, corrections are normal—short, sharp and scary. Any weakness is a chance to buy, if you aren't flush with stocks. The time to sell will come, but not yet.

What to buy? Anything I have suggested in my columns since last July that isn't up more than 20%. That's a long list. Go back through your old issues of *Forbes*. I have not recommended the smaller regional utilities before, but they seem ripe now. The utility stocks have done terribly since last September in anticipation of rising rates. From top to trough the Dow Jones utility index lost more than 15%. Enough already.

Are you an incurable bear at these prices? If you want things to sell, focus on areas where the complacency quota is highest. Like gold stocks. It's darned near impossible to find anyone who admits publicly to being an outright, full-fledged gold bear. Gold stocks have had a hot run. Let me be the first to say two things: First, sell. Second, I don't think gold has seen its long-term low yet and won't until 1996 or 1997, and that below $300.

To me, gold's rise since last spring is a mere correction in a 15-year-plus bear market that still has far to go. This gold rally is like the fool's traps of 1982 or 1986–87.

Gold demand comes from two sources: speculation and fabrication. The first needs inflation fear to drive it, or a crazy story. I have said many times in recent years, there is no global inflation pressure and won't be for years. Europe's and Japan's cycles, which are now out of whack with ours and lagging badly—with excess capacity—will see to that.

The crazy story is that the Chinese and Indian economies will grow super-fast forever, and the Chinese and Indians will buy up all the gold in sight. It kind of reminds me of the 1980s super-Japanese stories. This is a classic greater-fool theory.

It's supposed to lead to greater future fabrication demand (gold for Chinese jewelry). In the US jewelry demand is rising. It always does, lagging a business upturn. But in Europe and Japan the upturn will take years, and the negative impact will far exceed the Chinese supermen.

Now, let's look at the supply side for gold. The main speculative supply source is Canada, the only government to regularly sell from its gold inventory. The price rise since fall occurred only because Canada held back. That will change.

The big news? Expect gold production capacity to rise sharply and costs to fall this decade—amazingly, to some degree because of the gold bugs. No, not the die-hard gold fans, but a new production technology based on thiobacillus ferro-oxidans, a bacteria that—to shorten a long story—does the costly part of processing while "eating" hard-to-handle ore. The first large-scale plant based on this started last month (Ashanti Goldfields). The bugs are apt to do to gold what Nucor's mini-mills once did to steel. It is low cost and environmentally benign, overcoming the two major obstacles to supply increases.

More bearish signs: Gold sells well above production costs—most commodities don't. The shares are nicely above last summer's peak prices, while gold's can't get back close to August's $420—in terms of trading, that's bearish; they should cross back. Gold is like a rocket that lost its last thruster. Relative to other commodities and their vendors, gold shares are at historical record-high valuations.

For commodities or shares in firms vending them, your best bet for the next few years is where commodity prices are below production costs and likely to rise as supply contracts: aluminum, cattle, cocoa, cotton, oil, sugar—or zinc and lead.

P.S.—a final confirming note: There has been recent heavy insider buying among utility shares and insider selling; in gold shares. ∎

Fessing Up
April 11, 1994

Reader Edward Davidson from Tucson writes nicely, but firmly, and twice, that I do too little to review prior picks from old issues. Guilty. My first priority has been and will remain to show you what to do right here, right now. Then, too, after 135 columns spanning ten years, with more than five stocks per column, I often boggle at just where to start stabbing at the past in terms of updates. Still, Davidson makes a good point.

In my January 17, 1994 column I did review my first-quarter 1993 picks. But readers like Oregon's Robert Antic and Virginia's Albert Hobbs wrote asking why I hadn't fessed up to Tiphook, one of my worst disasters ever, which was in last year's second quarter and bombed from 12 to 2.

Well, the answer is I haven't yet gotten to reviewing my second-quarter 1993 picks. But since at least two of my readers were burned in Tiphook, here goes.

I am very sorry I ever recommended it. It's an English ADR from my June 7, 1993 column. It was Europe's dominant container-leasing firm and got clocked by the economic slump there, which hasn't improved. Its debt spiraled, and Tiphook is now clearly on the verge of bankruptcy—and selling its best lines to Transamerica at fire sale prices. I continually underestimated how tough the turnaround would be and how slowly the economy would rebound. Call a loss a loss. This is the right time of year to sell, as tax-loss pressure will build on this one toward year-end.

The interest in Tiphook surprised me because I had an even worse mistake in 1991 (September 30), yet it seems like nobody ever noticed it. Gitano was in the same place on the page with the same linage that Tiphook got. I recommended it at 19 and it was just taken over at 1. Ugh. Why the follow-up interest in Tiphook but not Gitano? Beats me.

Understand please, I cannot in every column follow up on all my previous recommendations. But if you want me to update you on any of them, write to me care of *Forbes*. I will read it and at least reply to you, although perhaps briefly. Depending on other reader interest and demands on the column space, I may be able to do the update when you want.

Or, if you want to just write to tell me I'm dumb as dirt and twice as testy, that, too, is okay by me. Putting out my neck as often as I do and as publicly, I expect a certain amount of punishment. At least regular readers know that far more of my picks have worked out than haven't. ∎

The 7% Rule
May 9, 1994

Buy now. After the February and March stock market decline, plenty of pundits are bearish, including several fellow columnists. Count me among the bulls. This is the safest time to buy stocks since late 1990.

Bear? Or Correction?

Investors tend to confuse bear markets and corrections to their detriment. A bear market is an extended period of sustained market losses, usually over 20 percent. It is slow and agonizing. A correction is almost the opposite. It's short, sharp, and scary as hell—lasting a few weeks to even a few months—and can drop as much as 20 percent. Lots of investors feel the sharpness of a correction and wrongly assume it's a bear and sell at a relative low, only to watch stocks rebound and continue surging in the ongoing bull market. Major mistake. The 7% rule is aimed more at keeping investors in the market and not hitting the panic button far too soon.

Longtime readers know I have been unabashedly bullish since my December 24, 1990 "Buy Now" column. I have also often said to expect largely unpredictable, short, sharp corrections coming anytime, from anywhere, leading to later higher prices. We just had such a jolt. Take advantage of it while you can.

The broad big-cap indexes peaked on February 2—smaller cap indexes on March 18. By March 31 they were all down 7% to 8% before dividends.

It's an old saw but true. Bull markets die with a whimper, not with a bang. A plunge off a broad peak such as we just had is scary, but it's the way corrections act, not how bear markets usually begin—time to buy, not sell. That leads to my 7% rule. Buy whenever stock indexes fall 7% or more in just two calendar months.

Consider the last 20 years. Using my 7% rule on the Dow industrials, S&P 500, Nasdaq and NYSE composites—I find among them 84 instances of two-month 7% drops. In the next three months the indexes rose about 70% of the time. Nothing earthshaking. But after 12 months, the indexes were up 78 of the 84 times

(93%). Sometime between 3 and 12 months later a two-month 7% drop was followed by higher prices in an overwhelming 82 of the 84 occurrences.

My favorite index of the four cited is the NYSE Composite, because it's broad and better built than, say, the Dow industrials. In 21 two-month 7% drops, it failed only once to generate gains 12 months later. The median price gain in 12 months was an incredible 22.4%. (Numbers in this column are without dividends, to focus on price changes—total returns are higher than numbers cited.)

The data also show my 7% rule is even more consistent on value stocks than growth stocks.

My forecast remains intact: A bull market until 1995 or 1996. We just had the long-awaited correction—a big enough one to indicate higher prices 3 to 12 months out—consistently so among the nongrowth stock, value sector. ∎

Fashion Report
June 6, 1994

The recent market correction offers a great chance to buy heavily capitalized value stocks—stocks of big companies selling at low multiples of sales, earnings and book value, and at high dividend yields. Recommending this group is a switch for me. For the last three years I have said the best values were in small-cap value stocks, which have led the market since early 1992. There is still opportunity there. But for the remainder of this bull market we may see market leadership change to the big-capitalization value stocks—laggards, relatively speaking, since 1987.

Each quarter my firm does a computer run that slices the investment universe into three segments: the 250 stocks with the greatest market capitalization (currently $3.5 billion and up); the next 750 mid-cap stocks (down to $650 million); and the next 1,500 small-cap stocks (market caps of $650 million to $90 million). We then break each of these three segments into two groups: cheap value stocks and pricier growth stocks. This exercise thus creates six groups, each of which we look at as a market style—small-cap value, say, or big-cap growth. We then calculate the total dollar value of each style as a percent of the whole stock market. The result, which we call a group's "market share," represents how fashionable each style is.

This is a good tool for contrarians. We have run these market shares back 20 years. When a style has a very low market share compared with its historical average share it always catches up, kind of the way long and short skirts go out of style but eventually become fashionable again.

Three years ago, among the six groups the small-cap value stocks had the lowest market share relative to their history. The group has since caught up. Now the big-cap value group has the lowest market share. The big institutions haven't allocated funds to this sector for years. Yet as my fellow *Forbes* columnist David Dreman has pointed out many times, the companies in this group have a lot going for them—good dividend yields, earnings leverage from an improving US economy, additional leverage from recovery in Europe.

I'm not suggesting that you get rid of your small-cap value stocks, just that you should now begin to add big-cap value stocks to your portfolio. ∎

A Bullish Spread

July 4, 1994

A big reason I'm bullish and see the recent stock market drop as a correction, not the start of a bear market, is the yield curve spread. That is the spread between 20-year Treasury bond rates and 90-day T bill rates. Bear markets prefer flat yield curves; rarely has the bear reigned when long-term rates were more than 1% above short-term rates. Right now the spread is big—300 basis points—three full percentage points.

Here's why a steep yield curve is good for stocks: With long-term interest rates much higher than short-term rates, banks become eager to lend. They can make fat profits borrowing short and lending long term. Rising rates don't choke booms so long as long rates and short rates both rise and the spread between them stays wide. Take 1929. In 1928 short rates rose above long rates—staying so for two years—making bank lending unprofitable and serving as an early warning of 1929's pain. Spreads have always been a good guide.

Haven't there been exceptions—times when stocks crashed even though the yield curve was steep? Sure, but they were exceptional periods. For example, Hitler's rise and then World War II bombed the dickens out of stocks, even though yield curve spreads stayed bullish. So if World War III is ahead, or if the Martians are about to land, all bets are off. Otherwise, make some money. Buy some stocks. ∎

What's in a Name? Too Much.

August 1, 1994

Many years ago ago my good friend Monte Stern gave me a plaque with a John Shedd quote. I keep it by my desk and see it now, as I write. It says: "Opportunities are seldom labeled."

So I learned to seek out unlabels: stocks whose names are simply initials that tell you nothing. The stock market always pays up for visibleness. Sort of like a name-brand drug versus the equal but cheaper generic. Why pay the premium? "Initials" stocks are often overlooked, creating great value.

Here are some stocks whose names are mere initials, meaningless to all but those who already know about the company. All are great buys. Now.

CPI Corp. does not produce inflation. Instead, think color photofinishing and color portraits. It runs almost 1,000 Sears portrait studios and 700 processing laboratories. Its P/E is 22 but earnings are depressed. Down from 34 in 1990 and at 50% of annual sales, 40% above book value and with a 3.3% dividend yield, CPI is very cheap. Earnings plus depreciation total an amazingly high 20% of its $250 million market cap (i.e., a 20% cash flow yield), I expect CPI stock to hit 30 by 1996.

QMS, Inc. was a hot growth stock in 1987, selling at twice its annual revenue. Now it's at 28% of revenue. It makes products to enhance computer printers. Since 1987 its revenues have grown about 15% annually and the stock has fallen. It is down from 26 in 1991. At book value, with well-positioned products, great cash flow and a strong balance sheet, this dog will have its day.

PHH Corp. is the big gorilla in corporate auto fleet leasing and relocation services. Great firm. Known it for years. Grows moderately but steadily. Great value, too. A P/E of 9, just over book value, 27% of annual revenue. PHH has lots of debt, but its non-earning cash flow—principally deprecia-tion—will carry it. It sells for less than one times cash flow.

In my March 14 column I said utility prices would rise. Bad timing. But I still expect good things. You can construct a nice utility portfolio that is cheap and has above-average yield, and all based on nothing but initials. Try BCE Inc.; DPL Inc.; DQE; FPL Group; IES Industries; MCN Corp.; MDU Resources; NUI Corp.; SCEcorp; TNP Enterprises; UGI Corp.; WPL Holdings; and the CIPSCO and NIPSCO twins.

On the bigger-cap side you have stocks like MBIA Inc., which stands for Municipal Bond Investors Assurance Corp. Believe it or not, it actually gets paid to provide insurance for the payments on muni bonds, the history of which is almost flaw-less. Investors have made good money within a few years whenever it has sold for 10 times earnings or less, like now at a P/E of 9 and 1.5 times book value.

Or IBP, Inc., the world's largest beef and pork processor. Bloody business, but the company, is simply the biggest and best at it. Growth is moderate and steady and valuations are always low: a P/E of 15, 2 times book value, and 12% of annual sales.

Or AFLAC Inc., the largest insur-ance underwriter of medical benefits for cancer—a big and growing market. But it doesn't sell like a growth stock; it's just 1.8 times book value with a P/E of 13.

WPP Group is an English over-the-counter ADR. It's also the world's largest marketing services firm, with quality gross billings of almost $10 billion. The initials hide class names like J. Walter Thompson, Ogilvy & Mather, Hill & Knowlton and much more all over the world. As overseas economies continue their infant recovery, WPP's profits should, too. It now sells at 15 times earnings, 45% of annual revenue and at book value.

TJX Cos. is retailer TJ Maxx, plus a bunch of specialty retailing chains that col-lectively used to be Zayre. The balance sheet is clean, earnings are rising, and you should make money in the next two years. It sells at 12 times this year's earnings, 38% of annual sales and 2.8 times book value. You get 2.8% back in dividend yield.

PS Group isn't for faint hearts. High risk, maybe high reward. I almost hesitate to mention it. But it's a fascinating specu-lation—perhaps the most leveraged way to profit if the airlines ever recover. It's a leading airplane leaser, often to marginal airlines. Running just about break-even now, I think its depreciation is sufficient to carry its debts, even if business turns down again. PS is off from 72 in 1991, or 86%. It sells at a tiny market capitaliza-tion of just $60 million—also 45% of book value and 42% of annual sales. I hope for some recovery, future dividends and a stock price over 30, where it sold steadily from 1982 to 1992. It's some comfort that Warren Buffett now owns 20%—its largest shareholder. ■

Avoiding Whiplash
August 29, 1994

No one sets out deliberately to buy a stock or a mutual fund group at the top and panic-sell at the bottom, but it happens all the time. You know the stocks are high, but you can't miss out on the excitement. You know the stock is cheap, but you've lost money on it and you are just sick of it, so you dump at the bottom.

Market whiplash. You bought bio-tech when it was hot, then sold out this year in disgust. Costly mistake.

The smart players avoid whiplash. They know they can't time markets. They know, too, that no one style of investing pays off all the time. So they spread their bets by style of stock, go for good long-term returns and to hell with volatility.

They spread their bets over a variety of investment styles. This means having a chunk of capital in small stocks and a chunk in big stocks. It means diversifying those two groups further into half growth and half value stocks. And it means owning some foreign stocks. This isn't the path to instant riches, because when one group shines, another will hold you back; but it's the path to steady growth. It's a sure way to avoid whiplash.

This requires owning lots of stocks, but individual investors can get virtually the same whiplash-proofing by using mutual funds.

Realize that each fund has its own style whether it means to or not. The key is to balance styles against each other. As a rule that is right 95% of the time, if big growth stocks are the market's hottest area for a few quarters, small value will have been the worst area. And vice versa. Ditto for big-cap value and small-cap growth. If one leads, the other lags.

Say you saw the article in the July 18 *Forbes* on Kent Simons and Lawrence Marx, who run Neuberger & Berman's successful Selected Sectors Fund. You liked their philosophy and background. You buy the fund for your 401(k). Good choice. But remember: Marx and Simons go for big value stocks, and they won't always lead the market.

Next step: Hedge your bet by putting some money in a good small-cap growth fund to pair against Simons and Marx's predilection for big value stocks. It's unlikely the two funds will do equally well at any one time, but it is also unlikely you'll be left behind when the market changes gears.

One fund that would make a good match with Selected Sectors is Fidelity's Select Biotechnology. The latter is a splendid fund that has lagged for several years as biotech stocks went out of favor. Buying Fidelity Biotech is a way of betting that favor will smile again on this kind of stock—which it certainly will. But you might prefer a small-stock fund that invests over a wider spectrum.

Where do you get this information? *Forbes* Annual Mutual Funds Survey and Morningstar can be a big help. Morningstar's in-depth style analysis is the cat's meow: accurate, updated and easy to use.

Forbes is tops for making down- market behavior friendly to fathom. I would buy no fund that rated lower than "C" in a down market, no matter how good it was in an up market.

For those who don't want to spend hours poring through *Forbes* and Morningstar, here's an easier way to whiplash-proof your portfolio: Pick a big fund family with funds of varying styles. Most load families let you switch among their funds load-free. Spread 80% of your equity money equally four ways in the family's funds: one pan in its big value fund, one big growth, one small growth and one small value—four funds, 20% each. Put another 20% into its foreign fund. Instant, cheap and relatively painless diversification.

For those who would like a more active and sophisticated variation and profit from most folks' tendency to whiplash themselves, you can do this: Check which of those five funds had the highest return in the last five years; pare that one back from 20% to 8%—and spread that 12% you took from it equally among the others. You now have four funds with 23% and one at 8%. Next year do it again—and every year—always setting the fund with the best five-year record at 8% of your portfolio. Four funds with 23% and one with 8%.

Why cut the winners? Simple experience. Market leadership rotates, which is why some people get whiplashed. If a group of stocks has been a winner for five years, it is almost certain to lag in the next five years. It's about to become the place not to be.

Based on my analysis (and paralleled by a similar Morningstar study), this approach would have done about 4% per year better on average over the last 20 years than simply being fully diversified in funds. And it would beat any single style in total return. ■

Three's the Charm
September 26, 1994

Expect President Clinton to do great things for stocks in 1995. Am I kidding? Nope.

My studies show that it is near impossible to find a third year of a President's term that is stock market bearish—they tend to gangbuster.

When investors think of presidential election cycles, they tend to think of the fourth year as when the President "guns" things to promote his reelection. But the third year is the best year for stocks. The first really good stock market data starts in the 1920s. Since "cool" Cal Coolidge we have had 17 presidential terms. Except for the Depression, when every year was a bust, the third presidential year has only seen one decline in the S&P 500—in 1939 and then less than one-half of 1%. Since 1939, not once.

On average the S&P 500 has gained 18.6% in third years. The smaller half of stocks on the NYSE did even better—up 25.6%. We have merely three months until Clinton's third year.

This is not a political column. I don't like Clinton and think his policy prescriptions are almost all bad. But Presidents, whatever their stripes, tend not to make or break stock markets.

So far as third presidential years go, Democrats are better for stock markets than Republicans. The Democrats' third year S&P 500 gain averages 21%, versus 16.4% for Republicans. All this bodes well for the stock market in 1995—if not for the country in the long run.

Warning: September and October of a President's second year often see falling prices leading to an above-average third year. If so now, it's a double buying opportunity.

Why are third years so strong? I don't know. My guess is that midterm elections cause all of the mess you see right now. In second years, incumbents of the President's party usually distance themselves from him. Those of the opposition bash him. And all challengers bash everyone and everything. The President bashes back. You can't find anybody to say a good word about anyone. All the babble bashing

> ## Bad Politicians, Great Stocks
>
> In Ken's view, far too many people are blinded by their ideologies. If they dislike a president, they think he must be bad for stocks. Ken has, interestingly, at varying times been accused of being a strong Republican, and at other times a strong Democrat. He's neither—adamantly so. In actuality, his favorite president, hands down, is Millard Fillmore. Figure that out, and you'll understand Ken's personal ideology.
>
> And, as Ken likes to say, fortunately bad politicians don't mean bear markets.

weakens faith in our institutions and with that often comes stock market corrections.

But by the third year we kind of tire of all that. Politicians make less noise because they needn't run again soon. We get back to Main Street, which looks pretty good about then. In 1995 this should be even more true. The Republicans will gain enough House and Senate seats in November to ensure a healthy gridlock. Congress won't be doing much so it won't do much damage.

Whatever the mess in Washington, Main Street is booming and the boom is still young, while inflation is nowhere to be seen. We had a nice correction in stocks this year. Little noted: Insider buying is at big bullish levels. And investor sentiment is glum, which is good.

Buy some stocks. Make some money. ■

Be a Buyer, Not a Seller
October 17, 1994

Can you get really rich playing the stock market? The answer is, no.

The most exceptional stock market operators have generated multi-decade annual returns in the 15%-to-25% range. In theory this kind of return could land you on the *Forbes* 400. If you start with $40,000, need not pay any taxes and compound at 25% per year for 40 years, you get to $300 million. But I never heard of anyone pulling that off. For one thing, you do pay taxes on both income and capital; gains that would severely handicap even so impressive a showing.

George Soros? Michael Steinhardt? Richard Rainwater? Didn't they get on the *Forbes* 400 via stocks? They didn't get there just by investing. Their first few tens of millions were via percentage-of-profits contracts on huge hedge funds—managing money. I am not taking anything away from them—better men than I, but remember: They didn't get as rich as they did just by investing their own money.

Warren Buffett also did more than just buy and sell stocks. His career has been analyzed by Robert G. Hagstrom Jr. in a hot-off-the-press authorized Buffett book, *The Warren Buffett Way* (John Wiley & Sons).

I was asked to critique a late draft because it has a fair amount about my father, Philip Fisher, and his impact on Buffett—an influence to which Buffett paid tribute in the *Forbes* of October 19, 1987. To me this Buffett book is simply the most important new stock book of the 1990s, to date. Buy it and read it. But when you do you will understand that Buffett was a lot more than just a money manager. You will also learn a lot about the art of investing and business in general.

As the book shows, Ben Graham taught value, whereas my father preached quality. That is, Graham taught that any stock is a bargain if it is cheap enough, while Phil Fisher believes in identifying exceptional management and investing in it. Buffett merged both approaches as no one ever has. As (*Forbes* editor) Jim Michaels said in last year's *Forbes* 400, Buffett seems increasingly to lean toward my father's views. A noted buyer, not a noted seller, Buffett has bought few stocks and sells virtually never—straight Phil Fisher, as opposed to Graham, who argued that you should sell if you couldn't find 30 cheap-enough stocks because the market wasn't cheap enough.

If you conclude from this that the secret to getting rich in the stock market is to pick a few great stocks and stay with them a la Phil Fisher or Warren Buffett, think again. Concentrating on just a few stocks is easy. It is also an easy way to get nowhere, because it works only on the unlikely chance that you have an uncanny knack for picking real winners. It can equally well produce subaverage results or even disaster.

So, unless you are good enough to attract lots of investment partners, as Soros is, or unless you have a highly developed and rare ability to identify long-term winners, forget about getting rich in the stock market.

Should you, therefore, give up on stocks? No. Because if you have some money and want to protect it from inflation and get a reasonable return above inflation, stocks are perfect. They won't put you on the *Forbes* 400, but if you are already there a diversified portfolio can keep you there. If your means are more modest, a portfolio of stocks can help ensure you a comfortable retirement and even leave something over for your next generation.

Which gets me to another principle on which my father and Warren Buffett would agree: Stay fully invested in good stocks and don't try to time the market. ∎

The Babson Four-Step
October 24, 1994

Sadly, the National Bureau of Economic Research buried some of the best forecasting logic ever. Since 1921 basically all NBER research has been aimed at issues and indicators of a rising versus a falling economy. Everyone else has forever followed the NBERs lead. Wrong turn.

You can fathom economics and markets far better if, instead of thinking rising and falling, you think of four phases. As the century dawned, Roger W. Babson, my alltime favorite forecaster, devised his four-phase system, which the NBER later obliterated. His was a more sophisticated concept and a better one.

To sum it up quickly, the Babson method says: A given economic indicator can be viewed in four different ways, depending upon whether it occurs in a period of 1) overexpansion; 2) decline following a period of overexpansion; 3) steep recession; or 4) improvement following a recession,

Phenomena mean various things at various times. Something bullish right after a recession—like rising prices— can be bearish in an overexpansion. Sometimes expanding business makes interest rates rise—sometimes not. And sometimes rising interest rates kill bull markets, and sometimes not.

For example, after the economy bottomed in 1991 came a surge in initial public offerings. Many folks saw that as excess speculation, leading to a bear market. But no, as Babson wrote, after a recession, before we reach overexpansion, there should be a big boost in IPOs; if not, he knew the expansion would peter out. I think we are currently in a Babson Phase 4—improvement following a recession— have been for three years.

It is the period of overexpansion— Phase 1—that starts the danger for stocks. And we won't see it until we see rising inflation, as opposed to anticipatory fear of it; this plus industry operating close to full capacity and starting to add new plant. Not yet.

Babson looked like Colonel Sanders of Kentucky Fried Chicken fame and was more than a bit eccentric. Doctors prescribed fresh air, as Babson had suffered from tuberculosis since his youth, so he made his employees work during Boston winters with the windows open, bundled in overcoats and mittens.

Including periodicals, his name spans three full drawers in the Library of Congress card catalog. His best stuff? The many books he wrote with the words "business barometers" in the titles. If you find one, read it. While not a witty writer, he thought well—until he got old and cranky. His original firm became the core for what is now Standard & Poor's.

It would take too long here to detail all the ways markets look different by Babson's approach. And I would never sound-bite him. But you are ahead just knowing the economy moves in four phases, not just up and down.

My reading of Babson is that until we reach signs of overexpansion, stocks are fairly safe. ■

A Reading List for Serious Investors
November 21, 1994

Want to get some good investment books tor Christmas instead of yet another designer necktie? Try this: Scribble "Ooh" on this column, and leave it over the next week conspicuously displayed in a few carefully picked places, like your family's kitchen. Maybe you will find under the Christmas tree the very best new investment books. Or, if you are the impatient type, you can go out and buy them for yourself. Each year I browse for brand-new copyrights, picking the best for you. I found more new releases in 1994 than usual, and many of them were terrible. A few, truly great. Here are my picks:

The Warren Buffett Way by Robert G. Hagstrom Jr. (Wiley) is, as I said once before, simply the most important new stock book of the 1990s, to date. If you think you know all about Warren Buffett, you have a lot to learn from this book. I can't say enough good things about it, so I won't say much more than "read it." Peter Lynch did a great foreword, and it alone is worth the $24.95.

Jeremy J. Siegel's *Stocks for the Long Run* (Irwin Professional). He is a Wharton professor, which to me puts two strikes against him, but he has written a simply great book. He will convince you that bonds are riskier than stocks, teach you history you won't get elsewhere and throw new light on topics like diversification, value, style and economics—without being at all dry.

James P. O'Shaughnessy's *Invest Like the Best* (McGraw-Hill) is awesome if you aren't scared of computers. It comes with a companion disk of a stock-screening database. Load up, read the book and learn to closely mimic almost any pro you admire. He shows you the simple truth: Most of any money manager's results come from style biases—factors he builds into his portfolio, knowingly or not. O'Shaughnessy shows how these can be analyzed, replicated and how you can piggyback almost any manager. It's a workbook and takes time, but you learn lots.

Douglas J. Donnelly's *The Money Monarchs* (Business One Irwin). He analyzes the styles of ten leading money managers, showing what makes one zig this way while another one zags that way. Yes, I'm one of the ten analyzed, but, so help me, this isn't why I recommend the book. It's just good. If you hire money managers, own mutual funds or pick your own stocks—amateur or serious pro—you will learn lots as this fine book compares and contrasts different methods to skin the same old cat.

Jake Bernstein's *Market Masters* (Dearborn) is similar, with a twist. It interviews and analyzes eight great traders, as opposed to stock-pickers. If you decide when to buy or sell, you are trading and will benefit from these market masters' wisdom.

John C. Bogle's *Bogle on Mutual Funds* (Richard D. Irwin) is one-half of what you need in terms of books on mutual funds. The book bills itself as being to funds what Ben Graham's 1949 classic, *The Intelligent Investor,* was to stocks. Well, no, but it's still pretty darned good. Bogle, chairman of the giant Vanguard mutual fund family, teaches you how to pick funds and why buying a hot history is costly, all without being self-promotional. He exposes how much of what the fund industry does helps it, not you. There simply is no better book on funds anywhere. It will be definitive for years.

Norman G. Fosback's *Mutual Fund Buyer's Guide* (Probus) is another good fund manual. Punchy, to the point, concise and contemporary, it's more than a buyer's guide because it loads you up on techniques, trading systems and tactics—all in a very few pages—plus lots of data. Combine Bogle, Fosback and *Forbes'* Annual Mutual Fund Survey and you have every tool you ever need to succeed in mutual funds.

And here's one old and formerly out-of-print classic that has been formative to great investors for decades. If you haven't read it yet, hasten to do so: *Reminiscences of a Stock Operator* by Edwin Lefevre, first published in 1923. This year it was finally reissued, with a great new foreword by futures writer Jack Schwager—as the forerunner to a new classic series by John Wiley & Sons. ∎

Inflationary Ghosts
December 19, 1994

Inflation fears have spooked the markets. Are these fears justified? No. Most folks expect inflation because everyone else thinks it's coming. Crowd-think is almost always wrong.

The inflationists point to booming commodities, but without money creation, these booms bust fast. Just noise. Commodities always bounce. That isn't inflation, which comes from loose money, nothing else.

But isn't the money supply loose now, very loose? People who think so cite booming bank reserves, which they think must lead to increasing bank loans (the definition of money creation), leading to inflation.

As Albert Einstein said, "In the middle of every difficulty lies opportunity." Few folks know it but history blasts today's conventional monetary wisdom. Historically, when the monetary base has exploded, the quantity of money (M1, M2, M3—your pick) actually started falling while the monetary base was still rising. It has done so consistently in recent decades—a counterintuitive head fake that is quite anti-inflationary.

How can the monetary base bulge and money not? Because of human nature. Bankers panic, too, lending less readily than anyone would normally expect, afraid of the eroded future value of repayments. En route, normal operating cash flow builds reserves rapidly, but loans don't grow much, so money creation idles.

Read Milton Friedman and Anna Schwartz in their classic, *A Monetary History of the United States.* As they explained, the ratio of money to the monetary base varies over time, tied to bankers' changing liquidity preferences. The quantity of money, not the monetary base, leads to inflation. The quantity of money has been flat for years. M1, M2 and M3 actually fell this year. Aside from a few (but far from most) commodities that are rising, and that aren't very vital to overall price levels, most prices are behaving very well. Inflation is dead, but its ghostly vision terrorizes 1994's markets.

I expect a very big 1995. The fears will fade and investors will concentrate on the values available in the market today. ∎

1995

List After Bullish List

"
Avoiding stocks just because the market isn't cheap is a dumb idea . . .
The market rises just as often when it is 'not cheap' as when it is. This
may seem counterintuitive but it's not. There's a lot of ground between
'not cheap' and 'overpriced.'"

"Compared With What?" February 13, 1995

"
Hot new gurus aren't as good as the old gurus; the old ones got all
the wisdom first. If you must have a guru, pick one who already has
made mistakes and shown grace in making them. Otherwise, you are
most apt to need to pick another one soon. "

"Warren Buffett Versus the Beardstown Ladies," June 5, 1995

The title of Ken's first 1995 column summed up his outlook for the year—"A Year of the Bull" (January 16, 1995). He said, "I expect stocks to shock almost everyone in 1995 with a 20% to 40% rise." And shock most people it did. The Dow, flawed index that it is, crossed both the 4,000 and 5,000 marks in 1995.[1] The S&P 500 returned 37.6 percent—its best year since 1958.[2] And as Ken forecast the year before, US stocks led the charge, more than doubling the return on foreign shares.

In "A Year of the Bull," Ken offered up a laundry list of reasons to be bullish about stocks. In fact, he offered up quite a few lists throughout 1995. Appropriately, here's a list of those 1995 lists.

First, Ken's reasons to be bullish in 1995:

- "Too much pessimism. Forecasters are mostly bearish, and so are nine out of ten investors I talk to."
- "The yield curve is nicely upward sloping (long-term interest rates are well above short-term interest rates)."
- "Inflation remains low. Our current economic expansion has been moderate, which should help it to be long lived. Europe is now expanding after a long recession and a wicked market decline in 1994."
- "Bill Clinton is a lame duck. Congress is Republican."

- "Heavy net insider buying."
- "Valuations are the most moderate they have been since 1990."
- "And 1994 [was a bad year]."

The only way to gain an advantage over other investors and thus the market is to see things differently than others. It's not that other investors are always wrong. It's just that widely discussed information has no market-moving power, even if it's right. So Ken explained his "four basic tenets of contrarianism" in his March 13 column, "Advanced Fad Avoidance."

- "If most folks you know agree with you on a price move or some event's impact, don't take this as a confirmation that you are right. It is a warning; you are wrong. Being right requires aloneness, and willingness to let others see you as maybe nuts."
- "If you read or hear about some investment idea or significant event more than once in the media, it won't work. By the time several commentators have thought and written about it, even new news is too old."
- "The older the argument is, the less power it has. So, for example, inflation fears may have moved the markets in 1994, but sometime early in 1995 that view will run out of steam."
- "Any category of security that was hot in the last five years won't be in the next five, and vice versa."

Most investors shouldn't time the market, especially the small moves. The risks of missing out on a rising market usually far outweigh the benefits of avoiding a downturn. Avoiding even parts of bear markets requires a lot of skill, a healthy dose of discipline, and a dash of luck. For those inclined to try to avoid bears, Ken provided a few tips in his April 24 column, "How to Tell a Bull From a Bear."

- "Don't sell on corrections so long as you think the long bull market trend is intact; it doesn't pay. In a 5%-to-10% kind of drop, transaction costs eat up too much of the potential decline to make the effort worthwhile."
- "Don't turn bearish just because others have. Successful bearishness really does require being virtually alone."
- "To win as a bear, you must see things that aren't widely publicized. If you simply ignore the babble, important issues become more obvious. It's surprise that moves stock markets."
- "Never stay bearish longer than 18 months. 12 months in any but the most extreme situations . . . If you hit it right, and prices do fall, force yourself back in after a year. You may not hit the bottom, but will have missed plenty of the drop and won't miss the next bull rise."

Ken's columns and career have been greatly influenced by the work of others. In "Warren Buffet Versus the Beardstown Ladies" (June 5, 1995), Ken provides a few of his favorite investing quotes.

- "The first rule is not to lose. The second rule is not to forget the first rule." — Warren Buffett

- "If you don't know who you are, the stock market is an expensive place to find out." — George Goodman
- "Successful investing is anticipating the successful anticipations of others." — John Keynes
- "Wall Street's graveyards are filled with men who were right too soon." — William Hamilton
- "All you need is look over the earnings forecasts publicly made a year ago to see how much care you need to give to those being made now for the next year." — Gerald M. Loeb
- "A gold mine is a hole in the ground with a liar on top." — Mark Twain
- "Spend at least as much time researching a stock as you would choosing a refrigerator." — Peter Lynch

Though Ken expected the bull market to continue, his October 23 column, "Countdown to a Top," lists a number of risks with the potential to derail the bull:

- "The presidential campaign could turn ugly and the market may discount that unpleasantness."
- "Clinton must reappoint Alan Greenspan as head of the Fed or offer up a substitute. Either way you get uncertainty."
- "If reappointed, I think [Greenspan's] fangs may fast appear. He likes to bite."
- "And by late 1996 this economic expansion should get old and tired, and may fatigue itself into a rollover."

Even if a bear market isn't right around the corner, it's always a good idea to have a strategy ready for a bear market's eventual arrival. Next, a short list of things an investment manager can do to get defensive from "Bear Proofing your Portfolio" (August 28, 1995):

- "Buy bigger and less volatile stocks"
- "Raise cash"
- "Buy puts"
- "All of the above"

Lastly, Ken candidly expressed his desire to someday be *Forbes'* longest running columnist. "My goal? To be number one. To be still writing this column when the issue of August 30, 2016 comes out." ("Rummaging the Attic," December 18, 1995.) To do it, Ken would need to do the following:

- "Make big calls so I impact your investment performance"
- "Reverse course quickly when I'm wrong"
- "Fess up when I'm wrong"

Amen.

A Year of the Bull
January 16, 1995

This year will be a good year in the stock market.

With a few notable exceptions, a bad year has led to a good one—and 1994 was a bad year.

Measuring the market by the S&P 500 over the 69 years since 1925, there were only three periods when it didn't pay to buy after a bad calendar year. The exceptions were the four Great Depression years, the three years leading to World War II, and 1974, when a bad 1973 led to a horrible 1974.

So, for 61 of the 69 years, my pattern held: bad year followed by good year.

The cases in point overwhelm. On average these single year drops led to a year rising 24.2%. As John Templeton is famous for saying, the four most dangerous words in the English language: It's different this time. It's probably not different this time, so 1995 is likely to be good for investors.

Granted, I was too bullish in 1994. But while 1994 was bad, it wasn't that abnormal. Of the 18 years in which we have had midterm elections since 1925, the median return was positive—6.6% per year. But the market fell 8 of those 18 times, or 44% of the time. So 1994's odds weren't great.

Also going for the market in 1995: As detailed in my September 26, 1994 column, the year after a midterm election is almost always good, with gains averaging 18.6% since 1925 and only down twice—1953 and a sub-1% drop in 1939.

I expect stocks to shock almost everyone in 1995 with a 20% to 40% rise. Let me list my reasons.

- Too much pessimism. Forecasters are mostly bearish, and so are nine out of ten investors I talk to.
- The yield curve is nicely upward-sloping (long-term interest rates are well above short-term rates).
- Inflation remains low. Our current economic expansion has been moderate, which should help it to be long-lived. Europe is now expanding after a long recession and a wicked market decline in 1994.
- Bill Clinton is a lame duck. Congress is Republican.
- Heavy net insider buying.
- Valuations are the most moderate they have been since 1990.
- And 1994. ■

Compared With What?
February 13, 1995

"Stocks ain't cheap and you're not old enough to remember when they were." Thus did one old-timer dismiss my new year's impudence for suggesting 1995 should be an above-average year for stocks.

But I am old enough to remember other markets, other times. Not only old enough to

recall when stocks were truly cheap, but also old enough to know that avoiding stocks just because the market isn't cheap is a dumb idea. My 23 years in the investment business have taught me this: The market rises just as often when it is "not cheap" as when it is.

This may seem counterintuitive, but it is not. There is a lot of ground between "not cheap" and "overpriced." We are on that ground right now, with lots of room to go before stocks are "overpriced."

Think of stock prices over time as a bell curve and ask, "Where are valuations now, compared with the past?" Sometimes stocks become much too cheap or highly priced, but usually prices dance around the bell curve's bulge, not way out on either end.

Where are we now? Valuations are above average but not way out on the right side of the bell. By my count we are in the middle of the right half of the bulge, about "one standard deviation above the mean average."

How do I figure this? By applying a number of familiar yardsticks.

Measured by dividend yield we *are* out on the high-priced end of the bell curve,

So, too, on the basis of price-to-book value, which, linked to decades of above-average inflation, has lost much of its traditional usefulness for judging the overall market. But by price/earnings ratios we are not. The 250 biggest stocks' median P/E is 16.2—only a bit above the historical average. Ditto for price-to-cash-flow at 7.1 and price-to-sales at 1.1.

Averaged equally (giving a 20% weighting for each of the five above mentioned yardsticks), we are well within the bulge of the bell curve and a good way away from the far right.

Stocks not cheap? I predicted last month that stocks should rise 20% to 40% in 1995. I still do. Don't be frightened out of this bull market by meaningless babble about "not cheap." ∎

Advanced Fad Avoidance
March 13, 1995

"Will the Fed's recent rate hike finally break the market's back?" A perfectly reasonable question, which I heard during a recent Canadian speaking tour. What's wrong with the question is how often I heard it: over and over again.

I was giving talks to several audiences a day, organized by the Canadian retail broker Midland-Walwyn, on a tour that started in Halifax, and ended in Vancouver. What startled me was how much the questions were the same from one city to the next.

The investors who attended these sessions were intelligent and at least a little versed in the market, since they had money in the Canadian equivalent of an IRA. But there was so little variation in what was on their minds: the peso, Canada's "debt crisis," the US versus Canadian dollar, Orange County, Clinton versus Congress, the

financial impact of the Kobe earthquake—all the stuff of page one and talking-head shows. None of it was terribly original or unique as would be needed to surprise a market. Surprise is the only thing that moves markets.

This should be good news to anyone who likes to bet against prevailing trends. Sometimes I worry that there many people trying to be contrarian that they constitute a new herd. But the relentlessly similar questions I heard on this tour reassured me that there is still plenty of mob rule on Wall Street, and plenty of money to be made betting against it.

Here are four basic tenets of contrarianism that answer lots of contemporary questions genetically:

1. If most folks you know agree with you on a price move or some event's impact, don't take this as confirmation

that you are right. It is a warning; you are wrong. Being right requires aloneness, and willingness to let others see you as maybe nuts.

2. If you read or hear about some investment idea or significant event more than once in the media, it won't work. By the time several commentators have thought and written about it, even new news is too old.

   About here, I am often asked, "Do you urge avoiding the media?" Heavens, no. You have to read newspapers and watch television to know what is being talked about and therefore doesn't count. By exclusion you then save effort for that which may count.

   Case in point: high short-term interest rates, giving rise to a nearly inverted yield curve. Such a curve is always bearish when unnoticed. But I'm not bearish now: Today's interest rate concerns are too much discussed.

There's much truth in the old saw, the stock market climbs a wall of worry.

3. The older an argument is, the less power it has. So, for example, inflation fears may have moved markets in 1994, but sometime early in 1995 that view will run out of steam. Maybe it already has. Bearishness may yet be vindicated in 1995, but you will need new fuel to justify it.

4. Any category of security that was hot in the last five years won't be in the next five years, and vice versa. Emerging markets, junk bonds, Japan, gold stocks— you name it, extreme heat and cold can't sustain for more than about five years. So skip that which has been long sizzling.

Stocks, dampened by 1990's setback and a weak 1994, have been mediocre performers over the last five years. That leaves room for them to do fairly well in the next five. ■

How to Tell a Bull From a Bear
April 24, 1995

With all major stock market indexes hitting recent highs, lots of folks are nervous. Call it acrophobia—fear of heights. This nervousness is precisely the legendary "wall of worry" bull markets just love to climb.

Here's what history shows: Stock markets that hit new highs are more likely to keep rising than to fall. If you sell at the first new high or thereabouts, you miss the rest.

If you have read me only recently you may think me a Johnny-one-note bull. I'm really not. I made two big bearish calls in my 11 years as a *Forbes* columnist. Yes, I ran too early in 1987, but I'm not sorry I did. I am most proud of my September 18, 1989 column entitled, "The End Is Nigh"; which

preceded a broad market peak by only a few weeks.

But after each call, I returned to outright bullishness in time to catch the next upswing. So, no, I'm not a perpetual bull. I just don't see many signs that the current bull is dying.

Here are four rules for market timing:

1. Don't sell on corrections so long as you think the long bull market trend is intact; it doesn't pay. In a 5%-to-10% kind of drop, transaction costs eat up too much of the potential decline to make the effort worthwhile.

2. Don't turn bearish just because others have. Successful bearishness really does require being virtually alone.

If many media commentators, brokerage reports and friends are bearish, you shouldn't be: Don't follow the crowd. A good daily broad-brush thermometer on crowd psychology is ready to hand in *Investor's Business Daily*. Just look at lines one and two of the "Psychological Market Indicators" box in the S&P 500 section on the "General Market Indicators" page. Stay bullish, unless those psychological indicators become lopsidedly bullish.

3. To win as a bear, you must see bad things that aren't widely publicized. If you simply ignore all the babble, important issues become more obvious. It's surprise that moves stock markets. So, for example, ignore the current dollar dither. Too public. By contrast, central to my 1989 bear call was an inverted yield curve that got virtually no mention anywhere. That said a liquidity crunch was coming. But had that inverted curve been much discussed, folks would have been braced and it couldn't have clocked the market.

4. Never stay bearish longer than 18 months; 12 months in any but the most extreme situations. Most bear markets last about a year. If you are bearish and prices don't fall in a year, you are obviously seeing ghosts. If you do hit it right, and prices fall, force yourself back in after a year. You may not hit the bottom but will have missed plenty of the drop and won't miss the next bull rise. Note: This works for troughs, but not for peaks (as stated earlier in this column).

Right now there are lots of bears, but I can see little bad ahead that isn't much discussed—which is bullish under my Rule 3. ∎

Special Situations
May 8, 1995

Bet you can't name this stock: It's number one in a US industry in which most stocks have been red-hot for three years. Yet it's dirt cheap. I'm talking about Lockheed Martin. How many stocks in this market sell as Lockheed Martin does, for just 10 times earnings, 57% of revenues and 2.2 times book value? Once the market catches on to the implications of the merger between Lockheed and Martin Marietta, this stock is almost guaranteed to perform well.

At $23 billion in sales, Lockheed Martin is the world's largest defense contractor. Being in defense isn't bad: McDonnell Douglas, Northrop Grumman, et al., tripled or more in the last three years.

The merger allows Lockheed Martin to trim its work force, improving future profitability. My advice: Buy it before it gets hot.

Let's now move south. Are the Latin American markets a buy now after the beating they have taken? For me they are not. The median Latin American stock still sells above 4 times book value and at 1.45 times annual sales, well above US stock averages. I have urged avoiding emerging markets for years. They are just too popular, even after a big hit. They still are not really cheap.

But there are a few exceptions. Banco de Galicia y Buenos Aires, a darned good bank, at a good price; you can buy this $350 million market-cap stock for a P/E of 6, 50% of revenues and 75% of book value. The ADR is down 65% in 15 months. Banco should get much more visible in the coming years, as it just opened its first New York office.

Much smaller but similar is the ADR of Mexico's Servicios Financieros Quadrum.

It is down 86%, from a peak of 34. This bank's loan portfolio is above-average quality for Mexico. At 46% of revenues, 50% of book value and a P/E of 6, it is quite cheap. The banks are among the hardest hit of Latin American stocks, and these babies have been thrown out with the bathwater.

Coming back home, here's a theory I fashioned from financial history: There is a tendency for what's hot in the first quarter to unwind in the second quarter. For example, in 50 of the 68 years since 1926, small-cap stocks bested big-cap ones in the first quarter, tied to the infamous "January Effect." But in those same 50 years big cap did better than small cap in the second quarter. Ditto for growth and value types of stocks. Usually when one style is hot in the first quarter, it lags in the second. It's all part of averaging out.

In this year's first quarter big beat small while growth beat value. So be prepared for a setback in big growth stocks. These are great firms, but to use that cliche, some of their prices discount the hereafter. Far be it from me to criticize a stock owned by Warren Buffett—and Coca-Cola is a great outfit—but. The "but" here is that 4.5 times annual sales is an awful lot to pay for a stock. True, Coke's net profit margin is an awesome 16%, but it wasn't always so; a decade ago Coke wasn't netting even 10% on sales. As nature abhors a vacuum, so do competitive markets punish extra high profit margins. In my view Coke cannot forever earn 16% on sales.

I would rather own another great and growing firm, like Archer Daniels Midland. Here you get another real leader in its field, but at a mere fraction of the price for Coca-Cola: 13 times earnings, 70% of annual revenue and 1.6 times book value. Outstanding company and outstanding price.

Good news. Currencies confuse too many investors. The dollar, despite all the dither, isn't down. The yen and mark are up. Think on a trade-weighted basis; that is like a pie, with each piece's size based on how much we trade with each country. We trade much more with Mexico and Canada than with Japan and Germany. The peso and Canadian dollar are down, offsetting the mark and yen. If we were really down, commodities priced in dollars would have risen a lot. They haven't. Contrary to conventional views, there is no weak dollar-based inflation risk. This whole misperception is bullish for US stocks. Our better monetary policy is a big reason our stocks rise while foreign stocks fall. ∎

Warren Buffet Versus the Beardstown Ladies
June 5, 1995

After three hot quarters, tech stocks are too fashionable. I hear the Beardstown ladies now want into technology. My advice: Don't follow the crowd, not even the Beardstown crowd. It's still a crowd.

As a kid, I would hear from my mother, "Rarely criticize a woman, and never in public." With respect to mom's advice, I will couch my criticism of these Beardstown ladies and their homilies with a few brief but easy to remember sound bites of general investment wisdom:

- Stocks picked by committee are, by definition, too consensus-oriented to be exceptional.
- Hot new gurus aren't as good as the old gurus; the old ones got to all the wisdom first.

- If you must have a guru, pick one who already has made mistakes and shown grace in making them. Otherwise, you are most apt to need to pick another one soon.
- Beware of all hot performance claims that haven't been long laundered in public view. Or else, it may be you taken to the cleaners.
- Investing is a full-time job.

The ladies about whom that book was written are all wonderful, I'm sure, but they also flunk all my tests. I would seek advice instead from more publicly seasoned seers.

If you like my brief bits of investment wisdom, try Yale Hirsch's annual appointment book, *The Stock Trader's Almanac*. It packages brief quotes from famous financial figures, which is only part of its broad appeal. Here are a few of my favorites:

- "The first rule is not to lose. The second rule is not to forget the first rule."—Warren Buffett
- "If you don't know who you are, the stock market is an expensive place to find out."—George Goodman
- "Successful investing is anticipating the successful anticipations of others."—John Keynes
- "Wall Street's graveyards are filled with men who were right too soon."—William Hamilton
- "All you need is look over the earnings forecasts publicly made a year ago to see how much care you need to give to those being made now for the next year."—Gerald M. Loeb
- "A gold mine is a hole in the ground with a liar on top."—Mark Twain
- "Spend at least as much time researching a stock as you would choosing a refrigerator."—Peter Lynch ∎

This Time, It's Different
July 3, 1995

In its June 5 cover story, this magazine reported that Wall Street was awash in bullishness and wondered whether this might be a very bearish sign. I read the signs somewhat differently. Yes, investors are increasingly sanguine, and the market's march has trampled bears and caused lots of them to capitulate. This doesn't indicate much. Contrarianism works, but only at fairly extreme market turns. Except at such crucial junctures, the market and sentiment both bounce around a lot in ways that aren't terribly meaningful. Simply noise.

What I am saying is this. Most observers have merely moved from too pessimistic to more or less neutral. They have not reached the stage of euphoria. For example, TV's *Wall Street Week* "Elves," an aggregation often noted market technicians, are more bullish than they were, but remain, on balance, slightly bearish. They haven't called for a rising market in more than a year.

Dangers of Playing Contrarian

Ken is frequently—and wrongly—accused of being a contrarian. As he explains in his 2006 book, *The Only Three Questions That Count*, he's not a contrarian; he just frequently takes a different route than most. That might mean being bullish when others are—but just more or less bullish. Same for bearish. Ken would say being a knee-jerk contrarian has become about as profitable as blindly following the crowd. In other words, don't do either.

Numbers from *Investor's Intelligence,* a service that monitors adviser bullishness and bearishness, are about neutral also. *Investor's Intelligence* data are bullish when 50% or more of all advisers admit to being bearish and are bearish if fewer than 20% do. Right now 34% are bearish: smack in the middle. Flip side, the 38% portion of advisers who are now bullish is also in the middle of the bullishness range. (You can find this service on the General Marker Indicators page of *Investor's Business Daily.*)

Before this bull market ends, maybe in 1996, sentiment will really turn all-out bullish, throwing aside restraints. The sentiment numbers will tilt toward extremes. We won't see so many stories about how the market can't keep going up and will start seeing ones about how it's different this time.

I'm not sure what those reasons will be for why "it's different this time." Might be a Republican White House and Congress. May be that the baby boomers will really save and flood us with money. May be that Grumpy Greenspan is reappointed, having piloted us to a soft landing. Of course, it won't be different. What isn't different is that to be a bear and right, there must be darn few other bears.

But that time isn't yet; investors remain skeptical, even if afraid to be outright bearish. So I'll stick with my January forecast, that the market will be up 20% to 40% this year. We're close now. I wouldn't be surprised to see only a few percent more in 1995; but if so, there should be more advance ahead in 1996, and perhaps with it we'll get top-like optimism. ∎

Wall of Worry
July 31, 1995

"I just don't get why the stock market is so strong," my client said. Lots of other folks are asking the same question: Why?

It's simple. After 1994 there was just too much company on the pessimistic side; too many people, pros and amateurs alike, thought like my client. When few people expect markets to rise, they usually do. The pessimism came partly from 1994's sour stock market. Also from inflation fears, but these proved empty. There was also a wrong and pervasive fear that valuations were too high. As I said in my February 13 column, valuations are above normal, but not so far above normal as to be scary, if you average the various ways value can be analyzed. Only truly extreme valuations drive the market. The rest is just noise.

As I said in January, too, politics are right. Bill Clinton is a lame duck and markets like it when Presidents can merely quack. The third year of a President's term is almost always up, and usually big. Why investors never get this one escapes me. It's virtually bankable.

Also, insiders were big net buyers. They knew corporate profits were on a roll; it pays to follow their buying, and doubly so when sentiment is pessimistic. Finally, it's usually a mistake to bet big against an environment in which long-term interest rates are at least a point above short-term rates. They were and still are.

Because so many people have begun to sweat as the averages moved into high ground this summer, I remain optimistic. It's the wall of worry bull markets love to climb. Investor sentiment is no longer so pessimistic as it was, but it isn't optimistic, either. Sentiment is merely now in the middle of what could be considered its normal range. Until it tilts to real optimism, this bull market should continue.

What about the increasing fear that we are about to tip from a soft landing into a full-fledged recession? Don't let this one spook you. It's just more wall of worry. The economy rarely tips into recession without the stock market's fading first. Stocks lead the economy and not the other way around. This is twice as true when long-term interest rates are headed down and stocks are rising—it's not the stuff of recessions.

Political climate? I'm no great political forecaster, but I do know that the 1996 election is still too far away to affect the market—and won't at least until the February primaries.

Subject to short, sharp corrections, the market should do just fine through early 1996. ∎

Bear-Proofing Your Portfolio
August 28, 1995

The big bear market I see ahead will be harder on mutual fund investors than past bear markets. And there will be a bear market—there always is— even though I still believe the current bull market has a while to run.

Now is the time to prepare, and here is why. Investors have always tended to pick funds that show up as recent hot performers. But more so now. Since the last bear market, this chase-the-hot-numbers syndrome has been fueled by an explosion of new funds and, worse, of services that make it so easy to chase performance. Morningstar, which I regard highly, has unfortunately made it easy to chase heat because its figures are so widely and quickly available, and it crowns "champions." Very dangerous.

People pick funds as if they were driving a car forward while looking in the rearview mirror. They see behind, but not ahead. So they buy funds that did well in the bull market that is about to end. That car, which they drive by rearview mirror on a straight, smooth road, is about to hit an unpaved, twisty road.

Recently a friend called to say he had bought Heartland Value, with its sizzling recent returns. It was about to close its doors to new money, and he had gotten in in time and was so excited. He knew Heartland buys small-cap value stocks, the

kind I have often suggested. Besides, it was one of only three Morningstar small-cap value "style-box champions," which to him was a sort of seal of approval.

I respect Bill Nasgovitz, the fund manager there. Bill does great on straight, smooth highways. But he hasn't been so hot on bumpy, windy roads—bear markets. Heartland was down 17% in 1990; and in the volatile 1986–89 period, it lagged terribly. Now, because folks are chasing hot five-year returns, Heartland runs more than $600 million. But in the last downturn, it had only about $25 million— peanuts in mutual fund land. With the increase, it is now too big for its style.

Heartland buys tiny, thinly traded stocks, just the sort that get hammered hard in bear markets. There are basically four things a manager can do to get really defensive: buy bigger and less volatile stocks, raise cash, buy puts or all of the above. But for a fund like Heartland, these would all be maiden voyages. Risky.

Heartland has traditionally gotten an "A" rating from *Forbes* for up-market performance and a "D" for down-market returns. *Forbes'* are the best and easiest to use down-market ratings you can find. But I see few people paying attention to down-market ratings now because this bull market has been running so long there isn't much recent real down-market-ness to measure. The real jags of 1974 and 1982 may seem like ancient history. But they will return.

In recent years in the *Forbes* annual mutual funds issue I have said you should never buy a fund with a down-market rating lower than "C." But now, in the later stages of a bull market, pull in your horns a bit and tighten that up to nothing less than a "B." And add a few more protective caveats.

I would also avoid any fund that now has lots of money but had less than about $150 million when 1990's downturn hit. If a fund is headed by someone who hasn't run a lot of money through a tough bear market, I would just forget about it right now. And I would avoid any fund with a high expense ratio. I would skip those over 1% (the average is about 1.25%). You can pay for a high expense ratio with hot returns in a bull market, but it's an added burden in a down market.

I don't mean to pick on Heartland or on Morningstar, but I mention the former because it is not the kind of fund to own in a bear market, unless you are very long-term oriented and have rocklike guts. And I mention Morningstar's figures because unless you know what you are doing they can mislead you. ∎

Babbling Bears and Other Menaces
September 25, 1995

The bears had a lackluster 1994 and so far a terrible 1995, having bet on a multiplicity of negatives, which haven't quite happened.

Of course, there will eventually be a bear market—a big one—and I suppose the bears will be boasting that they saw it coming. Meanwhile, they will keep on growling that they will be vindicated soon and weren't really wrong. For the life of me, I can't see how anyone who was so wrong as to be bearish going into 1995 should now much be relied on to forecast 1996 with any better accuracy. The 1994–95 bears have cost their followers a bundle—probably much more than can be made up in a normal bear market. Good grief.

So have the pundits who urged you to put money into foreign stocks, especially in emerging markets. Fully 95% of all paid consultants articulate this nonsense. They didn't get started pushing folks this way until after years of foreign equities besting US stocks. But they got in just in time for the reverse to begin. Rearview-mirror driving. They praise diversifying but focus you on markets that have been long hot.

Now I may be wrong, but to my knowledge, the most successful investor of the last 50 years, Warren Buffett, has never ever put any appreciable money into any foreign stock. Lately, I have been scratching my head to figure just what it is that all these smart people know that Mr. Buffett can't quite get. And I can't figure it out. I decided I'm not clever enough to compete with them in loading up on all these great foreign opportunities. So I will stick to mostly what I know, finding deals here at home, where I know how to get around. And I will ignore all the long-term bears, who are no more likely to be right in the fall of 1995 than they were in the autumn of 1994. ∎

The Liquidity Trap
October 16, 1995

Stunning investment lessons come from simply mulling shifts atop the *Forbes* 400. For example, Ross Perot demonstrates one fundamental don't-do-it. Don't cash out for long. It's deadly.

Perot got on the *Forbes* 400 by starting, building and selling EDS, a phenomenally successful firm. In 1987 he was worth $2.9 billion and was number three on the list. At that time he held a huge position in bonds and Treasury bills. His liquidity helped finance his presidential run but dropped him to 33rd place on the *Forbes* 400. Had he in 1987, instead of staying in cash and near cash, simply invested in an S&P 500 index fund, he would still be about number three on the *Forbes* 400 and would be worth $7 billion—nearly three times what he is worth today.

Moving up in the *Forbes* 400 is not the only thing in life worth doing, but I mention all this to make a point: If you want your net worth to grow, "stay equitized." Bonds are okay if you are very old or can't afford any risk, but if you want to be in the action, buy a piece of the action, which is what common stocks represent.

With bonds, in the end either the taxman gets you or inflation does. If bonds yield 7% and you are in a 40% tax bracket, your real yield is a smidgen over 4% and that leaves you something over 1% after inflation—not even a millionaire could live on that kind of income. That bonds are costly relative to stocks in the long term has been shown repeatedly by numerous studies, the most famous of which was *Stocks, Bonds, Bills and Inflation* by Roger Ibbotson and Rex Sinquefield. It was sponsored by the Financial Analysts Research Foundation and is available at most major libraries.

How about cash or short-term bonds as a hedge against a market crash? Doing so for a year or so is fine, but only if you are really good at market timing—and who is? Most folks use this as an excuse to commit financial suicide. Even in a market crack, most folks do better riding through it than trying to time it. Ross Perot should know. He got killed in the market in 1970, but held on and was paid well for it. ∎

Countdown to a Top
October 23, 1995

Folks ask me how long this bull market will run. What they really want to know is whether the upside is worth the risk of getting trapped at the top. In short, is it too late to play?

I'm flattered people ask, but I don't really know when this bull market will die. My best thinking is: It shouldn't end before about March, and may well run strong through the elections and year-end. How much further can it go up? Anywhere from 10% to 35%— maybe to the 650-to-750 range on the S&P 500. After that? A bear market of normal size—down 20% to 30% over roughly 14 months, with the worst damage done on the growth stock side of the market.

How will we know when the end is nigh? Bear markets come in different ways.

There are a bunch of possible risks, some of which must evolve before a bull market ends. In March the presidential campaign could turn ugly and the market may discount that unpleasantness. Also in March, Clinton must reappoint Alan Greenspan as head of the Fed or offer up a substitute. Either way you get uncertainty. If Greenspan goes, what kind of person will succeed him? Someone new, and new at this function, often scares stocks. If he stays, that could mean trouble, too.

Greenspan wants Clinton to reappoint him, so the Fed chief won't tighten money much until after March, and until then the bull market will live. But then, if reappointed, I think his fangs may fast appear. He likes to bite.

And by late 1996 this economic expansion should get old and tired, and may fatigue itself into a rollover. Enough prosperity long enough, and folks finally want to play more than they want to work. As I have long said, there is less inflation than people think. So, with absolutely no pricing cushion, a recession can ravage corporate earnings. As always, the stock market will discount any such event.

So, sometime next year there's good odds the bull market will end, maybe in March, maybe much later. I have no reason to expect worse than a normal bear market. Why do I say it will hit growth stocks hard? Because bear markets rarely repeat stylistically. In 1990 value stocks were ravaged, but not growth stocks. With the money now heavily into growth stocks, time is ripe for this next bear market to change leadership and trap the new growth stock money. I see the recent toppy action of leading growth stocks as a further forewarning. ∎

Bear Hunting But Just Finding Bulls

As it turns out, nothing too negative that wasn't already widely known and discounted in stocks popped up for over four years. Ken was looking for negatives to chase him out of stocks. Failing to find any, he just remained bullish. And that's a good way to get long-term market-like returns: Be bullish, unless you see something extraordinarily negative few others do. It sounds easy, but is exceptionally hard. All through the extraordinary bull run of the 1990s, there was a non-stop chorus of bearish sentiment—but Ken was bullish throughout. And what a great time to be a bull.

Apples and Oranges
November 20, 1995

Nothing personal, Mark [Hulbert], but I'm in total disagreement with your September 25 column, "Carl Jung Had a Name for It." You note that money managers snootily scorn investment letters, and say that, by your count, only about 20% of either group beats the market.

To begin, I question your statistic. Your 15-year count is from 19 investment letters.

For ten years you recently ranked only 5 of 48 investment letters beating that market—10%. How can 5 out of 19 anything be significant?

Besides, Mark, apples and oranges. Money managers actually manage money. Investment letters don't. They are not directly comparable. Investment letters run paper portfolios, and their results gloss over real costs like "impact"—which is huge. By impact I mean the effect the letter's recommendation has on the price of the stock. An investment letter "buys" at 10 and "sells" at 12—and it is not a real 20% gain—not even close. Subscribers help push it up; their own buying produces the gain. This is only an illusion of profit. Maybe a 5% to 10% effect per in-and-out. This impact is felt more on small, illiquid stocks than it is with big ones. And high turnover strategies suffer much more than long-term holders.

Thus your top-rated investment letters are mostly what is now called "momentum investing"—price chasing, high turnover and mostly relatively illiquid stocks. This system works better on paper than in reality. For example, you regularly praise *Value Line Investment Survey* as tops among all investment letters for 15 years. Maybe so, but in mutual funds and money management *Value Line* is respectable but distinctly ho-hum. Its flagship, Value Line Fund, aimed at the broad market and rail by the same bag of tricks as the investment letter you so praise, has lagged the S&P 500 in seven of the last ten years, including the last three. In 1994, for example, you show the Value Line letter basically matching the Wilshire 5000. But the real world fund—same methodology, same firm—lagged the index by 4.4%.

You are right of course that only 20% of real-life money managers beat the market. But most who don't beat it are competent and pretty close in the pack. They aren't screaming disasters—or rarely so. But your investment letter lesser guys often are, and sometimes are even charlatans. I recall your blasting Joe Granville, claiming his portfolio eventually lost most of its value. He is still in the letter business. If a money manager lags its benchmark by too much, it gets fired fast. To wit, Concord

Capital ran $2.7 billion, lagged a bit too much for five years and was fired by every single account. I could go on forever with examples.

Now, most letters try to run money because the practice is almost infinitely more profitable than running an investment letter. But most fail. Take Mike Murphy of *California Technology Stock Letter.* The press loves him, and Hulbert has rated him number two for ten years. According to Nelson's Directory, he ran a paltry $40 million in 1990, down to a subpaltry $2 million as 1995 began. Little wonder: His fund was down 43% in 1994 and down 5% in 1993. If he's such a hot investment letter, why is he such a rotten money manager? Money management is competitive; you make the numbers or you are out. Investment letters are much less real. Their success depends heavily on advertising, public relations and direct mail marketing hype.

Now there are some fine guys doing both. For example: Martin Zweig, Louis Navellier, Al Frank. But the spread between paper and reality remains. If you like Navellier, my advice is: Cancel his letter and hire him to run money. You pay more, and you both will make more.

We are late in a bull market. When it turns, the spread between paper and reality widens even more. Bear markets drain liquidity and it's harder to in-and-out, because when you try to sell these small illiquid stocks you bang down your own stocks. Navellier may play a bear market well. His readers won't, because they can't move as fast as he can. Late in a bull market most investors should switch to big, liquid stocks. Money managers will increase liquidity. Investment letters won't.

In short, Mark, no matter how perceptive some investment letters may have been, this is a rotten time to start following them. ∎

Rummaging in the Attic
December 18, 1995

Some *Forbes* columnists have long runs. I have been writing in this space for 11 years but I'm only number ten in terms of longevity. Fellow columnist David Dreman outranks me, as do such long-departed stalwarts as Lucien Hooper and Heinz Biel. My goal? To be number one. To be still writing the column when the issue of August 30, 2016 comes out. That's still 21 years and hundreds of columns away.

As a man with a deep interest in the history of markets this matters to me. This spring I hired a summer intern, Paul Meegan from the University of Washington, to plow through every *Forbes* issue ever published. Meegan found 75 columnists who lasted more than six months. The longest running? Oldtime readers may recall the late Heinz Biel whose column lasted 32.14 years—November 1, 1950 to December 20, 1982. A German immigrant, Biel's resume included a PhD in economics from Gottingen University and 17 years in securities research (with time out for a World War II stint for Uncle Sam).

Biel, well known among professionals but less so to the general public, penned 726 columns, 90 more than Lucien Hooper, who lasted 29 years, until January 1, 1979. Hooper, a Maine native and graduate of Harvard College, served as president of the New York Society of Security Analysts and of the national society. He was once financial editor of the *Boston Commercial*. A generation of investors was nourished on Lucien's shrewd Yankee appraisals.

Forbes' third-longest-running columnist, and my personal favorite, Joseph Goodman of Philadelphia, wrote from July 15, 1935 until his death 23 years later. Sidney Lurie was Paine-Webber's obscure research chief when *Forbes* took him public in 1954. His column lasted 21.75 years. John Shultz, a "chartist," put in 16.45 years, until 1976. David Dreman, with 15.5 years, is now the senior columnist, and number six of all time. And I'm number ten.

A daunting task for me to outlast all these worthies. It means I must go another 21 years without blowing it badly enough to get booted. I think a lot about that challenge. To meet it I have concluded I must do three things:

1. Make big calls so I impact your investment performance;
2. Reverse course quickly when I'm wrong;
3. Fess up when I'm wrong.

For your sake, I have tried to envision how *Forbes'* longest-running columnists would view today's market. From my favorite, Joe Goodman, this key market-timing wisdom: "The best one can hope for is that the turn in the main trend can be detected two or three months after it has taken place."

Keeping that point in mind, I think Goodman would cite 1995's strength, and urge readers to hang on for the ride and plan to miss the top and then sell soon on the way down. In maturing markets like today's he urged boosting quality. His reason? Twofold. First, to avoid the stocks that would be ravaged the most in a bear market. Second, so selling would be easy at the right time. He would trade some late market gusto for liquidity.

In the issue of January 1, 1936 Goodman wrote: "When a bull market turns bear, sell the stock that has gone up the most, as it will react the most. Also sell the stock that has gone up the least. It couldn't go up; therefore, must go down." He would now move you out of what have been the hottest speculations and the biggest dogs, toward bigger stocks.

Goodman called only big moves. He wouldn't trade the squiggles. That meant riding with a big trend even if that trend encountered setbacks. "After the stock market has a steady rise, everyone fears a reaction," he wrote. As for waiting for a reaction before buying in a rising market: "As a matter of fact, few people have the courage to buy when the market breaks."

My reading of Lucien Hooper also leads me to think he would have you fully invested now. In the issue of December 15, 1958, well into the big post-World War II bull market, he wrote:

"Investors have found through experience that they make more money with the seat of their pants than with the soles of their feet." So, don't get nervous and sell out too soon. Peaks can always take longer than you think.

Around the same time, Sid Lurie wrote: "That the market is 'high' by all traditional standards of measurement doesn't in itself mean that a decline is inevitable." Biel, the PhD economist, urged ignoring all economists' forecasts. A believer in presidential stock market cycles, he would be a bull now, expecting a rise into next fall. And so do I.

The worst run of forecasting by *Forbes* columnists was at the market peak in 1972. All five of the stalwarts then writing missed it. But then that should have been a warning in itself: When everyone is bullish, watch out! ∎

1996

The Nifty Nineties

"
Predicting tops is not part of my investing method. I don't even try. . . . People who forecast market tops depend on foreseeing forces that will both materialize and make the market tumble. If the forces don't appear, neither does the top. And even if they do appear, there may be other, unforeseen events that arise and offset the negative developments they did anticipate."

"The Orderly Retreat," June 17, 1996

"
If capitalism works, if supply and demand determine prices, and if liquidity flows from sector to sector, it defies logic to presume one broad class of common stock is permanently better than others."

"Small Isn't Always Best," November 4, 1996

Nineteen-ninety-six was a bittersweet year for many *Forbes* readers. Stocks had a great year. But 1996 was also the year of Steve Forbes' first failed run for the presidency. Despite Forbes' strong showing in the Republican primaries, Senator Bob Dole won the Republican nomination, eventually losing the presidency to President Clinton, who won his second term. Republicans lost a few seats in the congressional elections but maintained control of both the House and Senate. The result was more political gridlock—and investors cheered.

Ken was bullish heading into 1996, but he was watchful for sign of a bear. "Last year, I stuck my neck way out by predicting a gain for the market of between 20% and 40% . . . In 1996, I'm less certain, but expect a rise of 10% to 20%, with more risk than in 1995." ("Year of the Aging Bull," January 22, 1996.) That forecast proved a tad pessimistic but nearly right on the money.

You could draw a chart of the 1995 stock market with a ruler. It was pretty much a straight line up all year—hardly any volatility at all. But a chart of the 1996 market required a serrated edge, at least in the first half of the year. Stocks began 1996 with a series of fits and starts. The trend was up, but it was a bumpy road. That is until midyear. Stocks experienced a 7 percent correction in July that left the market up just 3 percent for the year, but surged from there.[1] From late July through year-end, the S&P 500 gained nearly 20 percent with barely a hiccup along the way, finishing the year up a solid 23.0 percent.[2] Foreign shares were up less than a third as much.

Ken recommended remaining invested throughout the choppiness. Investors were still too bearish. The soaring market in 1995 only reinforced their views stocks were overvalued. As usual, guarded investor sentiment gave Ken comfort. "Without some worry, I worry. I don't much care what the worry is, I just want there to be a fair amount of it." ("Acrophobia," March 25, 1996.)

Though he saw risks to the rising market, in Ken's view the biggest risk was calling a market top too soon. In fact, Ken advocated never calling a top until after it has passed. Ken reiterated Joseph Goodman's Three-Month Rule: "The best one can hope for is that the turn in the main trend can be detected two or three months after it has taken place."(Joseph Goodman, *Forbes,* October 1, 1937.) Ken has said several times that Joe Goodman, who wrote for *Forbes* from November 1, 1935 until December 15, 1958, was his all-time favorite *Forbes* columnist—and perhaps the most underappreciated of all columnists ever.

Too many investors expect bear markets to unfold quickly, like in 1987. But that type of drop is the exception. Bear markets usually roll over slowly. Calling a bear market too early could mean missing out on gains if the bull continues. Instead, the three-month rule forces investors to wait until three months after the top has passed. "Three months after a top you have six months more information than you had three months before the top." ("The Orderly Retreat," June 17, 1996.) The three-month rule worked out perfectly in 1996. The July market correction lasted nearly a month. Investors with itchy trigger fingers might have bailed out of the market too soon, viewing the downturn as the start of a new bear market. But those following the three-month rule got a profitable dose of discipline. Three months after the July peak, the S&P 500 was 2.5 percent higher and moved substantially higher from there.

Ken recommended focusing on US shares in prior years, but was warming up to foreign investments. Central banks in Europe and Japan waited too long to ease monetary policy to stoke struggling foreign economies but had finally done so in a big way. "As usual with central bankers, they finally knee-jerked and over-reversed course. They now print money desperately and hard, to pound life into their lifeless patients." ("Good for Europe, Bad for America," July 15, 1996.) All that extra money would eventually have a positive economic impact, but not immediately. Much of it was parked in capital markets first. "Monetary policy works, absolutely, but with an unpredictable time lag . . . When you print money and your 'Main Street' economy can't absorb it, the excess liquidity spills over into your financial markets and then to the global markets." This excess liquidity overseas had been adding fuel to US stocks. In 1996, foreign economies were on the mend, possibly sucking some money out of the US. This forecast missed the mark a bit. US shares would lead for the remainder of the bull market. European stocks did exceptionally well too, but not as well as the US. Japan languished in its "lost decade" of economic and stock market malaise.

Ken again recommended shifting toward larger stocks. "In the real world the market moves in cycles: Big stocks lead for a while, then smaller, but neither has a permanent edge. Sometimes value stocks lead the market and sometimes growth stocks do. They all have alternating periods in the sun and in the rain. Since early 1994 big stocks have led every year. I missed the start of this, but around the beginning of 1995 my column began advocating the bigger stocks. I now think big stocks should stay in front through the end of the next bear market." ("Small Isn't Always Best," November 4, 1996.) Bullseye here. The massive stocks market gains to come would be dominated by ultra-huge stocks.

In his December 2, 1996 column, "For Your Christmas Shopping List," Ken introduced his readers to an emerging finance field. "To me, finance's frontier is what academics call 'behavioralism'—the psychology of what people do with investment tools." Today, Ken is recognized as a pioneer in behavioral finance. Ken and Dr. Meir Statman of Santa Clara University wrote "Cognitive Biases in Market Forecasts," which won the *Journal of Portfolio Management* outstanding Article Award for 2000–2001.

Year of the Aging Bull
January 22, 1996

"This year will be a good year in the stock market." So started my January 16, 1995 column. Ditto, I say, for 1996. Last year I stuck my neck way out by predicting a gain for the market of between 20% and 40%. And I didn't hedge.

In 1996 I'm less certain, but expect a rise of 10% to 20%, with more risk than in 1995.

Here's my reasoning:

First, in the fourth year of a President's term the market rarely falls—only three times in the last 110 years. The last exception was 1940, when Nazi ranks swept through Europe. The other two times, 1932 and 1920, were both pretty darned exceptional in American financial history, particularly 1920. But this year should be remarkably unexceptional.

These few exceptions notwithstanding, since its inception, the S&P 500's mean average return in a President's fourth year is 14.3%. Before that, fourth years appear to have done about as well, albeit measured by less reliable indexes.

There are sound explanations for this strength in the fourth year of presidential terms. Facing the electorate, the politicians tend to be on good behavior. This year it helps that the President and Congress are of opposing parties. Keeps them both from being too arrogant and defaulting to something stupid.

Arguing also against bearishness is the old but wise saying: "Bull markets die with a whimper, not with a bang." Clearly 1995 was a bang-up market, to the end. It takes a real top a long time to form—rising less and gently, suckering in lots of money over many months so it can punish the most people and dollars later. It falls gently at first, too. It doesn't want to scare you away, but instead to charm and lull you into complacency.

A spike-top, which is what everyone always fears, doesn't have enough time to suck in enough sacrificial victims.

Finally, I think the government economic data are now all screwed up, broken badly. If you doubt the wisdom of abolishing the Commerce Department, watching government economic data over the next few years in their various new formats will convince you. Way off base. So the economy will be stronger than the indicators will indicate; and stronger than today's consensus forecasts, which are downwardly biased by the use of those data. Contributing to a pickup in the economy will be demand from Europe and Japan. Both are just starting to turn up after a long wicked period. Then, too, consumers have been on a diet of late, which increases their propensity to binge in 1996. With a good economy and inflation tame, earnings will be very nice indeed, buoying stocks.

Risks? Yes. The yield curve is too flat, and Grumpy Greenspan, who I always fear, can easily create a credit crunch like that of 1989–90. He's a real sadist, that Greenspan.

Another worry is that a year of goodness has warmed hearts, and folks are slightly too sanguine, although not yet enough so, I think, for a real top. That should come late this year.

But following the advice of the late Joe Goodman, *Forbes'* third-longest-running columnist ever, I won't try to call a market top until shortly after I think it has happened. There should be plenty of time to get out with profits mostly intact.

My advice: Stay fully invested, but replace smaller stocks with bigger ones—to most folks' surprise, the Goliaths tend to do best in late bull markets and, being highly liquid, they are easiest to sell when time comes to unload. ∎

Bet on the Bull
February 26, 1996

Several fairly sophisticated investors asked if I am "afraid for 1996," because January began with a dip, ended with a zip, and the economy and the economic indicators look terrible. My unequivocal answer: No, I am not worried. It's still a bull market.

There are three "January" indicators. "As goes January, so goes the year." As it happens, January ended on a strong note. "January's first week tells it all." That one turned out bearish. "Small stocks usually do best in January—if they don't, look out below." Bearish also.

Two out of three bearish, but so what? The "first week" argument is weak. Five trading days, or five anythings, are meaningless statistically for forecasting. As for the small-stocks theory, in my view it's not relevant at this stage of the bull market.

Since early 1995 I've urged concentration on bigger stocks. As time passed I urged more strongly. To me, this long bull market ends with a last leg in which bigger value stocks do best—as has happened so far this year.

Reader Richard K. Fischer of Roanoke, Va. is the most recent to write noting that an indicator I cameoed on August 3, 1992, under the title "My Favorite Indicator," is bearish. This is the Commerce Department's former Series No. 940, the "Ratio of Coincident Index Indicators to Lagging Index Indicators." I said it had "given excellent advice on the stock market's direction for 40 years." Yet since 1994 it has been bearish—so how can I remain bullish? Good question. The answer is a sad one.

Slowly, as I said in past columns, the Commerce Department has destroyed Uncle Sam's economic data. They now have a zero link to reality. I no longer use any of it for forecasting at all. It's sad—the data were so useful. But they are all wrecked, including my blessed No. 940—which is not only broken but also now produced by the Conference Board. For example, even the basic GDP model is useless. GDP was completely reconstructed in 1995, making it highly misleading, like all of Uncle Sam's new data. Most folks won't know the difference and will get suckered by upcoming numbers. As you see Commerce Department data releases, or other government data, in the months ahead, don't be suckered. Ignore them.

And don't you be misled by the various excuses people have for not owning stocks. This is still a bull market. ∎

Acrophobia
March 25, 1996

Right now the stock market has about as severe a case of acrophobia as I have seen. So relax. This year shapes up as a good year overall, despite fear that the market is too high.

Reader Pierson E. Clair asks how I reconcile my January bullish forecast against fellow columnist Charles Babin's bearishness of February 12. Babin writes: "Without exception, bull years like 1995 have marked a stalling point in the stock market cycle."

Hey, that's part of why *Forbes* runs more than one stock market columnist. To give readers exposure to different points of view. If every one were a bull, there would be nobody to sell stocks and there would be no stock market. Same with bears. A market needs buyers and sellers. It needs pessimists and optimists, both at the same time.

As usual, the bears come in all stripes and colors. Charlie Babin marshals some historical data (although I disagree with his interpretation). Other bears cite other factors. But the bears are united by a common feeling: that markets like last year's are just too good to last.

Maybe, but any rise over any period, by itself, has almost zero predictive value. Yes, it's safe to say that after the market has gone up 40% in one year, it's not likely to do as well the next year, but that doesn't mean it can't have a nice rise—one from which anyone would want to profit. Knowing the market will eventually "regress to the mean"—the mean being about 10% per year—says nothing about when.

Yes, there are tops and bottoms. But you can't read them in the numbers. Trying to do so is a mistake. You can only try to read them in mass psychology. Sometimes folks get lulled by a rise and lured into complacent, excessive buying, which makes a top. Other times the crowd gets acrophobia, like now, which propels stocks higher. As the saying goes: "Bull markets climb a wall of worry." Without some worry, I worry. I don't much care what the worry is, I just want there to be a fair amount of it. That there is today—worry that the market is too high. Until it passes, the bull market isn't apt to die.

One of my favorite indicators is the "all-star roundtable" in each year's first-of-the-year *Barron's*. In it about ten biggies share their forecasts as a crowd. This particular crowd hasn't been right in memory. Which is why I use the issues as a contrary indicator. This year? Bearish, almost to a man (and a woman), centered on acrophobic rationalizations.

I conclude that the bull market, though subject to classic corrections, is still snorting. ∎

The Election and Stocks
April 22, 1996

Since politics does influence markets, I'm making a detour into political prognostication to explain why I think the stock market is going to be extremely strong as Summer spins to Fall—even if Dole does poorly against Clinton. My analysis extends from the substantive but little-known work of the Business Institute for Political Analysis, part of Washington, DC-based BIPAC, of which I'm a board member and enthusiastic supporter.

BIPAC notes there will be 43 vacant House seats up for grabs this fall—an unusually high 10% of Congress. This is where most of the action will be, because it's far easier to win an open seat than to beat an incumbent. Of these seats, 28 are now held by Democrats, 15 by the GOP. Most of the Republican seats are safe. Of the 28 to-be-vacant Democratic seats, 15 are in the South and are vulnerable.

Consider Representative Sam Gibbons of Florida's 11th district, elected in 1962, when you had to be a Democrat in the South. Despite being number two on the pork-pushing Ways & Means Committee, he got just 52% of the vote last time around. He's retiring. His district has shifted Republican with the South. The next representative from Florida's 11th district probably will be a Republican.

BIPAC also ranks by vulnerability incumbents who are running for reelection. I carry the analysis further by analyzing their money-raising powers and spending habits. The 40 most vulnerable Democrats are mostly long-timers and in the habit of spending their opponents to death with big chunks of PAC-based "access" money. But this year, with the Dems no longer controlling Congress, the flow of money into these coffers will slow. These old dogs won't all be able to run the spending-intensive campaigns they got used to.

I see a similar pattern in the Senate, which also adds up to an enlarged Republican majority in the upper house. What this means, I think, is a strengthened Republican majority in both houses. Thus, even if Clinton beats Dole, we may have a near-veto-proof Congress based on a pork-providing deal here and there—and a real chance for economically sensible legislation. That prospect can't help but be good for stocks. Especially for the big companies. ■

Pity the Poor Bears
May 20, 1996

Like the Fifties, the Nineties have exceeded most expectations. Both decades started with terrible investor sentiment. In the early 1950s consensus held that while we had shaken depression during the war, it was all artificial and we would eventually regress to a late 1930s-type doldrums because capitalism was fundamentally flawed. Skepticism rose further with the Korean War, inflation fears and the relatively minor 1953–54 recession.

But on July 15, 1954 *Forbes* columnist the late Sidney Lurie was boldly bullish in what I consider one of the most visionary columns ever run anywhere. It was here that Lurie, who would go on to become *Forbes'* fourth-longest running columnist ever, first used a phrase that was soon to become famous, as he forecast that the 1950s would eventually be recorded as the "Fabulous Fifties." He saw that computers, automation and a plethora of new products of every kind spawned by research would change the world and produce progress, not regression, in "a truly New Era." One reason I like reading the old *Forbes* columnists is it reminds me I have some truly huge footprints in which to follow.

As with the 1950s most commentators went into the current and final decade of this century in a glum mood. Pummeled by the 1970s' massive recession and hyperstagflation, pundits viewed the 1980s as artificially propped up by budget and trade deficits, debt and takeovers. Starting with a 1953-like relatively mild recession, and terrorized by inflation fears fueled from the past, most forecasters believed the 1990s must be below average because the 1980s were above average. Instead, the post-1982 markets were mostly a correction of the 1965–82 weak markets. The 1990s, while not appreciated, have been perhaps the most normal times of the last 50 years, while pundits have frantically sought abnormalities, most of which are ghosts. Our markets haven't been kind, by and large, to pessimists.

The financial markets have done fine. America has bested most nations, instead of lagging them. As in the 1950s, America is again clearly the world's leader in almost every way. And the long-term bears are getting poorer and poorer.

Overall these times are very normal on Main Street and starting from such a dour mind-set really quite wonderful on Wall Street. As early 21st century historians ponder the 1990s, they are as destined to be recorded as the "Nifty Nineties" as the 1950s were the "Fabulous Fifties." And, for many of the same reasons Sid Lurie cited way back when.

Don't get me wrong. I expect bad things to happen. Cancer, taxes, Bill Clinton. Maybe a market peak late this year and a normal recession in late 1997. And on with the "Nifty Nineties." Until I see actual signs of a major market peak right behind me, I'm bullish and want to own big, cheap stocks. ∎

The Orderly Retreat
June 17, 1996

One reason I don't anticipate a stock market top right now is that predicting tops is not part of my investing method. I don't even try. I have found that it is far better and more profitable to wait until I can see that a market peak has in fact been formed, and then beat an orderly retreat. There's almost always plenty of time, especially if you're in the right kind of stocks.

People who forecast market tops depend on foreseeing forces that will both materialize and make the market tumble. If the forces don't appear, neither does the top. And even if they do appear, there may be other, unforeseen events that arise and offset the negative developments they did anticipate.

Almost all market observers try to predict the spike top. Spike tops terrify because the drop is a cliff—as in 1987. Spike tops are often foreseen, but almost never actually seen. If you track the market with multiple stock indexes, as I have always advocated, you'll be hard put to point to a single spike top this century. Not even 1929 was a true spike top.

What generally happens when bull markets come to an end is the formation of a long, slow, rolling top that lulls away fears and sucks in megamoney on both sides of the top. Then the market rolls softly south, as observers think it's a mere correction before the next up-leg. They keep throwing money in—easing the fall, but not braking the downward momentum, which later gains velocity and viciousness. But the point is this: In the early months after the top has been reached, there is still time to get out of big, liquid stocks.

How much time? As Joseph D. Goodman wrote in these pages—October

---

Patience Is a Virtue

Not calling a top until after it has formed is a consistent theme in Ken's writings. Historically, most bear markets do roll over—they don't spike-top. All that time rolling and grinding gives you a chance to develop conviction that what you're seeing is a top. What you don't want to do is predict a top beforehand, get out, and get left in the dust as the bull keeps marching. And, here in June 1996, though many notable voices were seeing a bear market—including Greenspan who famously (and far too early) cautioned against "irrational exuberance"—the bull had another nearly four years to go.

1, 1937: "The best one can hope for is that the turn in the main trend can be detected two or three months after it has taken place." (Goodman was *Forbes'* third-longest-running columnist ever, and my all-time favorite.)

That's my goal. Three months after a top you have six months' more information than you had three months before the top. And right now, looking back, I see no evidence that the market has formed a top. Almost every single stock index except the Dow Jones utilities is hitting new highs as I write. Don't expect to hear a bearish market call from me for at least three months. ∎

Good for Europe, Bad for America
July 15, 1996

When Europe awakens, its economic revival could trigger a US bear market. In the early 1990s, led by the then self-righteously austere Germans, the Europeans and Japanese wouldn't grow their money supplies. They now suffer for that folly. Their economies are like birds without wings; they just won't fly. Weak demand, no GDP growth, high unemployment and sagging productivity.

All well known. But as usual with central bankers, they finally knee-jerked and over-reversed course. They now print money desperately and hard, to pound life into their lifeless patients. It will work.

To me this reversal is a major event, and more so because no one has noticed. It's the events the media miss that cause market surprises. When that loosening of money starts to revive European economies, that's going to be very bad news for our financial markets.

Money printing statistics vary country to country, but are very big. In Germany, for example, look to M3. It is up 12% year over year—whereas it should be up about 3%. But Germany's economy languishes. Why? The lagged result of earlier excess monetary austerity and too much government in the economy. Whereas two years ago Europe and Japan were too tight, they are far too loose now.

Why is this worrisome for our financial markets? I'll explain. Monetary policy works, absolutely, but with an unpredictable time lag. The lag for big shifts is even less predictable. When you print money and your "Main Street" economy can't instantly absorb it, the excess liquidity temporarily spills over to your financial markets and then to the global markets. So recently, as Europe and Japan pumped money and their economics wouldn't absorb it, our markets got a temporary dose of liquidity. It will dry up when Europe's economies finally awaken. Once Europe ignites, the central banks must rein in money growth to avoid inflation. Worse, that European money now in our markets will return home.

It's funny, but central bankers have rarely understood monetary policy. Milton Friedman wrote on that when I was a kid. Liquidity has flowed between major nations this way for 100 years. The $64 question is: When does re-pay day hit? I don't know. As I said, the time lags aren't predictable. The money flow will reverse, maybe in 3 months, maybe in 18. It depends on how long it takes for the European economies to perk up.

For now, I remain bullish on big, relatively cheap stocks that haven't moved too much and have exposure to a European pickup. ∎

Time to Take a Trip

August 12, 1996

It is now time to start buying large European and Japanese stocks. No big rush, but over the next two years big, cheap, cyclical stocks in major markets overseas should outshine our homegrown variety.

Despite the July drop, I haven't yet turned bearish on America, but am getting more bullish on the rest of the developed world. If nothing else, the July volatility suggests that there are better prospects elsewhere.

Note: A few years back, when foreign was faddish, I was urging you to stay at home. But in 1997 I don't see the US having the cyclical advantages I see overseas.

Last month I detailed how European and Japanese central bankers were printing money like crazy and how that would eventually get their economies going. The implication, in my mind, is bullish for them. But there are lots of other signs I like, too. Japan's unemployment rate hit an alltime high in May. In France it is just shy of a record. This is the yeast bull markets rise from.

Buried in a recent Dun & Bradstreet survey is the news that US business executives are much more optimistic than foreign counterparts. In America, about 45% of executives expect higher sales ahead, about the same as last year. But in Germany, only 17% are optimistic, down from 40% last year. Again, this is pessimistic porridge for a contrarian.

Then, too, there's the question of risk. Most of the diversification benefit from foreign investing comes in a skinny slice of time. The coming years, 1997 and 1998, look like one of those slices. While foreign looks good, the US may get dicey. Over the S&P 500's entire history, exactly 45% of all negative years were in the first year of a US President's term. Another 35% of all the index's downers have been in the second year. The first half of a President's term has had at least one negative year an amazing 82% of the time. So, Clinton or Dole, risk rises here in 1997 and 1998 while it dwindles abroad.

I'm not recommending emerging markets—a very different cycle. I'm recommending only ADRs of huge, cheap, dominant firms that will benefit from a cyclical pickup in business activity. ∎

PSRs Revisited

September 9, 1996

A number of readers have written to ask if there has been more research on price/sales ratios since my first book introduced PSRs to the world in 1984. If you need refreshing, the price/sales ratio is the relationship between a company's sales and its market capitalization. Let's say sales work out to $100 a share and the stock price is 100—rather high in my book. That's a 1-to-1 ratio. If the stock price were 50, the PSR would be 50%. A low PSR is good because it means that a small improvement in profit margins can bring a lot to the bottom line, improving the firm's future P/E. Low-PSR stocks are held in low regard by Wall Street. Those with improving profit margins usually catch the Street by surprise.

A recent book covering PSRs is *What Works on Wall Street*, by James P. O'Shaughnessy (McGraw-Hill). He doesn't give me the credit I think I deserve for introducing the concept, but, what the heck, it's still a great book.

O'Shaughnessy tests most screening tools—everything from low P/Es to momentum measures like relative strength—over more than 40 years. His finding: Low-PSR stocks swamp not only high PSRs but all other cuts and by a lot. Ditto, using only small stocks or big stocks. Low PSRs beat the next-best horse across all races, and by about 1.5% per year or more. That was true, too, in most multiyear subsets of the 40-plus years, whether the subsets were long ones or short ones.

O'Shaughnessy then shows that you do better still combining PSRs with other ratios in a more complicated multivariate attack. While true, I doubt most folks will ever do this. If it's complicated, most investors won't stick to it. But there is lots to learn here.

In a similar vein, professors William C. Barbee Jr., Sandip Mukherji and Gary A. Raines wrote a barn burner of a paper in the March/April 1996 issue of the *Financial Analysts Journal*—at your library—entitled "Do Sales-Price and Debt-Equity Explain Stock Returns Better than Book-Market and Firm Size?" Their answer? Yes. Challenging the academic establishment's current conclusion that price-to-book is the best way to view reality, this trio's academic work shows that price/sales ratios are "a more reliable explanatory factor" for stock returns than other measures. They use all the standard academic tools and rules to show that if you like academia, you will love PSRs.

My own firm's recent PSR research has focused overseas. Here, too, low-PSR stocks nicely beat higher PSR stocks and beat other valuation cuts. We have focused research overseas because it hasn't been done yet publicly, and because, as my most recent columns have predicted, 1997 and 1998 will offer better stock market returns in Europe and Japan than in the US. ∎

The Election and Stocks
October 7, 1996

Here is my advice on how to play the November election. The best outcome for 1997 markets would be an increase in the GOP's hold on Congress even with the reelection of Clinton. It is also the highest single likelihood. It offers slow change, no chaos, no antibusiness legislation and no big surprises—a great market backdrop. Yes, such an outcome means legislative gridlock in Washington, but markets much prefer gridlock to massive change. In big change is big risk.

The worst outcome? A Clinton win with the Democrats gaining both houses of Congress. This could cause the stock market to take a 10% to 15% hit and maybe much more later. It would probably result in big changes and unchecked antibusiness legislation. This outcome looks highly unlikely, but not impossible. More possible and not too bad is a Clinton win with the Democrats winning one house in Congress. Still gridlock.

To be objective, a Dole victory with a stronger Republican majority in Congress would be poor for stocks. Just before and after the election, stocks would be very strong, almost euphoric. But they would then be hurt heading into 1997 because a Republican sweep would also lead to change—a different sort of change, but any big political change will be unsettling for stocks.

I'm Republican to the core. I want Dole and big Republican gains in the House and Senate, which would be great for America in the long run. But facts are facts. The outcome I most desire personally would cause a lot of turbulence in financial markets as they adjusted to a new set of circumstances.

Those are the scenarios. Which is most likely? Who holds Congress is more key to 1997's markets than the presidency. Here I feel reasonably optimistic: I believe the Republicans will continue to hold Congress, and that means we don't have to worry about business-bashing legislation. That should help buoy a nice stock rally. All the more so if, as I sense it will, the GOP gains seats.

The prospects for added GOP congressional strength come from (1) the fact that since 1950 the reelection rate of House incumbents has averaged above 92% and never has been below 87%, and (2) the open races happen to be in places that heavily favor the GOP. The open seats are where most of the action is. Add up both parties' shaky incumbents and the open seats, and I see Republican gains in both House and Senate.

After that rally, what? I have been saying for some time now that the action soon shifts from US stocks to overseas stocks as the recovery abroad gathers steam. It follows, therefore, that a preelection rally on Wall Street would be an excellent opportunity to raise cash for investment overseas. ■

Why the Rich Get (Relatively) Poorer
October 14, 1996

Rich Americans have, in general, been terrible investors. Compare the first, fifth and this, the fifteenth, annual editions of the *Forbes* 400. Initially it took $100 million to make the bottom of the *Forbes* 400. Now it takes $415 million.

In theory, it shouldn't have been all that hard to stay on the 400 list. A person on the bottom of the first list could have remained there to this day by simply compounding his wealth at 10%. Seemingly not so difficult. After all, that is less than two-thirds of the S&P 500's 15.6% average annual return during the same period.

Yet how many of the original names remain on the *Forbes* 400? Precious few, even allowing for deaths. Not one of the original ten richest remains in the top ten now. Folks like the Hunt brothers and sisters, who have seen their assets stall or fall.

Of 1986's top ten, only two remain there, John Kluge and Warren Buffett. Even the great Kluge, who has done far better than most of the *Forbes* 400, hasn't kept pace with the S&P 500 in the last ten years—11.2% versus 13.8%.

Lester Crown in 1986 was number eight on the list, worth more than $1.3 billion. But he was in real estate and is now worth only $2 billion—a compound ten-year return of only 4.4%. The names go on and on with similar results. The conclusion is inescapable. The superrich have done poorly as investors.

You can see this in any time period as long as it is fairly long. Recall that to remain low man on the *Forbes* 400 totem pole for 15 years meant you didn't keep up with the market—you did less than two-thirds as well as the S&P 500. But the same was true for each of the 5-year periods within those 15 years. In any of them the guy starting last on the list fell off if he did worse than 63% as well as the S&P 500 and rose nicely on the list if he beat the market. Most folks fall.

In a way, all this is healthy: It keeps great wealth from becoming permanently concentrated in a few hands. In a way, too, it is inevitable. You make big money in a business when it is hot; when it turns cold, you can't just get out and do something else. That is one nice thing about the stock market for the average investor: He has almost total liquidity and can shift quickly with the winds of fortune in a way the superrich can't.

And that leads to another conclusion—that keeping up with the S&P 500 is vastly harder than almost anyone imagines. Not only do stocks as a category tend to have higher returns than individual businesses, but they get you there at lower risk, because the stock market allows for much more diversification than the average rich person has.

And stocks are less messy. So many of the superrich own big, illiquid chunks of businesses. When bad management or other sticky personnel problems pop up, they can't just sell and move on. They have the necessity to step in personally and set things right. They don't just own the firms; the firms own them.

For 12 years I have recommended specific stocks in these pages—twice pausing for brief bear markets, but always aiming to own stocks. This issue, I urge you to visit a used-book store. It can refer you to a bookfinder, who can scrounge up old issues of the *Forbes 400*. These will be valuable someday, perhaps in price, but surely in what you can learn from them.

The lesson, of course, is: No company is forever. Most businesses have periods of rapid growth, then slow down or even drop down. Only the economy grows forever, even if irregularly. Doubt me? Get out your financial calculator and do what I have done: Calculate rates of return for 400 members from years past. Learn who did what that worked and who did what that didn't.

What you'll find is that building a business is the best way to get rich, but for staying rich, you can't do better than own common stocks. If I had to bet on the long-term winner of the *Forbes 400*, I would pick Warren Buffett, not Bill Gates. ∎

Small Isn't Always Best
November 4, 1996

In this, the 18th annual small companies issue, recall that small is often said to be beautiful—that small stocks do better in the long pull than big stocks. This is true—sometimes. I do not think this is one of those times. The outlook for smaller stocks looks rather ugly to me right now.

There are lots of lousy but well-accepted academic studies of paper portfolios to show that small stocks do best, by several percent per year. Unreal. These studies ignored total transaction costs—spreads, commissions, the effect on the market of heavy buying and selling. I should know. My firm runs a large small-cap portfolio. If small stocks do 2% per year better than big stocks on paper, you end up several percent behind after all costs. The transaction friction is that bad.

Small stocks aren't worse than big stocks; they just aren't better. If capitalism works, if supply and demand determine prices, and if liquidity flows from sector to sector, it defies logic to presume one broad class of common stock is permanently better than others. After all, we have a huge world of securities' creators whose job it is to make sure they swamp any such image with new supply.

In the real world the market moves in cycles: Big stocks lead for a while, then smaller, but neither has a permanent edge. Sometimes value stocks lead the market and sometimes growth stocks do. They all have alternating periods in the sun and in the rain. Since early 1994 big stocks have led every year. I missed the start of this, but around the beginning of 1995 my column began advocating the bigger stocks. I now think big stocks should stay in front through the end of the next bear market. Small stocks should not shine again until then.

But the revival of small caps is a long way down the road. First will be a bear market in which big value stocks should drop least and small growth stocks should do worst. Yes, a bear market. For the benefit of readers under 30 I mention that there really are such things as bear markets. July was a modest foretaste.

No, I am not yet bearish on the US market, as recent readers know and don't know exactly when I will turn so. But I am pretty certain it's too late to start buying small stocks. Unless your time frame is short enough to aim at in-and-outing the rest of this bull market, it may be too late to buy big stocks, too. Going into a bear market I would rather own stocks that don't fall, and my best sense of how to sidestep the next bear market is with big, cheap foreign stocks, which as I have said for several months now, should benefit from an economic pickup in Europe and Japan in 1997 and 1998. ■

For Your Christmas Shopping List
December 2, 1996

Christmas is coming. Call 1-800-575-9255 right now. Have them rush you a *Financial Insiders Catalog of Wall Street Creations*. It's the darnedest collection of neat financial gift items anywhere—all available by credit card and 800 number.

Maybe you like bull-and-bear accessories like neckties, business card cases, bookends, letter openers or towels. All here. Stock certificates, classic financial artwork—even investment greeting cards.

Haven't yet found all the presents you want for investor friends and associates? Call 1-800-272-2855. Order the Traders' Library Catalog for a wide selection of hard-to-find investment books. It has lots of those I have suggested over the years, including: *Reminiscences of a Stock Operator*

by Edwin Lefevre; *The Warren Buffett Way* by Robert Hagstrom Jr.; *Investment Psychology Explained* by Martin Pring; the legendary *The Intelligent Investor* by Benjamin Graham and *Security Analysis* by Graham and Dodd.

Calling 1-800-927-8222 will get you the Traders Press catalog, stuffed with investment-oriented gift novelties and books. I have bought more from this catalog over the years than from the first two. All three of these catalogs are great and free.

For years my pre-Christmas column was a "best of" critique of the year's new investment books. Not this year. Couldn't find any. Most investment books I have seen since 1994 remind me of Bill Clinton: a good-looking cover, great sound bites—but when you get inside, no real content.

But there are a couple of exceptions. Aswath Damodaran's new *Investment Valuation*, from John Wiley, deserves real estate on any great investor's bookshelf. It is a virtual bible on valuation, focusing primarily on techniques on how to value firms, and in more depth than most investors will ever need; but it also covers real estate, bonds and options. If you hate math, this book gets tedious in places—just skip those. If it isn't in your bookstore, order it.

Hate math? Then you will like James Dines' self-published new book, *Mass Psychology*. To me, finance's frontier is what academics call "behavioralism"—the psychology of what people do with investment tools, as opposed to traditional finance, which simply analyzes the tools themselves. Yes, no-load funds beat load funds, but investors in load funds beat investors in no-loads. A paradox? No, but it took academics more than 30 years to figure out that people who pay loads are less likely to engage in costly in-and-out trading. Sometimes how tools are used is more important than the tools themselves. Dines jumps into the psychology of it all, warning that many of us harbor a deep-seated desire to lose. His exposition on gambler psychology and investing is classic. ∎

The Top Is Nigh
December 30, 1996

Our stock market looks sick. It feels just like 1972. My best guess has the S&P 500 peaking in 1997's first half, then falling, with a small negative total year return, perhaps down 5% to 10%.

After that? Look out. The parallels between 1972 and 1996 are uncanny, and, all the more powerful, no one has noticed. For those who have forgotten, 1972 led to 1973–74, when the S&P 500 dropped a sickening 37%.

It worries me that the pundits so uniformly love having Clinton in the White House and the GOP controlling Congress. Note that these were many of the same folk who once shunned the market because they feared gridlock between Congress and Clinton. What they feared in 1994 they love in 1996.

The honeymoon is just too sweet. Since November 5 Clinton has adorned so many magazine covers that it is almost guaranteed the media will turn against him by midterm. Falling presidential popularity is always a powerful bearish motivator.

I have long said that bull market peaks take a long time to form. No exception now. Smaller-cap indexes like the Russell 2000 or the S&P 500 remain at or below their May levels. Just as they did in 1972, which saw thin leadership, with only the biggest stocks hitting new highs after the spring. In 1972 there were the Nifty Fifty. This year's market also has been led by high-quality, big-cap growth stocks, although valuations aren't quite as high as they were in 1972.

Make no mistake, 1972's massive movement to "one-decision stocks" had the identical intellectual foundation that supports today's case for the big growth stocks.

Then, too, stocks exploded after our election, just as they did after 1992's voting. More than coincidence, this is bearish. I find only two times this century when a market boom right after a presidential election wasn't a market warning sign aimed 1 to 12 months out. Those two exceptions, 1924 and 1944, had the White House and Congress held by the same party—unlike now or 1972. Of course, the Whitewater to Watergate parallel is obvious. Tricky Dick. Slick Willie.

More parallels. I see 1994 being to 1996 what 1970 was to 1972—a brief pause en route to the last leg of a big, long bull. In 1972 Treasury bill yields were at their lowest in ten years—ending the year almost exactly at today's level. Then and now, the yield curve was flattening, with long bonds appreciating. No, the yield curve is not flat, but neither was it in 1972. People have failed to notice that the decline in interest rates flows from the barely noticed liquidity that has been quietly pouring into America from overseas.

The big difference between then and now is that 1972 was part of a secular inflationary upswing and 1996 isn't. Another big difference, I suspect, is that in 1973 foreign stocks fell with ours, while in 1997 and 1998 I think they will be on a different cycle. European and Japanese stocks can make forward, positive progress while our stock market backslides. Months ago I predicted that the world's excess liquidity, which has been flooding into the US market, would slosh abroad again in 1997. No one paid attention. At least now, a recent article in the *Wall Street Journal* has noticed that the money inflow has fueled our recent rise. Soon investors will notice the flow back to Europe.

I expect to try to make money throughout the upcoming bear market. Note I said "upcoming." As of this writing, the bull market is still intact, and I have said I won't turn bearish until after I think I have seen the top. It may be very soon. I'm not selling good, huge stocks. But it is much too late for small stocks. It is not too late—as I have advocated since August—to buy big foreign stocks. Right now I'm 55% US stocks, and that only from among the 50 very largest, and 45% foreign. ■

1997

Rational Exuberance

> " *In some respects I have been lucky and it scares me. . . . Getting these short-term swings right is often just luck. I'm always grateful for luck, but know enough not to confuse it with skill.* "
>
> "MY ANNUAL REPORT," FEBRUARY 24, 1997

> " *I haven't a clue when [the bull market] will end, and neither does anyone else. Better than futilely trying to foresee a top, wait for a clear signal the market has topped. That won't get you out at the absolute peak but will get you out soon enough to stay intact.* "
>
> "WHEN SHOULD YOU GET OUT," SEPTEMBER 22, 1997

In many of his columns, Ken highlights the folly of calling a bear market too soon. Investors dream of getting out of the market at an exact top and getting back in at the bottom, but that's a fool's game. Forecasting the market that accurately is nearly impossible. The odds of making that call perfectly with any consistency is on par with winning the lottery—only it'll cost more than a dollar if it's wrong. Given the choice between getting out of the market too early or too late, Ken will take too late every time. Getting out too early can mean missing out on substantial upside before a bear market develops. Getting out too late may mean giving up a little, but usually only a little if done right. Bear markets typically develop slowly; they seldom drop off a cliff initially.

If anyone is equipped to make an accurate prognostication about a market top ahead of time, surely it's the US Federal Reserve chairman, right? Not so much. Then-Fed Chairman Alan Greenspan closed 1996 warning of unsustainably high asset values in his famous "irrational exuberance" speech. As you might expect, stocks reacted negatively to such a warning from the world's most powerful economist. But only briefly. Greenspan would have done well to abide by Ken's forecasting guidelines. The S&P 500 lost a few percent in the days following Greenspan's speech but regained their upward momentum. The S&P 500 gained 33.4 percent in 1997.[1] Between the date of Greenspan's speech and the end of the bull market in March 2000, the S&P 500 gained 115.6 percent.[2] Calling a bear early can be expensive.

Ken was wary of a coming market top—in the US not abroad—but his forecasting rules kept him and his readers in the market. That was fortunate since by midyear Ken was bullish again. Interestingly, Ken's firm's clients were at least partially responsible for changing his tune. He noted that too many were also worried about a near-term bear market for one to be around the corner. "When we sign on a new account, we ask certain questions, and it is surprising how many of the new clients are worried about an impending top . . . The market is giving lots of people—too many people—fear of heights. Fear is bullish." ("The Top? Not Yet," July 28, 1997.)

Ken repeated his call for big stocks to do best in 1997 and coming years. And when Ken said "big" he meant "mega-big" as in bigger than the weighted market capitalization of the overall market. Most investors set somewhat arbitrary parameters to distinguish big stocks from small stocks. They call any stock over $10 billion or $20 billion big—or some other number that usually doesn't change with the market. Ken's research showed the proper way to distinguish big from small is to look at the overall market's weighted average market capitalization (the sum of each stock's market capitalization times its weight in a capitalization weighted index) of the whole market. Stocks bigger than the weighted average market cap act big, and those smaller act small. Ones that are just a little smaller than that act a little small, and ones a lot smaller act a lot small. To Ken it was a simple, linear function. In 1997, a firm had to be worth about $50 billion to be considered big by Ken. A scarce few firms fit the bill. But those biggest of the biggies were some of the best performers in 1997 and for the remainder of the bull market.

Incidentally, Ken nailed this one cold when very few foresaw it. Many forecast big stocks doing well, but by not measuring size correctly, ended up buying stocks they thought were big but actually acted a little small compared to the market—the way a $20 billion to $40 billion market cap stock would.

Another factor contributing to Ken's changed view of a near-term bear emanated from overseas. In prior years, Ken saw massive amounts of money creation by foreign central banks boosting US shares. Foreign central bankers were trying to grease their economic wheels with loads of cash. It takes a while for that extra money to get their economies going again. In the interim, some of those funds made their way in US assets. After all, interest rates in the US were higher than many other major countries, so investors could borrow money abroad, invest it in the US, and earn a profit on the spread as long as the US dollar didn't plummet. As foreign economies improved, Ken feared those funds would leave the US. But in 1997, Ken recognized foreign economies weren't recovering as quickly as he expected, and that foreign capital would stay in the US—for a while anyway. "In the short term this foreign interest rate arbitrage feels mighty good to us. Manna from abroad. One day, the manna will stop flowing. Monetary policy works, albeit with unpredictable time lags." ("Beware of Foreigners Bearing Bucks," October 20, 1997.) With foreign manna parked in the US, Ken altered his previous forecast and looked for US shares to lead foreign. They did in 1997 and for the remainder of the bull market.

Stocks market gains may have been centered in the US in 1997, but most other action was overseas. In the UK, political change was afoot as the Labour

Party wrested control from conservatives for the first time in 18 years. The UK also lost Princess Diana when she was tragically killed in an auto accident in Paris. In Asia, the Asian Financial Crisis was unfolding, shaking foreign markets. But US stocks were largely unscathed.

Sometimes global markets move together. Sometimes they don't—1997 was a year in which some markets floundered and some flourished. A main reason for Ken's global view today is global markets are never perfectly in sync, so there's always some diversification benefit to investing globally, even if that benefit fluctuates over time.

Decoupling
January 27, 1997

My December 30, 1996 column got one very strong reaction. Several readers wrote, "Fisher, if you think US stocks will soon enter a bear market, you're a fool to think foreign stocks won't suffer similarly."

You can call me a fool for not accepting the common wisdom that markets move in sync, but I stick to my guns. I continue to expect rising stock prices in Europe and Japan in 1997. And a bear market here. Major foreign stocks can rise 10% to 20%. US stocks may drop 5% to 10%, and more in 1998.

No, I haven't sold my big, high-quality US stocks, but the end is nigh. And then? A classic bear market—of an ilk many 40-year-olds have never felt.

But back to that question about markets moving in sync. Yes, global equity markets have been getting more closely correlated in the last few years. But that comes and goes. Over the long sweep our linkage with overseas markets has varied from very high to very low about every four years on average. I expect our market to soon decouple from the rest of the Western world. It will be like when the Japanese market had a resounding crash after 1989, dropping 60%, but the US market just went up and up. Now I think it's the US' turn to take a beating.

Why? I expect our interest rates to rise in 1997. Grumpy Greenspan will get grumpier and can tighten without fear of upsetting a White House that doesn't have to run for reelection. But in spite of higher interest rates the hundreds of billions of dollars of newly printed foreign money that flooded into our financial markets will return home to be deployed in their "main street" activities as I first detailed July 15, 1996.

Meanwhile, our politics will trend ugly. They always do in the first year of a President's term. We haven't seen the last of the Clinton Administration scandals. As speculation turns to desperation, our bull market will keep acting badly, roll over, and finally we will get a rather normal recession.

Meanwhile, overseas looks great. After years of severe monetary austerity and the weak economy and belt-tightening that goes with it, Europe is now showing signs of life. Japan will soon. That will be reinforced by all that newly created money they parked here in 1996 going home to work. Still, they all keep printing money.

In December alone, interest rates were cut in Australia, France, Italy, Portugal, Spain and Sweden. Japan cut its prime rate to 2.5%. In Germany, reserve requirements were loosened. Not only are rates lower abroad than here, yield curves are steeply upward-sloping, with typically more than a 3.5% spread between short-term and long-term interest rates. Bully for them. Our yield curve is much flatter. Eight times out often it is smart to have your money where rates are lower and yield curves are steeper.

Monetary policy works, but with a lag, and because of this lag a lot of the foreign money took a sojourn in the US. When it goes home, as it will when foreign economies recover, it will strangle us, pushing us into recession. This is going to be one of those times when US markets and foreign markets decouple. ∎

My Annual Report

February 24, 1997

Forbes wants you to have a periodic accounting of our recommendations. This issue it's my turn to bare my record. On a few occasions I haven't felt too good about my reckoning, but this time I display it proudly.

Spanning 14 columns in 1996, I recommended buying 61 new stocks and selling 11 stocks that I had earlier suggested for purchase. Had you done it all, and in equal dollar amounts, you would be up 13.9%, versus 12.1% for the S&P 500 for the same holding periods, with dividends reinvested. Had you simply made my 61 "buys," you would be up 12.7%, versus 11.3% for the S&P 500.

My 1996 market forecast, made in the January 22, 1996 issue, projected the market to be up 10% to 20% for the year. The S&P 500 ended up 22.96%. The Russell 2000, the standard measure of small stocks, was up 16.49%. I was a bit too cautious, but the results were within the range I predicted. I was among the relatively few who thought we could have a super 1996 on top of the super 1995.

And my forecast that big stocks would nicely beat small stocks in 1996 was very good. Recommending only big stocks helped a lot. But I was wrong in thinking that big value stocks would outperform big growth stocks. The reverse occurred.

In some respects I have been lucky, and it scares me. In my column of January 22, 1996 I recommended Merrill Lynch at 51. I used it to replace Raymond James Financial, a previously successful pick that has since done much less well, I used Merrill again on June 17 at 66—the only stock used twice in 1996—this time as a replacement for Bear, Stearns. And it worked again very nicely. Getting these short-term swings right is often just luck. I'm always grateful for luck, but know enough not to confuse it with skill.

But I am proud about picking Merrill in the first place in my column of September 26, 1994, at 40, Brokerage stocks were out of favor; nobody expected the bull market to last. I saw Merrill as the leader in an industry that would flourish as king as the bull market continued. Right after I picked it, Merrill plunged briefly into the low 30s and readers rapped my knuckles. That was just bad luck, I wrote back to hold on. I can't tell you exactly where the bottom will be for a stock, but I think I'm usually pretty good at knowing when a stock is a relative bargain.

I still like Merrill and won't sell it until I think this bull market is finally over. When is that? In my December 30 column I predicted the market would peak sometime in 1997's first half, followed by a normal bear market. We're not quite there yet.

> ### Mistakes Are Part of the Game
>
> This column makes an important point. In investing, you can make errors—sometimes lots of them—and still end up ok or even great over time. Here, Ken shares some of his big losing picks from the previous year. Yet, even with those, he still ended up nicely outpacing the S&P 500 in 1996 (the way Forbes calculates it) because he recommended a diversified bunch. Investors, even great ones, can and will make errors. It's to be expected. The goal is to have your mistakes not hurt you too badly in the long run. (For more, see Table 1 in the Introduction.)

I have learned that the smarter you feel the dumber you think. Feelings of infallibility goeth before a fall. That my 1996 picks beat the S&P 500 by a bit tells you nothing about whether I will have good advice for you in 1997. All I can promise is that I will not let my recent successes go to my head.

And that I will continue to learn from my mistakes. My worst 1996 pick, sort of, was Eastman Chemical at 72. It had fallen 23% by year-end. I failed to see how much rising oil prices would eat into Eastman's profit margin. I expect more oil price hikes ahead and Eastman will continue to suffer, so I would take my losses.

My most costly 1996 advice was on July 15—suggesting selling Liz Claiborne at 34 after recommending it at 18 in 1995. It had risen another 74% by year-end. I thought it was fully priced. Bad call. Too early. Sorry,

My next worst 1996 pick was suggesting Casio Computer at 97 on August 12. It dropped 20% by year-end. Would I sell it now? Call me Crazy Ken, but I love Japan now. There are oodles of doomsayers about Japan—which suggests Japan is very close to the end of its major long-term bear market and is a real buying opportunity. I like the fundamentals there. Its monetary policy is sound. Casio will do well in the upturn, as will Kubota, Matsushita and Sony, all of which are down single-digit percentages since I recommended them in *Forbes*.

I like all the first-class global Japanese names. My advice right now is to have 25% of your portfolio in Japan. ∎

Golden Opportunity
March 24, 1997

Call me goofy, but I suddenly like gold stocks. I'm not a goldbug. In my March 14, 1994 column I bad-mouthed gold and gold stocks as they were climbing toward $420. I said the price rally was a "fool's trap," and predicted gold could go below $300. I'm no longer betting on that $300 bottom. Back then, I said gold wouldn't bottom until 1996 or 1997. Well, it's about time. Gold looks mighty bottomish to me between $340 and $360. It could be back to $420 in a year.

The G-10 nations are on a money-printing binge. This spells inflation a bit down the road. Despite weakness in recent weeks, oil is up while gold is down over the last one, two and three years. Oil and gold can't head in different directions indefinitely.

It also impresses me that the goldbugs are so quiet these days. The big names of yesteryear are invisible or have capitulated.

Note how former Federal Reserve Vice Chairman Wayne Angell, currently chief economist at Bear, Stearns, a longtime lover of the glittering yellowish stuff, has just turned cold on gold. Angell now calls the dollar "better than gold," and predicts lower gold prices. Yet no one notices that he caved in. When capitulation goes unnoticed, it is a powerful long-term trend signal. And when the last optimists give up, it's time for gold contrarians to turn optimistic.

At half the price of one or two years ago, you can get—all in one—what may be the world's best gold mining outfit, a real emerging markets stock and a true value play. Ashanti Goldfields is aggressive, efficient, innovative and, with its leaching methods, arguably gold's technology leader. Ashanti has smart management. It has extensive reserves, low-cost production, growing revenue, and excellent balance sheet and cash flow.

Ashanti was formerly a one-mine outfit in Ghana. It is 20%-owned by the Ghanaian government, but it is aggressively branching outside Ghana, buying African gold operations, properties and upgrading them. It will produce more than 1 million ounces of gold this year and has more than 20 years of proven reserves, and keeps adding to them. Being "out of Africa," it always sells at a steep discount, but never more so than now. Ashanti is cheap at 12 times earnings, 9 times cash flow and 2 times book value. It even has a dividend yield—1.7%. I expect 35 within four years, a near triple.

Also out of Africa, but South Africa instead of Ghana, is $14 billion mining brute Anglo American, A conglomerate and holding company, it is largely linked to precious metals pricing. Chairman J. Ogilvie Thompson and his crew are predatory. That's good. Anglo's most recent blitz was wresting control of publicly traded Lonrho from its management. The violent acquisition gives Anglo American monopoly control of the world platinum market and 30% of Ashanti Goldfields.

The European Union's antitrust commission is apoplectic about Anglo's platinum monopoly and is holding extensive hearings to figure out what to do. I have always liked owning a stock under government attack for antitrust. If there's something the bureaucrats want to take away from a company, it must be something worth owning.

Anglo American is also gold and diamond mining, mining finance for other firms, steel, paper, chemicals, real estate and 51% of Amcoal, which by itself earns $100 million annually. Anglo grows moderately, and is well financed. It sells for only 13 times my calculation of next year's earnings (including non-consolidated subsidiaries), less than 2 times book value and has a 1.1% dividend yield. When gold is back to $420 and rising from there, price Anglo at 90. That's 50% better than the current price.

Oh, I forgot. Anglo also owns 32% of $13 billion DeBeers, the world's dominant diamond producer, which owns 39% of Anglo American. Same management. DeBeers is cheap and worth owning in its own right. ∎

Bet Against Buffett? Not Me.
April 21, 1997

If you are waiting for small stocks to have their day, I have bad news for you: You have a long wait. And I have further news: You had better revise your definition of what constitutes a large stock versus a small stock.

For several years I have urged readers to stick with big-cap stocks. That has been good advice. For example, my December 30, 1996 column said that the best US stocks to own are those "from among the 50 very largest." I expect this trend will continue.

As of this writing there are just 35 stocks with a market capitalization (price times shares outstanding) bigger than that of the S&P 500. I call them super caps. You may think of outfits with market caps of $10 billion as big, but my firm's research shows that even such biggies tend to perform more like small caps than super caps for years at a crack.

So, forget small cap versus big cap. Think instead of super caps versus everything else.

Look at the S&P 500 without the super caps. My studies show that when small beats big or vice versa for multiyear spans as is happening now, these 465 perform more like small stocks than large stocks. Take 1996: The S&P 500's ten largest stocks, super caps all, returned 29.5%, versus the S&P 500's 23%. If you owned all 35 super caps last year, equal-weighted, you beat the S&P 500 by 1.1%. The S&P 500's 465 smallest stocks returned 17.4%. And the small-cap Russell 2000 came in at 16.5%. In short, the super caps beat big caps, most of which acted like small caps.

Don't sweat a billion bucks or so. Warren Buffett's bets on Gillette and McDonald's, which would be numbers 40 and 41 on the list at $33 billion, are both big enough to act super. But during these periods $10 billion-size stocks act about 70% like small stocks; stocks with caps of $5 billion act about 85% like the smallest stocks.

Based on my cycle analysis, I expect big to keep beating small until the bottom of the next bear market. And I expect the super caps will keep beating the market. As the bull market turns bearish, the super caps will drop, but less drastically than all smaller stocks.

No, not forever. Only until we have completed a full bull/bear market cycle. From 1974 until 1982 small caps were the stars. They will be again. But that time is a whole bear market away. Until then, small-ness hurts.

So, are the super caps well represented in your portfolio? If not, you are unlikely to beat, or even match, the market. Note that Warren Buffett's Berkshire Hathaway is a super cap, and owns primarily super caps or near super caps including: Coca-Cola, Disney, Gillette, McDonald's and American Express. Do you want to bet against Buffett? ∎

Nowhere to Go But Down
May 19, 1997

Short Toyota; buy Nissan. Toyota is so overpriced today, it sells for more than General Motors, Ford and Chrysler put together. The market says Toyota is worth $106 billion. General Motors is priced at $42 billion. Ford at $39 billion. And Chrysler at $20 billion. Nissan is valued at $15 billion.

If you don't like Nissan, if you agree with the *Forbes* article skeptical of its comeback efforts, short Toyota anyhow and buy the US big three. Toyota is so overpriced as to be almost ridiculous.

Yes, I know. Toyota has a hot lineup and better and faster engineering than anyone else. It is generally better managed than most competitors. And more aggressive. I won't argue these points. However, you can overpay for a quality image, and Toyota's virtues are overrecognized and overpriced. Stocks often look their best just before they fall.

Wall Street usually adopts a favorite or two among the autos, often based on a hot run of models. But the leader flips to laggard just when it ramps up its PR machine and its boss starts gracing magazine covers. In autos a big ego goeth before a fall. For me the clincher was Toyota's April 7 *BusinessWeek* cover spread. We all know that magazine's history of bad calls.

Toyota is a distant third in global auto market share, just ahead of Volkswagen. Nissan is fifth. Toyota's president, Hiroshi Okuda, says he wants to dominate the world auto market. Fine, but that is already in the stocks. Ford and GM both sell at 28% of annual sales, eight times earnings and two times cash flow. With Ford you get a 4.8% dividend yield. GM yields 3.5%. Chrysler yields 5.3% and sells at a P/E of 6 and 38% of revenue. All three stocks are flat over the last year.

But Toyota sells at 105% of revenue, 38 times relatively normal earnings and 16 times cash flow, with almost no dividend. Is Toyota that much better an outfit? Worth more than the big three all put together? No way.

Toyota's US market share is relatively stagnant right now. I see Nissan as the swing factor. Both Nissan and Toyota sell about half their cars outside Japan. But Nissan's cars are lower-end, and we've had world auto markets recently that favor high-end cars. As Europe and Japan revive, which is only starting now, more ordinary people will be able to buy cars, and that bodes well for Nissan. Nissan's low-end line will pick up relative to Toyota and reduce the spread between them, making Nissan look better and Toyota worse.

Nissan isn't profitable now, but it will be. It sells for the same price it did ten years ago, which is pretty rare. Nissan is 55% as big as Toyota in revenue but sells for 14% of Toyota's total market cap. Buying Nissan while selling short Toyota dollar for dollar leaves you net neutral to Japanese auto sales and is a simple bet on the low end of the auto market as the non-US market revives.

Right now a good overall auto exposure might be 6% of your global equity portfolio: 2% Nissan, 2% Ford, 1% GM and 1% Fiat. If you are comfortable selling short, you can boost your dividend income and cut your overall risk using 2% GM, 2% Ford, 1% Chrysler, 2% Fiat, 3% Nissan and shorting 4% in Toyota.

Moving from stocks to buy to books to buy, get yourself a copy of Tony Spare's terribly titled new book. *Last Chance Financial Planning Guide* (Prima Publishing). I think it should have been *Wit and Wisdom From One of the Street's Savviest Survivors.* I have known Spare more than half my life—since my father taught him at Stanford. About half that time we have argued. He is ornery and stubborn. But I've always respected and admired him. His first book was informative but boring.

In this new book, he is brilliant from the first paragraph. Tony questions much of Wall Street's conventional wisdom for 225 pages. That's good. When Tony Spare speaks, I listen. You should, too. ∎

Do It Yourself
June 16, 1997

Investors simply give away too much money—in needless fees for needless services. For example, they often pay advisers 1% per year to be switched around among no-load mutual funds, which themselves cost 1.5% per year. Don't forget: Funds pay brokerage, too. Fees on fees, plus fees—all cutting into good years and bad.

An adviser using no-load funds can easily cost you 3% of your portfolio every year. Then come wrap programs, which are as bad. Here, a broker picks a handful of specialist investment advisers and helps you allocate among them. The brokers claim to be market-wise consultants but they rarely add value.

The very first wisdom I learned from Warren Buffett, when I was 21, was that 3% per year into fees when stocks do 10% in the long term starts you 30% in the hole. You net 7%—bond-like. My rule of thumb: Every 1% in fees means you need to be another 10% smarter than the market just to keep up with it. Nearly no one is 30% smarter.

I have a radical suggestion but it is a very old idea: How about picking your own stocks, buying them through a sound discount broker and avoiding heavy trading? Just cut out as many of the middlemen as possible.

With even $100,000 you can save a lot of these costs. If you own about 30 stocks, you can get about 85% of the diversification you would have with five mutual funds. Do your own diversifying: Buy a few foreign stocks, some big-cap value stocks, some big growth stocks and a few small stocks. Shy of severe bad luck, you will do just as well as with a high-priced adviser and a handful of mutual funds. And you will save a bundle. ∎

The Top? Not Yet.
July 28, 1997

Seven months ago my December 30 column said that "my best guess" was for a peak "in 1997's first half." Happily, I did not urge you to sell but urged you to remain fully invested until it looks like a top has already come.

I'm glad I advised holding on to stocks because that peak now looks a good deal further away than the first half of 1997.

What has changed my mind? My own clients, to a large degree. When we sign on a new account, we ask certain questions, and it is surprising how many of the new clients are worried about an impending top. In fact, many have hired us to help them decide when to pull the cord on their parachutes. The market is giving lots of people—too many people—fear of heights. Fear is bullish.

The June 30 quarter saw an S&P 500 return of 17.5%—big by any count—the fourth-largest quarter since 1970. There is no history of quarters this big reversing immediately. But more important, my intuition tells me if this were the top, the customers wouldn't all be so darned worried about it.

Markets don't do what most people fear. They do something else. By the time we get to the actual top, most folks will have become complacent. I'm now in my fourteenth year here. Only six *Forbes* columnists have lasted longer. My favorite is Joe Goodman—spanning 1935 to 1958. Joe's columns persuade me, as I have said many times, that you don't try to call tops until just afterward—not before. Tops are usually gentle enough that you can get out, not at the top, but close enough to the top to satisfy anyone but a pig.

My advice remains: Be 100% in stocks, with a 55% weight to the US—and that among our 35 largest stocks. Not only do these giants perform now, but I think they will fall least when the next bear market does arrive.

The other 45%? I have it overseas in large European stocks aimed at a big cyclical bounce and in Japanese global

Something Else

Ken makes a comment in this column that "markets don't do what most people fear. They do something else." That alone is one of the greatest arguments against being a contrarian. It's not that markets do the reverse—they just do something else, wholly unexpected. If folks fear stocks will fall big, they might just fall a little or stay flat. If everyone agrees stocks will rise, they might rise, but hugely, surpassing all expectations. That's how markets work.

exporters. All these stocks can be sold easily at the right time—huge and liquid.

Yes, one day there will be a bear market again. Prepare now by doing the time-consuming paperwork with your broker to buy index puts—basically an insurance premium with a specified deductible to insure against portfolio loss. Index puts cost about the same as the transaction costs to sell out of, and later get back into, equities. The day will come when I urge hedging with a put—maybe on the S&P 500 or a small-cap index like the Russell 2000—depending on conditions then.

But that's for the future. For now, the bull marches on. And we should enjoy the party. ∎

Bigger Is Beautiful
August 25, 1997

One reader wrote recently asking if I still like Liz Claiborne, which I recommended on April 24, 1995. It has since tripled in a straight line. She thanked me.

Fortunately for her, this reader missed my July 15, 1996 column. Liz Claiborne had doubled, and I urged selling it at 34. At that time I recommended culling out smaller stocks and shifting to the bigger ones.

I apologize to readers who may have missed out on some of the run-up on Liz Claiborne, but I stick with my general advice: Stay with US super-cap stocks and large foreign stocks. I expect huge US stocks to outshine smaller stocks through the end of the next bear market, whenever that is.

Huge stocks have the qualities the market now prefers. Yes, there will be a few small stocks that really shine, as Liz Claiborne has, but big stocks, overall, should do better on the upside as well as on the downside when this bull market finally ends. The big ones have both quality and foreign revenue exposure, which the market now warmly regards. They also have the liquidity, so they can be sold easily. How big is big enough?

For me, a US stock must have a market capitalization of close to $50 billion (price times shares outstanding—what the market values the whole firm at). There are only a few dozen such stocks. I detailed all this in my April 21 column. Several readers asked what I meant by a stock "being bigger than the market." How can one stock, they ask, be bigger than the market when the market must total more than any one component? Think averages. Is a single stock's size—its market capitalization—bigger or smaller than a correctly calculated average of all stocks? If it is

> ### Small OK, Big Better
>
> Though the late 1990s was a great period for large-cap (even mega-cap) stocks, that doesn't mean small stocks did poorly in absolute terms. They just did poorly relative to the overall market, and certainly poorly relative to larger-cap stocks. This highlights the importance of being style agnostic. Some money managers adhere to one size and/or style. But that can mean getting lackluster returns for years when some other area outperforms. A small cap value investor wouldn't have posted negative returns in the late 1990s, but certainly got his lunch eaten by investors who went bigger. Styles trade leadership. Don't get stuck.

bigger, that will tend to help it if big stocks drastically outperform small stocks—and vice versa. For several years now the market has rewarded large size and punished small. Where is the cut-off? The problem is, and this is where I confused readers, to figure it correctly you can't use a simple "mean" average—what most folks think of as average. There are many kinds of averages. The right method for this averaging function is what statisticians call "dollar-weighting"—which is how I get to the seemingly large $50 billion number. But it works. ∎

When Should You Get Out?
September 22, 1997

I like getting letters or email from readers. Sometimes they ask smart questions. Like this one:

Reader Bill Alkire of Ashburn, Va. writes asking if the volume of stock buybacks won't keep fueling this bull market?

My answer is: No. Stock buybacks are rather a long-term warning signal, a sign that a top is not far off. When prices and optimism are high, there are lots of buybacks. When prices are low and folks are fearful, buybacks and takeovers are rare. I detailed all this ten years ago in my second book, *The Wall Street Waltz*. History repeats. Corporate chief executives as a group differ little psychologically from the rest of us. They buy when prices are rising, sell when prices are low.

Reader JW Smith of Cupertino, Calif. wants to know when the bull market will end.

Doesn't everyone? My advice is not to ask the same question everyone else is asking. I haven't a clue when it will end, and neither does anyone else. Better than futilely trying to foresee a top, wait for clear signals that the market has topped. That won't get you out at the absolute peak but will get you out soon enough to stay intact. I don't mind losing a little by waiting until after the fact so I can be more certain I'm right. Market peaks roll over—they don't spike top. I want to stay with a bull market as long as I can, even if it means possibly giving up some paper profits. So long as I can avoid one-half to two-thirds of a subsequent bear market, I will make out handsomely in the long run. I know it takes discipline to act accordingly, but I know no more profitable or safer way to proceed.

Longtime reader Stanley Light accepts my after-the-fact axiom about market tops but worries that if I turn persuasively bearish he won't get the word in time. Light thinks in Internet terms. In the market, minutes, days and weeks don't really count. Don't sweat the small stuff. Try to catch the big swings. Acting on split-second information and trying to catch an absolute peak is a sucker's game.

Markets drop slowly at first. Take 1980's peak, for example. Was it in 1980, or in 1981? The S&P 500 peaked on November 28, 1980 at 140. But the Russell 2000 small stock index, which was at 77, didn't peak until the next June 15, at 85. By then the S&P 500 was down, but only to the mid-130s. Later came the damage, leading to a total 27% drop ending August 1982. Or 1972's top. The S&P actually peaked on January 11, 1973 at 120. The next October it sold above 110, down less than 8%—ten months later. It took until late 1974 to drop to 62. Roughly, two-thirds of a typical bear market's drop is in the last third of its duration. We have time.

Bryan Willey e-mails that I recommended Philips Electronics on August 12, 1996 at 30 and wonders now about my "opinion of its valuations." Well, obviously, it's not the steal it was at 30, but I wouldn't sell. At 70% of sales, a P/E of 17 and yielding 2.3%, it's not cheap, but it will rise in the European bull market I see ahead in 1998 and 1999. Look for 100 by year 2000.

Jim Harrison e-mails about Montedison, which I recommended November 4, 1996 at 6 as a stock to ride for the European bull market. He noticed that it has gone nowhere. Well, Europe is taking longer than I expected and Montedison is doing worse. But I wouldn't give up. Its chemicals and pharmaceuticals will come roaring back. You should see 12 within a few years.

Write me. Or e-mail me (I prefer letters). I personally respond to everyone who writes. Whatever bothers and worries you often plagues other readers, too. I don't consider reader-comments a bother; I like them, as you can see. ∎

Beware of Foreigners Bearing Bucks
October 20, 1997

Money is simply pouring into the USA. Foreign money is what fundamentally drives this stock market. As long as it pours in, this bull keeps galloping.

So it's important to keep your eye on this figure. Easier said than done. The Treasury's accounting of cross-border flows, like all governmental economic statistics, is terrible. In July the Treasury released ridiculous revisions of prior revisions. For example, from nowhere they find $210 billion of previously unnoticed foreign-held US greenbacks—hard, paper money—more than all the currency US residents hold here. Do not believe the government's economic statistics.

Probably at least several hundred billion bucks have come here unaccounted for this year. For example, in most major countries you can borrow at the bank, turn around and buy foreign-held US Treasurys and make a whopping spread. But that usually isn't counted as foreign investment.

Take Germany. To stimulate its strangled economy, the central bank has kept monetary policy loose and rates low. You can borrow readily for three months at 3.5%. That's supposed to encourage Germans to borrow and invest. Instead, it encourages them to borrow at 3.5% and put the money in US three-month Treasury bills. They pick up 1.5% easily. As the dollar rises, they get a double kick. Germany says its money supply grew about 10% over the last year—a lot. A lot of those newborn marks are visiting the US.

The potential to arbitrage against US interest rates exists almost everywhere except in England, Italy and Spain. Foreign rates are so low relative to US rates that this will go on for a while: Borrow and buy. Americans who sell foreigners a Treasury use the proceeds for something else—maybe on Main Street or maybe for other bonds or stocks.

In the short term this foreign interest rate arbitrage feels mighty good to us. Manna from abroad.

One day the manna will stop flowing. Monetary policy works, albeit with unpredictable time lags. Foreign central bank money creation will eventually get foreign economies going, and then we will have rising commodity prices and, later, rising inflation. And the dollar will eventually fall enough to spook speculators away from this game.

When I first saw this trend late last year, I thought it would likely have reversed by now—and that Europe's major economies would be humming now. That's why I began recommending the shifting of funds from the US stock market to European stock markets. I was too early. The present game may go on for a while longer. ∎

Go Slow: Inflation Ahead
December 1, 1997

In the issue of November 17, editor Jim Michaels notes that the edition included the word deflation at least a dozen times. He noted that, based on deflation, four commentators were recommending bonds. I disagree with the deflation thesis. When everyone expects deflation, it won't happen—or it's already priced into securities.

If money is created rapidly, we can't get deflation. Globally, central banks are printing money like drunken sailors. I never believe any country's published economic data, but this process is ubiquitous; I don't need precise data to see it. Yet it is seldom cited, increasing its force as a surprise factor to impact pricing. Deflation is a nonstarter. As Milton Friedman has said so well for so long, inflation is always and everywhere a monetary phenomenon. Deflation, too. You can't have it when the printing presses are on overtime.

This money creation should keep the bull market alive for a while. It will end when inflation gets ugly. That's what's in store, not deflation. I don't know when—but it's coming.

I don't buy the deflation trend, and I don't buy the small-stock trend, either.

Readers now ask if the third quarter's small-stock rally isn't the new basic trend.

I don't think so. The really important trends aren't the ones the media get quickly. They get the big trends late, very late. The recent strength in small caps is ephemeral, a bounce-back that I think is already over. That the media was so quick recently to jump on the small-cap bandwagon suggests to me that big stocks will outperform the small fry.

Late in bull markets and then afterward in bear markets, small stocks usually lag most of the way. If small stocks really have just begun a big, long move, then the bull market has a long, long way to go, in which case you can also make good money in big caps. But hey—while intact, it's an old bull. I can't see it running far enough to make small stocks pay off. Forget that talk.

If you want diversification away from big-cap leaders, don't go to small caps. Try large Continental European stocks and huge Japanese global exporters. They are pumping money out in Japan and the Continent, and it's going to revive those economies for a while and strengthen their stock markets. ∎

Buy High, Sell Small

December 15, 1997

The recent turmoil notwithstanding, I continue to like the very largest US stocks, many of which are lots like 1972's infamous Nifty Fifty. Some readers complain, "How can you own these grossly overpriced stocks like Gillette and Microsoft?" Some readers recall that years ago I favored small, cheap stocks. Have I gone nuts?

I hope not and don't think so. The obvious rarely gets you anywhere in the stock market, and the high prices of these stocks is obvious. People don't expect these stocks to do so well, so they can.

Furthermore, the bull market has gotten very old and a bear market is coming. No, I'm not bearish. In fact, the recent market volatility has made me more bullish rather than bearish looking at 1998. But big stocks do better than small ones late in bull markets as well as in bear markets. You can count on quality to hold up pretty well in the early stages of a bear market. Take 1973–74. Nine months into that decline, on September 30, 1973, the overpriced Nifty Fifty glamour stocks were down only about 3% on average, while the S&P 500 was down 8%. Only at the very end of that crash, in 1974, did the Nifties take a bath.

I don't think there was one big bear market this century where the 35 largest stocks as a whole did worse than the market.

Late in a bull market I like huge stocks, cheap and expensive ones alike. You can own Gillette and Microsoft and cheaper huge stocks like General Motors and Mobil Oil. I'll take them all if they're $50 billion in market cap or bigger.

For all of this fall's turbulence, we are not yet in a bear market. When we are, here's what I recommend: Buy a put on a small-cap index. As small stocks fall more than huge ones do, the put rises in value more than huge stocks fall, and we make money overall.

I hear from readers who rebel at my notion of avoiding small stocks. If a bear market is close, small is dead. If it is years away, okay, but even then huge stocks will rise with less risk than small fry. For now I continue to urge readers to have 55% of their equity money in the 35 largest domestic stocks and 45% in overseas companies.

I am distressed to report that some readers write to complain that 25% a year isn't the kind of return they are after. They want 25% in just a few months. One more sign that this bull market is not going to live forever. Keep in mind, I have no idea where prices will be in February or March. Prices bounce too much. I look one to five years out. If you want short-term advice, look elsewhere. ∎

Rat Hunting

In this column Ken writes about readers who don't just want above-average equity returns annually, but want to see a huge return in just months. Beware anyone claiming they can get you hugely above-average market returns. That's a sign something sinister may be afoot, and one of the five signs of financial fraud Ken writes about in his 2009 bestseller *How to Smell a Rat*. If you have any money to invest, you could be a con artist's target. Don't fall prey. Read the book.

1998

Rubles, Corrections, and More Bull

> " *Some readers chastise me for losing my 'value roots.' Guilty as charged. I have simply changed my mind, learning that no investment style is for all times.* "
>
> "The Dance of the Elephants," April 6, 1998

> " *The most basic of all market notions is that the market (The Great Humiliator) is a discounter of all known information. It succeeds by making sure that whatever we all know is either wrong or already priced into securities.* "
>
> "News You Can't Use," September 7, 1998

Investors began 1998 in a salty mood. Nineteen-ninety-seven was a great year for stocks—the third in a string of over 20-percent years for the S&P 500. With such an impressive stretch under their belts, you'd probably expect investors were feeling pretty good going into 1998. Hardly—1997 was good, but it was heavily front-end loaded. In a year when the S&P 500 rose over 30 percent, the fourth quarter was only a tad better than flat, rising just 2.9 percent.[1] And foreign stocks didn't fare nearly as well. Foreign stocks were up only 2.1 percent in 1997, and global markets peaked mid-year, driven lower in the second half by agony in Asia.[2] The Asian Financial Crisis had folks feeling forlorn about the state of the world. Many saw this as the inevitable top of what had already been a great bull market. From the October 1990 bear market trough through 1997, the S&P 500 was up nearly 300 percent—not the biggest bull in history but well above average.[3]

Instead of buying into the general gloom, Ken continued to write of the vast reasons he saw for optimism. In his view, the Asian Financial Crisis wasn't the precursor for Armageddon. Rather, it was just the Great Humiliator at it again. As he writes in his first column of 1998: "The market's prime goal is to always embarrass as many people as possible. . . . For the Great Humiliator to fulfill its goal, it must simply move in ways that surprise." ("The Bull Market's Not Over,"

January 12, 1998.) The best way for the market to surprise too-gloomy investors? Keep rising. In Ken's view, wary investors had it wrong. Turns out, he was right.

The global economy looked much different in 1998 from how it does now. Today, emerging economies, combined, account for a larger portion of global output than the US.[4] But in 1998, emerging economies were still very much emerging. As Ken writes in his February column, "The US exports to all of non-Japan Pacific Rim actually total less than two-thirds that of US trade with Canada." ("A Passing Storm," February 9, 1998.) In his view, problems in emerging Asia weren't likely to cause a global meltdown. So in light of pervasive pessimism and unwarranted investor fears, Ken called for a continuation of the already robust bull market—a forecast that turned out well. The S&P 500 would rise 28.6 percent in 1998.[5]

But it wasn't a smooth ride. The S&P 500 surged right out of the gate, crossing the 1,000 mark for the first time in February and gaining 14 percent in total in the first quarter alone[6]—nearly a straight shot up. But things then got considerably more dicey. If 1997 seemed eventful, 1998 was about to knock folks' socks off. The Asian Financial Crisis would spread west, contributing to a financial crisis in Russia that saw the government default on its debt and the ruble devalued—the famous "Russian Ruble Crisis." The ripples then made their way to the Americas, contributing to the failure of then-massive US hedge fund Long-Term Capital Management (LTCM). With nearly $130 billion in assets (almost all of it borrowed) at the start of 1998, LTCM was thought to be so big, its failure could reverberate through the global financial system. Latin America was struggling too, with many developing countries there entering recession. All this against a backdrop of US political scandal. The Monica Lewinsky situation was rapidly unfolding in the media, eventually leading to President Clinton's impeachment vote in December 1998.

So after a fairly smooth ride in the first half, the back half of 1998 was considerably choppy. A market correction beginning in July saw the S&P 500 drop—fast—over 18 percent.[7] By early October, the S&P 500 was essentially flat on the year despite the strong early run. Foreign stocks fared worse, falling by more than 20 percent during this period.[8] Ken's advice during tumult: "Stay Cool"—the title of his September column. In it, Ken describes his 2% Rule: "US bear markets, top to bottom, decline irregularly, but at an average rate of about 2% per month. If a decline exceeds that [which the late-1998 decline did], you can soon count on a pullback and a better chance to get out." Ken went on to recommend remaining invested in his October column, "Don't Let 'Em Scare You Out of Stocks," and his November column, "Get Fully Invested." Ken's advice proved prescient as US stocks recorded their best fourth quarter ever, rising over 21 percent.[9]

Ken's bear market calls have received much attention over the years and contributed to his success as a columnist and investor. But staying in the market at the right times can be even more important than getting defensive during bear markets. After all, investors can achieve long-term stock market returns by riding through the tough times, but they can't if they miss out on the upturns. Few people think of it this way because people are wired to hate losses more than they like gains. In other words, people would usually rather miss out on some of the market's upside than suffer downturns. But as Ken would tell you, this is exactly wrong. Avoiding downturns is a worthwhile endeavor if successful, but not at the expense of missing out on strong markets. This wisdom of staying invested at the right time was particularly evident in 1998.

Incidentally, 1998 was the year Ken gave up on forecasting gold. In his September column with reference to gold he states, "I don't think I know what I'm doing there. Better to exit." Another good piece of advice—stick with what you know.

The Bull Market's Not Over
January 12, 1998

The aftermath of the recent Pacific Rim-led hysteria makes me much more optimistic about stock market prospects globally. This market acts as if it wants to run far further than any of us ever imagined.

My logic? Well, the market's prime goal is always to embarrass as many people as possible. It can probably best do that now by rising smartly for several years, surprising and convincing everyone that we really are in a new era and stocks can never again fall big. For the Great Humiliator to fulfill its goal, it must simply move in ways that surprise.

A 1998 bear market won't surprise half the forecasters. A modest rise won't surprise many folks either. But three more years of up market is inconceivable to almost everyone I hear or read. So, to me, it's most likely.

Folks forget, and I've used this many times over the years: The stock market simply does not fall in the third year of a president's term. The third year is 1999. The fourth year of a president's term is almost as consistent historically. So if, as I suspect, 1998 rewards, the Great Humiliator is set for a three-year run that will surprise everyone.

One long-time reader e-mails me: "I read your view that bull markets bend over slowly, but it seems we are in uncharted territory. I am not a skittish investor, but things seem a little unsettling now." That a Pacific Rim currency crisis could crash the civilized world makes less sense than that it could build the proverbial wall of worry that another leg of a bull market would love to climb.

Note that even as the panic evolved, bonds rose and utilities steadily hit new highs. Finally, the S&P 500 rebounded to a new peak. But there wasn't euphoria en route. To me, new highs tied to fear say more juice ahead.

So I remain 100% invested, with 55% in America's 30 or so largest stocks, ones like Du Pont and Wal-Mart that have risen so much for so long that everyone will be surprised when they rise more. I am 37% in huge foreign stocks that dominate their businesses. And I'm 8% in beat-up, tax-depressed gold stocks—pick any ten. If you like my bullish rationality but remain a bit fearful, go for yield with cheap stocks. ∎

A Passing Storm
February 9, 1998

The Asian madness is just that: An excuse for a big market correction. Ride it out. The US exports to all of non-Japan Pacific Rim actually total less than two-thirds that of US trade with Canada. When Canada stumbled a few years back, few folks in the US even noticed. So why should we go into a panic over the Pacific Rim's troubles?

To see the world's overall financial shape, use two basic measures: First, what is happening with the global money supply? It is increasing nicely. This is bullish. Second, check the global yield curve, which measures the intent of central banks. It should have long-term interest rates comfortably above short-term rates. And almost everywhere they are, except in Thailand and Indonesia, and the UK, which, of Western nations, has far and away the most to lose from the Pacific Rim debacle.

The world is in good shape. This storm will pass and we will wonder what the fuss was about. It offers a grand chance to buy big, cheap overseas concerns that won't be badly hurt by Asia and will be nicely higher in price in a few years. I remain optimistic on Europe and Japan. Between these two, I keep a 37% weight overseas.

Since I have been recommending foreign stocks, lots of readers ask me how to study them. A good start is in any major city or university library. Better and easier is the Internet. For example, with Hoovers. com or Newsalert.com you can enter a stock's ticker and learn quite a lot for free. Then, on Morningstar.net, you can access Quicktake stock reports and find out still more.

Finally, every major stock has its own Web site. Some are quite useful. If you haven't gotten computer-friendly yet, you should. There is just too much useful data there for you to pass it up. Starting now, I will include a stock's Web site address with my comments so you can look it up and learn.

And, oh, by the way, if for any reason you want to contact me, my e-mail address is always here under my picture. My Internet home page is www.fi.com. Thanks for writing. ∎

Report Card
March 9, 1998

Last year wasn't my best as a *Forbes* columnist: My recommendations returned 23%, versus 33% for the S&P 500. My domestic picks did beat the S&P 500, but my substantial number of foreign stocks kept me behind that big stock index. Simply said, I went overseas too soon. In the December 30, 1996 issue I urged a starting weight of 55% US stocks—and that only from among the 50 very largest—and 45% foreign stocks.

I got the first part right: The 50 largest US stocks, equal weighted, beat the S&P 500 by more than 1% in 1997. In the April 21, 1997 issue I raised my size threshold again, to only the 35 largest stocks. That helped. They beat the S&P 500 by 5.21%.

But I got the second part wrong: EAFE (Europe, Australasia and the Far East) returned under 2%. Several of my Japanese stocks turned out badly, such as Nissan, Kubota and Matsushita. I still like all three stocks and am happy holding them. Fortunately, of course, I never did recommend any Asian emerging markets stocks and missed that bitter sting completely.

In Europe I hurt myself with Mot Hennessey (LVMHY). It had fallen 38% by year-end from my July 28, 1997 pick. I still like LVMHY.

I had a few okay performers overseas. Akzo Nobel was up 26% from my June 16, 1997 recommendation. I still like it. Telefonica España rose 32% from January 27, 1997, and I recommended it again January 12, 1998. But overall, what I touched overseas hurt. I picked several natural resources stocks. They all bombed: Anglo American, Ashanti Goldfields, Broken Hill Proprietary and DeBeers. The world feared a growing deflation risk.

Then, in December, I suggested you put 8% of your portfolio into beat-up gold stocks. I don't think deflation is coming. I think gold will do fine in 1998.

Having eaten this substantial portion of crow, I turn happily to my domestic recommendations. I made double bets on some domestic stocks, like Merrill Lynch, Viacom, Ford, Travelers Group, Motorola (MOT) and General Motors (GM). With only MOT and GM lagging, these six did 7.9% better than the S&P 500 from the time of recommendation. Also, I recommended six domestic and foreign stocks to sell and very simply, by luck, every single one went my way, and more so than EAFE.

Overall, and adjusted for Schwab discount brokerage commissions, my 1997 advice lagged the S&P 500 by about 10%. I'm sorry I was early on Europe—but early may be okay looking forward. I continue to recommend a big foreign weight.

In recent years my *Forbes* picks beat the S&P 500. But I used only US stocks. Having gone foreign too early in 1997, I still want foreign diversification. After years of the US besting foreign, some day that will reverse. So I'm aiming at the Morgan Stanley World Index and expect it will be a higher hurdle than the S&P 500 in coming years.

For now I remain bullish, here and overseas, urging a 55% US equity weight, with that restrained to owning all of and only our 35 largest stocks. Supercaps only. Put 37% into the kind of huge continental European stocks and Japanese global exporters that I was too early on in 1997. ∎

The Dance of the Elephants
April 6, 1998

Readers regularly write for current advice on some stock I recommended years ago. This month it was Allmerica Financial, the Singer Co. and Cummins Engine. Last month it was Applied Magnetics, Blount, Jenny Craig and Seagate. I know I sound like a broken record, but I always give the same advice: Sell smaller stocks; buy superhuge ones. Broken record or not, that's been the way to make money and that's the way it's going to continue to be for quite a while. Size is basic now.

Take Applied Magnetics, which is down from 60 fifteen months ago. I recommended it in my very first column 14 years ago. I recommended it twice more with success. But I've not recommended it in years—or any other small stocks.

When I say big, I mean giant. Market caps no less than the S&P 500's $60 billion weighted average size. There are only 35 of them. They constitute my domestic portfolio. Yes, these big stocks are pricey. They were pricey 24 and 36 months ago. That didn't keep them from beating the market. Readers ask if I have a favorite. Okay—General Electric. Why? Because it's the biggest.

Some readers chastise me for losing my "value roots." Guilty as charged. I have simply changed my mind, learning that no investment style is for all times. Late in a bull market and in a bear market, size pays and protects. If I have lost my value roots, Warren Buffett has also lost his. Go complain to him.

David, the seventh grader, contacts me on Dad's e-mail. Seems his teacher broke his class into fours to pick stocks to be judged on their outcomes in two months. He asks my advice. My advice is: His teacher needs lessons in investing. Two months is a meaningless time frame—two to five years is mine. Also, the teacher should know that picking stocks by committee is dumb. My two-month forecast? I don't have one and never did.

I continue to like European and Japanese stocks—big ones here, too. I suggest having one-third or a bit more of your portfolio in big continental European stocks and Japanese global exporters. Take it easy. Think big, both here and abroad, and don't get too fancy. The tide has been running in favor of the biggest global companies and that tide shows no signs yet of reversing. ∎

This Bull Ain't Tired
May 4, 1998

Table 15.1 explains another reason I remain bullish and expect the bull market to last through 2000. It shows that stock market risk is mostly in the first half of a president's term. In third years, stocks love to rise. Except for Herbert Hoover's years in the White House, and 1939—the year World War II broke out—every presidential third year has been positive.

Fourth years are good, too—not quite so buoyant, but basically the same as third years. Except for the Great Depression's 1932, 1940 is the only fourth year that fell—back-to-back with 1939 and 1931. Imagine. For negative third or fourth years you needed the Great Depression or a world war. Even prior to the S&P 500, there are few exceptions—only weird ones.

Why does this happen? My sense, based on history, is that the market likes a president at his lowest level of power. And that happens on the back end of his term. So don't look down at how far the market has come—that will just make you dizzy. Instead, look at how much further it may have to go.

TABLE 15.1   Presidential Term Anomaly

President	First Year		Second Year		Third Year		Fourth Year	
Coolidge (R)	1925	NA	1926	11.6%	1927	37.1%	1928	43.3%
Hoover (R)	1929	−8.9%	1930	25.3	1931	−43.9	1932	−8.9
FDR 1st term (D)	1933	52.9	1934	−2.3	1935	47.2	1936	32.8
FDR 2nd term (D)	1937	−35.3	1938	33.2	1939	−0.9	1940	−10.1
FDR 3rd term (D)	1941	−11.8	1942	21.1	1943	25.8	1944	19.7
FDR/Truman (D)	1945	36.5	1946	−8.2	1947	5.2	1948	5.1
Truman (D)	1949	18.1	1950	30.6	1951	24.6	1952	18.5

(Continued)

TABLE 15.1   *(Continued)*

President	First Year		Second Year		Third Year		Fourth Year	
Eisenhower 1st term (R)	1953	−1.1	1954	52.4	1955	31.4	1956	6.6
Eisenhower 2nd term (R)	1957	−10.9	1958	43.3	1959	11.9	1960	0.5
Kennedy/Johnson (D)	1961	26.8	1962	−8.8	1963	22.7	1964	16.4
Johnson (D)	1965	12.4	1966	−10.1	1967	23.9	1968	11.0
Nixon (R)	1969	−8.5	1970	3.9	1971	14.3	1972	19.0
Nixon/Ford (R)	1973	−14.7	1974	−26.5	1975	37.2	1976	23.9
Carter (D)	1977	−7.2	1978	6.6	1979	18.6	1980	32.5
Reagan 1st term (R)	1981	−4.9	1982	21.5	1983	22.6	1984	6.3
Reagan 2nd term (R)	1985	31.7	1986	18.7	1987	5.3	1988	16.6
Bush (R)	1989	31.7	1990	−3.1	1991	30.5	1992	7.6
Clinton 1st term (D)	1993	10.1	1994	1.3	1995	37.6	1996	23.0
Clinton 2nd term (D)	1997	33.4	1998		1999		2000	
Median		4.5		5.3		23.4		16.7

Thomson Reuters

1998 Looks Like 1958
June 1, 1998

Last month (May 4) I described how stock markets hate to fall in the third and fourth years of Presidents' terms. I explained that this boosted my optimism for 1999 and 2000. Some skeptics wrote that all my nifty history just can't recur after this "unprecedented" post-1982 bull market. Well, yes, the last 15 years were huge, with an S&P 500 average annual return of 18.4% through 1997. But I am not so sure it is unprecedented.

The 16 years from 1942 to 1958 averaged 18.9%, almost identical. Both long periods had five slightly negative or subpar years. Both began and ended at generally similar valuations. Take 1942. The market's price-to-sales ratio was 0.75. It hit 2.05 by 1959. Since 1982 it has risen from 0.80 to 2.17.

Differences? Sure—40 years' worth. For example, interest rates rose in the 1950s but fell in the 1990s. Some folks will note 1957 was a minor down year—1997 wasn't—and 1957–58 had an extremely mild recession. But 1957's hiccup played the exact same role then that 1997's Asian "crisis" did in today's more global world.

No, I'm not saying 1998 will rise 43%, as 1958's market did. I'm just saying the market should continue positive.

The parallels continue. The 1942 bottom discounted, in advance, winning World War II. The 1982 bottom discounted winning the much longer-lasting Cold War.

Here's another parallel, my favorite: Markets fear strong Presidents. The weak one now sitting in the White House is to its taste. Both boom periods began with a political party's strongest President of this century (FDR and Reagan)—followed by their weak former vice presidents (Truman and Bush), who could get elected just once. The weak Presidents then handed the White House to the opposition, who held it for two terms (Ike and Clinton).

Ike's first two years had a flurry of activity, like Bill's. The last six years for both are noted for what they didn't or couldn't do. After Ike's heart attack he did little. The big headlines were the Suez crisis and Sputnik. Clinton is as lame a duck as you can get—hence his popularity. Ike played golf. Bill just plays. Ironic—that two so different men play such a similar role for the market.

My study tells me the third- and fourth-presidential-year precedent I detailed last month should be fine in 1999 and 2000, and that the current market isn't abnormal; it has a good road map. Among US stocks, I own only the 35 largest ones now—totaling 57% of my portfolio (per my April 6 column). Nothing changed there. There are so many foreign stocks I like, you could buy almost anything I mentioned last year and I'll stand by it now—that's 33 stocks in your old *Forbes* copies (which you should always keep). ∎

Dumb Is Beautiful
August 10, 1998

For almost two years now I've urged owning only the 35 very largest US stocks so far as our domestic market is concerned. Readers regularly grouse that my US super-cap strategy is too simple. That is a big part of why it works: The Great Humiliator loves to surprise, and what could be more surprising than that? The S&P 500 rose 17.7% this year, through June 30. The Russell 2000, the standard small-stock measure, was up just 4.9%. In the second quarter, the S&P 500 rose 3.3%, while the Russell 2000 fell 4.6%. This size effect runs right up to the very largest stocks. The largest 35 stocks are whupping the S&P 500 now.

These super-caps (from December 31, 1997), on average, are up 24.3% through June 30, wasting everything. In June alone the top 35 averaged a 6.6% gain, versus the S&P 500, up 4%, and the Russell 2000, up just 0.3%.

Dumb? If so, I like it.

I'm content to be dumb. My critics are content to be wrong. Most of them cite the numerous academic studies covering the span since 1926 that show that small stocks do better than big ones over the very long haul. It's true. Since 1926 small stocks averaged better than big stocks. Yet in most of those same years, big stocks beat small stocks.

My critics and academics confuse averages with what happens most often. The real long-term results from small caps come from seven very spectacular years (1933–34,

1943–44 and 1975–77). All of them were huge bounces off major bear market bottoms, which is hardly the case with today's market. Without those seven stunning years, small stocks have lagged big stocks by 1.5% per year since 1926, and 61% in all years.

And, of course, with higher risk.

It is only off the bottom of a real bear market that you should concentrate in small stocks. In the last two-thirds of a bull market and throughout a bear market, big stocks best small stocks, and the very largest stocks shine brightest. Late bull market optimism usually encourages people to think small stocks will lead the way. But it's usually futile. In my study of late bull markets, it has happened only once, 1967–68.

There will be a time for small stocks again. When? Not until the end of the next bear market—and it hasn't begun yet. Right now, stick with the 35 largest US stocks. Which ones? You can't go too wrong with all 35. If you don't like a few of them, throw them out, but it is in this group that you should remain concentrated. ∎

Complain All You Want
September 7, 1998

I'm amazed how many of my readers are upset by my view that a smart investor need own only the 30 to 35 largest stocks. Yet the 35 largest stocks are nicely besting the S&P 500 even though the S&P 500 has had a great run this year, even allowing for the big summer correction.

My sticking to the biggest may not be popular but it sure has made sense. And it is based on solid research. Everything I do comes from original research, financial and social history, and market theory. I guess I should be comforted by some of the complaining letters I get: If too many of you agree too easily, I must be wrong.

I continue to believe that 1999 and 2000 will be good stock market years, and that this summer's correction was just that, en route to more bull market ahead. This correction is about as normal as you get. Key features consistent with a correction but not with a bear market include the dollar's strength coupled with the strong bond. Then, too, there is no real new news, just the same old stories recirculated from months back with an extra dose of hysteria. Finally, there are too many folks, too early, seeing this as the turning point for it to be so.

Among domestic stocks you need only focus on the 30 or 35 largest ones. I remain 63% US stocks—the biggest—and 37% foreign stocks; and abroad, too, I prefer the huge European firms and Japanese global exporters.

I throw in the towel on gold and admit my foray into it was a mistake. In January I recommended putting 8% of a portfolio into any ten beat-up, tax-depressed gold stocks. The strategy hasn't worked, and I don't think I know what I'm doing there. Better to exit. ∎

Hold Tight

This column was published just days after the correction bottomed, before stocks resurged, then nearly retested the low again in October. Sentiment was as black as could be, as it typically is during a swift, deep correction. But the right thing was to hang on through the wild ride—as Ken recommended—and remain invested. The bull market was still far from over.

Stay Cool
September 21, 1998

Correction or bear market? Either way, stay cool. The time for tough decisions comes in a few months, but it isn't now.

My best guess is that this is a correction in a bull market, but with portfolio management you're never 100% certain. The key is to conduct yourself so that when you're wrong, you don't pay too heavy a price.

Even if we are now in a real bear market, it's wrong to sell now. That's because even powerful bear markets have rallies, and one is coming. When it comes, we will have a better sense of whether this summer marked a real turning point for the worse.

In situations like this I invoke my 2% rule. As detailed in my second book, *The Wall Street Waltz*, the 2% rule says: US bear markets, top to bottom, decline irregularly but at an average rate of about 2% per month. If a decline exceeds that, you can soon count on a pullback and a better chance to get out. This summer of 1998 drop was too much, too soon. It's oversold. So stay cool. If you want to sell, you'll have a better chance.

Yes, 2% is just an average; bear markets have ranged from about 1.5% to 3% per month. But every one I have found was within that band, except 1987, which is the exception that proves the rule. It came and went so fast that if you sold after it started, you felt foolish fast.

Way back in the 1940s and 1950s, my hero Joe Goodman, the third-longest-running columnist in Forbes history, advised: Never call a peak too soon. Never call one until at least three months after you suspect it has happened. There is plenty of time to get out if the rallies are disappointing. The stock market—that great deceiver—likes to play dirty tricks on us. A big, broad, jagged rolling top fakes out almost everyone over a year or two. If we decide that it is indeed a top, we usually have at least several chances for getting out with no more than a 6% to 10% decline from the top. When will we know? Maybe November. Maybe not until next February.

In the months ahead I'm watching and waiting for Goodman's three-month rule to collide with my 2% rule. Then we face Yogi Berra's famous rule that, "When you get to the fork in the road, take it."

Among domestic stocks, continue to own America's 30 to 35 largest stocks. They keep besting smaller stocks and should basically continue to do so until after the next bear market bottom.

You can look up the last two years of my old columns on the Internet at my Forbes archives page at www.forbes.com/fisher. You can even click on to my Forum page there and tell me what you don't like about this or any other column. I'll even answer. ∎

Don't Let 'Em Scare You Out of Stocks
October 5, 1998

Last issue I said I thought we had a correction, not a bear market. I still think so. Here are my reasons: First: It's rare that bear markets start out with a big break like the one we've had. They usually begin gently to lull people into complacency.

Second: The US bond market is strong and interest rates are benign.

Most bear markets are preceded by a nice long period of either rising short-term interest rates, rising long-term rates or both.

Third: In the past when bear markets began without rising interest rates, the dollar was weak. The dollar has been strong. Bear markets rarely develop when there is lots of liquidity around. And there is now, because the Federal Reserve is creating lots of it by printing money aggressively. Even more liquidity is coming here from overseas where the dollar is strong.

Fourth: Recall history and my "third-year-of-a-president's-term" rule, showing how 1999 should be a good year (see my May 4 column). Bear markets generally take a long time, and there isn't time for one between now and a good 1999 market.

Fifth: All the media talk is similar to what we've heard for almost a year now. Asia. Now Latin America and Russia. Monica. High P/Es. All old. As I wrote on March 13, 1995, in one of my all-time favorite columns, old and widely circulated arguments lose their power. As I said: "Bearishness may yet be vindicated, but you will need new fuel to justify it."

Sixth: People have a hard time fathoming how big the economies are in the US, Western Europe and Japan. And how small everything else is. In the rest of the world there are many bodies and little economies. If you take all those countries and aggregate their real international trade, Russia and China included, it looks like several dozen major US firms.

A major downdraft in all those places at once would look about like a major industrial sector rotation here (of which we've had many over the decades). It would likely cause the Fed to cut interest rates early next year, and we would move on. Shy of a Russian revolution that put nuclear weapons into the hands of wackos, there really isn't a there there.

Seventh: Politics look good. The elections now seem assured of providing us more gridlock. Bullish. So don't let the correction scare you out of stocks. ∎

Pick a Strategy and Stick With It
November 30, 1998

Electronic reader feedback is teaching me new and useful lessons about how investors react. Yeah, I always drew reader mail, but reader e-mail simply pours in now—more every month since my e-mail tag first appeared here last year. The letters are revealing. While revealing, the e-mail is not always flattering to you or to me.

I've learned from it that many readers simply won't believe I mean what I say. A common question is: "Yeah, I know for two years you have urged that among US stocks we should only own the 35 largest ones, but what do you think now about Standard Commercial, which you recommended in 1992?"

My response is always the same: Read what I say. This is not, in my opinion, a time to buy small-capitalization stocks.

Or readers ask my views on a bigger stock that is less than half the market's $65 billion average size—say, $27 billion cap Colgate-Palmolive. Too small. When I say stick to big stocks, I mean superbig.

This morphs into the lesson that most folks can't stick to any focused strategy, whether theirs, mine, their friend's or anyone's. They seek consensus, which is no strategy and no real diversification. Why ask me? Great investors always have a clear strategy and adhere to it for years. Learn from them. If you have a strategy that works, ignore me and everyone. Stick to it.

Some longstanding "value" readers get upset because: "You've lost your value roots." The fact is that years ago I learned that different investment styles—big caps, small caps, value, growth—each have their seasons. There are times when one style works best and times when another does.

My research tells me that this is still a time for the superstock strategy.

So my advice is: Think flexibly but strategize rigidly. That is, decide which investment style is right for the present, and, once you have decided, stick with that style and the strategy that flows from it.

My strategy remains to be 100% in equity, with 67% in the 35 largest US stocks and 33% in a collection of big European stocks, with a few Japanese global exporters. ∎

Style Rotation

Rotating styles is a theme that comes up repeatedly in Ken's columns over the years. And following his advice to hold big cap, then super cap, stocks served his readers well in the late 1990s (had they heeded him), as the largest of the large cap decidedly outperformed not only the market as a whole, but simply clocked small cap stocks. If you stuck with small caps because you prefer them to all others, you lost ground—big time.

Bullish for '99
December 28, 1998

Here I go again, still optimistic. I expect a strong 20% gain for the S&P 500 in 1999.

No, this bull market won't live forever. I'm no "permabull," as one of my e-mailing critics labeled me. Scan my 15 years of Forbes columns and you will find two extended periods of bearish calls. I'm very proud of them. But I don't think I'll need to make another one until 2001. I'm predicting two more good years.

Starting in September we have had three interest rate cuts.

Previously when we had three cuts the S&P 500 rose 19.4% on average over the next 12 months.

I expect more cuts in 1999. What makes me think so?

My reading of history tells me that in general three rate cuts is it—there is rarely a fourth or fifth. With an exception: Usually, when the rate cuts start in the second year of a presidential term—1998 is one—there have been additional cuts beyond the third. Sometimes five or six more. Rate cuts when inflation is low almost always promptly lead to higher stock markets.

Grumpy Greenspan will forge an unholy alliance with Bill Clinton.

Clinton badly wants Gore elected in 2000 and needs easy money to get him elected. Greenspan badly wants another term as Fed head, and Clinton makes that decision in the spring of 2000. Sacking Greenspan would cause a stir, but Clinton can be ruthless when political advantage is at stake. And history is littered with Presidents sacking seemingly indispensable Fed chairmen. Greenspan knows this and will play ball with the man in the White House.

Stocks almost never fall in the third year of a President's term. That's 1999. The third-year median return is 23.4%. Check out my May 4 column. Greenspan will cooperate to keep the string intact.

Market risk has been concentrated in the first half of presidents' terms. When we've had material corrections in the second year of a President's term, as per this summer, the third year has been particularly robust.

What about the Y2K problem? Forget it. It's just so much noise. I devoted a full column to it on July 6. You can get that column in my archives at www.forbes.com/fisher. Just click on the "Archives" button.

My allocation for 1999 remains 100% equity, with 67% of that in the 35 largest stocks and the other 33% spread over huge continental European stocks, with a few Japanese global exporters.

Merry Christmas. ∎

1999

IPOs, Y2K, Nasdaq, Oh My!

> " *The Great Humiliator has only one goal: to humiliate as many people as possible for as many dollars as possible over as long a time as possible. En route its favorite victims are professionals. As a group they can't be right.* "

"Bet Against the Experts," April 19, 1999

> " *Y2K is the most widely hyped 'disaster' in modern history. It is well documented: The only folks who aren't familiar with it are in the upper Amazon basin, rapidly fleeing the rest of humanity. I need not even define Y2K for you to know exactly what I'm referencing.* "

"Greater Fools," October 18, 1999

Many folks remember 1999 as a banner year for stocks. However, big stock returns did not necessarily translate into a fantastic year broadly for individual investors. How so? Nineteen-ninety-nine's big returns were concentrated in just a few categories: technology stocks, telecommunications stocks, anything Internet related, and just about any initial public offering (IPO). And IPOs aside, the bigger the stock, the better the return. The heavily technology-weighted Nasdaq Composite Index, which mostly kept pace with the S&P 500 during the earlier years of the bull market, skyrocketed an astounding 85.6 percent in 1999. As an extreme example of the 1999 fervor, telecommunications firm Qualcomm gained over 2,000 percent that year. The hottest IPO of the year was VA Linux—a firm selling computer systems that ran the Linux open-source operating system. The firm's IPO was priced at $30 per share. On its first day trading, it reached a peak of about $320[1]—a nearly 970 percent gain in under a day. Over $70 billion was raised through IPOs in 1999 alone![2]

The rest of the market had solid but not exceptional returns. The S&P 500 gained 21.0 percent in 1999—a good year historically but the worst since 1994.[3] Foreign stocks rose 27.3 percent[4]—better than the US, but again, not an abnormally outsized gain for a bull market. Returns for small US stocks were decidedly average with the Value Line gaining just 10.6 percent.[5]

Unlike most experts, Ken was bullish for 1999. In fact, it was the bearish experts in part that made him bullish. "In one recent study [Ken and Meir Statman] measured investors in three categories—retail investors, newsletter writers, and professional Wall Street strategists—and compared their sentiment about market direction to later results. Each of these groups is regularly wrong. But the worst of them are the professional strategists, by far." ("Bet Against the Experts," April 19, 1999.) Ken sought to capitalize on professional investors' consistent wrongness through capital markets technology. He plotted their yearly market expectations on a graph to come up with a professional forecaster sentiment bell curve.

The pros mostly looked at the same data the same way and drew similar conclusions. So their forecasts tended to be tightly grouped around some average forecast for stock market returns for the upcoming year. Because these folks were so frequently wrong, the consensus was gameable! You could cancel out their expectations as the least likely market outcome. That meant stocks would probably do something other than what they expected—maybe much better or much worse. In 1999, most pros expected a below average or negative year—a bullish signal for Ken. "This year the pundits were quite bearish. So, as a contrary bettor, I'm for a bullish stance on stocks in 1999. . . . Of course, there are also very few forecasters foreseeing a disaster year, so you must consider that possibility. But—it would be, in the light of history, extraordinary if 1999 were a negative year."

One fear on investors' minds in 1999 was the Y2K scare. As you might recall, to save then-scarce memory resources, early computer programmers used a two-number abbreviation for calendar years (e.g., 99 for 1999). Doomsayers feared rolling into the new millennium would throw computers out of whack, with all sorts of tragic implications. Ken first dismissed the notion Y2K could derail the stock market in 1997, but Y2K hysteria was again building in 1999. In fact, the S&P 500 suffered a nearly 10 percent correction midyear tied to concerns about Y2K's impact. So Ken revisited the topic in his October 18, 1999 column, "Greater Fools": "Those who still fret Y2K's market impact don't fathom the markets, and you simply should be dismissive of them all." Ken usually doesn't make very short-term predictions, but as stocks suffered from Y2K mania, Ken saw the potential for a strong end-of-year stock market surge as calmer, wiser heads prevailed. "There are just enough investors who do understand how markets work to potentially create a pre-year-end buying stampede. They will sense in coming weeks that a Y2K bust ran out of time and that with year-end the rigid Y2K nuts lose their reason for caution. Those sages may play Y2Kers for greater fools by getting their money into stocks before year-end." Ken's forecast could hardly have been better. The S&P 500 surged over 18 percent from mid-October through year-end, finishing the millennium at an all-time high.[6]

Ken's investing horizons were increasingly global in 1999. Foreign stocks underperformed US stocks again in 1998, but Ken saw an eventual change in market leadership. "After the long string of years in which US stocks have been beating foreign ones, the time will come when EAFE beats the S&P 500. I don't know when it will come, but I know it will come." ("Report Card 1998," January 25, 1999.) Ken also saw the benefits of global investing as one of many reasons not to simply invest in an index fund tracking the S&P 500. "If and when the US market lags, S&P 500 index fund holders will be sorry." ("The Case Against Index Funds," February 22, 1999.)

Loose money abroad was still flowing into the US, causing Ken to favor the biggest stocks here. Foreign investors simply favored the biggest, internationally active US firms. And the structure of the newly created European Economic and Monetary Union (EMU) ensured loose money would continue to flow.

Each country in the EMU has its own fiscal policy, but there's one overarching monetary policy for all member countries, directed by the European Central Bank (ECB). There's no back-out provision to the EMU structure. If one country wants to leave, the whole EMU could fall theoretically apart. So the ECB has an incentive to keep the economically weakest countries from jumping ship. That means keeping interest rates low when those economies are struggling. Low interest rates in Europe keeps money flowing to the US.

Ken recommending big US and foreign stocks was a far cry from his initial emphasis on US small-cap value stocks. In his June 14, 1999 column, "Adaptability," Ken explained the change: "In the 1980s small-company stocks trading at low multiples made sense to me. My early research on price/sales ratios—long before others thought about them—made me feel I held an edge with that discipline. But religious-like faith is for God. Treating value investing as if it were unshakable dogma is wrong."

"My big-company portfolio is no more permanent dogma than my earlier emphasis on smaller companies. It is opportunistic and temporary. One day I hope to urge small value stocks—at the right time—and, at other times, other styles. I hope to be a bear when the time is right."

In the meantime, his big cap bias in 1999 helped his stock picks to outperform similarly timed investments in the S&P 500 by 9 percent (which he'll divulge in an early 2000 column). A huge spread, but in the entirety of the time *Forbes* has been tracking picks up to the time of this writing (1996–2009), it was just Ken's fifth-best performance. His stock picks have beat by the S&P 500 double digits on four occasions. See Table 1 in the Introduction for a refresh.

Report Card 1998

January 25, 1999

If you had bought every one of this column's recommendations last year, you would have done just as well as if you put your money, on the same dates, into the S&P 500 index—no better, no worse. That's after docking all my recommendations, but not your hypothetical index investment, for a 1% commission cost.

This is not a record to boast about, but it is not one to be ashamed of, either. My material exposure to big foreign stocks reduces portfolio risk below that of an all-US portfolio.

I started 1998 by recommending 100% equity—55% of that in America's 35 largest stocks, 37% in "huge foreign stocks that dominate their businesses" and 8% in "beat-up tax-depressed gold stocks—pick any ten."

Being 100% equities was great. And gold stocks were up 20%—but not for long. By spring gold sagged. By September 7 I told you to bail out. I hit gold's bottom almost perfectly. Ugh!

My foreign stocks reduced risk, but they sure didn't boost return. You measure foreign stocks against the Morgan Stanley EAFE Index. My foreign picks beat EAFE on average by 2%. Fine. But at 20%, EAFE lagged the S&P 500's 1998 return by 8.5%. So the international diversification and risk reduction came at a price.

Let me restate what I said a year ago. After the long string of years in which US stocks have been beating foreign ones, the time will come when EAFE beats the S&P 500. I don't know when it will come, but I know it will come. So, keep up that diversification. For 1999 I think your stock portfolio should be 33% invested abroad.

Among my early foreign picks, Nissan and Rio Tinto did very badly, dropping 37% and 14%, from recommendation to year-end. I think these are just pricing

and timing issues. With patience, they should be okay. If Nissan doesn't get its act together, it will get taken over for its brand names and distribution channels.

Much like a gold stock, Rio Tinto suffered from the disinflation trend that clocked all the other commodity metals producers. Still, I'd keep a little inflation hedge in my portfolio, and this is one I'd pick. By 2004 it should hit 130, which is 25% per year.

In July I picked Fiat and Volvo. They sank. These autos are driving me crazy, but I'm keeping my seat belt on. Norsk Hydro, recommended in April, fell 31%, simply reacting to falling energy prices. I would hold on for now.

I had foreign winners, too. From last January, my pick of Telefonica de Espana was up 52%. Nokia rose 56% after I said in the September 7 column that it could rise at 30% per year for several years. Still, I would hang on to both of these.

I got lucky in the June 1 column when I told you to sell my prior successful recommendations of Banco Santander and Montedison. They fell fast, 44% and 35%, respectively. On November 2 I said buy them back, and they're up 14% and 29% already.

Overall, my country allocations were fine, aimed at continental Europe and Japan. Happily I avoided all the lesser-developed countries. Many investors got caught trying to call the bottom in these very volatile markets, seeming not to know that they take much longer to make bottoms than the developed Western markets.

My initial 55% weight to the US was too light. But my call to stick with only the 35 largest US stocks was again, as in 1997, a good call.

All year I caught flak from cynical readers who thought this was really dumb, leading up to my August 10, dig-in-my-heels column titled "Dumb Is Beautiful." Those 35 largest stocks, equal-weighted returned 40% in 1998, nicely beating the S&P 500 by 11.5%. During the year I boosted my US weight to 67%, which also helped a lot.

The summer's correction jolted millions and caused many, maybe most, columnists nationally to bolt bearish. I didn't

and was vindicated by December's new highs on the S&P 500. I am very proud of that string of columns, and particularly my September 21, "Stay Cool" column. Check it out at the *Forbes* Digital Tool archives, www.Forbes.com/fisher. You can see all my 1998 columns there. While there, visit my "Forum" site, and, as I said on September 7, complain all you want. ∎

The Case Against Index Funds
February 22, 1999

Several readers read my January 25 column "Report Card" and e-mailed asking, "Since this column's 1998 advice only matched the S&P 500's return, why not simply buy an index fund and tune out?"

It depends. An index fund is nothing more than a tool, and isn't inherently good or bad. Like a hammer, it depends on what you use it for and how good you are with it.

Note first, my advice is much more diversified than the S&P 500, which is valuable. Here you get global diversification to reduce risk.

Matching the S&P with globalness beats just owning the S&P. You get good US and good foreign returns. If and when the US market lags, S&P 500 index fund holders will be sorry. This column's 1998 advice beat the overall world stock market by more than 4%.

Similarly, the S&P 500 is more specialized and less diversified than you may think. It doesn't act like all stocks, but like a specific subset of US stocks: huge growth stocks. It has an average dollar-weighted market capitalization of $90 billion. That is, it acts like a $90 billion US stock. Huge. And like a growth stock, selling at 8 times book value, 30 times earnings and 3 times sales. The rub?

Sometimes huge stocks pay off. Sometimes they don't. Sometimes growth stocks pay off and sometimes they don't. Sometimes US stocks pay off and sometimes they don't. It's not impossible to have a year in which all three factors reverse, and small beats big, value beats growth and overseas markets beat the US market. The S&P 500 is unique enough to be potentially risky, part of why it has done so well.

Then, too, comes behavioral finance with powerful arguments against index funds. If you turn to me, or others, for advice, you must feel some need for advice. There is more than ample evidence that folks who are in need of advice will misuse index funds. They either try to time the market or they panic in a downturn. Index funds are easy to buy and too easy to sell.

If you're a great market timer, which few folks are, then you may well use index funds to buy low and sell high. But normal folks who discover index funds late in a bull market won't use those funds to be long-term investors, even if they think they will. Instead, most of them will sell out late in a bear market, hurting themselves.

People forget that late in a bear market a general consensus builds that stocks will never again be worthwhile. It gets very easy to sell out then, and there is nothing easier to sell than an index fund.

The normal investor's brain works with what behavioralists call "mental accounting." There is a decision "tree" or mental process associated with every single investment you have. If you have 50 stocks, it takes a lot more internal crunching and mental agony to sell out than if you have just one stock, an index fund.

I would hate to see you sell out at the bottom and take a real loss a few years from now. At the right time, I hope to advise you out of stocks. But for now, stick to my basic allocation, which is to be 100% invested in stocks, with 67% of that from among the 30 largest US stocks. The other 33% should be in huge high-quality foreign stocks with a handful of global Japanese exporters. ∎

Why Big Gets Bigger
March 22, 1999

Through February, the 25 US stocks with the largest market capitalizations, namely, those at $91 billion and up, have gained a collective 2.8% in value. The Standard & Poor's index of 500 stocks is up 1%. Meanwhile, the Russell 2000 roster of small stocks is down a full 7%.

Wall Street's favoritism for huge stocks shows no signs of abating. Indeed, there is a powerful new force at work that should cause this trend to continue: the new euro currency.

In the first two months of 1999 the euro was down 7.5% against the dollar, from a value of $1.17 to $1.10. Unless you've been on Mars, media babble has probably brainwashed you to believe the euro is a competitive threat to the dollar. But how can that be if the euro falls like a rock? Fact is, the euro isn't a threat. It ensures a strong dollar and drives money into America's largest stocks.

The euro "contract" includes a no-back-out provision among its 11 members. If even one country pulls out for any reason, the whole deal falls apart. Imagine, for example, that one euro economy sinks into recession. Its politicians then blame the Eurobank, claiming monetary policy is too tight. If that country withdraws, the whole euro contract becomes void and must be renegotiated—a nightmare for the remaining 10 members and potential death to the Eurobank. It's hard to get agreement among 10 nations, and harder still to do it fast. Like all central banks, the Eurobank is self-interested. It cannot allow that to happen.

So the Eurobank must temporarily make monetary policy accommodative to what it perceives as the weakest economy among its members. As long as it does so, it prints more money than America does and the euro is a weak sister to the dollar. How long is that? Remember, each of these 11 countries still has its own cash and monetary systems in place. Until those disappear, in two years, it is easy for a country to pull out. The euro is only a potentially strong currency starting in 2001, at the earliest.

Until then, euro-denominated interest rates will be artificially low. Europeans will borrow at their banks at cheap euro rates, turn around and buy US Treasurys at higher US interest rates, and pocket the spread—around 1.5 points today—as a free ride. Any currency profit they make from the weakening of the euro is icing on the cake.

This borrowing process injects liquidity into US markets just as if the Fed were printing new dollars. And the buying makes the dollar strong. This is just what has been driving the bull market.

I first wrote about this invasion of foreign money into America in my October 20, 1997 column, long before the euro existed. Of course, there's a similar invasion from Japan.

Some of that money, either from the foreign borrowers or from those who sell US Treasurys to the borrowers, goes into stocks. Which US stocks do foreigners buy? The most global firms, the ones they know, which are also the very largest stocks. So, as I've said for years, for now limit your US holdings to the largest stocks. ∎

Bet Against the Experts
April 19, 1999

When it comes to market forecasts, will you do better listening to your friends—or to high-powered investment pros? Your friends. This year they are probably bullish.

Meir Statman, a finance professor at Santa Clara University, works with me on research that explores how investors behave. In one recent study we measured investors in three categories—retail investors, newsletter writers and professional Wall Street strategists—and compared their sentiments about market direction to later results.

Each of these groups is regularly wrong. But the very worst of them are the professional strategists, by far. For decades, traders used odd-lot statistics to bet against the sentiment of retail investors. They would have done better to bet against professionals.

Statman and I did not rate individual market seers; we lumped them all together. But there is no reason you can't pick out your own favorite experts to bet against. One of mine is the *Barron's* Roundtable, an annual talkfest by a roomful of Wall Streeters that appears in January and February. The repartee is entertaining but the sentiment is wrong. This year the pundits were quite bearish. So, as a contrary bettor, I'm for a bullish stance on stocks for 1999.

Another great source is Merrill Lynch's compiled Wall Street Sell Side Strategists Indicator. Done monthly, it has a contrary and statistically significant result. Now the strategists are bearish. So be bullish. My firm compiles its own data on strategists. As 1999 began, only 14% of portfolio strategists foresaw an above-average year. Fully 86% envisioned a below-average or negative year. Again, be bullish.

Of course, there are also very few forecasters foreseeing a disaster year, so you must consider that possibility. But as I detailed in my May 4, 1998 column, it would be, in the light of history, extraordinary if 1999 were a negative year for the S&P 500. It doesn't ever fall in the third year of a president's term.

The Great Humiliator has only one goal: To humiliate as many people as possible for as many dollars as possible over as long a time as possible. En route, its favorite victims are professionals. As a group, they can't be right.

So, you should expect this to be an above-average year. My global total return allocation remains 100% equity with 67% of that in the US, and that solely from among America's 25 largest stocks (see my March 22 column for the list). The other 33% should be in good, big, foreign stocks with a concentration on continental Europe and a few Japanese global exporters. ∎

Not Your Average Joe

May 17, 1999

Some readers are asking when, if ever, I will turn bearish. I've done so twice during my tenure here. But I couldn't now if I had to. Longtime readers know I won't call a peak until at least three months after I think it has already happened.

I am the seventh-longest-running columnist in *Forbes'* history. I stole my three-month rule from Joe Goodman, who ranks third, with a 23-year tenure that began in 1935. In my opinion he was the best ever.

Tremendous timer, super stock-picker—and a stunning simplifier. Goodman knew bull markets have long, rolling tops, and bear markets are painfully slow. If he got you out three months after a top, you missed most of the drop, and he would be a hero.

He knew it was vastly easier to see a peak afterward, more so if you don't clutter your brain with prior biased forecasts. Joe simply waited until he could look back and see higher prices three months earlier.

Then he looked for problems that weren't widely appreciated. If he found them, he turned bearish. Following this practice helps me avoid getting spooked by corrections. I last used it in my September 21, 1998 column explaining why you shouldn't bolt that market. I hope to live up to Joe's standards when the next bear market comes.

When will that be? I don't know. I'm thinking that it won't be until 2001. But I could be wrong. Until then, his three-month rule will keep us where we should be. In the meantime you might enjoy some other classic Goodman pearls:

1. Don't be a bull or bear all the time.
2. There is a time to buy, a time to sell and a long time to do nothing.
3. Never buy a stock that didn't rise in a bull market. Smart guys are out of it.
4. Don't buy the sympathy stock. Don't buy a weak railroad because a strong one has started to move. Everyone does this, and it is rarely profitable.
5. When a bull market peaks, sell the stock that rose most. It will fall fastest. Sell the stock that rose least. It didn't rise, therefore it must fall.
6. Early in a bear market, the high-class stocks show the most class.
7. In a high market, confine yourself to high-quality stocks.

Hence, my advice now is to be 100% in stocks, 67% of that in America's 25 largest stocks, and 33% in high-quality foreign stocks. ∎

Bear Coming

In fact, Ken did advise readers to get bearish in early 2001, after having gotten bearish on the Tech sector in his *Forbes* column just days before the global Tech peak. He couldn't have known now that 2001 would be the right time to get bearish. Rather, he was explaining that unless you're darn certain, you're better off bullish. That thinking is part of what kept Ken bullish all throughout the back part of the long 1990s bull when so many others had turned bearish—far too early.

Adaptability

June 14, 1999

Should a money manager stick with one style forever? Or change with the times?

Reader Ken Koester of Edina, Minn. grouses that I have drifted from one discipline early in my tenure here—an emphasis on smaller companies trading at small multiples of their sales—to a very different one now, which emphasizes big companies at big multiples.

Koester wants to know if I can explain myself. I can.

In the 1980s small-company stocks trading at low multiples made sense to me. My early research on price/sales ratios—long before others thought about them—made me feel I held an edge with that discipline. But religious-like faith is for God. Treating value investing as if it were unshakable dogma is wrong.

Subsequent research showed me fundamental causes behind long periods when value leads, other periods when growth leads and yet other times when the market cannot be neatly assigned to either of these themes. Now size alone is more important.

By 1996 I was urging my readers to choose, for their US portfolio, among the 50 stocks with the largest market capitalizations. Applied today, that formula would leave you a list starting with Microsoft at the top and ranging down to American Express in position number 50.

But, as the market has climbed, I have whittled the list down to 25 companies, ending with Hewlett-Packard. Lots of research went into all of this beforehand. Changing wasn't drifting; it was planned.

Late in this bull market and early in the next bear market, big stocks should lead, and biggest do best. (For more on why, check the March 22 column.)

My big-company portfolio is no more permanent dogma than my earlier emphasis on smaller companies. It is opportunistic and temporary. One day I hope again to urge small value stocks—at the right time—and, at other times, other styles. I hope to be a bear when the time is right.

If I am not wedded to either value or growth, what are my principles? Besides researching new discoveries that drive me to change still more, here are five:

1. No investing style can be best permanently. When a consensus forms believing one style to be best, investment bankers create enough new securities to make sure it disappoints.
2. The consensus of professional market strategists tells you what won't happen, cutting down your menu of what might.
3. Foreign investing provides real diversification, but only if you don't buy the same stocks everyone else buys.
4. Markets trading at unusually high multiples of earnings are inherently low in risk and never lead to disaster years.
5. An important but little understood cause of bear markets in history is the fear of redistribution of property rights.

So, in this bull market, keep 67% of your equity money in America's 25 largest stocks. Keep the other 33% in big continental European and Japanese stocks. ∎

Investing for Acrophobics
July 26, 1999

Last month I mentioned in passing that when the market is trading at a high multiple of earnings, it's low in risk. I got a ton of puzzled responses. "Was it a typo?" "Didn't you mean, 'high risk'?" One reader opined I was "funnin'" you and never meant it. No.

The past 127 years of US trading show that ultra-high-P/E markets have been nicely lower in risk than lower-P/E markets. That is, they offer higher returns, and a lower frequency of declines. Readers of my *Forbes* forum site at www.Forbes.com/fisher not only know that, but also possess most of the raw data and statistical results. But you don't need a lot of historical statistics to become convinced of this relationship. It follows from simple market logic.

Start with the fact that the market is a discounter of all known information. This is the most basic rule of finance. Known risks and rewards are already figured into market prices. If everybody thinks something will happen—say, that small caps will bounce next January—then it won't happen because it will be figured into prices earlier.

High P/E Myth

Fear of high P/Es is everlasting and pervasive. Few question it—believing a high P/E means something has a "too-high" price relative to its earnings. Folks forget the P/E has two moving variables, as Ken deftly explains here. You simply can't expect a P/E, on its own, to direct you to stocks that are over- or underpriced. If only it were that simple . . .

Most investors believe high-P/E markets are unusually risky. And almost everyone knows when the market's P/E is high—now, for instance, with stocks trading at 34 times trailing earnings, a ratio about double the average for this century. But since the market has already reacted to whatever we all are fretting over, high-P/E markets can't be high risk. They would become high risk only if we didn't know when we had them—or if most folks switched to thinking they weren't risky.

Fear of heights, or acrophobia, has been bred into us over the eons and is hard to shake. For most longtime investors, admitting that high P/Es aren't risky also means admitting having been wrong. That's tough to do.

But not only have ultra-high-P/E years in America had better overall results than lower-P/E years, they have also never had disasters—not once has a January 1 market P/E above 19 led to a double-digit loss that year or over the next two years. All big calendar-year busts followed a January 1 P/E of less than 19.

The crash year of 1987 is no exception to this rule; the S&P 500 finished the year up 5% from January 1. How about Japan, which floated on seemingly high P/Es in the late 1980s and then crashed spectacularly? There aren't long enough, good enough Japanese data to know what is or isn't historically a high P/E for Japan. You can't construct a normal bell curve from Japan's P/Es—or, for that matter, from most other countries' historical P/Es. So, I'm just talking about the US market.

Generally, whenever we have had ultra-high-P/E markets, earnings exceed expectations for a while. That's happening this year. Eventually, the earnings growth brings down the P/E ratio. And from that point on is when you might see bad things happen.

So don't let the market's high P/E keep you from enjoying the rest of this bull market, which I suspect will last until at least November 2000. Remain 100% in stocks, with 67% of that in the 25 largest US stocks and 33% in big foreign stocks. ∎

The Broken Bond
August 23, 1999

How would you feel if your portfolio were down 10%? If you're like most folks, it depends on what you own. If you own stocks and the S&P 500 plunges 10%, you sweat, fret—and wonder if it's time to bail out. You might even vow to never, ever own stocks again. Remember last summer?

Why is it then that bondholders are not so sensitive to bear markets?

Through 1999's first half, the 30-year US Treasury bond's total return was minus 10.7%—with the S&P 500 up 12.4%. Yet you don't read manic media babble about bonds as some bottomless bog. Those who last year spurned stocks for bonds, which they considered ultrasafe, have yet to barely whimper. And those sage seers who pushed bonds at you have not had heaps of hate mail. The deflationists still rail—and still urge owning bonds—with no acknowledgment of their debacle. No regrets.

Why do folks commonly fail to note the losses they have on bonds? Or the risks?

People think differently about bonds and stocks, more differently from the real differences between the two deserve. The big differences are these two: 1) Bonds have a fixed maturity and yield. The S&P 500 doesn't. Sit passively with Treasurys and your pre-inflation principal should be returned on a certain date. 2) Bonds usually have slightly lower volatility than stocks.

The similarities are considerable. With either you aim (or should aim) at total return, the sum of price changes and yield, after inflation. With either you try, or should try, to achieve the best expected return per unit of risk. Both suffer big losses for years.

But bondholders have a tough time assessing risk. For reasonably long-term investors during much of the 20th century, bonds have been higher in risk than stocks. You can measure this many ways statistically: frequency of loss, amount of losses over rolling time periods of varying durations, retention of purchasing power, correlation of returns with returns on other assets. Too many bond investors fail to grasp these essentials.

Worse, lots of folks have big bond losses and don't even know it. They don't ever check since they don't expect losses with bonds. You will be a much wiser investor if you accept the fact that stocks aren't as risky and bonds much more risky than most people think they are. Don't make the

Bonds Are . . . Riskier Than Stocks?

It's an amazing feature among investors that many, if not most, forget that bonds can and do have negative returns, just like stocks. Ken shows in Chapter 10 of his 2008 bestseller *The Ten Roads to Riches* that, given just a bit of time, stocks actually have had better and more consistently positive returns than bonds.

mistake in 1999 that so many folks made last year and let your fear of stocks, and lack of fear of bonds, deceive you into a bad asset allocation. The right allocation now for bonds remains zero. Stick to my prescription of recent years of 100% equity with one-third of that in quality foreign stocks. ■

Small Stock Fantasies
September 20, 1999

After a disastrous last few years, smaller stocks staged a big rally starting in March.

That brought on a plethora of press about the new dawn for small caps.

It was just a suckers' rally and with no fanfare actually ended in late May, a mere countertrend to the market's main theme since 1995—bigger stocks besting smaller ones. In June big stocks dominated again. In July it was a toss, but in August small stocks were a disaster, lagging big ones by 3.2% and losing 3.8% overall.

Believers of the small-cap fantasy are losing money now. Late in a bull market and throughout bear markets, small stocks almost never lead for long.

Helping fuel this revival of interest in small companies is a big misperception— that today's market is just like the 1973 top, led by the Nifty Fifty. Untrue! The largest stocks in 1973 weren't expensive. The S&P 500 on January 1, 1973 was only 18.4 times trailing earnings, just one slice above the market's 127-year average of 15.5. Price/earnings ratios are much higher now, which, as I detailed in July, is good. The 1973–74 bear market was caused by global economics, not high P/Es.

And don't deceive yourself that the Nifty Fifty were that era's huge stocks. Unlike today's leaders, which, in a healthy and normal development, are our biggest names, the Nifty Fifty were mostly companies with smallish market capitalizations. The original December 1972 list of 50 leading glamour stocks included a few biggies like Coca-Cola, Disney, Merck and Xerox, but it also had Avery Products, Avon, CR Bard, Clorox, Colonial Penn, Damon, Dr. Pepper, Jack Eckerd, Fluor, Long's Drugs, Masco, Natomas, Ponderosa, Rite Aid, Simplicity Pattern and Standard Brands Paint.

Ironically, this famous high-P/E list of one-decision, buy-and-put-away-forever stocks changed drastically over the years. Fully 378 names eventually shifted on and off the Nifty Fifty. Amazing.

I don't have any illusion that any stock or even any style of investing is of the one-decision variety. But right now I stick with a long-standing decision, reiterated in my last column, to own huge stocks and avoid bonds. My portfolio remains 100% in stocks, with 67% in America's 25 largest stocks and 33% overseas. So far this year, Japanese and European stocks have been strong. This is no countertrend. Hang on to them. ■

Greater Fools

October 18, 1999

What can we learn about this year-end from 1942? First: that Y2K won't hurt the stock market. It may even drive a nice rally.

What does 1942 have to do with Y2K? Well, 1942 shows how the market works, which isn't in a way that now allows a disaster from Y2K. Those who still fret Y2K's market impact don't fathom the markets, and you simply should be dismissive of them all.

There are two principles here. First, markets don't wait for known events; they move ahead of them. Second, folks who wait for events to drive prices often get trapped and trampled by stampedes.

Which was a bigger risk: Y2K in 1999 or Adolf Hitler in 1941? Yet, in 1942, long before anyone could possibly know with any certainty that we would win the war, the S&P 500 rose 20%. In 1943 it rose 26% more—in 1944, 20% more; in 1945, another 36%, before peaking early in 1946. That last year was largely driven by folks who held back cash waiting for certainty—and then threw in their money, very kindly bidding up prices for those who had bought earlier.

How did the market know to rally in 1942 and 1943, long before definitive news? It's what markets do. They decline before a war or recession or something else ugly starts. Usually, they move with a long lead. They rise long before events improve. Hence the age-old adage, "The market knows." The market is also a "discounter" of all known information. That means whatever we all know, fret, read and cluck about is well priced into markets.

It is what we don't all know, fret, read and talk about that moves markets. It isn't that those things can never be discerned. Often they can. But overwhelmingly folks are blind and ignorant about real market movers.

For example, few can see the huge, unaccounted-for flows of foreign money pouring into America that I first told you about in 1997—that have largely driven our bull market since 1996. They just don't know it is happening. (See my columns of October 20, 1997 and March 22, 1999.)

Y2K is the most widely hyped "disaster" in modern history. It is well documented: The only folks who aren't familiar with it are in the upper Amazon basin, rapidly fleeing the rest of humanity. I need not even define Y2K for you to know exactly what I'm referencing.

My July 6, 1998 column detailed why Y2K could not hurt the stock market. But now, with December 31 so close, I'll go a step further and say that the market likely will rise as another Y2K force takes over.

There are just enough investors who do understand how markets work to potentially create a pre-year-end buying

Y2What?

Readers today naturally know the world did not come to a screeching halt as, worldwide, clocks ticked to January 1, 2000. But in the back half of 1999, Y2K fears were everywhere. Ken was right, though—the fears couldn't touch stocks. Those fears had been around too long. Ken rarely makes very short-term forecasts, but he was spot on here in predicting a big year-end surge. US stocks soared 17 percent and global stocks 19 percent from this column's publication to year end—an annualized 121 percent and 133 percent respectively![7] Just amazing.

stampede. They will sense in coming weeks that a Y2K bust ran out of time and that with year-end the rigid Y2K nuts lose their reason for caution. Those sages may play the Y2Kers for greater fools by getting their own money into stocks before year-end. I am never sure where the market will go in the very short term, but there is more likelihood of a big pre-year-end up move than any other possibility.

So, remain 100% in equities, with 67% of that in America's 25 largest stocks. The other 33% should be in big continental European and Japanese stocks. ■

Never Say Dow
November 15, 1999

Quick! Where is the S&P 500? You don't know? But I bet you know all about the Dow 30. You hear it daily. You see it in book titles and magazine headlines. Here is the market's version of Gresham's law: Bad indexes drive out good ones. The Dow Jones industrial average is a completely useless, misleading index of market performance. It is useless for analyzing history or making forecasts. Use the S&P 500 instead.

I learned this very young as, "Never say 'Dow' unless talking about a chemical company, a publisher or an Asian philosophy."

There are two reasons for this. The first is that an index of 30 stocks is necessarily a narrow and arbitrary gauge of market activity. For 40 years, from 1939 to 1979, the Dow omitted International Business Machines. This one choice, made more or less on a whim, has had a permanent impact on the Dow's level, since that happened to be a period when IBM was a powerful growth stock.

Today the Dow includes some comparatively small stocks, like JP Morgan (with a market capitalization of $21 billion) and Caterpillar ($19 billion), while omitting some very important ones: Bank of America ($100 billion) and Cisco Systems ($219 billion), to name two. Only belatedly, on November 1, did the Dow add Microsoft ($472 billion, America's biggest stock) and Intel ($237 billion).

The other deficiency in the Dow is a structural one. It's price-weighted. That is, you add up the prices of the 30 stocks, then divide by an adjusting factor, to get your index value. When Charles Dow first calculated his index, he divided by the number of stocks he was tracking to get an average stock price. Over the years he and his successors had to adjust this divisor to preserve continuity in the index as the component stocks have been split and some stocks have replaced others. Currently, the divisor is down to 0.197.

What's wrong with a price-weighted index? In the weighting of the components it ignores the variations in the market values of the different companies. Instead, it gives the most weight to companies whose share prices happen to be high. A company with a share price of $100 would have twice the weight of a company with a share price of $50.

This is why you won't see Berkshire Hathaway (recent price, $55,500) among the Dow 30 anytime soon. However well this company might represent a cross-section of the market, it would make a joke of the index by overpowering the other stocks in the computation of the average.

With the price weighting you have the absurd result that the performance of the index hinges on what stocks split and when. If IBM splits 2-for-1, its weighting in the Dow is cut in half. This is absurd, because stock splits are purely cosmetic; they have no bearing on any investor's net worth or dividends. The Dow is completely useless for analyzing history. Mathematically, year by year, the outcome is purely random, depending upon which stocks split when. So you get periods like the early 1940s, cited in my October 18 column, when the S&P 500 and the Dow show very different returns. Or this year Through September the Dow was up 12.6%. Were it cap-weighted, as it should be, like the S&P, it would have been up only 4.5%. Ridiculous. The Dow is similarly useless for making forecasts. Ignore any forecast of the Dow or anyone whose analysis is based on the Dow.

Dow or S&P, what you really want to know is where I think the market is going. It's a little early for me to make a specific forecast of returns for 2000, but I will hazard that it will be a fine year for the S&P 500 and an even better year for foreign stocks, as measured by Morgan Stanley's cap-weighted EAFE index. ∎

The Index Sirens
December 13, 1999

Active managers can't beat indexes, right? So go passive, right? You've read that lots. Like many things widely bandied about, it contains just enough truth to trick you. But it is wrong. It is a wicked lie.

Fact is: For decades active managers of US equities have badly lagged the S&P 500. Hence the index craze. But the evidence is not quite supportive of the theory that indexers always and everywhere beat active managers.

Look overseas. Were indexing a sure winner for foreign equities, you would passively buy a fund replicating Morgan Stanley's Europe, Australasia, Far East index, otherwise known as EAFE. But the fact is that most US managers of foreign equity funds have beaten foreign benchmarks. Take Morningstar data for US mutual funds with 100% of their holdings in foreign stocks. On a three-, five-and ten-year basis, 57%, 57% and 79% of them beat EAFE.

In this case the active managers' superior performance has a lot to do with investing flexibility, something an index can't deliver. Remember back in 1989, when Japan seemed to reign supreme?

EAFE was weighted 50% in Japan stocks. Fortuitously, few American money managers followed that lead. Instead, they held on average just half of EAFE's Japan weight. When Japan imploded, they blew EAFE away.

Another example of index illusion has to do with US small-cap funds. Small-cap value funds mostly haven't kept pace with their benchmarks, like the Wilshire Small-Cap Value index or the Russell 2000 Value—but small-cap growth funds have dwarfed their small-growth benchmarks. Why? As with EAFE, it has more to do with style biases in the indexes and market fads than with managers' skill.

The simple reality is that most US managers have lagged the S&P 500 mainly because on average big caps have done better than small caps for an extremely long time. Morningstar data show that, for every quarter of the past decade when big caps prevailed, US funds lagged the S&P 500. But when small caps beat big caps, funds beat the S&P. The bigger the spread between big and small, the bigger the performance differential between funds and the S&P.

Why? The S&P 500 is capitalization-weighted. The 25 largest stocks are so huge they pull up the other 475 to its average cap of $120 billion. But managers pick stocks and then buy relatively similar amounts of each, tending much closer to equal weighting of their different positions. Equal weighting the S&P would reduce its average cap by 80%, to $22 billion — close to the average fund's $23 billion cap. I happen to favor big-cap stocks now, but note that these won't always be the better performers.

Active or passive, you still need a portfolio strategy. Mine remains 67% US equities, solely from the 25 largest stocks, which you can't do with an index — and 33% in continental Europe and Japan, also unindexable. ∎

2000

Tech Bubbles Over

"All correctly constructed major equity indexes will have almost identical returns over the next 30 years. One will wax while another wanes, but over such a long time span they'll come out roughly even."

"What to Do About Tech," May 29, 2000

"A key lesson from behavioral finance is that people hate losses much more than they like gains. Normal folks feel the pain of loss about 2.5 times as keenly as they enjoy a gain of the same size. So when Uncle Sam takes from some to give to others, confidence falls and financial markets suffer."

"Gephardt for Speaker," September 4, 2000

Ken was on a roll as 2000 began. He had more or less correctly called the last two bear markets and kept his readers invested for the entirety of the bull markets in between. His forecasts for annual returns during the bull market years were darn good too. "Twice, in 1995 and 1999, I've had the single most accurate projection of any nationally published forecaster. While some of my forecasts were wide of the mark, my method has never put me on the wrong side of the market." ("Break Their Crystal Balls," April 3, 2000.)

But some of Ken's most prescient forecasts were yet to come. One of the most notable was his column "1980 Revisited" in which Ken correctly called a top in the Technology sector. The tech-heavy Nasdaq Composite's amazing 1999 returns carried over into the first months of 2000. By early March, the Nasdaq was already up over 24 percent while the broader S&P 500 was down almost 7 percent over the same period.[1] Investor demand for technology shares seemed insatiable—an environment that seemed to Ken a lot like the fervid demand for oil stocks two decades prior. "Tech stocks are in a late stage bubble. It should break later this year. . . . Right now technology stocks are just where oil stocks were in 1980. . . . This time it isn't oil's price that's supposed to triple in four years but rather the population of Internet users." The massive run-up in share prices was just one similarity Ken noticed. Technology stocks' share of the overall market had grown similarly to Energy stocks leading up to 1980. Both had price-to-book values around two times the market average near their peaks. And Energy stocks accounted for 20 percent of the IPOs in 1980, boosting the overall supply of stocks by 2 percent—almost exactly the same as Technology in 1999.

With a Technology top not too far off, Ken expected the Nasdaq to end 2000 down 15 percent and the S&P 500 to be flat. Remember, Ken advised getting out of the market only if you expect it to be down a lot, and never calling a bear market too early. So he recommended staying invested in stocks but lightening up a lot on Technology. That turned out to be great advice. The S&P 500 closed the year down a bit more than Ken expected, falling 9.1 percent in 2000. But the excess drop occurred because Technology's slide started sooner and was worse than he envisioned—the Nasdaq finished the year down 39.3 percent even though it started 2000 strong[2]—so a stock portfolio with relatively little Technology exposure held up okay.

Think of it another way. As 2000 began, Technology was just over 30 percent of the weight in the S&P 500—its biggest sector.[3] A 40 percent drop in a 30 percent sector would send an index down 12 percent if all the other stocks were exactly unchanged. Since the index was down 9.1 percent, the reality was the non-Technology stocks in the S&P 500 were actually up a hair in 2000. The decimating damage to stocks on a broader basis didn't really begin until 2001.

As Ken would recount in his annual assessment of his *Forbes* picks, the stocks he recommended in 2000 beat the S&P 500 by 10 percent.[4] A dearth of Technology recommendations was a key factor in the strong result relative to the market.

In his April column, Ken mentioned his readers were less than thrilled with "1980 Revisited." Too many folks believed in the Internet revolution story to their cores. This, of course, made Ken all the more confident in his forecast. "Last month's technology column generated more hate mail than any column I've done since 1990 and 1991, as our market was bottoming and heading sky-high. If you want to make me cocky, keep the hate mail flowing hot and heavy. I love it." ("Break Their Crystal Balls," April 3, 2000.)

Ken has always said investing takes some skill and some luck. The reasoning behind Ken's forecast for a Technology drop reflected his skill, but the timing of the column involved a fair amount of luck. He'd be the first to say he didn't know exactly when the Technology top would come—he thought it might not be until the second half of 2000. And he had no control over the *Forbes* publishing date. What turned out to be nearly impeccable timing was mostly luck. "1980 Revisited" was published on March 6, 2000. The Nasdaq peaked just a few weeks later on March 24, 2000 and began a massive slide from there.[5] In 2010, the Nasdaq is still about 50 percent below where it was in March 2000.[6]

On a separate note, Ken's October 30, 2000 column was graced with one of his most incendiary titles: "Wife Haters." The title might be provocative, but the advice is good—Ken explains why his columns and investing philosophy skew heavily toward owning stocks, except when he expects a bear market.

Unfortunately, conventional investing wisdom says the closer you get to retirement, the more bonds you should own since bonds offer fixed coupon payments and can be less volatile than stocks. But that thinking ignores stocks' long-term growth potential. Over long periods, stocks almost always do better than bonds, and by a wide margin on average. Investors' asset allocations should be more about their and their spouses' life expectancies, not when they retire. Investors may think they're doing the right thing by being "conservative," but depending on how you define conservative, they may be doing a serious harm to their portfolios' long-term performance. And the spouse that lives longer may suffer most for it.

"Take a normal fellow worth half a million at age 70 who thinks he might live ten years and is mostly in bonds. Conservative? No, foolish. His wife is 63. She comes from a family like mine where few folks die before 90, meaning her longevity stretches past 30 years. Her husband must hate her severely, because bond-like returns on half a million, offset by withdrawals to live on, will leave her in poverty long before the 30 years are up. Aged poverty is brutally cruel."

Thinking about long-term asset allocation goals in terms of how long the money should last (as opposed to an investor's age or retirement year) is something the financial planning industry and lawyers quibble about endlessly in terms of what's right and wrong. Every bear market convinces many that Ken's advice on this is wrong, and every bull market moves the needle back the other way. Ken's point is there are many investors who have, for whatever reason, been in fixed income since age 60 and are now 90—and they are living in relative poverty. These folks are the real victims, with no one to champion their cause and are largely forgotten.

Ken's goal of becoming *Forbes'* longest-running columnist got a little closer in 2000 as he jumped to number six on the esteemed list. Ken paid tribute to the previous number six in his December 25, 2000 column "Ode to John Schulz." His praise of Schulz would be well heeded by the blogosphere today—where vast commentary on anything and anyone is available—but it's rarely verifiable, and anonymity and unaccountability seems to rule the day. Of Schulz, Ken noted: "First, he admitted when he was wrong, which was refreshing. Second, he was crystal clear about his views. You never suffered qualified statements or wishy-washy forecasts. His neck stuck out. Third, he questioned every trend, keeping him from being wrong more often than he might have been. Fourth, he turned a phrase well." Sounds a lot like Ken.

Against the Odds

January 10, 2000

Is your goal to maximize return? It shouldn't be. Why not? Portfolio management isn't just collecting stocks and hoping they rise. Lots of investors, including professionals, ignore risk control, which is portfolio management's very heart.

Many try to beat the S&P 500 by shooting wild and hoping to hit big. They may figure that putting all their chips on the Nasdaq 100 is smart because tech is doing so well. But what if tech stocks collapse? Neglecting risk control is a big mistake. In this game, whatever you do, you always know you may be wrong and that you're up against the odds.

Rather than trying to maximize return, you should try to do something a little different: maximize the likelihood of beating a given benchmark, like the S&P 500. And the way to do that is with a two-pronged portfolio. First, a core strategy, which you think will drive returns if all works well.

It could be as simple as, "I like tech." Or, "The economy will reward cyclicals." So you put the bulk of your money in tech or cyclicals.

But you must also have a fallback, or counterstrategy, to protect you if your core strategy flops. The rest of your portfolio goes in what will do the very best if your core strategy is completely wrong and does the very worst.

Say you pick tech as your core strategy. You buy the Nasdaq 100, which this year has by far outstripped the S&P 500. Your counterstrategy might be companies whose products have an inelastic demand, so they can raise prices if things get rockier. Tobacco, oil and drug companies are examples. They will keep you above water if tech takes a dive.

This is much more than diversifying. Since 1997, my benchmark has been the Morgan Stanley World Index. My core strategy since then: That copious money creation in Japan and Euroland flows into America, seeking our higher interest rates, driving up the dollar and a bull market focused on our most global US stocks, the very largest ones.

My counterstrategy? If I'm wrong and money returns home from America, Japan's large exporters and European stocks will head for the sky.

Hence, I've been 100% in stocks, 67% in the very largest US stocks—slightly overweight, since America's equities comprise 50% of the world market—and 33% in Japan and western Europe. In 1997 and 1998 my core strategy worked. Then, in mid-1999, lots of money headed home to Japan and Europe, and my counterstrategy drove returns.

Either way, I always have some laggard stocks. If my core works, my counterstrategy lags and vice versa. Having some laggards

---

Never Maximize Return

This short column has some real insight gems for how to build a portfolio. Namely, if you try to maximize return, you as often (or more often) end up maximizing losses. It's more rational and, in Ken's view, a better risk-management strategy to maximize the likelihood of outperforming an appropriate benchmark. For readers who want to explore more of what that means and how it can be done—both strategically and tactically—they can read Ken's 2006 tome, *The Only Three Questions That Count.*

---

is okay, particularly if they're part of your counterstrategy. Don't fret about them. Instead, contemplate the fact that they may be playing an important and beneficial part in how the portfolio works, despite current poor performance. Consider them the cost of insurance, a form of risk control and therefore basic to portfolio management. ∎

Good and Lucky
February 7, 2000

Each New Year, *Forbes* makes me give you a report card on how my column's stock picks did the prior year. How did I do in 1999? My picks were good—and lucky. With investing, skill can take you only so far. My December 28, 1998 call for a 20% 1999 S&P 500 return was America's most accurate nationally published S&P forecast. That was good, and very lucky. The S&P returned 21%. No one else was within several percent of me or the S&P on the high or low side.

Let's turn to my individual stock picks. *Forbes* calculates them each year as if you had invested equally in each of my stock selections, less a 1% phantom brokerage cost, and compares that with investing in an index on the same dates, same amounts. In 1999 I beat the S&P 500 by 9%.

Of course, I don't manage my column against the S&P 500. I use the Morgan Stanley World Equity Index. You get global diversification that way. Here, I did less well. Still, my picks beat that index by 5%, the exact margin I beat it by in 1998. With foreign stocks besting domestic ones, I got lucky and even squeaked 1% ahead of the Morgan's Europe, Australasia, Far East (EAFE) index, which has no US stocks.

Throughout 1999 I advised the same basic asset allocation—100% in equities. That was right. But urging you to be 67% in US stocks and 33% overseas meant too little overseas. I was wrong on that.

I had some lucky monster hits. Sony rose 284% from my recommendation; Nokia, 176%; Hitachi, 117%; Koninklijke KPN, 114%; and Cisco Systems, 103%. I had 24 picks that had risen more than 30% by year-end.

Certainly, I had dogs, too. My Philip Morris pick had lost 42% by year-end. Montedison was down 38%; Eli Lilly, 32%; Pfizer, 31%; and Bank of America, 27%. Seven stocks lost between 10% and 21%. As I detailed last month, in portfolio management you blend strategies, necessarily including some stocks that end up lagging. I don't sweat that. I'm lucky I didn't have more 1999 losers.

My March 22 column centered on the new euro, which I said would continue weak. It was down 7.5% against the dollar then and ended 1999 down 15%. Lucky. That column urged, among domestic stocks, to restrict yourself to the 25 largest stocks. I offered a list. While that wasn't great advice, it wasn't terrible and didn't cost you much.

Big stocks led small ones until late 1999. But on September 20, I re-urged restricting US portfolios to the 25 largest stocks. This was ill-timed and about as unlucky as I got last year. Led by a surge in the back half of December, the Russell 2000 small-cap stock index beat the S&P 500 by 3.5% for the fourth quarter. For the year, the two indexes were within a quarter percent of each other, with no yearlong trend favoring big or small. It was a toss.

On August 23 I noted that the US 30-year Treasury bond, which most folks envision as safe, isn't so safe and had a negative 11% year-to-date return. Meanwhile the

S&P 500 was up 12%. I said that spread would widen and the bond would weaken. Lucky. The 30-year US bond's 1999 total return ended at negative 15%.

On October 18 I repeated my advice of July 6, 1998 and December 28, 1998: that you need not fret Y2K. But I twisted it into a surprise market positive, predicting how and why Y2K would drive a "big pre-year-end up move." Hostile e-mail and forum postings came from "technology experts" who knew I was wrong. They didn't know I was lucky.

Perhaps my greatest 1999 contribution to you was analysis and advice that can't always be quantified: about how index funds can backfire; how to see investor sentiment; how and when to turn bearish— or not; why I keep changing, why you should; why high price/earnings markets don't signal you to be bearish; why the euro is weak; when small caps do and don't fit in; and why you should always ignore the Dow indexes in favor of the S&P 500.

My forecasts for 2000? In terms of indexes, I foresee 20% for EAFE and 10% for my benchmark Morgan Stanley World. For the S&P 500, a 0% return. Not a bear market, but flat. The Nasdaq 100 should lose 15%. And finally: I won't be as lucky as I was in 1999. Since I expect foreign stocks to best domestic ones, my allocation now changes. While still 100% equity, it shifts from 67% US and 33% foreign to 60% in continental Europe and Japan, with only 40% in the US. I'd love my picks to make 15% in 2000. ∎

1980 Revisited
March 6, 2000

Tech stocks are in a late-stage bubble. It should break later this year. I usually dislike "bubble," a word bandied about too often by extremists. But I watched a bubble like this one 19 years ago, and I have seen how it ends. Right now technology stocks are just where oil stocks were in early 1981.

Recall how unstoppable energy appeared in 1980. That was a time of high and rising inflation, booming commodity prices, OPEC's success as a cartel and the Iran-Iraq war. By late 1980 oil was $33 a barrel, with consensus forecasts of $100 four years out. No one envisioned oil's falling.

It's happening all over again. This time around it isn't oil's price that is supposed to triple in four years but rather the population of Internet users.

Here are some other disturbing similarities. Tech's share of the S&P 500 has grown from just 6% in 1992 to 19% in 1998 and 30% in 1999. Energy's S&P weight climbed from 7% in 1972 to 22% in 1979 to 28% at year-end 1980. You know about technology's great returns: rising 44% in 1998 and 130% in 1999. In 1979 energy stocks were up 68%, and in 1980, 83%.

Then the bubble popped. The energy sector's weight fell to 23% by the end of 1981, mostly in the second half of the year. Energy stocks lost 21%. The S&P 500 lost 4.5%. In 1982 energy stocks fell another 19%, while the S&P rose 21%. Since 1980 the energy sector has returned 9% per year. It has lagged three points a year below the next-worst-performing S&P 500 sector. Yet energy consumption has grown steadily.

Check out America's 30 largest stocks. They represent 36% of the US market's entire value. Exactly half are tech stocks. At year-end 1980 exactly half the 30 largest stocks were energy stocks. Of course, if you believe in the demand for and future of technology, today's weights may make sense. But if you believe in the increasing supply of the stocks, it doesn't.

Here's another eerie similarity: Back then energy stocks sold at twice the S&P's average price-to-book ratio. Today tech sells at 2.5 times the market's price-to-book.

Look at initial public offerings in 1980 and now. That year was a busy one, with energy making up 20% of the offerings. That boosted the overall number of US stocks by 2%. In 1999 tech comprised 21% of the offerings and, again, increased total stocks by 2%. While that may not sound big, it is. Newly public companies are where the bubble breaks, when they run out of cash.

Most energy initial public offerings were formed to develop some esoteric energy technology or to drill for oil in bizarre places. They were hardly the vertically integrated giants, like Exxon, which extract, refine and sell oil. And they weren't huge: None of 1980's 50 largest energy stocks was a 1979 or 1980 initial public offering. Eventually most went bust. But now 11 of our 50 largest tech stocks are 1998 or 1999 initial offerings, which means the damage will be greater if any fail.

Most new techies are as shallow in their areas as 1980's offerings were in energy. Who has the most Internet sales? Amazon? No. Intel, selling chips to its customers, did more online business in 1999 than all the dot-commies put together. Federal Express had more business on the Web than America Online and 17 times more business than Yahoo.

Most Internet stocks are merely marketing firms with no clearly defined or provable strategy. Most Net vendors have no real gross margin on sales, and that lack is a disaster waiting to happen—later this year.

As with 1980's energy initial offerings, these new tech companies burn feverishly through cash, hoping to catch on with the public. Later this year, just as happened two decades ago, dozens will run out of cash—there are 140 now with less than 12 months' cash supply. Folks will then worry about who will run out of cash next, causing many more sound stocks to fall. Selling will run rampant in tech from small to large, even hurting the most solid tech stocks.

Tech Top

This column, urging readers to get bearish on Tech, was published just 4 days before the Tech peak. Spooky. As to nailing the timing so precisely, Ken would say, "Good and lucky. But mostly, lucky." He was confident a Tech bubble had formed and would burst, and soon. But he could not have predicted how close he came to calling the exact peak—by mere days.

I have no clue which ones will implode first. Some will float more stock and lengthen their lease on life. But the large group of them without a viable business model are top candidates to go down hard. I don't see this immediately ahead; but instead in the second half of 2000.

Last month I forecast a flat S&P 500 in 2000, with tech stocks down 15%. I stand by that forecast. As 2000 progresses, you should lighten your holdings in technology, keeping the biggest and most solid companies. This is a year for moving forward with foreign equities while lowering US expectations. ∎

Break Their Crystal Balls
April 3, 2000

How is it best to forecast? Carefully analyze what the market pros say. Then know that won't happen. Think I'm kidding? The broad consensus of professionals as a group is always wrong. So figure out what it is and discard it. Consider all other possibilities and use historical analysis, market theory and good data-crunching to eliminate as many others as you can. What you can't eliminate is most likely.

Although not perfect, my record using this method has been pretty good. Twice, in 1995 and 1999, I've had the single most accurate S&P 500 projection of any nationally published forecaster. While some of my forecasts were wide of the mark, my method has never put me or you on the wrong side of the market. For 2000, I see a flat S&P.

How can you game professionals' forecasts? You can't access most of them, but an easy proxy is *BusinessWeek*'s annual market forecast page in each year's final issue. It gives 50 pros' forecasts for the S&P 500 for the next year. Usually, almost all of them are wrong.

Why? By the time forecasts are made public, the opinions behind them are priced into the market, meaning they can't work. The market is the Great Humiliator, and it enjoys chomping professionals more than you because we pros are visible, supposedly knowledgeable and on record.

Envision a bell curve. As 1999 started, 47% of the forecasters in the *BusinessWeek* survey foresaw the S&P returning between 0 and 10%. And 30% expected a return between 0 and –10%. So 77% were saying: "Up a bit or down a bit." There were continuous calls above and below these, but big holes existed, with no forecasts at all from 15% to 23.5%, and from –10% to –20%. Above and below the holes were thin streams of outliers. That left those two big holes as the only real possibilities.

I used history to eliminate the negative hole. For example, the third year of a presidential term never goes massively negative. And years starting with an ultrahigh P/E have never gone double-digit down. With a few more ditties like those, I wiped out the –10% to –20% hole. Hence, 1999's most likely outcome was in the 15% -to-23.5% range.

But 2000 brought the biggest shift in professional sentiment in a decade, swinging massively bullish. Fully 46% of all forecasters came out for a 10%-to-20% S&P return. A smattering anticipated negative returns. There are a whopping six holes in the forecast range: 21% to 28%, –2% to 4%, –4% to –10%, –20% to –30% and no one above 28% or below –30%. To soothe the Great Humiliator, the outcome must be in one of the six. But which?

I may be wrong. Picking among six is much tougher than picking between two. I ruled out the two entirely in negative territory. The reasoning is similar to 1999's. The fourth year of a presidency never goes down big. And the ultrahigh P/E argument remains valid. The only hole I couldn't knock out was the one around a flat, essentially 0% return. That became, by default, my forecast.

The same methodology, which I call behavioral-based forecasting because it derives from forecasters' behavior, leads me to think Europe (except Great Britain) and Japan will do better this year than the S&P 500. And technology ("1980 Revisited") will turn negative later this year. I do this based on a lot more forecasts than just the *BusinessWeek* survey and for lots of indexes. But needing to survive the Great Humiliator, I'm a chicken and would never forecast without having everyone else stick their sentiments and necks out first.

Speaking of sentiment, last month's technology column generated more hate mail than any column I've done since 1990 and 1991, as our market was bottoming and heading sky-high. If you want to make me cocky, keep that hate mail flowing hot and heavy. I love it. ∎

Downturn Insurance
May 1, 2000

The market's recent turbulence frightens people. How to deal with it? Use portfolio management to gird your portfolio against market plunges. Don't just collect stocks. Most investors collect, meaning they buy what they like. It may be growth stocks or value stocks or blue chips or small fry. When most investors find a stock they like better than the current collection, they trade for it.

You can see why people prefer collecting: It's embedded in how our brains work from prehistoric times of hunting and gathering.

While collecting is a perfectly valid form of investing, it's not good if you're not good at it. Far better is portfolio management, which goes far beyond diversifying by introducing risk controls. This is a discipline that operates under four rules:

1. **Use a benchmark.** Pick one carefully and manage against it. Mine happens to be the Morgan Stanley World Index. Yours could be the S&P 500 or dozens of others. It is your road map and the securities set from which you choose.

    Imagine someone who last year bought a bunch of tech stocks and his portfolio was up 70%. Was he a good stock picker? Heavens, no. The tech sector last year, as embodied by the tech stocks in the S&P 500, was up 130%, which meant he left 60% on the table. Always thinking of the benchmark would have warned him of that.

2. **Analyze your benchmark's components.** For each stock, think about expected return and risk. That way, you know what to own and how much of it. Think about countries, industries, size and valuation. What you don't own is as important as what you do. In seminars, I'll show investors my country weights and those of my benchmark—and ask what my biggest bet is. They always answer wrong. They never see that my biggest bet is owning absolutely no British stocks, when the United Kingdom is 10% of the world. If I'm right and the UK does badly, beating the benchmark gets really easy. If I'm wrong and the UK does great, I'm in trouble.

3. **Know that you may be wrong.** Believers in value investing think theirs is the only way to go. Growth investors feel the same about their philosophy. No style can be right always. Any strategy can fail. And under whatever precepts, you have to control the risk on the picks you have made.

4. **Build insurance into your investments.** In case you're wrong. And that comes from blending negatively correlated items. In other words, seek something that would go up a lot should other things go down. Then, if your basic premise is incorrect, you don't get killed. Making up for a decimated portfolio is hard to do. Remember, when you buy insurance, you don't want it to pay off. You'll be happy not

to need it and just lose the premium. But the insurance really does reduce your risk.

Here's an example. Let's say you're in S&P 500 stocks and you fear the market is going to drop badly. You sell 4% of your big, high-quality equities and use the proceeds to buy Russell 2000 puts—enough to eliminate your downside.

That means, with a $1 million portfolio, you've spent $40,000 on the small-cap index's puts, leaving $960,000 in your large-cap issues. Like any casualty insurance policy, this strategy has a "deductible," which is about 5%. So with premium and deductible the Russell has to fall more than 9% for you to make any money from the insurance.

Why use the Russell 2000? In a bear market small stocks always fall more than big stocks and usually by a lot, at least ten percentage points. As a result, the value of your Russell puts rises more than your stocks' value falls. And you come out

doing about as well as if you had sold out and gone to cash before the downturn. Suppose the S&P 500 falls 30%. Your big stocks, 96% of your portfolio, also fall 30%, from $960,000 to $672,000. The Russell 2000 plummets 40%. You initially spent $40,000 on the put. After the deductible, you collect $400,000 on the put, leaving you a $310,000 gain. You now have $982,000, before taxes and commissions.

Of course, remember you could be wrong. Suppose no bear market develops and stocks soar 20%, much as they did in 1999's fourth quarter. Had you sold out beforehand, you would be miles away from your benchmark.

But with the put strategy, you lost only the 4% you paid to buy the protection. You're still competitive against your benchmark and have to make up only the 4%. That isn't the worst challenge in the whole world.

So let your neighbors do the collecting. You should play the odds. ∎

What to Do About Tech
May 29, 2000

Here are the most frequently asked questions I'm hearing lately, with answers:

Q: Should I buy, sell or hold tech stocks?
A: Do underweight them. Don't get out completely. But first of all, understand that this question is asked so often that it provides its own answer. When tech is finally right for the long term, almost no one will be asking. We are early in a big sector bubble bursting (see "1980 Revisited"). A collapse happens in stages, not all at once.

The first stage has a violent price drop, as we saw in April. Then over several

months the sector recovers 30% to 50% of its losses, and is quiet for a while. So everyone thinks the problem is over, and fools rush back in. Then comes another down spike—in tech's case led by companies recently taken public and already running out of the cash they raised. This plunge is often less violent than the first one; again, a partial recovery follows.

The cycles are repeated until most folks who had loved the sector are too fatigued to continue. They can't envision an upside anymore. This will happen for tech, maybe, in 2001. When people won't ask about tech, it's time to buy.

Until then, be underweight. What tech you do own should only be of the highest quality. If you're overweight in tech, use the recoveries to lighten up.

Q: What do you mean by "overweight" and "underweight"? And what do you mean by "quality"?
A: Always manage against a benchmark. Underweight means owning less than the benchmark's share of a sector. Overweight means more. For most investors the benchmark should be the Morgan Stanley World Index, which encompasses both US and foreign issues; it's now 24% tech. The all-US S&P 500 is 32% tech. The non-US market, measured by Morgan's Europe, Australasia, Far East Index (EAFE), is 16% tech.

Quality means the biggest and most basic companies. In tech this means stocks like Intel, IBM, Microsoft, Cisco and Hewlett-Packard. It doesn't mean dot-coms. Sectors blow from the bottom up in a process called sympathy selling.

Q: What's that?
A: As a sector falls out of fashion, small, garbage issues go first. Individuals who are heavily concentrated in tech stocks and/or own them on margin, or in funds getting redemptions, are forced to sell whatever they can to raise cash. Because the garbage doesn't fetch much, they must unload parts of their big, quality holdings.

Q: But if you're right, why own any tech?
A: Recall this important portfolio management rule: "Always know you may be wrong." With only 15% in tech, you will do fine if you're right and tech tanks. Yet if you're wrong, and tech soars and the rest of your portfolio does fine, you can still make up for your tech error via your portfolio's other 85%. But if you own no tech and tech soars, it's particularly hard to make up for that lack of good performance.

Q: But I might lose money with tech, right?
A: Only if you are right that tech is going to collapse. You're thinking: "Maximize return, minimize loss." That doesn't work unless you're a genius, meaning you don't need advice from me. The way to maximize long-term returns is to forget about performance in the short term and figure out how to beat your benchmark's performance. Tortoises win, not hares.

Q: Why is the Morgan Stanley World Index the best benchmark for most investors?
A: Because it is the least volatile equity choice. All correctly constructed major equity indexes will have almost identical returns over the next 30 years. One will wax while another wanes, but over such a long time span they'll come out roughly even. The World Index offers the smoothest ride during that 30 years. ∎

How to Get Richer

July 3, 2000

Want to know how to become richer than your neighbors? The answer comes from the history of *Forbes'* global billionaires. Imagine you're number 200 on the list contained in this issue, and you have one simple goal: for your ranking to keep rising so you become wealthier than your fellow billionaires. How to do it? Simple. Just keep pace with the stock market. Anyone who does that will watch his relative wealth rise.

Take the first *Forbes* list in 1987. It didn't have 200 billionaires. Forbes found only 140 of them and couldn't find 200 until 1990. Now there are at least 450.

But that lowliest global guy out of 140, with a mere billion 1987 bucks, would have $8.2 billion now had he simply bought an S&P 500 index fund—and he now would rank 29th. Taxes, you say? Okay, lop off 30% for capital gains tax. He has $5.7 billion and ranks 51st.

This is more impressive than it seems. Maintaining your rank is terribly tough. For example, not one of 1987's top ten remains among the top ten now. In 1987, when Japan's property values were astronomical, real estate magnate Yoshiaki Tsutsumi was the richest person on earth, with $20 billion. Then Tsutsumi's wealth fell every year and he slipped off the top ten in 1996. He is 119th this year among working billionaires, with only $3.5 billion.

Few of the top ten from only a few years ago remain on that roster now. And only one of 1990's top ten is still there—the Waltons of Wal-Mart fame. Not only that: Few of the original billionaires are billionaires now. In 1990 the 200 billionaires were worth a total of $463 billion. Investing in the S&P would have put that at $2.65 trillion after taxes today. But today the 200 richest are worth only $1.1 trillion. Suppose you were number one in any year along the way. Had you invested in the S&P 500, you'd still be first (aftertax) now.

The same principles apply to nonbillionaires. And to keep pace with the market, you need to adopt the fundamentals of portfolio management. As an asset class, stocks are and will continue to be the best investment vehicle.

Skeptical? You scoff that my investment alternative works only because the S&P 500 did so well. And 25% of the billionaires are non-US, so the S&P 500 shouldn't be relevant. Okay. The numbers change, but the considerations are the same if we use the standard non-US equity index, Morgan Stanley's Europe, Australasia, Far East Index (EAFE). Ditto for Morgan's World Index, which includes the US.

In the long run it doesn't matter. While US stocks bested non-US stocks recently, finance theory holds that over time they must be almost identical. And during the last 30 years the S&P 500, EAFE and World have had average annual returns within one percentage point of each other.

This notion is not new, nor is it confined to billionaires. I made the same point in my October 14, 1996 column, demonstrating that it worked the same way for the Forbes 400 richest Americans. That list goes back to 1982. ∎

From 140 to 794

As of 2009, there were 794 billionaires on *Forbes'* global billionaire list. Number one was Mr. Bill Gates of Microsoft fame with $40 billion, followed by Warren Buffett with $37 billion. Ken has been appearing on the billionaire's list since 2007, and as of 2010 was ranked number 721.[7]

The Luck God

October 2, 2000

Want to train yourself psychologically to be a better investor? Learn to shun pride and accumulate regret. Forget fear and greed, the classically cited prime movers for the stock market. No, it's pride and regret that drive us in all our market actions, according to recent studies in behavioral psychology.

Pride is: "I bought it. It went up. I'm smart." Regret is: "I bought it. It went down. The broker sold it to me." Pride is: "Want to see me do it again?" Regret is: "It was just bad luck; could have happened to anyone." Pride associates success with skill and repeatability. Regret links failure to bad luck, victimization or randomness. Success was our doing; failure really wasn't.

In all our financial actions humans strive to accumulate pride and shun regret. That boosts our confidence, motivating us to keep trying. Long before markets existed this was hardwired into how our brains process information. It was a marvelous motivator for the hunter-gatherer world we evolved from. But for markets it's backward. It causes us to be overconfident and to make foolish decisions even though we lack the training, experience or raw skill.

Overconfidence? Recall that 80% of all motorists think they are above average behind the wheel. Likewise, studies show the average guy really believes he can do about 5% per year better than average guys in making market decisions. To know statistically how much of our success resulted from skill or luck requires so many data points that, for example, I'll never know that until I'm so old it can't matter.

Normal investors assume they can make the right decisions based on minimal training and background. But we wouldn't behave like that if we needed cancer treatment. With markets, though, we can't stop ourselves. The market knows we are overconfident. It baits us with opportunity. We bite, are wrong and lose. We blame bad luck.

So for good luck envision the market as the Luck God. Reverse course. Purposefully shun pride and accumulate regret. Then the Luck God rewards you. It's spiritual.

To shun pride, assume that when you are right it was primarily luck, not smarts. The righter I am, the luckier I feel. Then focus long and hard, looking for when you're wrong and accumulate regret by assuming it was not bad luck or being cheated; it was your lack of skill.

Focus on learning from your failures. You may not know enough about finance, markets or history to be able to learn much from your mistakes. Yet if you embrace them, you get luckier anyway. You simply decide to be luckier.

It's all attitude and takes no time or IQ at all. In my investment career's 29th year and in my 17th year as a *Forbes* columnist, I know I improve my results more by shunning pride and accumulating regret than by working still harder or smarter in an already long day. ■

Wife Haters
October 30, 2000

Reader Joseph Stehling e-mails saying he used to agree with me about being fully invested in stocks. But now he wants "some advice on converting from stocks to other securities for money needed in retirement."

Most retired guys, like Joe, confuse strategy with tactics in thinking they should invest for income. Most of them invest as if they hate their wives.

How so? Because their short-term approach regularly leaves a wife—and women tend to outlive men—poor after her husband's death.

Let's first review some basics of portfolio management. You start by picking an appropriate benchmark that is primarily based on time horizon. Perhaps the S&P 500 or the Morgan Stanley World, if your investing time horizon is long. If you don't need the money to last decades, you could put more into bonds and, as a benchmark, use a hybrid of the S&P and T bill rates. More on that in a minute.

No, you need not be 100% in equities at all times. Picture a young person who has an all-equity benchmark because she has an ultralong time horizon. Nevertheless, she may lighten up on stocks periodically should she become bearish—a temporary tactic to help her with her strategy of beating her benchmark.

But don't let retirement confuse you. Benchmark selection doesn't start with whether you're retired or not, nor even with your age. One 65-year-old is really old and doesn't have long on this earth. Another one has 30 years to go. The gut issue is: How long are you likely to live?

It's mostly genetics. Average your parents' ages at death and then add four years. Average all your grandparents and add eight years. Each generation lives longer on average. Only natural deaths count; if one of them died in an auto accident, skip that person. Find the average of these two sets of numbers and you'll know how long you likely have. Of course, you may die tomorrow in a plane crash, but you had better plan on living fully as long as your ancestors did. If you're married, remember that the money must last for two.

Never forget that bonds and cash have never done as well as stocks over ultralong periods like 30 years. For 20 years, aftertax, stocks return five times better. So anyone with time frames that long needs an all-equity benchmark like the S&P 500. Even in ten-year periods stocks beat bonds or cash 89% of history. Then your asset allocation might be 85% stocks and 15% cash. Construct a benchmark that is 85% the S&P, 15% Treasury bills. It requires very short horizons not to need a primarily stock-based benchmark.

Once you pick your benchmark, manage against it (see my May 1 column). Your goal is to maximize the likelihood each year of beating it—measured by total return, aftertax. Doing this optimizes your

Love Your Spouse

This concept is one Ken talks about repeatedly—investors overwhelmingly fail to think about their time horizons correctly. Typically, people pick a point in time, like retirement. But if you want your assets to last at least as long as you do, your time horizon is your life expectancy—*or* that of your spouse—whoever's extends longer. Assume on the high side, just in case. Then, if you go first, your spouse will remember you fondly, not curse you for your poor planning.

likely future wealth relative to your future needs. Then it doesn't matter where the income comes from: interest, dividends or capital gains.

So now you make a rational plan for how much of your assets you can afford to spend each year based on modest long-term total return assumptions, and for how much you still want sitting there when you and your spouse die. It is simple seventh-grade math. Anyone with a calculator can do it.

You simply take that amount out of your assets each year and spend it. This is what behavioral finance calls "homemade dividends." It is the most tax-efficient process known to man. (If you're among the 80% who can't do seventh-grade math, you shouldn't be doing your own investing.)

Take a normal fellow worth half a million at 70 who thinks he might live ten years and is mostly in bonds. Conservative? No, foolish. His wife is 63. She comes from a family like mine where few folks die before 90, meaning her longevity stretches past 30 years. Her husband must hate her severely, because bond-like returns on half a million, offset by withdrawals to live on, will leave her in poverty long before the 30 years are up. Aged poverty is brutally cruel. ■

America Versus the World
November 27, 2000

For years this column's benchmark has been the Morgan Stanley World Index. Folks often ask me: "Why not the S&P 500 or the Nasdaq Composite?" I would rather be asked: "How should I pick a benchmark to manage money against and to measure myself against?"

The answer starts with your time horizon. Take a 50-year-old who expects to live to 80. For 30-year periods in all developed markets, equities have always done better than bonds or cash. That fact doesn't guarantee that stocks will beat bonds over 2000-2030, but it definitely means that this investor should have an all-equity benchmark.

Next, recognize that all correctly constructed major equity indexes (market-capitalization weighted) end up with almost identical 30-year returns. Investors never believe this, yet it's true whether the index is the S&P 500 (which covers US large caps), the Nasdaq Composite (technology), Morgan Stanley's EAFE (for Europe, Australia and the Far East) or my preferred Morgan Stanley's World Index (the broadest one). And it is even true for country returns: Japan's, Britain's, France's or anywhere that isn't tiny. They all have average annual returns for the last 30 years within 0.75 percentage points, plus or minus, of 13.8%. Like the S&P 500 at 14.1% or Nasdaq at 13.6%.

The reason the returns cluster tightly is explained by core finance theory. No category is permanently better than another. To say otherwise is to say you either don't believe in capitalism or don't understand its pricing mechanism. Security pricing is set by supply and demand. When most investors believe a category is somehow superior, that means there is excess demand for it. Then investment bankers busily begin to create new supply in that category. Why? Because we pay them a huge chunk of the new securities' value, giving them a big incentive to create more.

Increasing the supply isn't very difficult. It's simply a matter of printing more paper, with a bit of legal work and distribution costs thrown in. The process takes time to crank up, but can be continued infinitely. And investment bankers keep cranking until they can see no more excess demand. They've created enough supply to bring pricing back into line with all other categories. Often they overshoot the mark, driving a category's pricing through the floor—which is just what happened to tech early this year.

Hence picking a long-term benchmark isn't about getting the best returns; it's about stomaching volatility. Investors hate wild gyrations. The best benchmark is one that gets you to that 30-year future return with the smoothest ride. And that is the Morgan Stanley World, since the broadest index is the least volatile.

Sure, in the next few years one index will soar while another develops sores. So if our horizon is shorter, we must pick a benchmark by forecasting where we think returns may be. If your horizon is, say, 10 years, you may want a benchmark that lagged in the last decade and can regress back to that 30-year future average. You might now pick one like EAFE but not Nasdaq, which has seen its highs.

If your time horizon is very short, like a year, then you must pick a benchmark via simple forecasting, which is tricky (see my April 3 column). With shorter time periods you also include a cash or fixed-income portion in your benchmark (see my October 30 column). But for the long term, go with the Morgan Stanley World. ∎

Ode to John Schulz
December 25, 2000

This month I happily step up a notch, to replace John W. Schulz as the sixth-longest-running columnist in Forbes history. He and I both span almost 17 years, though his tenure ended on March 15, 1976.

One way I've survived was by studying my predecessors early on, noting what they did well. Schulz is interesting because he was often very, very wrong—much more than the magazine's other long-lasting columnists. As 1963 started, for example, he forecast a long flat market that would stay within a small trading range. The market shot straight up, big time, and didn't look back for three years. Then he was bullish right past 1972's supercycle peak. Then in early 1974, with the market about to implode, Schulz saw it as oversold and forecast a big up move. But he compensated wonderfully with other qualities.

First, he admitted when he was wrong, which was refreshing. Second, he was crystal clear about his views. You never suffered qualified statements or wishy-washy forecasts. His neck stuck out.

Third, he questioned every trend, keeping him from being wrong more often than he might have been.

Fourth, he turned a phrase well. In his last column, decades before the modern phrase "irrational exuberance" hit the scene, he laid down this simple truth: "The stock market is rarely 'sensible' in commonsense terms. Stock prices have always gone up or down in response to rationalizations rather than reasons, and to levels that, in retrospect, appeared to be unmistakably excessive and irrational." Few folks have said more with fewer words.

I've always tried to emulate John Schulz on all his finer points, but not on something else: the fact that he was a one-trick pony. Schulz was a pure "technician"—he based almost everything he did on charts of stock prices.

Schulz's very first words in *Forbes* (October 1, 1959, p. 38) were: "About charts. One of the questions I hear most often is, 'Can charts really predict stock prices?' Naturally there is only one answer: a flat 'No.'" Ironically, he then went on for all those years trying to do exactly what he first said would not work. And it didn't.

Any single discipline is too narrow. Charting isn't very good to begin with. There is virtually nothing in theory or empiricism to indicate anyone can predict stock prices based solely on prior stock price action. Nevertheless, a big world of chartists continues to exist, amplified by recent Internet day trading. Yet the world of investors with long lasting success is devoid of them. You need broad capability to take on the market.

Schulz lacked the sense of economics and statistics of Heinz Biel (*Forbes'* longest-running columnist—32 years, to 1982). He lacked the street smarts of Lucien Hooper (second-longest—29 years, to 1979), the intuition about market theory of Joseph Goodman (23 years, to 1958), or the research skills of Sidney Lurie (22 years, to 1976).

Still, Schulz endured, stating his buy and sell recommendations with clarity when other commentators often had marbles in their mouths. More than 100 other Forbes columnists were unable to endure so long. I hope to endure, too. ∎

2001

Bear Market!

You want a nice domestic telltale that shows how things are
trending? Read the media and talk to your friends—and you'll discover
that an ingredient for a bull market is missing: There is no wall of
worry, the fear (misplaced or real) that a recovering market can't last.
All bull markets must climb this wall. Although we have plenty of nasty
news surrounding us, the prevalent US outlook is that the worst is over
and good times are in reach. "

"THE LONE RANGER," JULY 23, 2001

" This lingering optimism causes some to misread my past epistles,
recasting them into reasons for sudden bullishness. Nothing I've written
suggests that we can look forward to a bull market immediately. The
difference between a few months from now and immediately can feel
near infinite as the last leg of a bear market warps our perceptions. "

"WACKY FORECASTS," NOVEMBER 12, 2001

Two thousand was a bad year for the market, but the downturn in the S&P 500 didn't really begin until September. In fact, the S&P was down less than 2 percent for the year as October ended.[1] But by year-end, the downturn was gaining steam, and Ken was turning bearish. "I'm outright bearish for the first time in a decade, as I said in my last column. Get ready: The bumps will be brutal ahead. I've never minded giving up the first 10% in a bear market because, after all, we suffer 10% corrections regularly within normal bull markets. But bear markets don't get easier as they progress. The latter stages are what really ravage you. The pain that lies ahead is the stuff psychiatrists' dreams are made of." ("Bear Market!" March 19, 2001.)

Ken recommended getting defensive. For the average investor, that meant selling all their stocks and holding bonds and cash. But as a professional, Ken had more tools and know-how, so his portfolio positioning was a little more complicated.

"My asset allocation for this market sounds weird: It adds up to 130%. Let me explain. First, 30% is in stocks, mostly European and top-flight US issues like big drugs, banks and consumer staples. Forget consumer cyclicals, such as

319

autos, in a time when people spend less. Pick any stock from my columns over the last two years. I'm also 38% in US government bonds and 2% in index puts, against the Nasdaq 100 and Russell 2000. Then I have 30% in cash."

"Here's where we go over 100%. The cash came from shorting indexes (borrowing and selling what I don't own), taking positions equivalent to 30% of my assets. I've sold short the Nasdaq 100 and the Russell 2000, meaning I own no net equity. That totals 130%." ("Bear Market!" March 19, 2001.)

As Ken forecast, 2001 was quite unlike the rolling top of 2000. Two thousand and one was a year of sharp drops and massive countertrend rallies. The S&P 500 started the year on a positive note, rising through January. Then the downward momentum began again and accelerated. From February through April 4, the S&P slid 19 percent.[2] Then stocks rallied. From early April through late May, the S&P 500 jumped 19 percent,[3] leading many to believe the bear market was over. Ken didn't buy it. Bond prices were falling as stocks rose. Ken saw money shifting from one asset class to another, not new liquidity entering the stock market capable of sustaining stocks' rise. "As stocks soared for a straight month, long bonds simply tanked. This doesn't happen at real bear market bottoms. It happens often during bear market corrections, which are temporary and misleading." ("Bear Market Corrections," June 11, 2001.)

When most people think of stock market corrections, they think of a short, sharp drop and a quick recovery during a bull market. But corrections aren't confined to bull markets. The same regularly happens during bear markets, but in the opposite direction. Bear market corrections are sharp stock market gains during the general downward trend. Like their bull market counterparts, bear market corrections are usually over quickly. Sure enough, the rally faded, and stocks began falling again in late May.

By early September, stocks were at their low point for the year. Then tragedy struck—the September 11 terrorists attacks. The first plane crashed into the World Trade Center at 8:46am EST. The stocks market didn't open that day or for the rest of the week. When the market finally reopened on September 17, the S&P 500 dropped 5 percent and continued to fall for the next four days, bottoming nearly 12 percent below their pre-attack level.[4] But the market gyrations weren't finished. The S&P 500 staged another rally starting on September 24 and was back above its September 10 value within three weeks. Stocks would rise through year-end, finishing 5.5 percent above September 10, but down 11.9 percent on the year.[5]

Ken remained bearish throughout, but at 2001's close was reevaluating this view. Recall, Ken believed in staying bearish longer than 12 months only in extreme circumstances, and in December, Ken's 12th month out of the market wasn't too far off. So he was left to decide whether conditions were extreme enough to justify continued bearishness. He decided they were.

"This is an extreme bear market, by any measure, lasting as it has, 21 months. The bull market ending March 2000 was the second longest of the twentieth century, exceeded only by the 1942–61 bull. Thus it isn't shocking to see a longer-than-average bear market following. Among other weird factors present now that make things different: a President not elected by popular vote, the catastrophic terrorist attacks, the disruptive euro conversion and the long time it took for negative sentiment to spread wide among investors." ("Bottoming Out," December 10, 2001.) Thus, Ken maintained his defensive positioning heading into 2002. He continued on a roll. But he would soon feel comeuppance.

Tech 2001

January 22, 2001

People keep asking if the technology drubbing is over—or will be soon. As long as folks keep asking, you don't have to. It isn't over until they stop asking. The end is silent. Make no mistake, this is the middle of the bursting of a classic sector bubble. That should now be obvious to most. Less obvious is how these things end.

It is somewhat paradoxical, but sometimes a big sector correction, such as the 27% drop in the Russell 2000 Small-Cap Growth index over ten months in 1990, takes less time than a small correction, such as the 17% drop over 15 months in 1997–98. Either way, the correction takes a long time as investors first absorb the initial downward shock, then overreact.

My March 6 column was devoted to showing you that the structural qualities of this sector bubble are almost identical to those of the 1980 energy bubble, and that the 1981–82 bursting was a great road map for the present situation. So far it has been.

My May 29 column detailed how the first downdraft is followed by a recovery of 50% or so of the lost ground. Three or four more downdrafts then alternate with partial recoveries, which abort in months. For tech, the first of those recoveries was June through September.

This goes on, hitting lower lows, until fully half those who jumped on the momentum play conclude they never need to own another tech stock for the rest of their lives. Longtime tech devotees won't bolt, but most newer adherents to the religion will become absolute atheists. They'll sell, suffering real losses. Only then is the slide at an end.

Thus far this drop, which started in March, is about ten percentage points steeper and running five months faster than its 1981–82 twin. But that will slow. Note that the 1981–82 drop took 25 months

to end. There is painfully plenty of time ahead—maybe another 5 to 15 months.

If you're still overweight in technology, use the partial recovery to lighten up. By that I mean: If you're managing your portfolio against the S&P 500, where tech is 27% of the US market, you might reduce your tech weight to something like 16%. If, as this column does, you manage against the world via the Morgan Stanley's World index (see "America Versus the World," November 27, 2000), where technology is 21%, then have 12% in tech.

Why have any technology stocks at all? Because among portfolio management's most basic rules is: Always know that you may be wrong and that you must come out okay even when you are. If I'm dead wrong and tech soars, owning none of it will make you very sorry. You would not be able to beat your index with just the nontech stocks, which will lack the needed oomph to catch up. If I'm right about technology, underweighting the sector will enable you to beat your benchmark.

Finally, among techs, own only the biggest and highest in quality. From the March peak through November America's 15 largest tech stocks (measured by their March market caps) were down 35%, versus 45% for the Nasdaq Composite. But more important, they didn't implode the way many of the tiny tech stocks did. And they won't.

When tech falls, the best stocks in the short term are those that have what is called an inelastic demand for their products. That means if they raise product prices, consumers buy less, but not much less. Think of drugs, tobacco and (to a lesser extent) energy. Linking tech with drugs is a perfect example of blending stocks that are short-term negatively correlated. When tech zigs, drugs zag. ∎

Lucky Again in 2000

February 19, 2001

*F*orbes compels a columnist to render an annual explanation of the prior year's picks. Compared to the indexes, I did fairly well in 2000, but I probably disappointed you, anyway. My beginning-of-the-year forecast for a flat S&P 500, while not up to some of my recent years' calls, was still the fifth most accurate S&P prediction of any nationally published forecaster. Lucky and good, not great.

Credit should go where it's due—the most accurate 2000 S&P forecast was for a −10% return, by Douglas Cliggot of JP Morgan Securities. The index lost exactly that in stock price terms. It was down 9% when dividends are included.

Among more than 50 nationally published Nasdaq forecasts, my −15% prediction was the seventh most accurate. Few expected Nasdaq to be negative, much less down its final 39%. I thought foreign markets would be positive—and was dead wrong. I predicted the Morgan Stanley World Index would rise 10%. It fell 13%.

On my individual stock picks: *Forbes* accounts for them as if you invested equally in each selection when it appeared, less a 1% phantom brokerage cost, then compares the result with investing in an S&P 500 index on the same dates, in the same amounts. In 2000 this column broke even, beating the S&P by 10%, almost the same margin as in 1999. The column was lucky. My firm's managed accounts didn't beat the S&P 500 by anything like that.

But this column has been managed for years against the Morgan Stanley World, and in going sideways it beat the World by 13%. That's too much by my standards. You may think it isn't enough.

Anything you do in managing against a benchmark is a risk, because you can always be wrong. Pile on the risky plays in hopes of beating a benchmark by 13%, and you instead might end up lagging by 13%. In 2000 that would have meant a horrifying absolute loss. I would rather aim to beat the mark by a modest amount—four percentage points a year on average over a long period. Few folks do nearly so well.

Note: As I detailed in my November 27, 2000 column, in the very long run all correctly constructed indexes have almost identical average annual returns—S&P 500, EAFE, Nasdaq, etc. So if I can beat the World Index by 4% per year forever, I will look pretty good even if compared to the Nasdaq.

Meanwhile, I had some dirty dogs in 2000. Nippon Telegraph lost 48% between April 3 and year-end. Kirin Brewery fell 30% and Ito Yokado, 28%. News Corp. was down 31% in just two months, starting October 30. SGL Carbon lost 27%. Telecom Italia and LVMH Moët Hennessy Louis Vuitton were both off 22%. I also had my share of big winners: Groupe Danone appreciated 43% from my April 3 recommendation. Japan Airlines was up 34%. KLM Royal Dutch Airlines, 35%. Elsevier, 27%. As explained below, however, I am very cautious now about all these stocks—winners and losers alike.

I had 23 stocks up and 23 stocks down. That isn't so bad in a year when, globally and nationally, more stocks fell than rose.

I had fewer midyear big calls than in most years. My March 6 column—devoted to detailing a tech bubble and peak—had, in retrospect, near-flawless logic, but its at-the-top timing was sheer luck. My May 29 column furthered the arguments of how to underweight tech and looked unlucky for several months. Now it looks good.

On August 7, I detailed how Bush would beat Gore in a narrow race reminiscent of 1960. I had no idea how close the race would be or how similar to 1960. Pure coincidence. Pure luck. On September 4, I told how the Democrats should win the House of Representatives. I was plain wrong in sizing up the close races.

My 2001 forecasts? I'm shifting to fully bearish for the first time in a decade. Next month I'll detail why the S&P 500 should be fairly flat this year. For a while it will do much worse. It should fall more, maybe down 25% to 35%, in the late third or early fourth quarter. Nasdaq should fare slightly worse, losing another 15% for the year—and at its nadir will be lower still than the S&P at the bottom. I think foreign markets will fare slightly better, with the World Index beating the S&P by just a few percent for the year. It's time to be defensive. ∎

Bear Market!
March 19, 2001

I'm outright bearish for the first time in a decade, as I said in my last column. Get ready: The bumps will be brutal ahead. I've never minded giving up the first 10% in a bear market because, after all, we suffer 10% corrections regularly within normal bull markets. But bear markets don't get easier as they progress. Their latter stages are what really ravage you. The pain that lies ahead is the stuff psychiatrists' dreams are made of.

If I'm right, the S&P 500, which lost 9% in 2000, will be off for 2001 by 35% come Labor Day. Nasdaq, down 40% last year, will drop another 50% before the market's bottom. Foreign markets will be off almost as much.

My guess: The bottom is August 30, although it also could be early July or late October. Then stocks should bounce back a bunch, but not until lots of folks have simply lost their minds.

We started a recession in December that won't end until next year, destroying about 4 million jobs. Ugly. (Market rebounds, anticipating better days, usually precede economic turnarounds.) Almost no one will call it a recession this year, certainly not Alan Greenspan or George W. Bush. Contrary to popular mythology, bear markets and recessions do sometimes occur even when interest rates are steadily declining and taxes are cut. That is just the kind we're in. Short- and long-term interest rates should fall in 2001.

While not perfect, your best single road map for this market is the 1981–82 bear market and recession, which were led by energy as a bursting sector bubble. Tech plays that role now. Early last year I drew those parallels and showed why Nasdaq should fall in 2000 (see last year's columns for February 7, March 6 and May 29). Little did I know how fast and far tech would decline.

The peak was March 24, 2000 at 1527 on the S&P 500. Folks were gaga for tech then. Today it's easy to see the signs of a classic manic top in technology then.

What is different now? My "Break Their Crystal Balls" column (April 3, 2000) detailing the consensus of expert forecasts is always wrong, so avoiding that advice is critical to foreseeing market direction correctly. The 2000 tech break and negative S&P return didn't make the pros fearful and defensive, as should have been the case. Late last year they turned massively more sanguine—the biggest swing in crowd sentiment in a decade. I've never seen anything like it. I'll lay out in future columns why this was extreme bear-market behavior.

Synthetic Cash

Ken refers to the portfolio (described here) he built for many of his firm's clients during the 2000–2002 bear market as "synthetic cash." The idea was to be market-neutral—to have a portfolio that acted cash-like, but got better than cash-like returns. And it worked well. But replicating it might be harder for individual investors, which is why he recommended *Forbes* readers simply hold bonds and cash. They wouldn't have as much upside, but should certainly protect against stock-bear-market-like downside. You can read more about Ken's defensive strategy during the 2001–2002 bear market in *The Only Three Questions That Count*.

The result was January's temporary rally, which was cut short in February when bad fourth-quarter earnings reports rolled in. And foreigners took money home.

Blind optimism caused the pros to miss the year-end signs of recession. A big one was in the commercial paper market: Rates soared for low-quality paper and opened the biggest gap with high-quality paper since 1990. Banks harshly pulled back their lending to lesser credits, as well. At the same time, the Conference Board's leading economic indicator series imploded, falling more in both relative and absolute amounts than it had going into 1990's recession.

Unemployment in January replayed a pattern seen at the outset of every modern recession. After years of steadily dropping, joblessness rose in one month enough to offset the whole prior year of declines. Many more such signs abound. Given the weight of the evidence, you can't conclude that we're in a mere slowdown, even though almost no one has the moxie to acknowledge we're in a recession.

My asset allocation for this market sounds weird: It adds up to 130%. Let me explain. First, 30% is in stocks, mostly European and top-flight US issues like big drugs, banks and consumer staples. Forget consumer cyclicals, such as autos, in a time when people spend less. Pick any stock from my columns over the last two years. I'm also 38% in US government bonds and 2% in index puts, against the Nasdaq 100 and Russell 2000. Then I have 30% in cash.

Here's where we go over 100%. The cash came from shorting indexes (borrowing and selling what I don't own), taking positions equivalent to 30% of my assets. I've sold short the Nasdaq 100 and the Russell 2000, meaning I own no net equity. That totals 130%. I suspect most of you can't do all this; go for cash and bonds instead.

Next month: Why Greenspan and Bush can't do anything about the recession. And don't want to. ∎

Bears, Bush and Greenspan

April 16, 2001

What can President George W. Bush do to stop the bear market and recession I've foreseen in recent months? Nothing. How about Alan Greenspan? Again, zip. Nor do they wish to, although they ritually say they want to forestall economic hard times.

Only one of these two gentlemen was elected, but both are politicians, hence liars. Political wannabes aren't always liars. But if they get into office they become liars—at least Presidents and Fed chiefs do. Of the two, Greenspan is the better liar. He has been at it since the 1960s.

Before Arthur Burns ran the Fed (for Richard Nixon), he described this more kindly than I would. He said, "Fed chairmen take a pill that makes them forget everything they ever knew, and it lasts until the job is over."

They all take the pill that prevents them from telling the truth. Greenspan's lifelong goal is to go down in history as the great inflation slayer. En route he must be reappointed as Federal Reserve chairman (his term ends in June 2004). He can't say the truth, which is that he needs a recession because it fights inflation. Recessions dampen demand, throw people out of work and shrink business pricing expectations. Increasing supply fights inflation much better, but then the Fed chairman can't control supply.

A President can never say he wants to see the pain of a recession inflicted upon the voting public at any time in his term. But if there has to be a recession, better that it be an early one. America forgets the pain by election time if the preceding two years are strong.

Each January the President and Fed chair meet. This year, it probably sounded like this:

Dubya: "Well, Alan, what should I expect during my first four years here? Huh?"

Alan: "First four years? George, there's gonna be a recession. It's already started, I think. Gonna be ugly."

Dubya: "Is there anything I can do about it?"

Alan: "Sure, wait until folks start to see it. Then blame it on Bill Clinton. Next year get your old buddy, Don Evans, who runs the Commerce Department, to lean on the National Bureau of Economic Research to have the recession officially clocked as starting December 2000—which is about right, anyway. That can't be your fault. I'll blame it on Clinton, too. I sure don't want it blamed on me. No one will be able to disagree with us. We let it run its course. It'll be over long before you run again. See how that works? Don't be a chump like your dad. Be smart like Nixon and Reagan."

Dubya: "Anything else, Alan? Huh? Huh?"

Alan: "Have your tax cut kick in mostly in 2003 and 2004. I'll pump up the money supply from mid-2003 until the election. And we coast to victory in 2004. Of course, you also reappoint me early in 2004, right? If not, I will jerk rates up so hard before June and the election, it'll make your squinty little eyes spin. Got it, kid?"

Dubya: "Got it. What would I do without you?"

In a way, even though many think these two have vast powers over the economy, they are only bowing to the inevitable. Neither one can do anything to stop the recession that started in December.

Tax cuts, retroactive or not, can't be implemented fast enough to stop an implosion that already has begun. Bush's puny

$5.6 billion 2001 tax reduction will have no effect on our $9.4 trillion economy. That is one-twentieth of 1%, or $40 per US worker. About enough for one good beer bash.

If Bush really wanted to try saving the economy he would do something bigger. Still, tax cuts have never been good short-term recession fixers. As I wrote in my last column, the best single road map to 2001 is the 1981–82 bear market. Note that Ronald Reagan's tax cut, the biggest in modern history, passed just weeks after 1981's market peak and couldn't slow that recession or bear market at all.

Interest rate cuts? Expect them. Short-term rates should be maybe 4.4% by year-end. Sometimes interest rates have a big impact, other times not. This time, not. We haven't had a real credit crunch, so rate cuts will have minuscule effect.

In Reagan's early 1980s recession, the Fed cut rates four times and that couldn't stop the carnage. In such a climate your investments must be maximally defensive—bonds, cash and put options should be prominent in your portfolio. ∎

Fall Till the Fall
May 14, 2001

It is still a long way to this bear market's bottom. I stick by my forecast of an S&P 500 bottom below 860 (it's now 1240) and a Nasdaq nadir of about 1200 (from 2080 currently). Why? Sentiment hasn't turned dour enough yet. My forecasting methodology is based on the broad consensus of market pros, but not in a way they may like: Whatever they say will happen simply won't happen.

This may sound odd, but it rests on pure finance theory and is empirically wonderful. Both in theory and in practice, the market is a discounter of all known information. Everything people read about in the print media, see on TV and talk about with their friends is the basis of investment decisions. The trouble is, you can't make excess returns based on what everyone knows.

If you try, you will sometimes be lucky, more often unlucky, and overall do worse than if you had done nothing. Making excess returns requires knowing something others don't know. Not easy. Well, what about the leading-edge pros? They generally have much more access to information than does a normal person. Hence the total information held by top pros is a concise, effective proxy for all known information. Thus their views are already discounted and therefore cannot occur. That doesn't tell you what the market will do, yet it gives you a huge leg up on figuring it out.

In my April 3, 2000 column, "Break Their Crystal Balls," I showed you how my approach works.

Basically, I plot where pros forecast the market to be for the coming year. Their calls tend to cluster in bunches, so I eliminate those forecasts and try to figure out which of the "holes"—where no one picked—will turn out to be right. This isn't easy: In 1999 forecasts were all over the place, and you ended up with four small holes; in 2000 you had to deal with six possible outcomes.

But as 2001 began there were only two possibilities. December's professional forecasts stretched all the way from a 7% to a 40% S&P gain. In other words 2001's outcome could only come in above or below that 7%-to-40% range, not within it. So I knew my bear market forecast would be just about the world's best—or the worst.

By now you have figured out the S&P won't end this year up 40%-plus.

What happened to professional sentiment in last year's fourth quarter is enormously telling. I collect and update professional forecasts by resurveying them during the year. In the fourth quarter, as stocks plunged, forecasters became much more optimistic. The fourth quarter's positive shift in professional sentiment for Nasdaq, for example, was the biggest such shift I've ever measured in any single market. This is all very bearish.

If we were simply going through a temporary bull-market correction, forecasters overall would become more pessimistic and advocate increased caution. Not this time.

Their behavior was the very sign of a bull market having turned to a bear market. Increased optimism in the face of a strong market jolt downward means the pros and their friends spent or caused to be spent every bit of cash they could. This leaves no future demand to push stocks up.

Before we get to the bottom, all that optimism will have been replaced—if not by extreme pessimism, at least by what we had before last year's shift to increased optimism began. That must happen before the bottom is reached.

As stocks fell in February, March and early April, sentiment did deteriorate as you might expect, but not nearly enough. Sentiment is still more bullish than it was last summer. To erode that and to really hit the bottom, quite a bit more mayhem must ensue.

En route there will also be some short, sharp upward moves. These are just corrections to this bear market, and temporary. Don't let them fool you.

It remains a time to be maximally defensive. I described what I'm doing in my March 19 column, including balancing stocks against short sales to be market neutral and buying index puts as insurance. Most of you will probably be best served with simple cash and bonds. The time to get back in will come soon enough but isn't now. Wait. ∎

Bear Market Corrections
June 11, 2001

Is it a new bull market? No. The rally that kicked off April 4 inspired widespread talk that the bear market is over and a new bull market has begun. The market's sideways move in May has done nothing to dispel that. Why don't I think we've seen the bottom? The spring rally has just about all the signs of a classic correction within a bear market.

The most significant sign: As stocks soared for a straight month, long bonds simply tanked. This doesn't happen at real bear market bottoms. It happens often during bear market corrections, which are temporary and misleading.

At real bottoms, when stocks start to rise, bonds rise, too. Stock and bond prices sure don't head in opposite directions. At times they are very, very highly correlated, as they were during the 1970 and 1990 bottoms. Other bottoms aren't so highly correlated, but they still move in the same basic direction, as in 1966, 1974, 1982, and 1987.

The only modern exception is 1962. But that was more the result of a foreign policy crisis—Soviet missiles in Cuba and a possible nuclear war—than the playing out of a normal, long economic and sentiment-oriented bear market, such as we've seen lately.

Why is a stock market bottom so linked to bonds? A new bull market in stocks is confirmed by bond prices because they compete so directly against each other for investor dollars—just as water quickly seeks its own level. When investors are optimistic, there's plenty of money available for buying both equities and bonds. In a bear market correction folks often shift money from bonds to stocks to catch the ride. That doesn't endure for long.

Here's another way to think of it. After genuine bottoms both bond yields and earnings yields go down. A declining bond yield, of course, is synonymous with a rising bond price. The earnings yield on a stock is the inverse of the P/E, and it goes down as the stock price rises. Unless real, net new liquidity pushes down both of these long-term yields, you won't get a new bull market.

This spring's correction has reversed all the psychological damage of the market's last major slide, re-buoying sentiment to its December levels. That is what corrections are all about. But just as bull market corrections are short and deceptively scary, bear market corrections are short and deceptively reassuring.

You know it is a sucker's rally when the mass of journalists tells you to buy into it. Journalists are more sanguine now. You can see this on the June cover of *Kiplinger's Personal Finance*, with its screaming headlines "Bye-Bye Bear" and "Sweet Ways to Make Money Now," along with a picture of a honey pot and bees. Egads! Don't they know? Honey pots attract bears.

This is not the stuff of bear market bottoms. At real bear market bottoms most journalists disbelieve for many months thereafter. They've become convinced by the downdraft's power that no real good can come to equities for a very long time.

At bear market bottoms you always have at least two despairing magazine cover stories on the "death of equities." So far we haven't had any.

In my 1987 book I described a simple formula for predicting a market bottom. You don't apply it until there is a real bear market, defined as 20% or bigger declines in the major stock market indexes. After this point is reached, wait until unemployment has risen one full percentage point from its low point before you call a market bottom.

We've had the 20% corrections: By the end of March the S&P 500, the Wilshire 5000 and Nasdaq were all off 20% or more from their highs. Unemployment was at its nadir of 3.9% last October. This April it hit 4.5%. Hence, we have another full four-tenths of a point to go. That will probably take until about September. And that means we face at least one more down leg in the bear market.

Note that rising unemployment will continue well beyond the bottoming of stock prices as it most normally does. Since we are well short of a market bottom, I expect layoffs to continue. They began in technology in January and

Countertrend Rallies

Many investors forget—fortunately because bear market periods occur less frequently than bull markets—that bear markets also have corrections. In an overall bear, the stock market can and does reverse trend, sometimes sharply, for a few weeks or even months. Bear corrections do the same thing as bull corrections: Fool investors into doing exactly the wrong thing at the worst possible time—like buying into a relative high right before the market crumbles away again, just as it did following the April 2000 mini rally, as Ken predicts here.

February, rippled into other industries in March, and in April and May spread beyond America to the world.

As I wrote in my March 19 column, the best single road map to this market is the 1980–82 bear market. Look at its corrections in 1981's fourth quarter and in 1982's second quarter. That is where we are right now. Prepare for the next downdraft. Stay maximally defensive. ∎

The Lone Ranger
July 23, 2001

This issue, which carries *Forbes'* International 500s listing of the top foreign companies, couldn't come at a better time. It reminds inward-looking American investors that they can benefit by checking out what's happening overseas. Yes, events beyond our borders affect the US market.

Even in the 19th century markets were more connected than is now commonly thought. All the big downturns were global, and still are. Consider 1929. In my second book (*The Wall Street Waltz*), I detailed how Americans could have foreseen the crash simply by noticing that all major foreign markets had already turned sour, and that this had been going on for months. Ours was the last stock market to fall.

Amazingly, to this day most US history books portray the 1929 market crash as if it were a US-only event. Looking overseas warns you when America is out of step—a condition that will not last.

As the US stock market rallied in April, pundits cheered the emergence of a new bull, ushered in by the Federal Reserve's interest rate cuts. Suddenly market wisdom could be simplified to: "The Fed is all that matters." Six rate cuts have fueled investors' enthusiasm. They have also blinded them to the reality that the rally is temporary.

I doubt if 1% of American investors ever examine charts of more than two foreign markets. It's time they broadened their vision a little. Lately the charts aren't pretty. Except for Australia, the big markets around the globe are sick. Sure, these markets had their own rallies, too, for a while this spring. But starting in late April they stagnated, staggered sideways, then headed south.

Foreign bourses are in a far deeper hole than the US': Morgan Stanley's Europe, Australasia, Far East index, known as EAFE, is down 16% year to date (this dollar-denominated index in part reflects the weakness of foreign currencies). The S&P 500 is off only 8%.

Even if you believe interest rate cuts are the only things that matter, you must fathom that the Fed is not the world's only central bank. But it is alone in easing rates. Historically most Fed cuts were in conjunction with other central bank cuts. Alan Greenspan is a Lone Ranger with no Tonto.

The Bank of Japan couldn't cut rates if it had to. Japanese rates have been effectively zero for some time, and Japan's economy still deteriorates. The European Central Bank eased once by one-fourth of a point to please Greenspan, then promptly announced this move was a mistake it wouldn't repeat. Note that the Eurobank does not have the Fed's dual charge of economic growth and price stability. Now that inflation is heating up on the Continent, the Eurobank has no incentive to reduce rates. The Bank of England can't cut rates much when sterling is weak relative to the dollar. For a long time the pound was worth $1.60, but now that's down to $1.40.

You can see the US recession, which is still in an early stage, spreading overseas. Not only is Japan slumping, Germany is, too, and the downturn moves across Europe. Meanwhile, America is in denial that there is a recession. The optimism here stems from the news that first-quarter US gross domestic product was up 2%, so it seemed our economy was doing fine.

You can't trust our government's economic statistics, however. In the early 1990s Washington bastardized the numbers, rendering them useless. I last explored this deplorable situation in my February 26, 1996 column. Five years later people continue to be duped. Instead of the distorted GDP stats, pay attention to the torrents of layoffs. These bloodlettings just keep coming, in the US and overseas.

You want a nice domestic telltale that shows how things are trending? Read the media and talk to your friends—and you'll discover that an ingredient for a bull market is missing: There is no wall of worry, the fear (misplaced but real) that a recovering market can't last. All bull markets must climb this wall. Although we have plenty of nasty news surrounding us, the prevalent US outlook is that the worst is over and good times are in reach.

How about that *Time* cover story with the picture of a bear? It urged buying stocks and thinking past the soon-to-end bear market. That isn't the way the wall works.

In my 30 years working in this industry and studying its history, I've never known of a new bull market that didn't face the wall. Genuine bull markets start out hesitantly. All the investment buying power isn't expended in one eruption but slowly and inexorably levitates prices. Remain defensive. The ride is rougher ahead. ∎

I Hate Funds
August 20, 2001

This issue, the Mutual Fund Guide, is a great one in which to tell you this: I hate funds. So should most of you. The average Forbes subscriber (net worth at last count, $2.1 million) is too wealthy for funds. Funds were never meant for you. They were meant for folks with a small pool of money in search of diversification. But at a price. A big one.

For years I've urged a global approach. I won't retread that now (see, for example, my November 27, 2000 column). But foreign and global funds are expensive.

The average global no-load fund has a 1.8% annual expense ratio—for portfolio management and overhead costs. On top of that are the soft-dollar fees, which are trading commissions, over and above competitive rates, funneled to brokerages for research help they give the fund. Average soft-dollar cost to fund customers: 0.3% of assets annually. It's a fee that rips you off but is legal. The fund should pay for research from its own revenue.

Then people go haywire and hire a person or service to tell them what funds to own, because there are so many, and sorting through them is confusing. The normal fee here is 1% annually. Add these three fees and you could be spending 3% a year to own a global stock portfolio. At that you need real genius to come out ahead. If stocks do 10% in the long term, and if inflation averages 3%, your real return is 7%. A 3% annual fee eats up almost half of that. You wind up with bondlike returns while taking stocklike risks. That's a sucker's game.

Then comes performance. Everyone knows the average mutual fund hasn't kept pace with the market. What they don't understand is why. It isn't about stock picking. It's structural. Here's why.

Funds tend to be overweighted in small companies, underweighted in large ones. There could be a lot of reasons for this, but a big one is probably just that it's hard for the portfolio manager to justify a fat money-management fee if he owns only big, obvious stocks like General Electric and ExxonMobil. So during an era like the past decade, when big outperformed small, it was inevitable that funds would underperform the large-cap S&P 500 Index.

You can quantify this disparity. A portfolio has what's called a weighted average market capitalization. A fund 80% invested in a $10 billion market-cap stock and 20% in a $100 billion market cap would have a weighted average market cap of $28 billion. For an index fund tracking the S&P 500, this calculation results in a $110 billion figure. For the average US equity fund, it's only $24 billion.

It is very restrictive for an actively managed fund to get its weighted average market cap up near $110 billion. There are, at the moment, only 15 companies with market caps above that figure. Funds own many more stocks than that.

And when small stocks beat big? Funds lose again, at least if they trade actively. Small stocks (that is, stocks of companies with market capitalizations below $5 billion) tend to have low share prices and high bid/ask spreads. If a fund goes in and out of a stock quoted at $20 bid, $20.50 offer, it will lose 2.5% to transaction costs. This is as bad as 3% fees.

So I don't like funds. The actively traded ones will cost you a bundle. The passive index funds are a lot cheaper, and of course an S&P 500 fund will track that index pretty well. But I don't like those, either. Why? Taxes. There are no tax advantages to funds, only disadvantages.

Fans of funds, including the editors of this magazine, make much of the fact that index funds are tax-efficient. That is, they have not had the habit of forcing out taxable capital gain distributions onto helpless shareholders. But they have been successful at this game in large part because they have been taking in new money over the past decade. Come a time of massive redemptions and the index funds might have to sell some of their low-cost-basis shares of stock, making taxable distributions inevitable. Also note that even a tax-efficient fund can't pass capital losses through to shareholders. If you can use capital losses on your tax return, own shares directly.

Anyone with more than about $350,000, which is most Forbes readers, can do better than a fund by buying stocks. Let me put in a plug for following this column's advice. It is global. As measured by *Forbes* annually and after adjusting for phantom 1% brokerage costs, it has beaten the MSCI World, EAFE and S&P 500 for years. It costs you almost nothing. This year? I've been cashlike all year. When I turn bullish, I will be recommending stocks. Not funds. ∎

Mad Magazine Investors

September 17, 2001

Clearly I've been wrong. I thought by now the stock market would have fallen much more than it has. My February 19 column said the S&P 500 would be " d o w n 25% to 35% in the late third or early f o u r t h q u a r t e r ." This year the index has lost just 12%. So what happened to throw off my prediction? A l m o s t everything.

All the i n g r e d i ents seem to be on hand for f u r t h e r trouble in the market. And yet investors have amazingly disregarded a lot of bad news. To start, corporate earnings

have been weaker all year than almost anyone expected. Layoffs are big and spreading globally. Europe and Asia are now falling apart. Non-US inflation has been higher than January expectations. Our Federal Reserve has cut interest rates, but abroad only Britain, Canada and the Philippines cooperate. The European Central Bank has told the US to go jump in a lake.

I still believe my forecast, although the drop is taking longer than anticipated. As I wrote May 14, professional investor sentiment remains far too optimistic for a new bull market. Still true. The market needs to hit the bottom before it can rise, and that won't happen unless everyone has given up hope. As I wrote July 23, the infamous Wall of Worry normally accompanying new bull markets doesn't exist. The sunny outlook has prevented more panicky selloffs. Stocks aren't rising, but they aren't falling much.

What confuses me most? People are so complacent. As I poll individual investor sentiment, I see an almost universal view that wasn't there six months ago: That the economy will get worse, and others will get hurt, but few folks being asked think it will harm them much. This sentiment reminds me of *Mad* magazine's Alfred E. Neuman: "What? Me worry?" I don't think it can last.

Maybe they're soothed by government data that claim the economy is up—1.3% in the first quarter, 0.7% in the second—feeding a delusion that any downturn won't be bad whenever it comes. We're not in a recession because we haven't had two quarters of decline, right? Wrong. Only morons believe these measurements reflect reality. The government data are all screwed up. The manufacturing, service and technology sectors are in the

---

Terror and the Stock Market

This column is dated September 17, but Ken typically closes his column about four weeks before the issue date. So Ken was writing these words well before the spectacularly tragic 9/11 terror attacks. As it happened, stocks fell huge just following the attacks.

But what many may not realize is US stocks rallied just as hugely after bottoming on September 21, and traded above September 10 levels for months after. But the bear market wasn't over—not by a long shot. The global bear finished with a triple bottom in 2003. All this is to say that surprising geopolitical events can have near-time market impact, but longer term, haven't shaken the overall market from its general trend. The Madrid train bombing (March 2004) and the London Underground bombing (July 2005) happened amid a global bull market. Neither one derailed the ongoing bull market. Bull or bear—the forces causing these are generally more powerful than even huge geopolitical surprises.

tank. Hence the overall economy is, too. Consumers spend at retail as if life will roll blissfully onward. As Alfred E. might say: "Hey—if you get laid off, you've suddenly got time to go shopping."

Even odder is what the market seems to like: smaller, low-quality stocks that suffer more than other stocks do when the economy is weak. Look at mobile-home maker Fleetwood Enterprises and auto-parts maker ArvinMeritor. Both have sick businesses, deteriorating sales and deteriorating earnings, and yet both rise like 1999 Internet stocks. Fleetwood is up 40% this year, ArvinMeritor 60%.

It isn't as if I automatically reject stocks like these. They have their place. I've used small value stocks for most of my early career and will again. But they don't usually rise in a bear market. Not in 1974, not 1982, not 1990.

I also don't understand why the dollar, though off a bit since July, hasn't fallen faster. We print more money than they do overseas, we drop our interest rates much more and yet the dollar doesn't drop very far. And I don't even understand why inflation isn't finally warming up in the US. It is overseas. But here, after many years of printing much more money than a monetary theorist would see as consistent with price stability, inflation is nowhere to be seen.

Domestic investors act as though the US is an island, immune to the world. From its peak in March 2000, we've clearly had a bear market both here and internationally. That's because all the world's major cap-weighted indexes fell more than 20% from their peaks. The MSCI World index, reflecting the entire global market, is down 27% from its peak. Generally, foreign has slid more than domestic. Recently China simply imploded. If you told anyone in 1998 that Chinese stocks would act this badly, they would have expected the apocalypse. Not in 2001. Europe is lagging us and headed down; Japan keeps sliding. There's clearly more ugliness to come overseas— and it will ripple back to us in time.

What to do? Well, I'm still ahead year-to-date, by having avoided the decline so far this year. I'm content to sit and wait defensively until I see more worry and pain. Maybe it isn't until the end of the year or, heaven forbid, until early next year. I say "heaven forbid," because an old rule of mine is to never stay bearish for longer than 12 months, and year-end gets us right there. But patience is a virtue. Right now call me confused but virtuous. What? Me Worry? ∎

What HP Says About the Market
October 15, 2001

I remain bearish, and this has nothing to do with the way the market has reacted following the national tragedy. I remain bearish because, in a perverse way, UBS PaineWebber's management and Hewlett-Packard's board told me to be. They seem to assume we've seen the market bottom and that better days lie ahead.

To show how they're mistaken, let's take UBS PaineWebber first. The firm launched a huge national ad campaign this summer claiming the market's "fair value" at year-end 2002 would be 50% above current levels, based on the rationale of its chief strategist, Edward M. Kerschner. Following the terrorist attacks, he remains bullish and lowered his target only slightly. (So far this year the S&P 500 is down 25% to 984.) Well, everyone is entitled to an opinion. But you would think readers would want to know how well Kerschner did with prior forecasts. If he hasn't done well, why pay heed now?

Early each year *Forbes* reports on how its financial columnists did the prior year. But *Forbes'* approach is uncommon. If readers knew how bad Kerschner's past forecasts have been they would pay zero attention to the UBS PaineWebber claims.

Take 1999. Kerschner originally forecast that the S&P 500 would end that year at 1250, up 1.7%. He was smack in the middle of the range of forecasters then, many of whom were knock-kneed nervous over Y2K. The S&P finished 1999 up 21%. As 2000 dawned, Kerschner forecast it would rise 8.9%, to 1600, again in the midst of most mavens. The index fell 9.1%. As 2001 began he foresaw a 30% rise, to 1715, once again within the pack. Three strikes and you're out.

As detailed in my April 3, 2000 column entitled "Break Their Crystal Balls," and this May 14 in "Fall Till the Fall," the middle of the range of professional forecasts never comes true. The reason is that the market is a discounter of all known information. Professionals as a group have access to a body of information that is pretty complete. Hence what they can agree on must already be discounted into market pricing and can't happen.

This is straight finance theory. No one who really understands markets would ever lay a market forecast in the middle of peers. In fact, average professional forecaster sentiment right now still is much too bullish for a new major bull market to develop yet. When we hit the real bottom, UBS management won't spend good ad money to support proven losers. The firm's willingness to spend big bucks on nonsense shows the ugliness will continue.

Then comes Carly Fiorina. After nearly 20 years at AT&T and Lucent Technologies, she arrived in July 1999 with great fanfare as the imported chief executive of Hewlett-Packard, charged to "reinvent" it. Two years

later little has changed; this onetime icon of technology is drifting aimlessly.

So what does Fiorina do two days after the stock hits a five-year low? Announce that HP is acquiring Compaq Computer for $25 billion in stock. For Fiorina's career this deal is a time-buying smokescreen. Now no one ever will be able to see if she accomplished anything fundamental for at least several more years. The time and energy spent integrating Compaq will take center stage and obscure her past mistakes at HP.

Trouble is, you don't put two sick outfits together and get a well one. The management that can't fix itself in two years can't fix another troubled giant in that time.

As I detailed in my 1987 book, *The Wall Street Waltz*, merger and acquisition activity in both dollars and deals parallels the stock market cycle. You don't see many deals, especially big ones, announced right around market bottoms. They dry up. Why? Because even the very best boards of directors are sheeplike. They get too timid to take real risks buying anything when prospects are bleak. That HP's board will back a failing chief executive by spending $25 billion of new equity for a troubled company says folks aren't scared enough for there to be a market bottom.

Takeover numbers in America and overseas increased throughout 1999 and peaked in the spring of 2000. They have fallen gradually since then, but not enough yet for a real market bottom. On the very day of HP's Compaq news, six more midsize deals were announced.

In the weeks around this market's final bottom, you won't see deals like Hewlett's. You won't see ads like UBS'. In fact, you will see scant anecdotal evidence of folks seeking opportunities. You will see fear.

That's why you should remain bearish for now. Buy Treasury bills. Buy put options. Avoid equities. ■

Wacky Forecasts

November 12, 2001

I am hearing two extremist views lately about where the market is headed. One is optimistic, the other pessimistic. Both are wacky. Still, in their own odd ways, they signal to me we are getting close to the market's bottom—although we aren't quite there yet.

Why are they wacky? Let's start with the optimists. They are just too darn eager not to miss a new bull market. At the real bottom they won't be so eager. Then, as I've written before, they will be scared about buying. So the ton of e-mails I received starting in late September, asking if the market's bottom hadn't already happened, shows me that it hasn't.

This lingering optimism causes some to misread my past epistles, recasting them into reasons for sudden bullishness. Nothing I've written suggests that we can look forward to a bull market immediately. The difference between a few months from now and immediately can feel near infinite as the last leg of a bear market warps our perceptions.

Then there are the war bulls. Some have dredged up my 1991 bullish comments about the Gulf war, which they took to mean that all wars are bullish. Now isn't then, though, and no two wars are necessarily alike in their impact on the market. A massive assault on fixed enemy positions is far different from the years-long police action we now face.

Other optimists deny gravity. They are certain that, even if stocks fall further, some group they like won't. Their favorites are tech, which has suffered since spring 2000, and insurance and airlines, most heavily affected by September 11. The argument: "Having fallen so much, these stocks can't fall more." Sure they can. If we are in the last stage of a bear market, everything drops—your favorites, too.

Let's turn to the pessimists. They contend for various spurious reasons that we're not in a cyclical bear market but a secular one. In other words, we're doomed to two or three more years of continuous downward movement. This view surfaces in volume late in every bear market. It is normal and precedes the final wave—the Death of Equities stories that we will soon see, about why stocks will never, ever be a good deal again. At that point the optimists fade away and the future looks grim to everyone, creating the bottom.

The pessimists, however, are simply beyond rational. Both 2000 and 2001 were negative years. History shows that, using correctly calculated, cap-weighted indexes, the US has suffered just three instances where the market fell more than two years in a row. And those times don't resemble our day. Take the most recent one, the war-jittery 1939–41 bear market. Equally evil, Osama bin Laden has not the multinational coalition behind him that Adolph Hitler had. The other two long

> ## No Bull
>
> Just as during a bull market you can hear an endless chorus of people claiming it's really a bear market, during a bear market, lots of folks will claim it's really a bull. This is the remnants of the euphoria that typically marks the top of a bull. And in the last quarter of 2001, as the market staged a countertrend rally, plenty of folks were (wrongly) clamoring the bear market had ended. Not so—and Ken maintained his bearish stance.

periods, 1929–32 and the 1830s, featured an imploding money supply. That's not the case today.

We've had many eras with two years down, three years up, two years down, one year up—a decade or more when stocks sawtoothed and overall ended up going nowhere. Some people are predicting that we're going into another such period, last seen from 1966 to 1982. Overall flat, yet capable of driving investors crazy. Maybe it will happen again, maybe it won't.

Yes, forecasts are wonderful—when they work. I've studied forecasting, its history and processes, more than you want to know. I've developed methodologies of my own. I've tested those of others. My conclusion: No methodology exists to deliver any accurate long-term forecast, ever.

Be extremely skeptical of anyone telling you what will occur in five or ten years. Plenty of seers do so and will. And some of them are famous names, legends even. John Templeton—soon to be 89—and one of the alltime great investors, recently has adopted the 1966–82 analogy. I've always been personally interested in Templeton because, among many other reasons, we share a birthday (not year). But the record of big-name investors morphing into perma-bears as octogenarians is long and near perfect.

While I may be wrong, this market is most likely going to find a bottom in late December tied in part to a wave of tax-related selling, the biggest one in decades. Then, too, comes a year-end euro currency panic as the paper is converted, revolving around Europe's vast underground economy, which will suffer huge tax penalties in the process. And, finally, sentiment should bottom when forecasters harden their hearts looking into 2002, delivering downbeat economic and market forecasts, not wanting to be wrong again.

I don't have my specific next-year forecast right now, and won't until January, but overall it will be positive. So yes, a bottom is coming, and not too far away.

Until then, hold tight. Remain defensive. ■

Bottoming Out
December 10, 2001

The year-end Investment Guide presents a great time to assess the overall market and where we are headed next year. I've been fully bearish throughout 2001, starting in January. The spring 2001 rally caused many to turn bullish. Not me. In the September 17 issue (which was in your mailbox two weeks before the issue date) I expressed confusion that a market bottom was taking longer to arrive than I first envisioned. I then said the bottom might not be "until the end of the year or, heaven forbid, until early next year." I reiterated my rule about avoiding being bearish for longer than 12 months. Because I turned bearish at the outset of 2001, that year-end deadline is approaching.

So start buying soon, right? Longtime reader Graham Munro of Toronto e-mailed asking about how to allocate his investments now that it's time to invest again: value versus growth, country weights, etc. I advised Munro to slow down. It may be time to break my 12-month rule.

Let me begin by quoting from my April 24, 1995 column: "Never stay bearish longer than 18 months; 12 months in any but the most extreme situations. Bear markets last about a year. If you are bearish and prices don't fall in a year, you are obviously seeing ghosts. If you do hit it right, and prices fall, force yourself back in after a year. You may not hit the bottom but will have missed plenty of the drop and won't miss the next bull rise." Well, until very recently, I've been right.

And this is an extreme bear market, by any measure, lasting, as it has, 21 months. The bull market ending March 2000 was the second longest of the 20th century, exceeded only by the 1942–61 bull. Thus it isn't shocking to see a longer-than-average bear market following. Among the other weird factors present now that make things different: a President not elected by popular vote, the catastrophic terrorist attacks, the disruptive euro conversion and the long time it took for negative sentiment to spread wide among investors.

Despite the anomalies, you have to trust that historical patterns will prevail. This bear market is already 21 months old. Very old. Old bear markets burn themselves out. Price declines and time eat away positive sentiment. Only when positive sentiment is gone can the market reach a bottom.

Western markets do not like to be down three years in a row. And after huge down moves the markets reach the point where even the worst pessimists can't justify lower prices. As a result, next year will most likely have a positive return. But it may well have a few negative months first. That's why I'm expecting the bear market to continue for a while. I envision this bear market may be running out as late as June. Maybe and probably sooner.

Of course, you can't calibrate the bottom's arrival precisely. I don't mind some risk of slightly missing the bottom. Meanwhile, I'm content to remain bearish.

Too many investors still remain optimistic for me to expect a near-term bottom.

Nevertheless, good investors must always ask themselves: What if I'm wrong? The trick is to avoid being stubborn. There are three signals that will show me I'm missing the market's recovery. Late in a bear market is one juncture where I evoke technical analysis, albeit in a very limited format.

I've got a phrase describing this approach: Three strikes and I'm in. If the S&P 500 climbs past three barriers, which the technical analysts call resistance levels, then it isn't just a sucker's rally. My bearishness would then be wrong. And I'll be back in.

The S&P, as I write, has been struggling to rise above 1100—which has been acting like a ceiling. That was last spring's low, before the sucker's rally. Getting past 1100 is the first step.

The second? Chart the fizzling of the rally in May through the market low point after it reopened in September, postattack: It fell from 1320 to 944. Recovering half that drop would be very odd for a short-lived rally at this late stage, implying a new bull is under way. So if the market rises much above 1130, that will be the second strike. This needs to last several weeks.

The third? Note that the market spent vast time this summer bouncing around 1200. Moving above 1200 for several more weeks is the third step. If I get back in before the market tops 1200 I won't mind missing the bottom by a little.

Right now, though, it's unclear if the market has the strength to surpass these mileposts soon. I'll publish my 2002 forecast in late January. Until then it's best to remain maximally bearish and defensive. ■

2002

Triple Bottom Blues

> " *Financial markets are long-term economic equalizers between competing uses of capital. Stocks versus bonds. Domestic versus foreign. Big versus small. In the long run it all balances out. In the short term the stock market is simply a fatigue-o-meter, measuring which group's sentiment is wearying fastest.* "
>
> "Fatigue-O-Meter," March 4, 2002

> " *Stock prices derive solely from shifts in supply and demand for stocks, nothing else. . . . In the short term, supply is heavily constricted, tied as it is to the regulatory process associated with its creation. In the long term, supply shifts freely and is the prime price-setting force. . . . In the short term, since supply is constricted, it is demand bouncing around that sets prices.* "
>
> "Buy Stocks Now," July 8, 2002

In his February 4, 2002 column, Ken summed up the year in a single sentence: "Much is weird this year." And he was right. The 2001 year-end stock market rally was petering out. From September 21, 2001—five trading days after the stock market reopened following the September 11 tragedy—through the end of 2001, the S&P 500 was up nearly 20 percent.[1] The rally had some believing a new bull market had begun. But stocks rolled over again as 2002 began. Ken started the year with a somewhat positive outlook, suggesting the bear market might bottom sometime in 2002, and the subsequent market rally could result in a positive year for stocks. But by his February 4, 2002 column "2002: Another Down Year," Ken was expecting just that.

The rally that closed out 2001 and another, smaller rally in early 2002 had folks believing a new bull market was at hand. That fact alone made Ken a disbeliever. "In all my studies of financial history, I'm unaware of a new bull market that began with Wall Street strategists and press commentators expecting rising prices that then materialized as expected. Historically, the reverse takes place: For many months prices climb the proverbial 'wall of worry' amid bad news, but pull back on any good news. Not now." ("Myopia," April 1, 2002.) Sure enough, stocks headed south again.

Weird things were also transpiring in the stock market's periphery in 2002. Infamous energy firm Enron had gone belly up in late 2001 in the wake of a massive accounting scandal. Enron had been the largest bankruptcy in history, but it wouldn't retain that distinction for long. In 2002, telecommunications firm WorldCom followed in Enron's loathsome footsteps. Like Enron's demise, an accounting scandal was the root of WorldCom's downfall. Predictably, legislators' knee-jerk reaction to these and other scandals was to legislate, and the Sarbanes-Oxley Act of 2002 was born. Sarbanes-Oxley has been highly criticized in the years since it was enacted because it foists substantial regulatory costs on US-listed companies, especially smaller firms that can't spread the costs out over a larger revenue base. Despite widespread acknowledgement of Sarbanes-Oxley's flaws, it remains in place in 2010.

The Fed continued to cut interest rates in 2002 in response to the slumping economy. When the stock market peaked in March 2000, the fed funds target rate was 6 percent. By late 2002, Greenspan and his cohorts had slashed it to 1.25 percent—an all-time low to that point. The Fed's discount rate, which unlike today was below the target rate in 2002, was down to 0.75 percent.

By midyear, all this weirdness was well known to investors, and most had soured on stocks. Ken saw this capitulation as a sign the market was ready to turn higher. Ken's recommendation was clear from his July 8, 2002 column, "Buy Stocks Now": "Among the most basic market rules is that the market discounts all known information. To be bearish, you must see bad things others don't. One and two years ago, I could . . . Now I can't. Simply agreeing with others about the world's evident evils won't hack it."

Ken had been bearish for nearly 18 months. He was right that a market bottom wasn't far off, but he was clearly too early turning bullish. Ken believed it was best to get out of the market a little late to avoid calling a bear market too soon, and get back in a little early to capture the initial market upturn—often the strongest part of bull markets. But in 2002, getting in early was costly. Not only that, but after years of being on a roll—right much more than wrong—Ken was clearly and publicly wrong.

The bear market not only continued through July, it sharply picked up steam. From the end of June to the market's near bottom on July 23, the S&P 500 fell over 19 percent.[2] Stocks rallied briefly from there, then turned south again, reaching the ultimate bear market bottom on October 9. "In shifting last month from bearish to bullish I was clearly too early. But I'm content. Investors are fearful. Many folks foresee a foul future. Few fathom fantastic returns. In my 30-year investment career, and in the history I've studied, such times are always rewarded, if not immediately, then before many months pass." ("Four Dangerous Words," August 12, 2002.)

To make matters worse, it wasn't a straight shot up from the October bottom either. Stocks faltered again into March 2003 before hitting their real global bottom and finally starting higher. Combined, these three troughs formed a triple bottom for the market.

In his following columns "A Beautiful Market" (September 16, 2002) and "Five More Reasons to Buy" (October 14, 2002), Ken outlined the 10 reasons he was optimistic about stocks looking forward. They were:

1. "Big bear markets (such as we've had since 2000) tend to be followed by big rallies."
2. "People protest too much that economic signs are horrible."
3. "The market is fixated on corporate scandals."
4. "Operating profits are strong despite weak bottom lines."
5. "High price/earnings ratios are not a predictor of price declines."
6. "Insider transactions have shifted from bearish to bullish."
7. "The total position of shorted stock increased to record levels."
8. "Small investors exit near market bottoms, and they are exiting right now in droves."
9. "We will soon enter the sweet spot in the cycle of politics and markets."
10. "The long bond's price has been rising."

The bear market was painful. From the March 2000 peak to the October 2002 low, the S&P 500 lost over 47 percent, making it one of the worst bear markets in history.[3] In 2002 alone, the S&P 500 dropped over 22 percent—the worst year of the bear.[4] Ken was bruised but unshaken by the timing of his market reentry. Fortunately, however, his renewed optimism (though early) would soon be rewarded. But as 2002 ended Ken appeared to be and was wrong for fully half a year. Very clear on his bullishness, 2003 would either put him back on top or make him appear quite the fool—maybe permanently.

Troubling Questions
January 7, 2002

Highly probable for 2002: an up year for US stocks despite a down first quarter. I'll flesh out this forecast in my February 4 column. In the meantime, stay defensive. While we're waiting for a time when it's good to get back in the market, here are answers to questions I hear over and over again from anxious investors:

Isn't the market's high P/E going to put a lid on gains for 2002?
No. The truth is that the market's price/earnings ratio is useless for forecasting. Fear of outsize P/Es is an example of what psychologists call the "illusion of validity." That's the tendency to accept data confirming what our senses tell us while ignoring comparable data that contradict our perceptions.

Our brains are set up to fear heights, so a market with a high P/E—the S&P 500's now is twice the historical norm—makes us afraid. But there is nothing in finance theory or history indicating P/E alone should predict anything, and much to indicate it shouldn't. For every historical instance of a high- or low-P/E market doing badly or well over the following one or two years, there is a comparable instance of the reverse.

My buddy Meir Statman of Santa Clara University and I detailed all this at length in the fall 2000 *Journal of Portfolio Management*. But *Forbes* readers saw it here years beforehand. On rare occasions the market's P/E is useful if linked to shifts in interest rates or market sentiment. By itself, though, P/E says simply nothing about market direction. Ignore it. Ditto for other standard valuation measures.

On the optimistic side, can we expect the market to do well simply because we are at war?
Maybe. History is mixed on this. If you bought into the Korean War, the investment paid off mightily, yet the same bet on Vietnam didn't do well. It depends on the type of war and how the conflict plays out. I'm not sure that lessons gleaned from past wars apply today.

Is this a new era of lower long-term returns because of terrorism and the hangover from the tech mania?
No. First, we're never in a new era. Fundamentally the market's basic functioning never changes. Second, as I said in my November 12 column, no right way exists to make accurate long-term forecasts. You may end up guessing right, but not for any sound analytical reason. You just were fortunate.

But isn't it obvious we can't do as well now as we did in the 1990s?
No. Folks said the same thing as the 1990s started. Right after the booming 1980s we faced a war, recession, rampant job downsizing and a glut of overleveraged companies. You always encounter negative outlooks after a terrific decade ends. The 1990s turned out pretty well, didn't they? The current decade may be great or one to hate. No one can foresee the fate of stocks five to ten years out.

The pricing of stocks and bonds is always a function of supply and demand. Short-term pricing is affected more by demand, which bounces around freely as a function of temporary psychological factors such as fads (tech in the late 1990s) and fears (reluctance to fly, post-September 11). In the short term the supply of stocks and bonds is constricted: Securities laws prevent anyone from pumping out fresh batches of paper at whim.

In the long term, however, supply is much more powerful in pricing than demand is. Supply is very elastic—meaning, companies are happy to issue shares if it means raising cheap capital relative to their sense of their future long-term borrowing costs. Since no one can predict far into the future those returns on capital, no one can predict where supply and demand for equity shares will come into balance.

Isn't the risk of another terrorist attack enough to keep stocks down? What if they nuked Manhattan?
The market is a discounter of all known information, meaning what you read and hear commonly has been already well priced into markets. No event in my lifetime has been more heavily broadcast than the September 11 terrorism. The chances of another attack have been much discussed and therefore priced into the market.

Clearly, the market has concluded that Osama bin Laden and the Taliban had no nuclear, nerve gas or biological capabilities. What they had were knives, boxcutters, gunmen on horseback and some crude Afghan labs less sophisticated than those in most Western high schools. The total effect of a few lucky suicide bombers will always be horrific but economically minuscule in our $20 trillion global economy.

It is natural for bear markets to create pessimism. Don't let this one psych you out. A great time for stocks is soon approaching. ■

2002: *Another Down Year*
February 4, 2002

Okay, I changed my mind. In my last column (January 7) I said the market would be up in 2002. It won't. Get over it. Expect the S&P 500 to lose another 5% this year, plunging until spring with a strong rally in the year's back seven months, one that won't quite make up for the downdraft. The bottom might be around May 1, at about 900.

I use a forecasting methodology I developed some time ago (see my April 3, 2000 column) based on market pros' calls about the year ahead—and the fact that they're always wrong since their expectations are already priced into the market. I get my number by choosing among the holes between where their forecasts cluster. This approach is both empirically and theoretically novel, and nifty.

As often happens, I'm surprised by the result. The fourth-quarter rally made American forecasters too sanguine for 2002 to be a positive year. When a bear market really ends, the initial upturn is met with disbelief, not acceptance. That US professionals are so optimistic after years of being wrong says there is more blood ahead. Much is weird this year.

As I've said recently, the US market doesn't like to drop three years in a row. Such a thing has occurred only twice since 1925 (in 1929–32 and 1939–41). But a spate of New Year's stories makes me confident everyone knows this, diminishing its validity. Nor has the market liked to fall both years of a presidential term's first half, which my forecast envisions. The market did that only in 1929–30 and 1973–74. So I'm expecting the market to do rare things. I'm knowingly making a long bet. These last two years were the worst two back-to-back since 1973–74. And 2001 was the worst year since 1974.

Usually after such ugliness you should expect good times soon. The good news is, during all of 2001's downdraft I was on the right side of the market. I had the luck to have America's best market forecast of any nationally published portfolio strategist in two of the last three years. For 1999 I called for a 20% increase and the S&P came in at

21%; for 2001, I expected a flat performance and the index fell 13% in stock price terms (12% with dividends included). Yet I was closer than anyone else. Most predicted solidly positive returns.

Strategists' current euphoria isn't warranted either. Having been too dour all through the 1990s, in 2000 forecasters tilted optimistic. In 2001 they doured down until the fourth quarter, when the upturn too easily intoxicated them. As 2001 ended, the average forecaster, the guy smack in the middle of the bell curve of professional prognostications, foresaw a market rising 17% in 2002. That is a nice notch above the market's long-term-average history. And in 30 years' data I've reviewed, it has never taken place.

In 2002 there are three holes in the pros' array of calls, meaning three likely S&P outcomes: to end above 40%, below –20%, or between –2% and –10%. I'm betting on the latter. A market rise of more than 40% would be weird. That has transpired just three times in the first half of Presidents' terms. If the market fell more than 20%, that also would be weird: Such deterioration this late in the market cycle defies experience.

One caveat is that my methodology might be thwarted by the sky-high turnover among professional forecasters in 2001, because so many had been so wrong so long. Strategists who departed include Christine Callies at Merrill Lynch and Greg A. Smith at Prudential Securities. Still, regardless of who is making projections, I believe pricing is always a function solely of supply and demand; that supply is rather rigid short-term and that demand can be measured through sentiment.

My approach implies Nasdaq will lose another 12% this year after bottoming in the spring at maybe 1350, 33% below the present level. Small-cap value should remain the best part of the market. Longtime readers know I run this column managed against the Morgan Stanley World Index, which should do worse than the US, losing about 9% for the year and falling maybe 28%, to 725, in the spring. Stay maximally defensive.

That was my advice throughout 2001. At the outset, before the pros' forecasts were in, I recommended three drug stocks: Schering, Akzo Nobel and Novo-Nordisk. Had you invested $10,000 in each of these, you would have lost 2.5% in 2001, factoring in a hypothetical 1% trading cost, or $750 on your $30,000 investment. You would have soundly beaten the market: Putting the $30,000 into the S&P would have lost you $3,420. Once I could do my own forecast, I advised staying out of equities, going for cash and bonds instead. This would have earned you around 4%. Not bad for a bad year. ∎

Fatigue-O-Meter
March 4, 2002

The stock market has gone nowhere for months, trying in vain to head higher. The S&P 500 is where it sat both in early September, before the terrorist attacks, and in mid-October after the market recovered from the shock. The foreign market, best evidenced by Morgan Stanley's Europe, Australia and Far East index, is smack where it was right after September 11. That's ugly.

What gives? In the US, most folks sense economic recovery at hand and believe a new bull market started in September. Still, can it be real if its initial thrust can't maintain upward momentum? I think not.

Recall December's optimism over the market, which then was up 21% from the September low. Wall Street's loud voice claimed that 2002 would be positive, that we would even have a traditional

"January effect," buoying stocks. Now if you expected a January rally, when would you buy? December, right? And hence we had a strong December.

The same thing happened last spring. When the spring rally grew fatigued, that didn't start a new bear. It was the same old one. The first few days of January fizzled into a non-January effect. Today's market is up just 14% from the September low. The market is simply tired. All this causes more fatigued bulls than bears and increases net selling pressure.

Financial markets are long-term economic equalizers between competing uses of capital. Stocks versus bonds. Domestic versus foreign. Big versus small. In the long run it all balances out. In the short term the stock market is simply a fatigue-o-meter, measur-ing which group's sentiment is wearying fastest. Right now the bulls are losing energy.

Two little-appreciated factors stand to move the bulls' needle even more to the fatigue side of the meter. The first problem lies in economies abroad, the second in domestic politics.

Oblivious, Americans don't fret about how foreign economic problems could melt down the US. They did manage to fear just that in 1997 and 1998. Those fears proved groundless, so US investors—who seldom look beyond their borders anyway—now completely ignore the potential for economic catastrophe overseas. But the economies that suffered in 1997–98 were small ones such as Indonesia's and Russia's. The big ones, like Japan's and Germany's, are weak now.

Non-Americans, particularly in the big economies, pray for a US recovery to yank them from their doldrums. They know they can't escape on their own. Unfortunately, there is scant prospect for a US recovery strong enough to pull foreign economies up. Instead the reverse is occurring: The foreigners are dragging us down.

Fighting the recession, Alan Greenspan has printed money with abandon. He can't continue this torrid pace. He has indicated as much. Europe and Japan haven't gone the Federal Reserve's monetary route, though. They understand the long-term inflation risks of creating too much money. While we don't like to think Europe and Japan are collectively as important as we are, we should. The result of our major trading partners' prudence and Greenspan's downshifting is that money tightens globally. And that's bearish for stocks.

Now look at the November 2002 congressional elections. I predict the Democrats will take the House this year and extend their Senate control. Investors, being more Republican than Democrat, will start to fear this outcome by spring. In the long term it won't much matter: US markets are bigger and more powerful than politicians. But the fatigue-o-meter is about short-term sentiments that can cause panic.

What's my political analysis based on? Years ago I was the western regional finance chairman for the Republican National Committee and know something about congressional race analysis. My House outlook stems from the larger number of Republican seats left open by retirements (2-to-1) and their locations. And more Republican retirements are on the way in coming months. What's more, Republicans will get far fewer new seats from redistricting than they have counted on, realizing maybe two net additions when they planned for ten.

In the Senate, six prime races will determine the outcome, with Democrats vulnerable in Minnesota, Missouri and South Dakota, while the Republicans can lose close ones in Arkansas, Colorado and New Hampshire.

President Bush's high popularity, tied to September 11, will flag as well. Fatigue always sets in when presidents get this popular for long. Besides, Bush is no great trail campaigner. Like most Presidents, he will cost his party in the midterm elections.

Remain bearish. Save your strength. ∎

Myopia
April 1, 2002

So? Have I been wrong? Do we have a bull market? The S&P climbed 7% between February 22 and March 8. I think this is just another sucker rally in a long bear market. I may be wrong. Yet the logical conclusion to draw from this winter's rally is that almost everyone is myopic now, unable to see anything except what stares them in the face. One of evolutionary psychology's great lessons is that people are naturally shortsighted.

Immediate events drive us emotionally in all our market conclusions and actions, far more than any inter-mediate or long-term force. Why do folks believe stocks will rise now? Largely because they've been rising. If you want to avoid getting hurt in the next big market move—up or down—learn to look beyond today's news.

Just lately, after we've been through Enronmania, all news is seen as good. Sentiment has soared. While that may seem to be a bullish signal, it really is bearish. The more we feel good about the US economy, the more risk stocks hold.

The myopia extends far afield of the market. We have one of America's most popular presidents ever, according to the opinion polls. Why? I don't know. Aside from having been there on September 11 and having later made only a few grave mistakes, like hiking tariffs on steel, George W. Bush has done little. Hence, there's little to make us think that he is wonderful. Most Americans do, though.

As I write in early March, the news is that February unemployment fell. Stocks responded by soaring. The news was good enough for most investors. They're myopic.

Federal Reserve Chairman Alan Greenspan on March 7 publicly declared an economic recovery was under way. Almost everyone feels that, if Greenspan is happy, they should be, too. What he says must be correct and good enough for them. Myopic.

In all my studies of financial history, I'm unaware of a new bull market that began with Wall Street strategists and press commentators expecting rising prices that then materialized as expected. Historically, the reverse takes place: For many months prices climb the proverbial "wall of worry" amid bad news, but pull back on any good news. Not now.

I've never seen a new bull market where so many normal investors, ones who rarely make right market calls, loudly proclaim they know this is real and, what's more, knew it all along. Myopic.

In my lifetime only one recession, the 1990 downturn, didn't do a double dip. The normal recessionary path is to fall a few quarters under heavy inventory liquidation, pick up for a quarter or two, then relapse. Take the 1969–70 recession. Two quarters of mild economic decline were largely made up for by two quarters of advance, only to relapse violently in late 1970.

Any economic bottom in 2001 was invisible. If real, it would be our first in which a recession ended before the bear market did. Normally stocks lead the economy, they do not lag it.

The latest market run-up, starting February 22, does not break the bear market pattern. Since the down market started in March 2000, there have been eight other upward moves of 7.5% or more lasting 11 trading days or more. This is number nine. The market is no higher than in December or January. But sentiment sure is higher. Talk about a bearish indicator.

The most bullish thing in this uptick is that for the first time in many months foreign markets have joined in fully. As I detailed in my July 23, 2001 column, after last spring's sucker rally, you can't have a real US bull market without major overseas participation. And thus this up move has a greater possibility than usual of lasting.

Yes, there is always a remote possibility of the market's doing something truly unique. Sometimes, obviously very rarely, that will happen. If such is the case now, the result is that any predictions going forward will be tougher to make. But what's more likely, with all these optimists around, is that the rally is temporary.

I detailed for you in my (December 10, 2001) column my "Three Strikes and I'm In" rule: The S&P must climb past three barriers for me to decide I was wrong and dive headfirst into stocks. Two (1100 and 1130) have already been passed. The third, as I wrote then: "Moving above 1200 for several more weeks." From here 1200 seems close, yet it actually is quite distant. My best guess is that the market won't get past the 1200 mark soon. Lots of indigestion lies ahead before we reach that level.

But I may be wrong. If the S&P heads above 1200 and can sustain that altitude for two weeks—and unless the Martians have landed—you will know I'm fully invested. Until then, don't be myopic. ■

Buy Now
April 29, 2002

That's a trick headline. I'm as bearish as I have been, without interruption, for 18 months. The headline refers to buying good investment books, not stocks.

In the 1920s, above *Forbes'* "Fact and Comment" column, BC Forbes first ran the line that Malcolm and Steve later used, "With all thy getting get understanding." While waiting for the right time to reenter the market, you should bone up on investing. For serious students of finance, the most important new book in years just came out: *Triumph of the Optimists*, by Elroy Dimson, Paul Marsh and Mike Staunton. The authors, all from the London Business School, are serious scholars who write in easily understandable English.

Yes, the price is high, but their book offers much more than anyone has before. Educational and enjoyable, this book is a tremendous reference, providing detailed data on 101 years of returns from all over the globe. Just spend an hour with it and you're guaranteed to learn something worth the $99. The optimists in the title are those in the 1950s who believed stocks would have a 9% real return over the next half-century—and were right.

I've studied market history much more than most folks and have written two books on the subject. Nevertheless, I learned lots from *Triumph*. For example, Dimson, Marsh and Staunton show how markets in what we now call developing nations have been important for a long time. My historical knowledge is mostly about America, Britain and some of developed Europe. I had no idea that the 1900 Russian and Indian stock markets were as big as they were (almost solely owned by non-Russian and non-Indian suckers). And I learned that the 17 biggest markets of 1900 had a combined global stock market share very similar to what they have today (about 85%, including Russia).

The authors teach that some things change and some things never do. Knowing the difference is critical to success. Another of their insights: Over the long term, different sectors tend to deliver equivalent returns regardless of differing growth rates, industry to industry or even country to country. You get more growth out of an electronics company than a can company, but the prices reflect this difference—so returns on the glamour sector are not necessarily better.

Two lesser new books, still worthwhile, are: *The Market Gurus* by John Reese and Todd Glassman (Dearborn) and *Dean LeBaron's Treasury of Investment Wisdom* by Dean LeBaron and Romesh Vaitilingam (Wiley). Both address markets through the minds of "gurus," investment leaders who've made a difference—30 for LeBaron, 9 for Reese and Glassman. (Disclosure: My fellow *Forbes* columnist David Dreman and I are included in the Reese-Glassman book. They are far too kind to me.) Interestingly, the two books have scant overlap, because the ways individuals have contributed to finance is vast and varied. They share only stories about Warren Buffett and Peter Lynch.

LeBaron, the retired money manager and one of the original quants (applying computer modeling to investment analysis), now calls himself an "investment futurist." Still, he largely focuses on past theory, with a sweeping view of how, over the last half-century, cheap computer time, cheap graduate-student labor and creative professors combined to deepen and enrich investment thinking. Reese and Glassman, whose Validea.com Web site (which is no longer active) ranked stock pickers, offer slightly more futurism, which you might expect from dot-comers. For instance, they detail my views that the public's knowledge of markets will grow vastly over the next 30 years. The race will go to those who learn more sooner and act on their knowledge.

Good new market books have been rare in recent years and cheesy ones plentiful. Most of the best are classics of long standing. By a wide margin the best source of used books is www.abebooks.com—a real marvel. I've bought thousands of books there over the years for very little. Screen for "stock market" books and you'll find 6,600, priced from $1, up to $8,095 for a first edition of Benjamin Graham's *Security Analysis*. If you expand your search from "stock market" to "investing," you'll find 12,000 books.

You want something else to buy while we're waiting on the market? My only neckties are novelty stock market ones (my favorite has a dial you spin to bullish or bearish graphics), chiefly from eBay auctions, at about $7 each. eBay also offers oddities like market games, cuff links—even books. For ties, keywords are "bull, bear, tie." Buy now. Unless I outbid you. ■

Controlled Risk
May 27, 2002

I compose this column from the computer center on board the *Crystal Symphony*, which is hosting the fourth *Forbes* Cruise for Investors as it sails the Pacific south from Acapulco. What's on these investors' minds? Repeatedly I have been asked how to make real money in what has been a very ugly stock market. These investors don't want to settle for T-bill returns, and they know that small market pockets are doing well, like domestic small-cap value or Russia, and want to know what can make good money right now. It's a wrong—but telling—question.

First, that I am being asked the question in volume is a sign the ugly markets aren't over. If they were, investors would be content simply to avoid having their financial heads chopped off. At and around real bottoms, optimism is basically wiped out and investors don't stretch for return; they duck for cover. Stretching reflects partial optimism, which reflects excess demand for stocks, which presages still more ugliness ahead.

The right questions are: What bet do you take? How much risk do you want to adopt taking it? What tactics do you like? You always have market risk (which way the market goes), factor risk (what type of stock you buy) and stock-picking risk (how your stock varies from its type). But these can be separated and controlled almost completely.

Suppose you like technology, want market risk and like passive investing. Then buy the QQQ (the exchange-traded fund—ETF—for the Nasdaq 100) at $30. It is a bet on market risk and tech as a factor risk but has no stock-picking risk. But if the market falls and tech does worse, you implode.

Now suppose you agree with my view that it's more likely tech will lag rather than lead the market this year. You'd like to make a clear, controlled, measured antitech bet. How?

Well, you could sell short the QQQ. But I wouldn't. Again, that combines tech and market risk. If the market rises, the QQQ will probably do so, too. I always know I may be wrong. Simply selling QQQ short could butcher me if I'm right about tech but wrong about the market—if the market force ends up a bigger factor than the tech play. Control your risks. How?

Buy the S&P 500 as an exchange-traded fund and sell short the QQQ. Now you are simply betting that tech lags the market, and you don't care if the overall market rises or falls. This I would do and recommend to you. You could, for example, buy $50,000 of the SPY while shorting $50,000 of the QQQ. Full-service brokerage commissions at Schwab run $840 for this round-trip. So if the QQQ lost another 15% while the SPY was flat, you would get $7,500 less $840. If you use Schwab's discounted Internet rates, the commissions drop to $140, saving $700.

Of course if I'm wrong and tech beats the SPY, my bet loses. But it is a controlled bet, and it is very unlikely you will lose any more than $7,000 from it.

Suppose you want more risk. Then boost your short position some while decreasing your long position. This leaves you with a lopsided bet on the tech/nontech spread. Note that SPY is about 18% tech itself, so for every $100 you buy of the SPY you are buying $82 of nontech stocks and $18 of tech. Now short, say, $150 of tech, and your net position is long $82 of nontech, short $132 of tech.

More extreme, wickedly efficient, but a bit more complex (if you don't mind greater complexity): Sell the QQQ short for $50,000, as above, and then against that buy three sector ETFs at $17,000 each: the energy sector, the chemical sector, and the REIT sector. These are all value plays and have a smaller average market cap than the QQQ. When selling something short, you inject into your portfolio the reverse of that which you sell. Since QQQ is huge in cap ($123 billion, correctly calculated) and growthy, selling it short injects into your portfolio smallness and value. Buying the three somewhat smaller value sectors and shorting a bigger growth area creates a synthetic small-cap value portfolio. And truly acts just like small value. Of course, if small value does badly, this bet will backfire. But it is a controlled risk.

Now add stock picking. Applied Materials makes wafer fabrication equipment. I think it will be dog meat the rest of this year. The Street expects a big earnings rebound—and fast. Intel's falling price indicates just the reverse. But I might be wrong. So sell AMAT short, but control your risk. Now you are going to flip the QQQ trade around. Go long the QQQ in order to offset your short AMAT bet. The net position has you betting only on whether AMAT does better or worse than tech. There is risk in this bet, but again—it is a controlled risk. ■

Buy Stocks Now

July 8, 2002

It is finally time to get fully invested, although maybe only temporarily. Investors have dug down into pessimism too far for stocks not to pop upward nicely. My shift may surprise recent readers, who have seen me unremittingly bearish for 18 months. But bear markets last only so long. Why now?

Buy Early

After having been bearish for over 18 months, Ken recommended buying stocks—albeit too early. The bear market wasn't done yet—it grinded through multiple bottoms before taking off like a bullet in March 2003 for a grand year. However, Ken would say you can't perfectly time a bottom and shouldn't try. If you envision a market bottom like a V (or a W, but with time that resolves into a V), it shouldn't matter too much which side of the V you get in on. In his view, the risk of missing bull market upside far outweighs the risk of slogging through some late bear market downside. It's not fun. In fact, it can be quite painful. But long-term market returns include bear markets too—so it's better for investors with long-term growth goals to be sure to capture every second of upside, as investors following Ken's call here to get bullish would have.

Seen another way, getting bullish in mid-2002 meant you had been bearish. And being bearish for 18 months during a big bear market can put some serious spread on the market—which simply helps long-term results.

Among the most basic market rules is that the market discounts all known information. To be bearish, you must see bad things others don't. One and two years ago I could. Now I can't. Simply agreeing with others about the world's evident evils won't hack it.

What's so horrific now? The global economy is no longer collapsing. Layoffs have largely laid off. Corporate scandals abound and everyone expects more ahead, and that is discounted into pricing. And we know the terrorists will be terrible—our government now guarantees it, even promising that there will be future attacks. No surprise, so terrorism can't impact markets much. And everyone knows the market isn't statistically cheap, so valuations won't impact pricing. What will? Something basic.

Stock prices derive solely from shifts in supply and demand for stocks, nothing else. We can't think that way because our information-processing capability was hard-wired between the ears eons before stock markets. None of us arises daily gleefully contemplating supply and demand. No, our psyches evolved to deal with hunting and gathering—and their functional replacements, like earnings (rain), interest rates (wind), politics (tribes), trends (seasons), demographics (squalling kids) and demagogues (neighboring chieftains). We don't focus on supply and demand for securities. That's alien.

In the short term, supply is heavily constricted, tied as it is to the regulatory processes associated with its creation. In the long term, supply shifts freely and is the prime price-setting force—and our brains can't and won't begin to comprehend that. In the short term, since supply is constricted, it is demand's bouncing around that sets prices. Demand is a function of our collective emotion.

Emotion gets only so gleeful or dour; when it is too extreme for long, we regress toward the middle.

Demand fell apart in May, having imploded after a very long, lousy market. Lots of capitulation came with the last down leg, starting in March. Hence, with demand too low, it will rise—and with it stock prices. How long? How far?

Uncertain! It may be an up-move of only a few to 12 months, then may roll over again into more ugliness. Or it may be a real new bull market. Either way, it should last long enough to vaporize the emerging consensus that stocks can't have a major up-move soon. Some people can't quite fathom this because it seems like circuitous reasoning. It is. But that is exactly what I am saying and it is exactly how markets work. Meanwhile, buy some stocks; make some money. Life is good. It just doesn't feel that way to everyone now. ∎

Four Dangerous Words
August 12, 2002

In shifting last month from bearish to bullish I was clearly too early. But I'm content. Investors are fearful. Many folks foresee a foul future. Few fathom fantastic returns. In my 30-year investment career, and in the history I've studied, such times have always rewarded, if not immediately, then before many months pass.

When I point out that this bear market has been the longest (and second biggest) since World War II, I'm lectured by folks who never foresaw this bear market yet who now cite many well-publicized reasons that the bottom isn't here yet. I like that. They cite causality that was never valid and the reasons it will be different this time.

Note John Templeton's legendary phrase that the world's four most dangerous words are: "It's different this time." It never is. It just feels that way. At and around bottoms people clutch at ghoulish visions while praying to craven mythology that never was realistic.

This time, for example, many cite the market's high P/E, fretting further that it is higher now than in early 2000. All true—and normal. The market's P/E usually is higher at a bear market bottom than its prior peak because as a rule earnings disappear faster than stock prices.

Counterintuitive, but history shows there is simply nothing about P/E levels, cut any way you want, to help predict market tops or bottoms, or market levels several years out. That we believe otherwise is mythology. If you want more on this, see my Fall 2000 *Journal of Portfolio Management* article (co-written with Meir Statman), "Cognitive Errors in Market Forecasts." Nor does finance theory suggest the P/Es should be predictive. Theory would have you flip it on its head, as an E/P, the earnings yield, and compare that with interest rates. Hereto, nothing much is revealed. For example, the E/P divided by the 90-day T bill rate is boringly in the middle of its historic range.

P/Es often skyrocket around bottoms and thereafter because of all the write-downs. Correctly calculated, the market's highest P/Es ever were in 1920, 1932 and 1982, three of the five best times to buy in the last century.

Some folks want the bad news to slow down before the market bottoms. It never has worked that way, so it won't now. More accounting scandals? Sure. Will they stop a bull market? No. We've been here before, just not recently.

Investors fear terrorists and war. Nothing new here. At all. Nuclear war? Old idea. The last time around we were worried about the Soviets—and didn't know that they lacked the thrust power to hit us. But we know the rogue states lack it. Dirty bombs? They were always possible. No one says the truth, that the terrorists we so fear are amazingly incompetent. So they got one lucky strike on us. Name one thing they do well that threatens us. Just ghoulish visions. If all the globe's suicide bombers targeted only American shopping malls from now on, we should rationally be much more frightened of our drunk drivers.

I see very nice returns in 2003 and 2004. The question is: Exactly where is the bottom? Most folks now say later rather than sooner, so I suspect it will be sooner. A bull market now would surprise more investors than a bad market. And if I'm wrong? You'll pay a small penalty for being a little too early, but someone who buys a little too late will pay the same penalty. Both sides of the bottom of a "V" look pretty similar 6 to 12 months later. ■

A Beautiful Market
September 16, 2002

This market is sheer beauty—the most stunning I've ever seen clearly. Maybe not as beautiful as 1974, but perhaps as a young man I didn't see that right. Of course, beauty is in the eyes of the beholder. But I think most of you will never see a market this gorgeous again, ever. Or if you do, you won't see many.

How beautiful? Count the ways. First, big is beautiful. Big bear markets are followed by big rallies. There are no exceptions. This bear, with a 48% decline in the S&P 500 at its worst point this summer, falls in the middle of the range of the seven big bear markets of the last century. With the exception of the Great Crash, which took the Dow down 89% between 1929 and 1932, big bear markets have sliced stock prices 42% to 55%. But if you think this is like 1929–32 you are delusional: Absent are the 1930s' massive global trade barriers, the massive worldwide destruction of the quantity of money and the massive economic dislocations.

Following all the big market drops came 12-month advances, ranging from 29% to 65%, with a 50% average. That's big. And beautiful.

I devoted last month's column to Wall Street's four most dangerous words: "It's different this time," and how folks are fixated on that now, and why that fixation is a bullish sign. More beautiful still is all the hate e-mail that column generated, reiterating how it really is different this time. The more people protest that things are horrible, the more persuaded I am that it's not different this time. Fear is beautiful.

All this hostility to corporate leaders—does that mean more trouble ahead for stocks? No, this is already priced in. Today's antibusiness emotion parallels that of the 1903 bear market, known as the Rich Man's Panic. Then Teddy Roosevelt, as trustbuster, played the role now being played by congressmen who, with perverse irony, lecture business on integrity.

The bears today bemoan falling profits. What they overlook is that operating income is rising. Operating income is the spread between sales and direct costs. (It is also known as earnings before depreciation, interest, taxes and nonrecurring items.) The operating margin is the most basic efficiency ratio for a company. Without writeoffs, earnings would rise nicely now. Profits are about the past. Operating margins are about the future.

As I said last month, and despite what everyone wants to believe, the market's overall price/earnings ratios tell you simply nothing about where the market is headed. But within the market, there is a tug-of-war between growth stocks (generally, those with high P/Es) and value stocks (low P/Es). This is a time when value stocks are winning the tug-of-war. ∎

Five More Reasons to Buy
October 14, 2002

Last month, I detailed five things, some of them counterintuitive, that make this a beautiful time to invest in stocks. Here they are: Big bear markets (such as we've had since 2000) tend to be followed by big rallies; people protest too much that economic signs are horrible; the market is fixated on corporate scandals; operating profits are strong despite weak bottom lines; and, finally, high price/earnings ratios are not predictor of price declines.

But there is ever more beauty. Let's now extend this list of positive indicators.

Six: Insider transactions have shifted from bearish to bullish. Normally insiders sell more shares than they buy, as they turn options into spending cash. In bear markets net selling increases. Earlier this year, insiders sold about four shares for every one bought. In July, that flip-flopped to two shares purchased for every share sold, according to Market Profile Theorems in Seattle. That's an extremely bullish ratio.

Seven: In the steep August rally the total position in shorted stock increased to record levels. Every share sold short, which must eventually be bought back, is a borrowing of future demand for stock, and that is beautiful. That short-selling rose as stocks did is evidence of the skepticism the rally received and normal for a new bull market.

Eight: Small investors exit near market bottoms, and they are exiting right now in droves. In July equity mutual fund redemptions brought the two- and three-month totals to alltime records or near-records. July by itself was the second-biggest month ever in redemptions as a percentage of fund assets, exceeded only by October 1987. This is a beautiful form of capitulation.

Nine: After the midterm congressional elections next month, we soon will enter the sweet spot in the cycle of politics and markets. Almost never is a third year of a president's term a down year. The last time it happened was 1939, and then the S&P 500 was down only 0.4%. The median third-year return of the S&P since inception is 22.8%. Coming right up. Beautiful.

Ten: The long bond's price has been rising. This is basic to new bull markets. Reacting to the bear market rally of April through June 2001—a sucker move most seers mistook for a new bull market—my June 11, 2001 column argued for staying out, detailing why for a new bull market you need the long bond to act well. Ditto for last fall's false rally. Now Treasury bond prices are strong. Yields, that is, are down. Why is this key?

Bonds compete in the capital market with stocks, and in this market a bond's yield corresponds to what is called the earnings yield on a stock. The earnings yield is the inverse of the price/earnings ratio. A P/E of 20, for example, is an earnings yield of 5%—for every $100 you invest, you buy $5 in annual corporate earnings. When bond yields fall, the prior balance between earnings and bond yields is knocked off kilter, pressuring stock prices to rise to return the balance. As the Fed creates new money in a noninflationary world, it goes first to the fixed-income market, buying bonds and driving bond prices up and yields down. It then rebounds into stocks, driving the price up and the earnings yield down. ■

The P/E Myth
November 11, 2002

C an you predict which way the market is headed by looking at the average price/earnings level? Some investors think that you can—or at least, that you are likely to do well buying when the ratio is low and selling when it is high. I have evidence to the contrary. The P/E level is useless for market timing.

But first, why do we so believe P/E predicts the future? It appeals to human senses of nature, fairness, value and simplicity. We believe, wrongly, that the supply and demand for securities follow the same curves as the supply and demand for petroleum or corn. ("I'd buy more of anything if it were cheap.") The truth is that demand for stocks is not in some neat inverse relationship to the price. On the contrary: It's when stocks are already high (as in 1999) that buy orders flood into Merrill Lynch and Schwab.

There's an emotional component to the belief that buying into low-P/E markets leads to success. When we buy "cheap" and are rewarded with rising prices, we feel smart and deserving of the capital gain. The fellow next door who paid up looks like a gambler and not deserving of a reward. Perhaps investors are afraid of high-P/E markets because of instinct. For eons only those with a healthy fear of heights passed on their genes while the daredevils did not. But that fear of heights shouldn't dictate your willingness to hold equities.

The thesis that stocks should be sold when P/Es are high is wrongheaded, for two reasons. First, the data don't support the thesis. Second, finance theory denies it.

In an article in the fall 2000 *Journal of Portfolio Management*, Meir Statman, a Santa Clara University finance professor, and I statistically showed that there is no linkage of market P/Es to subsequent returns in the market. This is true no matter how you measure the ratio (for example, above a random number, like 20, or in the top 20% of history) and no matter over how long (up to five years) you measure returns. The conclusion is based on 125 years of data. For every instance in which high-P/E markets do badly or well, however determined, there is an almost identical number and magnitude of times they did the reverse. Low-P/E markets lead to bad results as often as good ones.

Recently we did further research on the disconnection between average P/Es and buying opportunities. Make any P/E trigger you want—buy when it's below 20 and sell when it's above, or buy below 8 and sell above, whatever—and you won't wind up with a trading rule that works. Vastly more often than not, you'll wind up with a return that badly lags buying and holding. Why? You'll be out of the market for crucial rallies, and you will not be spared all of the corrections. With a trigger of 25, for example, you'd be out of the market in 1922 (when the market was up 28%) and in the market during all but four of every money-losing year ever. An analysis of returns in the UK, another market where historical data go way back, delivers the same result: P/E triggers don't work.

Finance theory also undermines the case for letting average P/E levels dictate your preference for stocks over fixed income. Stocks compete with bonds by offering an ever-varying "equity risk premium." If this premium were fixed, you could devise a target earnings yield on stocks. Flip that earnings yield, or E/P, and you would get a target P/E, and you could argue that stocks are "cheap" when they go below this P/E, expensive when they are above. The problem here is that the equity risk premium is driven not by some fixed mathematical formula but by shifting emotional preferences for or against uncertain earnings (with potential opportunity) versus safer fixed income flows. In short, investors' moods throw simplistic E/P rules out the window.

The very fact that people are worried about high P/Es suggests that the mood is about to shift in favor of equities. The not-quite-50% decline in stocks over the past two and a half years has wrung a lot of risk out of the market. ∎

Not Bonds, Books
December 9, 2002

The next bursting bubble? Bonds. Folks have flooded into the Treasury market. They are driven by panic in the stock market, mesmerized by a 21-year bull market in fixed income and misled by the mythology that bonds are safe. They aren't. You can get killed by them.

Until people realize that, bond managers will remain the new heroes. Pimco's Bill Gross, arguably the best bond manager of the last three decades, runs what just became the world's biggest mutual fund. For some reason, that suddenly qualifies him as a stock market sage. While claiming that anyone who is bullish on equities is self-serving, Gross himself self-servingly suggests that stocks will be disappointing for years while bonds will be okay (although, to his credit, he says that Treasurys are fairly priced and their big bull market mostly over).

The bond bull market of 1981–2002 was quite extraordinary. Long-term Treasury rates collapsed from 15.8% to 4%. You won't see that again, ever. On the contrary: Interest rates are destined to climb some of the way back up. And why shouldn't bonds get a bear market? If a 20-year stock run-up could lead to the last 3 years, why not ditto with bonds now? How much lower can yields fall while globally central banks print money at 5% to 10% annual rates and economies grow at 2% rates?

Sooner or later bondholders will demand an aftertax coupon exceeding inflation. If the real aftertax return is to be, say, 2%, and if inflation is 4%, and if your tax rate is 25% (it's probably higher), you need an 8% coupon on your long Treasury. That's just about double where long rates are now.

Treasurys are safe? Do the math. If over the next year the yield on long Treasurys climbs four percentage points from where it is now, your total return on such paper will be -40%. That is nearly as much as stocks fell since March 2000. I can't promise you that Treasury yields will double, but I can say the bond market won't be pretty over the next few years. As economies finally pick up some steam in 2003 and 2004, inflation fears will renew and the bubble-bursting will begin. Once the prick starts it will be steady and fast until all the hot air arguing for bond safety is fully dissipated and turned into cold fear.

Do not forget: Inflation is a creature of politics, and politicians never lose their lust to spend money. Yours. You know the old folk etymology of "politics" (Greek scholars, please don't write in with corrections)—that the word comes from "poli," meaning many, and "tics," meaning small blood-sucking creatures. The blood is money, printed by central bank chairmen. Ours, revered as he is, is getting old and has to work hard to get the reappointment he covets. President Bush can stall through summer 2004 his decision to reappoint Greenspan or not. That hinges, despite what you may think, on whether Greenspan motivates our Fed to be adequately accommodating to give Bush a suitable economic backdrop for reelection. I predict that Greenspan will so motivate the Fed.

You will find few five-year periods in Treasury history without a severe uptick in rates somewhere. Yet usually those bond bear markets saw stocks fare pretty well, particularly when they were preceded by a stock bear market. We just had a doozy of a stock correction. What to do? One approach is to take some of your money out of bonds and find stocks with better overall yields. By "yield" here I mean the earnings yield, or earnings divided by price.

Christmas approaches. A great gift for investor friends is Robert Menschel's new *Markets, Mobs & Mayhem* (Wiley). While not written for this purpose, its detailing of how panics of all forms end can help you see why stocks will do fine in the next few years.

The best older book I read this year is Thomas Gilovich's *How We Know What Isn't So* (Free Press, 1991). In simple English he exposes the cognitive traps that cause misperceptions of reality, which are rampant in markets. ∎

2003

Buy on the Cannons

> " *It is pointless to worry about what others worry about. If you do and base market judgments on those worries you will be wrong more often than right. . . . If others worry about something, you just don't have to because they are doing it for you. You should worry about something else—namely, whatever they're not worried about.* "
>
> "Greed Is Good," May 26, 2003

> " *Our brains weren't set up to do the stock market. We got our information processors from ancestors eons ago. We are only here because they did well then and passed their genes on to us. Financial markets came much later.* "
>
> "Volatility, the Good Kind," June 23, 2003

"Buy to the roar of cannons, sell to the sound of trumpets." Sound familiar? Once again, as in 1991, British financier Nathan Rothschild's 1810 quote proved prescient. The bear market reached its ultimate low in October 2002, but as mentioned before stocks didn't move straight up from there. The S&P 500 nearly retested the bear market bottom in March 2003—a low point that coincided almost perfectly with the beginning of the Iraq War. From the day the Iraq invasion began, March 20, 2003, through the end of the year, the S&P 500 skyrocketed nearly 29 percent.[1]

Ken's optimism grew in 2003 even as the stock market struggled early on. "Where will the market go in 2003? I see only two real possibilities: down a lot or up a lot. Since I don't envision down a lot, I'm bullish . . . I think the S&P 500 could have one of its best years ever." ("Next Year Will Be Better," February 3, 2003.) And it did. Despite a lingering hangover from the steep bear market and concerns about the impact of the Iraq War, the S&P 500 gained 28.7 percent on the year. Foreign stocks were up even more, rising 40.2 percent.[2]

One factor boosting Ken's optimism was underfunded pensions. No, that's not a misprint. Many view underfunded pensions as a negative for stocks because corporations are forced to increase their pension contributions to make up for the shortfall. These additional contributions decrease earnings. But most investors ignore the fact a sizeable chunk of new pension money is allocated to stocks, so the negative impact on earnings and, thus, stock prices is offset by new stock purchases. Not to mention the fact a fair amount of new pension funding comes from institutions other than publicly traded companies. Those contributions have no impact on public company earnings but still boost stock purchases. "Corporations, governments and foreigners will all add unexpectedly large amounts of cash to their underfunded pension plans, investing much of that money in stocks. . . . Investors have already figured pension problems into their earnings expectations; they have not figured the size of the stock purchases . . . more than half of this demand comes from buyers for whom there is no S&P 500 earnings effect." ("Buy Money Managers," March 31, 2003.)

Two-thousand-three was also the third year of President Bush's first term—historically an overwhelmingly positive period in the presidential cycle for stocks as Ken has noted in a number of his columns over the decades. The reason stocks do well in third years is grounded in behavioral finance, a growing field Ken has helped pioneer.

At its core, legislation involves taking money or property rights from one group of people and giving it to another. That might seem like a zero sum game, but our brains don't see it that way—the losers end up in a much sourer mood than the winners. Anyone not involved on either the winning or losing end is afraid they might be the loser next time around. So when legislative change looms, investors become more cautious.

The president's party typically loses congressional seats in midterm elections. "As a result almost all big schemes to redistribute wealth or property rights happen in the first half of Presidents' terms. Take from the rich, give to the poor. Or transfer from the poor to the rich. Or from these rich to those rich. Whatever the direction of the flow of wealth, it is an iron rule that the losers hate the transfer twice as much as the winners like it. . . . When government threatens property rights materially, it scares the foundation of free markets, hence stock markets." ("Three's a Charm," January 6, 2003.)

The 2002 midterms were odd in that Republicans actually gained congressional power. But Ken expected the third-year trend to hold true in 2003 as President Bush looked to extend Republicans' lead in Congress and win himself a second term in 2004. "[President Bush] can build political capital or spend it. Legislating means spending it, hurting his 2004 goals. I'd bet he keeps building capital . . . If he pushes legislation, those he takes from will hate it more than those he gives to will love it. The losers will be energized for 2004 revenge; the winners, placated, will lose the urge to vote or help Bush's campaign." Congress and Bush passed the Jobs and Growth Tax Relief Reconciliation Act of 2003, but otherwise all was quiet on the legislative front.

Typically, Ken doesn't make forecasts out more than about a year. Any longer and it's near impossible (in Ken's view) to know what market conditions will look like—because you can't forecast sentiment or equity supply longer term. Economists make all kinds of long-term forecasts, most of which are off the mark, and none divulge how stocks will fare. Like anything else, stock prices are determined by supply and demand. In the short run, the supply of stocks is fixed since it takes awhile for stock offerings to come to market, so demand is the primary driver of stock prices. In the long term, however, stock supply has a greater impact on prices. So though Ken didn't know where stock prices were headed longer term, he was sure the path there wouldn't be boring. Stocks rarely are.

"The bear market made it fashionable to say stocks might be flat for ten years or more. That's moronic. It has never, ever happened that stocks lie flat for a decade. Sometimes, rarely, the market is no higher ten years later. But there is too much volatility to ever have a ten year period without huge moves within it. Up or down, it's still volatility." ("Volatility, the Good Kind," June 23, 2003.) That comment turned out to be prescient as the 2007–2009 bear market erased the returns of the bull market from 2003–2007. But the period in between was far from flat. And after having a tough year—(bullish too early and very publicly in 2002), 2003 was another great year, for investors and Ken.

Three's the Charm
January 6, 2003

Readers reacted with hostility to my October 14, 2002 column, which cited, among ten reasons for stock market bullishness, the fact that third years of Presidents' terms are overwhelmingly benign. They told me this was silly, superficial and quirky, like the Super Bowl indicator. It was cute correlation without basic causality.

I disagree. It's basic and causal. As we enter this president's third year, you should contemplate that causality. Those blind to its power are blind.

First, note the history. Using full terms (for example, 1973–76 was the Nixon/Ford term), since the S&P 500's 1926 inception, there were more negative than positive first years (by 10-to-9)—and almost as many negative second years, (8-to-12). But the entire back half of all Presidents' terms suffered only five negative years: 1931 and 1932, leading to the Great Depression bottom; 1939 and 1940, leading to

World War II; and 2000, as tech's bubble first burst. All huge, weird sequences of events. Put another way, in modern history almost all negative years were in the first half of Presidents' terms. The exceptions involved massive negative events. The third year is best. The last negative third year was way back in 1939—down merely 0.4%. The third-year median return is not only positive but a big number: 22%.

Why? First, as you might instinctively know (but as economists established only two decades ago), normal people hate losses more than they like gains, more than twice as much. Second, a President expects that his party will lose congressional seats in the midterm election. (President Bush's accomplishment in bucking this rule was truly exceptional.) So, he knows that whatever would be his toughest legislation must pass either in his first two years in office or never. This is a basic fact about our political cycle.

As a result almost all big schemes to redistribute wealth or property rights happen in the first half of Presidents' terms. Take from the rich, give to the poor. Or transfer from the poor to the rich. Or from these rich to those rich.

Whatever the direction of the flow of wealth, it is an iron rule that the losers hate the transfer twice as much as the winners like it. Note that wealth here is not limited to cash; property rights are just as important. We take property rights for granted, but without them capitalism never thrives long. When government threatens property rights materially, it scares the foundation of free markets, hence stock markets. Examples? To name a few: In 1930, a presidential second year, we got the Smoot-Hawley tariff; in 1933, a first year, we got the Glass-Steagall divorce of commercial from investment banking; in 1969, a first year, came legislation that created

Term Cycle Voodoo

Lots of people know about the Presidential Term Cycle. Yet, as Ken has pointed out through the years, if information or even a forecasting tool is widely known, it loses power. So why does this one still have power? Because most people assume it doesn't work—that it's voodoo. In *The Only Three Questions That Count*, Ken shows how you can gain a market edge by finding patterns that are widely evident—so long as you can find causality when most others find only a joke. Those can be very powerful patterns—and in 2003, this third year of a president's term was very positive indeed.

the Environmental Protection Agency; in second year 1994, the Clintons attempted to nationalize health care.

Having bucked the trend and added midterm power, will President Bush now legislate heavily, voiding the third-year magic? Unlikely. He can build political capital or spend it. Legislating means spending it, hurting his 2004 goals. I'd bet he keeps building capital. Remember, he needs marginal 2004 voters. If he pushes legislation, those he takes from will hate it more than those he gives to will love it. The losers will be energized for 2004 revenge;

the winners, placated, will lose their urge to vote or help Bush's campaign.

By proving that he and Karl Rove can strategize better than anyone expected (amazed me!), Bush will want to do it again, building further election success. He will blame the lack of passage of consequential legislation on thin congressional majorities, while gunning for additional congressional power in 2005, when he has little to lose. That is when heavy legislation is likely, and 2006. Hence the third-year magic likely endures—2003 will be good, indeed. Particularly after three negative years. ■

Next Year Will Be Better
February 3, 2003

Each January, *Forbes* asks its columnists for a retrospective on the prior year's stock picks. How did we do? And what should you do with some of the winners and losers? In recent years, my picks beat or matched the S&P. Not so in 2002. My market timing was fairly good (I was bearish until the July 8 issue), but my stock selection was not. My picks declined an average 6% by year-end and would have left you 3% poorer than a hypothetical investor putting the same money at the same dates into a no-load index fund. Actually, all of this is better than my firm's individual clients fared.

Note that the performance measure *Forbes* uses assumes that an investor loses 1% to commissions and bid/ask spreads on each round-trip trade for my stock picks. The hypothetical S&P 500 index fund against which the stock recommendations are compared has no trading costs and no overhead.

My four short recommendations were better. They declined on average 23%, 20% more than the average decline of the S&P 500 from the same dates.

The good news: Early on, continuing my 2001 bearishness, I advised that you shouldn't own stocks—specifically, that the S&P 500 would be down 5% in 2002. While that wasn't nearly pessimistic enough, mine was among the few negative forecasts then in national print. Now the media are full of folks claiming they were bearish, but I find just seven nationally published forecasters who in early 2002 issued specific predictions for declines in the market. Only four were more bearish than me. None was bearish enough.

Credit where due: The closest call came from Joseph Barthel of Fahnestock, who foresaw a negative 20% year (the S&P 500 ended down 22%, not including dividends). Douglas Cliggott of JP Morgan Chase was 2002's third-most-accurate forecaster and 2001's most accurate, a stunning two-year display. Cliggott, now with Brummer & Partners, remains bearish, expecting another 16% drop for 2003.

The bad news is I shifted to a bullish stance months too early, with eight buy recommendations in that July 8 column.

I didn't see the factors causing market weakness through September. I'm unsure if I see them correctly now. While October and November were strong, December had a disastrous 6% decline, the S&P's third-worst December ever.

Also wrong, I forecast in March that the Democrats would gain House and Senate seats in November elections. The opposite happened.

While I'm not proud of my market laggards, six months is not very long for picks to work out. The worst was Ford Motor, recommended at 17 last July and trading just below 10 at year-end. I'd recommend that you hang on to this one; consumer purchases of big-ticket items like cars will be far stronger in 2003 than expected. While almost no one knows this, consumer confidence moves almost perfectly, in the short term, with the market. Hence, as goes the market, so will Ford. Other bloopers included Credit Suisse, at 28 when the magazine reached readers and 21 at year-end, and Ryan's Family Steak Houses, down 15%, the way *Forbes* calculates. These you should stay with, as well.

My winners included Household International, which spiked up when HSBC decided to buy it, which was pure luck, and Gap. You can sell it now; there are better opportunities.

Where will the market go in 2003? I see only two real possibilities: down a lot or up a lot. Since I don't envision down a lot, I'm bullish. Next month I'll detail why I think the S&P 500 could have one of its best years ever, maybe up 40%. ∎

The Bipolar Market
March 3, 2003

Last month, I suggested 2003 would be a great stock market year. Why? Because the forecasting methodology I've long used says 2003 will be great or terrible. Since I see abundant reasons it won't be terrible, I expect it to be great. Here's why:

Years ago, I fashioned this tool by building representative samples of professionals' expectations. Then I noted what they agreed would occur, and figured the best place for an investor to place a bet is on some other outcome. Financial markets discount all known information. That means what we all know and commonly discuss is priced into markets—having no residual power. You can't make money off it. So contemplate other possibilities and choose among them.

Suppose the consensus forecast is for So & So Co. to double its earnings next year. If you buy the stock now, do you have a big hit when the company delivers? No, that outcome was figured into the price you had to pay. You win when you know something others don't.

Sometimes you're right. Sometimes wrong. Last year I was wrong. My February 4, 2002 column said that there were three holes in the pros' array of calls for 2002, meaning three S&P 500 outcomes worth betting on: to end with a gain above 40%, with a loss of 20% or worse, or with a loss between 2% and 10%. I bet on the last option. The second proved to be the correct one. The methodology wasn't wrong, just my particular choice.

The same technique now offers only two outcomes. Up 35% or more. Or down 35% or worse. I'll bet the former. Why?

You bet based on what is historically reasonable and what you see that others can't. First, a fourth big down year would be rare and would make this bear market fully comparable in magnitude and duration to 1929–32, a uniquely bad episode in economic history. Next, as I've often detailed (over the objections of many readers), history and reasoning point to the fact that the market will not experience a fall during a President's third year in office.

The third reason I don't expect a 35% fall has to do with a quirk of investor psychology. Recently I discovered investor psychology runs a continuous spectrum from higher-end, more famous and formally trained professional forecasters from the very biggest firms, down to lower-end, small money managers with little or no formal training (and nonprofessionals). Upper-end pros tend to be "mean reverters," meaning above-average years make them more bearish and below-average years make them more bullish. They want to revert toward average. Lower-end investors (professional or not), tend to be trend followers. They expect good years to be followed by good, and bad years by bad. From upper end to lower end is an accordionlike flexible psychological continuum. So, a long bull market pulls all investors together—toward more similar views. But long bear markets spread out sentiment, with high-end folks getting optimistic (by mean reverting) while low-end folks get ever more bearish.

The longer a bear market, the more that spreads out. And they all get more sure they're right. If the market is down 35% this year, high-end mean reverters will get more optimistic still, and low-end trend followers will get more pessimistic. Then, in 2004, with sentiment pancaked even further than it is now, the market will have to rise or fall a lot more than 35%, which seems much too much to be realistic, either way. But if the market is up big later this year, the mean reverters will get less optimistic, the trend followers less pessimistic and 2004 won't have to be unrealistically extreme. Hence psychology argues for up, not down. (For more, see "Blowing Bubbles," by me and Meir Statman of Santa Clara University, in the *Journal of Psychology and Financial Markets*, 2002, Vol. 3, No. 1).

Fourth reason to expect a rebound in 2003: Professionals overwhelmingly forecast a big move up in both long- and short-term rates this year, and the possibility of this bearish development is already figured into stock prices. I expect rates to stay more or less flat. With economies weak, central banks have scant choice but to err toward looseness. (And with his reappointment in 2004 on the line, Alan Greenspan has no choice but to help Bush's reelection prospects with loose money.) Low rates will be a pleasant surprise, pushing stocks up.

Fifth, municipalities and states plugging gaps in their pension funds will be big net buyers of stocks and bonds this year, to the tune of $50 billion. No one expects this, and next month I will detail what's behind it. ■

Buy Money Managers
March 31, 2003

Here are another 70 billion reasons stocks should do well: Corporations, governments and foreigners will all add unexpectedly large amounts of cash to their underfunded pension plans, investing much of the money in stocks. This year,

I expect net equity purchases by these three groups of $70 billion.

If you are like the majority of Wall Streeters, you see pension shortfalls as a negative. They cause high pension charges—meaning lower earnings, after all, which could depress stock prices. I concede the point but believe that the supply-and-demand effect will overwhelm the earnings effect. Investors have already figured pension problems into their earnings expectations; they have not figured in the size of the stock purchases. Another important point is that more than half this demand comes from buyers for whom there is no S&P 500 earnings effect—namely, state and local governments or foreign pensions.

All this is about "defined benefit" plans, the traditional pension plans promising a certain monthly dollar benefit to retir-

ees. The alternative—"defined contribution" plans like 401(k)s—make no promises and expose the sponsor to no liability, and aren't pension plans.

Every year the actuaries for a pension plan estimate its future liabilities—future benefits already earned—plus expected future benefits. En route, actuaries make lots of assumptions about career spans, average future employee pay, inflation and retiree life spans.

They also estimate the future value of present assets, starting with a smoothed-out average, usually over the last three years, to mitigate the effect a volatile stock market may have on the calculation. Then they estimate a future return on their assets, typically about 9%. Three years of bear market declines knocked the three-year average down. With it, pessimism has lowered their return assumptions, ratcheting double-downward estimates of future assets. This is backwards. Depressed stock prices, if anything, should boost the likely future returns on the portfolio. The time to lower future return assumptions was five years ago, not now. But no one ever does it that way.

Anyway, estimated future liabilities are subtracted from future assets and any spread is "underfundedness," which must be made up by paying that amount into the pension slowly, yearly, over the life of the plan.

Those who disagree with me note that money is put into pension plans every year, but this year it will go unexpectedly through the roof. The newly injected cash buys mostly stocks and bonds (and a little real estate and other illiquid holdings). Corporate plans typically hold about 60% stocks and 40% everything else.

This year General Motors will inject $3 billion into its fund and use almost $2 billion of it buying stocks. The pension managers won't do this, but imagine they just bought GM stock. Earnings would fall, but GM shares would rise with increased stock demand. This is bullish, just as stock buybacks are bullish. To be sure, corporations buy each other's stocks for pension funding, not their own, but they create the same overall effect.

My firm estimates that this kind of buying will create $30 billion of 2003 corporate demand for stocks. Another $30 billion of stock buying will come in from public retirement systems (like CalPERS, but mostly from county plans). The pension cost recorded by states, counties and cities should triple in 2003 from the level the year before. Foreign pension plans will pour $10 billion into stocks this year.

So far, beyond one brief sentence in last month's column, there has been no national media mention of the size of public and foreign pension underfunding. Hence, it will surprise investors and be all the more bullish. This is a state or municipality's number one legal liability and must be paid. They will pay for it mostly by issuing municipal bonds, relatively painlessly. ∎

Crash and Opportunity
April 28, 2003

Reporting live from the war: Heavy casualties, with German forces hit worst—75% lost. American and British losses lighter. German life insurers decimated. I'm not gloating, just reporting the facts: In terms of market capitalization, the coalition of the willing is doing much better than the coalition of the unwilling. The US and the UK between them account for more than two-thirds of the world's combined stock market value. The German market is now worth less than Canada's. That was not true in August, when Iraq war talk began. Canada's stock market has been correlating with those of the two Uniteds, which are hovering at last summer's levels. German and French stocks, in contrast, have tanked. Badly.

The German and French markets combined are now worth less than the UK's 20 largest stocks, or the 4 largest American stocks Microsoft, General Electric, Exxon, and Wal-Mart. The unwilling are being marginalized.

I report from Munich. With the war starting I had to head to Europe to get some good old-fashioned anti-Americanism. I can't find much. There is more back home in San Francisco. Germans love Americans but dislike the French. Yet in foreign policy they allow themselves to be led blindly by the French. The French can't fathom why they're losing ground as they plant both feet firmly in the 20th century.

What about all those antiwar protests? They sure get a lot of television play. On March 29 I saw the biggest anti-American protest since San Francisco, in Edinburgh, Scotland—but it was all students and old 1960s socialists, openly organized by the Scottish Socialist Party. The Scots, for all that they are part of the British Isles, have less hostility to Americans than to the English. The two Uniteds are united. The unwilling are losing badly. The unwilling are unable. Disabled.

Germany's market is down 75% from its high three years ago—worse than 75% in real terms, since there has been a little inflation. That puts its bear market in a league with America's 1929–32 debacle. That period saw the S&P 500 down 86%, but the decline was partly offset by a 33% deflation. In real terms the US Great Crash came to 79%, in line with Germany's current crash. Very similar.

In 2000 financials were 33% of the German market, slightly more than tech was in America's market. But the German financials fell even more than the US tech stocks did. This sector is led by insurers instead of banks, and as stocks have fallen they have been forced to sell their own equity to meet regulatory requirements, driving their stocks lower still. These newly created shares provide newly created liquidity at depressed, fire sale prices. This vicious cycle won't end until global markets rise. But because of the forced equity sales, these insurers will have greater liquidity than their non-German peers after the dust settles, and they will be stronger for it. In sympathy with the insurers, everything else German is battered badly.

Pessimism is thick and pervasive. At a Munich-based German professional investor conference, sentiment is vastly more dour than in America. It's the war. Germans can't make sense of what is happening and see no way out. There is more talk here among professionals about surviving in money management than about the German stock market. How to cut costs. How to hunker down. How to survive regulatory scrutiny. Opportunity is obsolete in their minds. And Munich is ground zero as the insurance capital. The tower of dour.

But the *biergartens* are busy. Business on the streets isn't as bad as you read about. The economy is weak, but nothing near as weak as the stock market. The depression is more psychological than real. Older Germans, and most are, can't watch news of the war or even talk about it. They have talked themselves into a slump of despondency. Hence, there's opportunity.

As Iraq fades—and it will—so, too, will the coalition of the unwilling. With that, as markets rise in the two Uniteds, their overwhelming weight in the world will, through classic competitive sympathy buying, pull the non-United equity market up, too. And then Germany's market will rise, but more so. It will be led by the same insurers that dragged it down. Just as tech in America led the US market down but is now leading it up, the insurers that cost Germany so badly present great opportunity. Expect a reversal soon. ∎

Greed Is Good
May 26, 2003

If you didn't already know it by instinct, then the last four years should have taught you: When most investors are greedy, you should be fearful, and when most investors are fearful you should be greedy. Investors now get the first part of this rule, but not the last part. Fear is pervasive on Wall Street, so this is a good time to be greedy. Sell your timid Treasury bills. Buy stocks.

Financial markets are popularity contests. They discount commonly known information, whether the prospect of $1.10 a share in earnings for Microsoft this year or the risk that occupied Iraq will turn into a quagmire. Therefore it is pointless to worry about what others worry about. If you do and base market judgments on those worries you will be wrong more often than right.

Put it this way: If others worry about something, you just don't have to because they are doing it for you. You should worry about something else—namely, whatever they're not worried about.

In 1999 folks fretted over the Y2K bug in computer software. So that was one risk to the stock market you didn't have to spend any time on. In 2000 they worried about how to navigate the so-called new economy, hence one more thing safely ignored. Note, they did not worry about the economy going south. So you had to.

In late 2001 they began worrying about terrorists. Since then terrorist activity has declined. We didn't get the follow-on hit in the US we expected. Suicide bombings in Israel have declined from one a week to one a month. A year ago the big worry was corporate integrity. Since then a river of scandal (Enron, Arthur Andersen, Dynegy, WorldCom, Adelphia) has become a trickle of scandal (HealthSouth). The feared catastrophe that does not materialize creates an upward push on stocks when fear finally fades and demand for equities returns.

Of course, this year the masses worried about Iraq. So you didn't have to. Now they worry that in the war's wake the economy will weaken. So you don't have to. I'm not saying the economy will be gangbusters, only that it won't fall into recession.

What should you worry about now? Letting the new bull market get away from you. Almost no one worries about that. Here is why it's a real risk. First, invert the market's P/E into an E/P, an earnings yield to compare with interest rates. In 2000 it was markedly lower than fixed-income returns. Ten-year bonds yielded almost 7% and stocks' earnings yield was below 3.5%. Now, the bond yield is below 4% while the earnings yield on 2003 earnings is conservatively at 6%. Further, in the next decade the bond yield on current holdings can't grow.

The earnings yield will. Stocks aren't expensive.

Second, we've had three years in a row in which the return was below the market's long-term 10% average. In the S&P 500's history that has happened only seven times. On the previous six occasions the subsequent five-year return averaged 17% a year and was never negative; the ten-year performance averaged 12% a year and was never negative. Big performance numbers. You can't get them with bonds or cash. Cash yields 1% and change these days. The ten-year Treasury yields 4%. Whatever uptick you might or might not get over the next month on the T note, I can assure you that if you buy it now and hang on for ten years, you will get a 4% annual return.

You can expect far better from stocks over the next decade. Be greedy. Try to do even better still. ∎

Volatility, the Good Kind
June 23, 2003

Why is it hard for most stock investors to see a big rally ahead? Partly for the same reason most of them completely missed the last three negative years. Volatility blindness. Test yourself. What is the more likely return for the market in any given year—say, 2009: (a) something between 0% and 20%, or (b) something outside that range?

We're talking about total return, price appreciation plus dividends. The long-run average is 10% a year. Figuring that the results cluster closely around the average, most people would bet that (a) is the correct answer—that stocks return between 0% and 20% most of the time.

The truth is just the reverse. Since 1925 the market has fallen within the 0% to 20% band in 24 years, or 30% of the time. In 70% of the years the S&P 500's total return

was either better than 20% or negative. Big moves are the norm in the US.

The British stock market is less volatile; it falls outside the 0% to 20% range only 60% of the time. The French market is more volatile; it's outside the range 75% of the time.

Why do we expect so much more placidity from the market than it has historically demonstrated? Why, that is, do we have this cognitive blindness to volatility? It's natural. Our brains weren't set up to do the stock market. We got our information processors from ancestors eons ago. We are only here because they did well then and passed their genes on to us. Financial markets came much later.

In nature most phenomena follow normal distributions, meaning you can make a simple bell curve out of them and most occurrences cluster fairly consistently around the average—average rainfall, temperature, whatever. Equity returns, whether plotted daily, monthly or annually, do not follow a normal distribution. They are bimodal and skewed.

You can make the stock performance pattern look a little closer to normal by plotting it on a logarithmic scale, on which a +300% move looks exactly as big as a −75% move, a +33% move as big as a −25%. This is the so-called log-normal distribution talked about in finance textbooks. But even then the pattern doesn't fit very well. The stock market's history has been punctuated by too many big swings for it to fit under a log-normal curve. If stock market returns were normal or log-normal, the one-day move of more than -20% witnessed on October 19, 1987 would be well-nigh impossible.

Expecting normalcy where there was none, people were blind to how far volatility could carry the market up in the late 1990s and then down in the last three years. Now they are blind to the likelihood of a big upward move.

The bear market made it fashionable to say stocks might be flat for ten years or more. That's moronic. It has never, ever happened that stocks lie flat for a decade. Sometimes, rarely, the market is no higher ten years later. But there is too much volatility to ever have a ten-year period without huge moves within it. Up or down, it's still volatility.

Look at rolling ten-year periods in the history of the US market, and measure the size of the smallest round-trip, meaning moves from high to low and back within the decade. The quietest ten-year interval was 1963–72, when the swing was 34%. The biggest swing came in 1929–38, at 97%; the average swing was 57%. Those are big enough numbers to drive most folks crazy. Don't go crazy. After three bad years prepare yourself for upside volatility, the good kind. ∎

Dumb Bears II
July 21, 2003

"Supporting most bears right now is a bunch of bull: Namely, the notion that too much debt will bite us in the butt. Ever since last fall, the guts underlying gloom-and-doom market forecasts have been disproven, one by one. Excessive debt is the main argument that the bears still hug. Which is one reason the bull market has a long way to run;

the bears are basing their case on a wrong argument. Debt doomers come in varying styles. There is the banking-crisis style and the real-estate-implosion style—often linked, as in "falling real estate prices will bankrupt the banks, which will cause chaos." Then, too, are those noting the "tapped-out consumer," who can't or won't borrow more—thereby causing an anemic recovery, or no recovery; or, finally, the pseudo-sophisticate's favorite—the double "dip" recession.

Don't get me wrong. I don't recommend going into debt. Personally, I owe virtually no money. Certainly there are individuals, firms, industries and municipalities that are too heavily and stupidly leveraged and will pay for it dearly (as is always true).

However, in aggregate, debt levels won't hurt the economy or the stock market in the 1990s."

No, that "1990s" isn't a typo. The four paragraphs above were the beginning of my August 5, 1991 column, entitled "Dumb Bears." With this issue, as I start my 20th year as a Forbes columnist, I reach back 12 years to steal my own material, word for word—because so much of what I said about 1991 and 1992 plays well in 2003 and will in 2004. From a handful of those 1991–1992 columns I could lift paragraph after paragraph, and, with no more than the insertion of contemporary dates, they could serve for analysis of the here and now.

For your amusement, let me continue from the August 1991 column:

"And the tapped-out consumer? Historically silly. Consumers have always reacted conservatively to tough times—recoveries have never been fueled by consumer borrowing. Despite all you read, consumer debt as a percent of personal income has always been flat to down in the 18 months after a recovery's birth. That so many otherwise seemingly intelligent and educated seers seem to have so overlooked this fact is astounding. Consumer debt won't impede this recovery, just as it didn't fuel past ones."

Knowing that 1991 and 1992 were great times to buy and own stocks, you can be confident that now is a good time, too. Is it different now? Of course. But it's also much the same. The four most dangerous words in English: "It's different this time."

Bush I. Bush II. Take your pick of administrations. Bush I then had the highest popularity rating in the history of polling. Bush II now has the highest, longest average popularity of any President ever. It was and is the third year of a presidential term, when the market usually does well. So we are in a similar political cycle (although the first Bush didn't enjoy the advantage of a Republican Congress). More similar than different.

We fretted mightily over the market's high valuations then, and I wrote much about how that wouldn't stop the market. It won't now. We fretted over a weak economic recovery then, and now. Recall candidate Bill Clinton campaigning in 1992, with the slogan: "It's the economy, stupid"? The gurus then saw a below-average decade ahead, and they see the same now. Why? Because the prior decade had been too good for the next one to be anything but bad. The times ahead are going to be good. Enjoy them. ■

Professors and Markets

September 1, 2003

The professors are out in full force, warning you away from stocks. Their theory says that the "equity risk premium"—the extra reward you can expect from holding stocks rather than safer Treasury bonds—is at a low ebb. Don't be intimidated. These experts don't know any more than you and I do about what stocks are going to do over the next decade.

We have been treated to academic pronouncements at other turning points in investing history. In 1929, just before the Great Crash, the Yale economic genius Irving Fisher was famously quoted as saying that stocks had reached a "permanent high plateau." In October 1974, at what turned out to be the bottom of a bear market, academics could be heard explaining why stocks had to go lower. You may recall the Nobel laureates who presided over the demise of Long-Term Capital Management in 1999.

The academic theory is correct in saying that stock investors, in compensation for the extra risk they are taking on, need an extra return above that available on government bonds. That incremental return, historically, has been a big number, averaging about 5% annually.

But the problem comes in taking this theory into the future. Working from either fundamental data like earnings or from the notion that the market must revert to a mean following the 1982–2000 run-up, the academic analysts calculate that returns are now going to be disappointing. An article in the July 1 issue of *Fortune* homes in on a formula favored by noted University of Chicago professor Craig Asness. He says we now confront a meager 3% equity risk premium.

But let's be honest about what these professors of the dismal science are up to. If you're bearish, you can create an equity risk premium foreseeing low returns. To say you are bearish because your ERP calculation is bearish simply says you're bearish because you're bearish.

Try back-testing that Asness formula. I did. It would have produced gloomier forecasts throughout the 1980s and 1990s, actually being negative as both decades began. Why, if the formula flopped in the past two decades, won't it flop in the next one? These academic theorists are too cute by half.

Consider the total return on stocks since the beginning of the S&P 500 in 1926 versus that on the ten-year Treasury bond. On an annualized basis over rolling ten-year periods the extra return on stocks ranges from 18.5 percentage points above to 5 points below. There is no basis for saying that stocks' advantage over bonds is predestined to be 3 points or any other figure. Equity prices are determined by sweeping increases or decreases in the supply and demand for equity securities. There is simply no way to know what that will be seven to ten years from now.

Here's another would-be expert on the subject. July's *Investment Advisor* magazine bills Harold Evensky "the nation's most quoted financial planner." (Are we supposed to take that as a compliment? Isn't the most quoted expert the one most likely to follow the consensus, and isn't the consensus always wrong?) Evensky says in this piece, "I don't know anyone who has not accepted that returns will be lower in coming years, certainly not in professional circles." He is right. And that is one excellent reason to expect higher long-term returns.

I don't know where stocks will be ten years from now. But neither do the academics. Nor do you. We are all entitled to opinions, but they are nothing more than that. And we can all be wrong. What we can know is that right here and now, equities are doing just fine, beating cash or bonds this year handily. So don't be misled by the gloomy talk about the equity risk premium. ∎

Valuation Myths
September 29, 2003

Valuations are too high for a long bull market, right? Wrong! The S&P 500 has averaged a 12% total annual return over the last 40 years. It began this four-decade run with prices that average, from 1962 through 1963, 18 times expected earnings. That is about where we are today (if you look at earnings before nonrecurring charges).

Four decades ago the ten-year Treasury bond was yielding somewhere around 5%. That's about where it is now. If these levels didn't hurt buyers of stocks in 1962–63, why should they hurt today's buyers? Why won't the next 40 years be as good as the last 40? If you say you don't have 40 years, only 5, I would point out that 1963–68 was a good period in which to own stocks. Only 1 year? Okay, 1964 had a great return.

My point is this: For every period where high-P/E markets fizzled, there are comparable ones, of roughly similar frequency, where they did well. The market's average P/E ratio is a bad market forecaster. If you must do something with the ratio, turn it upside down, getting an earnings yield, an E/P. At the moment that number is 6% (again, on forward-looking earnings estimates). Then compare the E/P with interest rates. Over the long term a relationship between rate-adjusted E/Ps and future returns is discernible, and at least consistent with finance theory. But even this metric is useless in the short term.

Take advantage of the popular fear of P/E ratios. Bet against it. Few feared 2000's P/Es, because of the "new economy." Now that people think P/Es are too high, buy into the market.

Here's another red herring: volatility. Multitudes bemoan the fact that the VIX, the volatility index tied to put and call prices, is too low for stocks to shine. Supposedly the placidity of the market reflects excess optimism. Okay, a low VIX coincided with some dramatic market reversals, enough to convince the anecdotally inclined. But it also missed lots and has lousy overall statistics. The correlation coefficient between VIX and coming returns, over any period from a week to two years, is within a hair of zero. That means it explains nothing.

Yet another myth: Sentiment indexes are too optimistic for the market to go up. One such indicator is a survey of do-it-yourself investors by the American Association of Individual Investors; another is the *Investor's Intelligence* survey of newsletter writers. These indexes won't help you with the market, as Meir Statman and I demonstrated, at some statistical length, in the Spring 2000 *Journal of Portfolio Management*. The first survey tells you only what is happening now, not what is going to happen. The other indicator misses many turning points and flashes signals at wrong ones. That folks think these are predictive and bearish is useful if you know they really aren't. When they create fear, sentiment indicators are bullish.

September and October are the worst months for stocks, right? Nonsense and mythology! It goes both ways. Crashes have often happened then. But often not, too. As in other months.

This bull market's wall of worry will find more to fret about after October. Count on it. In the meantime real good news gets amazingly little press. Continental Europe's new but consistently advancing economic reformation gets scant notice in America. Throughout Europe, tax policies are becoming more benign. We rarely hear about how this shift could reignite growth.

Life will be good for the next few years, even in Europe. Get ahead of the market's response to the economic renaissance. ∎

Don't Sweat Small Moves

November 10, 2003

What counts is if the market rises or falls, right? Wrong! That's the wrong way to think. Divide the possible outcomes for the next year in stocks into four boxes: They go up a lot, up a little, down a little or down a lot. And only one of these four should have any impact on your thinking about whether to be in stocks or out. There is why.

It is easy to see that if you think the market is likely to rise a lot, you should own equities, and that if you think it is likely to fall far, you should be defensive. The other two are what confuse folks. Because the market is so much more volatile than we commonly envision, as detailed in my June 23 column, too few investors appreciate that they should simply ignore small moves—which happen often and mean little. If the market rises or falls 10% in the next quarter, it really isn't very important. It's the greater sweep over the next two or three years that matters.

Small up moves aren't worth worrying about; they are background music in a long-term trend that has stocks rising in two years out of three. Small down moves aren't worth being defensive against, because the transaction costs of moving in and out are much bigger than people think (include bid/ask spreads, market impacts of large orders, commissions and taxes). Even if you envision a small down move correctly, you can't save enough after transaction costs to make it worthwhile. And, of course, if your prediction is wrong and the market rises, you can pay a big opportunity cost.

So, exclude from consideration the gains and the small down moves. What's left are the uncommon bear markets. Since 1926 the S&P 500 index has suffered a loss (total return) of 10% or more in ten years, or 13% of that time. The percentage may surprise you, if the bear markets of 2000, 2001 and 2002 loom large in your memory, but it is the fact. The same frequency, more or less, is found in other Western markets. Focusing on that 13% can make sense. But thinking about getting defensive for any other reason is unwise.

How do you focus on that small percent of the time when the market might fall a lot? First, recall finance theory. The markets are discounters of all commonly known information. To make an excess return in the long term you must see something significant that others don't. Making decisions based on what you read commonly in the media and debate with friends is pointless, a fool's game.

Usually it's very hard to see something very terrible that others don't see. But this is the only correct basis for going defensive. The only one! Said otherwise: "What do you know that others don't know?" It's Wall Street's most basic question.

Rarely have I foreseen problems others haven't and urged defensiveness. In the 20 years I've written this column I've done it three times and three times only: in mid-1987, briefly; during 1989 and 1990; and for the first two-thirds of the recent bear market. I sure haven't done it perfectly. No one does.

But right now I don't see anything very bad, if you exclude the bad things that everyone sees and debates (the cost of the war, the trade deficit, massive debt). Hence, I'm not defensive. ∎

A Three-Year Bull Market

December 8, 2003

I see a silver lining in the cloud over the mutual fund business. Indeed, the after-hours trading scandal is bullish. It gives the first partial clues to how long this bull market may last—2006. How can that be? It has to do with the psychological forces driving the Wall Street prosecutions. The "all insiders are crooks" thinking is, for the moment, putting a lid on stock prices. When the psychological depression lifts, markets will climb higher.

In recent decades, behavioralists discerned a prime psychological force: the desire to "accumulate pride" and "shun regret" (detailed in my October 2, 2000 column). Accumulating pride is like this: "I bought it. It went up. I'm smart." Shunning regret is like this: "I bought it. It imploded. My broker misled me." The former associates success with skill and repeatability. The latter associates failure with victimization or bad luck. Doing both maximizes our motivation to keep trying. This kind of thinking goes back to the Stone Age, and it drives markets today.

The deep bear market of 2000–02 created a huge societal need to shun regret by finding scapegoats. First came the 2002 syndrome—that all chief executives are crooks, including Martha Stewart, et al. If our chief executives are bums, then we are not to blame for buying their stocks. But perhaps it slowly dawns on investors that, of the world's 20,000 public companies, we can pin something on executives at a few dozen firms at most. There are too few scapegoats to satisfy us.

So next we shifted to attack investment banker/broker dealers as slimy and as crooks. Now we're doing mutual funds. The very week that the lynching of Frank Quattrone dead-ended in a mistrial, the fund-trading scandal offered new opportunities to shun regret. New York State Attorney General Eliot Spitzer told us about short-term mutual fund trading done with the collusion of fund firms. A "sure thing" for a privileged paying few.

A lynch-mob mentality emerged almost overnight. The emotional value of the scandal: If money managers are crooks, then we aren't to blame for diving into their faddish tech funds at the peak of the market.

What Attorney General Spitzer doesn't want you to know is that hyperactive fund trading loses money on the whole. Sure, there were some lucky players; have a thousand gamblers toss coins and a few of them will get ten heads in a row. But I am convinced. After talking with a handful of securities lawyers who represent most of the mutual funds that the fund timers used, I know that as a group fund timers lost money. It will take three years of court cases for all this to come out.

Bullish Scapegoats

This period was indeed marked by a lot of regret-shunning and finger-pointing at various CEOs. Some were legitimate slimebags, as Ken described them. Many more were collateral damage, later vindicated (but you never hear about that later).

All that ill will against CEOs did help keep sentiment depressed in the coming years. If bull market tops are typically (though not always) marked by an excess of euphoria, misplaced dour sentiment can be useful in keeping a bull market alive.

Those who played the timing game with US and small-cap funds overwhelmingly lost money. A higher proportion of those doing it with foreign funds and aiming at overnight trades made money, but still, on balance, they lost. Fact: There is nothing about an overnight move on one side of the globe that tells you where the other side goes next. While counterintuitive, that fact is provable and long documented. If you place bets that Tokyo is going to go up on Wednesday because New York went up Tuesday, you lose as often as you win. Those who played this game were high-IQ morons. They saw themselves as clever folks taking advantage of loopholes. In reality they were more like some crazy guy running into a bank with a gun, yelling, "Steal my money—now!" They would have done better in Las Vegas.

Spitzer and company will hang high those few crazies who made money, those lucky head-flippers. What do we care? They're kangaroo-court victims but slimebags nonetheless. No one cares about slimebags. It will take three years of litigation to put all this behind us. That means three years before the psychological negativity now depressing prices fully lifts and with it fully lifts equities.

The bull market likely lasts longer than this nonsense. There is no real scandal. We're blind to American kangaroo courts because we believe in America. But kangaroo courts may keep a kangaroo bull market hopping maybe three more years. ∎

2004

If

" *There's no right way to make long-term market forecasts, as opposed to guesses. Those who say they 'know' where stocks will be in [ten years] are telling you more about what they don't know than what they do.* "

"My WAG Model," April 12, 2004

" *Ignore the long-term doomsters. The future is just beginning and will be awesome.* "

"Philip A. Fisher, 1907–2004," April 26, 2004

Ken's bullishness continued in 2004. "My 2004 forecast is for a very positive year … with the Morgan Stanley World Index (in dollar terms) up 20%—less blessed than 2003 but rosy nonetheless. The S&P 500 should do about 20%, too." ("A Lucky Year," February 16, 2004.)

Stocks rose in 2004 as Ken expected, but not quite as much as he hoped. A market pullback began in early March. It was shallow, with the S&P 500 falling only about 7 percent.[1] But it was long, extending well into August. Stocks finished the year strong, but not enough to reach Ken's 20 percent target. For the year, the Morgan Stanley World Index gained 15.2 percent, and the S&P 500 did a little worse, rising 10.9 percent.[2]

Ken also forecast a strong bond market and steady interest rates in 2004. Using the same bell curve analysis he used for stocks, Ken saw most forecasters expected substantially higher interest rates in 2004. "This year's forecasters universally called for rising rates, on both long- and short-term bonds. I say the crowd is wrong and rates will be flat to down from where they are now." ("The Benign-Rate Scenario," May 24, 2004.) But it wasn't just forecasters' opinions that shaped Ken's view on bonds. He also saw productivity gains keeping inflation in check and demand from Asia for US bonds buoying bond prices. Ten-year Treasuries began 2004 with a 4.27 percent yield and finished with a 4.24 percent yield[3]—almost perfectly flat as Ken predicted.

Stocks and bonds did well in 2004, but losses suffered that year were far more sorrowful than investment returns could ever be. In March, in one of the deadliest terrorist attacks since September 11, 2001, explosives planted on commuter trains in Madrid, Spain, killed 191. In December, a tsunami in Southeast Asia was far more destructive, resulting in approximately 230,000 casualties. And Ken suffered a great personal loss with the passing of his father, Philip A. Fisher.

In his April 26, 2004 column "Philip A. Fisher, 1907–2004," Ken pays tribute to his father—a legendary investor and author—and recalls some of the lessons his dad taught him. Among them (paraphrased):

- "Always think long term."
- "In your bones believe in capitalism."
- "Buy what you understand."
- "Be yourself."

His dad also recommended Ken read Rudyard Kipling's poem "If" every month. (Ken keeps it by his desk and a copy in his wallet. Ken believes, as his father did, its message is central to dealing with volatile capital markets—particularly so if you do it as publicly as Ken does.) Here it is so you can do so yourself.

If

If you can keep your head when all about you
Are losing theirs and blaming it on you;
If you can trust yourself when all men doubt you,
But make allowance for their doubting too:
If you can wait and not be tired by waiting,
Or, being lied about, don't deal in lies,
Or, being hated, don't give way to hating,
And yet don't look too good, nor talk too wise;

If you can dream—and not make dreams your master;
If you can think—and not make thoughts your aim,
If you can meet with Triumph and Disaster
And treat those two impostors just the same;
If you can bear to hear the truth you've spoken
Twisted by knaves to make a trap for fools,
Or watch the things you gave your life to, broken,
And stoop and build 'em up with worn-out tools;

If you can make one heap of all your winnings
And risk it on one turn of pitch-and-toss,
And lose, and start again at your beginnings,
And never breathe a word about your loss:
If you can force your heart and nerve and sinew
To serve your turn long after they are gone,
And so hold on when there is nothing in you
Except the Will which says to them: "Hold on!"

If you can talk with crowds and keep your virtue,
Or walk with Kings—nor lose the common touch;
If neither foes nor loving friends can hurt you;
If all men count with you, but none too much;
If you can fill the unforgiving minute
With sixty seconds' worth of distance run,
Yours is the Earth and everything that's in it,
And—which is more—you'll be a Man, my son!

—**Rudyard Kipling**

The Great Humiliator

January 12, 2004

How long should this bull market last? Until the last bear cries uncle. I'm waiting for most of the big-name investors who were pound-the-table bearish as 2003 began to either capitulate or be publicly ridiculed. That hasn't happened yet.

The market is the Great Humiliator. It wants to humiliate everyone but has a strong preference for the biggest and most famous.

That's how the 1990s boom played out. It didn't—couldn't—end until the seers who were bearish in the mid-1990s became bullish or were derided as quacks. Longtime bear Charles Clough, Merrill Lynch's chief strategist, was openly fired and replaced by longtime bull Christine Callies in June 2000. Almost perfect timing—backwards! That was when the two-and-a-half-year bear market was just getting under way.

Over those two and a half years every important bull either caved in and turned bearish or was painted as powerless by the press. Christine Callies took her turn on the execution block. Unbendingly bullish, she was booted for value-based permabear Richard Bernstein in January 2002. Poor Merrill! Self-lynched again.

Other bulls who either gave up or were sent packing: Edward Kerschner of UBS PaineWebber (cameoed in my October 15, 2001 column as a reverse indicator); Jeffrey Applegate, who was publicly squeezed from Lehman Brothers in November 2002; James Weiss at State Street Research.

To kill the bull market that started a year ago, the same eternal invisible hand must unseat most of the current bears. They must either do an about-face, turning bullish, or else be cast out as kooks.

Which bear will be undone first? Merrill's Richard Bernstein is an obvious candidate. Merrill is a long tradition. Bernstein has done some fantastic intellectual work on market sentiment. I respect him. We owe him. But he misunderstands some aspects of behavioral psychology that underlie his work. And he has been wrong in his predictions. The Great Humiliator won't care that we owe him for his earlier contributions.

Another likely victim is Robert Shiller, the widely revered Yale academic whose book *Irrational Exuberance*, appearing on the eve of the 2000–03 crash, was brilliantly timed. Professor Shiller's admirers forget, though, that he was bearish throughout the 1990s. Another famous bear is Jeremy Grantham of money-management firm Grantham, Mayo, Van Otterloo. Then my favorite: Bill H. Gross of Pimco, the world's most famous bond manager and maybe the best. Early in 2003 Gross authored a widely circulated white paper explaining why stocks were overvalued and should perform poorly. So far, no peep of rebuke! That's very bullish, because the bear market won't come until the media attack folks like Gross.

Others: Richard Pell of Julius Baer Investment Management, Douglas Cliggott of Brummer & Partners (formerly of JP Morgan), Carlos Asilis and Stephen Roach; newsletter writers Robert Prechter, Richard Russell and Martin Weiss; and fellow *Forbes* columnists James Grant and Gary Shilling.

Some bears maintain their pessimistic proclivities by claiming 2003 as a counterrally in a longer bear market. But my reading of history says the move to date is already too big for the Great Humiliator not to have his way. So buy and hold until you hear that beautiful hum—of bears either turning tail or being humiliated. None of them has gotten really ridiculed, yet. This is not to say that they won't stand their ground and may be vindicated years later. But until the public turns against them, this most enjoyable bull market has legs. ∎

A Lucky Year

February 16, 2004

At *Forbes*, the first column of the year is expected to be a confessional. How did we do last year? Which of our winners should be held, which closed out? And do we tell readers to stick by a loser?

This time the exercise occasions no great pain. Last year was probably my best in 20 years as a columnist here. I've done this report card column 18 times previously, starting in January 1986 with a review of my 1985 recommendations. In 2003, I was very lucky. If I believed the superstition that a coin that has come up heads repeatedly is particularly likely to land tails the next time, I would be very worried about 2004.

Beginning with my January 6 column, I remained unwaveringly bullish. My forecast at that point called for the stock market to be up 35% in 2003, which would make it one of the best years ever. I was the most bullish forecaster in America publishing in a periodical of wide circulation. I was too optimistic—but amazingly lucky.

The world stock market, which I take as my benchmark, was up 33%. The S&P 500 was up 29%. Pretty close. If there was someone closer, tell me about it (or tell *Forbes* at editor@Forbes.com).

My 2004 forecast is for a very positive year, too, with the Morgan Stanley World Index (in dollar terms) up 20%—less blessed than 2003 but rosy nonetheless. The S&P 500 should do about 20%, too. Next month I'll detail my reasoning behind this bullish forecast.

Last January I said George Bush and the Republicans would, in posturing for 2004's election, keep away from any drastic moves on Capitol Hill. Right! The Republicans gained strategically against the Democrats all year long. They won the bulk of major elections. Their good luck continued with a redistricting in Texas (the occasion of a court battle and much histrionics) that will give them more seats in Congress in the coming election. Whoever wins the Democratic nomination will have an uphill battle against the President.

In the March 3 column I detailed how the money market experts were expecting big upward moves in both short- and long-term interest rates and how the uniformity of their views was a signal the rate rise wouldn't happen. It didn't. Now the interest rate professionals are again saying rates will rise materially in 2004. But rates won't change much at all.

In the March 31 column I noted that consensus expectations foresaw pension-plan underfunding as hurting earnings and stocks.

My contrarian take was that this was all bullish. I argued that pension sponsors' putting cash into underfunded plans would provide a boost for the market. I mentioned General Motors. By year-end no scourge from pensions had developed to blight stocks, and GM's plan was fully funded.

Now let's look at the record on stock picks. *Forbes'* statisticians assume that you lose 1% to commissions and bid/ask spreads on your recommended trades and compare the result with the performance of a commission-free investment on the same date in the S&P 500.

By this measure my picks beat the market on average by 14%. This formula is too kind to my results last year, since I am trying to beat a global index. Last year the Morgan Stanley World Index did 5% better than the S&P 500, so I was beating my own target by only 9%.

My best recommendation was Research in Motion (currently at $77), maker of the BlackBerry, at $22, in the July 21 issue. BlackBerry may be the best electronic product of the last five years. If it can keep pace with Microsoft and others in the market for combo phone-palmtop appliances, it will own the world. But having come so far in 2003, I doubt the stock can beat the market in 2004, too. Out it goes. We can revisit it later.

I can't possibly have a better overall 2004 than my 2003, so I'll have to do worse. But I hope you'll keep reading—even if you are superstitious about lucky pennies. ∎

Bush's Bull Market
March 15, 2004

A particularly bullish tendency can be found in years when we reelect presidents. Markets hate uncertainty. An easy reelection makes investors feel less certain.

I said last month that the world stock market should be up 20% in 2004, and I'm sticking to the forecast. As I see it, there are only two plausible outcomes for stocks this year, either a loss or a very big gain. A loss is very unlikely. So I see a good 20% as the result to bet on.

My reasoning, detailed at some length in my March 3, 2003 and February 4, 2002 columns, has to do with betting against the crowd. I build bell curves of forecasts by market pros, and then work on the assumption that the end result will be anywhere but the middle of the curve—because markets have a way of surprising the pros. Not surprising every forecaster, to be sure, just the ones who stick close to the consensus.

This year the hump in the curve spans from flat to being up 20%. Expect the market to land outside that range. That means if you agree that we are not going to have a bear market in 2004, you should expect a very good year for equities.

I also expect less variation between markets than we saw in recent years. Why? The bell curves from various countries and sectors fit together that way now. The same line of reasoning tells me that global interest rates will be much more benign than forecasters expect. My most controversial forecast may be about currencies. The consensus is that the dollar will suffer a further weakening against a world basket of currencies. I expect the greenback to strengthen by year-end.

We may encounter some other surprises this year—surprises that will combine to help the stock market. One of them is a reduction in the risk of terrorism (the consensus is more or less that we're in for some mass destruction). Another positive surprise: Combined federal and state budget deficits will twist unexpectedly to a more benign total than today's consensus.

Politics favors a rise in the US stock market, and the US will tug overseas markets up with it. It's an election year. Election years tend to be positive for the stock market. In the history of the S&P 500 Index, which begins in 1926, there have been only three presidential election years that ended down: first as the Great Depression bottomed in 1932, then as World War II began in 1940 (and Roosevelt became the first President to seek a third term) and finally as the tech sector blew up in 2000. It takes a big problem, in other words, to derail the positive momentum of an election year.

When we have Presidents seeking reelection, it's more bullish than years of open races, like 2000 was. Markets hate uncertainty. An easy reelection makes investors feel less uncertain. Better the devil they know.

I am no fan of George W. Bush, but I predict he will be reelected easily. Even if I am wrong, we still have an election year, and it's still more likely to be a year with a 20%-plus gain than a year of loss. (And if you are a Bush fan, please don't hate me. I have bad things to say about most Presidents, Democrat or Republican; my eccentric pick for favorite President is Millard Fillmore.)

In the whole 20th century we refused reelection to only five residents of the White House: Taft, Hoover, Ford, Carter and Bush the elder. Also note that the Democrats are going to nominate a senator, and there have been only two Presidents of either party ever elected straight from the Senate floor: Harding and Kennedy. Recent Senate losers include Dole, McGovern and Goldwater. For that matter, who was the last Democrat elected who wasn't southern? Kennedy. And who last won advocating tax hikes? Gotcha!

There is more to favor a Bush win. He's in the majority party. He has an overwhelming campaign fundraising advantage. Our economy is now too strong to throw out an incumbent. Bush defines the Democrat more than vice versa. It's a cakewalk, becoming clear by November. By then you will see higher prices on stocks. ∎

My WAG Model
April 12, 2004

How well will stocks do over the next decade? There have been oodles of pundits suggesting that they will go nowhere. The proposition that they will just stay flat for ten years running is, of course, absurd; stocks gyrate wildly. The talking heads, rather, mean that average annual equity returns will be somewhere around zero. That's almost as absurd. My guess—and at least I'm willing to admit that it is no more than a guess—is that stocks' total return will average something better than 7% per year over the next decade.

There is no right way to make long-term market forecasts, as opposed to guesses. Those who say they "know" where stocks will be in 2014 are telling you more about what they don't know than what they do.

Future stock prices are determined by shifts in supply and demand for equities. None of us wakes up thinking about supply and demand for equities. If you do, you're weird. Our brains think about almost anything else when it comes to stocks.

But it's definitely true that supply and demand determine the prices of things, and that fact is as true of equities as it is of oil and hotel room rates. In the short term it's demand that is the driver of where stocks go, because supply, in the sense of how many shares are outstanding, is pretty much constrained. If Microsoft wants to sell 10 million new shares to expand, it has to file papers with the Securities & Exchange Commission and wait around for a while.

In the long term, supply is quite elastic, meaning that it can respond in a powerful way to prices. Keep the prices of equities low, as they were 25 years ago, and companies retire more shares than they issue. Raise the prices high enough, as happened five years ago, and all kinds of issuers come out of the woodwork with share offerings. In the long term, shifts in supply are nearly all-powerful in setting equity prices.

Note that, over the last 20 years the total return (share appreciation plus dividends) on US stocks averaged 12.4% a year, while the combined market value of US stocks climbed 22.6% a year, or 10.2 percentage points more. The difference is new supply. Had there been less of it, stocks would have done better. Had new issuance been more, they would have done worse. We have no capital markets science or technology with which to forecast long-distant shifts in equity supply. We simply have no clue. Hence we can't make precise long-term forecasts of returns.

So why do I guess stocks will exceed 7% per year on average through 2014? Stocks compete against bonds, specifically low-grade corporate bonds. Think like an accountant and recall where both sit on a balance sheet—one atop the other on the right-hand side. Enter my WAG model. All scientists know WAG models—the "wild-ass guess." And that's all this is. Now, measure the prospective return on low-grade bonds by the yield on Baa (low investment-grade) issues. In 78% of all ten-year periods since 1925, average stock returns have beaten the beginning Baa yield. The only times this wasn't true were long ago. The last was the period 1981–90, when the Baa yield started at 16.8%. Before that the exceptions were decades beginning in 1972 and 1973, near the big market top.

In some ten-year periods stocks beat the Baa rate by a lot, in some periods by a little. So, after a three-year bear market starting in 2000, I'm more than 75% confident stocks will beat the current 6.2% Baa yield over the next decade. With demand for stocks rising in the short term, I'm even more confident this is a great year for stocks. ∎

Philip A. Fisher, 1907–2004
April 26, 2004

Phillip A. Fisher died March 11 at 96 from old age. He was a great man. Not in his last years, ravaged by dementia. Then he was just a little old man. But he was my little old man. I will love him, forever! Among the pioneer, formative thinkers in the growth stock school of investing, he may have been the last professional witnessing the 1929 crash to go on to become a big name.

His career spanned 74 years—but was more diverse than growth stock picking. He did early venture capital and private equity, advised chief executives, wrote and taught. He had an impact. For decades, big names in investing claimed Dad as a mentor, role model, inspiration or whatever.

His first book, *Common Stocks and Uncommon Profits*, appeared in 1958. It was the first investment book ever to make the *New York Times* bestseller list. It's still in print at Wiley.

Phil Fisher was one of only three people ever to teach the investment course at Stanford's Graduate School of Business. He taught Jack McDonald, the course's current professor. For 40 years Jack has seen to it that you can't get past that class without reading Phil Fisher. Dad last lectured at Stanford for Jack four years ago. He had a knack for getting great minds to think their own thoughts—but bigger than they would have conceived otherwise on their own. Many disciples described this experience to me.

People presume I learned lots about stocks from him. Not really! He got me started and then I fashioned my own notions, as did everyone else he influenced. Much more important in making me who I am were his early 1950s bedtime stories. He conceived stunning adventure tales of pirates, explorers, kings and crooks.

The fictional hero was Jerry Clerenden. I couldn't fathom this at the time but I realized later that this character was created as the person Dad wanted me to be. His stories drove me to dream bigger visions than most children are allowed.

He was small, slight, almost gaunt, timid, forever fretful. But great minds drew insights out of him like water from a well.

His views are in his writings and those of others. I won't repeat. What remains unsaid? What would he think now if he were alive and in his right mind?

First, always think long term. A short-term horizon, if it is relevant at all, is a mere tactical tool to get to your long-term future. Thinking long term usually goes hand in hand with a low turnover of a portfolio. My father bought Motorola in 1955, when its main attraction was radio systems. He still owned it at his death.

Next, every single month read Phil Fisher's favorite poem, Rudyard Kipling's oft-quoted "If," to help you become Jerry Clerenden.

In your bones believe in capitalism and its basic ability, despite recessions and scandals, to better the human condition. From that belief you can conclude that, over the long term, the stock market works. It is better to come to this conclusion from faith than from studying a column of statistics.

Buy what you understand. You can hear Peter Lynch in that. And not too many stocks. You hear Warren Buffett in that. In his prime, Dad owned about 30 stocks. And diversify into different types, and not only your favorite types, so you have ones that work when your favorites fail.

Don't try to be Phil Fisher. Or Warren Buffett or Peter Lynch or anyone else. Be yourself, but be more energetic and imaginative than you thought you could be. Dream bigger.

I remember what my father said eight years ago to James W. Michaels, then the editor of this magazine: "What are you doing your competitors aren't doing yet?" At the time Jim Michaels had been in the job for 35 years, but he was no less imaginative than he had been at the start.

Try posing that question about some cherished company in your portfolio. What is the management doing that the competition is not doing? Great managements live the answer and in the process create great stocks.

Ignore the long-term doomsters. The future is just beginning and will be awesome. My father would say technology offers society a bounty in the decades ahead that is vastly underestimated even by technologists. Still, it is as powerful to invest in companies adopting technology as those creating it. With either, he would urge buying stocks of firms he called "fundamental." You don't buy assets or earnings but the overall endeavor. I'll have stocks for you next month. ∎

The Benign-Rate Scenario
May 24, 2004

I'm not wavering from my earlier (February 16) forecast that US stocks would be up 20% in 2004, even though the market has delivered a return of only 2% in the first four months. My reasoning had to do with the fact that most experts were predicting anything but returns near that 20%—and that markets always veer off from the consensus forecast. Now here's another reason for a bullish view: Interest rates should also be more benign than what's expected in the consensus view.

A bull market for bonds (low rates, that is) tends to go hand in hand with a bull market for stocks, and for good reason. A stock is a claim to a stream of future earnings. Discounted to present dollars, that stream is worth more when interest rates, and thus the discounting factor, are lower. To put it another way: The earnings return on risky equity has to compete with the coupon return on safer bonds. If bond rates are low, the earnings yield on stocks can be low, too, and that means the inverse, the price/earnings ratio, can be high.

Just as I do for stock markets, I build bell curves of professional interest-rate forecasts. This year's forecasters universally called for rising rates, on both long- and short-term bonds. I say the crowd is wrong, and rates will be flat to down from where they are now.

On ten-year Treasury notes the experts envision rates rising from January's 4.25% to somewhere between 4.5% and 6% by year-end. The average forecast is 5.2%. The

The Stock-Bond See-Saw Myth

Investors tend to believe when stocks go up, bonds go down, and vice versa—always. Not so. Very often, as Ken points out here, bonds can go up when stocks do (though usually less than stocks) and certainly lose value when stocks drop. However, stocks, historically, are more volatile year to year, so a good year for bonds might mean a terrific year for stocks.

crowd-is-wrong theory says that the note's yield will end the year anywhere but in the 4.5%-to-6% range, where the experts' darts are clustered.

I don't see how the ten-year rate can wind up north of 6%. There is too much productivity improvement. Another phenomenon is that Asian central banks are forced to buy dollars and dollar-denominated debt as a way of keeping their countries' exports affordable. That buying helps keep rates down.

It's happening. Despite beginning-of-the-year forecasts for massive short- and long-term rate increases, there hasn't been much movement. The 90-day T-bill is essentially unchanged since New Year's, and the benchmark ten-year Treasury is up a mere quarter percentage point.

Asia's effect is misinterpreted. Remember the formula from your college economics course: MV=PQ. Quantity of money times velocity of money equals price level times real gross domestic product. "Velocity" here means how many times a dollar changes hands in the course of producing a dollar of GDP. Money velocity is lower in Japan and China than here—for a lot of reasons, notably having to do with the greater deployment of credit cards and teller machines in the US. That means the quantity of money in Asia is relatively high in relation to GDP. Indeed, Japan's monetary base (currency plus deposits at the central bank) is now larger than America's, even though our economy is 2.5 times as big.

The relatively larger Asian money supplies mean that Asian central banks have a disproportionately large impact on the global money supply and thus on global interest rates and stocks. Last year China, for example, with a money supply almost as big as ours, increased its money supply 20%. It can't scale back that rapid growth without inducing a recession, so it won't scale back. This flood of paper is keeping a lid on interest rates, not just in Shanghai but in New York, too.

Efficient Chinese savers seek safe, fixed-income returns in both Europe and the US. Despite speculators' huge bets on a falling dollar this year, the greenback has risen 2.7% against global currencies and almost all major ones, except sterling. The benign effect of Asian money supply expansion is low interest rates and high stock prices in the US and Europe. Here are four ways to participate. They all relate to the auto sector, itself a prime beneficiary of low rates, which make its products more affordable to people buying cars on credit. ∎

Road Map 2004
June 21, 2004

While 2004's stock market has started off bleakly, abundant reason exists for optimism here and now. Stand your ground. Buy stocks. Historical patterns strongly lean toward the likelihood that 2004 will end with a gain for the stock market. As my March column detailed, presidential election years are almost never down years for the broad US stock market. Since 1899 there have been 26 quadrennial elections; in only 4 of these years did the market fall.

To refine history a bit more: In 18 of these elections an incumbent was running, and the index showed a yearly decline in only 2 of those cases. Now, to press the statistics to their limit: You could further look at the 13 election years in which an incumbent was reelected, and you would find that the market was up for all but one of the years and that the average total return for all 13 was 15.8%. So, better if Bush is reelected, but either way I am expecting an up move for US stocks between now and December.

You should not, of course, get carried away with historical statistics, which have, after all, a large element of randomness built into them. But there are good reasons that stocks should do well when politicking is at its peak. This has to do with the fact that markets (a) abhor risk and (b) anticipate what's around the corner by half a year or so.

Elections represent risk of change. Markets hate uncertainty for largely the same reason you hate losses more than you like gains. It is basic to behavioral psychology. If some group wins political power and all that goes with it, others lose power. But the losers hate it more than the winners love it, so overall we feel worse.

Anticipating the uncertainty, investors sour on stocks in the late spring of an election year, then turn bullish later. As November nears with a victor, the risk and the uncertainty diminish. We (usually) have a pretty good idea who's going to get the White House, and we can live with the consequences, even if the probable winner is not the fellow we want. This is the usual pattern, even though there are exceptions; the uncertainty in 2000 remained almost until Inauguration Day.

The average first-quarter total return for stocks in those 26 election years was a gain of 2.3%. The average for April plus May together was a decline of 1%. Over the next three months the market has averaged a 7.6% gain. September and October add 1.7% more. November plus December see a 3.3% gain on average.

This year comes close to fitting the pattern. There was some early bullishness followed by a weak month or two. More likely than not: We're going to see a summer rally and positive continuation to year-end. ∎

Value Made Easy
July 26, 2004

It is fashionable but wrong to think cheap stocks are now effectively non-existent. Cheap stocks are plentiful. Now there are a lot of ways to define cheapness, but here is a simple formula: A stock is cheap if its earnings yield—earnings divided by the share price—is better than the yield on medium-grade corporate bonds. Lots of companies meet that definition.

What about the prospect of rising interest rates? That would raise the hurdle for the earnings yield and put some companies out of the running as potentially cheap buys. Except for one thing: Earnings may rise just as fast as interest rates.

The Baa bond rate, the rate for companies at the low end of the investment-grade spectrum, is 6.75%. Any stock with a price/earnings ratio of 14.8 or less has an earnings yield better than 6.75% and is cheap by our definition. What happens if the Baa bond rate climbs a point to 7.75%? The stock is still a buy if by then its earnings have also climbed by 14.8% or more. I am less worried than most people about rising interest rates. But even if rates go up more than I expect, I think that many of today's bargains will in hindsight still look like bargains, because their earnings will climb faster than interest rates.

Here are five cheap stocks. Three of them are in the oil business, but my bullish case does not rest on any assumption about sharply rising oil prices.

Despite what you may think, oil stocks mostly move with the market. So, being bullish, right now I like America's fourth-largest integrated energy company, Marathon Oil. It lagged the sector for years, but I expect it to pick up as its margin improves relative to those of its peers It offers broad global exposure to the full spectrum of petroleum-related activities and has made a host of recent discoveries in Angola, Norway and the Gulf of Mexico, as well as a purchase in Russia. With 5,700 retail outlets, its refining and marketing operations are the largest in the Midwest. You are buying at a price that is equal to 30% of annual sales and 11 times trailing earnings and with a 2.9% dividend yield.

Tidewater, a drilling service firm and a dog for years, is soon to have its day. It's the world's biggest operator of offshore supply vessels, spanning most of the big offshore oil and natural gas basins in the world. Its nearly 600 vessels do everything from transporting roughnecks between oil platforms to towing mobile drilling rigs. It has renovated much of its fleet from smaller older vessels to larger modern ones, boosting efficiency. At 1.2 times book value, with a 2.1% dividend yield, it's cheap at a time when the oil companies are spending more on exploration.

Maverick Tube is the largest North American producer of tubular steel for oil and natural gas wells and pipelines. Its industrial unit makes coil tubing and pipes. You can get this company at 1.1 times sales (market capitalization of $1 billion compared with revenue of $900 million) and ten times likely 2004 earnings.

Virtually everyone expects interest rates to skyrocket. I've explained before (see my May 24 column) why that outcome is unlikely. If I'm right that rate increases will be modest, midsize banks will be conspicuous beneficiaries. Particularly nice is Hibernia. Long sleepy as Louisiana's leader, it has awakened from its hibernation. At 13 times likely 2004 earnings, and 2 times book value, it trades at slight sector discounts stemming from credit quality problems dating back to the 1990s. With its credit turnaround, a powerful brand name in its home state and a presence in the fast-growing Texas market, this is a bayou beauty. The managers are reducing loan portfolio risk even as they build up sales. If the stock doesn't emerge on its own, the company will be acquired by a national outfit seeking regional strength. Collect a 2.9% dividend until then.

Benchmark Electronics provides contract manufacturing services to electronics firms. It managed tech's downturn better than most peers, but the stock has suffered valuation penalties because of its linkage with troubled Sun Microsystems. Still, Benchmark has clipped the Sun exposure to one-third of revenues from more than half. That fraction will keep falling as dozens of new programs ramp for other customers. Benchmark is, for example, strong with medical technology outfits, making devices like pacemakers and test instruments. With revenue diversity will come a higher valuation. Beyond internally grown programs it has the financial strength to acquire diversification and customers where needed within contract manufacturing. At 60% of annual sales and 18 times expected 2004 earnings, this fast-growing tech stock can help your portfolio exceed its own benchmark. ∎

Stocks for an Iffy Investor
September 6, 2004

Unsure of the market's direction? Whenever I'm on edge about the stock market I take comfort in compartmentalizing the possible outcomes. The market can do any of four things: go up a lot, go up a little, go down a little or go down a lot. It's only in the last case that you should really regret not having gone to cash, and the last case occurs only rarely. Returns below 20% have occurred in only 6% of the calendar years since 1925.

Unless I think I see big, bad things others don't see, I can't justify a down-a-lot forecast, since the market is a discounter of all known information. That means that bad stuff we already know (war, deficits, you name it) is already priced into stocks, so you gain nothing by selling. That fact helps explain why I almost always own stocks.

What should you do if you are persuaded that the market is destined to decline just a little? Nothing. It costs too much (taxes, commissions, price spreads) to move out and in for a brief interval. Remember, too, that a downward blip tends to be over before long. Also remember that you might be wrong. Much more of the time than not, stocks rise. Often they rise when there seems no good reason.

Sometimes I'm wildly bullish, expecting the up-a-lot outcome. That is, I think I see big, good factors others don't see. But again, the only basis for such an extreme view is if you think you see something others don't.

I remain optimistic for a big upward move ahead. Partly it is because economic sentiment is dour, while the economy progresses quite nicely. But just as important, I am bullish because I see a lot of great stocks to buy. This year, with the S&P 500 off 3% since January 1, the bargains have gotten more visible. But even if you are much less sanguine than I, you should be in stocks. Just look for unappreciated quality. That way, if stocks do sour, you are likely to lose less than the market as a whole. If stocks soar, you participate.

What do I mean by quality? Firms that are leaders in their fields. Maybe, because of past problems, profits are down or margins are thin. But if the firm has a competitive advantage, it should be able to turn more of its sales dollars into profit dollars. Signs of market leadership: high market share, prestige customers, lower costs, unique distribution or regional dominance. ∎

Those Bearish Brits
October 4, 2004

One reason this stock market is so spiffy is that journalists are so dour on it. They reflect and, in fact, promote low investor sentiment. The setting is perfect for a nice rebound. The journalists I have in mind are primarily not from the US but from Europe. But since the stock market is largely global, America's market won't go far in any direction without the rest of the world in parallel. And the rest of the world has economic writers aplenty who are down on the stock market.

In America the scribblers are somewhat mixed, but overseas they're morose, depressed, sarcastic. Just back from the *Forbes* Cruise for Investors, I took some side time to visit a swath of British business journalists. Simply reading the British media, and there is a lot of it, you can't find one important writer who doesn't think stocks will fall and interest rates will rise markedly. They're consistently bearish. They think British markets will fare badly and American and the other European ones will fare worse. That's a bullish sign for me. I love it.

Several then wrote about my visit and my optimism and why they think I'm wrong. But none cited arguments that aren't cited by everyone and hence already discounted in pricing. It is fashionable in Britain to think that the media are always uniformly sour on stocks, but I've probed them regularly for years, and it isn't true. Memories are short. In 2000 economic writers were optimistic, specifically on tech. Even in 2002 they could hear a bullish argument. They can't now.

With time they will revert to more optimism, and with it provide motivation for readers to buy. You want to buy before their readers do.

The same is largely true across Europe. In Germany and France, in particular, writers are depressed. There is nothing so pleasing to see as depressed journalists. (Well, maybe depressed, unemployed lawyers are more fun to see. But that's a different story.) Another reason I like this spiffy market is that so many great companies sell on par to the market's average valuations. ∎

When Earnings Are Cheap
November 1, 2004

Whenever you have doubts about the US stock market, you should take a step back and look at the whole world. Markets elsewhere may give you some reassurance that the phenomenon you see at home is or is not a fluke. Foreign data help you check US reality.

Suppose someone tells you "X" causes "Y" in our stock market. And your observation of American history suggests it's true. If it's really true, and not some statistical coincidence, then it will work similarly— not exactly in the same way, but similarly— in Britain, Germany, France, Italy, Spain and Japan.

One phenomenon I have in mind relates to earnings yields and bond yields. The earnings yield on a stock is the earnings divided by the share price. It's the flip side of the price/earnings ratio. General rule: When earnings yields are higher than bond yields, stocks are cheap.

It works here and it works abroad. Between 1974 and 1982 the earnings yield was steadily above the bond yield, a great long core period to buy stocks. The same was true in Britain and much of the Continent. Contrast that with what was going on five years ago, when the earnings yield on the S&P 500 was only 3.5%, while ten-year government bonds were yielding 7.6%. Not a good time to load up on equities.

Stocks are, in fact, good to own— better than bonds—most of the time. But that is because future earnings growth has boosted the subsequent average earnings yield above initial levels and initial bond rates. Tracking it through history, usually the current earnings yield is a little below government bond rates. Earnings yields at or above bond yields are exceptional. When you see that inversion of the normal relationship, you probably should be buying stocks.

Which means you should buy now. At a recent 1120, the S&P 500 is going for 16 times this year's 2004 earnings (before nonrecurring items) of $70. Turn it around and you have an earnings yield of 6.2%. That's a terrific earnings yield, compared with the 4.2% you get on a ten-year Treasury. It's even pretty good-looking against the 6.2% return on Baa corporates, as reported by Moody's.

Now earnings yields are above bond yields all over the developed world — in Japan, for the first time in modern history. It gets better than this. The best time of all to own stocks is when the earnings yield is good, yet mainstream expert opinion says stocks are overpriced. You are buying, and you are betting against the crowd. When the crowd comes to its senses, it will bid up the prices of the shares you own. Put it this way: When the experts think stocks are appallingly priced, but stocks are, in fact, appealingly priced, then stocks are very appealing. ∎

The Coming Melt-Up
November 29, 2004

I'm looking for a melt-up. The postelection rally of November is just a down payment on what should be a terrific market for stocks in 2005. Next year will be a lot like 2003, when the S&P 500 index was up 28.7%, dividends included. I have to confess that in my columns last spring I was expecting a strong second half of 2004 and was wrong. But that makes me more optimistic for 2005. We get part of what should have been the 2004 rally added to 2005.

Nowadays everyone has heard that the first year of the term of a President, even a returning one, is typically weakest of the four. This oft-quoted statistical fact is misleading. It is true that the average of all first years is low (from 1929 to 2001, the 19 first years have averaged a total return of 7.5%), and in 10 of these the number was negative. But look more closely. In the 9 first years with gains, the gains have been big, averaging 28.4%. I think next year will fall into the gain column and that it will fit the pattern by being big — up 30% or more.

What's the significance of Bush's victory? The last century demonstrates exceptional variability of returns in the year after Presidents have been reelected. The negative years span from negative 35% to negative 10.8% in 1957. The lowest positive year was 12.5% in 1965. There was no middle ground between. You get the uglier numbers like negative 35% after Roosevelt's 1936 victory and 25% down after Wilson's 1916 reelection. And the 30-plus-percent up years after Coolidge, Reagan, and Clinton. Ugly or awesome? I bet the latter.

This past year has been the sleepiest since 1964. Expect volatility next year. Pleasant volatility — upward spikes. Why? In the November 1 issue I showed you that stocks are cheap when the experts tend to believe they're expensive — which is the situation now. Precious few forecasters expect a strong market over the next 12 months. This makes for a positive surprise and stampeding potential.

It is also bullish that the yield curve is so steep. The spread between long-term and short-term interest rates is 2.1 percentage points. When this spread has been above 2 points, stocks have tended to do well over the following 2 and 5 years. Some experts fret that we may be in for 15 years of below-average returns, which happened after 1965. But they overlook the fact that the yield curve was flat to negative at some point in every one of the 5 years from 1965 through 1969. A flat yield curve is a precursor to a tight monetary policy.

And tight monetary policy is bad for stocks. Why does this matter? The core business of banking is to borrow short-term money to lend back out as long-term loans. The yield curve reflects the gross operating profit margin on a bank's next loan—the steeper the curve the fatter the profitability. When there is no spread between short- and long-term rates future loan profitability is near zero. Hence this spread reflects the banking system's eagerness to make future loans. When the banks aren't eager lenders, it's very bad for business and stocks. Now they're eager beavers.   ■

Pray for Deficits
December 27, 2004

One reason I'm bullish is that the federal budget deficit is so high. Yes, you heard that right. If you prize prudence in financial matters, you may be surprised or offended to hear that federal deficits are associated, at least in the short term, with bull markets. But the historical pattern is unmistakable: When the federal deficit (as a percentage of gross domestic product) spikes, stocks do well in the intermediate term. Budget surpluses generally have led to dour markets. Pray for more and bigger deficits.

Our biggest recent spikes in the deficit relative to GDP were in the fourth quarter (Q4) of 1949 at 3%; Q1 of 1958, 1971 and 1975 at 2%, 2% and 6%; and more recently in Q3 of 1982 and Q2 of 1992 at 5%. In none of these six cases were the subsequent 12- and 24-month returns negative; the averages were 21% and (annualized) 12%. Surpluses have been followed, on average, by subpar returns. The deficit, now running at about 4% of GDP, is likely to turn down. In other words, we've got one of those spikes.

Counterintuitive though this relationship may be to you, it isn't inconsistent with economic theory. The original Keynesian motivation for a deficit was to increase the speed at which money changed hands (in the economist's phrase, "velocity"), averting stagnation. If normal folks and

Deficits Are Good ... Really

Many investors have a hard time believing periods of big deficits aren't disastrous and, in fact, can lead to great stock returns. But in Ken's 2006 book, *The Only Three Questions That Count*, he shows vast historical data supporting this view. More amazing, he shows big deficit peaks also led to great stock returns in other major developed nations. As Ken prescribes in "When Earnings Are Cheap" (November 1, 2004), if you observe something about US markets, you should confirm your findings by testing it elsewhere.

businesses wouldn't borrow money and spend it, the government would step in to prime the pump. While there can be negative repercussions from overspending, deficits do increase the velocity of money. And when that happens, some of the money ripples out into financial markets, sending prices up.

Here's another reason to be bullish: Stock buybacks in 2004 are at the highest level in almost 20 years, equal to well over half the federal budget deficit. In other words, it has not escaped the attention of corporate treasurers that stocks are cheap. Whenever a stock's "earnings yield" (the inverse of the price/earnings ratio) is high relative to borrowing costs, the corporation can increase earnings per share by buying in shares. That buying drives prices higher. You should buy before the treasurer buys more. ■

2005

Giving It Time

" *You should sell stocks only if you foresee trouble other people don't foresee; don't sell in fear of trouble that everyone else is already anticipating. The only reason for a defensive posture, in other words, is perceiving risks that are little noticed.* "

"THAT WALL OF WORRY," MAY 9, 2005

" *Real bubbles are never commonly referred to as bubbles in the press until after they've burst. . . . When something is commonly labeled a bubble that hasn't burst that means there is fear of it. There is little or no fear of a real bubble. Fear, priced into markets, reduces risk.* "

"BUBBLENOMICS," JULY 4, 2005

Politics were in full swing in 2005. But not so much here in the US as abroad. We inaugurated President George W. Bush for his second term, but bigger changes were happening overseas.

In Japan, the world's second-largest economy after the US, Prime Minister Junichiro Koizumi dissolved the lower house of parliament after a measure to privatize Japan's postal system (which serves as a post office, life insurer, and the world's largest bank by assets) was voted down in Japan's upper house. In the general election that followed, Koizumi's Liberal Democratic Party (LDP) won an overwhelming majority, gaining enough seats to override the upper house's vote. This referendum was seen by many as an important step in initiating much-needed pro-growth economic reforms in Japan (unfortunately, many failed to materialize). The LDP maintained its supermajority in the upper house until 2009.

In Germany, then the third-largest economy (China surpassed Germany in terms of economic size in 2007), Angela Merkel—also seen as a pro-economic growth reformer—unseated Gerhard Schröder to become the new Chancellor.

Back in the US, Hurricane Katrina tore through the Gulf Coast region, devastating much of New Orleans. As with the September 11, 2001 terrorist attacks, it belittles the magnitude of human tragedy to simply consider how stocks perform following such terrible occurrences. But folks often wonder what would happen to stocks if a terrorist attack or similarly destructive event crippled a major US city. Hurricane Katrina provides something of an example. Despite the hugely destructive and tragic events surrounding Katrina, stocks did well in the weeks and months following, especially global stocks.

Like 2004, 2005's gains didn't come until late in the year. The S&P 500 bounced around for months and was slightly negative in late October. But stocks rallied in November and December, and the S&P 500 finished 2005 up 4.9 percent[1]—a positive year, though not much to write home about. The MSCI World did a bit better, rising 10.0 percent, led by Canada, Norway, and notably Japan.[2] After years of poor returns, Japanese shares surged in 2005. The aforementioned reforms promoted by Prime Minister Koizumi stoked renewed optimism in the prospects for Japanese firms, and stocks there soared. Japan's Topix Index (again, a better barometer of Japanese stocks than the well-known Nikkei 225) gained 45.2%, but only 27.0% for US investors as the Japanese yen fell versus the US dollar.[3] But that was still good enough to make Japan the third-best performing developed stock market for US investors in 2005.[4]

Ken was rightly bullish for 2005—but he was too bullish. Given 2004's solid but unspectacular returns, Ken expected 2005 to produce more of a splash. "Now I expect to be blessed in 2005 with what I didn't get in 2004. I'll stick my neck out and predict a better than 25% gain for 2005 for both the S&P 500 and the Morgan Stanley World Index." ("Give It Time," January 31, 2005.) Too optimistic, but as he has said in his columns many times, portfolio strategy shouldn't depend much on whether you expect the market to be up a little or a lot—or even down a little. Only the anticipation of true bear markets necessitates getting out of stocks for most investors.

Widespread but misguided concerns about a host of factors contributed to Ken's bullishness. When investors fear factors that have little real market impact, stock prices can become temporarily depressed but should get a boost later as these fears prove feeble. So Ken spent a fair amount of ink in 2005 addressing issues like expectations for higher interest rates; trade, current account, and budget deficits; and rising oil prices, to name a few. All were widely viewed as harbingers of economic and stock market doom, but not in Ken's eyes.

Fed-controlled short-term interest rates might rise, he argued, but market-determined long-term rates wouldn't. Instead, monetary tightening would keep inflation expectations in check, and investors wouldn't demand significantly higher long-term rates. Folks were quick to point to problems with US deficits but failed to acknowledge the UK was running similar deficits without ill effect. And Ken shows statistically there is no connection between oil and stock prices, despite what many investors believe. "So why do we hear so often something like, 'The market fell today because oil rose'? Behaviorists call it confirmation bias. Our brains tend to see instances that confirm our prior biases and 'common sense' but tend to not see those that contradict." ("Stop Fretting About Oil," August 15, 2005.)

Stock valuations were another factor contributing to Ken's bullishness. Repeatedly, Ken has pointed out the futility of simply looking at P/E ratios to forecast stocks. But comparing stocks' earnings yield—the inverse of a P/E ratio, or E/P—to bond yields provides a useful measure of whether stocks are relatively cheap or expensive. In 2005, the S&P 500 earnings yield was nicely above long-term bond yields, indicating stocks were cheap. This cheapness had positive implications for stock prices. As Ken points out in "Do Your Own M&A" (June 6, 2005) and "Buy That Earnings Yield" (November 28, 2005), when earnings yields are high relative to borrowing costs, firms can borrow money at relatively low after-tax costs and use the cash to buy other companies or their own shares, benefiting their bottom lines. The spread between earnings yields and borrowing costs led to fantastic amounts of share repurchase and merger and acquisition activity in 2005. This not only benefits the share prices of acquisition targets and firms repurchasing their own shares, it shrinks the overall supply of stocks, which benefits stock prices across the board.

Ken's October 17, 2005 column "Three Questions That Count" is a prelude to his 2006 New York Times bestseller, *The Only Three Questions That Count: Investing by Knowing What Others Don't*. The column poses these questions:

- What do you believe is true that is actually wrong?
- Can you fathom the unfathomable?
- What is your blind spot?

The column provides a taste of why these questions are relevant to investors, but it's not a substitute for reading the entire book—which is excellent.

Give It Time

January 31, 2005

This is the time of year for introspection by *Forbes* stock market columnists. How did we do last year? What do we see ahead? In 2004 I made 51 recommendations. Had you put $10,000 into each, your $510,000 would have grown to a bit more than $574,000 by year-end, a 12.6% appreciation. This calculation assumes, moreover, a 1% haircut for transaction costs. Had you put the same money on the same dates into the S&P 500 (and with no haircut), your ending value would have been only $548,000. In other words, I was a good five points ahead of the market.

My worst pick was Equant (currently at $5), the Dutch telecom firm. I recommended it at 10 in the March 15, 2004 issue, which you would have had in your hands in time to place an order at the March 1 close. I saw Equant as cheap in an improving world. Its world didn't improve, and it got cheaper.

I'd give this one another go. If you own it, hang in there, and if you don't, try it at a price half of what it used to be. In other words this stock gets reentered as a 2005 recommendation (without a haircut) at the December 31 price. Equant has a strong position in seamless broadband networks for big corporations. The world has to go in this direction, and that will yield the profitability that doesn't exist now. Meanwhile, Equant is dirt cheap at 50% of annual revenue and one times book value. I think it just needs more time. If it doesn't pan out on its own, it will get bought out eventually. You can buy the stock as an ADR on the New York Stock Exchange.

My other clunkers included Snap-on, the vendor of mechanics' tools; Lifepoint Hospitals, a chain of 30 acute-care hospitals headquartered in Brentwood, Tenn.; and Tidewater, the supplier of services to offshore drillers. None of these did anything very bad, but they just didn't catch on. There are more exciting ways to light up your portfolio in 2005. So these three don't get included in my 2005 recommendations.

I recommended Ocular Sciences in the June 21 issue. It gained 39%, but I think it can do better for a while. While it isn't cheap at 35 times trailing earnings, its disposable contact lens business is really nifty and in my view underappreciated. This one gets reentered.

I recommended Benchmark Electronics, which provides outsourcing for electronics manufacturing and engineering. It, too, has done okay but needs more time. It is growing, is financially strong, adequately cheap and will become a leveraged play on the rebound of the tech sector. Stay with it.

The magazine's scorekeepers don't have any way to compare macro forecasts among different columnists (some of us make precise predictions early in the year, others don't), but we are supposed to address the matter in the look-back column. I confess to being too bullish. I forecasted a strong year for the market, with most of the gain coming toward the end. The fourth quarter was indeed strong, but I expected more and earlier and didn't get it.

Now I expect to be blessed in 2005 with what I didn't get in 2004. I'll stick my neck out and predict a better than 25% gain in 2005 for both the S&P 500 and the Morgan Stanley World Index, and also predict that the excitement will start right around the corner. Next month I'll explain why. ∎

It's a Beautiful World
February 28, 2005

L ast month, I promised to explain why I expect stocks to be up 25% this year. Well, they sure haven't started out robustly. But I'm not throwing out my rose-tinted glasses. My reasoning: First, forecasters have a very tight and strong consensus for low-single-digit stock returns this year, yet historically, the consensus has almost always been wrong.

So stock returns should be either into double digits or else negative. Now, the first year of a President's term has almost always been sort of 50-50, either negative or up a lot—nothing in between. Since I don't expect a negative year, I expect the market to go up a lot.

Next, positive first years of Presidents' terms average 28%. The numbers for second-term Presidents (11 cases since 1900) are also blessed, with 64% positive years and those years averaging a 24% gain. Third, the inverse of the market's P/E—that is,

the earnings yield—is now higher than ten-year bond rates in every important country. This is the case for the first time in decades. Stocks are cheap globally, just when people think they aren't.

Fourth, everyone expects interest rates to rise. Maybe short-term rates, controlled by the Federal Reserve, will. But long-term rates are dictated by a free market of traders, and these traders know that Fed tightening is good for keeping inflation, hence bond rates, down. Contrary to myth, stocks aren't very sensitive to short-rate shifts, but they are to long-term rates. That's bullish. Fifth, the balance of trade deficit, the balance of payments deficit and the budget deficit are not negatives. If they were, Britain, with deficits very similar to ours (as a percent of gross domestic product, and cumulatively for 20 years), would have a similarly weak currency instead of being one of the world's strongest. ∎

End Your Gloom
March 28, 2005

T hose who are financially gloomy usually fix on deficits: the budget deficit, the trade deficit and the current account deficit (often mistakenly called the "balance of payments" deficit). First, the trade and current account deficits are by definition basically the same, since they are coming from the same basic sources and accounting. The difference is always microscopically tiny as a percent of GDP—currently 0.1% of GDP, or $17 billion.

If you don't fear the one you don't fear the other.

Surprise: These two deficits have nothing to do with currency values. Ours came to 5.2% of gross domestic product last year. Britain's was 5% of its gross domestic product. If these deficits determine currencies, how can the British pound be so strong? Over the last three years the US trade deficit came to a cumulative 13% of GDP, identical to Britain's. Britain's three-year total is identical at 13%. So why is sterling so much stronger than the dollar? Do trade deficits lead to a weak economy? No, just the opposite, as was pointed out in the previous issue of this magazine (see "Trading Up," March 14).

How about budget deficits? As I noted in my December 27 column, they are in no way associated with poor returns in the stock market. Nor do they dictate currency weakness. The past three years of federal budgets have run up a cumulative deficit equal to 8% of GDP. Britain's three-year deficit total comes to 5%. If all three of these deficits are at basically similar levels in the short, intermediate and long term, which they are, they can't be causal, since the dollar has been among the world's weakest currencies in recent years, while sterling has been among the strongest.

If you want to explain currency moves, you'd do better to look at interest rates than at deficits. As 2004 started, Euroland's rates were nicely above America's, on both short- and long-term money. Arbitragers borrowed in America and lent in Euroland, pocketing the spread. Doing it all at once, they drove the dollar down and the euro up. Over the course of 2004 those rates flip-flopped, and now the game is taking place in reverse. That's why the dollar has been strong in 2005 (which seemingly few notice). ■

Surprise—America Owes Too Little
April 18, 2005

Here's another reason to be bullish: everyone is worried sick that America is overindebted, but it's not. This country could profitably take on more loans from abroad and invest the money in productive assets. We're underindebted.

The debt worriers have been with us for a long time, and they've always been wrong. Their economic prescriptions are born of a moral philosophy that says debt is bad and more debt is worse. They don't like to see the US importing capital from abroad at the rate of $600 billion a year. What the worriers fail to contemplate is the uses to which that capital is put.

What is the right debt level for society to carry? The answer is: that level where our marginal borrowing costs approach our marginal return on assets. This is, in fact, the same formula that a corporation would use. If you can borrow at 6% to build a factory that will yield a return of 12%, you should borrow.

The US is nowhere near there. As a result, we need more debt to get more income, so people can become wealthier.

The Federal Reserve counts $97 trillion of assets in the economy, offset by $44 trillion of debt, leaving (with rounding) $52 trillion of net worth. The asset figure, to be sure, involves some double-counting (General Motors' factory, an asset, is financed by bonds, counted again as an asset in your individual retirement account), but no matter: The key figure is the $52 trillion at the bottom of the US balance sheet. And we're getting a great return on that $52 trillion. Our national income is $12 trillion.

Yes, most of the income is labor income, not a return on capital as conventionally calculated. Yet think for a moment: Why are labor rates higher here than in Madagascar? It's precisely because we have so much invested in the form of roads, factories and job skills. I compare the $12 trillion income to the $52 trillion of net capital and conclude that capital is extremely productive in this country. I'm not worried about importing a little more of it and putting it to use.

Folks fret about our $2 trillion of consumer debt and $4 trillion of federal government debt. But these are small numbers in relation to our income, to our total debt (mortgage and business debts are far larger) and to our net worth. Stop worrying. ∎

The Wall of Worry
May 9, 2005

Maybe I was wrong. Maybe the stock market won't be up a lot in 2005. The year sure hasn't started robustly. It's always possible to be wrong. What do you do when your plans go awry?

First, don't panic. On September 6, I detailed why having been too bullish doesn't necessarily mean that you should change course. Those principles apply now.

The key is this: You should sell stocks only if you foresee trouble that other people don't foresee; don't sell in fear of trouble that everyone else is already anticipating. The only reason for a defensive posture, in other words, is perceiving risks that are little noticed. I can't find many.

So what might be bothering you? Inflation? Rising rates? A weak dollar? Look closely and you will find that such worries are (a) widespread and already priced into the stock market and (b) exaggerated.

Inflation is not as bad as you probably think it is. Over the past 12 months prices (excluding food and energy) are up 2.4%. As for rising rates: The rise is pretty much limited to the US and to the short end of the maturity spectrum. Rates are not going up abroad (for the most part) and are not going up very much on long-term bonds. The 30-year US Treasury yields 4.7%, down from 5.2% a year ago.

Don't worry about interest rates unless you have an adjustable-rate mortgage. Rising short-term rates by themselves don't have a predictive history for global stock prices.

Weak dollar? The dollar is actually up against all major currencies so far in 2005. Budget and trade deficits? They are for real, but they don't hurt the economy or the market, as I've pointed out in recent columns.

Or, that stocks might fare badly for a decade as is currently fashionable to presume? Relax. There is no rational way to make such statements. Those who do are telling more about what they don't know than what they do. Stock levels a decade out result almost solely from shifts in the supply of securities six to ten years hence. No one knows how to estimate that. So don't let the gloomsters baloney you.

If you want something to worry about, consider long-shot risks that other people are overlooking. One on my list is if George Bush appoints a disaster to replace Alan Greenspan. Another is if budding intracountry social tensions within the European Union cause an economic disintegration there. Others: a large terrorist attack; a new era of repression in China that depresses its economy. None of these is impossible, but I think the odds are sufficiently low that they do not justify an exit from equity investments. ■

Do Your Own M&A
June 6, 2005

Stocks may look expensive to you, but they look cheap to a certain class of investor now avidly buying up entire companies. This year through April, 225 public companies in the US have agreed to be bought out, at a combined cost of $246 billion. I am happy to report that several of these deals were for companies I've recommended recently, like Archipelago Holdings (recommended April 18 at $18, now at $30) and Premcor (December 27, 2004 at $41, now $65). Electronic trading firm Archipelago is further discussed in David Dreman's column "The Dinosaur at Wall and Broad"; Premcor is being bought by Valero, making it North America's largest oil refinery.

Most of the acquisitions are being done by other public companies: SBC is buying AT&T, and Federated is buying May Department Stores. But some companies are going private. The buyers are in what used to be called the leveraged buyout business and now goes by the name "private equity." Their targets include DoubleClick, Polaroid and Toys "R" Us.

Besides the takeovers, we have 339 companies in the first third of the year that have started programs to buy back some of their own shares. If all of the plans are completed, that will be another $132 billion of equity taken out of circulation. Last year total buy-ins, among both newcomers to the game and old players, totaled $333 billion. Note that these equity retirements dwarf the market for initial public offerings (so far this year, 60 companies raising $18 billion).

What explains this massive reabsorption of equity? Cheap money. The average corporation can borrow ten-year money at under 6%. If your share price is only 12 times earnings, you pick up 8.3 cents of earnings for every dollar invested in a share buyback. That borrowed dollar costs you only 4 cents or so in aftertax earnings. The spread between the 8.3 cents and the 4 cents boosts the earnings per share on the surviving shares. Indeed, you could buy your stock, cancel it and create EPS gains even at stock prices as high as 24 times earnings.

A firm more interested in expanding than contracting can buy another firm with borrowed money and get the same effect. All this explains the feverish level of takeovers. Half the global stock market is cheap enough for this. The phenomenon won't go away soon.

Focus your investing now on stocks that are likely to be bought, either in takeovers or in buybacks. The surest bets are companies with desirable strategic attributes for an acquirer, like high market share, low-cost production, regional dominance or brand name strength. ■

Bubblenomics
July 4, 2005

So, are home prices a bubble, ready to burst and implode the economy with it? No! Real bubbles are never commonly referred to as bubbles in the press until after they've burst. Real estate doesn't qualify. You can't pick up a reference to home prices in any newspaper or magazine nowadays without seeing the word bubble nearby. That is true here and around the Western World. Only here is it seen as American-only. In Britain, for example, they not only bubble-fret about their housing, but also ours.

The sign of a real, honest-to-God bubble is an entirely different kind of public discussion, one in which there is talk of a "new paradigm," or words to that effect. Recall tech's heyday, when absurd prices were justified by the theory of a global "New Economy" via eyeball-counting on the Internet. My March 6, 2000 column calling tech a bubble was out of the mainstream.

In the late 1980s not many people talked about Japan being a bubble. The common view was that its way of doing business was simply superior and that this nation would sooner or later replace America as the world's economic leader. Michael Crichton's 1992 bestseller, *Rising Sun*, was based on that notion. The book and the movie it generated look silly now.

When something is commonly labeled a bubble that hasn't burst that means there is fear of it. There is little or no fear of a real bubble. Fear, priced into markets, reduces risk. I have no clue where home prices will go from here; they might go sideways or drift down. But this isn't a bubble, because it's been widely called one for two years, in America and elsewhere.

What keeps housing so strong? Long-term interest rates, specifically rates for mortgages, remain low. If mortgage rates remain benign, housing may keep booming. But the housing sector is not in a bubble.

As 2004 and 2005 began, most experts believed long rates would rise markedly. Instead they've fallen, both years, in America and throughout the world. The real bubble must be the airholes in those brains that thought interest rates would rise. There is scant media discussion of how long-term rates are down globally, much less why. The reason is that inflation is lower than expected. Despite regional and sector ups and downs, prices, globally, are pretty flat. Expect more of this and with it a sweeter world than the bubble brains forecast. ∎

Stop Fretting About Oil
August 15, 2005

Have you allowed yourself to be scared out of the stock market by high oil prices? If you have, you're making a big mistake. You are falling prey to a media myth. It's fascinating how often the media get away with a story claiming X causes Y when an abundance of statistical evidence exists to disprove the connection. It is routine now to see stories blaming a drop in stock prices on a rise in oil prices. Don't believe these stories. There's no connection between the two.

The Oil Versus Stocks Myth

Amazingly, many investors firmly believe that high oil prices drive stocks down. However, this is easy to disprove, even if you aren't good with Excel. Consider that oil and stocks rose together for much of the bull market that started in 2003. And following oil's 2008 peak, oil dropped right along with stocks. Don't take that to mean oil and stocks move *together*. No—sometimes they move together, sometimes opposite, and sometimes they do entirely different things. There's no material long-term correlation—positive or negative. And if there's no strong long-term correlation, there can be no long-term causation either.

Anyone with access to Yahoo Finance for data and Excel to crunch it can answer the question: Do jumps in the price of oil correspond with dips in the price of stocks? The answer is no. Try it out. Plug into your spreadsheet the daily percentage changes in the S&P 500 over the first half of 2005 and the daily percentage changes in the price of oil. If the two sets of numbers marched in reverse lockstep—say, a 2% rise in oil matched a 1% decline in stocks—then the correlation between these two data sets would be –1. Anything close to zero means that there's no connection. The oil/stock correlation coefficient comes out as –0.08.

This correlation is smaller than it looks. You have to square it to get what's called R-squared, a quantity that shows how much of the jumping around in stock prices can be explained by movements in the oil market. Here, R-squared comes out as less than 0.01. That means you can explain only 1% of the action in stocks by looking at oil. It's as good as random.

So why do we hear so often something like, "The market fell today because oil rose"? Behaviorists call it confirmation bias. Our brains tend to see instances that confirm our prior biases and "common sense" but tend to not see those that contradict. As events transpire, we remain "stuck." When confronted by contradictory statistics, we buck them by "reframing." Instead of daily prices we claim some other time frame counts, like weeks, months or whatever—or that a price change has to be more than X% to count. At this point we are grasping at straws. Or, as the statisticians say, data-mining.

Data-mine all you want. You're not going to find a credible cause-and-effect relationship between oil and stocks.

There are a lot of myths about what drives stock prices. Here are some other factors uncorrelated with stock market performance: the market's overall price/earnings ratio (I've looked carefully at this one, across the globe and many time periods), high volatility as measured by the VIX index, gold, trade deficits, the dollar's level, consumer sentiment, investor sentiment as measured by the "Investors Intelligence" data. So don't panic when any of these go up or down. Buy good stocks and hold them. ∎

You Bought a What?!

September 19, 2005

Should I have written a column on annuities? I've been in this space for 21 years but have never seen the need to say the obvious, which is that an annuity is just a mutual fund dressed up with some punitively stiff fees. (I am talking only about the most common form of annuity—the deferred annuity sold as an investment account. The other kind, the instant annuity that converts a lump sum into a monthly lifetime payout, is another matter.)

A *Forbes* reader from Mutual, Ohio recently reminded me that it is sometimes useful to state the obvious, if that will protect investors from making serious mistakes. The reader told me that he had bought a variable annuity and wanted advice on what to do next. The damage, though, was done. Broker-sold annuities levy killer annual fees, in large part to compensate the brokers who sell them. You are required to keep your money in place for a while—seven years is typical. You can get out early only by paying a huge exit fee to make up for the vendor's lost chance to extract that annual fee.

Maybe I was too hard on the poor fellow who wrote in. I instructed him that he should never, ever again make any financial decision. Have a spouse or offspring do it. If no one loves you, have your county court conserve you. Buying a deferred annuity proves you are a serious dupe. Seriously.

The only ones benefiting from annuities are the insurance companies issuing them and the sales reps selling them. Sales reps usually lie. They never tell the whole truth. That is, they may mention the annual fees and the exit penalty, but they rarely clarify how strongly motivated the broker is to push you into this particular product. The sales commission, paid out of those annual fees you are committing to, can easily be 8% to 16% of the amount you invest. And almost never does the salesman disclose the fundamental fact that you'd be better off investing similarly outside the annuity—for example, in a plain old mutual fund.

The tax deferral that comes with deferred annuities is costly, unless you live for centuries. Under present law the tax rate on capital gains and dividends is 15%. The annuity defers this tax, but at the cost of more than doubling the rate. Profits from annuities are taxed as ordinary income, at rates up to 35%. Ouch!

The hot new type is equity-indexed annuities. These give you a sliver of upside potential while promising that your principal will not shrink. I do mean "sliver." And your principal may shrink. There's not much left for potential gain, not when you have paid for the put option (the supposed guarantee against loss) and paid for the broker's golf club membership and kids' college.

Instead of losing money while insurers use yours to buy stocks for themselves, buy good stocks directly and hold them. ■

Three Questions That Count

October 17, 2005

You want to maximize your chances of getting good results from stock picking? I have a system, and it boils down to focusing on just three big questions. They aren't what you might expect—say, questions about the market's price/earnings ratio or interest rate forecasts. Rather, they have to do with your own psyche. Overcome your psychological failings and you can be a better investor.

First question: What do you believe is true that's actually wrong? If you are captivated by some market myth, other investors probably are, too. Figure out what that popular but wrongheaded belief is and you can disassociate yourself from it. You can bet against it.

Example: Most investors believe that years when the market is trading at a high multiple of its collective earnings are bad years in which to invest and low-P/E market years are good times. This popular belief is contradicted by the evidence, as I have outlined in earlier columns. Yes, there are some high-P/E years that turned out to be disasters (2000 and 2001, for example). But there are just as many occasions when buying into a high-P/E market was the right thing to do, for example in 1932, 1998 and 2003.

So when you see folks freaked out by high-P/E markets, you can bet against them. You know something they don't know. You can invest knowing that the market P/E is irrelevant. (And it should be.)

Question two: Can you fathom the unfathomable? If you have the right instinct for turning market statistics into buy-and-sell signals, you seek correlations first, then causal relationships that would explain them.

For example, the main force driving cycles when growth stocks do well versus value is time-lagged shifts in the yield curve. The yield curve plots the yield on Treasury notes and bonds against their maturity dates. The historical pattern has been this: About 9 to 12 months after the yield curve gets flat, growth stocks start beating value stocks, and they continue to beat value until the curve gets very steep again. The causal relationship is very simple. A flat yield curve reflects a reluctance of banks to lend to commercial borrowers. And value stocks are very borrowing-dependent, while growth stocks aren't.

At the moment the yield curve has gone close to flat—the yield on ten-year Treasurys, 4.1%, is not much more than the yield on two-year Treasurys, 3.9%. So mid-2006 is the time to prefer growth to value.

Question three: What is your blind spot? I've been writing here for years about self-blinding psychological traits like confirmation bias and reframing (August 15), fear of heights, myopia and Stone Age hardwired thinking. It takes time and effort, but you can learn. For example, if you are myopic and suffer confirmation bias, you are a trend-follower and will miss upcoming changes like the capital expenditure and agricultural booms starting in 2006. ∎

The *Only* Three Questions

This column bears the same name (almost) as Ken's fourth book (and *New York Times* best seller), *The Only Three Questions That Count,* published late in 2006. The book showed investors how to build a forecasting methodology—using the three questions to take commonly available information and turn it into a market advantage.

Buy That Earnings Yield
November 28, 2005

If you are spooked by the recent increase in interest rates, or if you aren't sure what to make of Federal Reserve chairman nominee Ben S. Bernanke, you might be holding back from new commitments to the stock market. Rising rates kill stocks, don't they? So you decide to wait and see.

If that describes you, you have a lot of company. Corporate profits are up strongly this year, GDP growth came in at a robust 3.8% (annualized) in the third quarter despite Katrina, and still investors are fretting. Measured by the MSCI World Index, stocks are only fractionally higher than in January.

Stop fretting. Plenty of stocks are cheap enough to buy, for the reason I outlined in my June 6 column. Namely: For a lot of good companies the earnings yield, which is the inverse of the price/earnings ratio, is higher than the yield on high-grade corporate bonds. That makes such stocks cheap—cheap for the company, if it wants to buy in shares; cheap for a corporate acquirer financing a takeover with its own bonds; and cheap for a portfolio investor whose alternative is owning corporate bonds.

Forecasters have wrongly predicted steeply rising long-term interest rates for fully two years. Yet ten-year rates have hovered within a half-percentage point or so of 4.25%. This cheap money has prevailed even as the Fed has jacked up the cost of overnight loans. How can this be? High short-term rates have renewed foreigners' confidence in the dollar. Foreigners have a lot of money to save, and so long as they don't have to worry about a devaluation of the dollar, they are happy to save it here.

Today the lending business is globalized. Not so 40 years ago. Then, with fixed currency rates, national rather than global banks, minimal electronics and no futures to hedge, each country's long-term rates were set within that country's domestic market. Today the market forces that determine whether you can refinance your mortgage at 6%, or how much a corporation pays to borrow money to finance an acquisition, are truly international. Any firm whose stock is trading at a multiple of earnings below 22 can buy back its stock or be taken over, increasing the acquirer's earnings per share. ∎

The Integrity Premium
December 26, 2005

What would the S&P 500 be trading at if we had complete confidence in corporations' audited numbers? A lot higher than 1,300. Post-Enron, post-WorldCom, a pall of uncertainty envelops financial statements. There's what you might call the murkiness discount. You expect this kind of haircut in Shanghai or Rio, but we have it, too, right here in America. That isn't bad enough by itself to trigger a bear market. But this makes the stock market worth less than it otherwise would be.

The quality of corporate audits has imploded as the government has fostered a collusive auditing oligopoly that is now fully global. There is simply no real competition among auditors anymore. With very few exceptions the auditor of almost any public corporation can't be fired and replaced. Scott Paper just switched auditors but had a heck of a time. It is virtually impossible. As in any other field, an absence of competition begets a deterioration in quality. Today's corporate-audit quality is a joke. This despite the big fuss Congress made over restoring integrity with the Sarbanes-Oxley law.

Remember the Big Eight and a national array of smaller auditing firms competing regionally? By 2002 a merger wave had shrunk eight to five. Just two regionals, with a combined 1% market share, did any significant number of audits of public companies: BDO Seidman and Grant Thornton. Then the government, in its infinite wisdom, decided that since Arthur Andersen employed one or two bad auditors, the entire firm should be destroyed. Now we're down to four big CPA firms, and one of them, KPMG, is getting a lambasting from the IRS. So we sort of have the Big Three and a Half.

What does that mean? No competition. You can't float an offering today without a Big Four audit. PricewaterhouseCoopers, Ernest & Young, Deloitte & Touche and the wounded KPMG audit companies that account for 99% of this country's stock market capitalization. In Germany, New Zealand, Norway, Finland and Spain, two of these four have more than 75% of the auditing market. That concentration is also the case within the US, in many industries. Usually in a city the audit partner for a particular industry who works at the biggest auditor is a longtime buddy of his counterpart at number two. They talk. They curb their competitive spirit.

In any other field the government would break the foursome into the Big Fourteen. We'd have Touche competing with Delo and Delo with Itte. Not here. The regulator of the auditing industry, the Public Company Accounting Oversight Board, likes the clubby and confined marketplace. Because the oligopoly isn't going away, you should focus on stocks that are good enough and cheap enough that you can be comfortable with them despite zero ability to believe in audited profit-and-loss and asset-and-liability accounts. ■

2006

Celebrity Market
Indicators

" *Markets do really hate political change. It's not that Republicans are good for stocks and Democrats bad. After all, didn't stocks do well in the 1960s and the 1990s, when Democrats had the White House, Congress or both? And haven't stocks disappointed during the current all-Republican era? What worries investors is simply any change in control—always.* "

"The November Surprise," September 18, 2006

" *I also know I always may be wrong. CXOAdvisory.com, a site (owned by market research firm CXO Advisory Group LLC) that ranks 33 public prognosticators, puts me at the top with a 69% accuracy since 2000 on 58 market-timing calls. That means I've been wrong 31% of the time. So I always plan to own some stocks that will do well if what I expect to happen doesn't happen.* "

"The Rangel Factor," November 13, 2006

Two-thousand-six was a difficult year . . . for celebrities. That was good news to Ken. It's not that Ken has any ill will toward the likes of Paul McCartney (separated from Heather Mills in 2006), Whitney Houston (filed for divorce from Bobby Brown), Paris Hilton (arrested for DUI), Steve "Crocodile Hunter" Irwin (killed by a stingray), or Wesley Snipes (indicted on tax fraud charges). But the fact these were the stories making endless headlines in 2006 was a bullish sign for investors. "Today we have the Internet to bombard us with more news than ever. Still, it is bullish that the most exciting headlines have to do with Angelina Jolie's baby and Barry Bonds' home runs. There is again nothing to hurt stocks." ("No News Is Good News," July 3, 2006.) Ken was only partially right. One story with a celebrity bent did emerge and impact stocks in 2006. But not materially or for long.

After starting the year strong—the S&P 500 was up nearly 7 percent by early May[1]—a stock market pullback was sparked at least partially by a cocktail party conversation between newly appointed Federal Reserve Chairman Ben Bernanke and financial news anchor Maria ("Money Honey") Bartiromo. During the White House Correspondents' Association Dinner, Bernanke intimated to Bartiromo that—contrary to what investors inferred from his recent congressional testimony—the Fed might not be done raising short-term interest rates.[2] Bernanke's comments brought into question not only his stance on monetary policy but his skill in communicating sensitive information to the market. Days later, a stock market slide began that saw the S&P 500 lose 7.5 percent in just over a month.[3] Global stocks suffered even more, falling 11.3 percent over the same period.[4] Ken correctly advised *Forbes* readers to stay the course. "There are corrections and there are bear markets. What we're experiencing right now is a correction. Know the difference. . . . The damage may not be over, but it's not the beginning of a sustained bear market. You should be buying stocks now. There's more bull market ahead before any real bear market." ("The Short, Sharp Shock," August 8, 2006.)

Stocks did regain their upward momentum in earnest as Ken expected. From mid-June through year-end, the S&P 500 shot up over 17 percent, and global stocks gained over 20 percent, finishing the year up 15.8 percent and 20.7 percent, respectively.[5] This put stocks' gains within Ken's forecasted range. "My 2006 forecast is that the MSCI World Index will be up somewhere between 10% and 40% and that this gain will beat the S&P 500's gain." ("A Replay of 1995?" February 27, 2006.) Why the rather wide range of 10 percent to 40 percent? Again, most investors should own stocks whether they expect the market to be up a little or a lot. The exact magnitude of stock market gains doesn't matter much. So Ken increasingly began shying away from exact forecasts and instead focused on the bigger picture of whether or not investors should be invested in the stock market.

As he had for years, Ken touted the benefits of global investing in 2006 and expected foreign shares to outpace US shares. "Any single country is more hit-and-miss, for the same reason that any single stock is more volatile than a portfolio of stocks. American markets aren't as strong this year as foreign markets. I expect this disparity to widen for a while." ("Feel the Force," May 8, 2006.) Ken's foreign focus wasn't limited to stocks. He also highlighted the increased importance of a global economic perspective. "Even if you don't invest globally (which you should do, particularly this year) you will always be a better US investor if you think globally." ("Surviving Rate Rises," June 5, 2006.)

Lending is one area Ken specifically recommends a global rather than domestic focus. He highlighted a common barometer of lending conditions—the yield curve. As mentioned, a yield curve is an illustration of interest rates on bonds of different maturities. A steep yield curve—short-term interest rates lower than long-term interest rates—is typically seen as a plus for lending. Banks borrow money at low short-term rates and lend money at higher long-term rates. The difference between the two is mostly profit. So a steep yield curve gives banks a strong incentive to lend—excellent for economic activity. But in 2006, the US yield curve was inverted, meaning short-term interest rates were higher than long-term rates. This environment is often viewed as a negative for the economy and stock market—less profitable loans mean banks are less willing to lend and less liquidity to keep the economy going.

Borrowing and lending, however, was no longer confined to any single country. In an increasingly globalized financial system, firms and individuals can borrow in any number of countries. So Ken developed a global yield curve—a yield curve with interest rates weighted by the relative size of countries' economics—which showed lending remained profitable globally. "Some investors fear an inverted US yield curve. This is wrongheaded. It's the global yield curve that counts, and it remains adequately steep." ("A Replay of 1995?" February 27, 2006.) This was an example of new capital markets technology developed by Ken and the people at Fisher Investments.

All wasn't rosy globally, however. In September, a coup in Thailand ousted then–Prime Minister Thaksin Shinawatra. Just a month later, North Korea revealed it developed and tested a nuclear device. Neither event caused stocks to skip a beat.

With April 17, 2006 column "Lessons From Lurie," Ken moved ahead of Sidney B. Lurie to become the fifth-longest-running *Forbes* columnist—one step closer to his goal of becoming number one. Ken noted that Lurie gave us phrases like "New Era" and "Fabulous Fifties." A Lurie line Ken liked a lot and quoted in the column: "The market usually rings a bell before changing direction, but few people hear it." Perhaps Lurie was speaking from his grave and warning about 2007 ahead.

I Still Hate Funds

January 30, 2006

My last column about mutual funds (August 20, 2001) was an unemotional look at their pros and cons, concluding that individual stocks are a better investment for most *Forbes* readers. But look at the screaming banner the magazine put atop the page: "I Hate Funds." No surprise that I drew much wrath from the fund industry.

At some risk that an editor will attach another sensationalist headline to my ideas, I am going to venture into this territory again. The original purpose for funds was to provide a professionally managed portfolio to serve those with too little to diversify on their own. A fund is a good tool for someone with only $50,000 in the market. But the average assets of this magazine's subscribers are upwards of $1.6 million. You folks should buy stocks directly.

What's wrong with funds? Start with performance. Over the long term, the average fund in pretty much every category has fallen short of the S&P 500 index or whatever other benchmark is relevant. Yes, there are some winners, duly publicized in fund surveys, but you don't know about these in advance. Published numbers, moreover, overstate average results experienced by investors, because loser funds disappear.

Next problem: costs. The average expense ratio for the US equity funds tracked by *Forbes* is 1.23% a year. Foreign funds cost an average 1.46%. Then there are sales charges (both up front and imposed on redemption), plus all sorts of hidden costs. Funds can legally overpay brokers for commissions and then get kickbacks in the form of "soft dollar" services like free research (which the fund management company should be paying for out of its own pocket). The other trading cost is the spread between bid and ask prices. For a fund that trades heavily and owns stocks in smaller companies, portfolio transaction costs could easily add a few percentage points to your annual cost burden. Add it all up—the sales loads, the published expense ratio and the invisible transaction costs—and you could be spending 4% a year to have your assets in a fund.

Costs can be minimized in an index fund, but then there's a third problem: taxes. Funds cannot pass through losses to their shareholders. Say you have $1 million in the market and you earn 9%, or $90,000. Maybe you have $130,000 in appreciation on winning positions and $40,000 in losses on the other stocks. If you own these stocks directly, you can switch out of just the losers and use the $40,000 loss against other capital gains (say, from selling a house). If the stocks are tucked into a fund, you're walled off from the $40,000 deduction.

The first 35 pages of Don F. Wilkinson's *Stop Wasting Your Wealth in Mutual Funds* (Dearborn Trade Publishing, 2005) are worth the book's $20 purchase price. Read them.

A Title by Any Other Name

This column and the August 20, 2001 column ("I Hate Funds") bring up some interesting trivia about column writing. Though Ken (and most columnists) may suggest titles (which may get used), ultimately, the editor picks the title. So, like not judging a book by its cover, don't get turned off (or on) by a column title. It's just there to draw you in.

I suggested 53 stocks in 2005, including stocks re-recommended from 2004, and they collectively were up 14.3%, after a hypothetical 1% transaction haircut on new positions. Equal amounts invested in the S&P 500 (without haircut) at the same times were up only 3.4%. (In my column I choose not to write about companies I already hold in managed accounts.) My best picks were electronic exchange operator Archipelago Holdings, up 191%, and apparel maker Guess, up 113%. My biggest losers were hair care outfit Helen of Troy, down 34%, and Thomson, the consumer electronics company, down 25%. ∎

A Replay of 1995?
February 27, 2006

This should be another good year in the stock market. Maybe it will be a great one. Yes, I've been too optimistic since 2003. Last year I predicted the Morgan Stanley Capital International World Index would be up 20%. It was up only half that, at 9.5%. Still, relative to bonds or cash, equities have been the place to be. Stocks could end 2006 like 2005, up a little, or like 1995, when they went up a lot—37%.

Consider first the case for the extreme outcome, that stocks explode. In 2002, for the first time in a quarter-century, the market's earnings yield exceeded the yield on ten-year Treasury bonds. (Earnings yield is the inverse of the price/earnings ratio, where the earnings in question are projected for the current year.) This cheapness indicator has held true ever since, and it is true today for most of the world's big stock markets.

The S&P 500 should earn at least $75 in 2006, which is what it earned in 2005 (both numbers are before nonrecurring items). That $75 is 6% of the recent price on the index, near 1250. The 6% is 1.5 percentage points better than the yield on the ten-year bond.

What would it take to bring the relationship between bond yields and earnings yields back to normal—that is, where the latter is the smaller figure? Any of three things would do it: Stocks rise at least 36%; bond rates rise at least 1.6 percentage points; earnings fall 27%. Or some combination of the three. Since I don't think earnings will fall or long-term rates will rise much, I find an explosion in stock prices very plausible.

The other possibility: We don't return to traditional relative valuations. Maybe investors remain historically dour and skeptical. Then earnings yields would remain well above bond yields. Stocks would rise only a little, as they did in 2004 and 2005.

Foreign valuation spreads are more extreme, and so the likelihood of an upward surge overseas is greater. In Britain, France, Germany and Japan earnings yields exceed bond yields by between 3.25 points (Japan) and 4.35 points (France).

Forecasters, on average, foresee the US ten-year rate climbing to 5.1% by year-end from the current 4.5%. I don't think that will happen. But even if these experts are right, that's still not enough to close the earnings yield gap. Forecasters have wrongheadedly expected long rates to rise markedly for three years.

They miss the fact that US long rates are set in a global market. Foreign long rates keep falling, in response to an abundance of savings and a shortage of thriving economies in which to invest. As long as foreign long-term rates remain benign, the

US bond market won't crash. Still, stocks offer more potential in this benign interest rate environment.

Takeovers in January accelerated drastically above 2005's January level, which was twice 2004's record level. There's a simple reason: In two-thirds of the world's stock markets debt-financed takeovers are antidilutive. You borrow at the bond rate (less than the bond rate, when taxes are figured in) and acquire earnings coming in at the earnings yield rate. Takeovers shrink the supply of securities and thus push those securities' prices higher.

Some investors fear an inverted US yield curve. This is wrongheaded. It's the global yield curve that counts, and it remains adequately steep. Last year Britain had a slightly inverted yield curve all year—almost identical to ours now. British stocks were up but lagged the world's markets. That's what to expect in America now.

My 2006 forecast is that the MSCI World Index will be up somewhere between 10% and 40% and that this gain will beat the S&P 500's gain. Ditch your bonds and cash.   ∎

Take My Stock, Please
March 27, 2006

This is a great time to have part of your portfolio in the shares of takeover candidates. You don't even have to try very hard to wind up with at least a few. January's cash-based takeovers (24 deals with a combined $15 billion purchase price) tripled 2005's record level, according to Bloomberg. I expect February, March and all of 2006 to be no less robust. It's growing, not fading.

After stocks got very cheap in 2002, corporations became very avid buyers of them. They either buy in some of their own shares or buy other companies outright. When either kind of buying takes place at a low enough price, the result is a boost in the earnings per share of the acquirer.

A low price, in this context, means that the acquired stock has an earnings yield better than the aftertax cost of borrowed money (or the aftertax return on idle cash). At the moment, the market's earnings yield—that is, the inverse of the price/earnings ratio—is 6%. Pay a dollar and you get yourself an earnings stream that starts off at 6 cents. The aftertax value of cash is

more like 3 cents. Use borrowed money or loose cash at a cost of 3 cents to get 6 cents of earnings and you are ahead. This process can continue until either the stock market or global long-term interest rates are way up, or earnings fall apart.

If a firm is cheap enough, it must either borrow money to buy back its own stock, driving up its price to eliminate that cheapness, or it will fall prey to an acquirer who does a hostile takeover. This rule does not apply to companies with insiders in firm control (the New York Times Co., for example), but it does apply to the majority of companies, which do not have insider control (Knight Ridder, for example). You can play the takeover game by owning cheap companies that lack controlling insiders.

Did you read somewhere that hedge funds aimed at takeover stocks have fared poorly? Don't let that discourage you. Those hedge funds are playing the wrong game—the old 1980s arbitrage game of buying right after a deal is announced and profiting on the spread between the announcement price and the final deal price. This game is over because spreads are tiny and, in the era of Sarbanes-Oxley audititis, deals take forever to close. If you want to make money in takeovers, buy long before any announcement.

Just find stocks that could be taken over profitably and that you would be content to own even if they aren't taken over. If they're acquired, you win, and if they aren't, you don't lose. ∎

Lessons From Lurie
April 17, 2006

With this issue I overtake Sidney B. Lurie to become the fifth-longest-running financial columnist in *Forbes'* 88-year history. Lurie wrote "The Market Outlook" on these pages between 1954 and 1976. A lot of what he said back then about market psychology is still valid today.

Lurie, who died in 1985, had been research head at Paine Webber, where he wrote the world's first recurring brokerage house market letter, and, during most of his *Forbes* years, at Josephtal & Co. A generalist covering a wide array of topics, he was a marvelous writer and also a marvelous excavator of obscure facts.

He knew then what you need to know now, that it is pointless to make investment decisions unless you are doing so based on information you don't think others widely possess. Otherwise you would be better off in an index fund, since you will just get lucky sometimes and unlucky others. In a world with much less information flow than ours Lurie devoured obscure industry trade journals, often extracting a minor footnote about inventories or a new product and building a theme around it. In his very first column he said, "The market usually rings a bell before changing direction, but few people hear it."

He knew that to see the market right you also had to see it "colorfully," by which he meant big bright themes that might now look like a color PowerPoint pie chart. He coined the terms "Fabulous Fifties" and "New Era" to describe the 1950s (when the S&P 500 rose more than 19.2% annually), not believing that the market had to go down in the latter half of the decade just because it had done well in the first half. He said things like, "Don't get scared—yet!" He wasn't a permabull or permabear. He was always looking for the turn but could remain bullish or bearish longer than most investors because he knew trends usually extend to extremes.

On November 1, 1958, late in a very bullish year (during which stocks rose 43%), he said, "That the market is 'high' by all traditional standards of measurement doesn't in itself mean that a decline is inevitable." The S&P rose for the next three years. Today's bevy of believers in the inevitability of rapid reversion to the mean could learn lots from Lurie.

I remain bullish and believe that buying pressure will continue from companies using their excess cash and low aftertax borrowing costs to either acquire competitors or shrink their own capitalizations in buybacks. ∎

Feel the Force

May 8, 2006

Did you know that we are in the midst of a bucking bull market? Look only at the S&P 500, up 4.2% in the first quarter, and you might miss it. Pay attention, instead, to the Morgan Stanley World Index, the best measure of the developed-country markets. It was up 6.6% in the quarter. Never before said in print—you read it here first: Whenever the whole world stock market has gotten off to a good start, there has always been more good news for the remaining nine months of the year.

In MSWI's 37-year history there were 15 other times when the first quarter was up 4% or more. The second quarters were up 13 times. The collective nine months after those strong first quarters were negative only once. That was in 1987, a heck of a weird year that saw an extraordinary two-day collapse in the third quarter but still a return of 16.8% for the year. In fact, each of the 15 years saw double-digit returns. (A negative first quarter doesn't ensure a negative year; it merely increases the odds of such a misfortune, to about 50/50.)

What's putting the wind behind the racing stock market? The force is historically cheap global valuations relative to long-term interest rates. This relationship between rates and price/earnings ratios creates a bargain for corporate buyers of stock. Both corporations buying in a few of their own shares and acquirers taking over competitors in toto find their earnings per share enhanced. The accompanying buyback and takeover binges are shrinking the supply of equities. I've been describing this phenomenon since November 2004. But not thinking globally can cause you to miss feeling the force when you're in a country that is lagging, as America is now.

If you ask what happened in America when first quarters were up more than 4%, you get a basically bullish picture, but it is easy to miss, more ragged and inconsistent than the whole world's. And why wouldn't it be? Any single country is more hit-and-miss, for the same reason that any single stock is more volatile than a portfolio of stocks. American markets aren't as strong this year as foreign markets. I expect that disparity to widen for a while.

As I detailed in my February 27 column, stocks are cheaper overseas than in America relative to each country's long-term interest rates. Our interest rates, over both long and short terms, are higher than rates in most other nations. Our yield curve is much flatter, which is a drag on stocks (but not an indicator of a decline or economic weakness, unless the whole world's curve is flat). Also, sentiment has been more dour outside America than in, allowing for more sentiment pickup overseas.

So follow the world market's first-quarter signal. Take heart. Buy into this beautiful year. Keep thinking and buying globally, with a mix of good domestic and foreign stocks. ∎

Surviving Rate Rises

June 5, 2006

Should you fear rising long-term interest rates? The ten-year Treasury, which started 2006 at a 4.4% yield to maturity, now hovers near 5.1%. As I have been arguing for a while (most recently, in my March 27 column), the bullish case for equities hangs to a large degree on the fact that corporate share purchases—in the form of either cash takeovers or stock buybacks—have the effect of boosting earnings per share of the company buying the shares. And this phenomenon, in turn, depends on the fact that long-term interest rates are low. A chronic upward trend in long rates would do a lot of damage to stock prices.

The rise in long rates raises two questions. First, at some times in recent years when America's long-term rates ratcheted up a bit, foreign rates didn't, later pulling US rates back down with them. Is that what is happening now? No. Long rates have been marching upward pretty much everywhere that counts. So this easy out from the rate threat is not really available.

But there's another safety hatch. The second question: Is the rate rise big enough to indicate a trend?

I may be wrong, but I think no trend is at work. The jump in rates is just statistical noise.

If you can stand to figure percentages of percentages, look at the uptick this way. A rise from 4.4% to 5.1% is a 16% increase in the interest rate on Treasury notes. Since May 2003 we've had four prior upward moves bigger than that, each of which later largely or completely reversed itself. For example, between March 2004 and July 2004 rates rose 30% from 3.7% to 4.8% before falling back to 4% by November. Between December 2004 and March 2005 rates rose 16% before more than fully reversing. In mid-2005 they rose 20% and then mostly reversed.

Even if you don't invest globally (which you should do, particularly this year) you will always be a better US investor if you think globally. Overseas, too, the foreign long-rate increases aren't so big as to indicate more than noise. In Britain, for example, ten-year rates are up 14% from their low early this year but had a 9% run in the middle of last year, 14% the year before and 33% in 2003. All these jumps fully reversed themselves.

By my calculations, global long-term rates would have to almost double, to 7.2%, to choke off this bull market. Such an upward spike in rates—such a collapse in global bond prices, in other words—is unlikely. ∎

No News Is Good News

July 3, 2006

You could, if you were predisposed to pessimism, find much in the news to despair over: global warming, abuses by the military, loose borders. But think, also, about the bad news that you are not seeing:

recession, runaway inflation, oil embargo, unemployment. You shouldn't let gloomy thoughts stop you from buying stocks.

When I see the headlines these days about illegal immigration, I am reminded of some gloomy news from 28 years ago. The cult leader Jim Jones had led 900 followers to their death in the Guyana jungle. The fact that this tragedy occupied front pages for a long stretch was evidence that there wasn't something more substantial and negative for editors and the public to fixate on. The murder/suicides took place in November 1978. The next year the S&P returned 18%.

At least the doings at the Peoples Temple was news. There isn't any genuine news in immigration—nothing happening any differently at our borders now than one, three or five years ago. The only different thing is that Congress and the President are all for expensive legislation that won't accomplish much. But then, there isn't anything new to that.

Other 1978 headlines: We surrendered the Panama Canal, *Hustler* magazine's Larry Flynt was shot, Cleveland defaulted on its debt, Pope Paul VI died, and Pete Rose got at least one hit on each of 44 successive days of baseball. There was a lot of hand-wringing about giving back the canal. And some jokes about Flynt. (The jokes about Rose

came later.) But there was nothing to hurt stocks.

Today we have the Internet to bombard us with more news than ever. Still, it is bullish that the most exciting headlines have to do with Angelina Jolie's baby and Barry Bonds' home runs. There is again nothing to hurt stocks.

I'm pretty confident our upcoming elections won't damage stocks. Control of Congress may shift, further lowering the probability of an extension, past 2010, of the 15% dividend and capital gains tax rate. But it's unlikely, and that risk is already priced into stocks now. This year's elections probably won't budge the market.

So count the immigration saga as an absence of news, and remember that, for investors, no news is almost always good news. Pray for a wall of coverage on the latest social commentary issued by a movie or rock star (among the hundreds to choose from). It would be great if toward the end of 2006 we could get a newsmagazine cover on some nonevent like anomie in our youth or a crisis in American culture. ■

The Short, Sharp Stock
August 14, 2006

There are corrections, and there are bear markets. What we're experiencing right now is a correction. Know the difference. As this column went to press, the Morgan Stanley World Index had fallen 11.5% from its May 9 peak to its June 14 bottom—and then risen. The damage may not be over, but it's not the beginning of a sustained bear market. You should be buying stocks now. There's more bull market ahead before any real bear market.

What makes me confident that the decline will be short and small? Corrections

and bear market beginnings act very, very differently. Having the one means not having the other. And this decline has the distinct fingerprint of a correction.

Corrections are preceded by spike tops. You see a rally (such as we had in the first four months of this year) followed by a sharp cliff that takes the market down 10% to 20% in a very short time. The retreat is over very quickly, in one to four months. Usually, there's a story to go with it. In the correction of 1999 the explanation was the upcoming Y2K crisis, which didn't happen. In the current spill a common rationalization is that the new Federal Reserve chairman, Ben Bernanke, is bad news for equities. It reminds me of the five-week 10.4% correction of 1979 that accompanied Paul Volcker's ascension to that job. The Bernanke scare is just another one of those silly stories that accompany corrections. In time the explanation wears thin and the bull runs.

The adage is true: "Bull markets die not with a bang but with a whimper." The crash of 1987 is the last century's only real exception, and in many ways it was simply an oversize correction. It was big, fast and over fast. By contrast, the bear market of 2000–2002 accumulated slowly. For 11 months around the market peak in March 2000, the Morgan Stanley World Index never wandered outside a 9% band. But that slow and painful downturn was the prelude to much worse. At the bottom the world index was off 51% from its peak.

Buy stocks now, before it is well understood that the recent correction is a short-lived phenomenon. ∎

The November Surprise
September 18, 2006

Nowadays the stock market has lots of political fear priced into it. Shrug off the fear and buy. You'll find stocks a little cheaper than they should be. The fear is of a Democratic congressional sweep. The Dems taking both houses (gaining 6 Senate seats and 15 in the House) could destabilize markets. And markets do really hate political change. It's not that Republicans are good for stocks and Democrats bad. After all, didn't stocks do well in the 1960s and 1990s, when Democrats had the White House, Congress or both? And haven't stocks disappointed during the current all-Republican era? What worries investors is simply any change in control—always.

Iraq, gasoline prices and the Middle East have the incumbent party on the defensive now, but here's something to appreciate: As congressional elections heat up, popularity shifts toward that party with the structural advantage. By that I mean which has fewer Senate seats up for reelection, which has fewer open seats (without an incumbent running), how seemingly close districts vote on other issues, which has more money and which controls the bulk of the state houses. These are all advantages. At the moment Republicans have the edge. In 2008 Democrats will, because there will be vastly more Republican Senate seats up for reelection. I might not be bullish in mid-2008, but I am now.

The Bob Ney House seat in Ohio is a good illustration. The scandal involving his connection to lobbyist Jack Abramoff had the Democrats hoping to knock him off. Because it's a heavily Republican district otherwise, with Ney's announcement to not seek reelection, this seat will stay Republican because of structural advantage. This is one Democratic hope bashed.

A basic rule of politics and a little-known fact: The Senate changes hands so much more easily than the House that in 100 years the House has never changed hands unless the Senate has, too. For the Democrats to win the House they must win the Senate, which means they must win almost every close race—something that almost never happens. I count only seven this year. There are more Democratic than GOP Senate seats up in 2006. And two more open Democratic seats than

Republican; that's more for the Democrats to defend. Joseph Lieberman's getting reelected in Connecticut means one more seat the Democrats need to win than before. Another GOP structural advantage.

My forecast is for the GOP to lose three seats in the Senate and six in the House. Sometime before the election the market will perceive this likely outcome and will move upward in response. ∎

Fear Will Fade
October 16, 2006

Readers didn't much believe me last month when I said the Republicans wouldn't lose Congress in November. If I'm right and these skeptics are wrong, fears of a big political fallout will fade—which is bullish—and you should buy now before the fear fades. No surprise that readers have this view, since the media are close to unanimous in decreeing that the probability of a Democratic victory is high.

But in a national election, structure trumps popularity. Structure means things like which seats don't have an incumbent running, which party has more Senate seats up for reelection, which party has more money in the bank. These factors count more than the fact that George Bush is unpopular. I predict that the GOP will lose seats but not enough seats to lose either house of Congress.

What if I'm wrong? There are only three possibilities. One is that the Democrats win one house but not both. Another is they win both houses but with weak majorities. The third is a Democratic landslide.

With the first two, the outcome is gridlock, the mirror image of what we had in the late 1990s, when Republicans had Congress and Bill Clinton was President. The market loves gridlock. Nothing gets done. That is, we have no tax or regulatory upheavals.

For structural reasons, I believe there is zero chance the Democrats will win by an amount greater than gridlock—by enough, in other words, to override a Bush veto. There just aren't that many iffy seats. Not even close.

Still, suppose I'm wrong. Look ahead. We are only three months away from the third year of George Bush's term. In the entire history of the S&P 500 there have been only two negative third years of any President's term. They were both long ago: in 1931, in the midst of the 1929–32 crash, and in 1939, as we entered World War II. Both very weird and unusual times.

All other third years were double-digit positive, except single-digit positives in 1947 and 1987. The average return in third years is 20%. In fact, there have been only five negative S&P 500 years in the back half of presidential terms. Market risk is highest in the front half of Presidents' terms, which is historically when most attempts at redistributive legislation have occurred. Once the midterms are over, it gets better. It will be no different in 2007. If the S&P 500 is up, the world market will be, too. Good times are close at hand. The time to buy is now, before the perception of political risk fades. ∎

The Rangel Factor

November 13, 2006

Suppose I'm wrong. I've been bullish for a long time; I've been on the right side of the global market as it has risen year after year since 2003, beating bonds or cash. For all the reasons I've rattled off over the last two years I still think there is a big bull move ahead. But suppose I'm wrong.

Bears think the consumer is tapped out, the economy about to crumble, corporate earnings at an unsustainable share of national output, the commodity boom snapped, the housing bubble burst and the Federal Reserve trapped between rising inflation and a wobbly world economy. You might have that nightmare in which the Democrats sweep Congress and you wake up one morning to find Charles Rangel sitting at your kitchen table filling out your 1040. The New York liberal might be the next House Ways & Means Committee chairman. Suppose, that is, that my last column, predicting that the GOP would hold both houses, is just wrong. (For which I can thank Mark Foley.) How bad will a Democratic win be for investors?

Not bad enough, I submit, to sell stocks now. Market timing is a dangerous game, best limited to the rare occasions when you have good reason to expect a significant bear market—meaning a decline of 20% or more. This column has gone truly defensive only on a few occasions, in 1987, 1990 and 2001. But I just can't justify the cost of in-and-outing to sidestep small corrections.

Could we have a big bear market now? I don't think so. Bear markets come from a combination of positive sentiment with bad surprises virtually no one anticipates (like the 1973 oil crisis). Today too many gloomsters and not that many big-time boomsters (like me) are around for this combination to occur.

I also know I always may be wrong. CXOAdvisory.com, a site (owned by market research firm CXO Advisory Group LLC) that ranks 33 public prognosticators, puts me at the top with a 69% accuracy since 2000 on 58 market-timing calls. That means I've been wrong 31% of the time. So I always plan to own some stocks that will do well if what I expect to happen doesn't happen. Right now that means stocks that would do relatively well in a slightly bearish market, stocks that have some defensiveness to them. ∎

When Turkeys Fly

December 11, 2006

In my September 18 column I predicted that the Republicans would lose 3 seats in the Senate and 6 in the House, and that the stock market would move up in anticipation of this outcome. I have to eat some crow on the political soothsaying (actual losses: 6 and 29), but I'm not backing down on my bullish forecast. The S&P 500 has climbed 6.2% since that column came out and is on its way to a double-digit gain next year. Reason: 2007 is the third year of the presidential term, and third years tend to be bullish.

In not a single one of the 16 third years beginning in 1943 did stocks fall. While the market rose only 5% or so in 2 of these years (1947 and 1987), all other third years saw double-digit gains. Interestingly, foreign markets did well in these years, too. Beginning in 1943 third years of US presidential terms all showed gains for the Morgan Stanley World Index, gains that averaged 20.5%.

Since this rally is getting a little old (it started in March 2003), 2007 may be the year that scrapes the bottom of the quality barrel. Turkeys will fly. This will be a change from recent years, when the trend favored quality value—prestigious companies trading at affordable multiples (like ExxonMobil and Altria).

If the market is up big, as I expect, market leadership will shift away from these recognizable names. Many of the best-performing stocks will be those that folks haven't bid up yet because they can't fathom one single reason to do so. The bottom of the barrel! Boring becomes best. Bad becomes beautiful. ■

2007

Another Broken
Record

"
*When earnings yields are bigger than bond yields, institutional
investors can make a profit by using borrowed money to acquire shares
of stock. The process can continue for years, until equity prices are bid
higher or the cost of money gets higher.*"

"Takeover Targets," March 26, 2007

"
*It is a demonstrable fact that people are more displeased by a loss
than they are pleased with a gain. In fact, behaviorists have quantified
this phenomenon: To offset an unexpected loss of magnitude x, the
average American needs a windfall gain of 2.5x. Apply this rule to the
zero-sum nature of tax and economic legislation and you have a recipe
for unhappiness with every enactment.*"

"Thanks for Not Legislating," June 4, 2007

Ken expected good things from stocks in 2007, and he got them—for most of
the year at least. Despite that, the market peaked late in the year, and Ken didn't
foresee that. His 2007 forecast was identical to 2006. "I'm starting to sound like
a broken record. My 2007 forecast is for the global stock market, as measured by
the Morgan Stanley World Index, to be up somewhere between 10% and 40%,
while the S&P 500 will be up but by a lesser amount." ("A Broken Record,"
January 29, 2007.)

Stocks moved higher in choppy action in 2007, suffering two steep pullbacks
through August. But two months later in October, both the S&P 500 and MSCI
World Index reached all-time highs. Stocks then retreated in the final months
of the year, bringing 2007 returns for the MSCI World Index and the S&P 500
to 9.6 percent and 5.5 percent[1]—barely shy of Ken's forecasted range.

Compelling stock valuations relative to borrowing costs continued to drive
Ken's bullishness. Stocks had been cheap relative to bonds before, but never

for as long as they were heading into 2007. "This is the very first time in history we've seen a prolonged interval of equity arbitrage. That's where you borrow money to buy equity, earning more from the equity than you own in interest on the borrowed money. . . . Equity arbitrage has cropped up before. . . . What's unprecedented is the worldwide breadth of the phenomenon and its duration—55 months and counting." ("Never Before!" May 7, 2007.) As long as this phenomenon continued, the supply of stocks was likely to keep shrinking as it had for several years up to 2007, lifting stock prices.

Even as stock market indexes were reaching record levels, investors remained cautious and sentiment was subdued—a far cry from the investor euphoria that usually precedes a bear market. "My prediction is that before this bull dies we'll see a *Wall Street Journal* front-page piece on why it's different this time and the bull will buck for several more years." ("The Media Monitor," July 2, 2007.)

In Ken's view, not only were common investor fears already factored into stock prices in 2007, many were outright wrong. Take the US savings rate for example. US savings rate data simply don't capture the way most Americans save. "The official numbers have some big deficiencies. They don't count capital gains, and they don't count contributions to retirement plans. . . . Amazingly, when money comes out of a 401(k) plan, the resulting consumption is counted against savings." ("Don't Worry," April 16, 2007.) Simply, Americans tend to save by investing, and that type of saving isn't counted in the savings rate.

Political inaction was another positive for Ken. Democrats controlled Congress but not by a wide enough margin to override a veto from the Republican White House. The resulting stalemate meant little risk of big legislation. "The Democrats have no margin to pass material legislation. In that regard they are in the same position as the GOP in 2005–06. The Democratic Congress has scarcely legislated at all. Markets love that. Gutless is great." ("Thanks for Not Legislating," June 4, 2007.) As far as Ken is concerned, politicians with tied hands are the best kind, and they were tied tight in 2007.

Talk of a credit crunch was also widespread. Credit had tightened by some measures, but borrowing rates were actually lower for highly rated firms by year-end than they had been when the year started. Housing was another concern, but in 2007, national housing prices were only slightly off their 2006 peak with most of the price declines unsurprisingly concentrated in markets that had previously been hottest. As it turned out, Ken was too sanguine on these issues as both would deteriorate markedly during the financial crisis the following year, but in 2007 they were widely known and overhyped in his view.

In November 2007, a seemingly innocuous accounting rule was put in place that would end up having a much bigger impact than anticipated. Statements of Financial Accounting Standards No. 157 (aka FAS 157) required financial firms to utilize mark-to-market accounting to value their assets, or the value they could fetch in an immediate sale. Mark-to-market accounting works great in liquid markets like those for stocks or US Treasuries, but it becomes problematic when applied to the illiquid assets on banks' balance sheets, as investors would unfortunately learn in 2008.

Two-thousand-seven was also the year Ken passed another of his idols, Joseph. D. Goodman, to become the fourth-longest-running *Forbes* columnist, ever. "For me, this lap on the track is sweet and bitter. Sweet because I relish a quest to become *Forbes'* longest-running columnist, ever. Bitter because I've always believed Joe was the best *Forbes* columnist, ever. He was also the first. He made and broke the mold." ("The First and the Best," August 13, 2007.) One of the many Joe Goodman quotes Ken cited was, "The market always does what it should do, but not always when." Perhaps he was speaking to the 2007 peak, just days ahead.

A Broken Record
January 29, 2007

I'm starting to sound like a broken record. My 2007 forecast is for the global stock market, as measured by the Morgan Stanley World Index, to be up somewhere between 10% and 40%, while the S&P 500 will up but by a lesser amount. By either measure the stock market will trounce both bonds and cash. The problem: This was precisely my last year's forecast.

In 2006 the World was up 20.1% (including dividends). The S&P 500 was up 15.8%. The ten-year bond delivered a total return of 2.4%, and cash was boring. It was what I initially envisioned as a good to great year—better than most folks expected. And that is just what I see now.

Some of the same forces are driving stocks. By a yardstick that I consider very important, namely the spread between bond yields and stock earnings yields (the inverse of the price/earnings ratio), global stocks are 75% too cheap. The S&P 500 should earn $90 before nonrecurring items this year, which comes to 6.4% of the index's price of 1414. Compare that with a ten-year bond yield of 4.6%. Historically, the equity yield is below the bond yield. In 2000 this relationship was reversed: Stocks had an earnings yield of 3.5%, while the bond yielded 6.5%.

The discount on stocks won't all get made up in one year. But a chunk of it may. We still cling to skeptical sentiment we learned to embrace between 2001 and 2003. But this spread between low-yielding bonds and high-yielding equities is driving both cash-based stock buybacks and debt-financed takeovers of companies by competitors or private equity players. Until that gap gets closed the bull market will live on.

Then, too, as I detailed on October 16, we haven't had a negative third year of a President's term since 1939. And only two

single-digit positive years. Third years are sweet. The question is how sweet.

As each year starts *Forbes* requires its stock-picking columnists to deliver a retrospective on the previous year's recommendations. The statistics department calculates what would have happened to a fictional $10,000 put into each pick, less a 1% trading haircut, versus $10,000 put into the S&P 500 at the same time with no haircut. I've gone through this kind of report card for 11 of the 22 years I've done this column.

The retrospective, too, is sounding like a broken record. My prior ten years' report cards are detailed in Appendix L of my book *The Only Three Questions That Count*, just out from John Wiley. My columns did 11.7% annually for that decade versus 6.8% for the S&P tracker. I lagged the S&P in only two of those years, 1997 and 2002.

For 2006 I recommended 54 stocks, one more than in 2005, and my picks returned 15.7%, versus 8.7% for the S&P 500 tracker, an eerily similar seven-point spread.

In 2006 I did well primarily because my picks had a slight value bias in a year when value beat growth and because they included foreign stocks in a year when the dollar was weak. Someday I'll have to return to leaning primarily on US stocks, as I was doing in the late 1990s, but that day hasn't come yet. This year, once again, foreign stocks should do better than US ones. Quite apart from what happens to the dollar, foreign stocks will be helped by their low starting valuations. The expected 2007 earnings yield on the Morgan Stanley World Index is 7.6%, a whopping 3.6% spread over the ten-year, GDP-weighted global long-term government bond rate— twice that for US equities.

My best-performing stock was Finland's Metso (currently at $50), up from

$33 in the July 3 issue. This industrial-machinery firm is excelling as the global economy expands. While up a lot, it's still too cheap at 13 times 2007 earnings, and I'd hold on to it.

From January 30 the Dutch heavy-machinery maker CNH Global and steel-maker Mittal Steel were up as much but not as fast. But these two are now, in my view, fully valued, and I'd ditch them.

On April 17 I said Inco, the world's second-largest nickel producer, was cheap at $49 and plausible as a takeover. I was very lucky on this one: Companhia Vale do Rio Doce bought it at $75 on October 24.

My worst stinker was also from the April 17 issue, Bausch & Lomb (currently at $52), which I recommended at $68, immediately before a spate of bad news and eye illness associated with its contact lens solutions. While my timing was terrible, I still like the basics. The stock is now goes for 14 times expected 2007 earnings. Hold fast.   ∎

Housing Boom!
February 26, 2007

Don't buy it. For months now the debate has been over whether America will have a hard landing or soft landing, the answer hinging on how big 2007's housing disaster turns out to be. Well, there won't be any housing disaster. We won't have a landing at all, soft or hard. Right now the US and global economies are both accelerating.

You can see right through the housing crash story by looking at the prices of housing stocks. The market knows what the economic worrywarts do not, which is that the housing sector is already making a comeback. In the last six months housing stocks are up 24%, well ahead of the overall market. If housing were destined to fall apart in 2007 these stocks wouldn't be so strong now.

Did you know that housing sales are up in the last few months, not down, and that inventories are lower than six months ago? We're accelerating, not landing. This is true not just in housing but also pretty much across the board.

The consensus forecast is for single-digit S&P 500 earnings growth tied to a slowing economy. Disbelieve it. Experts' forecasts have been too low for four years and will be now. First, the accelerating economy

Right More Than Wrong Still Means Wrong Occasionally

Ken would say, to win in investing, you needn't always be right—that's impossible. You just must be right more often than wrong. But that means being wrong occasionally—and this is one instance. Though housing stocks were indeed up in the six months prior to February 2007, they started dropping not soon after.

Contrast that with Ken's view on stock-supply-shrinking buybacks and M&As—2007 was indeed a record-breaking year for such activity as he predicted. And that likely did help buoy stocks, which overall had a fine year despite housing.

will deliver earnings that exceed expectations. Second, the analysts polled for these consensus numbers never factor in the effect of corporate purchases of stock for cash. Whether a company is buying in its own shares or taking another company, the acquisition of equity stakes (if done cheaply enough) raises earnings per share.

Not since the late 1950s have sustained fundamentals (low long-term interest rates and low price/earnings ratios) so strongly favored corporations shrinking equity. My firm's count of last year's buybacks and takeovers, less new stock issuance, was $585 billion, or 4.5% of gross domestic product. That will be even higher in 2007 as more players learn this game.

Along with sales growth comes productivity growth. Companies are hiring but not in proportion to the gains in their top lines. The result is higher productivity, which feeds into rising profits and living standards. The Federal Reserve probably won't cut interest rates soon, but it doesn't need to. The economy is humming along without any artificial boost. This is a time to own stocks. ∎

Takeover Targets
March 26, 2007

Four and a half years and still going strong. The bull market that began in late 2002 is far from over. Pessimists will tell you that the good times have to stop, that after four years the market just has to be due for a correction. But that's because the pessimists don't look at what is driving this market.

The driver is the relationship between earnings yield (the inverse of a price/earnings ratio) and bond yields. When earnings yields are bigger than bond yields, institutional investors can make a profit by using borrowed money to acquire shares of stock. The process can continue for years, until equity prices are bid higher or the cost of money gets higher.

We're in the middle of such a process. The phenomenon can go on for quite a while. It did in the early 1960s, when a combination of cheap money and low stock prices gave rise to the conglomerate boom, personified by Harold Geneen of ITT.

Who are today's institutional buyers? They are of three kinds. Some are private equity investors, firms like KKR and Blackstone that use mostly borrowed cash to buy whole companies outright, even,

as we are now witnessing, a giant electric utility. Next are publicly traded corporations using debt (or a combination of debt and other financing) to acquire competitors or related firms; an example is Tata Steel's deal to buy British steelmaker Corus, announced January 31. In the lingo of analysts, the deal will be accretive. That is, Tata's earnings per share will go up as a result.

Finally, astute chief executives who don't want their companies to be taken over can leverage up their own balance sheets in order to buy in shares. Done cheaply enough, the buy-in raises earnings per share and thus the share price, making the company less tempting to takeover artists. Two companies that have successfully undertaken large-scale buy-ins over the past several years are Avon Products and Texas Instruments.

Some, not all, chief executives are either slow to figure out what is going on or else too conservative to want more debt on their balance sheets. I will cite two companies that ought to be buying in their own shares. My purpose is not to scold management into acting but to tip you off to shares you can still buy cheap.

By the time the companies in question (or hostile acquirers or Blackstone) get around to buying, you should be looking at a nice capital gain.

The first is Lone Star Technologies (currently at $47, LSS), which makes the steel pipe used to drill oil and gas wells. It's a perfect takeover target in a naturally consolidating field. One plausible buyer (pending any antitrust concern) is Tenaris SA, an Argentinean firm in the same field that recently announced takeovers of two Lone Star competitors, Maverick Tube and Hydril.

Lone Star trades at 12 times its likely earnings this year. Tenaris or another acquirer could pay a 25% premium to get Lone Star, pay the tab with BBB-rated bonds paying 5.8% (which would cost only 3.8% aftertax) and pocket an earnings increment of $45 million a year. Now, Lone Star's boss, Rhys J. Best, is about the best guy you could get to run an oilfield steel firm like this. But he's simply too conservative financially. I think he should borrow $700 million and buy in a third of Lone Star's shares. He'd still be left with a balance sheet no more leveraged than that of the average S&P 500 firm. Buy now, before Best reads this column.

Here's another steel man I admire: Keith Busse. He was a protégé of the late steel industry genius Kenneth Iverson of Nucor Corp. But Keith must not know finance or he would get his stock up more. He is the founder and chief executive of Steel Dynamics, which is a smaller version (4.7 million tons a year) of Nucor, a low-cost minimill operator. Insiders own 17% of Busse's firm, but that isn't enough to stop a takeover.

Steel Dynamics trades at ten times likely earnings for 2007. An acquirer paying a 25% premium using borrowed funds should be able to boost its own after-tax earnings by $175 million a year. The steel industry is globally fragmented. Takeovers are accelerating as firms strive for share. Cross-border takeovers are common now (witness Mittal's purchase of Arcelor). Anticipating a hostile tender offer, Keith Busse should have his company borrow money and use the proceeds to buy in shares.

Keith has

been doing just the reverse: paying down debt, a bad strategy for 2007. Keith Busse is as courageous as anyone you will ever meet and fears no fight, but if he doesn't get his stock up he will have a fight he can't win. Buy that stock before the fighting starts. ∎

Don't Worry
April 16, 2007

American savers, end your guilt trip. You have been told, by economists and by official government statistics, that you are inadequate, that the US savings rate is negative. Wrong! It's a myth that Americans don't save.

The official numbers have some big deficiencies. They don't count capital gains, and they don't count contributions to retirement plans. Most of Bill Gates' wealth consists of realized and unrealized capital gains. In the stats published by the US Commerce Department Bill Gates is a spendthrift. His consumption is more than his salary.

What's true of him is true of any American with net worth tied up in a home's value, a 401(k) or stocks. A lot of people built wealth by owning a home and watching it appreciate. In my New York Times bestseller, *The Only Three Questions That Count*, just out from John Wiley & Sons, that's a form of savings. The government, though, counts only how fast you pay down your home's mortgage.

Americans are really the world's biggest and most productive savers. Collectively, we are not tapped out, we are tapped in.

Think about this when the gloomsayers tell you that a softening of housing prices will turn into a collapse in consumption and thus into a recession.

Recently America's capital gains have bounded ahead at about $3 trillion a year—stock price appreciation, home price appreciation and the rest. Those who own these appreciating assets think they've saved. If this were how the officials measured wealth accumulation, we would have a 23% savings rate. That is, gross domestic product is about four times the capital gains number. I doubt any other country matches this savings.

There's another bug in the official savings formula. It excludes contributions to defined contribution plans, like 401(k)s. Amazingly, when money comes out of a 401(k) plan, the resulting consumption is counted against savings.

When I say that Americans are productive savers, I mean that we don't stuff money under mattresses and hide gold in the vegetable garden. The savings are matched with investment in PCs and power lines, delivery trucks and drug patents—things that give rise to increased economic output. ∎

Never Before!

May 7, 2007

The world has a way of worrying right now. Subprime! Iran! High oil! Ben Bernanke's inflation babble! Profligate consumers! Soft landing! The yen carry! These are small, petty, garden-variety suicidal excuses to miss the reality that this is a uniquely spectacular time.

This is the very first time in modern history that we've seen a prolonged worldwide interval of equity arbitrage. That's where you borrow money to buy equity, earning more from the equity than you owe in interest on the borrowed money. The arbitrage comes in three forms: corporations buying other corporations for cash, corporations buying some of their own shares for cash and private equity investors buying corporations using mostly borrowed money. The arbitrage has to do with the fact that the earnings yield on equities (earnings divided by price) is often more than the aftertax cost of money (which is, roughly, two-thirds of whatever your long-term interest rate is).

Equity arbitrage has cropped up before, for fairly long stretches, in single countries. It has occurred globally, for example in 1974 and 1982, but only for a short while. What's unprecedented is the worldwide breadth of the phenomenon and its duration—55 months and counting.

Far from being about to exhaust itself, the leveraged buyout/buyback binge is, I believe, accelerating. Why? Because it takes awhile for corporate bosses to catch on. After a few years of seeing LBO-meisters get rich, they realize that they had better do some borrowing and buying of their own, or else someone else will do it to them.

What does this mean to small investors? That you should own equities. The acceleration in buyouts and buybacks will keep creating a booming world stock market by shrinking the supply of equity while boosting earnings per share.

This year the global equity supply will shrink by 5%, or $1.75 trillion. That dwarfs the things that people worry about, like the US deficit, the cost of the Iraq war or the likely losses of principal on subprime mortgages. Buy good stocks and enjoy the ride.

P.S. In the March 26 issue I recommended Lone Star Technologies (currently at $66.50) at 47 as a takeover target. I never expected the tender offer to come so fast. On March 29 US Steel announced it would pay $67.50 for the outfit. Pure luck! I wouldn't waste time hanging around for the extra buck. You'll get it but can do better elsewhere. ∎

Thanks for Not Legislating

June 4, 2007

Here's one more reason to remain bullish in 2007 and into 2008: We've got a do-nothing Congress. Stalemated legislators are good for the market. Have you ever seen a more gutless Congress than the one now in session? Well, okay, maybe the last one, the Republican one, was almost as gutless, but it's all the same bull market. The less that lawmakers can do, the less damage they can do.

Last November, as the Democrats won control of Congress, you heard endlessly about how many things they would change this year. Health care, oil, impeachment, the Iraq war, taxes and on and on. A big first 100 days!

Now consider how much time House Speaker Nancy Pelosi (D–Calif.) has spent traveling, even in those first 100 days. And why shouldn't she? She can get more done outside the Beltway than inside it. The Democrats have no margin to pass material legislation. In that regard they are in the same position as the GOP in 2005–06. The Democratic Congress has scarcely legislated at all. Markets love that. Gutless is great.

People of all ideological persuasions feel frustrated when Congress doesn't enact the laws that they think will improve society. But every change helps someone at someone else's short-term expense. Every winner is matched with a loser.

Now, it is a demonstrable fact that people are more displeased by a loss than they are pleased by a comparable gain. In fact, behaviorists have quantified this phenomenon: To offset an unexpected loss of magnitude x, the average American needs a windfall gain of $2.5x$.

Apply this rule to the zero-sum nature of tax and economic legislation and you have a recipe for unhappiness with every enactment. You are pleased that Congress is handing you a subsidy for your solar panel. Your neighbor is twice as displeased about the taxes he will pay as a result.

In years when Congress is active, political risk aversion rises and, as it does, demand for stocks and bonds falls. Political risk aversion and stock demand are inversely correlated.

For this year and next anything important that Congress passes, and there will be precious little of it, can be vetoed with impunity by our lame-duck President. What a beautiful world. Celebrate gutlessness! If you haven't already done so, buy stocks. ■

The Media Monitor

July 2, 2007

Here's a good reason for believing that the bull market will continue: Journalists don't think it will. Business commentators keep trying to see a peak or to imply that the market is high. Since this bull market began in 2003 they have been bearishly biased. And that's bullish. They have been looking back at 2000's peak, clearly a deadly time, and making comparisons with now. They are fighting the last war.

Yes, the Dow Jones industrial average and Morgan Stanley World Index are at all-time highs, as we are constantly reminded. But many indexes aren't—notably the Nasdaq, the Japanese markets and pretty much any growth stock index. And note that the headlines about new highs never mention inflation. Prices are up 20% from the spring of 2000, the last time records were being set, and so it would take an S&P at 1800 to set a real record.

Something else about that last war: Stocks were expensive seven years ago, compared with long-term borrowing costs. Now, on that metric, they're at near-record cheapness. Since 2000, S&P 500 earnings are up 57%. Shouldn't stock prices be up, if not in tandem, at least by a good amount? Yet the media see earnings growth as bearish. It seems that earnings, as a fraction of economic output, are abnormally high and so due for a collapse.

Take the *Wall Street Journal*'s May 23 front-page story "Why Market Optimists Say This Bull Has Legs." It is cast as a story about why optimists see more gains ahead but really spends much more ink on why gains aren't ahead. The story suggests that regression to the mean from high earnings levels will drive this market lower. The experts saying this, however, have been saying this for several years. The day will come when profits shrink, yet there is no evidence for why this day is imminent. The *WSJ* article does not identify a trigger. My prediction is that before this bull dies we'll see a *Wall Street Journal* front-page piece on why it's different this time and the bull will buck for several more years.

Bad Sentiment to Worse

What was notable about this bull market as it neared its peak (which was coming soon) was the utter absence of euphoria for stocks. Typically, bull markets peak on euphoria—easily seen in media headlines. This is what Ken's noting in this column—the media were fairly uniformly dour. Contrast this to the mania that coincided with the Tech bubble peak in 2000, when it was common to hear talk of the "new economy" where "earnings don't matter." Stocks weren't seen as risky then. What was seen as risky was missing the next hot IPO. Sentiment was similarly euphoric near the 1987 and 1990 peaks.

While it's never truly "different this time," one feature different about this bear market was it started on bleak sentiment that just got bleaker.

■

The First and the Best
August 13, 2007

With this column I pass Joseph D. Goodman to become the fourth-longest-running financial columnist in *Forbes'* 90-year history. Joe wrote for a 23-year stretch that ended in 1958. For me, this lap on the track is sweet and bitter. Sweet because I relish a quest to become *Forbes'* longest-running columnist. Bitter because I've always believed Joe was the best *Forbes* columnist, ever. He was also the first. He made and broke the mold.

Stock columnists weren't common when he began writing here, three years away from the bottom of the 1929–32 market crash. Joe was way ahead of his time. Handpicked by his friend and this magazine's founder, BC Forbes, he kept up the column for four years after BC's death, in 1954, until his own death, at the age of 64.

Joe was stunning with market direction, sector picks, stocks—and words. He called the 1937 peak; he envisioned World War II well before it was in the market. He was bullish in 1949, at a time when stocks were very out of favor but poised to quintuple in the space of seven years. In the June 15, 1956 issue of *Forbes* he nailed the top almost perfectly, just a few months after its peak. By early 1958, as the market was bottoming, he was bullish again. When he died he went out on top, riding high.

He created lines that became famous in finance:

> *If your stocks worry you, sell to the sleeping point.*
> *Be bullish in a bull market, but don't be either a bull or a bear all the time.*
> *A bull makes money, a bear makes money, but a hog makes nothing.*
> *The market always does what it should do, but not always when.*

He had his own way of seeing things. He said that you should buy a stock that won't go down in a bear market because it will probably lead the next rise. Just so, he feared stocks that wouldn't rise in a bull market. They didn't look like bargains to him; they looked like trouble.

Some pros go by the adage "I get rich selling too soon." He worked the other side of the price chart, aiming to sell two or three months after a bull market was over. I learned from reading Joe not to precall market peaks—those who do are often run over. There is always plenty of time to get out. For two decades I've seen Joe Goodman as a virtual mentor, even though I never met him (and was 8 when he died). ∎

The Fall 2007 Rally
September 17, 2007

Don't let this fall's rally whiz right by you before you take a close look at stocks from Asia. The midsummer correction—at one point on August 16 the Morgan Stanley World Index was down 12.5% from its 2007 high—provided a great time to get into stocks on the other side of the dateline. If you don't own this region, now is the time to get in. When the rally resumes, Asia will lead. These stocks are to this market what tech stocks were to the mid-1990s.

What makes me so sure that we're in a rally, not a long-running decline? Four things. The first has to do with the shape of a bull market termination. The final peak does not arrive sharply. It tends to have a gentle upward slope, as the final but diminishing round of suckers is drawn in. And then the decline (usually) begins with a gentle slope, too (October 1987 was the exception proving the rule—over almost instantly), as some buyers continue to come in even after the bull market is over. The bull market leading up to the July 16 peak was too sudden and the plunge too sharp to presage a real bear market.

Second, bear markets don't start from old news. In this case the old news is that many subprime borrowers are going to default on their mortgages. While this misfortune is still unfolding, the basic facts have been out for a while. A fundamental rule of markets is that old news runs out of power. It takes new information to move stock prices.

Third, it usually takes a severe credit crunch to set a genuine bear market in motion. This credit crunch, at least for corporate borrowers, is not severe. You measure crunch by the spread in yields between junk bonds and Treasury bonds of like maturity. In 2000 that spread widened by three to four percentage points, a harbinger of both a broad tumble in stock prices and an economic contraction. In that case, moreover, the widening spread came atop rising Treasury interest rates— weak corporate borrowers had two strikes against them. Contrast that with what's happening now. Junk spreads widened by only a percentage point before going back the other way, and much of the widening was from a fall in Treasury rates, hardly bearish. This is a phony credit crunch.

Fourth, the media always jump on a short-term correction but rarely wake up to a long-term bear market in its early phases. One form of this media attention is trotting out the perma-bears to deliver their "I told you so" speeches to the TV cameras, with scenes of the New York Stock Exchange running in the background. Generally speaking, the friendly interviewer conducting the show neglects to ask the bear when he first turned bearish and how much the market is up since then. As with all corrections, a few months from now we will be wondering what the fuss was about. ∎

Credit Goblins
October 15, 2007

So many people are bearish, so many experts are wringing their hands over subprime lending, so great are the fears of a credit crunch, that you should be . . . bullish! It isn't just the media's dirge about mortgage defaults that will supposedly ripple everywhere. Normally sounder-thinking Main and Wall Streeters are worrying themselves to death about the economy. It took just one lightning-quick month, beginning in mid-July, for the popular consensus to go from optimism to pessimism. A rapid switch like that never happens around market tops, only corrections. The bears are wrong.

In the September 17 column I detailed why we have no real credit crunch, scarcely even a hunch of a crunch. By the time Halloween is over, the credit crunch bogeyman will have disappeared along with the ghosts and skeletons.

The bigger picture, which has been apparent for three years, is that corporate earnings are very strong in comparison with stock prices and the aftertax cost of borrowed money. This phenomenon is fueling takeovers, leveraged buyouts and share buybacks. Bears don't see any good in this. They posit that corporate profit margins are abnormally high—therefore destined to revert to a lower level—and that the cost of borrowed capital will soar in the coming credit crunch.

Wait a minute. What credit crunch? Since June interest rates are down, not up. Not just short-term rates, not just government rates, but long-term corporate rates.

Compare the earnings yield on stocks (the inverse of the price/earnings ratio) with the yield on ten-year corporate bonds rated BBB. That credit rating is at the lower end of what bond traders call "investment grade." At the moment the ten-year BBB yield is 6.2%, or 3.7% aftertax if you assume a corporate federal-state income tax rate of 40%. Compare that cost of money with the earnings yield on the S&P 500. The index should earn $95 a unit this year, before nonrecurring items. That's 6.2% of the index's price of 1531. In other words, corporations can earn more money on borrowed capital than the money costs them. Despite what you hear, recent buybacks and takeovers weren't primarily funded by junk. By December, buybacks and takeovers will both be back and stocks will be soaring. ∎

Put Some Money in Japan
November 12, 2007

Academics say that the stock market is random—that there is no pattern to price movements. Now take a look at the chart, which plots a foreign exchange rate along with a price index for the global stock market. Random? Not a chance. This year these two price series have marched almost in lockstep.

When the euro appreciates against the yen, stocks tend to do well. When the euro falls, stocks tend to do badly. The correlation between daily changes in closing price in the two price series is 0.93, on a scale where 1.0 would tell you that one change is always a fixed multiple of the other. The stock price used here is the Morgan Stanley World Index, which tracks 1,869 stocks in the world's developed markets.

What's going on? The connection starts with the weak Japanese economy. To give it a spark, the Japanese central bank keeps interest rates extremely low. These low rates have not inspired the Japanese to put capital into either machinery or houses. Instead, the capital is being swept abroad. Speculators in Europe and North

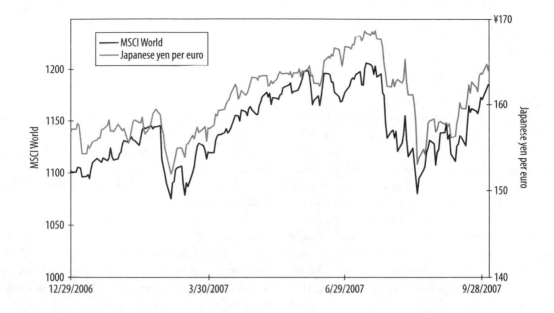

FIGURE 24.1   Yen/Euro Versus World Stocks

Source: Thomson Reuters.

America borrow in yen at those low rates, convert the yen into euros and other currencies, and invest in higher-yielding assets elsewhere. This is called the yen carry trade.

The borrowed Japanese money buys gold, stocks, bonds, you name it. But the net flow of capital is, ultimately, heavily into stocks. On days when the process moves in the forward direction, the euro is bid up, the yen is bid down, and stocks in the US, Europe and Australia are bid up.

I expect this flow of capital to continue. But what if it went into reverse? What if the Bank of Japan suddenly raised short-term interest rates, choking off the yen carry trade? Then folks would sell stocks globally. They would sell euros, Aussie dollars and US dollars in order to buy yen and repay the loans. That would send capital flooding back into Japan—making Japanese stocks strong relative to all else.

It is noteworthy that, in two corrections this year (starting in February and July), Japanese stocks outperformed. They also outperformed when the Bank of Japan twice raised rates a hair. Overnight money in Tokyo is now priced at 0.5%.

Again, I expect the flow of capital out of Japan to continue, and I remain very bullish about non-Japanese stocks. Right now you should be particularly heavy in emerging markets, in Germany, in energy, industrials and materials. But a smart investor hedges his bets. To hedge against the possibility that yen carry trades reverse, you should also have money in Japanese stocks. At the moment I have 12% in Japan versus the world's weighting of 10%. If you don't want to fret over single stocks, just buy the MSCI Japan iShares. This fixed basket of 354 stocks has a 0.54% expense ratio. ∎

Another New Era

December 10, 2007

What does "new era" mean to you? There was a New Era Philanthropy that turned out to be a scam. There was a New Era in technology at the turn of the century that said the Internet was worth an infinite amount of money. That turned out to be flimflam. And then, sometime near the market's double bottom in October 2002 and March 2003, the bears came up with their own New Era: We were entering a New Era of below-average returns. Bunk, just like the other two eras.

Since the epoch of supposedly sub-par returns got under way, the global stock market has been enjoying markedly above-average returns. This has been true over the past five years taken together (when the Morgan Stanley World Index has averaged an 18.3% annual return) and also in every calendar year except 2005, when the return was shy of its historical (post-1926) performance by a whisker.

What gives? At first post-2002 bulls were dismissed by academics and Wall Street sourpusses as not with it. Well, those who uttered the bearish New Era babble were the ones who weren't with it and should be relegated to the Siberia of commentators. But note that five years of above-average returns haven't yet generated any groundswell of thinking that we're now in some New Era of above-average returns.

That's bullish! It means sentiment hasn't turned euphoric, as it did in the late 1990s. Thus, there's room for more of a bull market ahead. I want to be the first to say we definitely are in a New Era of above-average returns. I'll keep buying stocks until we hear multiple pundits say we are entering a new period of high returns. That will be a time to sell.

When will this happen, that the consensus will turn almost uniformly bullish? I don't know, but I doubt it will be before 2009 starts. Hence, I'm expecting another above-average year ahead, an easy one.

Here are a few factors I don't fear as we enter 2008, either because they won't happen or don't matter: further collapses in the mortgage market; a credit crunch; Hillary as president (or whomever we elect—more on that next month); $125 oil; inflation; rising long-term rates; folly from the Federal Reserve (though I expect folly there); Iranian idiocy (a pleonasm); or anything you read in *BusinessWeek*. What *do* I worry about? I told you last month. My biggest fear is of a rising yen and for the reason I detailed. To wit: The US and European markets are being propped up by speculators who borrow in yen.

But otherwise, buy stocks and be happy. It's still easy—five years into this bull market—to find above-average companies selling at below-average valuations. And this when valuations are in general low compared with the cost of long-term capital. ∎

2008

The Unbubble

> " *Election outcomes don't affect markets the way you'd expect them to. . . . In inaugural years we discover that Democratic presidents are phonies and never meant most of what they said in their populist, anticapitalist campaigns. . . . Inaugural years for Republican presidents remind us that they are phonies, too; they don't do much for the economy or for investors.* "
>
> "BULLY FOR OBAMA," MAY 19, 2008

> " *The bubble, as an investing phenomenon, has been well studied ever since the 17th-century tulip bulb frenzy. Its counterpart in bear markets is not well understood. . . . In a bubble, anyone who argues pessimistically is seen as crazy. In today's reverse bubble, when you argue optimistically you're seen as the crazy one. . . . Bubbles are hard enough to see, but reverse bubbles are completely invisible.* "
>
> "THE UNBUBBLE," SEPTEMBER 29, 2008

Two-thousand-eight was the worst year for US and global stocks since 1931—and a year that, by Ken's admission, he was terribly wrong. In 2008, the S&P 500 lost 37.0 percent, and the MSCI World dropped 38.5 percent[1]—awful by any standard. But stocks didn't head straight down all year. Stocks drifted lower during January and February as concerns about a credit crunch, real estate, subprime mortgages, and other issues mounted.

Ken has said in many columns—the old stories everyone is talking about don't cause bear markets. It's the things most people don't see coming that really sink stocks. In Ken's view, the many looming problems being bandied about in the media were already reflected in stock prices at 2008's start. So he was bullish and saw the market drop through the first few months as a typical market correction tied to unsubstantiated fears instead of the start of a true bear. "Yes, we've heard all the problems. Over and over again. They're well broadcast. And that led to a weak stock market in 2007." ("We're Too Gloomy," January 28, 2008.)

After all, this wasn't the first time the economy and stock market had overcome issues similar to those present in 2008. In his February 25, 2008 column, "1998 Redux," Ken drew parallels between 1998 and 2008. "Early January 1998 saw stocks implode on news of the late-stage aftermath of the so-called Asian Contagion. Currencies and then debt markets started disintegrating in Asia, and that should supposedly have brought the world economy down. The parallel today is the American subprime contagion. Back then the dollar was strong, US stocks led foreign, and technology led on the upside and the downside. Now it is a weak dollar, foreign stocks lead and emerging markets dominate instead of tech." Despite these issues, the S&P 500 was up nearly 30 percent in 1998.[2] Ken expected similar resilience in 2008.

But troubles that seemed confined to relatively small financial firms mostly tied to mortgage origination began spreading to larger firms. Rising default rates, the impact of mark-to-market accounting rules (derived from the recently implemented FAS 157), and tightening credit conditions for select firms brought the health of some of the biggest investment and commercial banks into question. The first US firm of meaningful size to run into trouble was Bear Stearns—then the fifth-largest independent investment bank in the US.

In March, Bear Stearns was on the brink and was sold to JPMorgan Chase in a last-minute, late-night deal negotiated by the Fed and Treasury. Investors rejoiced. From March 10 through May 19, the S&P 500 rose over 12 percent and was down just 2 percent for the year and less than 7 percent from its October 2007 peak.[3] In addition, GDP growth in the US was positive for the first half of the year. Still, stocks renewed their downturn. By mid-July, the drop in both US and global stock prices topped 20 percent,[4] qualifying the decline as an official bear market.

"In my 36 years as a professional investor I have not seen a period like this. Investors are afraid, journalists are morose, and the same old stories keep replaying endlessly. That's not normal. In the world I've known most of my life, old stories quickly lose their power over capital markets and get replaced by new surprises. That which everyone fixates on gets priced into the stock market quickly and can't drag on. But here, 19 months after we first started hearing about subprime mortgages, housing woes and weak financials, the stories moving stocks are little changed. . . . To me it still seems more like a long, big correction than a bear market. But technically I'm wrong." ("Five Blue Chips," September 1, 2008.)

Ken has always been quick to admit when he has been wrong, a lesson learned from other longstanding *Forbes* columnists, most prominently John Schulz (see the chapter on 2000). But admitting you've been wrong doesn't necessarily mean you will then be right. Ken has always said that being wrong and then reversing course only works if you're right that course reversal is called for—otherwise you get whipsawed, among the worst of all fates. In 2002 when Ken turned bullish too early after 18 months of bearishness, he looked foolish at first and later turned out right. This time, having been wrong, he held the course of continued bullishness and continued wrong, delighting Internet bloggers who panned him as a permabull and pummeled him as out of touch.

Unfortunately, the worst for the market was yet to come. Like Bear Stearns, conditions were weighing on investment bank Lehman Brothers. But rather than negotiating a deal to marry Lehman with a healthy firm, Lehman went bankrupt—with no last-minute deal making by the Fed or Treasury. Concerns other firms might suffer a similar fate, and confused why there was no last-minute intercession as there had been for Bear Stearns, investors truly panicked and began fleeing credit markets. Had Fed head Ben Bernanke and then-Treasury Secretary Hank Paulson stepped in as they had for Bear, who knows what would have happened? Or, had they merely explained why they made a distinction, investors might not have had so much cause for blind panic. Instead, investors were mightily confused, and US insurance giant AIG was the next panic victim. By then, stock prices were plummeting precipitously. Between September 19 and November 20, the S&P 500 lost an astounding 39.7 percent of its value, accounting for 60 percent of the entire 2007–2009 bear market decline.[5]

From Ken's perspective, the panic was as irrational to the downside as bubbles are to the upside. So in his September 29, 2008 column he deemed the panic of 2008 "The Unbubble." "The bubble, as investing phenomenon, has been well studied ever since the 17th-century tulip bulb frenzy. Its counterpart in bear markets is not well understood. We've got an unbubble going on right now. People are dour and pessimistic. They are acting as if we were in a depression when we are not. . . . In a bubble, anyone who argues pessimistically is seen as crazy. In today's reverse bubble, when you argue optimistically you're seen as the crazy one—you 'just don't get it.' And because there is no word for irrational pessimism, folks are blind to it."

Just as a bubble pops and prices fall, a bursting unbubble can boost prices quickly. That exactly what happened in 2009, but not before the market inflicted tremendous pain—2008 was miserable for most investors. The financial panic that unfolded caught even the most esteemed and seasoned veterans off guard, Ken included. Fortunately, 2009 would shape up to be a much more prosperous year.

In capital markets, it doesn't pay to be a long-term bear. Most who needled Ken for being too bullish in late 2008 and early 2009 found by late 2009, the tide had turned against them.

We're Too Gloomy
January 28, 2008

Let me make you a solemn promise for 2008. This year, and for the rest of your life, the US market and economy won't head markedly one way while the foreign world collectively goes the other. We're too intertwined globally. Since the foreign economy is twice America's size, and is strong, America should do well in 2008—better, at any rate, than people expect.

Yes, we've heard all the problems. Over and over again. They're well broadcast. And that led to a weak stock market in 2007. In my January 29, 2007 column I predicted that the market (as measured by the Morgan Stanley World Index) would be up 10% to 40% for the year and that "the S&P 500 will be up, but by a lesser amount." The world was up a shy 9%. My *Forbes* stock picks, which were chosen expecting a more vibrant market, did not do well.

Since 1995 *Forbes* has asked its columnists to compare the performance of their picks with the market. This was my third worst of those 12 years. If you had bought all 60 of my 2007 recommendations you would be up 0.9% right now, assuming you lost 1% to transaction costs. Similarly timed investments in the S&P (without a transaction penalty) would be down a collective 0.5%.

Most of the lackluster performance of my picks came from a very wrong decision in February to jump into housing stocks. Beazer Homes, my worst choice, was down 79%. Best choice: Agrium, up 100%, as agricultural stocks did well.

I think we need a whole new type of stock for 2008. Hence, I'm not urging readers to hold on to my 2007 picks, be it Beazer, Agrium or any of the others.

I'm still bullish. Why? The larger non-US economy is doing great. America isn't doing badly. In each quarter we get a gross domestic product stronger than expected, followed by new expectations of terrible results for the next quarter.

This is basically bullish. We aren't likely to get much gloomier. Eventually we'll come around. So 2008 is more likely to be a robust market than a bust one. Stocks are cheap, particularly compared with long-term interest rates globally, as I've said for years.

We've had only three negative fourth years of a President's term in the S&P 500's history: in 1932 as the Great Depression bottomed, in 1940 as World War II began heating up in Europe and in 2000 as the tech sector disintegrated and we had the first constitutionally challenged presidential election in a century. Indeed, the 2000 market was positive until shortly before the election and was positive for the year if you exclude the technology sector. Nothing so severe is likely in 2008.

Fear a Democrat this year? We've elected them many times before. And stocks were almost always positive then. I'm betting so for 2008, although foreign stocks could beat domestic ones. My advice is to stay fully invested on a global basis. ■

1998 Redux
February 25, 2008

The worrywarts seek a parallel to today's market and think they see it in 1930: credit crunch, rising unemployment, financial institutions in trouble. So we must be in for a ferocious bear market. I seek a parallel and find it only ten years ago. And that makes me bullish.

Early 1998 saw financial crises eerily similar to today's and a lot of handwringing about institutions collapsing and setting off a domino chain of other collapses. But guess what? The S&P 500 was up 28% that year.

Early January 1998 saw stocks implode on news of the late-stage aftermath of the so-called Asian Contagion. Currencies and then debt markets started disintegrating in Asia, and that should supposedly have brought the world economy down. The parallel today is the American subprime contagion. Back then the dollar was strong, US stocks led foreign, and technology led on the upside and the downside. Now it is a weak dollar, foreign stocks lead and emerging markets dominate instead of tech.

This year January started rough. So what? Despite folklore, history shows January market movements foretell nothing about the rest of the year.

In early 1997 this column started saying that all you needed to beat the S&P 500 was to own any half of its very largest stocks. That worked for 30 months. My definition of large was a stock whose market capitalization was greater than the weighted average of the index. (This sounds convoluted, but it's mathematically simple: Take every market cap, square it, sum the results and then divide that sum by the combined market cap of all the stocks.) Then, the weighted average market cap of the 500 stocks was $55 billion, and 30 stocks topped that, ranging from General Electric down to Bell South. In 1998 these 30 stocks climbed an average 39%.

Nowadays my hunting ground is the whole world, where there are 24,000 stocks to choose from. The weighted average market cap of the MSCI World Index is $81 billion. In one of the stranger coincidences in finance there happen to be 81 companies whose market caps exceed that $81 billion figure. This is where you should concentrate your money. After all, we just started the final leg of a seven- or eight-year bull market (beginning in late 2002), and final legs of bull markets are dominated by big stocks.

In 1997 credit spreads had started widening as everyone feared Asia's finances and its low-quality debt. The result was that the biggest, safest firms were disproportionately allocated credit and lower-quality borrowers were cut off. We're seeing a replay now. Last summer junk borrowers were squeezed out of the market, especially the commercial paper market. General Electric and ExxonMobil can borrow all they want.

With big stocks continuing strong and weak ones getting squeezed we could see a bifurcated market in 2008. Don't be surprised if the biggest stocks do well while indexes of small stocks like the Russell 2000 do badly. This contrast will drive technical analysts nuts because they are trained to hate markets where there are more decliners than gainers. Ignore the technical analysts. ■

Crunch Mythology
March 24, 2008

If you believe the popular economic myths of the day, you think there's a credit squeeze—less total credit available. This is nonsense. There's indeed less credit available to poor risks, individual and corporate. But that just means there's more for the good borrowers. Blue-chip companies are flush with capital and borrowing power. This is bullish, both for the economy and for stocks, especially stocks of big companies.

Fact: The largest firms have much more credit access in all forms than they did 12 months ago. These are the very firms that can spend it the most and the fastest.

Fact: Total corporate borrowing—that is, total US corporate debt issuance—was higher in 2007 than in 2006. In January 2008 US corporate borrowing was $101 billion, up slightly from the same month a year ago. The majority of this debt was of investment grade, meaning that it was rated BBB or better; within this segment the borrowings were up 12% from a year ago. Some credit crunch!

If there were a squeeze, interest rates would be shooting up. They aren't. Over the past year the yield on investment grade corporate bonds has gone down. At the superprime end, debt rated AAA, the yield is down from 5.18% to 4.63%. Globally, there are only 14 corporate borrowers with that rating (among them ExxonMobil and Novartis). But there are more than 350 A-rated or higher. Recently rates are down, a little, on AA, A and BBB bonds, too.

A parallel myth is that corporations have stopped doing takeovers and stock buybacks. Tell that to Microsoft. It's just that we've changed from a lot of small deals to fewer bigger ones. By the fourth quarter "credit crunch" headlines were ubiquitous, yet fourth-quarter 2007 announced takeovers were $478 billion, the fourth-largest quarter ever. The volume was a $116 billion gain from the third quarter. Share repurchase announcements in January totaled $59 billion, up 16% from a year ago. That's a $700 billion annual rate. The prior four months were also up—collectively, by 63.5%, to $276 billion ($828 billion annualized).

Where do we get all these myths about crises and collapses? From pontificators. The sort of folks who frequent Davos.

Yahoo will cost Microsoft $40 billion or more if it goes through—essentially half cash. It will issue long-term debt for the first time in its existence. Surprise, it will be AAA rated. In one bite, IBM announces a $15 billion stock buyback. Some credit crunch. Think big.

As I detailed last month, the market has shifted, as it did in the mid-1990s, into a period where the biggest stocks do best. We're in the first full correction of the new leg of the bull market. The Asian debt contagion then is the American debt contagion today. This debt crisis is, like the last one, a false alarm. By midyear we will awaken to an ever shrinking supply of equity and a growing economy. The market will be led by big companies. ∎

Cash Rich

What was unusual about the coming recession was, as Ken points out in this column, big firms were indeed flush with cash. Overall, throughout the recession that began late 2007, non-bank balance sheets were extremely healthy. Firms already flush with cash started hoarding even more as the year wore on, in anticipation of bad times to come. So when the world returned to growth in 2009, firms had a record amount of cash on hand.

Dear Abby

April 21, 2008

I'm getting a lot of hate e-mail these days. This onslaught is not entirely a bad thing. It reassures me that my bet against the crowd is a wise one. I'm bullish and have been steadily since the July 8, 2002 issue. In my January 28 column I reiterated the upbeat outlook and reminded you that the fourth year of a presidency only rarely delivers losses to stockholders. Now, with stocks globally (as measured by the Morgan Stanley All-Country World Index) down 8.6% so far this year, people are telling me I'm an idiot. Someone posted to *Forbes* Web site, "Hi Ken. It's been an absolute pleasure watching you vie for the 2008 Henry Blodget Award. Keep up the good work!"

Gloat for now, but please note that 2008 isn't over. I still think the year will end in the plus column. And I'm never happier than when I'm alone.

My critics call me a perma-bull. They forget I called the last three full-fledged bear markets right here in *Forbes*—reasonably well and better than most—and mostly alone (June 15, 1987; November 27, 1989; February 19, 2001). I know I may be wrong now. But I see what's happened since January 1 as just a major correction, very comparable to 1998, with a few things flip-flopped, as described in my February 25 column.

On March 13 Goldman Sachs demoted market strategist Abby Cohen for having been bullish too long. That day marked the bottom of the back half of what I think is a double-bottom whose first bottom was in January. I see Goldman's move as bullish. That once famous market timer Joe Granville materialized out of nowhere saying that we are beginning a bad bear market. I'd bet against Joe any time. Gloomy people are saying that we are in the midst of the worst financial crisis since the 1930s. They said the same thing in 1998. Bullish!

You can't find a time in the 20th century when, less than five months into a real global bear market, people were talking bear market and recession in any visible numbers. But they always talk disaster during corrections. Check out "Russian Financial Crisis" on Wikipedia. The second sentence says 1998 was a "global recession . . . which started with the Asian financial crisis in July 1997." Wrong. There wasn't a global recession then. There isn't one now.

An old saw says, "You should be fearful when others are greedy and greedy when others are fearful." Clearly folks are fearful now. So you should be greedy. Another saw: "Buy when there is blood on the streets." There's plenty of blood, or at least depression, on Wall Street. So keep buying. As I've detailed in recent months, the market should be led by its biggest stocks. ∎

Bully for Obama

May 19, 2008

I get the sense, talking to investors, that a lot of you are terrified of what an Obama presidency would do to your portfolio. You shouldn't be. Election outcomes don't affect markets the way you expect them to. We have a long history of elections and S&P 500 returns, and the pattern is pretty clear. First, years in which Democrats capture the White House are usually bullish years for the stock market. Second, inaugural years following a Democratic win in November are better than Republican inaugural years. There is a reason for this pattern. The market expects the worst of a Democratic President and then discovers that he's not so bad for investors. It tends to rebound after the initial premonitions that a Democrat will win. On the other hand, Wall Street expects the most of a Republican and is disillusioned after the election.

The average performance for years with Democrats elected is dragged down by two exceptional years. One was 1932, as FDR won and the Great Depression bottomed. The S&P slipped 8.9% that year (including dividends). The other year was 1940, another FDR win, this time with war underway in Europe. The market was off 10%. Take away those two bad years and you find that election years with Democrats winning have always been positive for the market.

If we elect Obama and history's pattern prevails, expect 2008 to be positive but below average and 2009 to be above average. If we elect McCain, 2008 won't be so bad, but 2009 will be a disappointment. Republican inaugural years (there have been ten since 1925) have delivered an average 0.5% loss for the market. Only three Republican inaugural years were positive; seven were negative. Loser years include the first years in both of Eisenhower's and Nixon's two terms and in Reagan's first term, George W. Bush's first term and, of course, Hoover's single term.

In inaugural years we discover that Democratic presidents are phonies and never meant most of what they said in their populist, anticapitalist campaigns. They could never get reelected if they really delivered on their campaign promises. Inaugural years for Republican presidents remind us that they are phonies, too; they don't do much for the economy or for investors. We get disappointed and pummel stock prices.

The three-month period ending in January gave us the first big global market correction since 1998. Investors and the media still fear their own shadows. Stocks should rise regardless of who winds up in the White House. ∎

Election Cycle

As Ken wrote this, it wasn't clear President Obama would win his party's nomination. However, he won and went on to take the presidency—and the election year was indeed poor for stocks. There were other forces besides typical election-year fears that helped drive down stocks of, course. However, 2009, the inaugural year, did follow history's pattern perfectly (and then some) as Ken predicted—it was a hugely above-average year for stocks.

A Stock for Eco-Nuts
June 16, 2008

Now that we've had a full-fledged correction that scared the dickens out of everyone, stocks look wonderful. But I've said all that in recent columns. I particularly love megacap stocks—those, by my definition, with market capitalizations of more than $80 billion—and again for reasons I've clearly stated recently. But here are two smaller ones I like, too.

The Chilean firm Enersis is the largest private-sector electricity generator in South America, serving Argentina, Brazil, Chile and

Colombia. Generation is 40% of its revenue; electricity distribution is the rest. As South America modernizes and develops, Enersis will grow. It's controlled and majority-owned by Spain's giant utility Endesa, which I've recommended many times over the decades. So you know it will be well run. At 1.4 times annual revenue and 19 times likely 2008 earnings, and with a 2.4% dividend, it's more than cheap enough for a nicely growing firm. The American Depositary Receipts for it trade on the New York Stock Exchange. Its market cap is $12 billion.

If you're an eco-nut, buy France's Veolia Environnement, which is postured as the quintessential green company. If you're not an eco-nut, buy it before all the eco-nuts do. In a few years you can sell it to them. Veolia's basic businesses are hardly glamorous. It makes fuel cells, runs mass transit systems and desalinates water. It also turns scrap metal into steel and uses solid waste to generate electricity. Its revenue last year was $44 billion. Its market cap is $33 billion.

Guilt is terrible. It leads people to irrationality and terror. The political and social forces behind the movement to combat global warming and turn energy green are, to me, a form of paganistic spiritualism displacing conventional religions. But they are real forces nonetheless. I believe green investing will soon become a hot social trend throughout capital markets on a scale that "socially responsible investing" never began to approach. It is only a matter of time before big public pension plans, endowments and foundations start carving out specialized allocations for green investing. The cost of guilt will translate into a premium price on green stocks. Veolia will be in every green portfolio.

Veolia is internationally diversified. It gets 55% of its revenue outside France. Revenue breakdown: 33% water treatment, 28% waste management, 21% energy optimization (greenie buzz lingo for heating and cooling gadgets) and 17% outsourced public transit systems. The stock is cheap at 80% of annual sales and 16 times likely 2008 earnings. Its dividend yield is 2.1%.

If recycling waste doesn't make you all warm inside, earning your capital gain will. You can do that with this next stock, too.

Jeffrey Immelt wants General Electric to be the prime choice for greenie investors. This has been his ambition for a while; *Forbes* described it in a cover story three years ago. He is way too late to this party, and in any event most of his company's revenue sources have nothing to do with saving the planet. But GE is still a great firm, and it's soon to be a great stock. Dominant in pretty much everything it does, GE has nonetheless lagged the global stock market since 2004 and is down 23% since last fall. That's because Immelt missed earnings expectations in what the media described as GE's worst blowup since 1987. That year, by the way, was a great time to buy GE.

The unpleasant earnings surprise is a small blip in GE's century-long growth story, and this is a good stock for the megacap era I expect over the next few years. It costs 13 times 2008 earnings and yields 3.7%.

The Finnish handset maker Nokia is a megacap, with a $112 billion market valuation. It has pretty well wiped out its competitive threats, one after another. Years ago those threats included Qualcomm, with its CDMA channel-access technology, Motorola, Siemens and more. Since 1999 they have all shrunk in importance, while Nokia has tripled in size. There is more ahead, but in the correction Nokia's stock melted. It's down 25% this year.

The world's cell phone explosion is far from over. Nokia will be the prime beneficiary. Now, at 1.4 times annual revenue, at ten times 2008 earnings and with a 2.7% dividend yield, it's a buy.

Last on this month's list of premier megacaps is Intel. This $137 billion (market value) firm is far and away the world's largest and leading chipmaker. You can get it for only 16 times 2008 earnings. It yields 2.3%—better than the S&P 500 index. How many premier-quality technology companies can you find that yield more than the market average? ∎

Don't Fret About the Fed
July 21, 2008

There is a spreading fear that we are in for a period of tightening by the Federal Reserve Board. It has gotten to be obsessive. On a recent round of New York media interviews, I encountered two almost unanimous views: that the Fed would hike rates later this year, and that Barack Obama would be elected President. Both events are viewed as all but certain, and as all but certain to do great damage to the stock market.

Put aside your fears. The market will recover.

It is presumed that increases in the Fed's target rate for overnight loans are bad for stocks because high interest rates make the future earnings from corporations less valuable today. But the connection is not so neat.

Since 1970 there have been eight stretches in which the Fed was tightening and eight in which it was loosening. These periods ranged from 6 months to 56 months long. Recently I made two tables, one showing stock returns (as measured by the MSCI World Index) over various periods beginning at the starting points of the tightening periods, the other showing returns beginning at the starting points of the loosening periods. The periods covered 3, 6, 12, and 24 months. I've asked both large audiences and individuals to tell me which set of returns was for the tightening times and which for the loosening. They've been stumped. There's no pattern. They look almost identical.

For example, 24 months after tightenings started, returns averaged a cumulative 16.9%; 24 months after loosenings they averaged 19.7%. But look at medians instead of averages and the results flip-flop to 18.1% for tight money and 12.4% for loose money. You can't find any pattern over shorter holding times, either. Despite what your gut tells you, central bank action holds no useful information about where stocks are going.

In my May 19 column I detailed why you needn't worry about an Obama presidency. Another observation: US stocks do better than foreign ones (in dollar terms) in the last five months before a presidential election. Since 1928 this has happened three-fourths of the time; the advantage to domestic stocks, averaged over all 20 elections beginning with Herbert Hoover's, is 9.1 percentage points. And when it hasn't happened, the other quarter of the time, US stocks haven't lagged by much. When they've led it has been by more than 13%. Simple explanation: Markets dislike uncertainty, and uncertainty declines as Election Day nears. No guarantee the pattern will hold in 2008, but that's the way to bet. ∎

Five Blue Chips
September 1, 2008

The stock market's drop since last November is enough to qualify it as a bear market. I'm not sure there is a meaningful distinction between being down 19% and being down 22%, but 20% is the normal definitional cutoff, and the big indexes have pretty much all pierced 20%. Wrongly, I've been upbeat throughout.

There have been three other bear markets since I started this column 24 years ago: 1987, 1990, and 2000. This is the first time I haven't anticipated the fall. (See my columns of October 5, 1987, May 14, 1990, and March 6, 2000.) I hate that. I let you down.

I also admit confusion. In my 36 years as a professional investor I have not seen a period like this. Investors are afraid, journalists are morose, and the same old stories keep replaying endlessly. That's not normal. In the world I've known most of my life, old stories quickly lose their power over capital markets and get replaced by new surprises. That which everyone fixates on gets priced into the stock market quickly and can't drag on. But here, 19 months after we first started hearing about subprime mortgages, housing woes and weak financials, the stories moving stocks are little changed.

Normally the market peaks before bad news emerges. That's what happened in 1929, and that's what happened in 2000. In the latter crash global stocks had fallen by 16% over nine months before the Federal Reserve's first interest rate cut. This time multiple cuts of the discount rate and the bad news about the housing sector came before November's market peak.

The fact is, the global economy isn't so bad. We have very low growth, with deep pockets of weakness, but last year's consensus held that the pockets would ripple out everywhere, and they really haven't.

Slow, erratic growth continues. The US' first-quarter gross domestic product was up 0.9% at an annualized rate, despite expectations that it would be down. The experts said the number would later be revised down, but it was revised up. They said the second quarter would show a decline in economic activity, but now it's showing an increase of 1.9%. This is the recessionless bear market.

To me it still seems more like a long, big correction than a bear market. But technically I'm wrong. Either way, what do you do now? Well, if you haven't gotten out yet, it's a bit late. Of the ten bear markets since World War II, six went down less than 30%. Another, in 1987, lasted just a few months. Now is nothing like 1968–70, 1973–74 or 2000–02, which were entangled with, broad global recessions.

I'd bet we're most of the way through to the end of this bear market. And after bear markets end, the initial upswings come fast and steep. It would be risky to get out now and end up being whipsawed—that is, exposed to most of the decline but absent for most of the recovery. Now is the time for patience. The shares of big, market-leading companies should be materially higher 12 to 24 months from now. There is too much pessimism and gloom for those shares not to pay off. ■

The Unbubble
September 29, 2008

What's the word for an unbubble? Maybe "cavitation" will do, if you're a hydraulic engineer. I'm talking about the opposite of a speculative bubble: the absence of interest in owning stocks, a vacuum of optimism, a black hole of negativism. People are irrationally depressed, and their depression feeds more depression.

The bubble, as investing phenomenon, has been well studied ever since the 17th-century tulip bulb frenzy. Its counterpart in bear markets is not well understood. We've got an unbubble going on right now. People are dour and pessimistic. They are acting as if we were in a depression when we are not. We are not even in a recession.

In a bubble, anyone who argues pessimistically is seen as crazy. In today's reverse bubble, when you argue optimistically you're seen as the crazy one—you "just don't get it." And because there is no word for irrational pessimism, folks are blind to it. Bubbles are hard enough to see, but reverse bubbles are completely invisible.

People see Fannie Mae's problems as huge, but in money terms the worst imaginable fix is smaller than the Anheuser-Busch takeover. When Kenneth Rogoff, a relatively little-known Harvard economist, recently pontificated that the worst was ahead, European media were transfixed. But when US gross domestic product rose in the second quarter above the quarter before, and inventories fell, both bullish facts were dismissed. Then when inventories piled up in July, it was a big, bad deal.

When the economies of emerging markets don't just grow but beat expectations, there's scarcely a mention. The fact that the earnings yield (the inverse of the price/earnings ratio) of nonfinancial firms is today higher relative to long-term interest rates than it's been in your adult lifetime is not reported either. Britain's flat second-quarter GDP was reported as a sign of recession. Before the reverse bubble ends, buy something. ■

Stocks to Survive On
October 27, 2008

Though I walk through the valley of the shadow of death I fear no evil. Seems that almost everyone else does, though. Most investors need their investments to last them a long, long time, yet they're acting like the next few months are everything. The shadow of death is an illusion. In the long term equities always do well. They will now, too, even if they fall further first.

My firm has 25,000 high-net-worth clients. A typical account would be that of a couple aged 65 and 60 who need their money to last the rest of their lives, 25 to 35 years. They have a long time to go, and they accomplish nothing by getting in and out of the market from fear now. Yet such folks are so overloaded by the doom and gloom they hear around them that many must be re-reminded of their primary purpose and long-term needs.

If you have a time horizon that long, even a 9% minicrash, such as we had on September 28, is something you can take in stride. Over long periods equities have always done well compared with other liquid alternatives. Even if you have a shorter time horizon, such as a decade, you know that stocks are more likely than not to recover from a market decline.

I hear 60-year-olds say nonsense like, "I won't be able to retire because of the market's downturn." That's ridiculous. History has seen many similar bear markets. Yet folks have kept retiring. The next bull market more than makes up for what we lost in the last decline. The average bull market, of which there have been ten since World War II, takes stock up 150% before the cycle turns. The average 12-month rebound from the bottom is 36%. No, I don't know where the bottom is. I just know that stocks don't go down and stay down.

We can argue about where stocks are headed, and there are always two sides to the argument. But put that aside. Think longer. Unless you are in your late 80s and were an adult as World War II ended, stocks are cheaper, adjusted for tax rates and interest rates, than they've been at any time in your adult life. That's a simply stunning statement looking forward. You're walking forward. Stop myopically looking at your feet and focus on the horizon. Just buy great franchises at cheap prices now and be patient. ■

Pessimism and the Rebound

November 24, 2008

"Human affairs are admittedly in a deplorable state. This, however, is no novelty. As far back as we can see, human affairs have always been in a deplorable state." So begins *The Basic Laws of Human Stupidity*, by the late economic historian Carlo Cipolla of the University of California, Berkeley. Those words also began my December 24, 1990 column, "Buy Now," which started a long string of bullish columns following 14 months of bearish ones.

Cipolla's words were a comic twist on the observation that society makes progress despite excessive pessimism and abundant stupidity. He also knew that social fads cause smart people to do stupid things. Bear markets, for example, force investors to the sidelines because human affairs appear to be in a deplorable state. These investors end up missing the initial surge of the next bull market. Human nature causes them to create myriad rationalizations about why bad will endure and progress remains dormant. But that always ends up wrong, because even while conditions seem deplorable, things do improve.

Fighting the last war is always a mistake. Those who got scared out of tech in 2000–03 are finding that those problems are no longer around today. Three years from now, we won't be worrying at all about the demons of the 2008 credit crunch.

When will we get the bounce off the bear market bottom? Did it start on October 28? I can't tell you. I can only tell you that if you're preoccupied with the deplorable state of the world economy you're going to miss most of the recovery in the market.

Sometime soon, and maybe now, we will have the definitive end of the 2008 crash. The stocks that rise the most in the initial stage of a recovery will usually be those from the sectors that got beaten up the most in the decline and have a speculative quality to them. Companies in this group include energy, basic materials, industrials and consumer discretionary. But until all the damage is long past, and the rebound in these stocks is almost over, they'll remain speculative. Most investors, and maybe you, are too frightened at times like these to buy such stocks.

So then think of stocks that are in basically stable and strong fields, with a defined franchise, that have been beaten up in the bear market and likely overly so. They may not have the highest returns, but they may have the highest likelihood of a very good return. ∎

The Coming Bull Bounce

The bear market did not end in November—but soon. Those lows were re-tested and a bit more in March 2009. However, in this column Ken emphasizes a point investors would not have heard anywhere else before—that those categories that held up best earlier in the bear, but fell most in the end typically are the ones that boom most off the bottom. And those are the ones you want to hold. This "bounce" theme would play out almost perfectly across the board in 2009—for sectors, industries, and regions, just as Ken describes here.

Media Mayhem
December 22, 2008

The economy is receding, but not as fast as the media tell you, with their headlines about layoffs and store closings. This combination of facts is bullish. I was far too bullish, however, in my September 29 column. It referred to this period as a reverse bubble, where only the bad in everything is noticed. Indeed, the bad has been noticed—and incorporated into stock prices and credit default prices. Between that column's publication on September 10 and when this one went to bed on November 25, the MSCI World Index fell 31.5%.

The bearish headlines have gotten bolder, and the panic has gotten worse (notwithstanding the late-November rebound). So I'm even more bullish now. Stocks are an even better buy. The S&P 500 is going for 12 times earnings (after nonrecurring items) for the 12 months ending October 31. This at a time when 10-year Treasurys yield only 3.08%.

On November 14 the headlines screamed, "October Retail Sales Down— Worst Ever Recorded." Stocks buckled. But virtually no one noticed that the "recording" had started only in 1992. Since then we've had just one recession. The same reporting failed to mention anywhere that October sales, excluding autos, gasoline and building materials, which everyone already knew about, were down only 0.5%, which was hardly remarkable.

Simply nowhere in the mass media have I seen it reported how strong third-quarter earnings were. Roughly two-thirds of firms reported higher earnings through November 25. Also, two-thirds reported earnings stronger than analysts' latest expectations. Yet we only heard about the laggards. Excluding financials, 67% of companies reported earnings better than the year before, and 68% exceeded expectations.

On October 13 the S&P 500's dividend yield was 3.74%. That means it exceeded the yield on the ten-year Treasury note for the first time since 1958. Did you see a headline about that?

Business inventories are at record lows for the start of a recession, and that fact should make the recession milder. These times will pass. Because stocks are so cheap, a big bull market will emerge. I don't know when. Depending on your willingness to take risk, you could own bigger, safer stocks or smaller, riskier ones. The riskier ones are likely to bounce more in the bull market. ∎

2009

---

25 Years and Counting

> "
> *The stock market is a discounter of known information. It is not a barometer of the current state of the economy but a guess about where the economy (and corporate profits) will be 6 to 24 months in the future. . . . Stock market bottoms happen, and then stocks jolt upward, while the economy keeps getting worse—sometimes by a lot and for a long time.*"
>
> "BE A BAD NEWS BULL," JANUARY 12, 2009

> "
> *Bear markets have been typically followed by bull markets in a V-shaped pattern. The steeper and bigger the decline, the sharper and bigger the subsequent bull move. The few exceptions to this pattern in the past century have involved the emergence of completely different bad forces than the ones that created and contributed to the bear market.*"
>
> "ANTICIPATE THE V," FEBRUARY 16, 2009

As 2009 began Ken was six months away from completing 25 years of columns, the basis of this book. He was also riding as low as he ever had in terms of being right. In 2008, he had been bullish when the right thing was to be bearish, and his stock picks lagged the market (one of only three years when he had lagged in the 13 years, as of this point, *Forbes* had been measuring.) But in 2009, he would be not only right on market direction and right on sectors (down to the fine details), but also his stock picks had their best year ever—more than doubling the S&P 500's return. Not a bad way to close a quarter century.

In the broader world, 2009 was notable for many reasons. Barack Obama was inaugurated as president, Iceland collapsed, the global recession lingered. And the March bear market bottom marked the beginning of a massive, global stock market rally.

The year began miserably for stocks. The rally that began in November 2008 fizzled in the first days of January, and stocks turned sharply lower as panic engulfed the stock market. By early March, the S&P 500 was down nearly 25 percent for the year. Global stocks were down similarly. Investors feared a rash of bank nationalizations both in the US and abroad, and the proclamations of another Great Depression grew louder. "There are endless comparisons with 1929–32, a crash that was followed by a partial recovery and then another bear market (with another economic downturn) in 1937. I don't think that comparison is at all valid." ("Blink and You'll Miss It," May 25, 2009.) During the tumult, Ken was focused instead on a single letter: V.

Ken's 2009 columns advise readers to expect a V-shaped market bottom, or a rebound that roughly matched the pace of the bear market drop. (The titles of his February 16, 2009 column, "Anticipate the V," and his November 2, 2009 column, "Viva the V," allude to this phenomenon.) "The fundamental force behind every V is always that the last phase of a bear market is driven completely by imploding panicky sentiment rather than the fundamentals people think they're thinking about. The sentiment implosion is a societal, psychological depressed-spring effect that makes the market bounce back as quickly and as far as it went down." ("Viva the V," November 2, 2009.)

Stocks' decline during the bear market had been tremendously steep, but so would the rebound in Ken's view. He didn't know when the market would bottom, but the subsequent bounce wasn't something to be missed. "No one can be sure when a bear market is really over. Those who think they have some formula for precisely calling bottoms are fools. What I am pretty sure of is this: When the market rebounds, a lot of its gains will take place in a very short span (like two months or less), and people who are too cautious will miss most of these gains." ("Anticipate the V," February 16, 2009.)

Sure enough, the stock market bottomed on March 9, 2009, and the bounce was spectacular. In the first month of the market rebound, the S&P 500 gained 27 percent. After two months, the S&P was up nearly 38 percent. By the end of 2009, the S&P 500 was up 67.8 percent from the March 9 bottom and 26.5 percent for the year.[1] The rebound in global stocks was even more dramatic, rising 73.0 percent from March 9th and 30.8 percent for the year.[2]

As for Ken's stock picks in 2009, as shown in the Introduction, he trounced the S&P 500 as well as the MSCI World by a massive margin. Investing in Ken's stock picks (with a hypothetical 1 percent haircut for fees) would have resulted in a 44.4 percent return, whereas similar-sized and timed investments in the S&P 500 would have resulted in a 20.9 percent return—a massive 23.5% outperformance.[3] (See Table 1 in the Introduction.) Simply, Ken's outlook for a V-recovery was spot on.

But, more than that, he made stock picks in categories he thought likeliest to bounce hugest in the new bull. "An almost universal stock market fact that few know and you will likely not have read anywhere, ever, is that categories of stocks that fared better than the market in a bear market's first half but lagged badly in its later stages tend to lead the next bull market bounce and for a long time. History holds almost no exceptions to this. This group now includes energy, materials, industrials and consumer discretionary." ("Anticipate the V," February 16, 2009.) Ken's "bounce theme" played out almost perfectly, as those categories did indeed lead the world into recovery.

As they tend to do, the bear market uncovered a number of fraudsters whose hoaxes weren't as easily hidden when stock prices were falling. The huge 2007–2009 bear market revealed one of the biggest frauds in history: Bernard "Bernie" Madoff. Ken's March 30, 2009 column "Get a Grip on Your Fears" addresses the topic of investing fraud in the wake of the massive Ponzi scheme Madoff perpetrated. It foreshadows his *New York Times* bestseller, *How to Smell a Rat: The Five Signs of Financial Fraud*, released by John Wiley & Sons in July 2009.

In the column and his book, Ken offers advice on how to avoid scammers. The single most important step investors can take is not allowing the people who make investment decisions to hold your assets too. "There is one foolproof, easy way to be sure this never happens to you. If you hire someone to make investment decisions for you, be sure it, he or she is separate from whoever has custody of your money. That's it." ("Get a Grip on Your Fears," March 30, 2009.)

In his final column of the year (and this book), Ken looks ahead to the future. In 2009, many pundits were forecasting a new era of sluggish economic growth and stock market returns. They argued all the problems that led to the massive bear would linger for a decade or more. The phrase "new normal" was coined to describe the supposed lackluster decade ahead. Ken addresses this notion head-on in his December 14, 2009 column titled, "The Old Normal":

"The slogan has taken on a life of its own and been widely adopted. It's also utter nonsense—rubbish of the first caliber. . . . In my 37 years in the investment industry, I've never, ever seen an early bull market without some variation of this theme that was widely embraced. Last time around, in 2003–04, it was a 'new era of lower expectations.' Then stocks rose for four years. . . . It all reminds me inherently and eerily of Sir John Templeton's line that the four most dangerous words in the English language are 'It's different this time.'"

Ken has described the period around the March 2009 bear market bottom as a transfer of wealth from those with little faith to those with more faith in the future. Ken definitely falls into the latter group. As you've read in his columns, Ken has expressed periods of pessimism. "There are times to go to cash, but these are rare. This column has recommended pulling back in three bear markets, beginning first in June 1987, then beginning in September 1989 and then in February 2001." ("Quarter Century Mark," July 13, 2009.) But these periods are brief in the grand scheme of things. Even when Ken has recommended getting out of the stock market, it's never permanently. He's always looking for the opportunity to get back in. After all, long-term stock market returns include both good times and bad. Over time, the bull markets have collectively trounced the bear markets. Being in stocks most of the time is the only way to capture stocks' long-term positive returns.

Stock market investing is inherently for optimists. Things won't always be rosy. The economy and stock market will flourish at times and languish at others. During dark times, there are those with little faith things will get better and those who are long-term optimistic. Hopefully, Ken's 25 years of columns have nudged you into the long-term optimists' camp, if you weren't there already.

How will the next 25 years compare to the last 25? Ken would say we'll see some differences but many more similarities. "It's different in details, but the fundamental principles of investing don't change." ("The Old Normal," December 14, 2009.) Stocks will go through bull and bear markets but likely achieve positive long-term growth. The economy too will grow with both booms and busts along the way. And as *Forbes* editor-in-chief Steve Forbes wrote:

"Thankfully for us—and you—Ken's next 25 years promise to be even more fruitful than his first 25 at *Forbes*"—"King Fisher."

by Steve Forbes, August 3, 2009

Be a Bad News Bull

January 12, 2009

Bad news is good. You can expect more of it. And you can expect the stock market to resume its recovery, which began November 20. Do you find this line of argument perplexing? You have company. A lot of my clients are baffled at the notion that the stock market should be climbing at a time when employment is declining.

But if you look back at the pattern in past stock market recoveries, or think about what the stock market represents, the combination of a bull market and a recession will not seem so strange.

The stock market is a discounter of all known information. It is not a barometer of the current state of the economy but a guess about where the economy (and corporate profits) will be 6 to 24 months in the future.

When we all know that the economy is deteriorating, that is already reflected in prices. The September-to-November crash anticipated the announcement in December that the economy is in recession. Now stocks are starting to climb, in anticipation of an economic recovery that probably won't begin until the second half of 2009.

Don't expect to see any real economic improvement or any good news in the labor market for a long time. In history the evidence is overwhelming: Stock market bottoms happen, and then stocks jolt upwards, while the economy keeps getting worse—sometimes by a lot and for a long time. Take the bear market preceding the roaring 1920s. Global stocks bottomed in June 1921, but global economies didn't hit bottom for fully two more years. Or the 1973–74 monster bear, when stocks bottomed in October 1974 but the US economy kept sliding through March 1975.

In the past 12 months the unemployment rate has climbed from 4.7% to 6.8%. It will keep going up for a while. During this time you will see a steady parade of bearish news. There will be a lot of people saying that the stimulus schemes undertaken by the departing Treasury Department were a failure and that the ones from the incoming Administration won't do much better—or work at all.

Look past the pessimism and remind yourself that it's better to be a little early than a little late in getting back into stocks. The upward move at the beginning of a bull market is almost always huge compared with the vacillations late in the bear market. If you try to pick a bottom, you will miss a good part of the action. ■

Anticipate the V

February 16, 2009

This year has gotten off to a bad start, with the S&P 500 (as of January 20) down 10.7% to 805. This just makes me more determined in my bullishness. I like stocks for 2009 precisely because they did so badly in 2008.

Did we hit absolute bottom November 20? Maybe, but I can't be sure; no one can be sure when a bear market is really over. Those who think they have some formula for precisely calling bottoms are fools. What I am pretty sure of is this: When the market rebounds, a lot of its gains will take place in a very short span (like two months or less), and people who are too cautious will miss most of these gains.

Bear markets have been typically followed by bull markets in a V-shaped pattern. The steeper and bigger the decline, the sharper and bigger the subsequent bull move. The few exceptions to this pattern in the past century have involved the emergence of completely different bad forces than the ones that created and contributed to the bear market.

For example, stocks rallied 324% from July 1932 to March 1937. After a recession-induced big bear market and partial recovery over the next 21 months, stocks encountered an entirely new kind of trouble in 1939. War in Europe sent the market down even lower than the recessionary low of early 1938.

That could happen again, with the economic equivalent of an asteroid coming out of the blue. But, absent such a surprise, we should get the normal V pattern. Its upward swing will swamp any late-stage bear market vicissitudes as they always do.

How were my results last year? In line with the market's—which is to say, not good. Starting with 1996, *Forbes'* statistics department has prepared an annual accounting of each stock-picking columnist's picks versus the S&P 500. Over those 13 years my column has lagged the S&P 500 three times, and 2008 was one of them. The others were 1997 and 2002.

During 2008 I recommended 57 stocks. Equal money in each of my picks when first published less a 1% haircut for transaction costs would have lagged equal amounts in the S&P 500 by 1.1 percentage points (without a commission haircut).

That lag came from the first column *(January 28)*, which had my two worst stocks. AIG collapsed 97% because of losses on credit default swaps at a time when accounting standards demanded quicker recognition of such losses. Brazil's Aracruz Cellulose lost 84% as demand for its pulp shrank in the face of recession.

My picks were a hair ahead of the S&P until December 29, when Rohm & Haas shriveled amid fears (unfounded, it now seems) that Dow Chemical might not complete its takeover of this company. Despite this setback, Rohm & Haas was my best pick, up 36%. Other double-digit winners for me last year were NTT Docomo, the Japanese phone company; Logitech International, a maker of cordless PC devices in Switzerland; Repsol, the Spanish oil company; and Travelers, Wal-Mart and John Wiley & Sons.

What stocks from last year's picks are still worth holding? An almost universal stock market fact that few know and you will likely not have read anywhere, ever, is that categories of stocks that fared better than the market in a bear market's first half but lagged badly in its later stages tend to lead the next bull market bounce and for a long time. History holds almost no exceptions to this. This group now includes energy, materials, industrials and consumer discretionary. ∎

The V Cometh

The next bull market would begin, globally, 21 days from this column's publication—the bottom of the V. And a big, awesome V it was. The initial surge was indeed historically huge and steep, which Ken foresaw, since the end of the bear had been unusually steep. Plus, those categories that did worst to the bottom were the ones that did best initially—and for the rest of 2009.

Get a Grip on Your Fears
March 30, 2009

You can't be a successful investor unless you can overcome your fears. So what's bothering you? Maybe, after reading one too many stories about investigations of Ponzi schemes, you are fearful that your entire portfolio may have been embezzled. Huge and scary! Yet I've seen nothing addressing this well and simply. There is one foolproof, easy way to be sure this never, ever happens to you.

If you hire anyone to make investment decisions for you, be sure it, he or she is separate from whoever has custody of your money. That's it. Have your assets held at a major-name custodian such as Schwab, Merrill Lynch, Fidelity, UBS or the like. Have someone else non-connected make decisions about what to buy and sell. End of embezzlement story.

Every story ever about faked accounts, including those involving Bernard Madoff and Allen Stanford (who, by the way, has been the subject only of a civil fraud complaint), combines custody with decision making. Once the portfolio manager has custody he can take the money out the back door. Some set up this way to embezzle. Others start out honest but later fall to the temptation to exaggerate their returns. Separating the two functions is a prophylactic. Without some grand collusion between the two firms, embezzlement is impossible.

Note that even when Lehman failed completely, those who had securities custodied there were fine. Yes, doing this means some types of commingled investments like hedge funds may be harder to do or impossible. But if you set up this way, you will never be Madoffed.

The other fear these days is that of falling stock prices. This is not an irrational fear; stocks that are off 50% from their highs (and a lot are, at this point) can keep falling. But you can temper your fear by realizing that low prices make stocks less risky, not more risky. Unless there has been a corresponding collapse in its business, a company whose $60 shares are now at $30 is less risky for the investor. ∎

> ## Ponzi Protection
>
> In writing this column, Ken realized that few people understood how simple it can be to avoid being robbed blind by the likes of Bernard Madoff, Sir Allen Stanford, and their ilk. And, contrary to what many investors might think, Ponzi schemers can and do hit smaller-sized investors—they don't care who they scam, they just need more money to keep the con from collapsing. So Ken quickly penned his sixth book—*How to Smell a Rat*—to help investors easily identify and avoid money managers who either were or could easily morph into Ponzi scammers.

Lift Up Your Eyes
April 27, 2009

Why aren't people buying stocks when stocks are cheap? Investors refuse to think a few years out to the resurgence of the economy because they're busy staring at their feet. Look up and out. This huge bear market has presented huge opportunities. Beyond simple cheapness, we're on the cusp of the biggest global monetary and fiscal stimulus relative to the world's GDP in history. There is a wall of money coming. And then a boom!

There are problems, yes. But there always have been problems. With a very steep global yield curve the core of banking is now again profitable. President Obama will learn to govern toward the center or America's center will reject him—and Congress. He will learn. Inventories are lean. People are as cautious as they can be. Don't think of where stocks will be next week, month or quarter. Think about where they will be in three years. Here are seven to watch.

Canadian Magna International may be the world's best-run auto parts firm. When this recession ends it will clean up. The stock will move long before that. With $24 billion in revenue and 74,000 employees, this is a fundamental global piece of an industry long in distress. Yet it has grown slowly but steadily over the years, gaining market share. It will continue to do so. With a $5 billion industry bailout underway, Wall Street doesn't expect much from any parts company. But at 5 times prospective 2010 earnings, 40% of book value, 2 times cash flow and 10% of annual revenue, Magma makes sense even for someone with low expectations for the sector. It has a 3.8% dividend yield.

Marathon Oil is the US' fourth-largest integrated oil and gas firm (one, that is, combining production with refining) and the fifth-largest refiner, with a million barrels per day of capacity. Its operations span the Americas, Europe and Africa. It also owns interests in Canadian oil sands. It was cheap before the bear market halved it. Now at 30% of revenue, 90% of book value, 7 times 2009 earnings and 3 times cash flow (in the sense of net income plus depreciation), and with a 3.6% dividend yield, it's too cheap to pass up.

Finland's Stora Enso is Europe's largest paper, packaging and forest-products firm. Thanks in large part to a collapse in prices for lumber, the stock is down 79% since the market's peak. The $3 billion market capitalization is 16 times likely 2009 earnings and less than 5 times the earnings Stora had a few years back. The price is also 15% of annual revenue, 30% of book value and 2 times cash flow. The dividend, now yielding 14%, will be cut. Still, Stora is a buy.

Germany's Siemens has an exceptionally broad line of leading industrial products. The bear market halved its shares. I bet you would expect this outfit to be getting killed in sales and profits, but it's performing very well. As the bull market takes off, you will lose the opportunity to buy it at 8 times likely 2010 earnings and 50% of revenue. The dividend, yielding 2.8%, looks safe for now.

If you believe India will grow a lot over the next two decades, which I do, you will believe in its dominant automaker, Tata Motors. Down 80% in the bear market, it makes an exceptional line of small, fuel-efficient cars (and also now Jaguar, which it bought from Ford in 2008). Decades from now this will be one of the world's big carmakers. Today's price is 30% of annual revenue, 100% of book value, 3 times cash flow and 13 times likely 2009 earnings. Yield, 6.5%.

Brazil's Net Communications Services is the country's largest pay-TV provider, with 3 million customers. It also provides phone and Internet services to millions. It may be the firm best positioned to leverage Brazil's explosive middle-class growth. If you like Indian and Chinese consumer stocks, you should like Brazilian ones like this. At 9 times my estimate for 2009 earnings and 4 times cash flow, it's cheap enough for a big, long run.

Brazil's largest petrochemical firm, with almost half the market, is Braskem. It specializes in polyethylene, polypropylene and polyvinyl chloride. While currently profitless, it is generating cash flow. It sells at one times cash flow, 40% of book value and 10% of annual revenue. The stock fell 78% in a year. Don't be fooled by its dividend, which yields 17% but surely will be cut. The stock sells for about 2 times 2010 earnings. ■

Blink and You'll Miss It
May 25, 2009

Investors battered by the bear market are asking: "How long will it take to get back up to where we were when the bear market began?" My answer: I don't know. There is no way to really know. Just guess. But when the recovery comes, it will come much faster than you expect. Bear markets are almost always followed by bull markets in a pattern with a V shape, as detailed in my February 16 column. The steeper the descent, the steeper the ascent. We had a steep descent.

Worried investors are thinking that the pattern will be different this time, that it may be a decade or more before the S&P 500 is back to its 1,565 high. The really worried ones think that this recovery may not occur in their lifetimes. But the grim notion that a crash is different, worse and near unique has been ubiquitous late in every bear market.

There are the endless comparisons with 1929–32, a crash that was followed by a partial recovery and then another bear market (with another economic downturn) in 1937. I don't think that comparison is at all valid. Next month I'll detail why. The key point is that investors fear a 1930s-like L-shaped bottom with stocks going nowhere for years. But the 1930s had no L. There were, rather, several Vs in succession. In the first three months after 1932's bottom the market was up 92%. We should be so lucky now.

If March 9 was the bottom, and that's an if, then at the recovery rate seen between June 1932 and March 1937, we would reattain the November 2007 peak in March 2010. The gloomsters pondering comparisons with the Great Crash just don't contemplate this fact. If stocks rebounded at a slower pace—in line with the average during recoveries over the past century—then we get back to the S&P 500 at 1,565 in May 2012. Think about buying stocks now that you will want to own in 2012. ■

The Obama Effect
June 22, 2009

Call me an eccentric, but one reason I'm optimistic is that Barack Obama is in the White House. No, I'm not enamored with him—never am with a politician. It's strictly a matter of numbers. Statistics favor a bull market in 2009. As I write this (with the S&P at 888), the market is flat in the year to date. There are seven months left for the pattern to be borne out with a rally.

Here are the stats: S&P 500 returns (including dividends) for the first year of first terms for Presidents fit a neat pattern. Since 1926 five of six Republican first years have been negative, the lone exception being 1989 under George HW Bush (when the market was up 32%). Of six Democratic first years, five show double-digit gains, the lone exception being 1977, under Jimmy Carter (off 7%).

The pattern is not so strange when you think about what the market is and is not. It is not a register of current business conditions. It is an anticipator. Anticipating the worst from a populist presidential candidate, Wall Street marks down stocks before a Democrat takes office—before, in fact, he is even elected. After the inauguration there's a good chance for a rebound.

With Democratic politicians the big fear is about how antibusiness and anti-capitalist they will be. Obama says lots of stupid, scary things. That fear hit markets early in the election cycle. But once he is in office the overwhelming motivation of a left-of-center President slowly morphs toward getting reelected. Achieving that means pandering more to the independent voters and liberal Republicans, less to the Democratic power base. Obama's concern now is the recession and the job creators that can take us out of it. That means slowly backing off soak-the-rich, anticorporate talk over time.

The reverse happens with Republicans. They come in riding high expectations for pro-business, pro-growth policies—and inevitably disappoint investors as they drift away from their power base. Optimism fades, depressing stocks. ∎

Quarter-Century Mark
July 13, 2009

This issue marks the 25th anniversary of my column. That's a long run in columnland. It's been a blast. Thanks for your attention. Reviewing my first year's columns, I pondered: What would I still say? What would I say now that I didn't then?

In the still-say mode: Avoid overpaying. Use multiple valuation metrics—not just the ratio of price-to-earnings but the ratios of price-to-sales and price-to-book. Compare a company with both the whole market and peers. Buy quality cheaply. The title of my second column was "Glamour Doesn't Pay," meaning that the higher growth rates of the most obviously desirable companies didn't justify their premium prices. Still true.

I've done well over time but made lots of mistakes, too. Learn from your mistakes. My December 31, 1984 column, "Big Bloopers of 1984," was a sort of mea culpa, along with lessons learned. The editor liked the notion well enough that a few years later he began requiring all columnists to issue annual retrospectives.

A constant in my approach to investing: You should think politically but unconventionally. Last month I was arguing why Obama will be good for stocks.

Think about size. There are times for big stocks, others when small ones are better buys, and times, like now, when size doesn't much matter.

In the didn't-say-then category: Invest globally. The column started out with a domestic focus. That doesn't work in a more globalized economy. Including foreign holdings gives you more opportunities and better diversification.

Originally I thought Republican. Now I'm an equal opportunity politician-hater.

There are times to go to cash, but they are rare. This column has recommended pulling back in three bear markets, beginning first in June 1987, then beginning in September 1989 and then in February 2001. Good calls, but then I was dead wrong with a bullish stance in 2008. Usually getting out is the bigger risk.

In the early days I promoted the idea of spending time in libraries to gain facts that other investors didn't have. Not many people did that kind of research, so it worked. We have a reverse problem now: too much information that's too accessible and not too reliable. There's a lot of mischief and manipulation on the Internet, masquerading as fact or as casual commentary. Beware. ∎

The Bear Market Is Over
August 24, 2009

That 9% minicorrection between June 2 and July 13 was nothing to worry about. Pullbacks are normal early in a recovery. I can find only one bull market, in 1935, that didn't have some material indigestion within its first 12 months. But bull markets roll on for years.

This rally has taken stocks up 55% from their March 9 low, as measured by the Morgan Stanley All World Index. That's far bigger than any global bear market sucker rally. Interestingly, the record rebound has gotten less ink than the corresponding fall in prices during the first quarter. Maybe the bulls should be making a bigger fuss about what's going on.

In my September 29 column last year I wrote about how we're in a reverse bubble. In this mirror image of a buying mania, people can see only the negatives. But the positives are there and will be reflected in stocks before long.

For example, few see that housing affordability is now excellent: The median

home price in the US is 2.8 times median family income, down from 3.9 times three years ago. Another positive is that global leading economic indicators in total (such as real money supply and the yield curve's slope) are the highest they've been in a decade. Productivity is up 2% from a year ago, an impressive growth rate within a recession's decline.

The financial crisis is over. Most rate spreads between risky paper like junk bonds to Treasurys have reverted to precrisis levels. US bank cash on hand, at a trillion dollars, is (adjusted for inflation) three times what it was before the crisis. Cash in the form of US money market funds comes to 42% of the stock market's capitalization. That ratio is more than twice what it was in 1982 and 2003, as stocks were about to take off.

I have been saying for a while that stocks are dirt cheap, as measured by the degree to which prospective earnings yields exceed long-term interest rates globally. Stocks are also low in relation to commodity prices. In 2000 the S&P 500 matched the dollar price of 5 ounces of gold; now it costs you only an ounce. The price of the index in baskets of wheat and pounds of copper is down similarly. And what do the bears say? That earnings will be low this year. Old news. So what? I expect S&P earnings (before writeoffs) of $70 next year. The market is trading at 13.6 times that sum. ■

Buy Into Fossil Fuels
September 21, 2009

Rich Karlgaard's recent column on energy and the Waxman-Markey carbon trading bill should be required reading for every high school and college kid. They should have to read it three times. Adults should have to prove they've read it before being allowed to vote. The column outlined the harsh reality of renewable energy. In this country 89% of electricity comes from three fuel sources: coal, natural gas and nuclear fission. That fraction won't change dramatically in the next decade. If you want your air conditioner to work in 2014, you'd better hope that more fossil fuel plants get built.

I'm riding down the road in a friend's electric Tesla Roadster. Sounds clean, doesn't it? But we are burning 49% coal, 21% natural gas, 20% nuclear and little else. Wind power? Zip! How will we run Teslas without fossil fuel? We won't. How will emerging markets, with a combined GDP already bigger than America's, grow without more fossil fuel? They won't.

Nuclear power might provide for our needs (and, if you believe in the global warming theory, protect our atmosphere). If the French can get 70% of their electric energy from nuclear safely and cleanly, then we can. But will we? Politically, it will be difficult. Many of the same people screaming that fossil fuel creates global warming are also adamantly against adding clean nuclear power. There are a lot of nuclear reactor applications pending in the US, but the permits will be few, and slow in coming.

That situation, and the fact that other energy-hungry countries will also be demanding fossil fuels, tells me you should be overweight in energy stocks. That means at least 12% of your equity in energy companies, and most of that in companies with a fossil fuel emphasis. ■

Viva the V

November 2, 2009

Viva the vrrooom! We're in the midst of a really big and steep V. As detailed in my February 16 column, "Anticipate the V" (and updated in my May 25 column, "Blink and You'll Miss It"), big bear markets are almost always followed by big bull markets in a V-shape pattern. The steeper the descent, the steeper the ascent.

Most investors give too much credence to the theory that prices are rational; they presume that a market collapse must have been justified by serious economic trouble. As a result they presume that we can't have a big bull run after prices crash. History proves that presumption to be false.

This time the V is almost perfect—so far. As I write, the MSCI All-Country World index is exactly where it was on September 29, 2008. From there to the March 9 bottom was five months and ten days. From the bottom up to here is not quite seven months, a slightly lopsided V.

Note: The V works for the whole world stock market, not necessarily every country's. Any one market, including America's, can take on an odd shape. Always think globally first.

The fundamental force behind every V is always that the last phase of a bear market is driven completely by imploding panicky sentiment rather than the fundamentals people think they're thinking about. The sentiment implosion is a societal, psychological depressed-spring effect that makes the market bounce back as quickly and as far as it went down.

All the while people fret about sucker rallies and expected pullbacks, the V keeps its shape. I described that sequence for the 1930s in my May 25 column. Now take a look at the bear market bottom on December 6, 1974. A year and five months later the stock market was almost exactly where it had been a year and five months before December 6.

If history repeats, the current V recovery is far from over. If it keeps up for another six to nine months the global stock market will be 20% to 25% higher by January 1, 2010. We had a long (16 months) and deep (down 60%) bear market. Now we're getting a big, long bull run. Stay with it. ∎

The Old Normal

December 14, 2009

I can't call on my institutional clients without hearing anguished questions about the "new normal." In case you have been fishing in the upper Amazon basin, the "new normal" is Pimco's way of declaring that the decade ahead will be lackluster. The slogan has taken on a life of its own and been widely adopted. It's also utter nonsense—rubbish of the first caliber.

The basic notion is that all the new insurmountable problems we now face (deficits, unemployment, exhausted consumers) will keep us in a dismal economy and poor stock market for ten years. But to me it seems pretty clear that we are now experiencing the same old normal we've always seen.

In my 37 years in the investment industry I've never, ever seen an early bull market without some version of this theme that was widely embraced. Last time around, in 2003–04, it was "a new era of lower expectations." Then stocks rose for four years.

As a rule, the bigger and scarier bear markets have been, the bigger the floodgates have opened toward this sentiment—this view that the new problems are just too big and bad to overcome. It all reminds me inherently and eerily of Sir John Templeton's line that the four most dangerous words in the English language are "This time it's different." It's different in details, maybe, but the fundamental principles of investing don't change.

Not to impugn Pimco's integrity (which I consider the highest), but this view is convenient for that firm. Its business is mainly in fixed income. As the economy strengthens—whether a little or a lot—it is likely that long-term interest rates will rise. That will make Pimco's bond portfolios go down in value. There's not much that bond managers can do in a long bear market for bonds and still look smart. If they go to cash, even with excellent timing, they get no big hero's reward of the sort equity managers can get.

Take note: Pimco, a division of Allianz, is getting into the equity business right now. Watch what its managers do, not what they say.

While obviously far from March's lows, stocks (globally) are still very cheap by historical standards. They are also cheap compared with bonds. Be bullish. Skip the biggest US banks. Focus instead on materials, industrials and technology. More important, invest heavily overseas, where opportunities are the best. ∎

Notes

Introduction

1.   Through 12/31/2009. Performance is hypothetical and reflects *Forbes* magazine's calculation of simulated trades based on Ken Fisher's *Forbes* picks in *Forbes* magazine versus the S&P 500 Index during the same period. The hypothetical performance is based on transactions not made and is not an indication of actual performance by Ken Fisher or Fisher Investments. *Forbes'* calculation methodology is based solely on calendar years and assumes readers buy $10,000 of each Ken Fisher stock pick published in *Forbes* and immediately subtracts a 1 percent hypothetical brokerage commission. That is compared to putting $10,000 into an S&P500 Index fund at the same date with no hypothetical commission and no other fees. Hypothetical performance does not include the impact of taxes or any other costs, if any.

For example, in 2004 Ken Fisher recommended 51 stocks in *Forbes* throughout the year. If $10,000 had been put into each stock the total invested would have been $510,000, which would have appreciated by year end 2004 to $574,000, a 12.6 percent appreciation. The same amount of money invested in the S&P 500 Index at those various times without a hypothetical commission would have totaled $548,000 for a return of 7.6 percent at the end of 2004. Using this methodology Ken Fisher's *Forbes* stock picks tied the S&P 500 in 1998, lagged it in 1997, 2002, and 2008, beat it in 1996, 1999–2001, 2003–2007, and 2009 and overall beat it by an average annualized 5.23 percent for calendar years 1996 through 2009. Past performance is no assurance of future returns. Investing in securities involves the risk of loss.

2. Ibid.
3. James J. Green. "Doing it Right." Investment Advisor. June, 1, 2007.

1984—A Not So Orwellian Year

1. Global Financial Data.
2. Ibid.

1985—A 30% Yawner

1. Global Financial Data.
2. Ibid.

1986—Global-dy Gook

1. Global Financial Data.

1987—Crash!

1. Global Financial Data.
2. Ibid.
3. See note 1.
4. See note 1.
5. Bloomberg Finance, L.P.

1988—Ear to the Ground

1. Global Financial Data.
2. Ibid.
3. See note 1.

1989—The End Is Nigh

1. Global Financial Data.
2. Ibid.
3. See Note 1.
4. See Note 1.

5. See Note 1.
6. See Note 1.

1990—A Sneaky Bear Market

1. Global Financial Data.
2. Ibid.
3. See Note 1.
4. See Note 1.
5. See Note 1.

1991—Unbelievable Bull

1. Global Financial Data.
2. Ibid.
3. See Note 1.
4. See Note 1.

1992—Times They Were a Changin'

1. Global Financial Data.
2. Ibid.
3. See Note 1.

1993—A Taxing Year

1. Global Financial Data.
2. Ibid.

1994—The Calm Before the Storm

1. Global Financial Data.
2. Ibid.
3. See Note 1.
4. See Note 1.

1995—List After Bullish List

1. Global Financial Data.
2. Ibid.

1996—The Nifty Nineties

1. Global Financial Data.
2. Ibid.

1997—Rational Exuberance

1. Global Financial Data.
2. Ibid.

1998—Rubles, Corrections, and More Bull

1. Global Financial Data.
2. Ibid.
3. See Note 1.
4. See Note 1.
5. See Note 1.
6. See Note 1.
7. See Note 1.
8. See Note 1.
9. See Note 1.
10. See Note 1.

1999—IPOs, Y2K, Nasdaq, Oh My!

1. Jake Ulick. "1999: Year of the IPO." *CNNMoney*. December 27, 1999, http://money.cnn.com/1999/12/27/investing/century_ipos/ (accessed December 18, 2009).
2. See Note 1.
3. Global Financial Data.
4. Ibid.
5. See Note 3.
6. See Note 3.
7. See Note 3.

2000—Tech Bubbles Over

1. Global Financial Data.
2. Ibid.
3. Thomson Reuters.
4. See Introduction, Note 1.
5. See Note 1.
6. See Note 1.
7. "The World's Billionaires." *Forbes*. March 10, 2010. http://www.forbes.com/2010/03/10/worlds-richest-people-slim-gates-buffett-billionaires-2010_land.html (accessed March 25, 2010).

2001—Bear Market!

1. Global Financial Data.
2. Ibid.
3. See Note 1.
4. See Note 1.
5. See Note 1.

2002—Triple Bottom Blues

1. Global Financial Data.
2. Ibid.
3. See Note 1.
4. See Note 1.

2003—Buy on the Cannons

1. Global Financial Data.
2. Ibid.

2004—If

1. Global Financial Data.
2. Ibid.
3. See Note 1.

2005—Giving It Time

1. Global Financial Data.
2. Ibid.
3. Thomson Reuters; Global Financial Data.
4. See note 1.

2006—Celebrity Market Indicators

1. Global Financial Data.
2. Ibid.
3. See note 1.
4. See note 1.
5. See note 1.

2007—Another Broken Record

1. Global Financial Data.
2. Ibid.
3. See note 1.

2008—The Unbubble

1. Global Financial Data.
2. Ibid.
3. See note 1.
4. See note 1.
5. See note 1.

2009—25 Years and Counting

1. Global Financial Data.
2. Ibid.
3. See Introduction, Note 1.

Acknowledgments

It's often said if we ignore history we're doomed to repeat it. This seems like an awfully pessimistic view of the past. A key lesson I learned working on this book is that history will inevitably be repeated—and that's good. Human nature doesn't fundamentally change, and thus neither does investing. There will be differences to be sure, but the differences will undoubtedly be outweighed by the similarities. Save a few tumultuous years, most investors probably wouldn't mind repeating the 1980s, 1990s, and, despite claims a flat decade for stocks, even the 2000s (which in reality have been anything but flat).

Frankly, I don't deserve credit for much in this book. My comments added flavor, not substance. I simply peddled paprika, but Ken cooked the meal. So first and foremost, I'd like to thank Ken Fisher for his 25 years of work that constitutes the heart, soul, and most of the pages of this book. But my gratitude toward Ken goes deeper than that. The lessons I've learned under his tutelage have enabled me to view investing and the world in a clearer light.

Along with Ken, I'd like to thank Sherri Fisher, Jeff Silk, Andrew Teufel, Damian Ornani, and Steve Triplett.

Many thanks also to Steve Forbes and the outstanding staff at *Forbes* magazine. *Forbes* has been the preeminent financial publication for nearly a century. That level of quality and consistency is remarkable.

Lara Hoffmans' contributions to this book once again showed her incredible skill and patience as a writer and editor. She deserves as much if not more credit for this book as I. My thanks and sympathies go to Evelyn Chea who had the unenviable responsibility of correcting my many, many grammatical and other slip ups.

Special thanks go out to Thomson Reuters and Global Financial Data for providing the data for our research.

As always, I'm incredibly grateful to my family for their love and support. Mom, Dad, Kevin, and Natasha—thank you. I'm particularly grateful to and for my beautiful wife and daughter, Kim and Olivia.

About the Author

Aaron Anderson is a Capital Markets Research Analyst who holds BS degrees in Geophysics from the University of California at Santa Barbara and Applied Economics from the University of San Francisco. His first book, *Own the World*, was published in 2009 by John Wiley & Sons. He writes a regular column for MarketMinder.com titled *The Global View*. Aaron, his wife Kim, and daughter, Olivia, reside in Danville, CA.

Index